UNPUBLISHED MANUSCRIPTS
IN BRITISH IDEALISM

Volume 1

UNPUBLISHED MANUSCRIPTS IN BRITISH IDEALISM

Political Philosophy, Theology and Social Thought

Edited and Introduced by

Colin Tyler

Volume 1

ia

imprint-academic.com

First published by Thoemmes Continuum 2005

This edition published in the UK by
Imprint Academic, PO Box 200, Exeter EX5 5YX, UK

and in the USA by
Imprint Academic, Philosophy Documentation Center
PO Box 7147, Charlottesville, VA 22906-7147, USA

ISBN 9781845401252

A CIP catalogue record for this book is available from the
British Library and US Library of Congress

To Peter Nicholson,
With thanks

Table of Contents

Acknowledgements

A very great deal of effort and time has gone into this edition, and I must begin by thanking Dr Christopher Bearman who bore a significant part of the burden. Dr Bearman did the initial transcriptions and first checks for all of the material except Bosanquet's undergraduate essays, as well as helping with the initial annotation. He showed great fortitude, especially when faced with Edward Caird's truly appalling handwriting. The edition would have taken far longer to produce without his hard work and expertise.

I am also very pleased to acknowledge, in regard to this and two other projects, the financial support of both the AHRB and the Department of Politics and International Studies at the University of Hull. The Department provided vital seed-corn and other supplementary funding. Yet, the vast bulk of the work was funded by the Arts and Humanities Research Board, under their Resource Enhancement Scheme (Award: B/RE/AN3141/APN17357).

'The Arts and Humanities Research Board (AHRB) funds postgraduate and advanced research within the UK's higher education institutions and provides funding for museums, galleries and collections that are based in, or attached to, HEIs within England. The AHRB supports research within a huge subject domain – from 'traditional' humanities subjects, such as history, modern languages and English literature, to music and the creative and performing arts.'

The edition and two associated projects could not have been produced without the generous financial support of the AHRB.

Similarly, I am very pleased to acknowledge a number of institutions for giving me access to the manuscripts and for allowing me to include them in this edition. I am pleased to thank: the Master and Fellows of Balliol College, Oxford for permission to quote from the papers of TH Green; the Robinson Library of the University of Newcastle for permission to quote from Bernard Bosanquet's undergraduate essays; the Master and Fellows of Trinity College Cambridge for permission to publish both Bosanquet's and Caird's respective reports on GE Moore's Fellowship dissertations, and the letter by David Ritchie. Finally I am very pleased to thank the Special Collections Library of the University of Glasgow for allowing me to quote so extensively from the papers of Edward Caird.

I enjoyed greatly working in each of these libraries over the past eighteen months, and thank the following archivists in particular for their assistance and in many cases patience: Drs Penelope Bulloch and Alan Tadiello at Balliol, Drs Helen Arkwright and Melanie Wood at the Robinson Library, Newcastle, Drs David McKitterick Jonathan Smith at Trinity, and Dr Weston and Robert MacLean from the Special Collections Library of the University of Glasgow.

Philip de Bary has been a patient and helpful editor, as always. I am very grateful to him. I also wish to thank Alberto de Sanctis and particularly Dr Ben Wempe for pointing out the close connection between Green's published writings ca.1866 and the manuscripts which I have called here 'Rudiments of "The Philosophy of Aristotle" and Related texts'. I am also pleased to thank my colleague Dr Rudi Wurzel for his help transcribing and translating the German in these volumes. I have benefitted enormously from the comments of Peter Nicholson, and the help of Dr Manfred Kolte (Goethe und Schiller Archiv) and my colleagues Professors Jack Hayward and Philip Norton.

This is an appropriate place to acknowledge my debts to the Bentham Project, and particularly Professor Philip Schofield. I spent three years at the Project as a Research Fellow before coming to Hull in 2000. I enjoyed my time working on the new edition of Bentham's works, and do not doubt that often I would have felt lost in this current edition if I had not had the experience of working for the Project.

John Bowring records (Bowring (ed.), *Works of Jeremy Bentham*, vol. 11, p.80) that Bentham had a favourite 'puss', whom he called the Reverend Doctor Sir John Langborn. Apparently the Reverend Doctor helped Jeremy with his (Bentham's) work (as did certain mice). While I do not have Bentham's genius, I do have a much-loved cat. I thank Lucy for doing precisely what every academic's cat should do – namely, sitting in the middle of any papers that I happened to working on at the time, demanding attention.

I reserve my greatest thanks for Pip. On a prosaic level, she helped to prepare the texts for submission to the Press. On the far more important emotional level, she listened sympathetically to my whinging, made me take some breaks, and supported me in innumerable ways throughout what became a long period of rather intense and tiring work.

Finally, this edition is dedicated to Peter Nicholson. Everyone who works on the idealists owes Peter a huge debt. Peter introduced me to the idealists nearly fourteen years ago. I have learnt so much from him, and not least the crucial importance of scholarship. I hope that my work on this edition approaches his standards.

Obviously, I alone am responsible for the shortcomings that remain in these volumes.

Colin Tyler
University of Hull, 2005

Symbols and Abbreviations

[ ]	Editorial insertion
| |	Space left in manuscript
[?]	Transcription disputable
[...?]	Indecipherable word
[word?]	Word inserted for sense by editor as manuscript indecipherable
['word']	Translation
['word'?]	Suggested translation
MS alt.	Author's alternative
MS reads	Reading of the manuscript that has been altered in the edited text for the purpose of meaning
MS del.	Word deleted by author
MS orig.	Original manuscript reading superseded by author's alternative
Nettleship, *Memoir*	RL Nettleship, 'Memoir of TH Green', in Green, *Works*, vol. 3
DSF	TH Green, 'On the Different Senses of "Freedom" ...' , in Harris et al (eds.) *Lectures on the Principles of Political Obligation and other writings* (see bibliography for full details). Section numbers given.
LLFC	TH Green, 'Lecture on "Liberal Legislation and Freedom of Contract"', in Harris et al (eds.) *Lectures on the Principles of Political Obligation and*

	other writings (see bibliography for full details.)
PE	TH Green, *Prolegomena to Ethics* (see bibliography for full details). Section numbers given.
PPO	TH Green, 'Lectures on the Principles of Political Obligation', in Harris et al (eds.) *Lectures on the Principles of Political Obligation and other writings* (see bibliography for full details). Section numbers given.
Works	TH Green, *Works*, followed by relevant volume number (see bibliography for full details).

The following symbols and abbreviations occur only in Green's lectures on the Romans, on the Galatians, and on the Fourth Gospel.

[...]	Text leads on/follows directly from the relevant point in Green's *Works*
{word}	Curled brackets replace HN's square brackets
HN	Henry Nettleship
RLN	Richard Lewis Nettleship

Introduction

The archives of TH Green and Edward Caird contain a large amount of material, much of it unpublished.[1] In Green's case, the unpublished material varies greatly in both textual coherence and finish. On the one hand, Green's undergraduate essays are neatly written for the most part, and possibly for that reason all of them have now been published.[2] The notes for the lectures that he gave as Fellow and then Whyte's Professor of Moral Philosophy at Balliol, on the other hand, are often rather chaotic, for example with two different discussions running on facing-pages of his notebooks without any immediate indication as to their intended relationship. Fortunately, in many cases it is possible to disentangle these discussions and to reconstruct the intended structure of Green's argument with a reasonable degree certainty. Nevertheless, doing so can be a long and laborious task. The situation with Edward Caird's papers is rather different. These are generally relatively complete and coherent. Unfortunately, unlike Green, Caird had appalling handwriting, meaning that one must spend a long time deciphering Caird's manuscript before one can criticise his arguments.

While a significant proportion of Green and Caird's manuscripts remain unpublished, the same cannot be said for the papers of Bernard Bosanquet and David Ritchie. In Bosanquet's case, little that is 'new' survives in his archives at the University of Newcastle, and there are no developed pieces of any length and coherence from his mature period. Similarly, few of Ritchie's philosophical manuscripts appear to have survived, and, according to Ritchie's son, his father's personal papers were also destroyed.[3]

For the present edition, I have chosen to include those pieces from the archives that I believe reveal most about the political philosophy, theology and social thought of Green, Bosanquet, Ritchie and Caird. I hope that other scholars will also find things of interest in the manuscripts. I have tried to exercise as light an editorial hand as is consistent with producing readable versions of these texts. I have silently expanded the authors' respective contractions, including converting numbers into words and ampersands into 'and', and so on. I have added notes where there might be some doubt as to the intended meaning of such contractions. (For the most part, these notes have been required only where names have been contracted.) I have added definite and indefinite articles rarely, only doing so where otherwise the sense of the manuscript would be needlessly difficult to follow. All editorial additions are clearly marked as such, in line with the symbols and abbreviations listed at the beginning of this volume. Authors' notes appear with the editorial notes at the end of the relevant texts.

The remainder of this introduction describes the state of the individual manuscripts of Green, Bosanquet and Ritchie, and seeks to justifying the dates that I have ascribed to them. Where possible, I have provided some wider background to the texts. No attempt is made to assess the coherence or significance of the various arguments they develop. Discussion of Caird is reserved for the second volume, where all his texts appear.

Finally, I have endeavoured to provide translations for all of the Greek, Latin and German. Readers should to treat these as guides to meaning rather than as definitive translations, especially in the first two cases. Of course, in all three cases, the foreign text aims to be an exact reproduction of the manuscripts. This is especially important to notice in relation to New Testament quotations, where Green does not use the Authorised Greek text.[4]

Part 1: Thomas Hill Green
1. 'Rudiments of "The Philosophy of Aristotle" and related texts.' (1866–67)
(Title and location of manuscript: 'MS4 Two sheets of an apparently early essay on Hegel – other fragments on philosophy.' Green Papers, Balliol College, Oxford.)

The bulk of this first item appears to be a collection of rudiments of Green's important essay on 'The Philosophy of Aristotle', which was first published in the September 1866 issue of *The North British Review*.[5] In addition to the overlap of content between many of the rudiments and the final article, there is some verbatim overlap of text (for example, see rudiments 3 and 11).[6] That the bulk of the material in this group comes from this time (ca.1866) is indicated by the consistency in style and concern, and a consistency of allusions (not least the many quotations from Wordsworth).

The first line of Rudiment 12 (part of what Nettleship describes on the cover of MS4 as 'Apparently Early Essay on Hegel') is quite odd in this regard ('It is now thirty-five years since Hegel…'). Green appears to have in mind 1831, the year of Hegel's death. In fact, Hegel's first published use of the phrase 'was vernünftig ist, das ist wirklich, und was wirklich ist, das ist vernünftig' ['the rational is the actual, and the actual is the rational'] appeared in 1821, in the preface to the *Grundlinien der Philosophie des Rechts* (the preface is dated 25 June 1820).[7] An allusion to the *Philosophy of Right* would make this a very early piece in Green's literary canon, as the fragment would then date from either 1855 or 1856. In fact Green entered Balliol in October 1855, when he was nineteen years old. We do know that Green had begun to study philosophy for himself while at Rugby,[8] and it is conceivable that Jowett introduced him to Hegel before mid-1857 when Green began to study philosophy formally as part of the literae humaniores syllabus.[9] Nevertheless, it seems unlikely that Green would have had access to many of Hegel's own writings at this time, given that very little was available in English and Green began to study German in earnest only in 1863.[10] So the date of 1866 seems secure.

Rudiments 15 and (certainly) 16 appear to date from slightly later, in that they seem to be Green's notes for his inaugural lecture as a Fellow of Balliol, a position which he took up following the death of the Rev. James Riddell in September 1866.[11]

To avoid the impression that these rudiments are intended to form a coherent discussion, I have numbered each fragment separately. Footnotes record the differences between my transcription of Rudiment 12 and the version published by Wempe,[12] differences which I have verified against the original manuscript.

2. Political Philosophy' (ca.1869–71), and,
3. The Nature of Historical Narrative in Thucydides and Herodotus (ca.1869–1871).
(Title and location of both manuscripts: 'Notebook on divinity labelled by CBG.' Green Papers, Balliol College, Oxford.)

These clear short and continuous texts appear to be lecture notes. Green wrote them in the back of the same 'Divinity' notebook,[13] and they appear to originate from around the same date. There are two pieces of evidence from which we can date these notes. First, AC Bradley added a note to the 'Political Philosophy' manuscript (Green's own title) which reads: 'Given in lectures on [Aristotle,] the

[Nichomachean] Ethics, Book V, when I heard them. A.C.B.' The lectures to which Bradley refers were most likely given in the lead-up to his examination for Classical Moderations, which took place in 1871. Second, the text which I have called 'The Nature of Historical Narrative in Thucydides and Herodotus.' bears a striking resemblance to Bosanquet's 1869 undergraduate essay 'The Conception of Historical Causes in Thucydides Compared with that in Herodotus.'

4. 'Metaphysic of Ethics, Moral Psychology, Sociology or Science of Sittlichkeit.' (ca. late 1860s – early 1870s)
(Title and location of manuscript: 'MS10A: ... (At Other End, Lecture on Moral Philosophy)', Green Papers, Balliol College, Oxford.)
This untitled manuscript is written in a notebook, all of the pages of which are secured except for the first, although its placing is unequivocal as it had formed the back cover. All pages are numbered apparently in Nettleship's hand. The state of the text implies that it is a set of lecture notes (cf. Green's lecture notes on John, Galatians, and Romans).[14] I have added the title and subheadings. The text is very confused in places and has required much editing at those points (indicated in the editorial notes).

This long manuscript itself is undated, although it is similar in style and content to Green's philosophical writings between approximately the late 1860s and the early 1870s (cf. 'Popular Philosophy in its Relation to Life', published in 1868 and particularly his introductions to David Hume's *Treatise of Human Nature*, published in 1874).[15] That the manuscript was written prior to 1874 is indicated by the fact that Green uses the 1824 edition Hume's works[16] rather than TH Grose's version, to which Green added his long introductions.

This item is interesting on a number of levels, not least because it links directly Green's philosophical position and in the early stages at least his religious concerns, with his criticisms of the British empiricist and ethical traditions. It points towards the reconciliation of Green's critical concerns regarding the dominant form of British philosophy and the idealist alternative that he was to set out at greater length and in a more systematic fashion in the *Prolegomena to Ethics*. He discusses a range of topics, from the limitations of an ethics of moral sense and the inadequacies of utilitarianism to the universality of the moral law; from freedom, responsibility and the

will to punishment; and from the nature of God to social theory.
5. '*Pleasure* as the Chief Good.' (mid-1870s?)
(Title and location of manuscript: 'MS9: Fragment about *Pleasure* as chief good.', Balliol College, Oxford.)

Glued onto the reverse of the outer sheet of this manuscript is a note apparently in Lewis Nettleship's hand, which reads, '9/Fragment about *Pleasure* as the chief good.' The various sheets are wrapped in two pieces of paper, both of which are blank except for the following notes, both apparently in Nettleship's hand: 'Various loose sheets on Moral Philosophy.' '9/4 loose sheets on Moral philosophy.' Nettleship numbered the four pages '1 RLN' and so on, although actually they appear to run pp.1, 4, 3, and finally p.2 and are presented thus here. There is little evidence from which to date this manuscript. In view of the level of sophistication shown in Green's argument, I suggest that it was written in the mid-1870s.

6. 'Notes of Lectures on the Epistle to the Romans [Remaining text]' (ca. 1871)
7. 'Notes on the Epistle to the Galatians' (ca.1873)
8. 'Lectures on the Fourth Gospel (Remaining text)' (ca.1877)
(Title and location of manuscripts: 'Notebooks for divinity lectures on:/The Fourth Gospel/Epistle to the Romans/Epistle to the Galatians.' (Copies by Charlotte Green et al) Green Papers, Balliol College, Oxford.)

Green was appointed as a temporary tutor at Balliol for a brief period in 1860. He was made a Fellow in October 1866 and gained the Whyte's Chair of Moral Philosophy in the first half of 1878. Even though Green was 'probably the first layman who had held the office of tutor',[17] Nettleship records that taking up the tutorship in 1866 meant teaching 'the *Ethics* of Aristotle', as well as 'lectures on the New Testament'. A little later, Nettleship observed that,

'[Green's] view of christianity is to be gathered partly from courses of lectures on parts of the New Testament, delivered at frequent intervals during his tutorship, partly from occasional addresses of a distinctly religious character. The former, of which some extracts are printed in this volume, were not intended to be original contributions to biblical criticism. He took the material for them chiefly from German works, especially those of F.C. Baur, and his main purpose was to enforce certain truths contained in the books of the New Testament, and at the same time to point out where they seemed to him to have been misunderstood or perverted by the writers themselves or by subsequent interpreters. Probably many of his hearers were incapable of appreciating at the time the deeper ideas which he endeavoured to elicit from the epistles of Paul and the fourth gospel, and for that very reason they were likely to be disproportionately impressed by the unfavourable light which he sometimes threw upon the controversies of the early church. But if in these critical and expository lectures his intense sympathy with the spirit of Jesus and Paul was less obvious than his impatience of the mystifications with which party prejudice or ecclesiasticism had overlaid it, in the addresses on *The witness of God* and *Faith* his positive convictions found unabated expression.'[18]

Nettleship entitled the lectures on the particular books of the New Testament, 'The conversion of Paul' (on Galatians), 'The Pauline conception of justification by faith' (on Romans), and 'The Incarnation' (on the Fourth Gospel).[19] In the preface to the third volume of the *Works*, Nettleship states that, 'the extracts printed are taken from his notes supplemented by those of AC Bradley in the Galatians, RW Macan in the Romans, and CE Vaughan in the Fourth Gospel; these gentlemen completed their academical courses severally in 1873, 1871, and 1877.'[20] Yet, Lewis Nettleship failed to make clear that it was not he but his brother, Henry, who prepared the long versions of these lectures.[21] The present volume publishes for the first time the remaining portions of the lectures on John, and the Romans, and the complete lectures on the Galatians.[22]

Part 2: Bernard Bosanquet
1. Undergraduate Essays (February to December? 1869)
(Title and location of manuscript: 'Undergraduate Notebooks A and B'. Item I, Bosanquet Papers, Special Collections, Robinson Library, University of Newcastle.)
    Helen Bosanquet observed the following early in her biography of Bernard.

    ... TH Green is reported to have said of him that he [Bernard] was "the best equipped man of his generation." He used to say himself in after life that he owed much of his philosophy to the very practical and concrete nature of Green's own work and teaching. There still remain in corroboration of this two MS. books of Essays which he wrote for his tutors as an undergraduate, and those he wrote on subjects set by Green have many of them a direct bearing on social and political problems of the day.[23]

These notebooks now reside in the Bosanquet Papers held at University of Newcastle. Both ruled notebooks have black hard-covers and no margins. A card has been attached subsequently to the cover of notebook A, on which is written, not in Bosanquet's hand: 'Bernard Bosanquet Balliol 1869. Notebook A: Essays on mainly philosophical & literary subjects. Some Latin proses and a copy of Latin verse.' The title page of this notebook is signed in Bosanquet's hand: 'B Bosanquet/Ball.Coll./Febr 1. 1869'. A similar card is attached to Notebook B, reading (again in the different hand): 'B Notebook on Plato & Aristotle. Bernard Bosanquet 1869 Balliol.' On the title-page is written in Bosanquet's hand: 'B Bosanquet/Balliol. October./69./B2/Essays/Ethics Lect. Oct./69/Read./Symposium/Pheaetetus/Phaedrus.'

Notebook A includes twenty-four essays written in English and fourteen Latin exercises, as well as two sets of Logic exercises, sixteen of which are published for the first time in this volume. Notebook B contains thirteen essays, three of which are published here. (The full list of the essays in English forms the appendix to this volume.) I have included every essay for which Green is identified as tutor, and any others dealing with political philosophy, theology or social thought. Together, these essays provide numerous insights into the nature and development of Bosanquet's early thought. For example, included here is the essay on 'The Conception of Historical Causes in Thucydides Compared to Herodous', which Bosanquet seems to have written on the basis of Green's lectures on historical method among the ancient Greeks (Green's notes are also included in this volume). Also included is the essay which Bosanquet discussed several decades later in 'Unvisited Tombs': namely, 'The Proper Functions of Universities'.[24]

2. 'Report on a Dissertation entitled "The Metaphysical Basis of Ethics" by Mr. G.E. Moore.' (19 September 1898)
(Title and location of manuscript: Add. Ms. a. 247(1)–(7), Wren Library, Trinity College, Cambridge.)
George Edward Moore's 1898 Dissertation represented his second

attempt to gain a fellowship at Trinity College Cambridge. His first attempt had been made the previous year, with Edward Caird serving as an examiner (his report is included in volume two of the present edition). On the second occasion, Bosanquet was a referee, and his highly critical report is included here. In spite of Bosanquet's very serious reservations, Moore was awarded the Fellowship in November 1898. That the decision was a controversial one is clear from Bertrand Russell's letter to Alys Russell (his first wife) on 15 November 1898:

> Moore seems to have had a very close shave for his Fellowship: [James] Ward thought him too sceptical, said he reminded one of Hume and Bradley, and therefore (!) had better give up philosophy. Ward admitted his arguments to be unanswerable, but said, if such points were raised, the poor philosophers would never get anywhere. Bosanquet, who was referee, said much the same, but betrayed, according to Moore, a crass ignorance of the subject, even of its literature. I am confirmed in all I have ever thought: for this is the impression which a really first-rate young man ought to make on men of 50. Whitehead also takes this view. But it is awful; to think he might have failed to get his Fellowship.
> ...
> Thine devotedly,
> Bertie[25]

The twenty-five year old Russell's petulant loyalty to Moore did not diminish once he had actually read Moore's dissertation.[26] He wrote to Moore on 1 December 1989 in the following terms.

> ... I cannot conceive an answer to your arguments for the priority of the concept and truth to existence – the few comments of Ward and Bosanquet (especially one about the judgement of similarity) show a gross misapprehension of your meaning.
> Yours fraternally
> Bertrand Russell[27]

A significant portion of Moore's 1898 dissertation was published in *Mind* as 'The Nature of Judgement',[28] supplementing his earlier article on 'Freedom' which was submitted as part of his 1897 Fellowship application.[29] A fair (and examinable) copy of neither dissertation has been found, although very rough manuscripts of

both versions do survive in the archives of the Wren Library of
Trinity College, together with Bosanquet and Caird's reports and
Moore's response to Caird.

Part 3: David George Ritchie
Letter from Ritchie to Henry Sidgwick. (12 July 1895)
(Title and location of manuscript: Add. Ms.c. 95/50(1) to (2), Wren
Library, Trinity College, Cambridge.)
   The final text in this volume is a fascinating private letter from
David Ritchie to Henry Sidgwick. In it Ritchie answers Sidgwick's
hostile review in *Mind* of his 1895 book *Natural Rights*.[30] The text
is written in Ritchie's careful and generally clear hand.

Colin Tyler
University of Hull, 2005

---

[1] For the current, imperfect catalogue of those of Green's papers that are archived
    at Balliol College and the Bodleian Library, Oxford, see Geoffrey Thomas, *The
    Moral Philosophy of TH Green* (Oxford: Clarendon, 1987), pp.376–86. There
    is no similar printed catalogue for the extensive archive of Edward Caird's
    papers that is currently held in Special Collections Department of the University
    of Glasgow. It is possible to search their catalogue remotely via the internet
    however. Balliol College do have a list of the very small amount of material
    that they hold relating to Edward Caird. Carol Keene and William Mander
    have published a vast amount of FH Bradley's archive already in Carol A Keene
    and William J Mander (eds.), *The Collected Works of FH Bradley*, 12 vols.
    (Bristol: Thoemmes, 1999), vols. 1–5.

[2] These essays are printed in four books: Green, *Works*, vol. 3, pp.3–45 and vol.
    5, pp.1–104; TH Green, *Lectures on the Principles of Political Obligation and
    other writings* (Cambridge University Press, 1986), pp.302–09; and Alberto de
    Sanctis, *La democrazia 'puritana' di Thomas Hill Green: Con alcuni scritti
    inedite* (Florence, 2002), pp.203–20. An English translation of de Sanctis' book
    is forthcoming in Imprint Academic's British Idealism Studies: Series 3 Thomas
    Hill Green.

[3] Peter Nicholson, *The Political Philosophy of the British Idealists: Selected stud-
    ies* (Cambridge University Press, 1990), p.322.

[4] Two versions of the New Testament are preserved in Green's archives at Balliol:
    Das Neue Testament...stereotypirt nach der Hallischen Ausgabe (London:
    Samuel Bagster, n.d.), and *Novum Testamentum* (Oxford, 1844). See Thomas,
    Moral Philosophy of TH Green, p.386.

[5] TH Green, 'The Philosophy of Aristotle', *North British Review*, vol. 45
    (September 1866), pp.105–44; reprinted in *Works*, vol. 3, pp.46–91. Wempe
    also dates this manuscript to 1866. Ben Wempe, *TH Green's Theory of Positive*

Freedom: From metaphysics to political theory (Exeter: Imprint Academic, 2004), pp.22–3. Craig Smith dates it to 1864, although without citing any evidence, in his 'TH Green's Philosophical Manuscripts: An annotated catalogue', *Idealistic Studies*, vol. 9 (1978), p.180.

6   I am very grateful to Ben Wempe for pointing out this latter overlap (personal communication).

7   Hegel expanded on this claim – which is one of the fundamental principles of his system – in the 1827 (second) edition of his *Encyklopädie der Philosophischen Wissenshaften im Grundisse* (§6 zusätze). Yet, he introduces this later discussion by referring the reader to the *Philosophie des Rechts*. Hence, Green could not have failed to be aware of this earlier discussion. Alberto de Sanctis has raised the possibility (merely as a possibility) that Green could be referring to Hegel's development of this idea in *The Philosophy of History*, giving Green's manuscript a date of 1866 (personal communication). In its favour, it should noted that the thirty year old Green would have had access to Sibree's English translation of *The Philosophy of History* (published in December 1857). It would seem odd however, for Green to quote from one book (*The Philosophy of Right*) if he wished to allude to another (*The Philosophy of History*).

8   'Of the beginnings of his interest in philosophy [at Rugby School] only one or two traces remain; he refers himself in 1852 to a "tough bit of Aristotle" set in an examination, which he was the only one to make out, and a schoolfellow [Henry Sidgwick] tells of his attempt to impart some "elementary metaphysical conceptions" in connexion with a bridge on the Newbold Road; "he endeavoured to make me understand that we each of us saw a different bridge."' Nettleship, *Memoir*, pp.xiv–xv, quoting MS letter from Henry Sidgwick to Charlotte Bryon Green, 1 August 1882, Green's Papers, Balliol College.

9   Nettleship, *Memoir*, pp.xvi–xvii. I am grateful to Peter Nicholson for his thoughts on these issues (personal communication).

10 An English summary and analysis of the *Philosophy of Right* was published in 1855, although this did not include a translation of the relevant passage from the preface. TC Sandars, 'Hegel's Philosophy of Right', in *Oxford Essays. Contributed by Members of the University* (London: John W Parker, 1855), pp.213–50.

11 Once again I am grateful to Ben Wempe for this suggestion (personal communication).

12 Wempe, *TH Green's Theory of Positive Freedom*, pp.22–3.

13 The title-page of the notebook from which is comes reads (not in Green's hand): 'T.H. Green: IV A8: Notebook – Divinity. Pages at end on Political Philosophy.'

14 'Notebook: Notes for lectures on early Christianity', Green's Papers, Balliol College, Oxford (see Thomas, *Moral Philosophy of TH Green*, p.385).

15 TH Green, 'Popular Philosophy in its Relation to Life', *North British Review*, vol. 48 (March 1868), pp.133–63; reprinted in Green, *Works*, vol. 3, pp.92–125. TH Green, 'General Introduction to Vol. 1' and 'Introduction to the Moral Part of the Treatise', in TH Green and TH Grose (eds.) *A Treatise of Human Nature...and Dialogues Concerning Natural Religion by David Hume*, 4 vols. (London: Longmans, Green, 1874), vol.1, pp.1–71, and vol. 2, pp.1–71, respectively; reprinted in Green, *Works*, vol. 1, 1–371.

[16] David Hume, *Philosophical Works*, 4 vols. (Edinburgh: Adam Black, William Tait, and Charles Tait, 1824; 2nd ed. 1826).

[17] Nettleship, *Memoir*, p.lxi. See further *ibid.*, pp.lx–lxxiv.

[18] Nettleship, *Memoir*, pp.xci–xcii.

[19] TH Green, *Works*, vol. 3, pp.186–9, 190–206, and 207–20, respectively.

[20] Nettleship, 'Preface', in Green, *Works*, vol. 3, p. vii.

[21] Henry Nettleship's involvement is noted in the Balliol catalogue (see Thomas, *Moral Philosophy of TH Green*, pp.380, 386).

[22] Even though the latter are headed 'Notes on the Epistle to the Galatians', the manuscript appears to be as complete and finished as the other two sets of lectures on the New Testament.

[23] Helen Bosanquet, *Bernard Bosanquet: A short account of his life* (London: Macmillan, 1924), p.28.

[24] Bernard Bosanquet, 'Unvisited Tombs', in his *Some Suggestions in Ethics* (London: MacMillan, 1918), pp.69–70.

[25] Nicholas Griffin (ed.) *Selected Letters of Bertrand Russell. The Private Years 1884–1914* (London: Routledge, 1992), pp.184–5.

[26] Russell's reaction may well have been influenced by his own treatment at the hands of his examiners (including Ward) for a Trinity Fellowship in 1896. See Ray Monk, *Bertrand Russell, 1872–1921: The Spirit of Solitude* (London: Jonathan Cape, 1996), pp.104–5. On Russell and Moore at this time, see further *ibid.*, pp.116–7.

[27] Griffin (ed.) *Selected Letters of Bertrand Russell*, p.186.

[28] George Edward Moore, 'The Nature of Judgment', *Mind*, vol. 8, no. 30 ns (April 1899), pp.176–93.

[29] George Edward Moore, 'Freedom', *Mind*, vol. 7, no. 26 ns (April 1898), pp.179–204.

[30] Henry Sidgwick, Critical Notice of D.G. Ritchie, *Natural Rights*, *Mind*, vol. 4, no.15 ns (July 1895), pp. 384–8. David George Ritchie, *Natural Rights. A criticism of some political and ethical conceptions* (London: George Allen and Unwin, 1894).

Part 1
Thomas Hill Green

[Rudiments of 'The Philosophy of Aristotle' and related texts.][1]
[ca.1866-7]

[Rudiment 1.]

Disrepute of 'philosophy'. Two reasons.

(1) So much of its results already worked into life.

(2) Its claims and office misapprehended.

(1) really increases need of it. Each result of spiritual activity, when worked into life, if not recognized by spirit as spiritual, increases burden of latter.

Theology and physical science.

Futility of attempt to retain psychology and logic, as distinct from physical sciences, while 'ontology' is abandoned.

Common sense, religious feeling, and positive science – these three hold divided empire over the consciousness of our time. Each hostile to the rest, they yet make common cause against the enemy of whom, though he scarcely holds up his head in England, it is rumoured from Germany that his method is not strictly inductive, that he claims to know God through no higher revelation than his reason, and that though he neither robs temples nor erects barricades, he in a way of his own turns the world upside down.[2] A consideration of the causes and history of this three-fold hostility, may give us a clearer view of the claims and office of that form of spiritual activity which provokes it.

[Rudiment 2.]

Where the sciences end, philosophy begins. The object it deals with is that result of experience, which the sciences have elicited. This material, as left by the sciences, is not yet consciously appropriated by the thinking spirit. In order that it may become so, the spirit must trace its own activity in its creation.

[Rudiment 3.]

Between the wisdom of the world and philosophy there is an ancient feud.

1

[Rudiment 4.][3]

There is a sense in which, as the domain of positive knowledge advances, the difficulties of metaphysical philosophy increase. The metaphysician, as he is told depreciatingly but with truth, adds nothing to the sum of existing knowledge. He establishes no new facts by induction, he has nothing to do with evidence, he does not seek by the discovery of uniformities in 'contingent matter' to make that intelligible which was unintelligible before. His concern is with the analysis of that which is already known, and with the new synthesis which results therefrom. Penetrating the intelligible world, he seeks to disentangle its elements, and to 'put them together' again no longer as a material presented[4] from without, but as the complex realization, the organized body, of the spirit which contemplates them. (He is not a mathematician, or chemist, a physiologist or psychologist, but he re-adjusts (or ought to readjust) the processes pursued by all in a new order of unity and necessity, as successive determinations of the Divine spirit, whose thoughts he 'thinks after Him'.)[5] (He professes none of the sciences in particular, but he ascertains what is given, what received, by thought in each, and the dependence of the received on the given.) The ridicule which the assertion of such an office excites is a witness to its difficulty and remoteness from ordinary interests.

The H. theory of sensible world (l l) and the S: practice of def: are said to have formed the philosophic parentage of Pl:-[6]

[Rudiment 5.]

H.'s[7] philosophy result of activity of self-conscious thought. Impossible till this had attained great distinctiveness.

Yet leaves no room for it. Makes man a mere work of nature – passive, not constructive. Then why not in a 'state of nature'?

Why has he take to account of his own general good, and social good?

To say to the man of morbid self-consciousness, 'don't think but act', is as if in dealing with a patient whose enfeebled circulation results from a bad digestion the doctor were to try to stop the digestion altogether in order to strengthen the circulation.

If his pleasure is merely that of the most gifted of animals, his misery is a peculiar and absolutely original privilege.

'Custom hangs upon him with a weight' not 'almost' but altogether 'deep as life'.[8]

[Rudiment 6.]

In popular language, Platonism is the antithesis of all science of facts. The mystic to whom the real world seems a barrier between himself and the source of light, the ideal-monger, from whom it exacts longer methods than suit his impatience, the juggler, calling himself a spiritualist who finds it a limitation on the possibilities of frightened curiosity, which yield his harvest, all alike shelter themselves under the name of Plato.[9] It is a strange fate to have befallen the memory of one whose master had brought down philosophy from heaven to earth.[10] The modern Platonists perhaps are scarcely conscious of the discipline they must have undergone to be Platonists in Plato's own time. The spiritualist must have been ready to define spirit. The mystic must have been ready to give a reasoned account of his mysticism, the idealist to qualify himself for the realization of his ideals by discipline in the sole existing sciences.

[Rudiment 7.]

The universe involves a relation of two elements – necessary and contingent. That the contingent is not merely contingency is implied in the fact of its being in relation to the necessary. It is, in truth, that which is evermore being systematized and so becoming necessary. We may, however, abstract the necessary element from the contingent, and treat it as a system not yet applied to that which it systematizes, remembering at the same time that in its truth it implies such an application, i.e. that when thought *out* it is found to necessitate it.

This gives the distinction between Logic or Metaphysic on the one hand, and the philosophy of Nature and Man (Spirit) which is the true *applied* Logic on the other.

The same doctrine may be otherwise put thus. The universe is a system of thought. It cannot then be said that Logic has to do with thought as form, the sciences with things as given matter. For all thought is such, only as a thinking about some-*thing*, and all things are such, only as *thought* about. 'Formal' thought is nothing without a matter. We may distinguish however between thought when its matter *is* its own, and thought when its matter *becomes* its own: in other words between *pure* and *applied* ideas.

The former may then be regarded as *formative* to the latter.

Now the *applied* ideas as resulting from a reduction of the unknown to the known, partake of the infinity of the unknown. You may have one without another. No one of them is absolutely necessary to all thinking. The *pure* ideas on the other hand, involving no assimilation by thought of that which had not previously been thought, are brought by thought to all its acts, i.e. are necessarily involved in all thinking.

Logic is the science of these pure or necessary ideas as involved (1) in intuition, (2) in conception, (3) in judgement, (4) in reasoning.

[Rudiment 8.]

Is moral sense, according to Hume, *source* of virtuous action?[11] If it is, how is this compatible with statement that motive to a virtuous action is never regard to virtue?

If it is not, why contrast it, as the active, with reason as the inactive.

The self

Popular philosophy, with its division of the soul into reason and feeling, as mutually exclusive parts, was too strong for him.[12]

[Rudiment 9.]

'The good life, as uniform, excludes passion, as variable.' This arises from too abstract notion of unity,[13] as mere __, and not manifold in unity.

All thinking search for unity. Eleatics found this in abstraction of being of whatever we know, we say that it 'is.' This one *being* is same in all things; it alone is real, variety a delusion.[14] But Being, from which all variety is excluded, has no qualities – is nothing. As 'Unity' has no meaning except as relative to variety, so if we exclude 'God' as ἀμετάβολος ['unchangeable'] from all relation to variety, we shut him out from the world, and if – reason...from passion, it is mere name.

Rational life not a uniformity, but a harmony. Manifold in unity. Drama represents such a harmony.

Dramatic imitation, and flute-music excluded on same principle, viz: that the good man, like God, is ἀμετάβολος ['unchangeable'].[15]

Drama represents a variety of passions;

Flute-music expresses – [a variety of passions]

All passion implies violent transition from previous state: if the passions various in kind, so much the worse.

Passion as the manifold opposed to reason as uniform. But the uniform has no meaning, except in relation to the manifold.

So reason with Plato tends to become an empty form, of which no positive functions can be predicated.

Parallel in Eleatic 'One'.

Does the drama tend to unify the manifold of passion? Yes, in so far as it exhibits the strife of passion tending to one result – realization of idea.

'Purifies passions by pity and terror.'[16] Assimilates them with ideas. You can't *think* about passions, in which you are personally interested. You can about those with which you merely sympathize.

Thus, by thinking about latter, the former take more intellectual character.

[Rudiment 10.]

Question as to idea of goodness in individual –
  – as to authority of outward standards
  – as to freedom   aspiration.

_____

takes sensuous[17] experience as ready-made.[18]

Subjects 'moral feeling' to some analysis but in last resort takes it as giving consciousness of 'felt-thing'.

As thus extended, it may be made to carry anything, for every object of thinking, man may become object of 'feeling' – but in any case feeling must remain (1) merely subjective – valid for the feeling individual only, (2) merely passive.

Self – love as an effective [....?] self [....?....?....?] principle.'

Conscience and suffering.

[Rudiment 11.]

'Nature never did betray the heart that loved her';[19] no more did speculative philosophy. As we have seen it is no business of hers to edify; she has risen to ask what really is; she cannot return to the lower ground where the question 'what should be' has a meaning. She seeks not to produce pleasure or to lighten pain, but to know pleasure and pain in their truth. Yet since to know pleasure in its truth is itself the purest pleasure, since the recognition of the Spirit, of the world as Spiritual is the condition of that free movement which is essential bliss, the philosopher may say of this recognition in its gradual progress, as the poet of idealized nature, and for the same reason ' 'Tis her privilege to lead from joy to joy.'[20] (As the poet, traversing the world of sense, which he spiritualizes by the aid of the forms of beauty, finds himself ever at home, yet never in the same place, so the philosopher while he ascends the courts of the intelligible world is conscious of a presence which is always his own, yet always fresh, always lightened with the smile of a divine and eternal youth. Everything is new to him, yet nothing strange. For him nature works; and man, for him kings reign, and princes decree justice. The results of art and science, of religion and law, are all to him 'workings of one mind, features of the same face'.[21] Yet are the workings and the features infinite. No longer a servant, but a Son, he rules as over his own house: in it he moves freely, and with the confidence which comes of freedom.) He builds on no hypotheses, which the advancing tide of discovery may overflow: he has no crystalline vault above him[22] which scepticism may crack, and chaos could come again, self-conscious thought is his heaven above, and his earth beneath. It is the principle upon[23] which, the element in which, he re-fashions the world – a principle which has no fear of being superseded, for it knows itself to be the creator of every rival that can dispute its priority; an element which, as limited only by itself, can expand to the fulness [sic] of all reality. With such a heaven, etc., he can pass unheeded[24] the scorn of common-sense and the commiseration of an hysterical religiosity. He resents neither the one nor the other, for seeing each in its truth, he knows that common-sense would not be common-sense if it did not scorn, nor religiosity religiosity if it did not commiserate [with] him. He turns the other cheek, and goes on his way, confident that if true to his calling,

    'neither evil tongues,
    Rash judgements nor the sneers of selfish men
    Can e'er prevail against him.'[25]

[Rudiment 12.]
    It is now thirty-five years[26] since Hegel in the well-known words, 'Whatever is real is rational, Whatever is rational is real', announced the result of all preceding philosophy, the principle of

all that was to follow.[27] Throughout a heroic[28] life, which should be to this[29] age what the life of Socrates was to his own; in writings which are to the philosophy of the[30] world all and more than all[31] that those of Aristotle were to the philosophy of Greece, he unfolded and enforced this truth.[32] But, like Aristotle, he left no successor. He articulated the message which had been forming itself for utterance in the mouths of Kant, Fichte and Schelling,[33] and his countrymen, as if stunned by its greatness, at first wondered and applauded then roused themselves to discuss and in discussing to mutilate it, not hitherto to apply it in its fullness. It has been mistranslated, against the constant protest of its author, out of the terms of reason and into those of sense, of sentiment, of the common understanding. (Mistranslated, as by Heine, into the terms of sense,[34] it becomes the tempter's truism, 'whatever is pleasant is an object of desire';),[35] and by each mistranslation it becomes practically pernicious and scientifically insufficient. Mistranslated, as, into terms of the common understanding, it becomes the doctrine of Feuerbach, 'what is human, etc.,' which leaves religion unexplained.[36] Mistranslated into terms of sentiment, it becomes the maxim of moral emasculation, 'Idealize what is real; try to realize what is merely ideal', which leaves evil and ugliness unexplained. Mistranslated as by Heine into terms of sense it leaves morality unexplained, the divine truth becomes the tempter's truism, 'Every[37] pleasant [thing] is to be desired, whatever is to be desired is pleasant.' Such was the natural sequel of the enunciation of a principle which the spirit of man had been so far educated as to suggest to its own highest interpreter, but not yet to interpret for itself. The physical sciences were still immersed in matter – 'in disconnection, dead and spiritless'[38]—: the political world seemed to be still dominated by arbitrary will, the religious by superstition. Thus though Hegel by the method – which, though often subjected to the cheap ridicule of ignorance, has never been exploded or superseded – reduced the facts of the world to stages in a system of thought, the facts were still too repugnant[39] to the actual consciousness of the age for the reduction to retain its interest.[40] The exhibition of the real as rational and rational as real was simply the scientific form of the anticipatory belief in the redemption[41] of the world, which Christianity had introduced. Yet as the Christian belief first attained in the Hegelian philosophy a distinct rational consciousness of itself, so this consciousness has in its turn to wait appropriation and application by mankind. (The trumpet has spoken, but there has been no armed throng to answer.[42] The full philosophical equipment has not been found in the youth of Germany.)[43] The spiritual hunger was there, but not the positive knowledge or the hold on reality.

[Rudiment 13.]

No one, who has ever fairly let down his bucket into that well, has failed to draw it up full and running over. But the every-day critic, who vanquishes Hegel in a sentence, has come to the well without either rope or bucket. His knowledge of other philosophy is commonly scanty, and limited by false antitheses between Aristotle and Plato, between experience and intuition; of philo-Genesis[44] of Hegel himself he knows nothing at all; a strict speculative method he not only has never been trained in, but expressly repudiates, under the popular notion that philosophic truth is to be got at by impromptu guess-work. Thus he has nothing to draw with, and the well is deep. He looks in, and is for a moment attracted by a luminous [?] dark gleam of distant water, but it is beyond his reach. He soon tires of an ineffectual gaze, and turns to the surface-waters, where the multitude slakes its thirst. This is quite natural, but he need not go on to proclaim, as a quietus to all subsequent explorers in the same depths, that he is 'unsatisfied' and therefore the well is empty.

[Rudiment 14.]

We may admit the pretension of philosophy to be the reproduction in man of the infinite all-comprehensive thought of God, without allowing that it involves on that account an indifference to practical interests. Such conception of the divine life in man is only worthy of that primitive system which identified the Godhead with the bare abstraction of Being. If the divine nature, to be infinite, must be void of distinctive relation, and attribute, as involving limitations, then Buddha was right in the annihilation holding...to be the true entry into it. If God cannot delight in the work of his own hands, because such delight implies an external object which breaks his identity into difference,[45] then the most absolute indifference is the closest assimilation to him. But if speculative thought has now substituted for the idea of a limitless, lifeless, substance, (to the adequacy of which it is itself the witness), that of a spirit, limited but knowing itself in its limitations, abandoning itself to find itself in another, vibrating from one pole which is itself yet ceases to be so, to an opposite which becomes itself, and back to this which in turn ceases to be itself to the other which again becomes so,[46] the philosopher loses not the divine likeness when he gives himself to temporary interests, that he may carry them back to the universe of his own thought, or when he lives from day to day [so] that the days may become moments in the eternal being. His father works hitherto, and he works. In his spiritual manhood he no longer asks the childish question, why God made an evil world? His knowledge of the 'What' in its fullness renders unmeaning all questions as to the 'Wherefore'. The world is made, or rather is eternally in making, and it is for him to penetrate and reproduce God's workmanship.

[Rudiment 15.]

Every one must confess that if asked in ordinary society what was the merit of such a man[47] towards his age, it would be difficult to return an explicit and intelligible answer. He was a philosopher. Did he then discover an application of the doctrine of averages, or a syllogistic figure? or a new instance of mental association? or a new motive to an accustomed virtue? Did he find a new excuse for an old sin, or make two names applicable where one had been applied before? Did he show that morality means the price of corn, and religion the fear of thunder-storms? He did none of these things, and not having done them, his greatness is indemonstrable to the many. The vague dignity, which still attaches to the name of philosophy is thus seen to depend on those applications of it by which it is identified with any kind of scientific or empirical speculation. The philosophy which is neither physical nor psychological, neither moral nor political, what is it? The questioner, like jesting Pilate [John 19:5], will scarcely stay for answer. Not from indifference to truth, but because he believes the answer to be superfluous the truth is sufficiently assured to him by other methods, while the round-about road of Metaphysic leads nowhere if not to the abyss.

[Rudiment 16.]

We only know that a light, which might have broken the thick darkness now hanging over English philosophy, has gone out, and question ourselves more closely as to the nature of the fire which we wait for, and which we had looked to him to kindle.[48]

It is something more than a formality when an untried teacher recalls the memory and example of one who not only preceded him in his office but was a guide in the path of science which he hopes to pursue. Within the limits of that peculiar vacancy, of which the familiar friends of my predecessor must at this moment be conscious, it is not for such of us as but watched him at a distance, to intrude.

[1] [TH Green, 'The Philosophy of Aristotle' first appeared in *The North British Review*, vol. 45, no. 89 (September 1866), pp.105–44. References in these notes are to Green, *Works*, vol. 3, pp.46–91. Rudiment 16 must have been written slightly later than 'The Philosophy of Aristotle', as may have Rudiment 15 (see notes 47 and 48 below). For the full caveats about this title, see the editorial introduction, pp. xviii–xix.]

[2] [Likely to be a reference to either Kant or Hegel. For example, Immanuel Kant, 'Religion within the Boundaries of Mere Reason', in I Kant, *Religion and Rational Theology*, ed. AW Wood, trans. AW Wood and G di Giovanni (Cambridge University Press, 1996), pp.55–215. Georg WF Hegel, *Lectures on the Philosophy of Religion Together with a Work on the proofs of the existence of God*, trans. Rev. EB Speirs and J Burdon Sanderson, 3 vols. (London: Kegan Paul, Trench, Trubner, 1895), esp. vol. 1, 'Introduction'.]

[3] [Various sentences from this rudiment appear – either verbatim or in a modified form – in Green, 'The Philosophy of Aristotle', *Works*, vol. 3, p.55. I am grateful to Ben Wempe for pointing out this and other instances where these rudiments appear in 'The Philosophy Aristotle' (see the remaining notes to these 'Rudiments').]

[4] [MS orig.: 'grown'.]

[5] [The exclamation 'O God, I am thinking Thy thoughts after Thee' is found in Kepler's *When Studying Astronomy*, and refers to the discovery of the laws of astronomy. Johannes Kepler (1571–1630), German astronomer and devout Lutheran.]

[6] ['The Heraclitean theory of the sensible (in itself not so much a theory as a prophecy), and the Socratic practice of definition, are said by Aristotle to have formed the philosophic parentage of Plato.' Green, 'The Philosophy of Aristotle', p.55.]

[7] [Presumably a reference to Heraclitus of Ephesus (ca.540–ca.480BC), philosopher.]

[8] ['And custom lies upon thee with a weight,
Heavy as frost, and deep almost as life!'

William Wordsworth, 'Ode. Intimations of Immortality from Recollections of Eraly Childhood', his *Poetical Works: Cambridge edition*, revised by PD Sheats (Boston: Houghton Mifflin, 1982), p.355 (stanza 8, ll.28–9). Poem first published 1807.]

[9] [Plato (ca.428–ca.348BC), Athenian philosopher. The 'barrier' refers to the curtain which obscures the torch-lights from the view of the prisoners in Plato's famous cave (*Republic*, 514b–515a); on the utopianism of the *Republic* see *ibid.*, 471c–2a.]

[10] ['...As in a special sense their originator, Socrates is the father of metaphysic and logic.

'This may seem strange credit to take to one who is popularly known as having brought down philosophy from heaven to earth, as having discarded all speculation about the "nature of things," and directed man to know himself.' Green, 'Philosophy of Aristotle', p.47.]

[11] [David Hume (1711–76), Scottish historian and Enlightenment philosopher.]

[12] [A modified version of this sentence appeared in Green's 1868 essay 'Popular Philosophy in its Relation to Life', in his discussion of Joseph Butler: 'His value as an ethical writer is due to the same cause which makes his speculation perplexed and self-contradictory. A shallower and narrower view of the moral life would have fitted more neatly into the received theory of knowledge of the soul, which alone he had at his command. *Popular philosophy was too strong for him. Its division of the soul into reason and feeling as mutually exclusive "parts,"* its doctrine that the reality of spiritual processes may be known by observing what goes on "within one's own breast," are incompatible with any just view of the process by which the actual moral world has been created, and which it involves; for it is of the essence of this process that, in a true sense, the whole is in every part of it, and the "heart" of the individual, though the deposit of its results, belies the source whence it came.' (*Works*, vol. 3, p.104, emphasis added).]

[13] [MS del.: 'uniformity'.]

[14] [The Eleatics were pre-Socratic philosophers whose principal members were Parmenides (b. ca.510BC), Zeno of Elea (b. ca.490BC) and Melissus of Samos (fl. ca.441–440BC). The Eleatics denied the reality of change and plurality. The notion of 'the One' was developed with greatest force by Melissus of Samos, who claimed that there existed only one temporally and spatially infinite substance, and that there was no void.]

[15] [Plato, *Republic*, 376c–83b, 398c–403c, 573c–608b.]

[16] [Aristotle, *Poetics*, 1449b28–9. Cf. Edward Caird, *Hegel* (Edinburgh and London: Blackwood, 1883), p.26.]

[17] [MS del.: 'sensible'.]

[18] [The words appear thus in the manuscript.]

[19] ['Knowing that Nature never did betray
The heart that loved her; 'tis her privilege,
Through all the years of this our life, to lead
From joy to joy:...'

William Wordsworth, 'Lines, Composed a Few Miles Above Tintern Abbey, on Revisiting the Banks of the Wye During a Tour, July 13, 1798', in his *Poetical Works*, p.93 (ll.122–5).]

[20] [See the preceding note.]

[21] [Wordsworth, 'The Prelude', in his *Poetical Works*, p.167 (Bk 6, l.636). The passage from the opening bracket to this point appears in Green, 'The Philosophy of Aristotle', p.90.]

[22] [This phrase is conventionally taken as an allusion to Ezekiel 1, esp. v.22: 'And the likeness of the firmament upon the heads of the living creature *was* as the

colour of the terrible crystal, stretched forth over their heads above.']

[23] [MS orig.: 'from'.]

[24] [MS orig.: 'put aside'.]

[25] ['The mind that is within us, so impress
With quietness, and beauty, and so feed
With lofty thoughts, that neither evil tongues,
Rash judgements, not the sneers of selfish men,

...

Shall e'er prevail against us, or disturb
Our cheerful faith, that all which we behold
Is full of blessings. ...'
Wordsworth, 'Tintern Abbey,', in his *Poetical Works*, p.93 (ll.126–34).]

[26] [Strangely, this is apparently an allusion to Hegel's death in 1831.]

[27] ['What is rational is actual and what is actual is rational', GWF Hegel, *Philosophy of Right*, trans. by TM Knox (Oxford: Clarendon, 1967), p.10. First German edition published 1821. Cf. Green, 'The Philosophy of Aristotle', p.47.]

[28] [Wempe omits 'heroic'. Ben Wempe, *TH Green's Theory of Positive Freedom* (Exeter: Imprint Academic, 2004), p.23. All references to Wempe in these notes are to the transcription he gives of the first of these fragments (*ibid.*, pp.23–4).]

[29] [Wempe reads: 'his'.]

[30] [Wempe adds 'modern' here.]

[31] [Wempe omits: 'all'.]

[32] [Socrates (ca.470–399BC), Athenian philosopher and Plato's teacher. Aristotle (384–322BC), Macedonian philosopher and Plato's pupil.]

[33] [Immanuel Kant (1724–1804), German idealist philosopher. Johann Gottlieb Fichte (1762–1814), German idealist philosopher. Friedrich Wilhelm Joseph Schelling (1775–1854), German idealist philosopher and one-time friend of Hegel.]

[34] [Heinrich Heine (1797–1856), German writer, whose thought was influenced by Hegel's Berlin lectures which he attended as an undergraduate. The thought of Saint-Simon turned the poetry of his middle age (ca. 1827–33) towards, in one scholar's words, the 'exaltation of the senses' (SS Prawer, *Heine The Tragic Satirist: A study of the later poetry 1827–1856* (Cambridge University Press, 1961), pp.22–35).]

[35] [Green appears to have added the parentheses when it became clear that this sentence would be only a first draft. The second version appears shortly afterwards in the text.]

[36] ['What, then, *is* the nature of man...? Reason, Will, Affection. ... Man exists to think, to love, to will. ... [W]hat is the end of reason? ... Freedom of the will.' Ludwig Andreas Feuerbach, *The Essence of Christianity*, trans. by G Eliot (London: John Chapman, 1854), p.5. Ludwig Andreas Feuerbach (1804–72), Bavarian theologian and materialist philosopher. An atheist, the central claim of his *Das Wesen des Cristenthums* (*The Essence of Christianity*) (1841) was that the various conceptions of God are projections by men of what they

believe they themselves would be if perfect.]

[37] [MS orig.: 'what is'.]

[38] [William Wordsworth, 'The Excursion', in his *Poetical Works*, p.459 (Bk. IV, l.962).]

[39] [MS del.: 'alien'.]

[40] [I have revised the punctuation of this sentence as Green's manuscript reads very oddly: 'Thus though Hegel by the method, which though often subjected to the cheap ridicule of ignorance has never been exploded or superseded, reduced the facts of the world to stages in a system of thought the facts were still too repugnant [MS del.: 'alien'] to the actual consciousness of the age for the reduction to retain its interest.']

[41] [Wempe omits 'of the anticipatory belief in the redemption'.]

[42] ['So the people shouted when *the priests* blew with the trumpets: and it came to pass, when the people heard the sound of the trumpet, and the people shouted with a great shout, that the wall fell down flat, so that the people went up into the city [of Jericho], every man straight before him, and they took the city.' (Josh. 6.20)]

[43] [Wempe moves the parenthetical sentences to the end of this fragment.]

[44] [MS del.: 'German'.]

[45] [MS orig.: 'duality'.]

[46] [MS del.: 'the philosopher need not fear to alienate himself from the divine by enthusiasm'.]

[47] [Possibly a reference to James Riddell (see next note), although Green may mean, say, Hegel, Socrates, Plato or Aristotle.]

[48] [Probably a reference to Rev. James Riddell (1823–66), fellow of Balliol from 1844, classical scholar, whose works included editions of Homer's *Odyssey* and Plato's *Apology*. Green replaced Riddell on the college teaching staff following Riddell's death in September 1866. This was also the month in which Green's 'The Philosophy of Aristotle' was published in *The North British Review*.]

Metaphysic of Ethics, Moral Psychology, Sociology or Science of Sittlichkeit.[1]
[ca. late 1860s – early 1870s]

[§1 The Interrelation of Ethical Subjects and Objects.]

Nature = system of sensations.[2] That which makes the sensations a system is reason, that[3] in consciousness which combines, and constitutes permanent objects.

A stone = certain mode of consciousness[4] of ours, which reason, other mode of consciousness, combines in a thing as its[5] cause. But the sensations which we refer to it are not of a kind to make us think of it as itself sensitive. Object in this case neither feels nor thinks. Neither feeling, nor reason, which together constitute it, are in it.

An animal, in like manner, = certain sensations, etc. But in this case the sensations referred to object are such that we think of the object as itself sensitive. – Object, here, feels but does not think. In case of man, the reason, which in correlation[6] with feeling constitutes him, (as it does stone or horse) is also in him, forms his consciousness. In virtue of this, he knows his own nature. Nature is *revealed* to him, which it is not to animal.

If this be true account of nature, it would seem that relation between reason and sense *constitutes* nature as well as moral world. True, but not relation between reason and sense as in us.

Nature is *there – given*. We find it, don't *make* it – *we*, that is, in our limited human personality. The reason that makes it must be communicated to us, if it is to be 'revealed' to us.[7] But the natural world is made apart from this communication – is there, whether we understand it or no. Not so with moral world. It is by reason, as communicated to man and not otherwise, that this world is constituted.

Moral relation not one of matter to sense, but of sense to self-conscious reason, the latter being not (as sense in relation to matter) passive, but [originative].[8] From this relation moral 'facts' all result.

The constructive action of reason upon sense in moral life of mankind is a gradual process. A formal unity pervades it, but its results (a) [in] different ages and nations, (b) in different individuals of same age and nation, vary greatly. Thus (1) moral 'facts' are not in themselves *fixed* in way in which *natural* are, and as they all consist in, or arise out of, relation between self-conscious reason as in man and the sensible (2) each man etc.

In what does (1) Moral Philosophy differ from (2) Physical Science? Answer to this question gives true point of view from which to regard modern speculation on Ethics.

Three popular answers:

(a) 'Physical Science deals with world revealed to us by our senses; these are its test, to these it appeals. Moral Philosophy, with some inner consciousness, the facts of which (if so determined and Universal) can only be ascertained by each man's individual experience. Hence cumbered with diversity of views, which can never be got rid of.'

(b) 'Object of (2) consists of uniform coexistences and sequences which by experiment can be precisely ascertained. Object of (1) cannot be got at[9] by experiment; it is thus impossible to ascertain precisely what does happen in any test of moral action. Further in moral action there is an element of wilfulness, a possibility of unmotived[10] origination,[11] which if you could ascertain all conditions of a given act, would make it impossible to conclude that what results from these conditions in the given case would result in another.'

(c) 'There is no such element of wilfulness in object matter of Moral Philosophy. This matter consists of facts[12] of social life, which only differ from the 'natural' in their greater complexity, and in difficulty of applying experiment to them, which however only differs in degree from that of applying it to phenomenal living animal.'

As to (a), mere sense 'moral,' no world, can ascertain no 'facts', for it is not a consciousness of relations, and without these no 'world', no 'facts.'

Sense, indeed, itself a relation, and one of passivity on part of animal towards something without, but it is not intelligently conscious of such relation, and the intelligent consciousness of it cannot be explained as relation of passivity. It implies putting together [elements] which to us, as *passive*, are detached.

The 'facts' of physical world are not then 'sensible', as if not 'revealed' by sense, but intelligible. The intelligible physical fact, however, is a relation of something to sense. It is a fact, in understanding of which (as in all understanding) we are active, but in constitution of which we are passive.

The moral 'facts', however, we constitute as well as understand. They are *not*, indeed, merely facts of each man's consciousness but result of action of that self-consciousness, which is in each man that contemplates them; they are to be found in actual history and achievement of mankind.

But (2) each man can understand them only in their relation to himself, and this relation varies accordingly as self-conscious reason in him is developed so as to be adequate to this reason as expressed in highest actual moral life of men.

It cannot be said to moral, as to physical philosopher 'here are certain definite, though complex, facts, quite independent of variable human consciousness; analyse them.'

The human consciousness, which seeks to analyse the 'moral facts' (sc. that which is merely given, as opposed to what is constructed, in that motive)[13] has made – is making – them. In attempt to analyse justice, honour, etc., the just or honourable man necessarily reads himself into them.

No datum derived from other science can be applied here (as mathematical data in case of natural sciences).

The direction must be simply 'think not about your own experience as series of observed facts – but re-think the process by which human thought has expressed itself in the moral ideas and institutions which are heritage of civilized man.'

This operation of re-thinking not properly (a) one of observation nor (b) is its object one's own experience as such, but the experience of mankind. This indeed can only be dealt with as reflected in consciousness of the 'moral thinker', but value of his philosophy will depend on degree to which his personal consciousness gathers up results of moral progress of the world.

Moral theory thus not without test. Is it adequate to actual moral achievement of mankind? Still in appealing to individuals (say, the 'Epicurean pig')[14] one cannot correct his interpretation of this achievement by pointing to definite fact inconsistent with his interpretation, for every 'moral fact' to him coloured by his interpretation.

As to (2) regular sequence between motive and act in moral world, otherwise we could know nothing of that past. No unaccountable, unmotived, origination of any human event, coming in between event and its assignable antecedents. But same self-consciousness present in motive as in act. This constitutes *formal* freedom, which becomes real in so far as the self-consciousness, instead of being simply passive and perceptive (which it never is absolutely) in regard to motive (as when motive is sensual pleasure) originates it, as when it constitutes a law to itself in shape of idea of duty, or recognizes state-law as its own.

This principle of freedom, though it does not make moral action arbitrary or unaccountable, makes it progressive. The determining motive of action to a man at any time is his past history as gathered up in self-conscious thought, which is essentially originative. Thus the motive does not act naturally or mechanically, reproducing what has been produced before. It gives new results. Hence impossibility of prediction. This impossibility greater in proportion as freedom is *real* in sense given above.

(Possibility of conversions, etc., arises from this that though self-indulgent man goes on uniformly taking sensual pleasures into his self-consciousness as motive, his thinking self, appropriating the moral ideas everywhere active about him, may re-act in new way on these pleasures.)

From the above appears fallacy of (c). Moral 'facts' differ from physical not merely in complexity, but in this, that they are 'phenomena' of a 'thing-in-itself' – the self-conscious and self-realising reason, which they don't fully represent, which stands towards them in attitude of perpetual negation. This negation, this self-withdrawal of the man from his acts, does not constitute a fixed measurable[15] fact, like relation of a force to its effects, yet it is the essential differentia of moral life in [the] individual and in humanity.[16] It is the rational source of all religion, as well as of 'new births' in nations and men.

The idea of God comes from, or rather is identical with, consciousness of self. Difficulties the same in regard to one as to other. His acts are and are not the man, just as the world is and is not God. Even the difficulties as to relation of God to *nature* (as distinct from what we call 'moral and spiritual world') same in kind as difficulties in regard to relation of self-conscious reason to animal organism in us.

Simple feeling of dependence sometimes assigned as origin of religion, but this not enough, because it implies no conscious communion with object towards which this feeling directed.

Its true source is the consciousness of the self (1) as objective, (2) as not only distinct from, but inadequately expressed by, actual human life.

God thus recognized (1) as 'alter ego' – object of most intimate communion, (2) as definitely known only through the moral life, as actually so far attained by man, (3) as yet 'transcending' this.

Earliest form of recognition of self as object is fetishism, which [was] refined into nature-worship. Then 'Gods in nature' petrified into 'substances' or 'forces', and man finds divine object, which is reflex of his self, in the originator of a moral life.

It is not that man leaves behind 'theology' and 'metaphysics', but that he finds the 'God' and 'thing-in-itself,' which in these several phases he found in nature, no longer there but in a self-conscious subject which finds expression in his own moral life, yet under such conditions of development through animal organism as forbid him absolutely to identify his actual moral self with it.

The 'new births', etc., not properly 'mysterious' or unaccountable.

Practically true that there is hope of 'conversion' for the most sensual man. But this does not mean a possibility of absolute breach in the continuity of his life, or any event in it for which no intelligible antecedent can be assigned. It means that even the most sensual notions do not determine a man simply and directly, but, as taken into a self, which is perpetually detaching itself from the ἐπιθυμητά ['object of desire'] which it adopts as its filling (hence vicious man never satisfied); that, further, there are ideas, institutions, 'providential arrangements' operative in the world, which in contact[17] at some point with sensual man's experience, may suggest new object of desire, which his will, in perpetual detachment from its habitual ἐπιθυμητά ['objects of desire'], may adopt instead.

Here on one hand is regular sequence of causes (recognized idea or the like, special relation of this to personal experience of sensual man, consequent new motive) but condition of its producing supposed result is the perpetual detachment of man from, and his reaction upon, his habitual motions.

[§2 Motivation and Responsibility.]

Spontaneous origination intervening between a man's state at any given time and his next act, but the given state is a state of self-consciousness: and therefore originative – a state in which [there is] perpetual reaction of self upon surroundings.

Series of human action regular, but origination in it at every stage.

(1) If human action not determined by motives, why educate? Yet unless the man, determined by the motive, is active in the

constitution of the motive, how account for the progressiveness of the moral education; for the fact that while motives are the same (if by them we mean outward inducements) their bearing upon the man changes so that a[n] idea of[18] pleasure, which determines his action directly at one time, at a later stage though still a pleasure affects it only as stimulating an impulse of resistance or self-mortification.

If man does not make the motive which determines, why punish? Possible answer to (2), in order to supply a new motive, viz: fear. Does then punishment act on man like whipping on a dog?[19]

If not merely so by excitement of remorse for past, then man must recognize the motive that has determined him to the action for which he is punished as [of] his own making.

If, again, by excitement of feeling of shame at prospect of doing punished act again, then he must both regard the act, the possible repetition of which makes him blush as one would be caused by himself, and have power of constructing a motive out of the physical pain of punishment quite other than the pain itself.

Is it consistent to maintain at once the regular sequence of the moral past, and the impossibility of predicting the moral future?

It is the distinction between that which is made, and that which is in making. Things natural, even where we ascribe growth and development to them, not properly *in making*. Change in nature merely consists in varying combinations of a fixed and permanent material, under action of uniform forces, so that what is added here is subtracted there.

We may say of next act of a man at any stage of his life (under mechanical metaphor) that it will be result of the mutual action of his circumstances (i.e. his past history and inducements operative about him) and the originative reason (which, otherwise than mechanically, takes the circumstances into itself, or bestows itself upon them).

The latter, to greater or less degree (what does this mean?) an unknown quantity: hence result cannot be certainly anticipated. So with nations.

When the act has been done, however, if we have full information about it, we can infer from it its cause; or, more precisely, we can ascertain between its nature and degree of the modifying action exercised by the 'originative reason' on the circumstances.

The thing which has been is *not* that which shall be. While it is only from his past that we can learn what is in man, yet we may know that what we thus learn of him is not all that is in him.

Nay, it is only from past of man that we can learn what is in God; but expression which this past exhibits of that θεῖον τι ['divinity'] in man, is not its full expression. It has wrought in him hitherto, but it is still working.

[§3 Moral Psychology as the Basis of Social Norms.]
(1) Metaphysic of Ethics. Consideration of nature of reason as self-related; thus as giving a law to itself, as originating action in expression of itself, and as source of objective moral world and of recognition on part of individual subject of that world as 'alter ego'.

Corresponds to consideration of the source of that Synthesis in Knowledge of Natural world, which appears in the true Categories – in holding-together of objects (sensations transformed into objects) as qualifying each other, as forming quantities, as measuring each other, e.g. as many in one, as modifications of a substance, as ordered by a cause. All these are modes in which reason imparts its own unity to sensations gradually taken into itself as its object.[20]

Metaphysics of Ethics goes very little way, for so soon as question arises, *what* is the law which reason gives to itself, *what* the action which it originates, it can only be answered by passing from reason in its abstraction to reason as manifested in real motives and acts. These, indeed, misunderstood except in relation to self-determining 'reason', but it, again, only *defined* by them.

On mere conception, however, of equality of reason, as self-determining principle, in all men, with its corollaries, rests whole science of jurisprudence. It takes no account of basis of motives as constituted by feelings, of qualifying circumstances, of degrees of virtue. It simply applies to the various occasions of life the *abstract* idea of independence of each person, with everything he can appropriate,[21] against every other.

(2) As applied to natural impulse of correlated absorption and production, it issues in various forms of desire and feeling, which are to be considered by 'Moral psychology.' (Theory of moral sentiments.)

(3) These again have given rise[22] to social relations, out of which arise (a) rights and obligations, the subject matter of 'science of right', specific duties and the agencies which *moralize* the individual.

For consideration of these there should be a 'science of society.' 'Moral Philosophy' in England has confined itself almost wholly to (2).[23]

'Conscience' = reason in form of moral sentiment: reason as operating in the personal feelings of individual, and qualified by them. Hence dark or light.

Jurisprudence (proper) considers various forms which obligation in each to abstain from interference with outward freedom of another takes according to circumstances. It is a science of obligations. On other hand Political Economy is a science of facts results. It assumes impulse to appropriate, and freedom of appropriation secured, which in society means free interchange. Given this principle, it enquires which result according to various complicated conditions of production and interchange. Every question of Political Economy proper resolves itself into an equation. You can no more 'violate laws of Political Economy' than you can violate laws of nature. You may (1) mistake those laws, and expect a result to follow from certain arrangements that can't follow; or (2) you may deliberately interfere with freedom of contract: this however violation of *right*: not of laws of Political Economy; or (3) you may legislate upon supposition that impulse of appropriation is, or ought to be, under certain conditions interfered with. This no 'violation of laws of Political Economy' which merely mean chains of results[24] following upon that impulse – which, given the impulse, follow by natural necessity.

However, just as though you can't violate laws of nature, yet there are certain duties which arise upon knowledge of those laws, which may be broken, so upon knowledge of laws of Political Economy, (which are properly natural laws) there arise new views of duty in certain respects – e.g. modification of duty to be 'ready to give and glad to distribute.' These duties may be disregarded, and such disregard is a 'violation of law' in moral sense.

[§4 Freedom, Desire and Will.]

Jurisprudence regards freedom as merely negative. Its 'obligations' are all ultimately obligations to *abstain*.[25]

It regards freedom (1) as freedom to act, not as freedom to will; hence (2) as realized simply in the state of universal abstention – state in which no one is his brother's keeper – not in an inner life of rationalized desires, and hence (3) as not implying 'Duty', i.e. a law for the will, not merely for the *act*; an 'obligation' to respect not other men in way of abstinence from interference but oneself in the way of actualizing one's possibilities; a 'right' not as against other men, but as against one's own nature, as a *mere nature*.[26]

Freedom as (1) means freedom for me to do or not to do, *if I desire* or will to do or not to do. In thus considering freedom of mere agent apart from motions or character of agent, which determine[27] his freedom, we are really considering self-determination of reason in its *abstraction*. There is a[28] universality in this, just as in considering the categories apart from actual knowledge, or God apart from world. The necessity *for us* of such abstract consideration derives from impotence to present objects to ourselves except under 'forms of intuition'[29] as separate (apart in space or successive in time) when we *know* them not to be so. This source of all the paradoxes of Philosophy.

Jurisprudence, thus resting on an hypothesis which is in a way false on account of its abstractness, has to be (and as matter of fact is) corrected by 'moral and political' considerations. Its ultimate lesson is 'what a man does, is to be done to him.' In violating right of another, he loves his own. An act, if the doer knows its nature, is his own: no further consideration of responsibility admissible by jurist. Practically, however, these rules modified by more general considerations. Hence, we come to regard punishment as reformatory, etc. The power to do or not to do, *if I desire*, actually determined by the desire – sc. the *strongest* desire. A certain appearance of moral freedom arises from conflict of desires in stage of imperfect habituation. Hence that young seem more 'free' than the old. Really suspense of equal conflict between desires quite different from alternative of doing or not doing between persistence of one desire and the direction of the bodily powers to act.

Doubtless we not always act from strongest desire. Question is whether this desire is an *appetite* or a *will* – whether the man is simply passive in regard to it or whether an active self-consciousness – a subject which at once knows itself and seeks to utter itself – constitutes it.

The moral philosopher, then, adopting latter alternative, unlike Jurist will concern himself not with freedom in its abstraction – not with reason as unapplied, or with mere form of self-determination – but with reason as really manifested in desire and constituting a *will*.

Thus applied, reason becomes to itself a something which 'should be' in opposition to something which 'is'. As merely self-contained, it could not give conception of the 'Sollen', nor again would a mere impulse[30] of production and appropriation give notion of something not yet, but *to be*, appropriated or produced.

We can only describe the conception in question as resulting from application of reason, which gives its own object, to this impulse, which thus becomes impulse to create or appropriate that which will satisfy a subject, that can only be satisfied with itself.

[§5 Freedom and Duty.]

Opposition (1) between consciousness of freedom in the self, with correlative conception of duty, and the wants and feelings, which alone define the self, and which yet all depend on relations to that which is without, ἕτερον ['the other']. Primitive consciousness of freedom = judgment 'I can.'

'This merely means that I am conscious of volition[31] and not of its causes.' If so, it would merely be the consciousness that I *can* do, what *I do*. Really it is consciousness that I *can* do what I *should do*. The presentation by man to himself of an object, not as already existing and to be *received*, but to be created, goes along with consciousness of freedom, and shows that this is not ignorance of the ἕτερον, which determines him, but witness of a real self-determination.

'May not the presentation, etc., be imaginary?' How then account for constructions of man, as exhibited in the arts and social institutions?

But very fact that freedom expresses itself in judgement. I *ought to*[32] *do*, shows that it is only in process of realisation. It gives *imperatives*, not judgments of fact. 'Do Duty for its own sake. Be free for sake of being free. Be determined by universal Law' all come to the same. – 'Fulfil that idea of what should be, just because it is that idea of what should be. If you allow its place to be tacitly taken by a generalization from satisfied wants, or if you look to its fulfilment as resulting in satisfaction of wants, you lose that freedom and become determined by the ἕτερον ['other'] which these wants constitute. If again you allow it to ordain now this and now that, it ceases to be the expression of that unchanging self; and becomes expression of mere present want, sc. determination by a ἕτερον ['other'].'

Ἀπορία [?] ['a difficulty']. 'Describe Duty or Freedom as Duty or Freedom to do *something*, and they cease to be Duty or Freedom for own sake. (Again, let 'universal law' prescribe *something*, and this must be relative to the particular circumstances and thus not fit to done universally.) (The something must be a *good*, sc. a satisfied want.) Without such definition of Duty and Freedom by an end external to each, they are unmeaning.'

The difficulty arises from actual 'Dualism' of the life we live as men. Our wants *do* to *us* in greater or less degree constitute an alien world, and in proportionate degree the definition of our conception of the πρακτον ['thing that should be done'] by the satisfaction of desire, makes that conception an alien law, in obeying which lose our freedom.

To the 'selfish' man, i.e. the man who just gratifies his strongest appetite, because it [is] such, without considering its relation to organization of human life, and without consciousness of satisfying others in satisfying himself, his desires are purely 'alien'. 'There is no reason in them.' His life one of 'heteronomy'; but, [...?] 'animal he is himself author of that "heteronomy"'.[33]

Just so far as man becomes 'unselfish', this 'alienation' ceases. The world, to which he is related through his wants, becomes *to him* what it is in itself, a rational world, and thus not 'alien.'

'This world, etc., rational in itself; yet we have to make it so; this implies that it is not so to begin with, *not so in itself.*'

But habitual language about art involves just the conception of nature being beautiful in itself and not made so by us. We make nature what it is in itself, sc. beautiful.

As nature has ugliness or beauty,[34] only so far as we think ourselves into it, so the appetites and world to which we are related through them only become[35] a ἑτερον ['other'], and again cease to be so (become a reconciled ἑτερον) so far as we think ourselves into them and recognize them as a result of such *hineindenken* ['adoption of their perspectives'].

As we yet hold nature to be 'in itself' beautiful, and perpetually correct, or rather elevate, our representation of its beauty upon this supposition, so we hold appetites, etc., to be *in themselves* harmonious with reason.

This not to be understood as meaning that they are so *to begin with*, or *naturally*, as purely animal and not yet artificialized.

Wordsworth: 'The Blackbird among leafy trees,' etc.[36]

In this state (just as nature by itself neither beautiful nor ugly), they are like as alien to reason nor adjusted to it for the beings (?) that experience them. Language, however, inevitably confuses state which is as yet one neither of freedom nor bondage, with that of bondage overcome. Hence precept to 'become as little children' [Mark 10.15; Luke 18.17], and fiction of a primitive state prior to contract, etc. Hence, too, doctrine of 'Fall' with its theological consequences.

Question how we come to recognize objects as without us, sensations being in us, has been crux in theory of knowledge. Only to be accounted for by original separation [of] object [of?] thought as charged with sensations from, and presentation to, itself.

As only by such separation, is there an outward nature for us at all, so only by it are the appetites alien. It is not only our freedom that makes us conscious of slavery, and consciousness of self that makes us conscious of an opposite; the freedom creates the slavery, – only because identified with the self as object is the ἑτερσν ['other'] or what it is.

In knowledge, self-consciousness creates a world of permanent objects without asking any question as to its relation to them.

So practically it creates, a world of persons and institutions, which are objects of permanent interest and affection, apart from (to some extent antecedently to) questions that arise out of distinct reflection on itself.

This reflection parent at once of vice[37] and of philosophy: of sin, as suggesting question, how much more pleasure (or the like) can I get; of philosophy as withdrawal of the man from his sensitive life into attitude of contemplative acceptance.

One thing to be pleased, another to discuss one's pleasures: the latter confessed to be sign of demoralization, though demorali-sation of harmless men.[38] It is the pale shadow, in speculative men, of the violent πλεονεξια ['greed'] which invents new pleasures, instead of taking things pleasant as they come.[39] Without reflection on self, as an endless susceptibility[40] of enjoyment, no such invention, and in consequence no *vice*.[41]

Do we not all, as matter of fact, live for pleasure? Yes and no. The attainment of every object for which we live has a certain relation to the passivity of the individual which = pleasure. Thus anticipation of attainment of object is inseparable from anticipation of pleasure. To be determined by the *anticipation* of pleasure – by pleasure as thought upon – different from purely passive determi-nation of the animal by επιθυμητὸν ['the desired object']. Relation of animal to its object one of passivity; relation of man to what gives him pleasure *so far as it gives him pleasure*, one of passivity. (Stoic says of Epicurean in A. Gellius, IX.5 – 'ἡδονὴ τέλος, πόρνης δόγμα οὐκ ἐστιν πρόνοια οὐδὲν, πόρνης δόγμα.' ['Pleasure an end, a harlot's creed; there is no Providence, not even a harlot's creed.'])[42] But relation of man to such object *in thinking about it*, and it is the thought of it that determines him, not one of passivity.[43] Is it, however, the *thought of the pleasant* that in all cases (or in any case) determines our action? i.e. the thought of an object as related to my individual passivity.[44]

Fallacy[45] covered under expression of 'acting for removal of uneasiness.' Everything to *be done* causes uneasiness till it is done. Hence every act contemplated beforehand, occasions uneasiness, which is removed in the act. This uneasiness measures strength of impulse to act, but [is] not itself the impulse. This opposition to thought of it as (a) an expression of an ideal (sc. universalised idea); (b) to thought of it as affecting other men; – (c) as corresponding to law, or the will of God; – (d) as worthy of oneself.

(a) Motive of the artist, in wide sense, (b) of the good citizen and member of family, (c) is motive to life of conformity and religion in restricted sense, (d) is motive in the philosophic life which gathers up[46] all the previous objects as constituting its own realized in self.

In all these cases, doubtless, the man has individual interest in attainment of object; it is object of desire to him, but it is so because thought of in its relations ad universum, not in its simple relation to him as capable of pleasure. The conception of an act, in its real relation as to as to be done determines that desire; not the desire the conception of it so to be *done*.

To say that the pleasure accompanying the act is the motive is a false abstraction theoretically of activity from passivity; of consciousness of *mere* individuality from that of individuality as determined by relations ad universum.

It corresponds to false practical abstraction by simple ακολασὶς ['licentiousness'] of his momentary individual consciousness from consciousness of general good and general law, and surrender of himself to the former.

Itself theoretical; (as theory maintained by excellent men; by men who contradict their theory by embodying it in great books, for no one ever wrote a book for *mere pleasure* of it);[47] but has practical results. (a) It sophisticates enjoyment. The man who has got to think of himself as living for a sum of pleasures, can no longer enjoy himself healthily, no longer throw himself into the moment. (b) Deadens the moral and artistic initiative. (3) Makes virtue sentimental, and thus selfish.

What is this consciousness of self, which is not you or nature?

It must then always be relative to consciousness of self. To this, however, not necessarily as passive subject of pleasure, but as source of objective moral order: i.e. as presenting an idea or form, which is moral in sense that it is realized in, or filled up by desires. Relative to this end, benevolence is on [one] hand rational and moral, which it would not be if merely instinctive; yet 'disinterested', because the ulterior interest, which [determines?] it, is interest in an object which is mine but not special to me. In being governed by such an interest, thought yet free because it is interest in object which it has itself created.

As it is not the ἐπιθυμητὸν ['object of desire'],[48] but thought of sc. ορεκτὸν ['presented'] as become a selfish object, that can alone determine man, so all theories that find the true moral motive in a feeling – an instinctive propensity – however benevolent make morality selfish.

If it were possible for the feeling to [seem?] merely instinctive, it would not be so. The benevolent feeling can never be merely instinctive – certainly not when men have begun to philosophize about it. It can only determine us as reflected on – sc.: as the anticipation[49] of a pleasant experience – and thus becomes a selfish object. Moralists, aware of the sickliness that self-reflection thus gives to benevolence, try in vain to show that, like hunger, it rests in its object as end (hunger, however, destroys its object). If so, it would not indeed be selfish, but would be no basis of social order, would not be constructive.

How measure relations save by resulting pleasure? by *resulting freedom*. As the real freedom of the act gives it its moral value to the doer (its subjective value), so its tendency to promote such real freedom gives it its *objective* value.

The 'real freedom of the act to the doer' means the determination of act by an idea, which is not representative of a passive pleasure (of an object received as from without) but which creates its own object. Thought of ideal to be realized, of good of family or state etc., is or thought which creates its own object.

The relations by which ordinary acts are to be measured are their consistency with the institutions by which such 'real freedom' has been so far rendered possible to mankind.

[§6 'Stages in the Self-assertion of Reason.']
'Selfish' or 'sentimental' theory of morals may take either the 'Epicurean' or 'Friend of Man' form.

Benevolent sentiment, reflected on, becomes at once selfish and consciously a bondage. I am a friend of man as it happens, but with a bilious attack may cease to be so. The sentiment is a personal peculiarity of myself and so far from being law to myself,[50] as might seem at first sight, in being determined by my personal peculiarity (my 'empirical ego') I am confined[51] (1) by the presence of personal peculiarities of every one else, (2) by physical conditions of that peculiarity in myself. It may be the idiosyncrasy of all mankind; still as merely personal sentiment of each, it is to each *accidental* and therefore a bondage.

Reason, to be free, demands a law (1) *universal*, not merely valid *for me* from time to time (however regularly the times be repeated); (2) which it gives, not receives.

How can any law satisfy condition (1) which is other than merely negative; or (2), unless obedience to it excludes pleasure, i.e. all satisfaction of desire, all personal sentiment.

Admitting that such 'hunger and thirst after righteousness' [Matt. 5.6] is real, (1) it can only act in highest natures at intervals; in children etc. not at all. 'Pure will', as excluding every motive but such hunger unattainable; and (2) if attained would be will to do what? Will to gratify *im*pure will in every one else?

Stages in the self-assertion of reason. In theoretical abandonment of its claim, in doctrine of its mere passivity in moral action, it is still asserting itself, showing that it can't be pleased without accounting to itself for its pleasure.

Moral sense = pleasure arising on mere survey of an action.

Different views as to source of this pleasure.

'Pleasure in contemplation of harmony between social and self-regarding impulses.' Shaftesbury.[52]

Fellow-feeling acting upon sense of propriety 'Act so that you may have the feeling that others can sympathise with you.'

Desire for *personal* completeness. Pleasure resulting from consideration that an act tends to your own highest perfection. Wolf.[53]

All come to this, 'act for the sake of a personal feeling.'

Hobbes's[54] view [is] that 'pleasure on survey' of act is ultimately anticipation or recollection of pleasure resulting from act itself as satisfying appetite or desire.

'Handle so, daß die Maxime deines Willens jederzeit zugleich als Prinzip einer all-gemeinen Gesetzgebung gelten könne.'[55] ['So act that the maxim of your will could always hold at the same time as a principle in giving of universal law.'][56]

The 'maxim' is the αρκη πρὸξεως ['guiding power'] to individual. The maxim must not be any particular desire, or it will violate above rule. The good Will = *Pure* will = will that excludes every-thing empirical, i.e. every motive derived from generalizing desires. If determined by 'Desire' only, by such desires as = the yearning to fulfil the 'Moral Law.'

'Abstract duty.'

Duty is to manifold things-to-be-done as 'mind'[57] to manifold acts and objects of thought. Not an abstract residuum.

Negation, yet determined by relation to the manifold of which it is negation.

Worship. Can't worship what you don't know. Yet again not that which you know in sense of perfect appropriation.

Is ἀγαθόν ['the good'] an object of reverence?

Adam Smith's[58] fellow-feeling, or sense of what people will think of me, as good practical motive in most cases as one could wish.[59] Given idea of Duty, and Self-given Law, as *form*, this may fill it up: but without it (1) lacks universal authority, (2) is *alien*.

It presupposes recognized social relations, for which as mere feeling it *can't account.*

Through fellow-feeling individual appropriates reason as expressed in institutions and practical ideas of mankind. Its pronouncement may often be truer than that of what he calls his reason.

Fusion of the theoretical and practical.

This *theoretical* difficulty of reason overcome by recognition of its own work in the objective social world, which de facto partic-ularises our 'Duties', determines our desire and sentiment: recog-nition not of acquiescence but of cooperation and continual evolution.

The relation of individual to society subjects him to a law which is at once universal, as result of unity of 'Ego' giving freely to itself in 'manifold of desire', and at same time articulated into specific duties as various as 'positions in life' (and thus *pleases*).

This law at same time interests the individual personally, because it is the organization of his personal desires; yet so organizes them, as to convert them into activities. These activities so absorbed in their objects, that the subject has no separate consciousness of their relations as *pleasant* to him. He has no time to consider whether he is pleased or not, and thus practically delivered from 'false abstraction of passivity from activity.'

[§7 The Purification of the Will.]

'Pure will' equivalent in philosophical language to 'Faith' in religious, taking 'Faith' as cleared of theological accidents, and in its deeper meaning as neither acquiescence in a doctrine nor trust in a person, but as the act by which individual surrenders himself to God in absolute abandonment of personal interest.

'Whatever is not of *Faith* is sin.' [Rom. 14:23]

Whatever is not of the 'Pure Will' is immoral.

'How possible to "eat and drink" or do any acts of ordinary life in Faith?' Hence breach between Faith and Works. Works, as they can't express faith in this abstract sense, stand over against faith as something indifferent and accidental.

The antithesis, which primarily represents a permanent difficulty of thought translated into feeling becomes mischievous. 'Faith' becomes the simple feeling of personal vacancy, of personal irresponsibility, which, laying hold on notions that actions are indifferent, may become licentious.

With Kant, conception of 'pure will' basis of most exalted morality – one which puts to shame the 'accommodations' of the religious world – but which at same time, owing to false abstraction of 'pure' from 'empirical', of 'universal' from the particulars in which it is realized and which are only *definitely* particular through relation to it, of reason as form from the sensible as matter having independent existence of its own, becomes unreal.

Difficulty arises from intensification of individual self-consciousness. Not merely 'moral philosophy', but practical questions of political right and wrong, in modern times turn on notion of 'conscience', a notion which don't appear in Plato and Aristotle, but first comes in with Stoicism.

With Plato and Aristotle reason is in the state or in the world. It is the *whole*, and the whole is not conceived of as articulated into persons, each properly recognizing the *whole* or reason that is in the whole, against his own.

Conscience is reason as operative in individual and thus at once in collision with personal feelings and coloured by them (for latter reason apt to be delusive).

Rightly in collision with feelings, as merely personal, sc. as not adjusted, and consciously adjusted, to the organic system of social life as a whole.

But it does not follow that '*pure* Reason' as operative in human world, is separate from, or *pure* of, Desires.

On the contrary, *reason*, in its human, as opposed to merely *natural*, expression, just = desires as an organic system pervaded by self-consciousness, or desires as of self-conscious individuals, each recognizing himself in the other; just because this system is developed through such individuals, perpetual collision between wilfulness of individual, or desire not fit to be generally desired,[60] and will of whole, organized system of desires.

In stage of collision between 'conscience', or consciousness of will as properly 'pure' of desires, and desires which as matter of fact seem to determine ordinary action, these latter are taken in abstraction from rational system of desires, which constitutes social organism.

(Practically so far as the moral education of individual is incomplete, they are really to a great extent thus unadjusted, and hence strife of conscience and natural tendencies proper state of mind for most.)

But desires of individual not properly or in themselves thus abstract. On contrary, vehicles through which common social life, which is work of reason, imparts a real (in opposition to formal) rationality to individual.

Result of the theoretical claim of 'conscience', of its abstraction of itself from desires, is a more 'conscientious' form of the old morality.

You follow desires, because they are 'in themselves' rational and connect you with a 'rational' world. The more reason to do your diligence that the social world with which they connect you may be actually rational and that they are really harmonized with the common life, not of a kind, in however slight degree, to weaken or disturb that life.

'Unity of reason giving body to itself in manifold of Desire.'[61] What meaning? Reason, in morals = active principle, which distinguishes itself from itself in such a way, as to construct objects in which may be expression of itself, in which it may find itself, which may be permanent as it is permanent.[62]

Matter which it thus fashions into expression of itself = desires.

Owing to certain explicable necessities of language, we speak, and hence think, of this principle as if it existed to begin with in 'purity', in abstraction from desires (to begin with).[63]

(Practically for us as individuals it does so exist in each of us.) But 'reason' does not mean a belonging of each of us. In individuals, when in condition of sleep, and babyhood, and barbarism, though it is only through its action that we can account for their transition from these conditions.

It is a principle necessary to account for social world as 'force of gravitation' for physical. Just as this 'force' does not exist apart from matter in which it acts, so reason.

As reality, in the one case, is the matter as pervaded by the force and being what it is in virtue of such pervasion, so in other, desires as pervaded by reason, which means that they are desires of Universal.

But there is this difference that nature is complete, social world incomplete. The reason that is in it in constant effort towards more complete expression. Explanation of this that, though not = sum of wills of individuals, it yet works through such wills. Social order established by caprice; once established, it is independent of this, and beneficently regulates it; still retains imperfection derived from mode of its original institution.

Thus social world (with its laws, institutions [and] other influences) presents a realization, particulization, articulation of Reason. Reason in it *im*pure, and so much the better.

In the individual, when reason first becomes clearly conscious of itself, when he comes 'to have a conscience,' and places itself in conscious antagonism to desires, these already practically rationalized so far (1) as they have become affections for rational persons and (2) as they have been neutralized by mutual contradiction, and subdued in settled, passionless, habits of action.

Thus the antagonism practically takes form of distinction between disciplined and undisciplined desires. The discipline becomes more complete as individual more independent – as social take place of merely family 'duties.' 'To each such "duty" and disciplined *"desire"* corresponds, which prompts the act. Therefore (a) the will in thus acting, is "impure" in Kant's sense; (b) "demand of Reason", stated above is unsatisfied.' (a) true, but not (b). The πρακτόν (or particular duty) is just the 'universal law' of society in its definite relation to the individual.

But is it so to him? Is he not determined simply by the desire, without considering it as vehicle through which the 'universal reason' acts upon him? And if so, is he not necessarily selfish, according to above doctrine, that every desire as such, however benevolent, because necessarily reflected on, is selfish?

Answer: he is doubtless determined by desire, and without considering it, etc., but this desire is a personal interest in a *general* good – a good which only interests the individual as general – and the self to which it is relative, which is conscious of gratification in the gratification of the benevolent desire, is a *thinking* self, which 'finds itself' not perhaps in the 'cause of humanity' in its breadth, but in that cause as represented by good of society immediately surrounding.

When 'conscience' becomes[64] still more keenly conscientious – and asks how any will determined by personal interest[65] can be purely rational or good, the answer is at hand in recognition of desires, which practically determine the virtuous man, in their true character as...

He may then retain Kantian canon as his rule of life, but without supposing that when his 'maxim' is other than the pure desire to fulfil universal law, it is therefore unfit to be 'Princip eines all-gemeine Gestazgebung.' ['Principle that gives universal law(s).']⁶⁶[66] So far as his 'maxim' is a social interest, however limited by particular circumstances of his own sensitive nature or that of others, it is so fit; nay is *result* of the 'all-gemeine Gesetzgebung' ['giving universal law(s)'] which has constituted human society.

Not to be supposed that after such wakening of 'conscience,' as is represented by Kant's demand, it is practically in same state as before.

Legal and moral obligation not to be opposed as if there were not a moral obligation to obey the law. The *act* which law enforces, ought *not* to be *legal* act, in sense in which this is opposed to moral, as the act done from fear [is opposed] to act done from good disposition. Nor are they to be opposed as if one proceeded from without (from society), other from within (self, or conscience). Each proceeds from relation to society, though from society not as outward force but has having recognised claim, and though the moral object is only so far properly moral as the motive which society furnishes is taken by individual [and] made his own;[67] yet no less motive to 'keep one's hands from picking and stealing'[68], though[69] proceeding from society, is by good citizen made his own: otherwise would not be obligation but (as it is to rogue) compulsion. But since magistrate can neither ascertain disposition from which act proceeds, nor determine it (i.e. not *directly*, by simple command enforced by fear); though he may vitiate it by making fear inducement to act of which value lies in its not being done from fear; he properly confines himself to prohibition or injunction of acts, the commission or omission of which would interfere outwardly with freedom of others – i.e. would prevent free development and expression of good disposition.

(An act, which affects disposition of other directly, is of a kind which has no character apart from disposition of doer. Thus relation of act as outward – to person affected by it is correlative to possibility of treating it – as magistrate does – apart from disposition of doer.)

This limitation does not at all imply that law (or State as author of law) has 'nothing to do with morality': on contrary, (1) outward freedom which it secures is of value just as necessary condition of inward freedom; sc. of state in which reason, as principle of self-determination in individual (as his will) adopts as its own,[70] a rational motive – a motive upon which every one might act consistently with organic well-being of society. (This means that reason as self-consciousness or will of individual is at one with reason which orders that moral world. But how can it be other, on supposition that supreme reason does order the world? Answer, that out of evil act – sc. out of act not proceeding from will adjusted to supreme will – this supreme will elicits good, but it is not good for the doer; and doer not properly free.)[71]

(2) Limitation of its office is prescribed just with view to its moral end. Its end being disposition of freedom as above defined, the more reason why it should not present *inadequate* motive; sc. motive in which fear is ingredient. (Those who regard moral end as sum of pleasures get no precise rule for limiting office of state: never can say what extent of action on its part does or does not tend to promote greatest sum of pleasures.)

(3) The removal of obstacles to free development, etc., means really much greater action on part of government (supreme or municipal) than exists. Does not at all mean that it leaves every one to do as he pleases, so long as he does not pick pockets, etc. Great obstacle to such free development is disease, and as conditions of disease (specially in connection with mode of work and housing) come to be better understood, office of state, under limitations aforesaid, seems almost indefinitely to extend.[72]

(4) How about relation of state to education and religion? Ought (1) to keep its hands off promotion of opinion, so far as opinion affects or is affected by good disposition. May provide for teaching natural science. Mode in which a man receives his views about the stars does not affect his disposition. No danger of his doing right act from unworthy motive because state teaches him

this. But an opinion about God and the manner of his revelation does so relate to the moral life, that such an opinion adopted from any but the highest reason – as it is when there is any interested motive to its adoption – is a *vitiated motive*. This the ultimate ground of objection to all State religions. But (a) religious societies, left to themselves, may vitiate highest motive through fear more effectively than the state: and (b) may not minimum of vitiation.

Rel: to education.

[§8 Mind, Power and Virtue in Hobbes, Locke and Hume.]
   Hobbes. Powers of mind: (a) Cognitive, Imaginative, or Conceptive. (b) Motive.[73]

'Imagery or representation of qualities of things without us we call our Conception, Imagination, ideas, knowledge of them.'[74] Corresponding faculty called Cognitive or Conceptive power.

'Originally all conception proceeds from action of thing itself, whereof it is the conception. When Action is present, conception it produceth is also called Sense; and thing producing action object of sense.'[75]

'Subject wherein Colour and Image are inherent is not the object or thing seen. Such colour or image is but apparition unto us of motion or alteration which that object waketh in the Brain or Spirits or some internal substance of the Head.'[76]

Qualities which we think to be in the world are *seemings* only. 'The things that really are in the world without us are the motions by which these seemings are caused.'[77]

Imagination = 'conception remaining and by little and little decaying from and after act of sense'[78] (as motion of water remains after wind has ceased to blow.)[79]

'The succession of conceptions in the mind ... if orderly, as when the former thought introduceth the latter, is Discourse or Discursion'[80] (which with Hobbes seems to = reason. Ratiocination, which = syllogizing, presupposes formation of propositions).

'The cause of coherence or consequence of one conception to another is their first coherence or consequence at Time when produced by Sense.'[81]

A specific sort of 'Discursion' (or Reason) 'when appetite giveth a man his beginning.'[82] Suppose Honour be object of appetite. – Thence 'a man cometh to the thought of Wisdom, which is next means thereunto:'[83] Thence to thought of Study, which is next means to Wisdom. (This is Hobbes's form of 'Practical reason.')

'No conception that hath not been produced immediately before or after innumerable others by the innumerable acts of sense.'[84] Hence, any conception occurs just it chance to us to see or hear such things as may bring it to our mind. Man (unlike beasts) has invented[85] a device for regulating to some extent this chance; viz: *names* – a name 'is the voice of man arbitrary, imposed for a mark to bring into his mind some conception concerning that thing on which it is imposed':[86]

'When a man reasoneth, he does nothing else but conceive a sum total from addition of parcels; or conceive a remainder from subtraction of one sense from another; which (if it be done by words) is conceiving of the consequence of the names of all the parts to the name of the whole; or from the names of the whole and one part to the name of the other part.'[87]

'Reason, as a faculty of the mind, is nothing but reckoning (i.e., adding or subtracting) of the consequences of general names agreed on, for the marking and signifying our thoughts.' [88]

This renders science possible.

Simple consciousness, such as is neither *cognitive nor motive* not recognized by Hobbes, who by identifying pleasure with appetite makes even that motive. Thus with Hobbes only ground of distinction within the receptive (as opposed to motive) consciousness, between simple feeling (that of which we can only say that it is pleasant or painful) and cognition or conception, is that the latter is referred to outward thing as its cause. In like manner distinction between 'two kinds of conception' turns on question whether 'outward object' is actually present or no. If it is present, the conception is called *sense*: if not, imagination.

Question not yet asked, 'How do I know of an outward object at all?', to which only answer can be 'because consciousness tells me'; which necessitates further question, 'How can consciousness tell me of that of which the only thing that can be said is that it is that of which I am not conscious?'

The 'powers motive of mind'[89] (though powers to move outward things through the body) are themselves but effects of action of outward thing. Our whole experience thus accounted for as result of something, of which only possible account involves a contradiction.

As soon as phenomena of social life[90] has to be accounted for, Hobbes has to introduce another principle, which gives new character to motion resulting from outward thing. It is 'conception of powers in oneself' as a new object to which appetite and aversion are directed that alone with Hobbes can account for social strife that ends in Sovereignty and obligation. Appetite must become self-love: pleasure and hope (which = pleasure in expectation of pleasure) must become pride (pleasure in one's own power), in order to account for 'state of war', as much as for 'way of peace.'[91]

'Power motive of the mind is that by which the mind giveth animal motion to the body wherein it existeth: the acts hereof are our affections and passions.'[92]

'Conception and apparitions are nothing really but Motion in some internal substance of the head; which motion, not stopping there but proceeding to the heart, must there either help or hinder the motion which is called vital: when it helpeth, called pleasure, which is nothing really but a motion about the heart, as conception [is] motion about head. Object causing it called pleasant: and considered with reference to this object that pleasure called Love. This same motion is also a "solicitation" to draw[93] the thing or "beginning of animal motion towards the thing" – and as such called appetite. Thus pleasure, love, appetite, which is also called desire, are divers names for divers considerations of same thing.'[94]

Conversely when the motion in the heart 'weakeneth or hindereth vital motion', it is called pain. Then, considered in relation to object it is called Hatred;[95] and as provocation to virtue from that object, *aversion*. Aversion, 'in respect of displeasure expected' is called fear.[96] (Does not define *hope* here, but later on calls 'hope expectation of good to come, as fear expectation of evil'.)[97]

'Every man for his own part calleth that which pleaseth him *Good*, and that evil which displeaseth him; insomuch that while every man differeth from another in Constitution they differ also from one another concerning common distinction of good and evil.'[98]

'We so far conceive that anything will be hereafter, as we know there is something at present that hath power to produce it....All conception of future is conception of power able to produce something. Whoever therefore expecteth pleasure to come must conceive withal some power in himself by which the same may be attained.'[99]

Hence a set of secondary passions, consisting (a) of desire for or pleasure in our own power, or signs of our own power, direct or indirect (b) of aversion from, or pain in, etc.[100]

Will = last appetite or last fear.[101]

'Alternate succession of appetite and fear during all the time the action is in our power to do or not to do is that we call Deliberation.'[102]

'In Deliberation, last appetite, as also the last Fear is called Will – Will to do, or Will to omit. ... All one to say *Will* or last *Will*.'[103]

'Voluntary actions and omissions are such as have beginning in the Will.'[104]

'Involuntary, such as a man doth by necessity of nature. e.g. when he is pushed, and thereby doth hurt to another.'[105]

'Mixed...as when a man is carried to prison, going is voluntary, to the prison involuntary.'[106]

The pleasure then = appetite, not satisfaction of appetite.

'appetite, fear, hope and rest of the passions *not* called *voluntary*, for they proceed *not from* but *are* the Will, and the Will is not voluntary; for a man can no more say he will will, than he will will will, and so make infinite repetition of the word.'[107]

'Appetite and fear all expectations of future.' Human nature c.12,[108] but proper antithesis to appetite is aversion, to fear *hope*.

Distinguish (a) Simple feeling of pleasure or pain. (b) *appetite* – impulse of animal system to fill or relieve itself, implying no notion of an object. (c)[109] pleasure determined by notion of object producing it, which may be called 'Love', according to widest sense of that term. (d) *Desire* for a pleasure, implying notion of the object producing it.

These mixed up by Hobbes under terms, indifferently used, appetite, pleasure, love. Question whether (c) and (d) are possible without self-consciousness. If the object producing pleasure is distinguished from that pleasure itself as permanent thing from passing feeling, its effect, then action of self-consciousness, as that which can alone account for such distinction, is implied in question.

(Don't dogs exhibit such love and desire? In default of language we have no real means of interpreting actions of animals; but unconsciously interpret them by light of our own experience. No observation of animals can give any sure argument for or against any theory of human experience.)[110]

Anyhow, when (c) is 'pride' – when notion of object producing pleasure is notion of one's own powers – when (d) is 'desire for one's own happiness, conception of self, as permanent subject of experience, is explicitly active: and plan of accounting for man's experience simply through his passivity is obviously departed from.

With Hobbes, will = last appetite, but still it is appetite consciously referred to a self or I. You may avoid question of relation of will to appetite (question whether appetite is voluntary or no – whether I will will) but it will return as question of relation of I to the will. So far in Hobbes nothing to account for obligation or consciousness of obligation.

It is true [that] ἡδυ ['pleasure'] and λυπηρὸν ['pain'] do not in all cases give 'animal motion to the body' immediately. They often set in motion a train of 'reason' or discourse, sc. a succession of images of ἡδεα ['pleasures'] and λυπηρά ['pains'] – such as (in language of later philosophy) are *associated* with ἡδυ ['pleasure'] or λυπηρὸν ['pain'] first presented – such as are remembered as having preceded it. In such succession, ἡδεα ['pleasures'] and λυπηρά ['pains'] may alternate. Each of these being in turn object of appetite or fear, the succession constitutes what Hobbes calls deliberation. As the balance of appetite or fear prevails, after succession of images has been traversed, we act or abstain.

The result of such deliberation is simple appetite or aversion – and *last* appetite or aversion – not any judgment that *I ought*.

This judgment only comes as a *secondary* result of appetite and aversion, when these have led to the establishment of *sovereignty*.

Quite true that obligation and 'sense' of it arise from social authority, – authority thing of those *other* than the individual obliged. Question as to validity of all *physical* theories of Ethics is (1) whether appetite and aversion, however indefinitely extended by association, can account for sovereignty; and (2) whether, granted that they can, such sovereignty would be other than simple force – whether it would be authority, sc. force recognized as having right, which can alone be source of judgment 'I *ought*.'

Apt to be supposed that fault of Hobbesian theory lies in deriving judgment 'I ought' from relation of individual to society, instead of finding it in 'innate sense'. This was the antithesis fought about in last Century: the innate sense in question being supposed to be in such a way inside the man as not to depend on relation to others. So long as antithesis was put in this way, Hobbesian theory (or some mode of it) sure to prevail. True corrective lies[111] in better appreciation of work of reason as at once rendering society possible[112] and forming that 'conscience' in individual in virtue of which law of society becomes his own.)

How does Hobbes get sovereignty? Direct appetite for that which 'promotes life', upon introduction of faculty of anticipation, becomes appetite for present power (necessarily in oneself) of producing or getting *in future* that which 'promotes life.' Such power again must mean power superior to that of others, for 'equal powers opposed destroy one another.'[113]

Hence desire of every one to get better of every one, with its correlative 'mutual fear.'[114]

'Men's[115] appetites carry them to one and the same end, which oftentimes can neither be enjoyed in common nor divided.'[116] Hence 'battle',[117] or mutual 'offensiveness.'

'Man by nature hath right to all things, i.e. to do whatever he listeth to whom he listeth, to possess, use and enjoy all things he will and can.'[118]

But this right 'in effect no better than if no man had right to anything' because forces of men are on the whole equal and neutralize each other.[119]

'Irresistible Might in state of nature is Right.'[120] But according to 'supposed equality of strength', such might does not exist in any man. 'Reason therefore dictateth to every man for his own good, to seek after Peace as far forth as there is hope to attain the same, and strengthen himself with all help he can procure for his own defence against those from whom such peace can't be procured.'[121]

The several precepts which reason dictates for this purpose = law of nature.[122]

'Reason is the same in all men because all agree in the will to be directed in the way to that which they desire [to] attain, viz: their own good.'[123]

First precept of law of nature that 'every man divest himself of right he hath to all things by nature.'[124]

'A man's own consent may abridge him of the liberty which *law of nature leaveth him*, but custom not.'[125]

'Sum of law of nature' is to be sociable to them who will be sociable and formidable to them who will not.' Which also 'sum of virtue.'[126]

At first sight it might seem as if, according to Hobbesian view, the state of nature, or universal war, was opposed to law of nature, which 'declares the way of peace' as the irrational to the rational.[127] But not so.

Reason, in that sense in which according to Hobbes it 'declares way of peace,' is source of State of war: It is reason as succession of images, converting simple appetite into appetite for power, which causes state of war: and the same, at a later stage, when experience of state of war has so modified succession of images as to make fear predominate over hope in deliberation upon probable results of state of war, 'prescribes way of peace.' What Hobbes describes in detail as laws of nature are various forms of this 'way of peace'.

(Hobbes's system perplexed by his following the Jurists in applying language of 'right' to state of things in which as yet there was no right; because no sovereignty. Thus 'a natural right of all men to all things', which 'is in effect no better than if no man had right to anything,' because there is equality of powers, which neutralize each other.[128]

'Precept of *Law of Nature* – that every man divest himself of the right he hath to all things by nature,'[129] sc. in *state* of nature. Thus really means with Hobbes that the 'appetite for power', so long as it seeks direct satisfaction, turns out to be an impotence: thus, deliberation (as defined above) leads to a general fear of such direct satisfaction and consequent establishment of power which shall prevent direct satisfaction. This Hobbes (retaining language of Civilians) represents as transfer or delegation of *rights of all to sovereign*.

'Because the right of bearing the Person of them all is given to him they make sovereign by covenant only of one to another and not of him to any of them; there can happen no breach of covenant on the part of the Sovereign and consequently none of his subjects, by any pretence of forfeiture, can be freed from his subjection.'[130]

'The opinion that any monarch receiveth his power by covenant, proceedeth from want of understanding that covenants, being but words, have no force to oblige, constrain, or protect any man, but what it has from the public sword; i.e., from the untied hands of that man or assembly of men that hath the sovereignty, and whose actions are performed by the strength of them all in him united.' (Leviathan, II.18.)[131]

Locke's 'understanding and will' correspond to Hobbes's 'powers cognitive and motive' (§§5).[132] It is power to begin action from preference. The latter *is* freedom. (So Hegel in other sense says that question whether will is free as superfluous as question whether matter is heavy. No other than question whether self-determination is self-determination.)[133] Unmeaning then to ask whether will is free. Proper question is whether man is free or wills, to do a certain act; i.e. whether he begins the motion which constitutes the *act upon preference*.

Then Locke departs from his original identification of *will* and *freedom*; and makes will = *preference* or volition, *liberty* power to do or forbear upon such preference (§§15): from this point of view says that question whether will is free = question whether one power has another power: in other words to treat will which is a power as if it were an agent; or a relation as it if were a substance.

Question then is, whether the agent, man, is free. Free to *act* he certainly is, for that is no more than saying that he *wills*: whether he is *free to will* is another question. He is not so free. He cannot help preferring.

'Freedom consists in our being able to act or not to act according as we shall choose or *will*.'[134]

What determines the will to rest or motion? To *rest* – sc. to continue in any state or action – motive is present satisfaction in it: to motion – some uneasiness.[135]

First, will = simply, power to begin action. Then question occurs, what determines this power. Answer, *Preference*, which now is treated as Will. But what determines preference or will? Answer Present Uneasiness, or 'Uneasiness of the mind for want of some absent good' which = desire (§31). Yet will and desire may run counter (§30). Explanation of this, (though Locke does not explicitly give it) that we are 'beset with *sundry* uneasiness, distracted with *different* desires.' The *most pressing* uneasiness prevails'; in other words, desire which is *at present* strongest, though this may conflict with desire which under other circumstances would be stronger (§40).

But what 'moves desire'? What is object which we are uneasy till we have attained? Answer: 'happiness and that alone.' Happiness 'in its full extent' = utmost pleasure we are capable of = greatest good. It is not such happiness, happiness in general that moves any particular man's desire, but only 'that part of it which makes part of his happiness or which he desires. Sc. each man's desire is moved by that which he desires.

No meaning in such language unless 'happiness in general' mean something else than sum of each man's pleasures, which however must come to be pleasant to him, or more properly, to be so related to him that its absence is painful, before it can move him to action.

That determination to act results from present uneasiness is certainly true if it means no more than that, given an object of desire, there is uneasiness till it is attained. Question is, what is object of desire and whence given?

Is that object of desire itself the pleasure that ensues on attaining object of desire? Clearly that object must be desired *simply* first, in order that pleasure incident to its attainment may become object of desire afterwards.

(§58) 'Things in their enjoyment are what they seem: apparent and real good are in this case always the same....The greater pleasure or greater pain is really just as it appears.'

How then, if happiness = series[136] of pleasures, each in its turn present, does any man chose what is not his true happiness, his greatest good?

That there is such a 'true happiness' other than what actually pleases the man, and that it is object of interest to the man, implied in that suspense of judgment which according to Locke gives appearance of *freedom to will* (§56).

Variations of Hume from Hobbes: (1) that he takes feeling of pleasure as ultimate fact, without accounting for it physically as 'motion which promotes life': treats it as *psychologist* not as physiologist, (2) that he distinguishes *pleasure* from *desire for* the *object which excites pleasure*, (3) that he distinguishes 'direct passions' of appetite and aversion, hope and fear, from 'indirect' of *love* and *hatred*, which Hobbes identified with appetite and aversion, as well as from those of pride and humility, (4) that he reckoned 'benevolence' or pleasure in the pleasure of another, to be a coordinate indirect passion with 'pride', not derived from it. (So in animals, v.4 p.383.)[137] (5) Introduction of 'moral sentiment' – 4.206. [138]

'Direct passion.' vol.4 p.196. *Will*, ibid. [139]

Modifications of these 'impressions of reflection,' or 'sentiments', from association. Impression of pleasure copies itself in 'idea' of pleasant object. This 'idea' is so associated with idea of self, that the mind easily passes from one to other. At same time impression or sentiment of pleasure originally produced becomes another sort of pleasure, viz: pride, or satisfaction in self. p.207.[140]

In like manner through association of idea of a certain pleasure with a certain person, 'direct' passion or desire for that pleasure becomes indirect one of *love* for that person. p.218.[141]

Thus all possible 'moral sentiments' arise from modification of elementary impressions by association to these of ideas of past impressions.

Necessary, however, in order to give plausibility to his theory, that for such association he should substitute 'association to present impression of idea of (1) self and (2) other thinking persons.' Only through *this* association can the elementary impressions, which as Hume rightly holds, are not different in kind from those of animals, develop as those of the animals do not so as to become the impressions of the artist or patriot.

Interest in self and interest in others – pride [and] self-love and Love [and] benevolence (p.219)[142] alike *indirect* passions according to Hume, but *coordinate*.

Reason with Hume is faculty of calculating means to end given by *taste* or feeling. Does not really differ from Hobbes' account of it: the calculation of means is merely orderly succession of images of pains and pleasures *remembered* as antecedent to desired object. p.376.[143]

(1) Identifies desire with that uneasiness which, given the desire, possesses the subject of it till object is attained.

(2) then makes removal of the uneasiness itself the object of desire, though unless there were an object previously given, there could be no uneasiness.

(3) Then, treating the removal of uneasiness as pleasure (which he is warranted in doing, unless there is any alternative between pleasantness and painfulness of feeling), he makes pleasure the object of desire.

(4) Pleasure being = happiness, happiness is constant determinant[144] of desire.

(5) But as to pleasure, any more than any other simple feeling, there can be no distinction between reality and appearance. How then account (a) for opposition between series [of] greatest pleasures which a man actually prefers, and true happiness which he would choose if he were wise: and (b) for that suspense, in consciousness of individual between decision to take means for removal of most pressing uneasiness and decision to do what is for his greatest happiness.

As to (a), will be said 'that man chooses[145] wrong, because the pleasure which determines him, though greatest at time is not compatible with greatest sum of pleasure.' But how can the succession of greatest pleasures which that man without possibility of mistake chooses[146] when added up, be other than the greatest sum of pleasure possible for him? Answer, 'It is greatest possible sum for him, *his character being what it is*. But another turn might have been given to his character by education, so that the 'greatest pleasure' of his youth would have been compatible with more intensity or durability in the greatest pleasure of his age. Virtuous and vitious[147] man each obtain greatest sum of pleasure possible for them, but sum which virtuous man obtains is greater that what vitious man obtains, and with proper education vicious man might have been virtuous.' Perhaps, but no one can measure intensity of another's pleasure. Of durability there may be better tests, but how strike balance between durability – which can be partially known – and intensity, which can't be known at all?

Question, however, thrown back on education. How is this possible? It implies some conception of that good as other than individual's greatest present pleasure, which modifies simple and direct presentation of pleasures – makes what would otherwise have been the greatest pleasure not the greatest – either in the educator, or educated, or in both. How account for this? Suppose it only in the educator – how does he come by it, if he has uniformly and without possibility of mistake chosen greatest pleasure? Answer: 'that he has found out he might have had more pleasure by another course of conduct, and wishes to give another benefit of his experience.' Well: (waive question, how he comes to have this interest in another). The experience, of which he wishes to give another the benefit, implies a conception of himself as other than the subject of succession of pleasures, each of which has been greatest possible at time of its occurrence, and his 'wish,' etc., implies that this conception can originate action.

If this conception in teacher, why not in taught? That it may be so, implied in Locke's account of (b) (§§56).

The only other possible account of divided mind,[148] which can avoid representation of self-conscious reason as originative would be that in some cases pleasure, which would otherwise be greatest, is balanced by 'imagery' of pains associated with it: that after interval, balance turns one way or other: according to which way it turns, act is one of ακρ: or εγκρ:. But which ever way balance turns, act still determined by greatest pleasure. If 'imagery' of pains not strong enough to deter the man from act called one which shows want of self restraint – if this is uniformly the case with him – who can say that he has not attained greatest happiness which it is in his nature, and this being definition[149] of goodness, that he is not a good man?

No business to talk of his having 'vitiated his own palate' unless man determines pleasure, not pleasure man; unless self-consciousness given an object – which being given, pleasure indeed ensues on its attainment, as pain prevails till it is attained but not so as that pleasure should be original determinant.

It is this action of self-consciousness which makes pleasure motive (as Locke supposes it always to be) indistinguishable from object of appetite. In purely unreflective state, latter alone determines. There must be self-consciousness before individual, reflecting upon pleasure which ensues on attainment of object of appetite, can make this an object. This [is] that state of selfishness. If man determined by pleasure, however, attainment of his pleasure may involve that of another, he is selfish.

Question whether[150] man is free to will is not question whether there is a 'liberty of indifferency' – a state antecedent to that preference which determines act in which as yet no motive acts or in which there is no *strongest* motive – but, What and whence given is object that determines him?

This, again, is question that has to be answered in order to true notion of selfishness and unselfishness, or vice and virtue.

Hobbes accounts for all our experience by action of outward thing.[151] This produces motion that promotes life which = pleasure. He does not distinguish this 'motion' from desire for the pleasure that it constitutes. Thus action moved by this desire is, to him, simply result of action of outward thing.

Locke's essential principle that only in consciousness can he find anything while within consciousness he distinguishes between what is there whether we will or no – i.e. simple feelings, and the results of combining these – of bringing them into relation one to another, naming them, and analysing the significance of the names given. These results the 'work of the mind', of the reason.

Reason, then, having only such secondary office, cannot *initiate* – can't be αρκη κινηδεως ['an efficient cause']. This must be found in feelings.

This, however, (unless some account can be given of feelings) is to say nothing more than that consciousness precedes actions of a conscious agent.

We can only give account of feelings by reference to the objects that excite them.

Distinction between feeling excited by 'outward cause', as in case of animal appetites, and feeling of which object is itself a feeling, as desire for pleasure.

Latter presupposes a subject, present to the successive pleasant feelings, conscious of itself as subject pleased, and thus presenting succession to itself as object to be lived for.

In case of 'appetite', though it is determined by outward cause, this not constituted by self-consciousness of subject; though without such self-consciousness there could be no knowledge of that object. But in case of desire for pleasure, object actually constituted by self-consciousness.

Hunger would arise all the same whether I were conscious of food as outward thing or no: but pursuit of pleasure could not take place without consciousness of self as subject to be pleased and of object to be attained.

[§9 Moral Sense in the Eighteenth Century British Ethicists.]
The systems of Shaftesbury, Butler, and Hutcheson essentially the same:[152] differ from later doctrine of Hume and Adam Smith[153] in that they recognize an 'affection or desire for goodness as such': agree with it in denying (a) motive power to reason, and (b) that moral standard is to be found in 'reason of things', (though Shaftesbury rather ambiguous on latter point).

They (at least Butler and Hutcheson) wrote with two-fold antagonism (a) to the selfish moralists – Hobbes and Mandeville,[154] (b) to Clarke.[155] (The latter antagonism scarcely appears in Shaftesbury – too soon?) In Shaftesbury, and to some extent in Hutcheson, strong antagonism also to the 'theological' view, which made obligation to virtue depend on arbitrary command of God, enforced by rewards and punishments.[156]

According to Shaftesbury, Man is at once a self-contained system and a system relative to a wider system; that of society. He has, *qua animal*, two sets of affections (p.86).[157] That which constitutes the action of any sensibly good creature is its being done from an affection having for its direct object the good of this *wider* system. (pp.21 and 25 of vol. 2.)[158]

In man a *reflex affection* for this affection (p.28).[159] An action done from such affection is virtuous in proper sense.

This reflex affection called *rational*, as opposed to merely sensible. (p.36) 'Should the *sensible* affections stand ever so much amiss; yet if they prevail not, because of those other *rational* affections spoken of...the Person is esteemed virtuous.'[160] Clear that such 'rational affection' not merely a modification of sensible affection by calculation of means or cost, but different in kind. It has a 'rational object'; which is not the sum of satisfactions of animal desire, whether that desire be for 'public or private good', but a specific satisfaction in view of the right adjustment between the two sorts of *animal* desire (p.86).[161] This satisfaction is moral sense. But why call it *sense* in opposition to *reason* when (1) it gives an account of itself, and (2) is an apprehension of a 'universal', of a common relation.

With Hutcheson, in like manner primary distinction of 'acts of will,' 'according as one is pursuing good for himself and repelling the contrary, or pursuing good for others and repelling evils which threaten them.' But a notion of good over and above (1) the pleasure which results from satisfaction of either of these desires, and (2) all pleasure whatsoever even that of 'moral sense.'[162] This notion of the 'morally good' *causes pleasure* in attainment of the object thought good, but is not derived from the pleasure.[163]

If, however, we ask whence this notion is derived, Hutcheson answers not *from reason*: it is a *primary perception*.[164] But perception of what? If not of pleasure, nor of 'rational object'?[165]

Shaftesbury: father of Ethics[166] of the good heart.

Does 'affection having for its direct object,' etc., mean one determined by consciousness of the 'wider system'?[167] If *not*, in what does it differ from one which has this object *in*directly, though *directly* only that of the 'narrower system'?[168]

Difference between good and bad action lies in feeling (passion or affection) with which each is done. 'In a sensible creature that which is not done through any affection at all makes neither good nor ill in nature of that creature.' (Shaftesbury).[169]

An action good, if done from social affection. The man virtuous, if governed by affection for good action.

Difficulties which result from this view are: (1) distinction of the selfish from the unselfish. (2) What is to be said of that great class of actions, which we all commend, but what can't be said to originate either in social affection, or in affection for such goodness as consists in social affection, e.g. artist's enthusiastic pursuit of his art, or philosopher's of his philosophy: act of man who will go to stake for an idea not (in his consciousness) related to good of mankind, of man who is rigidly just without being a friend of mankind? (3) Possibility of freedom in any sense – in good action no less than in bad – if αρχη κινηδεως lies in 'passivity' of man which implies that is itself derived?[170]

Butler, on other hand, that coordination and opposition don't lie between self-love and benevolence, but between benevolence and other 'particular affections' to particular external objects. 'Every man hath general desire of his own happiness': Such desire is self-love; which 'belongs to man as a reasonable [being] reflecting on his own happiness': the happiness itself constituted by the particular affections, of which benevolence is one; these, 'though quite distinct from Reason, being as much a part of human nature.' (205 & 6).[171]

'Conscience', like self-love, a principle of reflection.[172] If Butler's language on the two subjects [are] to be made consistent, Self-love must be supposed to give the object with reference to which Conscience judges.

'Selfishness', then, can only lie in predominance of gratifications not involving pleasure of others over those that do – all 'gratifications' alike, in man as reflective,[173] being relative to supreme desire for his own happiness.

Apparently, Butler's perfectly virtuous man is that man who pursues his own pleasure (p.207) systematically, but in whom benevolence is [so] strong that its gratification balances (not *over*-balances) all gratifications not involving pleasure of another.[174]

Admitting this distinction between selfish and benevolent man, why is one approved, the other not? Why do I say that I *ought* not to be selfish, ought to be benevolent? Because of 'reflex principle of approbation and disapprobation'?[175] Does this = conception of one's *own* happiness or greatest pleasure?

Hutcheson says no.[176] Then what is it?

The judgment 'I ought' is a 'moral sentiment', sentiment of approbation, or disapprobation, as opposed to a judgment *given by reason*. Two questions. (a) Is it a motive to action? (b) Is it primary or derived? Agreed that *reason* cannot give motive.

(a) With Shaftesbury it is a reflex *affection for social affections* – and as an affection is a *motive*. With Butler motives to virtuous action appear ordinarily, as either self-love or benevolence, but in Sermons on Love of God, he recognizes a *love of goodness*, as such, which, like Shaftesbury's reflex affection, is a *motive*.[177] With Hume 'moral sentiment' is in the contemplator: not a motive; though desire to excite such sentiment in the contemplator may be a motive.

(b) Love for goodness, as such – if that be true account of moral sentiment – clearly can't be derived by any association of, or calculation of means to obtain, pleasures. It must then, either be denied or it must be admitted that reason *originates*; sc: creates an object by reference to which feelings are determined, but which is not itself a feeling. Received notion with followers of Locke – that reason is not thus constitutive. Hutcheson holds untenable position. Insists that moral sense is primary and that is not deter-mined by an object which reason gives. Makes it specific sense, specific as any of the '5.'[178] These, however, specified by *organ* or *object*. Moral sense clearly has no *organ*, and what is its object? 'Goodness of action.' But this goodness consists in action's satis-fying moral sense. A see-saw. First determine *object* by reference to *sense*, as if that were already determinate, then it turns out that sense on its part is only determined by reference to object.

Hence tendency to reduce moral sentiment to expectation of pleasure other than that which consists in satisfaction, of that sentiment. If object, which satisfies it, seems to give no pleasure to the contemplator apart from this satisfaction, this may be accounted for by number of links of association by which action, to which that sentiment is immediately directed, is connected with ultimate pleasure.

The 'intuitional moralists' of present day don't seem to have got beyond Hutchesonian 'moral sense.' 'Why ought I to do it?'[179] 'Because my moral sense approves it.' 'Why does it approve it?' 'Because it does.'

This sort of answer has its practical value because: (a) the uncritilised sentiment, resulting from education, represents a more comprehensive view of bearings of an act than any which individual could come to by his own reasoning; and (b) because to make enquiry into ground of that sentiment is commonly to begin making excuses in one's own favour for not doing that which 'sentiment' approves.

[§10 Self-love and Benevolence.]

Do 'social and self-regarding' affections differ only in their relations, as these may supposed to be seen by a philosopher or designing creator, or in the objects by which they are determined for the consciousness of those subject to them? Only on former supposition are they properly 'animal.' But, though Shaftesbury calls them so, the latter seems to be really his supposition. He calls them not affections *productive of* self-good and social good, but affections for – etc. This being so, they can't be separated from each other in same way as in a properly animal system (Adam Smith)[180] appetite for food and sexual appetite might be, of which one is operative at one time, another at another. Same self-consciousness determines both, presenting at once the man and the persons, an interest in whom is given in and with the existence of the man, to himself as an object determining his desire.

Butler argues that benevolence 'rests in its object as its end', just like any animal appetite; and that so far from its being 'interested', or a mode of self-love, self-love would be empty – would have no pleasures wherewith to satisfy itself unless the satisfaction of natural and disinterested desires – sc: desires which don't originate in desire to please oneself – furnished these.[181]

(Quite true that self-love and benevolence are not to [be] co-ordinated, as if they were competing, though reconcilable, 'principles of our nature.')

Undoubtedly benevolence 'rests, etc.' Benevolent man desires pleasure of his neighbour *not* as a means to a *separate* pleasure of his own; but on other hand consciousness of another as object implies consciousness of self. Benevolence not *more* interested than the appetites, if these mean desires for pleasure accruing on satisfaction of appetites, but pleasure of another must be presented by benevolent man to himself as his own good, just as satisfaction of appetite is presented by ακολαστος ['the licentious man'] to himself as his own good. Question is whether his own *good* means to him his own *pleasure*. Is the motive to benevolent man his own pleasure; not an ulterior pleasure other than that given in or with the pleasure of the other (and it was such pleasure that was contemplated by those who pronounced benevolence interested), but just the pleasure of seeing the other pleased? That such a motive may lead to course of action, generally recognized as selfish and bad, appears in the many forms of unjust generosity, spoiling children, etc., etc. Case of older man who spoils a younger by procuring him constant indulgence for sake of pleasure which he finds in seeing the other pleased. The 'benevolence' here not 'interested,' in the sense of Butler's and Shaftesbury's opponents, but still selfish, because determined by desire for pleasure. Is the only morally good benevolence then that which proceeds from sense of duty? And if so, are we not led to Kant's decried result that only benevolent act, of which we can be sure that it is morally good, is one of which the object is some one hated?[182]

Acts (e.g. of ordinary courtesy) which we do without thinking, under influence of social custom brought to bear on us through education, have been rendered possible by painful effort in the past which men, who acted for pleasure, would never have undertaken. Are not such acts morally good? Answer act can only be called morally good with reference to character of doer, and these do not shew *character* of doer. Don't shew whether forming principle of it is reverence for universal law. On the other hand, they are 'good' as tending to[183] a system of action in which everyone should be determined by idea of such law and accordingly free. Are only 'painful' acts, then, 'morally good' in above strict sense? Answer. No moral value in painfulness of act any more than in its pleasantness. Can only judge of man's life as a whole. Distinction between acts which society expects of a man, and acts which, however pleasantly and unthinkingly he may do them as a formed character, presuppose 'sense of duty' in his own person as influence for motive of his character. But since 'moral ideal' unattainable by individual, the 'morally good' man can never be one who acquiesces in merely doing what he does pleasantly. Not true that benevolence is worthless unless object of it is man whom I don't like, but true that it is morally worthless unless it issues from character which would equally do good to man towards whom an instinctive aversion is felt. An act to be morally good need not be prompted by present 'sense of Duty,' as implying 'impeded' activity. Presence of such sense very much depends on circumstances, but man whose life goes on so smoothly that sense of Duty' according to this meaning, never forces itself on him may be pretty sure that he is acquiescing in low ideal.

'Living for pleasure = wickedness: living pleasantly may be all right. How is anyone [to] ascertain about another (which doesn't[184] matter), or object himself (which does) whether he is only living pleasantly or living for pleasure?' Many people can have little difficulty, if honest, in deciding that they are living for pleasure. Doing no good to any one, not even helping to keep in play existing organisation of society, but incidentally doing a good deal of harm, and getting nothing done.

To others, only practical way of answering question is by direction[185] to new object – by putting them in way of getting something done, interest in which may save them from watching their own pleasures – at once from state of living for pleasure and from torturing themselves with question whether they are so living or no.

Unselfishness, according to Butler, does not as such render an action morally good. It is morally good so far as it suits our entire nature, i.e. so far as it satisfies supreme principle of reflexive approbation and disapprobation.

So with supposed act of benevolence, which spoils another. Not good, because not approved by conscience.

Two questions then arise. (1) Is an action morally good, merely because it accords with principle of approbation, etc., or must it *proceed from this*: must this give motive? (2) *What* is approved? Is it enough to say so-and-so is good because I approve it, and I approve because I do approve it?

Still, thinking man can't be satisfied with such answer - which in effect says that we approve action because it is good, and that it is good because we approve it.

To 'intuitionalists' are opposed those who, having said that we approve an action because it is good, in reply to further question why it is good, instead of saying because we approve it, say 'because of its results.' These are sometimes called 'experimentalists': sometimes 'rationalists', because they make reason not feeling the criterion. (Yet they suppose themselves followers of Hume, who was for ever reiterating that he made feeling, not reason, the criterion.)

On the ground of philosophy, every one in this sense must be 'rationalist' or experimentalist – must hold that what renders an action good is not its present relation to sentiment of doer, but (in some way or other) its consequences – its relation to a social system. Real question is as to source of that system and of that consideration of that system on part of individual which renders an action, suitable to the system, obligatory on him.

[§11 The Universality of the Moral Law.]
Universality of moral law means (practically) that individual must never make exception to it in his own favour (to please himself – or when he supposes that the exception is to please others – as in case of unjust generosity – it is always really to please himself). It does not mean that any rule of action can be drawn to suit all cases.

'Thou shalt not lie.'[186] This seems to admit of no exception, but only because by 'lie' we tacitly assume ourselves to mean such an untruth as violates moral law – i.e., as is told (in some way) in one's own favour. Put it in the form, 'Thou shalt never say what is *not true*' (i.e. what does not represent your own thoughts or may give incorrect notion to another) and it is easy to imagine cases where rule admits of exception.

(Nigger-driver;[187] on track of runaway. Ask other nigger which way he has gone.)[188]

In common life, odds so much on side of exception being in one's favour that rigid adherence to the general rule without thought of consequence is only safe course.

What then is this 'universal moral law', which admits of no statement? Kant's formula. Fitness of 'maxim' to be principle of universal law-giving (?) to be settled by consideration whether general carrying of it out implies contradiction, e.g. in case of property. 'What's his can't be not his, and everything must be his[189] or not his.'[190] But universal theft implies that everything is not – his to everyone and yet that every one has something for another to make his. But how about communism?

Really, 'fitness of maxim', etc., must be settled by consideration of what is 'good for society.' 'Then, say Utilitarians, you agree with us.'

Undoubtedly, there is practical Utilitarianism[191] in which all good citizens, who reflect, are agreed. Still all difference in world between Kantian view (however one may depart from Kant as to process of ascertaining 'fitness,' etc.) and Humian. According to Kant, source of all morality is immanent operation of this formative idea of Universal[192] law; which is antithetic to all sensitive experience, as the divine to the animal, though it acts upon it and only as acting upon it moves the individual. 'The only good is good will'[193] – disposition to conform to universal law – refusal to make oneself an exception – which may be most potent when formula in which individual would express the law is most inadequate or when (as sometimes nowadays) oppressed by perplexities of dialectic or complexities of society, he refuses to formulate it at all.[194]

How is [it] that there is moral right and wrong – good and bad: (a) Because there is idea of universal law, which taking to itself desire, may move action; so that when action is moved by this idea, it is good; when not, bad. (b) Because man is susceptible of pleasures varying in quantity, and may calculate conditions of pleasure rightly or wrongly, so as to gain or miss greatest sum.[195]

Doctrine (b) in *long run* can hardly fail to tell on life: though often doubtless man whose doctrine is (b) may act just as much from 'good will' as man whose doctrine is (a). Early Utilitarians were political reformers. Living for improvement of society, though their account of the end with reference to which they were trying to move society a mistaken one, they were yet, as much as any one, practically seeking to realize universal law. But as reforming zeal of Utilitarians passes away, its theory apt to get the better of its practices.

Why should I trouble myself about 'universal law' and not act as pleases me?

Difficulty inherent in nature of formative ideas. So with idea of uniformity of nature. 'The assurance that there is a law to be found if only we knew how to find it is source from which canons of Inductive Logic derive their validity': yet no adequate knowledge of what this law is without exhaustive knowledge of nature.[196]

As sensitive experience governed by this 'assurance' differs in kind from succession of sensations without it, so action governed by idea of 'something to be done universally' (as all human action is) differs in kind from action without it.

In each case the idea is 'regulative' not 'constitutive': sc. no object corresponding to it can be presented under conditions of space and time.

The idea of the world as a whole as a complete system can't be realized in any object that we can either perceive or imagine, or in any sum of experience. Every object perceived or imagined must be qualified by another object outside it: every sum of experience must [be] qualified next day by new experience.

Yet this unrealizable idea is source of all knowledge of objective reality. So with idea of God – as unity not merely of 'natural world' but of that moral world which man is in gradual process of making, as well: or rather, as unity of one world, in which natural is relative to the moral. This idea we can only define by negatives. Hence some reckon God the 'great unknown', the ὑποκείμενον ['underlying substance'] which remains when all definite attributes have been thought away. Others, out of presumed ignorance plus fear elicit result that we must accept traditional ideas of God as absolute and final revelation of him. In truth, the idea of God as in us is in process of definition by all knowledge of nature and development of morals; though never adequately. And this knowledge and development in virtue of the regulative idea is different in kind from what it would be without it.

So with idea of Duty.

How am I to ascertain whether an action is morally right? By reference to good of society. How measure this good? By amount of good will?

Is this a circle?

Objection to 'Moral sense' doctrine is that it makes this *sense of the good*, and then when asked what the *good* is replies 'that which this sense perceives'.

Thus that is good which seems so to individual, he knows not why. This does not explain *objectivity* of moral principle – its opposition to the personal likings – without which moral life not explained. It will explain beneficence, of the sort which consciously approves itself, on the part of one who is naturally a 'friend of man' at time when he is so: not idea of duty to be done to others by one who is in chronic ill-temper.

Not essentially different from doctrine which says that is good which pleases me. Utilitarian modifies this by saying – 'which pleases me because it pleases others.'

Either it is the pleasing me (my personal pleasure) that makes it good, though this pleasure as matter of fact implies pleasure of others: or, if *pleasure of others* is what makes it good, what is personal pleasure of John, Thomas, and William that it should make action good when my own personal pleasure can't.

If we say that his own personal pleasure is not the morally good to each man, but that disposition to please others = the morally good just on account of the sum of the pleasure of those others, then we are making the morally good that in the gross[197] which *in detail* is not morally good at all.

Meanwhile you are defining the good by the absolutely indefinite, and leaving unaccounted for that which has the permanent spring of moral elevation – the notion of Divine law, will of God, law of collective humanity, (called by many names) – of something to be done whether it pleases everybody or nobody.

It would seem then that the good disposition is disposition to promote good of society, is disposition to please others not on account of *the sum of the pleasures of others*. How else determine good of society?

'Will to do *something* universally (without making exception in one's favour); but what the *something* is can't be adequately defined.'

To Kant, as student of Hume, question as to possibility of morals (in proper sense) presents itself in same form as question as to possibility of knowledge. No association of feelings[198] can give synthetic judgment a priori – a judgement as to reality which shall be of general certainty: without which no mathematics: nor idea of permanent objective order, without which no knowledge of nature. Neither can it give idea of objective moral order – or (as Kant would rather say) idea of something *to be* done universally, whether it pleases me and multitude of others or no, and for its own sake. Yet without such idea moral experience of mankind impossible.

Kant admits a sympathetic interest (p.146) in good of others as a proper 'matter' of the moral maxim: he only insists that it must not be made *condition* of that maxim.[199]

According to him, however, the most that could be said of it would be that it was a not-immoral motive. In this it differs from 'reverence for law.' He is so far right about this, that we ought to be satisfied with ourselves,[200] unless there is such a 'reverence, etc.' to keep us to the moral law when 'sympathetic interest' fails.

But a great mistake to present them as competing principles proceeding from different sources within same character. Causality of reason upon feeling as much implied in the one as in the other. With one in whom 'elements were kindly mixed', under ordinary circumstances, distinction between them would never come into consciousness. But work of reason not complete till it has created a power in individual which will take that place of all impulses conditioned by animal nature. Life a lingering death of these – a dying into immortality.

Kant tends to above mistake: but remember that he was writing with reference to those who made that *sympathy* the ground and condition of obligation.

So far question concerns moral *maxim*. It is another question whether consideration of good of others is proper guide for determining what in particular, given that disposition to obey universal law, I ought to do. This is a question with which Kant scarcely deals. (a) What am I to do? (b) From what motive am I to do it? Kant seems to answer (b) without answering (a).

This procedure at first sight might seem illogical. Kant's vindication would be that it is characteristic of moral law to command not an act but a disposition; that thus the two questions coincide. It enjoins as motive conformity to a universal law (law that can be thought of as law for all rational beings): that *motive* is the *act* which it tells us to do: the inside though not the outside. It commands a '*wollen*' ['wish'], irrespective of *result* of 'Wollen.' Hegelian objection. Is not this same as say[ing] that mere aspiration suffices 'Die Lorbeers ['The laurels'], etc.'?[201] No: Kant did not mean inactive 'wollen.' But at any [rate] it means that act is all right, if only conscientious, whatever its consequences: this will[202] vindicate all the George IIIs and Newdegates.'[203] For Kant we may answer: What is called 'conscience' is often only an 'eigen dünkel' ['personal pride'] which is form of self-love. An act conscientious in true sense, in sense that if all men acted so, it would be perfect world, is all right. But may it not have bad results under given circumstances? Only if you consider results apart from *good will*. Each truly conscientious act *strengthens* and *propagates* good will.

But will mere conscientiousness guide a man right in complicated social questions, and is not every man as matter of fact constantly dealing with such questions (shall I join a trade's Union?)? Is 'duty' such a simple thing as Kant seems to suppose? (p.149)[204]

In most cases where we try to shirk it, it is very simple thing. 'Thou shalt not lie.' Supposed difficulty arises from wrong disposition – disposition to make oneself exception to law.

But undoubtedly cases arise where consideration of expediency can alone settle what I ought to do: though there is still not question about 'maxim.'

'Are not all established moral rules result of a controversy as to expediency which has been gradually settled by experience of mankind?'

Common Utilitarianism of good citizen admits of no adjustment between moral maxim and moral law. It does not allow that desire for personal pleasure is true moral maxim. If asked, when it happens not to please me to speak truth,[205] may I lie? – it would answer *no*. At same time its rule – 'live for happiness, which = maximum of pleasure, of others,' – implies that pleasure is the end, and therefore[206] logically the maxim, for everyone. Humish Utilitarianism avoids this inconsistency: according to it pleasure – sympathetic or other – is only possible *motive*, as well as standard.

This raises other difficulties. Respect for law must be reduced to fear: for 'moral' as distinct from 'positive' obligations, to fear mixed with sympathetic uneasiness caused by imagination of what others would think of us, if they only knew (difference between feelings of card-player who has lost and one who has cheated).

'Hope that is seen is no more hope; for that which a man seeth, why doth he yet hope for?' [Rom. 8.24][207]

'Duty that is done is no more duty; for that which a man doeth which should he have yet to do.'[208]

On other side, it may be objected to Kant's doctrine, (a) that there is inconsistency between exclusion of pleasure from moral maxim and law, and admitted fact that but for pursuit of pleasure and its results there would have been no laws, either of 'perfect' or 'imperfect' obligation, at all,[209] and (b) between asserted unconditional character of moral maxim and law, and fact that there are manifold cases where established rules of conduct fail us, and we have to fall back on considerations of expediency.

As to (a) – there would be no animal life but for chemical affinity, but laws of chemical affinity do not therefore = life. So with pleasure and moral law. Phenomena of human society are only explicable *teleologically*, e.g. they (1) form a process which is what it is in virtue of relation to a result which is other than any stage in the process taken by itself or all the stages taken together: nor is this relation merely one that we invent; it actually conditions every stage in the process: the process consisting in activity of self-conscious subjects.

(2) An elementary *conception* of that result conditions this activity in its primary ascertainable forms. Man acts from ideas – even if selfishly, *yet* from *conception* of self. (Thus Kant truly says that in acting from *idea* of freedom, he is *really* free.[210] It is only in investigation of nature that question whether reality corresponds to idea is applicable. In field of morals the idea *is*, or is in the process of forming, a reality.)

Only thus can characteristic movement in human society, which is *not* circular, be accounted for. Desire for new pleasures, self-assertion and correlative demand for recognition by others – remove these and αρχη κινησεως [efficient cause] of society, even in the least moralized forms of which we have any definite knowledge, is gone. Out of these, indeed, looking at them from outside, we could not construct moral law, as Physiologist[211] constructs an extinct animal out of 1,012 bones, but, having the moral law and having it as within our personal experience developed by successive negation from lower self-seeking principles, we can legitimately interpret history as like development.[212]

This leads us to (b). No doubt there are moral rules, which good man now takes for granted, which were once of debateable expediency – rules, which if some super-subtle philosopher calls in question, he feels are best settled – as Dr. Johnson settled question about matter by kicking a stone[213] – by kicking the philosopher:[214] e.g. rules of conduct that arise out of institution of monogamy. Those which arise out institution of property only differ from these as more elementary still. A mistake to represent 'a priori necessity' of these as if it depended on principle of contradiction.

'A-priori necessity,' (1) of moral disposition – necessity that individual should only do that which he can wish to be universal law – *a priori* to morality in same sense as is 'two straight lines can't enclose space'[215] is a priori to Mathematics: viz: that without it there would be no distinctively moral action: therefore can't be result of generalization from moral action.

A-priori necessity, (2) given disposition, of act that follows from it. All acts involved in maintenance of institutions and habits, so far found necessary to organization of society, are thus 'a-priori necessary.' About these, considerations of expediency only introduced as excuses for bad will.

But society still in process of organization.

'Handle so, daß die Maxime deines Willens jederzeit zugleich als Prinzip einer allgemeinen Gesetzgebung gelten könne.'[216] ['So act that the maxim of your will could always hold at the same time as a principle in giving of universal law.'][217] This according to Kant is a 'practishes grundsätz', as 'containing a universal determination of the will, which has under it a multiplicity of practical rules.'[218]   The same might be said of principle of 'eigene Glückseligkeit' ['one's own happiness'];[219] but it differs from the latter as being recognized as valid for all rational beings, and is thus not *merely* a 'grundsatz', but a 'practiches *Gesetz*' ['practical law'].

In what sense is it *necessary* '*a priori*'? Is it not in a different sense of necessity that we ascribe it to an αρχη κινησεως and to an αρκη γνωδεως: to the injunction of a disposition, and a proposition as to fact?

Necessity properly belongs to conceptions. Those conceptions have a priori speculative necessity which condition all experience, as ascertainment of facts, would be impossible. Those... practical...which condition all moral action:[220] of which therefore, it cannot be said that you first act morally by consideration of results of action and then gradually come to have the conception. As facts to a priori speculative conception, so are determinations of will to a priori practical conception. Consideration of what is involved in 'facts' makes *us aware* of former: consideration of what is involved in *determination of will* makes us aware of latter.

But observation of human action from outside can tell nothing of moral determination. It is not observation of how men *do* act, but consideration of how we ought to act, that does for a priori *practical* conception that which observation of facts does for a priori *speculative*, viz: bring it into clear consciousness.[221]

(Hence answer to question, Can moral philosophy rest on inductive basis?)

Principle which renders observation of nature possible can't itself be derived from such observation, but such observation exhibits it. It is manifested *in concerto* in every new discovery. The conception becomes fuller, more real, with every such discovery. But to conception of which expression is not a proposition, but an injunction, 'discovery' of facts of human nature stands in no such relation. It does not affect moral disposition. It does not relate to 'sollen' ['ought'], but to 'sein' ['to be']. Given that disposition to obey law, it *enlightens* men as to 'rules' which arise out of application of moral law to circumstances of life.

Consideration of position in which 'enlightenment' stands to 'good will' according to Buckle.[222]

Explain question about goodness and cleverness.

---

1   [I have adopted this heading as an apposite title for the manuscript as a whole. Green wrote the phrase at the top of an early folio, although it does not appear to be associated with any particular part of the whole.]

2   [MS addition: 'refer [?] [....?] object' (MS torn).]

3   [MS del.: 'synthetic power'.]

4   [MS orig.: 'sensation'.]

5   [MS reads: 'their'.]

6   [MS del.: 'as organiser of'.]

7   [MS orig.: 'we are to understand it'.]

8   [Paper torn.]

9   [MS orig.: 'dealt with'.]

10   [Green appears to use the word 'unmotived' as a synonym for 'unmotivated.']

11   [MS orig.: 'beginning'.]

12   [MS orig.: 'phenomena'.]

13   [Placing of this aside uncertain.]

14   [An allusion to John Stuart Mill, 'Utilitarianism', in his *Collected Works*, JM Robson et al (eds.), 33 vols. (University of Toronto Press, 1981–91), vol.10, pp.210–1.]

15   [MS orig.: 'ascertainable'.]

16   [MS orig.: 'nations'.]

17   'In contact i.e.'. Suppose that he comes in collision with law: or that the sensuous presentation of some religious idea attracts his desire.

18   [MS orig.: 'contemplated'.]

[19] [Cf. PPO §187, 200.]

[20] The reason which makes 'nature' (in virtue of which nature exists) is also in us as source of our knowledge of nature: but it is *not* as in man [MS orig.: 'us'] that it makes nature. But it *is* as in man that it makes moral world.

(a) How does reason give a system of *nature* to be known?

(b) How does reason give a 'moral universe', in being determined by which we are determined by ourselves: and thus determined not as we *must* but as we *ought*? (Ambiguity in *must*.) This involves two questions: [1.] what is duty? [2.] what is free action? [Placing uncertain.]

[21] [MS orig.: 'make his own,'.]

[22] [MS reads: 'given risen rise'.]

[23] [Number only partially formed in mss.]

[24] [MS orig.: 'consequence'.]

[25] 'Property has its duties as well as its rights.' If 'duties' = obligation, a truism. If = duties proper, not true. Really that 'duties' mean obligations *not enforced*. [Placing uncertain.]

[26] (1) and (2) properly deal with 'Sein.' [sc. external, 'legal' commands (sphere of obligation).]

(3) with 'Sollen.' [sc. inward, moral commands (sphere of duty).]

But duties always arise out of fact. Inquiry into *facts* of society *conditions* social *duties*. [Placing uncertain.]

[27] [MS orig.: '*define*'.]

[28] [MS reads: 'an'.]

[29] [Immanuel Kant, *Critique of Pure Reason*, ed. and trans. P. Guyer and A. W. Wood (Cambridge University Press, 1998), pp. 153–92 (A19/B33–A49/B73) ('Transcendental Aesthetic'). [First edition published 1781; second edition 1787.]]

[30] [MS orig.: 'instinct'.]

[31] [MS orig.: 'desire'.]

[32] [MS orig.: '*should*'.]

[33] [Kant makes this point often, although not in these words. For example, see Immanuel Kant, 'Groundwork of the Metaphysics of Morals', in his *Practical Philosophy*, trans. and edited by MJ Gregor (Cambridge: Cambridge University Press, 1996), pp.92–3 (Prussian Academy edition 4:444).]

[34] [MS reads: 'beauty or ugliness,' but Green indicates the reversal of the terms by placing the numbers '2' and '1' above the two nouns.]

[35] [MS orig.: 'either'.]

[36] ['"The blackbird amid the leafy trees,
The lark above the hill,
Let loose their carols when they please,
Are quiet when they will.

'"With Nature never do *they* wage
A foolish strife; they see

A happy youth, and their old age
Is beautiful and free:

"'But we are pressed by heavy laws;
And often, glad no more,
We wear a face of joy, because
We have been glad of yore.'

William Wordsworth, 'The Fountain: A conversation', in his *Poetical Works: Cambridge edition*, revised by PD Sheats (Boston: Houghton Mifflin, 1982), p.117 (ll.37–48). Poem first published in 1800.]

37 [MS orig.: 'sin.']

38 [MS del., before 'though': 'of speculative men'.]

39 [Green puts the final two phrases into separate parentheses.]

40 [MS orig.: 'possibility.']

41 [MS orig.: '*sin.*' Note from facing page:]

Distinction between personal Epicureanism and the Utilitarianism of 'Sociologist.'

A man *supposing* himself to live for pleasure, sc. to be passive, is apt to lose in moral originativeness.

To live in order to feel, or to live in order to act.

42 [Placing of this aside uncertain. Gellius introduces this quotation with the words: 'But our countryman Taurus, whenever mention was made of Epicurus, always had on his lips and tongue these words of Hierocles the Stoic, a man of righteousness and dignity: 'Pleasure ...'. Autus Gellius, *Attic Nights*, trans. JC Rolfe, 3 vols. (London: William Heinemann, 1947), vol. 2, bk 9, §5.8.]

43 Pleasure, like simple sensation, indefinable. *Passive* relation of the individual, as he is at any passing moment, to a passing object. Its physical conditions, like those of sensation, may be ascertained. But it is not any unimpeded flow of nervous currents (?) that = pleasure as a datum of our unconsciousness, any more than it is vibration in tympanum of ear that = sound as we are conscious of it. [Placing uncertain.]

44 [MS del.: 'No.']

45 [Placing of the next four sentences is uncertain.]

46 [MS alt.: '[...?] to reorganise'.]

47 [Probably Green has in mind John Stuart Mill. See Nettleship, *Memoir*, p.cxlv.]

48 [MS alt.: 'ορεκτσν'.]

49 [MS orig.: 'thought'.]

50 [MS orig.: 'free'.]

51 [MS orig.: 'imprisoned'.]

52 [Possibly a paraphrase of Lord Shaftesbury, 'Treatise 4. viz. An Inquiry Concerning Virtue, *or* Merit', in his *Characteristicks of Men, Manners, Opinions, Times*, ed. Philip Ayres, 2 vols. (Oxford: Clarendon, 1999), vol. 1 (hereafter, 'Inquiry'), bk 2, pt 2, §1, pp.241–2. Hereafter references give treatise, book, part and section numbers in square brackets, before the relevant page number(s) for this edition.]

53 [Probably Christian Wolff (1679–1754), German philosopher who, very controversially (and, for him, very dangerously) advocated a form of secular rationalism.
He published a great deal on most areas of philosophy. In his perfectionist ethics,
he argued that one's feelings of pleasure were an indicator of the degree of realisation of one's essence.]

54 [MS reads: 'H's'. Probably a reference to Thomas Hobbes, 'Tripos; in Three
Discourses. I. Human Nature: Or the fundamental elements of policy', in T
Hobbes, *English Works*, ed. W. Molesworth, 11 vols. (London: John Bohn,
1839–45) (hereafter, 'Human Nature'), vol. 4, chap. 8, §3, p.37. Cf. Thomas
Hobbes, *Leviathan*, in T Hobbes, *English Works*, ed. W. Molesworth, 11 vols.
(London: John Bohn, 1839–45), vol. 3, chap. 6.]

55 [Immanuel Kant, *Kritik der Praktischen Vernunft*, edited by K Vorländer,
[*Sämtliche Werke*, Zweiter Band] (Leipzig: Verlag von Felix Meiner, 1922), Erster
Teil, I. Buch, 1 Hauptstück, §7, p.39.]

56 [Immanuel Kant, 'Critique of Practical Reason', in his *Practical Philosophy*, Bk 1,
chap. 1, §7, p.164 (Prussian 5:30). This quotation recurs near end of this piece
(see p. 60 below).]

57 [MS del.: ' 'thought' .']

58 [MS reads: 'A.S.'s.']

59 [Adam Smith, *The Theory of Moral Sentiments*, ed. by DD Raphael and AJ
Macfie (Oxford: Clarendon, 1976), Part 1, §1, chapter 1, pp.9–10).]

60 [MS orig.: 'adjusted to the organic system'.]

61 [Cf. Kant, 'Critique of Practical Reason', in his *Practical Philosophy*, esp. pt 1, bk
1, chap. 1, pp.153–62 (Prussian 5:19–29) and pt 1, bk 2, pp.226–58 (Prussian
5:108–48).]

62 Remorse and sense of pollution. Man can't get rid of his act. It, and object against
which it was done, invested with permanence of the self, and pursue him as furies
– not to be rid of by resistance, but by recognition of their right. [Placing uncertain.]

63 Can have no image of such a principle: no more of rays of light, of undulations of
Other, of time. [Placing uncertain.]

64 [MS reads: 'become'.]

65 [MS orig.: 'desire'.]

66 [Kant, 'Groundwork', in his *Practical Philosophy*, pp.56–8 (Prussian 4:401–3),
81–5 (Prussian 4:430–6).]

67 [MS orig.: 'into himself'.]

68 [This phrase comes from the catechism in the 1662 service of confirmation of the
United Church of England and Ireland. The person to be confirmed professes to
have learnt two things from the Ten Commandments: namely, 'my duty towards
God' and 'my duty towards my Neighbour': 'My duty towards my Neighbour, is
to love him as myself, and to do to all men, as I would they should do unto me:
To love, honour, and succour my father and mother: To honour and obey the
Queen, and all that are put in authority under her: To submit myself to all my
governors, teachers, spiritual pastors and masters: To order myself lowly and
reverently to all my betters: To hurt no body by word nor deed: To be true and
just in all my dealing: To bear no malice nor hatred in my heart: *To keep my hands
from picking and stealing*, and my tongue from evilspeaking, lying, and slandering:

To keep my body in temperance, soberness, and chastity: Not to covet nor desire other men's goods; but to learn and labour truly to get mine own living, and to do my duty in that state of life, unto which it shall please God to call me.' 'A Catechism. That is to say, An instruction to be learned of every person before he be brought to be confirmed by the Bishop', in *Book of Common Prayer, and Administration of the Sacraments, and Other Rites and Ceremonies of the Church, and According to the Use of the United Church of England and Ireland...,* Rev. Richard Mant, DD (ed.), (Oxford: J Parker; London: FC and J Rivington, 1820), p.433 (composed 1661; adopted by the Church 1662) (emphasis added).]

69 [MS reads: ' through '.]

70 [MS orig.: 'is determined by'.]

71 Punishment. [Placing uncertain.]

72 (a) Confusion of 'State' with Society or nation.

(b) restriction of 'State' to supreme as opposed to municipal government. [Placing uncertain.]

73 [In fact, Hobbes claims: 'Of the powers of the *mind* there be two sorts, *cognitive, imaginative,* or *conceptive* and *motive;*' in Hobbes, 'Human Nature', chap. 1, §7, p.2. No attempt has been made to correct Green's quotations, most of which are inaccurate although rarely in such a manner as to seriously distort the meaning of the original.]

74 [Hobbes, 'Human Nature', chap.1, §7, p.3.]

75 [Hobbes, 'Human Nature', chap.2, §2, p.3.]

76 [Hobbes, 'Human Nature', chap.1, §4, p.4.]

77 [Hobbes, 'Human Nature', chap.2, §10, p.8.]

78 [Hobbes, 'Human Nature', chap. 3, §1, p.9.]

79 [Hobbes, 'Human Nature', chap. 3, §1, p.9.]

80 [Hobbes, 'Human Nature', chap. 4, §1, p.14.]

81 [Hobbes, 'Human Nature', chap. 3, §2, p.15.]

82 [Hobbes, 'Human Nature', chap. 3, §4, p. 15.]

83 [Possibly Hobbes, 'Human Nature', chap. 4, §4, pp.15–6, although Hobbes has 'appetite' where Green puts 'Wisdom'.]

84 [Hobbes, 'Human Nature', chap. 4, §1, p.19.]

85 ['invented' deleted in MS but replaced with an illegible alternative.]

86 [Hobbes, 'Human Nature', chap. 5, §2, p.20.]

87 [Hobbes, *Leviathan*, chap. 5, p.29.]

88 [Hobbes, *Leviathan*, chap.5, p.30.]

89 [Hobbes, 'Human Nature', chap. 6, §9, p.30.]

90 [MS orig.: '*social* experience'.]

91 [Thomas Hobbes, 'Tripos; in Three Discourses. II. De Corpore Politico: Or the elements of law, moral and politic, ...', in T Hobbes, *English Works*, ed. W. Molesworth, 11 vols. (London: John Bohn, 1839–45), vol. 4, pt 1, chap. 1, §1, p.87.]

92   [Hobbes, 'Human Nature', chap. 6, §9, p.30.]

93   [MS includes 'which' at this point.]

94   [Hobbes, 'Human Nature', chap. 7, §1, 2, pp.31–2.]

95   [Hobbes, 'Human Nature', chap. 7, §1, p.31.]

96   [Hobbes, 'Human Nature', chap. 7, §1, p.31.]

97   [Hobbes, 'Human Nature', chap. 9, §8, p.44.]

98   [Hobbes, 'Human Nature', chap. 7, §3 p.32.]

99   [Hobbes, 'Human Nature', chap. 8, §3, p.37.]

100 [Hobbes, 'Human Nature', chap. 9, pp.40–53 *passim*.]

101 [Hobbes, 'Human Nature', chap. 12, §2 p.68.]

102 [Hobbes, 'Human Nature', chap. 12, §1, p.68.]

103 [Hobbes, 'Human Nature', chap. 12, §2, p.68.]

104 [Hobbes, 'Human Nature', chap. 12, §3, pp.68–9.]

105 [Hobbes, 'Human Nature', chap. 12, §3, p.69.]

106 [Hobbes, 'Human Nature', chap. 12, §3, p.69.]

107 [Hobbes, 'Human Nature', chap. 12, §5, p.69.]

108 [Hobbes, 'Human Nature', chap. 12, §1, p.68.]

109 [Green has point (c) after point (d) in the MS.]

110 [Cf. PPO §§ 187, 200.]

111 [MS reads: 'corrective of lies'.]

112 [MS orig.: 'constituting order of socie[ty]'.]

113 [Hobbes, 'Human Nature', chap. 8, §4, p.38.]

114 [Hobbes, 'De Corpore Politico', pt 1, chap. 1, §3, p.82.]

115 [The next seven paragraphs are from folio thirty-three, where no indication is given of their intended placing in relation to the main flow of the text. They fit very well at this point, however.]

116 [Hobbes, 'De Corpore Politico', pt 1, chap. 1, §4, p.82.]

117 [Hobbes, 'De Corpore Politico', pt 1, chap.1, §5, p.82.]

118 [Hobbes, 'De Corpore Politico', pt 1, chap. 1, §10, p.84.]

119 [Hobbes, 'De Corpore Politico', pt 1, chap. 1, §10, p.84.]

120 [Hobbes, 'De Corpore Politico', pt 1, chap.1, §13, p.86.]

121 [Hobbes, 'De Corpore Politico', pt 1, chap.1, §14, p.86.]

122 [Hobbes, 'De Corpore Politico', pt 1, chaps. 2–4.]

123 [Hobbes, 'De Corpore Politico', pt 1, chap.2, §1, p.87.]

124 [Hobbes, 'De Corpore Politico', pt 1, chap. 2, §2, p.87.]

125 [Hobbes, 'De Corpore Politico', pt 2, chap.4, §11, p.109.]

126 [Hobbes, 'De Corpore Politico', pt 2, chap.4, §15, pp.110–11.]

[127] [Hobbes, 'De Corpore Politico', pt 1, chap.1, §1, p.87.]

[128] [Hobbes, *Leviathan*, ch.3, p.313.]

[129] [Hobbes, 'De Corpore Politico', pt 1, chap.1, §2, p.87.]

[130] [Hobbes, *Leviathan*, pt 2, chap.18, p.161.]

[131] [Hobbes, *Leviathan*, pt2, chap. 18, p.162.]

[132] [John Locke, *An Essay Concerning Human Understanding*, ed. PH Nidditch (Oxford University Press, 1975), Book 2, chapter 21, §5. MS del.: '§§9'. I have silently inserted single section marks (i.e., §) into the text where they are neglected by Green. Green's consistently use of double section marks (i.e. §§) has been retained in all other instances.]

[133] ['The freedom of the will is best explained by a reference to the physical world. Freedom, I mean, is just as fundamental a character of the will as weight is of bodies. If we say: 'matter is heavy', we might mean that this predicate is only contingent; but it is nothing of the kind, for nothing in matter is without weight. Matter is rather weight itself. Heaviness constitutes the body and is the body. The same is the case with freedom and the will, since the free entity is the will. Will without freedom is an empty word, while freedom is actual only as will, as subject.' Georg WF Hegel, *Philosophy of Right*, trans. TM Knox (Oxford: Oxford University Press, 1967), §2A, pp.225–6.]

[134] [Locke, *Essay*, bk 2, chap. 21, §27.]

[135] [Paraphrasing Locke *Essay*, bk 2, chap. 21, §29.]

[136] [MS orig.: 'sum'.]

[137] [David Hume, 'An Inquiry Concerning the Principles of Morals: Appendix II.2. Of Self-love', in his *Philosophical Works*, 4 vols. (Edinburgh: Adam Black, William Tait and Charles Tait, 1826), vol. 4 (hereafter 'Self–love'), pp.383–4.]

[138] [David Hume, 'An Inquiry Concerning Human Understanding: A Dissertation on the Passions', in his *Philosophical Works*, vol. 4 (hereafter 'Dissertation'), §2, paragraph 5, p.206.]

[139] [Hume, 'Dissertation', §1, pp.195–202. A 'direct passion', such as hope or fear, is one which is motivated in itself to secure an 'agreeable' feeling.]

[140] [Middle number indecipherable, but p.207 fits the passage.]

[141] [Hume, 'Dissertation', §3, paragraphs 1 and 2, pp.218–9.]

[142] [Hume, 'Dissertation', §3, paragraphs 3 and 4, pp.219–20.]

[143] [David Hume, 'Inquiry Concerning the Principles of Morals: Appendix I Concerning Moral Sentiments', in his *Philosophical Works*, vol. 4, p.376.]

[144] [MS orig.: 'motive'.]

[145] [MS reads: 'choses'.]

[146] [MS reads: 'choses'.]

[147] [In this and the following instance, Green adopts Shaftesbury's spelling of the word 'vicious'.]

[148] [MS orig.: ' 'suspense of choice' '.]

[149] [MS reads: 'diff^{ted}'.]

[150] [MS orig.: 'in what sense'.]

[151] [Hobbes, 'Human Nature', chap.1, §7, p.2]

[152] [Lord Shaftesbury, the Third Earl of Shaftesbury, title of Anthony Ashley Cooper (1671–1713), English politician and philosopher. Joseph Butler (1692–1752), English theologian, moral philosopher and Anglican Bishop of Bristol (1738–51) and Durham (1751–2). Francis Hutcheson (1694–1746), Scottish philosopher.]

[153] [MS reads: 'A.S'. Adam Smith (1723–90), Scottish philosopher and political economist.]

[154] [Bernard de Mandeville (1670–1733), English doctor who is most famous for the satirical *Fable of the Bees* (1705).]

[155] [MS del.: 'Cudworth'. Samuel Clarke (1675–1729), English philosopher and theologian. Ralph Cudworth (1617–88), one of the Cambridge Platonists.]

[156] [Shaftesbury, 'Inquiry', bk 1, pt 1, §1, pp.192–3.]

[157] [Shaftesbury actually outlines three such 'Affections or Passions': *'natural Affections*, which lead to the Good of THE PUBLICK'; *'Self-Affections*, which lead only to the Good of THE PRIVATE', and *'unnatural Affections'* which tend to promote the good of neither the public nor private good. (Shaftesbury, 'Inquiry', bk 2, pt 1, §3, p.237).]

[158] [Shaftesbury, 'Inquiry', bk 1, pt 2, §§1–2, pp.196–202.]

[159] [Shaftesbury, 'Inquiry', bk 1, pt 2, §3, p.202.]

[160] [Shaftesbury, 'Inquiry', bk 1, pt 2, §4, p.206.]

[161] [Shaftesbury, 'Inquiry', bk 2, pt 1, §3, pp.235–7.]

[162] [Francis Hutcheson, *An Essay on the Nature and Conduct of the Passions and Affections with illustrations on the Moral Sense* (London: J Darby and T Brown, 1728), for example, 'Preface', pp.xiii–xvii.]

[163] [Hutcheson, *Passions and Affections*, treatise 1, §1, pp.2, 13.]

[164] [Hutcheson, *Passions and Affections*, treatise 1, §1, pp.5–6.]

[165] Distinction between doing an act pleasantly and doing it for pleasure. Former, when 'activity is unimpeded.' When this the case, we don't regard act as done from 'sense of duty', because this carries notion of impediment in process of being overcome. Mistake to regard each act in isolation. Question is, what has been formative principle of character expressed in act. It may have been conception of ideal that could only be realized, of law that could only be obeyed, painfully. But just so far as the character has been completely fashioned, the painfulness is over. Nay, supposing happy temper and education, that painful stage may have been got over almost unconsciously. [Placing uncertain.]

[166] [MS del.: 'philosophy'.]

[167] [Shaftesbury, 'Inquiry', bk 1, pt 2, §1, pp.198–9.]

[168] [MS del. (next paragraph): 'If it does, in what does it differ from reflex affection for social affection? As 'animal affections' they stand on same footing (impulses to remove an uneasiness). It is only as rational – so far as one is determined by presentation of self, the other by presentation of wider system – that they differ.']

[169] [Shaftesbury, 'Inquiry', bk 1, pt 2, §1, p.199.]

¹⁷⁰ [MS del. (next paragraph): 'Shaftesbury does not acquiesce in notion that selfishness means merely *excess* of "self–affections." Every action prompted by affection for self-good in him is selfish and vitious however it may contribute to public good.' (II.25) [Shaftesbury, 'Inquiry', bk 1, pt 2, §2, pp.199–202.]]

¹⁷¹ [Joseph Butler, 'Sermon 11 On Love of Our Neighbour', in his *Analogy of Religion to the Constitution and Course of Nature: Also, Fifteen Sermons* (London: Religious Tracts Society, n.d.), pp.469, 470.]

¹⁷² [Joseph Butler, 'Sermon I Upon Human Nature', in his *Analogy of Religion*), p.365.]

¹⁷³ [MS orig.: 'Reasonable'.]

¹⁷⁴ [Joseph Butler, 'Sermon I Upon Human Nature', in his *Analogy of Religion* , p.371.]

¹⁷⁵ [Shaftesbury, 'Inquiry', bk 1, pt 2, §3, pp.202–3.]

¹⁷⁶ [Hutcheson, *Passions and Affections*, treatise 2, §5, pp.285–300.]

¹⁷⁷ [Shaftesbury, 'Inquiry', bk 1, pt 2, §3, pp.202–6.]

¹⁷⁸ [That is, the five senses (sight, smell, hearing, touch, and taste).]

¹⁷⁹ [MS orig.: 'is an action right?' '.]

¹⁸⁰ [Smith, *Moral Sentiments*, pt 6, §§1–2 (pp.212–237).]

¹⁸¹ ['But if there be any such thing as delight in the company of one person, rather than another;...if it be without respect to fortune, honour, or increasing our stores of knowledge, or anything beyond the present time; here is an instance of an affection absolutely resting in its object as its end, and being gratified in the same way as the appetite of hunger is satisfied with food.... The gain, advantage or interest consists in the delight itself, arising from such a faculty's having its object;' Joseph Butler, 'Sermon XIII Upon the Love of God', in his *Analogy of Religion*, p.501. This is the recurring theme of this sermon.]

¹⁸² Provisional answer below. [Followed by caret mark identifying the paragraph which follows here.]

¹⁸³ [MS orig.: 'being consistent with'.]

¹⁸⁴ [MS reads: 'don't'.]

¹⁸⁵ ['direction' deleted in MS with no replacement given.]

¹⁸⁶ [A conventional Judeo-Christian extension of the ninth Commandment: 'Thou shalt not bear false witness against thy neighbour.' (Exodus 20.16).]

¹⁸⁷ [MS del.: 'Slave'.]

¹⁸⁸ [For Green's attacks on slavery, see PE §§207, 245, 266, 270; PPO, §§ 114–115, 132, 140, 143–7, 154, 241, and DSF §6. Regarding Green's fervent support for the abolitionist North in the American War of Independence, see Nettleship, *Memoir*, pp.xliii–xliv.]

¹⁸⁹ [MS orig.: 'mine'.]

¹⁹⁰ [MS orig.: 'mine.' '.]

¹⁹¹ [MS reads: 'U'.]

¹⁹² [MS reads: 'U'.]

193 ['It is impossible to think of anything at all in the world, or indeed even beyond it, that could be considered good without limitation except a *good will.*' Kant, 'Groundwork', in his *Practical Philosophy*, p.49 (Prussian 4:393).]

194 'I have done my duty and shall perhaps be hanged.' Conscientiousness: how far justification [Placing uncertain.]

195 'Higher and lower pleasures': does this mean 'pleasures incident to a life organized with reference to attainment of 'good will'?

'Pleasures index to will of Good [sic].' [Placing uncertain.]

196 [Cf. John Stuart Mill, *System of Logic Ratiocinative and Inductive*, in his *Collected Works*, vol. 7, bk 3, chaps. 3–4, pp.306–22.]

197 [MS orig.: 'out of the *gross* of that'.]

198 [MS orig.: 'ideas'.]

199 [Kant, 'Critique of Practical Reason', in his *Practical Philosophy*, p.206 (Prussian 5:82).]

200 [MS del.: 'a man is not morally good'.]

201 [Probably a reference to the following: '*In magnis...voluisse sat est* ['In great things to have willed is enough' (Propertius, II.x.6).] is right in the sense that we ought to will something great. But we must also be able to achieve it, otherwise the willing is nugatory. The laurels of mere willing are dry leaves that were never green.' Hegel, *Philosophy of Right*, §124A.]

202 [In RLN's hand at this point: 'See p.55 R.L.N.' '3 New College Men' written above in same hand.]

203 [George III (1738–1820), King of Great Britain and Ireland 1760–1820, incapacitated by porphyria from 1810. Newdegate is probably a reference to Newgate prison, London's main criminal goal in the eighteenth century. Its filthy condition and the lawlessness within it made the goal a symbol of everything that was wrong with the British penal system. It was demolished and rebuilt between 1767 and 1785.]

204 [Possibly a reference to Kant, 'Metaphysics of Morals' [first edition published 1797], in his *Practical Philosophy*, pp.378–80 (Prussian 6:224–6).]

205 [MS orig.: 'conform to moral law'.]

206 [MS reads: 'and the therefore'.]

207 [On his death-bed, Green asked for Romans 8 to be read to him (Nettleship, *Memoir*, pp.clix–clx).]

208 ['Doth he thank that servant because he did the things that were commanded him? I trow not./So likewise ye, when ye shall have done all those things which are commanded you, say, We are unprofitable servants: we have done that which was our duty.' (Luke 17.9–10)]

209 [Kant, 'Metaphysics of Morals', in his *Practical Philosophy*, pp521–4 (Prussian 6:390–4).]

210 [Kant, 'Critique of Practical Reason', in his *Practical Philosophy*, bk 2, chap. 7, esp. pp.246–54 (Prussian 5:133–42).]

211 [MS reads: 'Ph.'.]

²¹² If Greeks had not idea of 'Duty', as defined by all the antagonisms of modern Ethical controversy, they had that of *unconditional good*. [Placing uncertain.]

²¹³ [Boswell recorded what became a famous incident which took place on 6 August 1763, involving his hilarious friend and mentor Dr Samuel Johnson (1709–84), English man-of-letters, wit and man of very limited philosophical understanding: 'After we came out of the church, we stood talking for some time together of Bishop Berkeley's ingenious sophistry to prove the non-existence of matter, and that every thing in the universe is merely ideal I observed, that though we are satisfied his doctrine is not true, it is impossible to refute it. I never shall forget the alacrity with which Johnson answered, striking his foot with mighty force against a large stone, till be rebounded from it, "I refute it *thus.*" ' James Boswell, *Life of Samuel Johnson*, new edition, ed. John Wilson Croker, 5 vols. (London: John Murray, 1831), vol.1, p.484. First edition published 1791. Cf. TH Green, 'Mr Herbert Spencer and Mr George Lewes: Their Application of the Doctrine of Evolution to Thought. Part 1. Mr Spencer on the Relation of Subject and Object', *Works*, vol.1, p.380, §7.]

²¹⁴ [Conjectural reading. MS reads: 'Ph.'.]

²¹⁵ [Euclid, *Elements*, Book 1, Axiom 9.]

²¹⁶ [Immanuel Kant, *Kritik der Praktischen Vernunft*, ed. K Vorländer, [*Sämtliche Werke*, Zweiter Band] (Leipzig: Verlag von Felix Meiner, 1922) (hereafter, KPV), Erster Teil, I. Buch, 1 Hauptstück, §7, p.39.]

²¹⁷ [Kant, 'Critique of Practical Reason', in his *Practical Philosophy*, bk 1, chap. 1, §7, p.164. This quotation also appeared earlier in this piece (see p. 28 above).]

²¹⁸ [Kant, KVP, Erster Teil, I. Buch, 1 Hauptstück, §1, p.23. Kant, 'Critique of Practical Reason', bk. 1, ch. 1, §1, p.153.]

²¹⁹ [Kant, KVP, Erster Teil, I. Buch, 1 Hauptstück, §3, pp.27–34. Kant, 'Critique of Practical Reason', bk. 1, chap. 1, §3, pp.155–60.]

²²⁰ [Both ellipses appear thus in the MS.]

²²¹ Further question, as to the practical '*rules*' which practical law contains under it. [Placing uncertain.]

²²² [Probably a reference to Henry Thomas Buckle, *History of Civilisation in England*, 3 vols. (London: Longmans, Green, 1902), vol.1, chap. 4 ('Mental Laws are Either Moral or Intellectual. Comparison of Moral and Intellectual Laws, and Inquiry into the Effect Produced by Each on the Progress of Society.') First published 1857–61.]

'Political Philosophy.'
[ca.1869–71][1]

First question is as to the 'origin of State' – to which is exactly correlative the question as to nature of political obligation.

(Better to speak of 'Society' than of 'state'. To Greek πόλις ['polis'] exactly = 'society'. All the rights and agencies of society summed up in πόλις. Not so now. We recognize social obligations which 'state' does not enforce, and *social* agency as *opposed* to *political*. 'State Church' not = society in its religious character.)

The question as to 'origin, etc.' may be treated in two ways. We may either (1) examine historically what was the earliest form in which men combined, or (2) take society in its developed form,[2] and examine what are its constituent elements. In the latter enquiry we may fairly be said to be enquiring into the *origin*...[3] if the developed form be φυσει προτερον ['underlying nature'] to the undeveloped.

(1) More or less pursued both by Plato and Aristotle – by Plato when he deduces society from mutual κρεὶα ['need' or 'advantage'] leading men to combine – by it when he traces progress from οἰκία ['household'] to πόλις ['polis'] in effort of man to attain αυταρκεὶα ['self-sufficiency'] (Rep: 2. 369B).[4]

Neither Plato nor Aristotle are much influenced by these investigations in their actual treatment of the state. Both treat it as a whole of which individual is part, τό ὄλον ['the whole'] being πρότερον τοῦ μέρσυς ['prior to its parts'].[5]

The opposite to their view may be called 'political atomism'. This held apparently by some of the Sophists; by Hobbes,[6] etc. in modern times. According to it, in language of Greek Philosophy, 'society' πόλις said to exist (α) νσμω ['by convention']. According to other view, taken by Aristotle and Plato, it exists (β) φυτει ['by nature'].[7]

According to (α), men mutually repellent, but this universal repulsion acts also as attraction; every one would like to injure every one else if he could with impunity, but the majority, finding balance against them in this work, institute Government to prevent any one from injuring any one. Civil government thus rests on mutual contract arising from mutual fear. It is expression of collective selfishness, and is as absolute as this selfishness is absolute. Tyranny Hobbes's Ideal.

According[8] to (β), as represented by Plato, State is a body of which individuals are limbs. Thus individual has no rights against State, any more than hand may say 'I am not of the body'. The natural result of this a sort of system of Caste. Man not regarded as coming into society by his own act, and making the best of himself therein in conformity with certain conditions, but as finding himself a member of an organism, in which he may have a position as necessarily subordinate[9] as appetite is subordinate to conscience. Supreme power as absolute in Plato's polity as in Hobbes's; difference lies in object for which it is exercised. Not to prevent one citizen from hurting other, but to see that every one does his proper work, in proper way, for good of whole.

(γ) Another form of 'atomistic theory' is that in which it is adopted by Rousseau. This makes Civil Government depend on *contract*, but the contract arises not from mutual fear, but from mutual love.[10] Men naturally attractive, not repellent, of each other. This theory would require that no individual should be governed except by his own consent, that no force should be employed by Government at all.

Fallacy[11] of this view that it represents that individual freedom as having existed prior to the institution of government which can only exist as the result of universal conformity to government.

This theory pretty much true, if instead of supposing such contract actually to have taken place, we say that society should approach a state in which Government should be carried on, as if result of such contract.

Individual can't have his rights recognized till he himself recognizes his obligations; must have force used upon him, if he uses it on others. (Two senses of individual liberty.)

Evidence of gradual tendency of society to constitution resting on free individual contract. Earliest recorded state the patriarchal.[12] Individual has no rights except as derived from a father, real or fictitious.

According[13] to original Roman ideas, citizen not free to make his own position – to make contracts at pleasure – but born in a certain *status*, in which he had to remain. Plebeian, on other hand, had no *status* at all; free to *contract* at pleasure. History of Roman law, that of substitution of law which Praetor administered to Plebeians (in respect of system of adoption, wills, etc.) for original law of the Gentes.

History of law evidences gradual movement 'from Status to Contract'.[14] Influence of Christianity, by opening personal relation between individual and God.

Aristotle's view occupies middle position between (β) and (γ). On one head regards πόλις ['the polis'] as resulting from ὁρμὴ ἐπὶ κοινωίαν ['an impulse towards community']; he distinguishes unity of πόλις from unity of individual,[15] and accordingly refuses to admit Communism.[16]   On the other, he speaks of state as ὅλον πρότερον τοῦ μέρους ['a whole prior to its parts'], and regards one class of mankind as φυσει αρχου ['natural leaders'], other as – ἀρχόμενον ['followers'?].[17]   On the whole, he seems to acquiesce in general Greek view, which gave each individual equal right as against every other, but not against mass, which gave self-determining power to body of freemen, *as a whole*, but not to units, and gave them this power as *citizens*, not as men.

According to (α), political *obligation* not so at all, but *compulsion*.

According to (β), [political obligation] consists in natural subordination, and has no limits.

According to (γ), [political obligation is] voluntarily taken by man on himself: only binding as long as his rights are observed (including if, without my having done any violence to other men, or done anything that tends thereto, violence is used towards me, I have a right to resist.)

Φὺσις[18] ['the essence of a thing'] = that element in things which exists independently of human action: things which we find readymade, ου [?] φυσει ['by nature']. This not exactly love with πόλις ['polis']; but it is so with οἰκία ['household'], and πόλις naturally developed out of οἰκία. φνσις τελος εστιν ['nature contains its end'?]. In one sense, end = beginning. When we see tendency to certain end, obliged to think of end as preceding means in creative thought.

False notion that because moral ideas are not innate, therefore not necessary, but conventional. But since there is tendency towards them, they are just as necessary and 'natural' as primitive relations out of which they grow.[19]

Transition from notion of *necessary* state to proper, normal, state required[20] sense of φνσις ['essence'].

Clear that as you approach condition of voluntary contract,

that agency of society which we call 'state' and which is agency of force, will interfere less and less. How far Greeks were from dreaming of such a condition is shown in fact that with them 'state' = 'Society'. Security against excessive interference with individual in division of powers of Society. Great division that of Church and State. Idea of 'Balance of Power in Constitution' among ancients?

According to Hobbes, individual can have no rights against sovereign, because only in virtue of submission to sovereign has he any rights at all.[21] Sovereign can do no wrong.

Individual, as such, not a *moral person* at all. Sole moral person people as a whole, or sovereign.

Really only because individual is a moral person – a permanent, conscious self, looking before and after, and law to himself – that relations of individuals lead to assertion of recognized sovereignty. Therefore individual has right to be free, so long as he does not interfere with freedom of others.

Mistake of Hobbes (1) that he supposes unjust law impossible; actual sovereignty[22] always the true sovereignty; (2) that he supposes a change of hands in which sovereignty is held to = abolition of sovereignty.

Volonté générale ['general will'] and volanté de tous ['will of all'][23] = νοῦς ανεν ὀρεξεως ['mind without desire'?] and that will of individual for his own good as including that of all others.

Rechtsphilosophie[24] ['philosophy of right'] = science of rights and obligations

Moral philosophy = science of ends and duties.

Political philosophy generally treated as the science which successive forms of social combination and the ideas of right appropriate to each.

---

[1] Given in lectures on [Aristotle,] the [Nichomachean] Ethics, Book V, when I heard them. A.C.B. [Andrew Cecil Bradley (1851–1935), an undergraduate at Balliol from 1869 to 1873, gaining a second in classical moderations in 1871 and a first in literae humaniores in 1873.]

[2] [MS orig.: 'as it is or ought to be'.]

[3] [Ellipsis in original.]

[4] [' "The origin of the city, then," said I, "in my opinion, is to be found in the fact that we do not severally suffice for our own needs, but each of us lacks many things. Do you think any other principle establishes the state?" "No

other," said he.' Plato, *Republic*, 2 vols., trans. Paul Shorey (London and New York: William Heinemann, 1946), vol 1 p.149 (Book 2, 369b).]

5   Common to speak of Plato as making analogy between State and individual. But he does more than this. He makes individual mere fraction of state, in such sense that full attributes of humanity only exist in state, and whole classes of individuals only possess certain of them.

Same difference as between nominalism and realism. According to realism 'universal' was an actual substance of which individual partook. According to nominalism, merely a *relation* of similarity between individual things. So according to Plato, state and whole, etc. according to modern notions, a relation in which individual units stand to each other. [Placing uncertain.]

6   [Thomas Hobbes, *Leviathan*, chaps. 13 and 17.]

7   [Aristotle, *Politics*, 1252a24–1253a39. Plato, *Republic*, 367e–376e.]

8   'Βαβυλων καὶ πᾶσα ἥτις ἐκει περιγραφὴν ἐθνους μᾶλλον ἢ πόλεως.' P. 3.3.5. ['Babylon, and any other city that has the circuit of a nation rather than a city;' (Aristotle, *Politics*, 1276a28–9 (III.i.12)) The relevant passage reads: 'But similarly it may be asked, Suppose a set of men inhabit the same place, in what circumstances are we to consider their city to be a single city? Its unity clearly does not depend on the walls, for it would be possible to throw a single wall round the Preloponnesus; and a case in point perhaps is Babylon, and any other city that has the circuit of a nation rather than a city; for it is said that when Babylon was captured a considerable part of the city was not aware of it three days later.' [Aristotle, *Politics*, trans. H Rackham (London: William Heinemann, 1950), p.183. The Greek in this Loeb edition reverses 'εθνους' and 'μᾶλλον'. Placing of note uncertain.]

9   [MS del.: 'inferior'.]

10 [Jean-Jacques Rousseau, *Du Contrat Social*, bk 1, chaps. 5–7.]

11 [Paragraph added on folio 4.]

12 [Green's discussion in the next two paragraphs is based on Sir Henry Sumner Maine, *Ancient Law: Its connection with the early history of society and its relation to modern ideas* (London: John Murray, 1861), chap. 9.]

13 [Paragraph added on folio 4.]

14 [Maine, *Ancient Law*, chap. 5.]

15 [MS del.: 'as consisting εξ ἐιδει δια φερὸ'.]

'οὐ ποιητέον μόνον ἐκ ἀναιρώπων ἐστὶν ἡ πόλις, ἀλλὰ και ἐξ ἐιδει διαφερόντων.' ['And not only does a city consist of a multitude of human beings, it consists of human beings differing in kind.' Aristotle *Politics*, 1261a24–5.]

'τὸ λὶαν ἐνοῦν ζητεῖν τὴν πόλις ουκ εστιν ἀμεινον ὀικὶα μὲν γὰρ αὐταρκέστερον ἑνὸς, πόλις δ ὀικὶας,' ['to seek to unify the state excessively is not beneficial. In point of self-sufficiency the individual is surpassed by the family and the family by the state,' Aristotle, *Politics*, 1261b11–12. In both cases, the English translation is taken from the Loeb edition, pp.71–3 and 75, respectively.]

16 [Aristotle, *Politics*, 1260a–1264b (Loeb edition, pp.68–99). See Green's 'Notes on Moral Philosophy', in his *Lectures on the Principles of Political Obligation and other writings* (Cambridge University Press, 1986), p.311.]

[17] [Aristotle, *Politics*, 1253a20–1, 1264a9–13.]

[18] [The next three paragraphs added from folio 6.]

[19] Eth.: 10.9.6/ 6.11.6/3.5.15/3.12.2/7.11.4/5.7.4. [Aristotle, *Nichomachean Ethics* (bk.chap.§). Green gives the individual references on separate lines. Placing uncertain]

[20] [MS unclear.]

[21] [Cf. Hobbes, *Leviathan*, chap.21.]

[22] [MS del.: 'law'.]

[23] [Rousseau, *Du Contrat Social*, bk 2, chap. 3.]

[24] [This short observation appears several pages after Green's notes on historical narrative in the Greeks, but is included at this point as it fits more naturally with this text. MS del.: 'Political philosophy'.]

[The Nature of Historical Narrative in Thucydides and Herodotus.]
[ca.1869–71]

What is meant by calling a narrative 'unhistorical'? Either (1) that between the several events it relates no connection in reason (i.e. according to known analogies) is traced or traceable, or (2) that agencies are introduced, of which we have no experience and for which we can't account, or (3) that there is no sufficient evidence for the events which it relates. (We may conclude that [there] is no sufficient evidence in various ways; commonly by observing that there are contradictions in the narrative, and thence inferring that it cannot be that of a direct witness. Does it follow, however, because there is no testimony[1] either of eye-witness or contemporaneous enquirer to a particular statement, that it is not to be accepted? If the event stated be such as might arise out of previous, and would account for subsequent, events, and if it be analogous to[2] known events in other series, may it not [be] accepted as real on this ground? If not, all historical theories at an end.)

Thucydides's [is the] earliest Greek '*history*', in the sense (α) that he first *rationalizes* the past, (1) by tracing regular sequence,[3] (2) by recognizing merely natural causes to the exclusion of super-natural and adequate causes to exclusion of accident, etc.; and (β) that in regard to contemporaneous facts, he only accepts them on evidence.

As to (1), his fundamental doctrine of uniformity of human nature [he] states in [Thuc.] 1.22.4.[4] The Peloponnesian war is the outcome of a gradual developement of Greeks, arising from a few simple causes. In it, for first time, all Greeks combined under one or other of two leading states ([Thuc.] 1.1.1). At first, a quantity of tribes in state of chronic migration and isolation. Then, as sea is more used, communication in way of trade and piracy. – Then, under Minos,[5] piracy superseded by regular trade, and larger federations or empires formed. The result (πλμωτερων ἤδη ὄντων ['navigation had become safer'])[6] is expedition against Troy under Agamemnon [Thuc. 1.2–8]. Then with χρημάτων προσδος ['wealth surplus'?] come tyrannies; great alliances and enterprises prevented by selfishness of tyrants. These put down by Sparta, and way cleared for great hegemonies of Sparta and Athens. Growing power of Athens produces Spartan jealousy, and hence the war [Thuc. 1.17–23].

Contrast Herodotus. – Instead of regular sequence, capricious interference of 'τὸ θειον' ['the Divine Being'] (φθσνερσι και ταρακωδως ['jealousy and strife']), which strikes down any power when it has reached a certain height. [Herod.] 1.32. 3.40.

Way in which Thucydides would have accounted for Persian war. To Herodotus simply a great manifestation of divine νεμεσις ['indignation'].

As [...?] contrast of human probabilities with hopes based on the supernatural in [Thuc.] 5.103. See also [Thuc.] 5.26. – 2.17 – 2.34, 2.8.2, etc. – 2.21.2, – 2.47.5, 9.1.1.[7] Main causes, whose agency he recognizes, (1) physical (α) the sea and opportunity of naval communications ([Thuc.] 1.7.1), (β) quality of soil, 1.2.4 and 5. (γ) geographical position. Corinth, 1.13.5.

No notice of that physical cause which operated most strongly in Hellenic developement – that division of country into small plains separated from each other by mountains. This specially adapted to formation of communities in shape in which alone self-government known in ancient times, i.e. in shape of independent cities with small circumscription of territory.

(2) Moral, (α) πλεσνεξια ['greed'], [Thuc.] 1.8.4–[1.]9[?]) power of individuals, Minos 1.4, Pericles,[8] 2.65.7, etc.

Adequate causes. Agamemnon gets together his armament not on account of the 'τονδάρεω σρκσι', but because he is strong and has a large fleet (1.9).[9] Peloponnesian war got up, because Sparta afraid of growing power of Athens [Thuc.] 1.23[.6]. cf: Herodotus on Democedes and Histiaeus.[10]

(β) As to evidence, though he exacts this rigorously in case of contemporaneous facts, (5.26.5, 1.22.5),[11] yet in reference to past, he merely subtracts from legend the marvellous and supernatural, and treats the rest as accurately true, 1.10.4, etc.

According to Thucydides the state, in which Greeks are found at opening of authentic history, result of a long series of migrations. What were these? Most of those of which we know (all which he mentions) placed after Trojan war.[12]

Eight migrations.
   H 7.73
      7.75
      5.66
      1.94
   Hom. Il. 10.426, 16.233[13]

Substantial truth of Thucydides's view lies in this (1) that in all important Greek states except Attica there was an immigrant conquering race overlying conquered. Course of Greek revolution turns on this. (2) The Greek national character that of immigrants.

According to Thucydides the Hellenic nation, as one and distinct, of late formation. Gradual conquest by 'sons of Hellen.' [14]

Remarkable, if this theory of Hellenization be true, that the earliest states to develope distinct Hellenic civilization, namely those of Asia, should have been the least Hellenized.

Thucydides (1) regards Pelasgians as only one among other pre-Hellenic tribes, (2) holds that originally there was no definite demarcation between Greeks and other races living round [the] Aegean.

---

[1] [MS del.: 'evidence'.]

[2] [MS del.: 'in accordance with'.]

[3] [MS orig.: 'developement'.]

[4] ['And it may well be that the absence of the fabulous from my narrative will seem less pleasing to the ear; but whoever shall wish to have a clear view both of the events which have happened and of those which will some day, in all human probability, happen again in the same or a similar way – for these to adjudge my history profitable will be enough for me. And, indeed, it has been composed, not as a prize-essay to be heard for the moment, but as a possession for all time.' (Thuc., [Loeb ed.], vol.1 pp.39–41. When inserted into the main body of the text, '[Thuc.]' denotes Thucydides, *History of the Peloponnesian War*, followed by the appropriate book and chapter references. 'Herod.' denotes Herodotus, *Histories*, followed by book, chapter and section references. When English translations are given in the editorial notes, the Loeb editions have been used: Thucydides, [*History of the Peloponnesian War*,] 4 vols., trans. C Forster Smith, (London and New York, William Heinemann, 1919–23), and Herodotus, [*Histories*] trans. by AD Godley, 4 vols. (London: William Heinemann, 1920–24). References are then given to the volume and page number of the relevant Loeb text.]

[5] [King Minos of Crete a quasi-mythical ruler of much of the Aegean (dates unknown).]

[6] [Thuc. 1.7.1. The Greek differs in the Loeb version (vol. 1, p.12).]

7 [Thucydides : 5.103 Hope when frustrated leads men to seek divine signals; 5.26 The Peloponnesian War was fated to last twenty seven years; 2.17 The Pythian oracle's strangely apt prohibition against citizens dwelling in the Pelargicum; 2.34 Athenian funeral customs; 2.8.2 The Hellenes look to the gods to protect them from the war; 2.21.2 Oracle-mongers advise the people; Sections 2.47.5 and 9.1.1 do not exist.]

8 [Pericles (c.490–429BC), Athenian statesman and eulogist of Athenian democracy.]

9 ['And it was, as I think, because Agamemnon surpassed in power the princes of his time that he was able to assemble his fleet, and not so much because Helen's suitor's, whom he led, were bound by oath to Tyndareus.' Thucydides, *History*, 1.9.1 (Loeb vol.1, p.15).]

10 [Democedes of Croton, physician to King Darius and Queen Atossa of Persia. Herodotus recounts that the king put Democedes at the head of military force to gain new colonies and power for Persia and handmaidens for Atossa (*Histories*, 3.125, 131–7). He also tells how Histiaeus, despot of Miletus, among many other things, attacked Atarneus in order to steal its corn (*ibid.* 4.28.]

11 [Thucydides claims accuracy for his history on the grounds that, 'I lived through the whole war, being of an age to form judgements, and followed it with close attention, so as to acquire accurate information.' (Thucydides, *History*, 5.26.5 (Loeb vol. 3, p.51)). There is no section 1.22.5, but 1.22.1–4 is apposite.]

12 [The ten-year long Trojan War is believed by some to have ended around 1,220BC.]

13 [Thucydides, *History*:

7.73: The proposed withdrawal of the Athenian forces to Sicily following their defeat by the Syracusans.

7.75: The actual Athenian withdrawal.

5.66: The Athenian attack on Orchomenus in Arcadia.

1.94: Pausanias' attacks on Cyprus and Byzantium.

Hom. Il.10.429 16.233: These two very narrow references to Homer's *Iliad* are puzzling 10.429 occurs during Ulysses and Diomedes' interrogation of Dolon which occurs during their night reconnaissance on the Trojan camp. 16.233 occurs as Achilles is preparing to pray to Zeus before sending Patroclus into the battle.]

14 ['Indeed, it seems to me that as a whole it [Hellas] did not yet have this name, either, but that before the time of Hellen, son of Deucalion, this title did not even exist, and that the several tribes, the Pelasgian most extensively, gave their own names to the several districts; but when Hellen and his sons became strong in Phthiotis and were called in to the aid of the other cities, the clans thenceforth came more and more, through reason of this intercourse, to be called Hellenes.' Thucydides, *History*, 1.3.2 (Loeb, vol.1, p.7).]

'Pleasure as the Chief Good.'
[Mid–1870s?]

From Kant's point of view, action determined by desire for pleasure is essentially immoral.[1] Morality = autonomy of rational will; determination of will by an object which it not merely finds but makes; by an interest arising out of reason as opposed to one which reason adopts, think about, and finds means to satisfy. Determination by desire for pleasure is just opposite of this, for reason has nothing to do with making pleasure. It is as animals, or parts of nature, that we are susceptible of pleasure. Thus in living for pleasure, man, instead of realising[2] that power[3] of acting according to conceptions given by reason which = his will, is 'admitting a nature into his will'. Just as every natural phenomenon is determined by something other than itself ('fremden ursachen' ['alien causes']), so the man is allowing himself to be determined by influence not proceeding from himself as rational.

From form in which Kant puts this doctrine, it excites such objections as these. (1) If to live for pleasure = to naturalize oneself, what harm in that? It is just what poets and artists (or those who write about them) tell us is the right thing to do. (2) Admitting the objection to finding our end of life in what our merely animal nature offers, is it not a 'false abstraction' to separate pleasures from objects exciting them and thus to call living for pleasure in the lump bad?[4] If the pleasures are those, e.g., of the artist or of the sympathetic friend of man, is it not a mistake to condemn them as immoral on account of their having some relation to our animal susceptibilities – a relation which every possible real object that man can pursue must have? (3) Does not Kant's whole doctrine of autonomy and heteronomy, on which his condemnation of pleasure-seeking turns, involve a contradiction? *Unless* will = self-determined reason, there is no meaning in calling its determination by desire[5] 'determination by alien cause', 'admission of nature into it', 'heteronomy', etc., etc. *If* it = self-determined reason, how is such alien determination possible for it?

Begin with (3). May naturally be asked: What after all does Kant mean by the will? (Defts. from Locke and others).[6] Do we

82

find in[7] such definition in Kant? In various places [he] tells us that 'will is faculty either of bringing into existence, or of getting oneself to do so, objects corresponding to "ideas" ("Vorstellungen")';[8] that it is 'faculty of acting according to consciousness[9] (Vorstellungen) of laws';[10] more fully (p.78 of Grundl:, on p.8 of my analysis) 'species of causality which belongs, etc.'.[11]

Perplexities in Kant's doctrine very much due to his falling in with common way of speaking of will as a faculty, which conveys notion of its being something other alike than man and than his activity – something which it is true, in so determined by self-consciousness as to be an effort after self-satisfaction, and self-satisfaction is pleasant, but the nature of the self-satisfaction is to be sought in those objects which satisfy – objects with which man so identifies himself in thought that he can only give reality to himself in obtaining or making them – not in the feeling which ensues when pursuit is over. The self-satisfaction which a man seeks, – though ipso facto pleasant supposing it to be even attained – is not properly said to be pleasure unless pleasant, form that object with which in the general tenor of his life he seeks to satisfy himself – as is the case with a man so far as he is what is called a 'mere voluptuary'. (The 'voluptuary' – man who lives for pleasure – though purely selfish, is not the only type of selfishness. A man is selfish so far as his own good, for which every one lives – the object of his dominant desire – is a good in which others cannot share. Just so far as a man, instead of finding pleasure in objects for which he lives makes pleasure his object, he is necessarily selfish, for pleasure is just that which is purely personal to oneself. No man can share another's pleasure, as such. What is meant, when a man is said to do so, is that having desired same object with the other, he is equally pleased in its attainment; or, that the pleasure of the other having been his object, he is satisfied when that object is attained. A man who lives for objects, though in seeking them he takes no positive thought for good of others, is not therefore selfish. An artist or man of science, who lives for his work without troubling himself with philanthropy, is yet not living for an object merely personal to himself. His special interest may be shared by no one, but the work done, the minute step forward in knowledge – i.e. the man's good as attained – is for all men. But a man may live for an object other than pleasure, e.g. his own glory, and yet be purely selfish, inasmuch as his good, though not pleasure, is yet one in which others can't share.)

These two doctrines, then, confront each other. (a) All good is
pleasure. Highest good = most pleasure. *Moral* good is pleasure
obtained in a particular way. Action or character mostly good if
of a kind thus to obtain it. (b) That is good which satisfies desire
(corollary of this that all good is pleasant.) That is morally good
which satisfies desire of a moral agent, Kant then not wrong in
treating desire[12]

Though it would be a mistake then – a 'false abstraction' – to
treat pleasures as all of a sort, it is not a mistake to speak of the
living for pleasure as a moral condition which is the same whatever
the difference of pleasures in relation to their exciting causes may
be. To desire pleasures – this, that, and the other – is one thing:
to live for pleasure quite another. The desire for them, in itself, has
no moral character either way, any more than the pleasures
themselves.[13] The only proper subject of moral predicates is the
man, who is good or bad according to the mode in which he
presents himself to himself as an end. If the man's interest is in
himself simply as a subject of pleasure, it makes no difference to
that interest how the pleasure is obtained. In this interest, just so
far as prevails, all desires for particular sorts of pleasure tend to
merge. It is an ideal opposite of interest in the purposes which one
has to serve as [an] agent in development of human society.
Mistake lies (a) in regarding it as a state in which certain men are
living,[14] whereas it is only a state to which they tend; (b) in
regarding it as only alternative to state in which sole interest is in
moral law.

What will be instances of interests of former kind? It may be
granted that interest in oneself simply as subject of pleasure and
pain is 'alien', or merely adopted from outside in sense explained.
So far as it exists (and doubt is not whether *all* interests, as Kant
following in wake of the 'British philosophy' supposed,[15] but that
in abstract moral law are [sic] reducible to it but whether *any* are
so), it means that, whereas in man upon the animal nature there
supervenes a principle which, distinguishing itself from this nature,
affords possibility of a higher order of things,[16] in which man is
loved by man, and nature known, used, and admired by him, this
principle in the individual is either remaining a mere possibility, or,
perhaps more properly, is undergoing some temporary perversion,
incidental to its ultimate realization, from interest in objects to
interest in effect of this interest upon animal susceptibilities – i.e.
in its pleasantness.

In truth, however, the mere 'living for pleasure' – determination by interest in oneself simply as subject of pleasure and pain – is a fiction of speculative men – of 'Hedonists' misinterpreting their own conduct, of philosophers like Kant who require an absolute antithesis to Will determined by mere form of law. The tendency to reduce of all interests to desire for pleasure in the philosophy to which Kant succeeded went along with its 'individualism' – its habit of inquiring into nature[17] of the individual man irrespectively of those relations in 'social organism' which make him what he is. In fact, the self which the individual man presents to himself and thro' which alone, so far as he is moral agent or nature and has will, objects move him, has its whole reality in relations to society 'Unus homo, nullus homo' ['one man, no man']. His interests, up to a certain point are determined by these relations. Consider life of a healthy peasant. He is interested in his parents, on whom, to begin with, he is physically dependent, and in whom, in virtue of his self-conscious nature, his interest does not cease as it seems to do with the animals when period of physical dependence is over. They become involved in the self in which he is interested, so that he cannot detach himself in thought from them, though no appetite connects him with them. Then he forms new ties – if no other, those implied in becoming a father, so that the self which he presents to himself as to be lived for in the future is conditioned by relations to children. To live for himself means to live for them.

'This account will not apply either to primitive man, or to any but a certain type of life in civilized society.' When 'primitive man' is spoken of, we have to ask whether or no this means a being that, by anything fairly called a process of development, could become the moral subject whom we now know as man. If we do, then he must have been capable of interests analogous to those described, as condition of his developing into what we now know. We have[18]

---

¹ [For a rather more nuanced statement of the claim that Green seems to have in mind, see Immanuel Kant, 'Groundwork', in his *Practical Philosophy*, pp.49–52 (Prussian 4:393–6) and 61–72 (Prussian 4:406–19), and Kant, 'Critique of Practical Reason', in his *Practical Philosophy*, pp.153–64 (Prussian 5:19–30).]

² [MS orig.: 'giving reality to'.]

³ [MS orig.: 'possibility'.]

⁴ [Cf. GWF Hegel, *Philosophy of Mind*, trans. W Wallace and AV Miller (Oxford: Clarendon, 1971), §§471–2. First German edition of third part of Hegel's *Encyclopaedia* was published in 1817; Wallace used the revised, 1830 edition.]

⁵ [MS orig.: 'pleasure'.]

⁶ ['This at least I think evident, That we find in our selves a *Power* to begin or forbear, continue or end several actions of our minds, and motions of our Bodies, barely by a thought or preference of the mind ordering, or as it were commanding the doing or not doing such or such a particular action. This *Power* which the mind has, thus to order the consideration of any *Idea*, or the forbearing to consider it; or to prefer the motion of any part of the body to its rest, and *vice versâ* in any particular instance is that which we call the *Will*.' John Locke, *Essay concerning Human Understanding*, ed. Peter H. Nidditch (Oxford University Press, 1975), Book 2, ch.21, §5, p.236. See Green, 'Metaphysic of Ethics, Moral Psychology, Sociology or Science of Sittlichkeit', p.p 41–3 above.]

⁷ [MS reads: 'find in any'.]

⁸ [Cf. Kant, 'Critique of Practical Reason', in his *Practical Philosophy*, pp.186–7 (Prussian 5:57–9).]

⁹ [MS orig.: 'ideas'.]

¹⁰ [Green's translation of a clause appearing at Kant, 'Groundwork' in his *Practical Philosophy*, p.66 ('the capacity to act *in accordance with the representation* of laws, that is in accordance with principles.' (Prussian 4:412)). Cf. Green, 'Lectures on the Philosophy of Kant', *Works II*, pp.83–4, §71.]

¹¹ [Immanuel Kant, 'Grundlegung zur Metaphysik Der Sitten', in Karl Rosenkranz and Friedrich Wilhelm Schubert (eds.) *Immanuel Kant's Sämmtiliche Werke*, 12 vols. (Leipzig: Voss, 1838–42), vol. 8, p. 78. Green's 'analysis' appears to be a selective translation of certain portions of Kant's ethical writings. It is preserved as Green MS10B. RLN describes this notebook on the inside cover as 'Kant (Moral philosophy)./(1) Analysis of Grundlegung zur Metaphysik Der Sitten. pp. 1–32./(2) [Analysis of] Kritik of Practical Reason. pp.33–67.' (The page numbers given by RLN and Green refer to the numbered pages of the notebook.) The relevant text on pp.8*: '(cf. "The will is a species of causality which belongs to living beings so far as they are rational. *Freedom* is a property which belongs to this causality so far as it can operate independently of determination by alien causes (fremden ursachen) while *natural necessity* is the property which belongs to the causality of all irrational agents – the property of being determined to activity by the influence of alien causes.")' Kant, 'Groundwork', in his *Practical Philosophy*, p.94 (Prussian 4:446). Green adds 'cf.' as he wishes the reader to compare this quoted passage with that given on p.8 and from which he has quoted earlier in this sentence: namely, Kant, 'Groundwork', in his *Practical Philosophy*, p.66 et sub (Prussian 4:412 et sub). (There are other 'analyses' in Balliol's Green Papers: most famously, his 'Analysis of Hegel' which is now well-known as a translation of much of Hegel's *Philosophical Propaedeutic* (see Ben Wempe, *TH Green's Theory of Positive Freedom* (Exeter: Imprint Academic, 2004), pp.23–49).]

¹² ['Kant … desire' deleted in mss, immediately after which Green starts the new paragraph ('Though...').]

¹³ [MS del.: 'This only belongs to activity determined by conception of self as individual.']

¹⁴ [MS del.: 'an actual state'.]

¹⁵ [Presumably, the 'British philosophy' is the philosophy of such as Locke, Hume and Hutcheson.]

¹⁶ [MS del.: 'world'.]

¹⁷ [MS del.: 'qualities, etc.'.]

¹⁸ [Subsequent sheet(s) lost.]

Notes of Lectures on the Epistle to the Romans.[1]
[Remaining text.]
[ca.1871]

[Edited by Henry Nettleship and Colin Tyler]

The date of the Epistle is inferred to be the spring of A.D. 58, from a comparison of the following passage[s]: Rom. 16.1 Φοίβην τὴν ἀδελφὴν ἡμῶν, οὖσαν καὶ[2] διάκονον τῆς εκκλησίας τῆς ἐν Κεγρεαὶς ['Phebe our sister, which is [also] a servant of the Church which is at Cenchrea']; ib. 23 `Ασπάζεται ὑμᾶς Γάϊος ὁ ξένος μον καὶ ὅλης τῆς εκκλησίας. `Ασπάζεται ὑμας Εραστος ὁ οἰκονόμος τῆς πόλεως, και Κούαρτος ὁ ἀδελφός['Gaius mine host, and of the whole Church, saluteth you. Erastus the Chamberlain of the city saluteth you, and Quartus a brother.'], compared with 1 Cor. 1.14 οὐδένα ὑμῶν ἐβάπτισα, εἰ μὴ Κρίσπον καὶ Γάϊον ['I baptized none of you, but Crispus and Gaius'.]; [Rom.] 15.23–25, ἐπιποθίαν ἐχων τοῦ ἐλθεῖν πρὸς ὑμᾶς ἀπὸ ἰκανῶν ἐτων ὡς ἂν πορεύωμαι εἰς τὴν Σπανίαν, ... νυνὶ δὲ πορεύομαι εἰς `Ιερονσαλήμ, διακονῶν τοῖς ἀγίοις. ['...and having a great desire these many years to come unto you;/Whensoever I take my journey into Spain.../But now I go unto Jerusalem to minister unto the Saints.' (Rom. 15.23–24, 25)], etc., compared with Acts 20.3. μέλλοντι ἀνάγεσθαι εἰς τὴν Συρίαν ['as he was about to sail to Syria'], and 22, ἐγὼ δεδεμἰνος τῷ Πνεύματι πορεύομαι εἰς `Ιερονσαλήμ ['I go bound in the spirit unto Jerusalem']; [Acts] 24.17 Δὶ ἐτων δε πλειὸνων ελεημοσύνας ποιὴσων. Εἰς τὸ εθνος μον παρεγενόμην ['Now after many years I came to bring alms to my nation, and offerings.']; 1 Cor. 16.4ἐὰν δὲ αξιον ᾖ τοῦ κἀμὲ πορεύεσθαι σὺν ἐμοὶ πορεύσονται ['And if it be meet that I go also, they shall go with me.']; 2 Cor. 8.1. foll., 9.1 foll..

The Epistle falls into three main parts; (1) ch. 1–8; (2) ch. 9–11; (3) ch. 12 – end.

The first part unfolds the conception of δικαιοσύνη Θεοῦ ['the righteousness of God'], as the opposite of the sin which adheres to man taken by himself; and the consequent conception of faith *ex parte hominis*, and grace *ex parte Dei*, in opposition to 'work,' as the channel through which this righteousness is to be conveyed.

The second part is concerned with the question how it is that the Gentiles, instead of attaining δικαιοσύνη Θεοῦ by clinging to the skirts of Israel, are attaining it apparently to the exclusion of Israel. Nay, the exclusion of Israel seems the condition of the inclusion of the Gentiles (11, 12, and 15). This part is not so much doctrinal as political; it has to do with the scheme of salvation not so much as related to the spirit of the individual as exhibited outwardly in the world.

The third part is chiefly concerned with questions of Christian morality.

The above account of the second part may be disputed. As a matter of fact, this second part has been the source from which the doctrine of election and predestination has been chiefly drawn. But on examination it appears that the doctrinal basis of the Epistle is complete without it. The idea that 'salvation is not of him that willeth', etc.[3] (9.16) is brought out sufficiently in the earlier part.[4] The passage about election merely comes in by way of practical explanation of the rejection of Israel, as showing from the history of the chosen people itself that a like process of rejection within the chosen seed had taken place before (9.7 foll.). In like manner St. Paul quotes from the prophets passages anticipating this very rejection and inclusion. But the real account to Paul of this fact, so perplexing to those who had become Christians from among Jews and proselytes, is to be found in the theory of salvation developed in the earlier part of the Epistle. The office of the Law, according to St. Paul, is to quicken the consciousness of sin, in order to open the heart of man to that righteousness which is not of himself but of God. The[5] Law is pure in itself, yet relatively to man is the source of sin (5.20). Its ultimate end is thus the true salvation; but its immediate effect is exclusion from the righteousness of God of those whom it leads to seek that righteousness through 'works of the Law'. Upon an ἐκλογή ['selection'] or κατάλειμμα ['remnant'] (9.27.), as e.g. on St. Paul himself, it has already wrought its full effect. 'They through the law are dead to the law' [Gal. 2:19]; it has put them at that (apparently) furthest distance from God, which is death; which by a sudden revolution becomes consciousness of their nearness to Him, if they will cease to strive to approach Him, and let Him approach them in the Spirit, whereby they cry 'Abba, Father.' [Rom. 8:15] But with most of Israel it was otherwise. – The Law was still deceiving them,[6] they were seeking δικαιοσύηνὲς ἐργων νὸμου ['righteousness by the works of the law']: Then, this operation of the Law, which (strictly speaking) whether unto death or unto life, could only tell upon the Jew, presents itself to St. Paul as the preliminary condition of salvation to the Gentiles.[7] 'The abundance of offence,' [Rom. 5.20] which it is the purpose of the Law to produce, extends to them as well as to the Jew. Thus in a way, the rejection of the Jew is the condition of the inclusion of the Gentile. It was necessary in the Divine scheme of the world, in order to put mankind in general into the state of mind which is open to the δικαιοσὺνη Θεοῦ ['righteousness of God']; that there should be that previous régime of the Law, which incidentally led to the fall of the Jews (11.15, 30, 31).

According to this view, then, the Epistle, like those to the Galatians and Corinthians, is occasioned by a practical difficulty, – the relation of the Christians to the Jews. In the Galatian Church the difficulty was whether the Gentiles could become Christians without becoming Jews. In the Roman Church it has got beyond that stage. The free admission of the Gentiles – not proselytes, and without the conditions to which proselytes were subject[8] – is an accomplished fact. It is not the question whether the adoption of the Gentiles into the old family of God shall be unconditional or not. It seems that the old family of God has ceased to be so; the Gentile family is taking its place. How can a believing Jew reconcile himself to this? Writing to a Church with which he had no personal connection, St. Paul could discuss this question upon general considerations as to the Divine scheme without the intrusion (as in addressing the Galatians and Corinthians) of the personal question.

Is the Epistle, then, addressed (1) to Gentiles, or (2) to Jews, or (3) to Jews and proselytes, or (4) to a mixed Church?

If the above account of its main drift be correct, clearly it cannot be mainly to unproselytized Gentiles, for whom it would have no direct interest. Contrast the way in which the Gentiles are dealt with in the Epistle to the Corinthians. Doubtless it has an interest for the 'Christian consciousness' now, not for the Jewish; why not? Because the present 'Christian consciousness' has to a great extent grown out of it. There is a state of mind which Christian men go through and which now naturally identifies itself with that of being under the Law. But this would not be so to the ordinary Gentile, unjudaized in St. Paul's time.

Yet, as apparently making directly against (2), comp. 1.13 and 14, τοῦτο δέ ἐστι σνμπαρακλη θηναι ἐς ὑμῖν διὰ τῆς ἐν ἀλλήλοις πίστεως... ον ἵνα τινὰ καρπὸν σχω λοιποῖς ἔθνεσιν καὶ ἐν ὑμῖν κάθως καὶ ἐν τοῖς,[9] and 11.13 ὑμῖν δὲ λέγω τοῖς ἔθνεσιν ['For I speak to you Gentiles'].

Throughout the 11th Chapter there is direct address to the Gentiles in the second person. In ch. 2 and 3, however (especially 2.17) there is a similar address to the Jews.

In the salutations *Mary* is the only strictly Jewish name [Rom. 16.6]; but this shows nothing; comp. the case of Aquila and Priscilla, Apollos, Acts 18.2 and 26, and Rom. 16.7, 16.11[10] (Andronicus, Junia,[11] Herodion, etc.)[12]

The only Roman names besides these known to be of Jews,[13] are Amplias and Urbanus ([Rom.] 16.8, 9).

In Rom. 1.5, 15.20, and Gal. 2.7 he writes as the apostle of the Gentiles.

The Epistle then was probably addressed to a mixed Church in which the Gentile element largely consisted of proselytes, and had thus been affected by Jewish ideas of the Law.

That the Roman church was not founded by an apostle appears from 1.11, 13; 15.20; comp. Gal. 2.7 and 9.

Δικαιοσύνη Θεοῦ ['The righteousness of God'][14]

[...]

[On p.191, l.7, after '(Rom. x.3)':]

[...] God as δίκαιος ['just'], must make man righteous: He is 'just and the justifier'.

It is only through His operation on us that this correspondence can exist on our part; thus it is a righteousness which He bestows. The perfect relation above described subsists, according to St. Paul from all eternity between the Father and the Son. But as between God and man, there is on the side of man a conscious alienation (ἁμαρτία ['sin']) from God. Through the Son's being, in St. Paul's language, made 'sin for us,' through his, in some way, partaking in our condition, being (Rom. 8.3) 'sent in the likeness of sinful flesh,' the spirit of sonship is communicated to us, and we are able to partake of the perfect relation which has subsisted from eternity between the Father and the Son, and thus becomes 'the righteousness of God' in him.

On the side of God there is no change in the relation. God is for ever δίκαιος ['just'], and in idea, according to the Divine purpose, man as in the Son is just towards God; but for the consciousness of man this perfect relation does not exist.

Thus the change in the relation between man and God, which St. Paul calls justification, is not a change in God, which is impossible, but a change in the consciousness of man.

[On p. 192, l.5, after 'hearts.":]

In the words [Rom. 2.15] μεταξὺ ἀλλήλων σῶν λογισμῶν κατηγορούντων, etc. ['their thoughts the meanwhile accusing or else excusing one another'], the judgment of each by the other in respect of their mutual dealings is distinguished from the judgment passed by each on himself as implied in the words συμμαρτυρούσης αὐτῶν τῆς συνειδήσεως ['their conscience also bearing witness' (Rom. 2.15)]. 2.16 ἐν ᾗ ἡμέρα, etc. ['In the day when God shall judge the secrets of men by Jesus Christ according to my gospel.']. In the ordinary texts v.v.13–16 are put in brackets[15] so as to make v.16 refer back to v.12; but it is more natural to take ἐν ᾗ ἡμέρα ['In the day when' (Rom. 2.16)] with what immediately precedes, the connection being 'as will appear in the day when,' etc. The judgment, which he speaks of as future, he brings into the present; the final judgment is merely the full manifestation of that actually going on in the condemnation or acquittal of the conscience by itself – in the silent intercourse of thought with itself in which the man accuses or else excuses himself.

[On p.192, l.16, after '(1 Cor. 2.14: comp. 15.44).':]

'Adam' is the personification of the 'fleshly' or 'psychical' nature. In receiving this from him we receive the principle of sin (and consequent death), but not the consciousness of it without the law. In [Rom.] 5.12 the protasis ὡς δὶ ἑνὸς ἀνθρώπον ['as by one man' (sin entered the world)] is not answered. St. Paul goes off upon death as evidence of *inherent* sin, existing before the law. The natural answer is οὕτω ... δικαιοσύνη καὶ διὰ τῆς δικαιοσύης ζωή,[16] latent in the words ὅς ἐστι τύπος τοῦ μέλλοντος ['who is the figure of him that was to come' (Rom. 5.14)].

[On p.192, l.40, after 'law.':]

Here (in Rom. 1.) St. Paul is regarding the history of the world specially from the Jewish point of view, turning the tables upon those who 'made their boast in the law' by showing that its function was not to produce righteousness but to intensify sin. In chap. 1 and 2 (1.19, 32; 2.15) where he is rather addressing the Gentiles, he enlarges his view of the law. The Gentiles too are under a law, a condemnatory law, that of the conscience.

1.32 ('are worthy of death.')
The Gentile conception of punishment in Hades converted into St. Paul's own conception of death as opposed to 'eternal life' (2.7). On death, as the result of the sin of Adam, comp. Wisdom 2.23 and 24; 'God created man to be immortal, and made him to be an image of his own eternity. Nevertheless, through envy of the Devil came death into the world, and they that do hold of his side do find it'. Comp. John 8.44.

In Romans 5.12 and 21 is it (1) *physical* death, or (2) moral, or (3) eternal, death that is intended? Primarily physical: but physical death, as the consequence of moral, becomes merged with it, as in 7.10 and 13, (which, along with 2 Cor. 2.16, 3.7, and 7.10, Meyer talks of 'eternal death,' denying that it ever means moral death).[17] In any case we may comp. Eph. 2.1 'dead in trespasses and sins'.

The meaning of Θάνατος ['death'] extended in correspondence with the extension in the meaning of σάρξ ['flesh']. As σάρξ ['flesh'], from being simply equivalent to 'body,' comes to mean that which in fact separates us from God, viz; the self-seeking principle, so death, necessarily attaching to σάρξ ['flesh'], comes to mean the consciousness of alienation from God; of his wrath.
σάρξ ['flesh'] = sin in principle:
παράβασις ['transgression'], sin in actuality:
Θάνατος ['death'], sin in result: but the *result* is not different from sin itself, but is sin in its full outcome.
Ἄχρι νόμου ['until the law'][18] (supposing there to be such a stage) as there was no transgression and hence no consciousness of sin: as, in other words, νοῦς ['mind'] and σάρξ ['flesh'] were not yet stimulated into conflict; so Θάνατος, physical death, was not yet regarded in its full significance.

Death (in that stage) being not yet (to consciousness) the symbol of alienation from God, is not spoken of as equivalent to such alienation; but in a later stage it is so spoken of (Rom. 7.10; comp. Gal. 2.19).

There is no sin without consciousness of sin – sin is a condition of self-consciousness, or it is nothing. A man may be 'alive without the law' [Rom. 7.9], but only in the relative sense of life; *alive* in contrast with that death as *conscious* separation from God, which comes of transgression, which comes of the law. But in this stage, sin is present *in principle* in the flesh. Καθ᾽ ὑπερβολὴν ἁμαρτωλὸς ['exceeding[ly] sinful' (Rom. 7.13)]. A qualitative difference (that expressed in 3.20) expressed quantitatively. The consciousness of sin grows in inverse ratio to the consciousness of the power of will.

But meanwhile νοῦς ['mind'] is awakened. Death, in its extremity as the most intense consciousness of sin, is but one step removed from true life.

The works of the law, as works *of the law*; cannot be done. The very attitude of seeking to do them as works of the law and thus establish an ἰδία δικαιοσύνη, as it excludes the 'action' of the 'quickening spirit,' renders it impossible. But when 'man through the law is dead to the law, that he may live unto God,'[19] then the law of the spirit of 'life' frees him from this impotence, ἵνα το δικαίωμα τοῦ νόμου πληρωθῇ ἐν ὑμῖν ['That the righteousness of the law might be fulfilled in us' (Rom. 8:4)].

The[20] reason why the law, though spiritual in itself, yet 'kills'; why its only function is to make sin more conscious of itself by giving it definite form and actuality as παράβασις ['transgression'], is to be found in σάρξ ['flesh']: 'the law of sin in our members'.[21]

How is the word σάρξ to be understood?

In Rom. 6.6 and 7.24 it = the physical body: yet this body, it would seem, may be destroyed in this life (τοῦτο γινώσκοντες, ὅτι ὁ παλαιὸς ἡμῶν ἄνθρωπος συνεσταυρώθη, ἵνα καταργηθῇ τὸ σῶμα τῆς ἁμαρτίας ['Knowing this, that our old man is crucified with *him*, that the body of sin might be destroyed' (Rom. 6.6)]: τὶς με ῥύσεται, etc. [(Oh wretched man that I am:) 'who shall deliver me from the body of this death?' [Rom. 7.24]). But again from Rom. 8.11 (comp. 2 Cor. 5.6) it would appear that the 'mortal body' may remain when we are no longer in the flesh. The quickening of the mortal body is spoken of as a result of the indwelling spirit yet to be achieved.

The explanation is that σάρξ, from simply meaning 'body,' comes in St. Paul's mind to mean that which in fact separates us from God, the self-seeking principle; and in certain passages he used 'body' in this moral signification of the self-seeking principle. From the 'flesh' or 'body' in this sense, more clearly put as the φρόνημα σαρκὸς ['carnal mind' (Rom. 8.7)], we are delivered in Christ through the Spirit dwelling in us; but there still remains something to be delivered from: the mortal body (Rom. 8.11) the tabernacle (2 Cor. 5.6): the being at home in the body which is absence from the Lord.

[P.193, l.23, after 'him.':]

The modern enlightenment would say that the Pauline conception begins with the distinction between mind and body; that then (with Aristotle) he alters the primary form of the distinction by treating the body as the organ or seat, not merely of life, but of feeling and appetite, as opposed to thought, reason, νοῦς: that feeling and appetite, next, though thus sharply opposed as 'flesh' to νοῦς, are yet regarded as in a state which the action of νοῦς (self-consciousness) can alone produce, i.e. as not in their animal simplicity, but become selfish through self-reflection – as the lust for personal enjoyment, which is the general source of the 'works of the flesh,' enumerated in Gal. 5.19; that the 'flesh,' though thus endowed with attributes which are as much mental or spiritual as anything in man, (a) is still identified with the 'body,' or 'members,' or 'outer,' in opposition to 'inner' man; and finally, by the old mistake about essence, which substantiates our generalization from individuals into a real universal, (b) this 'flesh' of each individual is converted into one abstract principle operative in manifold individuals, which again is personified as a perpetual Adam.

(a) The antithesis between σάρξ ['flesh'], as St. Paul understands it, and spirit is not of that absolute nature which on first thought seems to obtain between mind and matter. In speculative strictness, σάρξ ['flesh'] and πνεῦμα ['spirit'] may be opposed only as incomplete and complete. Σάρξ ['flesh'] is a self-conscious subject, as it makes an object to itself out of what satisfies its appetite, but is not good on the whole; νοῦς is the same subject as it ineffectually presents to itself an object which shall be good on the whole. Practically, the two objects, though the same self-consciousness is the source of each, are antagonistic. (Comp. Aristotle's ἀκρατία ['lack of self-control']).[22]

(b) The true notion of the universal is that it is that common relation between individuals which is the condition of their reality. The individual is no more real without the universal, than the universal without the individual. σὰρξ is equivalent to the relation of exclusiveness between the individual and other individuals, and between the individual and God, which makes satisfaction, otherwise *natural*, selfish. Into this relation we are born; it makes us what we are as men, namely sinners. The personification of it in Adam, the tracing of its source to a past event, is not essential.

Philosophically speaking, the same self-consciousness which makes the flesh sinful (converting simple animalism into selfishness) is the source of presentation of a law. (The law according to St. Paul, is not, it must be remembered dependent on Moses.) Thus the state of being 'alive without the law' is not to be understood absolutely; it must be taken to mean the state in which selfishness is *least* self-conscious, and in which, correlatively, there is least consciousness of law.

The most exact expression for that 'which lusteth against the spirit' is φρόνημα τῆς σαρκὸς [the 'carnal mind'] (Article 9).[23] [...]

[On p.193, l.38, note after (Romans vii.8–11)'[24]:]
In Coloss. 2.18 the νοῦς τῆς σαρκὸς ['his fleshy mind'], the source of sensual religion, leads to the envisagement of God's operation in an ascending hierarchy of 'angels' and the substitution of a certain abasement of feeling in the imaginary contemplation of these for the free and thoughtful worship of God.

[P.195, l.28–34, replacing 'The life ...'sanctification.":]
The sanctified life, or spiritual life, is already complete in that consciousness of adoption which comes of the recognition of Christ as under our conditions, namely as dying in the flesh and under the law: it is complete in it, as a necessary effect in a cause. Hence the use of aorists, as in Rom. 6.6 συνεσταυρώθη ['was crucified with him'], and 8.2 ἠλευθέρωσε ['freed'].

[On p.197, l.17, note after 'mankind.':]
The aorists which St. Paul uses in speaking of the 'liberation from the law of sin and death' (Rom. 8.1. etc.) though they carry the notion that 'life in the spirit' is already in principle complete in the primary consciousness of reconciliation to God, also express his

conception of this reconciliation as effected in a single act by Christ's death.

[On p.197, l.26–27, replacing 'In Romans viii.3, … sin.":]
[…] In Romans 8.3 this is modified into the expression 'in the likeness of sinful flesh and for sin'; περὶ ['concerning'] in contrast with ὑπὲρ ['of'] expressing the relation 'to sin' most generally. Comp. 5.14, 6.8; Phil. 2.7.

[On p.198, l.12, after 'past.':]
This is undoubtedly the requirement of the legal conscience. [Rom.] 3.21 foll. Δικαιοσύνη Θεοῦ ['righteousness of God'], as the perfect relation between God and man, has two sides. God is always δίκαιος ['just'] towards man, but man requires a change of consciousness in order to be 'just before God'. This change is effected by the Son's putting himself in man's place, so that man, even in the mortal body, may become one with the Son and thus share in his perfect relation towards the Father.

This is the most important aspect of the 'manifestation of the righteousness of God'. But another aspect is in view in [Rom. 3.] v.25. ἔνδειξιν, etc. ['to declare his righteousness for the remission of sins that are past'] refers to the 'manifestation' as a vindication of the righteousness on God's side, which might have been called in question διὰ τὴν πάρεσιν τῶν προγεγονότων ἁμαρτημάτων ['for the remission of sins that are past']. He exhibits ἐν τῷ νῦν καιρῷ ['at this time'] (v.26)[25] the justice which was always his, but had been hidden when 'at the time of that ignorance God winked' [Acts 17.30]. Thus the ἔνδειξις ['declare'] connects rather with δίκαιον ['just'] in the following clause than with δικαιοῦντα ['justifying'].

Again, it is as exhibiting[26] God's righteousness in this way that Christ in his death (which *as a sacrifice* is called αἷμα[τι] ['blood']) is a propitiation [Rom. 3.25]: namely, as paying a penalty for the προγεγονότα ἁμαρτήματα ['sins that are past']. God for the vindication of his justice, has to show that the penalty of sin was not dispensed with, even while for us (in its true form of conscious alienation from God) it was so taken away that we should be able to walk in newness of life.

This is effected, according to St. Paul's deeper view, by the appearance of God in his Son, under those conditions which are the result and penalty of sin; but which, owing to their manifestation, take a new character, and no longer separate us from him.

As the penalty of sin, (in shape of death) is viewed more outwardly and more inwardly according to indefinite degrees of difference, so it is with the death of Christ, as that which for us is the substitute for that penalty. Whenever Christ's death is spoken of as 'blood,' it is thought of as 'vicarious sacrifice': but then the meaning both of 'vicarious' and of 'sacrifice' fluctuates. The latter term, with us (probably through the exaltation of the idea of sacrifice which the representation of Christ's death as a sacrifice has brought about), has quite lost its original meaning, and come to mean perfect self-surrender.[27]

[On p.199, l.36, after value.':]

[...] 3.23. 'The glory of God'. The common interpretation of these words is 'the glory which God bestows'; compare one explanation of δικαιοσύνη Θεοῦ ['the righteousness of God']. This 'glory which God bestows' is thought of as the future glorification in heaven (comp. 2.7, 10).

The notion of δόξα Θεοῦ ['the glory of God'] includes that of a glory which God bestows, but there is no warrant for separating it from the highest spiritual life. It is parallel to St. Paul's notion of the blessed life (4.7 foll.). The idea of the 'glory of God' is best expressed by some such phrase as the 'Perfect Divine life,' which is only man's, indeed so far as it is bestowed by God, but in which he lives and communicates it to man. This notion will suit 5.2, 'we rejoice in the hope of the perfect life which is ours in principle, though not fully communicated (8.18). In 8.21 he speaks of the 'freedom of the Glory':[28] i.e. of the perfect life: in 6.4 of the 'Glory of the Father'.

The resurrection of Christ is the result, the completion of the communication to the Christian of the divine life; which communication is for us future, who have not attained the full freedom of the divine life, and shall not do so, according to St. Paul, until the quickening of the mortal body.

The same idea suits passages in St. John, e.g. ch.17. The glorification of Christ is the return to the divine life from which his dwelling in the flesh separated him; and the death of Christ is, throughout the fourth Gospel, spoken of as his glorification.

3.25 ἱλαστήριον ['a propitiation']. There is only one other passage in the New Testament where the word occurs, Heb. 9.5:[29] where it has the article and means the mercy-seat which was on the top of the Ark: and so in Exod. 9.5. In Amos 9.1 it is used by the

LXX for the altar; in the LXX generally, it is only used for some place or thing.[30]

Is there here a distinct reference to the mercy-seat, as that from which Jehovah communicated with Moses, and on which blood was sprinkled on the day of atonement (Exod. 25.22, Levit. 16.93, Num. 7.89)?

In this case there would be a double notion involved in the representation of Christ as ἱλαστήριον ['a propitiation']. (1) That of a medium of communication between God and man (Exod. 25.22), and (2) that of Christ's blood as the blood of sprinkling (Heb. 12.24:[31] comp. 1 Peter 1.2).

Others think that ἱλαστήριον need not mean the mercy-seat, but is merely the neuter of ἱλαστήριος, and means a propitiatory something.

How then is this something to be understood? What is to be supplied? Is the word to be taken specially of a propitiatory victim, or generally, of *means* of propitiation, by which the idea of Christ as a victim is avoided?

Ἱλαστήριον by itself could bear either interpretation but ἐν τῷν αἵματι ['by the blood'] shows that St. Paul was thinking of Christ as a victim. Compare on this view 4.25 ὃς παρεδόθη διὰ τὰ παραπτώματα ἡμῶν ['Who was delivered for our offences']. For the expression παρεδόθη ['to give up'], comp. Gal. 2.20, τοῦ παραδόντος ῥατὸν ὑπὲρ ἐμοῦ ['who gave himself for me'].

Can διὰ ['because'] express purpose? The wooden[32] commentators say that 'rose again for our justification' [Rom. 4.25] means 'rose again to produce that faith on our part which is the condition of justification': comp. the previous verses 17 and 23.

If, however, διὰ ['because'] expresses a purpose (as it does indirectly 1 Cor. 7.2 διὰ τὰς πορνείας ['because of fornications'] = *to prevent* πορνεῖαι ['fornication']) we may understand it as follows: As Christ's death is the condition of our deadness in sin and under the law becoming death to sin and the law, his risen life is the condition of our walk in newness of life. This new life is only possible for us so far as it has been already lived by the risen Son (6.5). The difficulty of this view is that δικαίωσις ['justification'] seems to be thought of as the initial act of the 'walk according to the Spirit,' not as the walk itself; as the pulling us into the new relation to God – or, strictly speaking, the consciousness thereof – which is the condition of the walk beginning. There is so much truth in the theological distinction between justification and sanctification.[33]

Taking δια ['because'] in the strict sense, 'rose again because we were justified,' we may understand the passage to mean that it was because the justification was complete in Christ's death that the new life began in his resurrection.' The death to sin and life unto God on our side – the death in which we are placed in a proper relation to him, become open to him, and are thus capable of a new life – has been anticipated (is only possible for us because anticipated) in Christ (Rom. 6.10 and 11).

Christ rose, because alive unto God, and we die and rise again in him, because he had died to sin. – His death to sin was our δικαίωσις ['justification']. So instead of saying that Christ rose again because he had died to sin, St. Paul says that he rose again because we were justified. The act of his death is presented as in its relation to us, while the rising-again (which has equally a relation to us) is presented *absolutely*.

The idea of Christ's death as a sin-offering, as a payment of the penalty due for the past sins of mankind, only appears incidentally in the Romans, but is more thoroughly developed in the Epistle to the Hebrews (9.15 foll.) in a way which would be natural to a writer who had St. Paul's writings before him. 'Wherefore he is the mediator of the new covenant, so that, a death having taken place for the redemption of the transgressions that are due on the ground of the first covenant, they that are called might receive the promise, etc.

In the English version the meaning of διαθήκη is changed from *covenant* to *testament*: 'or testament is of force after a man is dead.' [Heb. 9:17]

There is a great objection to shifting the meaning of διαθήκη. A better meaning is obtained by keeping to the sense of *covenant* throughout; and it combines two notions of the offering of Christ: the notion of it as a propitiatory sacrifice for the violation of the previous covenant, and that of the offering of a victim as a symbol of the ratification of a covenant. Comp. Genesis 15. which is interpreted to mean that Jehovah makes, not a covenant between two parties, but a promise (given by one). Comp. Gal. 3.16, 17, the law being in the proper sense a *covenant* between God and Israel. (Jeremiah 34.18.)

The offering of a victim in this case is the offering of a victim as ratifying a covenant, representing the death imprecated on the violator of it.

In the Epistle to the Hebrews the writer goes on to refer to Exod. 24.6 foll.. (Comp. [Luke 22.20] 'This is the new covenant in my blood') v.16 will therefore mean 'where a covenant is, there must of necessity be the death of the victim' which ratifies the covenant: the victim which ratifies the new covenant being Christ. [Gal. 3.] v.17 'For a covenant is ratified upon the terms of the death of victims,' or 'over the dead bodies of victims'; otherwise it is powerless while the victim that ratified the covenant liveth.[34] But can ὁ διαθέμενος ['the covenanter'] be taken of the victim that ratifies the covenant? Yes; for St. Paul is thinking of Christ as the victim, and so speaks of the victim as he would not otherwise do.

Can διατίθημαι in Luke 22.29 mean anything but *bequeath*? Even if it could not, the difficulty involved in the change of meaning of διαθήκη would not be removed.

Even where the death of Christ is spoken of as a propitiatory sacrifice, that notion is immediately fused and blended with the moral notion that the blood of Christ purifies the conscience from dead works. It is only because the idea of a propitiatory sacrifice immediately passes into the notion of a death unto sin in which we partake, that the sacrifice is never to be repeated, as having removed the consciousness of sin.

[On p.200, l.34–41, replacing 'just as there … life of Christ.':]
Faith in all its shades of meaning still expresses the attitude of moral receptivity, but varies according to the object received through it, viz. Christ's death, or the whole spiritual life of Christ; as the latter it becomes πίστις δι᾽ ἀγαπῆς ἐνεργουμένη ['faith which worketh by love'] (Gal. 5.6).

Whether ἐνεργουμένη ['worketh'] passive or middle the sense is the same: sometimes as in 2 Cor. 1.6 it apparently is passive; Rom. 7.5, Eph. 2.20 it is middle: in 2 Cor. 4.12 either meaning will do.

[P.201, l.31, after 'works?':]
One popular way of understanding the antithesis is to take it of the difference between the good disposition and the outward act; but there is no sign in the Epistle to the Romans that by the works of the law St. Paul meant mere outward observances.

Is not the state of mind called belief the same as the state of mind expressed in works, *minus* the outward proof and sign?

[On p.202, l.10, after '(iii.31).':]
The notion involved in speaking of the 'law of faith' [Rom. 3.27] is the same as appears in speaking of the spiritual walk, of

which faith is the beginning and condition, as being the fulfilment of the δικαίωμα νόμον ['righteousness of the law'].

Thus the law given by Moses is presented as a mere special and temporary mode of law. It is itself sequent to a previously given law of faith, for conformity to which Abraham received the promise of inheritance. It thus follows upon a first appearance of the law of faith received by Abraham, and prior to the acceptance of the law of faith by all men, and its condition: because its effect is to shut up all under sin, the consciousness of sin being necessary to the abandonment of personal pretension, which again is the condition of the recipiency of grace.

The notion of the merely 'interimistic' character of the law of works is developed in Romans 4 and Gal. 3. After saying that the law of faith is the true law, and that through faith we establish the law, he goes on to ask 'This being so, what shall we say that Abraham obtained in virtue of the fleshly rite of circumcision?' (Comp. Gal. 6.12, 13).

The practical answer is *nothing*.

The fleshly rite is taken as the symbol of the attempted righteousness of works, in respect of which he obtained nothing. That which he did obtain, the promise that he should be heir of the world, was given to him without any condition on his side but faith only, and when he was still in uncircumcision.

This notion is worked out more fully and technically in Gal. 3, where the same antithesis appears between the prior régime of promise, – already potentially the Christian regime (being of faith) though not universal, – and the subsequent interimistic régime of law. Thus the covenant given to Abraham is not an agreement between parties, but a promise *ex parte Dei*, Abraham's faith being the condition on his side. This cannot be set aside by the subsequent covenant of the law. In v.17 St. Paul says 'my meaning is that a covenant ratified before by God with reference to Christ cannot be disannulled by the law, it is no more of promise' (comp. Rom. 4.13).

Then comes the curious passage διαταγεὶς δὶ ἀγγέλων ['being ordained by Angels' (Gal. 3.19)], given by the interposition of angels. This in St. Stephen's speech (Acts [7.1–53]) is put as a rhetorical glorification of the law [Acts 7.53]. Here St. Paul puts it as a *depreciatory sign in the law*.

It was a received idea of the Alexandrian Jews that the Invisible could not communicate directly with his chosen people, and so employed the ministration of Angels.

v.20 'The existence of such a mediator as Moses implies two parties contracting, one promising something, the other covenanting to do something if the promise is fulfilled. But God is one, sovereign and absolute. The covenant of the law, as a transaction between two parties, could not express the one absolute essence of God: but a promise, as not implying any such covenant, was not incompatible with his absolute sovereignty'.

The law of works express the purpose of God, but St. Paul does not think of it as directly representing his nature. The purpose of it is to shut up all alike in the | | of sin, that they may be capable of receiving the promise in Jesus Christ.

So he speaks of the law as a παιδαγωγός ['schoolmaster' (Gal. 3.24)]. In this connection two notions are in his mind, neither of which is expressed by the word 'schoolmaster,' (1) The παιδαγωγός was a slave: (2) his office was not to teach, but to restrain merely.

For faith as to the fulfilling of the law, comp. Gal. 6.2, and 1 Cor. 9.21 ἔννομος Χριστῷ ['under the law to Christ' (1 Cor. 9.21)].

The other points which have to be considered are:

(1) The account given of the new life, its gradual fulfilment and realization, in ch. 8.

(2) The account of the providential scheme of election (chs. 9 and 11), St. Paul's view of the condition of the Gentile world (ch. 1).

(3) St. Paul's Christology.

(1) In the eighth chapter justification is especially presented as δικαίωσις ζωῆς ['the justification of life']. [...]

[On p.204, l.5, immediately after 'hope.':]
[...] so ἐλπὶς is used for the object of hope in Rom. 8.24, Col. 1.5.

[On p.205, l.2, after '17.':]
(The resurrection on which St. Paul is there dwelling is certainly not a *merely* spiritual resurrection. 'If the dead rise not, then is not Christ raised' [1 Cor. 15.16]. The resurrection of dead men is in principle involved in this: you cannot deny their resurrection without denying his, which involves it'. The resurrection of the dead spoken of is from physical death: his resurrection then, as involving it, must, it would seem, be a resurrection from physical death. Yet in v.17 it appears as that which delivers us from sin, viz. as a spiritual resurrection. Throughout the chapter, the resurrection spoken of is doubtless from physical death, yet it is only ours as in Christ (v.23).

[On p.206, text continues after end of extract:]

St. Paul's Christology

A great deal has been written about St. Paul's view of the pre-existence of Christ. In speaking of it it is as well to confine our attention to the Epistles to the Romans, Corinthians, and Galatians. (Comp. 1 Cor. 15, especially 21 and 27: Romans 5.15, 2 Cor. 3.17, 4.6: 1 Cor. 11.3: Rom. 1.4). In Rom. 9.5 the words 'God blessed for ever' are perhaps not to be taken in application to Christ as would appear from our (old) version.[35] In 1 Cor. 8.6 'by whom are all things and we by him' the phrase 'all things' probably does not refer to the material creation, but to 'all things' of the Christian life, the work of redemption. Comp. 2 Cor. 5.17, 18; 'if any man be in Christ … all things are become new'. The passage is not to be appealed to as supporting the notion of the pre-existence of Christ, i.e. of the πνεῦμα or eternal spirit, or again the existence from eternity of the ἄνθρωπος πνευματικός ['spiritual man'] or the spiritual man (as in Philo the ἄνθρωπος ἐπουράνιος).

In the heavenly man the glory of God is perfectly reflected: hence the spiritual man is spoken of as the εἰκὼν τοῦ Θεοῦ ['the image of God' (2 Cor. 4.4)]. Thus it is as the reflex of the Father's glory that Christ is spoken of as God's own Son, only that there are other notions associated with this in St. Paul's mind besides the perfect likeness of God, for it was the Jewish notion that the Messiah was the Son of God. Christ is spoken of as the spiritual man in 1 Cor. 15.21: Comp. v.45 foll. (ἄνθρωπος πνευματικός ['spiritual man'] as opposed to ἄνθρωπος ψυχικός ['natural man']). 'That is not first which is spiritual, but that which is natural'. [1 Cor. 15.46] How is this to be reconciled with the pre-existence of Christ?

The priority of ψυχικός ['natural'] to πνευματικός ['spiritual'] is priority of manifestation in time, opposed to the ideal or eternal priority of πνεῦμα ['spirit']. There is an equivalence between the terms 'Christ the Lord' and πνεῦμα ['spirit']: 'The Lord is the Spirit.' The presence, that is, of the spirit in man, in virtue of which he is said to be the temple of God, is equivalent to Christ in us, constituting our hope, by the ἀπαρχὴ τοῦ πνεύματος ['firstfruit of the spirit' (Rom. 8.23)].

Lord of Glory. The Son is the εἰκὼν τοῦ Θεοῦ ['the image of God']. With St. Paul the characteristic way of considering Christ is under the figure of light, the reflection of God's glory (2 Cor. 4.4). As the reflected light of God he gives the quickening of us, the making us holy by the πνεῦμα ἀγιωσύνης ['spirit of holiness' (Rom. 1.4)]. Δόξα ['glory'] means the reflected light. 'The woman is the glory of the man,' i.e. reflects the light of the man 'God is the head of Christ,' i.e. Christ reflects the light of God. Man too is the ›fl[ί,ì ['image'] and δόξα τοῦ Θεοῦ ['glory of God'], as the reflex of God; comp. Rom. 8.29 συμμόρφους της εἰκόνος τοῦ υἱοῦ ['conformed to the image of the son'].

The 'tabernacling' of this πνεῦμα ἀγιωσύνης ['spirit of holiness'] in the flesh constitutes the Messiah. He is, as it is elsewhere put, 'born of the seed of David after the flesh' (2 Cor. 8.ll).[36] Clement speaks of the ὁ Κύριος σοῦμὲν τὰ πρῶτον πνεῦμα ἐγένετο σάρξ.[37] This is exactly St. Paul's attitude.

Jesus being already the Son of God in the highest sense, in virtue of the indwelling of the πνεῦμα ἀγιωσύνης ['spirit of holiness'], is declared to be so by the quickening of the body in which he dwelt. It would not be Pauline to say *after he had died*. St. Paul looks upon the body as dead from the first, a body of corruption. Hence he conceives not only that those who are dead will be raised at the full manifestation of Christ, but those who are alive then will be changed, and thus become a spiritual body.

Rom. 1.4 ὁρισθέντος ['declared'] is not = 'constituted,' as if he then first became the Son of God, but implies the declaration or manifestation of him in the sight of man (comp. Acts 10.42 ὁ ὡρισμένος ὅπον τοῦ Θεοῦ κριτής, etc. ['he which was ordained of God *to be* the Judge of quick and dead.'])

Κατὰ πνεῦμα αγιωσύνης ['according to the spirit of holiness' (Rom. 1.4)]. By virtue of the spirit of holiness he is constituted the 'Glory of God'. Through the sign of the quickening of his body. Ὁξ ἀναστάσεως νεκρῶν ['the resurrection of the dead' (Rom. 1.4)]. St. Paul uses the expression of 'resurrection of the dead' generally, because he looks upon Christ's resurrection as a foretaste of the general resurrection'. So he is declared to be the Son of God exhibited in the resurrection of the dead through his own resurrection.

8.20, 21, ὅτι should probably be taken (as in the Revised Version)[38] as = 'that'.

Φύσις corresponds to 'nature,' as philosophically understood. 'Not willingly, but owing to him that subjected it' – Διὰ τοῦ ὑποτάξαντα ['because of him who hath subjected' (Rom. 8.20)] is to be understood of God: it conveys the same notion as in 11.32 'God included all under sin, that he might be merciful'.[39] Because subjection was of God, we are confident of its temporary character. Therefore the creature lives in hope of its own deliverance.

{On the question of 'election' I can find only the following notes.}
The doctrine of election, as conveyed in the words 'it is not of him that willeth,' etc., is involved in the doctrine of justification by faith.

It is not so involved, if it implies *particularity* of election. Ultimately, according to St. Paul, it does not. The term 'election,' taken strictly doubtless implies particularity. But salvation is in the strict sense elective only at a certain stage of God's providence.

In this stage it has to be elective, that it may be recognized to be as of Grace.

Thus the temporary particularity of election is to be accounted for in the same way as the 'inclusion of all under sin,' which was the purpose of the law.

The 'purpose of election' is that no *flesh* might glory in God's sight.[40] The elected people therefore, cannot be any one nation (comp. Luke 3.8).

What St. Paul has in view throughout is not any election of individuals, but the election of Gentiles into the place of the previously elected Jews. (Rom. 9.30 foll.). To this the whole previous part of the Epistle has been leading. He has shown that δικαιοσύνη κατὰ νόμον ['righteousness after the law'] was unattainable: that a perfect righteousness had been achieved by the Son of God, and so achieved in the flesh (within the condition of the flesh) as to be communicable in the shape of spiritual life to us.

Why has not Israel accepted that righteousness? (a) The title of Israel to be reckoned children of God was not constituted by their fleshly descent (vv.7–9); (b) as conveyed from the first it implied the election of some, the exclusion of others, according to the purpose of God (vv.9–15): (c) such election and exclusion belongs to the prerogative of God, as he says of himself to Moses and elsewhere, against which man has no right to complain (vv.14–21): (d) If it is part of God's plan to spare vessels of wrath and so to make known the riches of his glory on vessels of mercy, by making them his own after previous apparent alienation, why should he not? (vv.22–29).

The result is in fact stated in v.30, 'Then Israel could not help it.'[41] This consequence does not seem to suggest itself to St. Paul. Their rejection of the Gospel is their own fault for trying to do something for themselves, instead of receiving something from God. Salvation, according to St. Paul, is all of God working in and for us, but the receptivity of such operation on man's side depends on himself. He cannot find fault, for he is not called upon to do anything, but only to submit to the fact that he can do nothing: only 'to believe': and then for him Christ has fulfilled the law, and in fulfilling it has got rid of it. Man has not to ascend into heaven or go down into hell, but only to recognize what is already in his heart and make confession of it with his life.

[1]   {Partly from Mr. Green's own manuscript, partly from notes taken by Mr. Macan.} [Green's rather chaotic manuscript survives in his papers at Balliol ('Notebook: Notes for lectures on early Christianity'; see Thomas, *Moral Philosophy of TH Green*, p.385). Reginald Walter Macan (1848–1941), matriculated Christ Church, Oxford 1867, scholar at University College 1868–71, gained Firsts in Classical Moderations in 1869 and literae humaniores in 1871, held various academic positions at Oxford during his life, including Fellow and Tutor of University College between 1884 and 1906, before becoming Master from 1906 to 1923.] *{The words actually written by Mr. Green have been exactly repeated except in a very few cases where a slight alteration appeared necessary./Matter obviously parenthetical has generally been put into a note; matter apparently subordinate to or illustrative of the main current of the lecture has been written a little distance off the margin. H.N.}*

[2]   [Word marked for possible deletion.]

[3]   ['So then *it is* not of him that willeth, nor of him that runneth, but of God that sheweth mercy' (Rom. 9.16).]

[4]   [The preceding part of this paragraph has been marked 'Subordinate matter' in the margin.]

[5]   [This and the next sentence marked for possible deletion.]

[6]   ? The Law was still deceiving them. [HN's note?]

[7]   Just as he takes the Law given to the Jews as representing the Law generally. It is merely the more intense and distinct form of that law of conscience which has authority over all, and which all have come short of obeying (2.15–3.23.) It is a mistake to suppose that the 'Law' to St. Paul means merely the ceremonial law. It is the moral law, from which life in the 'Spirit' delivers us; delivers us by enabling us to fulfil it in a higher form (8.4, 13.10).

[8]   [Proselytes, or former heathens who have converted to Judaism, were subject to the seven conditions which bound Noah and his descendants; namely, the rejection of idol-worship, of blasphemy, of shedding blood or murder, of impure sexual relations, of rape, robbery and theft, and of eating the flesh of living animal, and the acceptance of the authority of judges appointed to implement these laws.]

⁹ [Green's Greek corresponds only very loosely to the Greek of Rom. 1.13–14 in the standard Biblical Greek. In the Authorised Version, these verses read: 'Now I would not have you ignorant, brethren, that oftentimes I purposed to come unto you, (but was let hitherto) that I might have some fruit among you also, even as among other Gentiles,/I am debtor both to the Greeks, and to the Barbarians, both to the wise, and to the unwise.']

¹⁰ [MS reads: '10.11'.]

¹¹ [MS reads: 'Junias'.]

¹² ['Aquila and Priscilla (Acts 18.2, 26); Apollos (Acts 19.1), Herodian (Rom. 16.11).]

¹³ The following passage bears on the number of Jews in Rome at this time, Seneca ap. Augustin De Civ. Dei 6.11 'usque eo sceleratissimae gentis consuetude convaluit ut per omnes iam tinas recepta est; victi victoribus leges dederunt.' ['But when speaking of the Jews he says: "Meanwhile the customs of the this accursed race have gained such influence that they are now received throughout the world. The vanquished have given laws to their victors".' Saint Augustine (quoting Seneca), *The City of God Against the Pagans*, trans. William M Green, 7 vols. (London: William Heinemann, 1957–1968), vol.2, bk.6, 11, p.361.] Sueton., Claudius 26, 'adsidue tumultuantes Judaie impulsore Chresto.' ['Since the Jews constantly made disturbances at the instigation of Chrestus, he [Claudius] expelled them from Rome.' Suetonius [*The Twelve Caesars*] trans. JC Rolfe, 2 vols. (London: William Heinemann, 1924), Vol.2, Chap. 26 pp.52–53 'Iedaios impulsore Chresto assidue tumultuantis Roma expulit'.] Comp. the advice given in 13.1 (of the time of Claudius). A special quarter was given to Jews at Rome by Augustus. More than 8,000 were then resident there,' Joseph. Ant. 17.11.1. [Josephus [*Jewish Antiquities*] trans. H St J Thackeray and Ralph Marcus, 8 vols. (London: William Heinemann, 1926–1965), Vol.8, Chap. 300, xi–I, p.511.]

¹⁴ The expression occurs 3.5, 22, 26: 10.3 as opposed to ἰδία [their 'own']; 2 Cor. 5.21 as opposed to ἁμαρτία ['sin']. In Phil. 3.9 we have τὴν ἐκ Θεοῦ δικαιοσύνη ['the righteousness which is of God']. Gal. 3.21 gives the relation between δικαιοσύνη Θεοῦ ['the righteousness of God'] and ζαοποιῖα ['to make alive']; Rom. 4.6 that between it and μακαρισμός ['blessedness']. Besides this we find the expressions δίκαιον εἶναι παρὰ τῷ Θεῷ ['those who are just before God'] Rom. 2.13; δικαιοῦσθαι ἐνώπιον Θεοῦ ['justified in his sight'] 3.20: and δικαιοῦσθαι παρὰ Θεῷ ['justified in the sight of God'] Gal. 3.11. If δικαιοσύνη Θεοῦ does not mean righteousness as an attribute of God, it is difficult to explain 3.5: if it does, it is equally difficult to explain 2 Cor. 3.21.

¹⁵ [Rom. 2.13–15 (but not v.16) are bracketed in the Authorised (King James) Version, with non being so in the 1881 Revised Version.]

¹⁶ [Possibly an allusion to '…even so might grace reign through righteousness unto eternal life, by Jesus Christ our Lord.' (Rom. 5.21)]

¹⁷ [Heinrich August Wilhelm Meyer, *Das Neue Testament Grieschisch nach den besten Hülfsmitteln kritisch revidirt …*, 2 vols. (Göttingen: Vandenhoeck und Ruprecht, 1829).]

¹⁸ ['For until the law sin was in the world: but sin is not imputed when there is no law.' (Rom 5.13)]

¹⁹ [Gal 2:19 'For I through the law am dead to the law, that I might live unto God'.]

[20] [This paragraph also appears in the published version, Green, *Works III*, pp.192–3.]

[21] ['For when we were in the flesh, the motions of sins, which were by the law, did work in our members to bring forth fruit unto death.' (Rom. 7:5)]

[22] [Aristotle, *Nichomachean Ethics*, 1145a15–1154b34 (i.e. Book 7).]

[23] [Article 9 of the Thirty-Nine Articles of Religion of the Church of England (1562) is entitled 'Of Original or Birth-sin', and reads: 'Original Sin standeth not in the following of *Adam*, (as the *Pelagians* do vainly talk), but it is the fault and corruption of the Nature of every man, that naturally is ingendered of the offspring of *Adam*; whereby man is very far gone from original righteousness, and is of his own nature inclined to evil, so that the flesh lusteth always contrary to the spirit; and therefore in every person born into this world, it deserveth God's wrath and damnation. And this infection of nature doth remain, yea, in them that are regenerated; whereby the lust of the flesh, called in Greek, *phronema sarkos*, which some do expound the wisdom, some sensuality, some the affection, some the desire, of the flesh, is not subject to the Law of God. And although there is no condemnation for them that believe and are baptized, yet the Apostle doth confess, that concupiscence and lust hath of itself the nature of sin.']

[24] [MS reads: '(Romans 7.11)'.]

[25] [MS reads: '(v.27)'.]

[26] [MS orig.: 'vindicating'.]

[27] *{The following seems to be a second version of the above.}* [HN is referring to the text printed in Green's *Works III*, p.198, l.14 et sub.]

[28] ['Because the creature itself also shall be delivered from the bondage of corruption into the glorious liberty of the children of God.' (Rom. 8:21)]

[29] [In fact, it also occurs at 1 John 2.2 and 4.10.]

[30] ['LXX' = the Septuagint, a term used for the translation of the Hebrew scriptures into Greek undertaken at Alexandria in the third century BC, because there were alleged to have been either seventy-two or seventy-five translators, who are said to have translated the Pentateuch in seventy-two days.]

[31] [MS reads Heb. 12:34 in error.]

[32] [On the facing page '? modern' is written against this passage [HN's note?]. Green's mss. simply reads 'wooden'.]

[33] Comp. 5.9; on the other hand 8.4. Why should not δικαίωτις refer to the fulfilment of the law in us?

[34] [The reference seems to be to Exodus 24. rather than 24.6. Cf. Hebrews 8.7–13.]

[35] *{see however the Revised Version. H.N.}* [Rom. 9:5 Authorised Version: 'Whose are the fathers, and of whom as concerning the flesh Christ *came*, who is over all, God blessed for ever. Amen.'; Revised Version: 'whose are the fathers, and of whom is Christ as concerning the flesh, who is over all, God blessed for ever. Amen.']

[36] [The phrase does not occur in the Bible. Green may have in mind: 'Behold Israel after the flesh: are not they which eat of the sacrifices partakers of the altar?' (2 Cor. 10.18).]

[37] [This quotation has not been found in St Clement of Alexandria. Very roughly, it translates as 'the Lord who drives his spirit to become flesh'.]

[38] [Rom. 8.21. Given, firstly, that RLN dates this piece to ca.1871 (Nettleship, *Memoir*, p.vi) and, secondly, that the Revised Version was published in 1881, this aside must have been added by HN.]

[39] [Rom. 11:32 'For God hath concluded them all in unbelief, that he might have mercy upon all'.]

[40] [Possibly 'right' rather than 'sight'.]

[41] [These words do not appear in Rom. 9.30, although. 9.31 may be intended. These verses read: 'What shall we say then? That the Gentiles, which followed not after righteousness, have attained to righteousness, even the righteousness which is of faith. But Israel, which followed after the law of righteousness, hath not attained to the law of righteousness.']

Notes on the Epistle
to
the Galatians.[1]
[ca. 1873]
[Edited by Henry Nettleship and Colin Tyler]

The Epistle falls into the following parts:[2]

(1) *Personal*. Ch. 1 and 2. The object being (a) to assert the independence of Paul's mission as derived from an immediate revelation of Christ in him, not from any teaching of those who were apostles before him: (b) to vindicate his consistency; to deny that he had ever wavered either as to his own freedom from the authority of the original apostles, or that of his converts from the bondage of the law. He could not have so wavered without being false to the revelation of Christ in him. The crucifixion of Christ, as he conceived it, was the extinction of the law, so that all who shared in it were *ipso facto* freed from the law. (This ends with 2.19).

(2) *Doctrinal*. Ch. 3 and 4. The opposition between Faith and Works, Grace and Law, Life in the Spirit and Life in the Flesh.

(3) *Hortatory and Practical*. Ch. 5, 6, 10.[3] 'Stand fast in the liberty wherewith Christ has made you free'. 'As you live in the Spirit, walk in the Spirit.'[4]

A postscript is added from 6.11 – end.[5]

One common idea, represented by the antithesis of κατ᾽ ἄνθρωπον κατὰ σάρκα ['after any human fashion or standard'][6] to κατὰ πνεῦμα, ['after the Holy Spirit'] runs throughout 1.11 and 12 γὰρ ὑμῖν αδελφοὶ, τὸ εὐαγγέλιον τὸ εὐαγγελισθὲν ὑπ᾽ ἐμοῦ ὃτι σὺκ ἔστι κατ᾽ ἄνθρωπον οὐδὲ γὰρ ἐγὼ παρὰ ἀνθρώπον παρέλαβον αὐτὸ οὔτε ἐδιδάχθην, ἀλλὰ δὶ ἀποκαλύψεως. ῭Ιησοῦ Χριστοῦ ['For I certify you, brethren, that the Gospel which was preached of me is not after man./For I neither received it of man, neither was I taught it, but by the revelation of Jesus Christ.' (Gal. 1.11–12)].

Οὐδὲ ['Neither']: he goes back from the Gospel to himself as its preacher: 'not only is the Gospel not κατ᾽ ἄνθρωπον ['after man'], neither did I, its preacher, receive it (as might naturally have been the case) from man.' His Gospel is not derived from any tradition

111

of Christ's words or of the events of his life, not from any instruction in doctrines, but is an immediate revelation. Hence his apostleship is independent, coordinate with the apostleship of those whose title to authority rested on personal intercourse with Jesus.

The word ἀπόστολοι ['apostle'] at the beginning of the Christian history is not to be confined to the Twelve, because it is applied to Barnabas and to James the brother of the Lord (comp. 1.19 'other of the apostles saw I none, but James the Lord's brother'). It is a term implying special authority derived from intercourse with Jesus (Luke 24.48; Acts 1.8, 22). On the ground of this the Jerusalemites[7] claimed a special authority, and Paul is always asserting his as coordinate on the ground of the special revelation of Christ to him, a vision corresponding to the eye-witness of the Twelve (1 Cor. 9.1). 'Have I not seen the Lord?' (comp. also 1 Cor. 15.8 'Last of all he was seen of me also': 2 Cor. 12.1).

παρέλαβον ['received']: the same expression is used [in] 1 Cor. 15.3; 11.23. with reference to what he had 'received' as to the Lord's supper and the resurrection. It is clear that though he made himself acquainted with the apostolic tradition after the ἀποκάλυψις Χριστοῦ ['revelation of Christ'], he did not conceive this revelation to be in any way conditioned by it. Presumably, he knew nothing of the tradition in detail until his visit to Jerusalem (v.18). His Christianity did not rest on evidence, nor on the example and history of Jesus.

Did he regard the revelation as momentary or continuous? In any case he regarded it as *repeated*: comp. 2.2 ἀνέβην κατὰ ἀποκάλυψιν, ['And I went up by revelation'] and 2 Cor. 12.1, 7. His life was governed by a succession of revelations. The expression ἐν ἐμοὶ (v.16) ('in my person',) is, it is true, different from ἐμοὶ, but it does not mean specially 'within me'; that is, St. Paul is not thinking specially the inwardness of the revelation. It was, as he conceived, a revelation consisting in this, that through it Christ's person became his, and his life became identified with Christ's (2.20) ἐν ἐμοὶ thus means much more than δι᾽ ἐμοῦ; comp. 4.19; Rom. 8.10; 2 Cor. 4.10; 13.3, 5. Coloss. 1.27.

Of this revelation the effect or expression was preaching to the Gentiles (ἵνα εὐαγγελίζωμαι αὐτὸν, etc.).[8] The life which Christ had begun to live in him, the life which he lived by the 'faith of the Son of God who died and gave himself for man' [Gal. 2.20], had for its consequence this preaching. (On the connection between the universality of the Gospel, its availability for the Gentiles, and the view of Christ involved in this 'revelation', more will be said when we come to 2.20). [Gal. 1.]16–17.[9] εὐθέως οὐ προσανεθέμην ['immediately I conferred not'] etc. Εὐθέως ['immediately'] is not to be connected with ἀπῆλθον ['went I up'] rather than with οὐ προσανθέμην ['I conferred not']. 'The immediate result was a break with flesh and blood' (comp. Matth. 16.17). The purport of the following verse is to show the slightness of his connection with the Jerusalem apostles (in confirmation of iv. [?] 12). He had no intercourse at all with them for three years after the 'revelation', during which he had been quite away from Christian influences in Arabia. When he went up to Jerusalem he saw only Peter and James, and stayed fifteen days: this he insists on in v.20. Then he went to Syria and Cilicia, being unknown by face to the churches in Judea: and after fourteen years he went up to Jerusalem, taking Titus with him, 'by revelation' [Gal. 2.1–2], that is, not by the commission of any other man.

2.2 αὐτοῖς ['them'] may be the leading Apostles, (going back to 1.19) or, the members of the Jerusalem Church (involved in 'Jerusalem' of the previous verse. Comp. 2 Cor. 2.13 where αὐτοῖς refers back to τὴν Τρωάδα ['to Troas' (2 Cor. 2.12)]). This, however, is limited by κατ' ἰδίας τοῖς δοκοῦσι ['but privately to them which were of reputation'], which is not past, but present, and on the strength of it men were disturbing the Galatian Church (comp. 2 Cor. 3.1).

μήπως ... ἔδραμον ['lest by any means ... had run[, in vain]' (Gal. 2.2)]: not 'in order that I might not' (which will not suit ἔδραμου, unless that be taken to be said *ex [....?] judicio*, 'in order that it might not be thought that I had'), but 'in anxiety lest I should be, or had been, running in vain': lest it should turn out that his effort to reconcile Jew and Gentile in Christ had been unavailing. V.3. *But* (in spite of this anxiety, and consequent wish to strain a point in the way of conciliation) not even Titus who was with me, (and in whose case, therefore, I might have more easily yielded than in that of Gentile converts in their Gentile homes) was compelled to be circumcised.

How is v.4 connected? (διὰ δὲ τοὺς, etc.).[10] The virtual answer may be found either in v.5 or in v.6. The thought may either be 'And the reason why I stood out against the circumcision of Titus was the action of those false brethren, who would have taken his circumcision as matter of right', or 'owing to the seductions of false brethren I got no support from the "pillars"'.[11] They did nothing to help me, or taught me nothing new: they merely agreed to let me alone, to maintain a friendly neutrality. They would confine themselves to the circumcision, but let me alone in dealing with the circumcision'. (Comp. Rom. 15.20, 2 Cor. 10.15).

[Gal. 2.]6 ὁποῖοί ποτε ἒοαν ['whatsoever they were'] has a temporal meaning: whatever they once were, when they were in personal intercourse with Jesus.

{[12]The account of these events given in the Epistle to the Galatians obviously fails to agree with that given in the Acts. Contrast Galatians 1.16 'to reveal His Son in me', which emphasizes the immediacy of the revelation, with Acts 9.17 foll., where Ananias is represented as the medium of the gift of the Holy Ghost. Again, in the Acts (9.15). Paul's mission to the Gentiles is communicated first to Ananias in a vision; but in the Epistle Paul speaks as if his mission to the Gentiles was involved in the original revelation.

In Gal. 1.17, Paul says he did not go until after three years to Jerusalem, and then (v.21) to Syria and Cilicia. In the Acts he is represented as first preaching to the Jews of Damascus (9.21) and then goes to Jerusalem, where again a medium (Barnabas) is needed for his admission to the Church. Acts 9.27 and 28 imply constant intercourse between Paul and apostles (comp. Acts 11.30; 12.25).

Contrast again Gal. 2.2 ἀνέβην κατ' ἀποκάλυψιν ['And I went up by revelation,'] with Acts 15.2, 4, 6. ἒταξον ἀναβαίνεον Παυλον καὶ Βαρνάβον ['they determined that Paul and Barnabas,'] and Gal. 2.10 μόνον τῶν πτωχῶν ἴνα μνημονεύωμεν ['we should remember the poor'] with Acts 15.29 ἀπέχεσθαι εἰδωλοθύτων καὶ πνικτῶν καὶ πορνείας ['That ye abstain from meats offered to idols, ... and from things strangled, and from fornication,']. Why cannot the visit of v.18 be the second visit of the Acts (Acts 11.25 foll.)? Such a supposition (a) contradicts the account in the Acts of Paul's previous intercourse with the Church of Jerusalem: (b) the purpose and nature of the visit described in Gal. 1.18 do not tally with those of the visit described in Acts 11.25: (v.) according to Gal. 1.21, the visit to Jerusalem is followed by a journey into the 'regions of Syria and Cilicia', which according to the Acts precedes the visit of 11.25.

The visit to Jerusalem mentioned in Gal. 2.2. must be that which Acts 15 is meant to represent. *(Reasons why it can't be the second or the fourth visit of the Acts. This point was apparently not worked out. H.N.)}

Result of the visit to Jerusalem. This seems to be that the decree mentioned in Acts 15[13] fairly represents the nature of the understanding arrived at between Paul and the 'pillars' of the church, in the sense (a) that the Jerusalemite disciples were ready to admit Gentile converts, without circumcision, into the same relation towards themselves as that in which the proselytes stood to the Jews, on condition of their observing certain specified conditions, and that to these conditions St. Paul used to advise his converts, as a matter of accommodation, to conform. (Comp. Gal. 2.3; 5.3; 1 Cor. 7.10: 9.20).

As to the ceremonial abstinence mentioned in the decree, Paul advised his disciples to conform in order to avoid offence. But the writer of the Acts, in representing the under standing as a decree, is adopting language which was only proper to a later generation. In representing Paul as accepting the understanding in this sense he contradicts Paul's own assertion of independence in the epistle. Nor, had the understanding been accepted by the other side, would the disturbance of the Galatian church have been possible.

Probably the Gentiles were admitted in a relation resembling that of the proselytes to the Jews. This did not settle much. There were laxer and stricter views as to circumcision: the decree adopts the laxer, but does not settle the relation of the circumcised and uncircumcised. The uncircumcised might be regarded as an inferior caste. The Jewish Christians might refuse to eat with them, thus incapacitating them for the *Agapê*, the great social institution of the early Church. It was also understood that the circumcision continued obligatory on the Jews.

James was presumably rigid in maintaining the separation between Jew and Gentile (Gal. 2.12), while Peter was disposed to give it up, but without having any clear principle to go upon. It was not with him as with Paul, to whom the abrogation of all Jewish privilege, the perfect fusion of Jew and Gentile in the body of Christ, was involved in the conception of Christ's death (a) as a death *under* the law, *through* the law, and *to* the law (b) as a death in which all believers partook, so that the law was extinguished for all alike. Of this death ('burial with Christ') baptism to St. Paul was the symbol, and this universally available right[14] was to him the substitute for circumcision in all cases.

Hence the dispute described Gal. 2.11 foll.. The whole point of Paul's onslaught lies in this, that no one, Jew as little as Gentile, could properly believe on Jesus without giving up the Jewish claim to a distinctive 'righteousness', of which circumcision was the sign. He withstood Peter because he was self-condemned. Emissaries of James with letters of commendation disturbed the church. In accusing them of dissimulation (ὑπόκρισις) Paul means that they acted a part not like their real mind.[15] They pretended to separate themselves by ceremonial from the Gentiles, who did not represent the mind of believers in Jesus. But there was doubtless a difference between their view of the Christian mind, and St. Peter's.

2.16, 18.[16] Belief in Jesus involves a breach with the law: therefore, if non-conformity to the law makes men sinners (as the Jew regarded the uncircumcised), belief in Christ makes us as much sinners as the Gentiles.

This brings us to the question of the sort of revelation involved in Paul's conversion.

The sense in which he believes[17] in Christ is[18] conditioned by the antagonism he felt and showed to the Christian teaching before his conversion.

For[19] the spiritual antecedents of his conversion see Rom. 7 and Gal.| |*[20] The account in the Acts shews that it was in the form presented by Stephen that the belief in Jesus specially provoked him. Further, we know from his Epistles what significance the death and resurrection of Jesus had for him when he wrote them; this, it may be said, had gradually developed: yet he always speaks as if his Gospel had been communicated to him in his conversion; at any rate he was clearly conscious of a perfect continuity of spiritual life from the time of his conversion.

The seventh chapter of the Epistle to the Romans gives an account of his spiritual conflict, which indeed we may not be justified in taking exactly to represent his experience before his conversion, but which probably reflects a consciousness derived from that period. According to this later view, the law issued in death.

Ch. 2.19, 20, 21. 'If breaking the law is sin, then Christ is the minister of sin'. For v.19 comp. Rom. 6.2, 6: 'the body of sin' is explained by the notion of the flesh as the seat of sin. (Comp. Rom. 7.4, 6: Gal. 5.4; Col. 2.20). What is said of 'deliverance from the law' is said here of the elements of the world. For v.20. comp. 2 Cor. 5.17: for v.21 comp. Gal. 3.21.

It appears from this that Paul's belief in Christ involves (negatively)[21] the abandonment of all claim to distinctive righteousness, and positively the duty of preaching a universal Gospel to the Gentile as well as the Jew. The belief in Christ is identical with life by faith in the Son of God, and this identical with the life of Christ *in* Paul himself. This life, further, arises immediately out of, or is the positive aspect of, death *to* the law, which again is death *through* the law, (produced by it).

Another expression for this life is 'righteousness', or 'righteousness of God', (just as another expression for 'death' is 'condemnation').

'The righteousness of God' means the perfect relation of man towards God. Just as the wrongness of the relation between man and God can only lie on the side of man's consciousness, so the change by which the relation is set right can only be a change of man's consciousness: a change by which the consciousness of alienation from God becomes the consciousness of adjustment to the Divine will. Hence the 'righteousness of God' subjectively considered (or 'ex parte hominis') is 'peace' and 'reconciliation': just as the opposite state is one of conscious alienation, which by a transfer to God of man's consciousness about Him is also spoken of as a state of being under God's wrath.

To understand how the law wrought death in Paul – a death which suddenly passed into a new life – is to understand his conversion, as described in this epistle. We must think of him, while in act and speech περισσότερως ζηλωτής ['exceedingly zealous for the traditions of his fathers'], as yet the subject of that inward conflict, the recollection of which caused him to write the seventh chapter of the Epistle to the Romans. It is an extraordinary delusion to suppose that that chapter describes the state of the Christian in the condition of St. Paul's experience *after* conversion.

In this state he was seeking to attain the 'righteousness of God' by doing the 'works of the law'. That effort, as he afterwards thought, involved a contradiction. Man can only attain the righteousness of God in virtue of the presence of God in him. But the Jew's effort after perfect conformity to the law was an effort to 'establish his own righteousness'. Really the Jew's effort, just so far as the Jew thought it successful, meant a self-satisfaction which effectually prevented the inward communication of God.

This is *one* effect of the law, the effect on the ordinary Jew: it may be called a death or alienation, but is not a conscious alienation, and probably not referred to here by St. Paul. Such a state *cannot* be suddenly changed into a new life.

It was another mode of death by the law that Paul experienced before his conversion. He had found that he could not establish his own righteousness: the law of God seemed to command without giving power to execute: thus its only effect was to give the knowledge of sin, which Paul tended to identify with sin itself. The notion of sin to him is so much that of conscious alienation from God that knowledge of sin and sin almost coincide: e.g. 'the strength of sin is the law' [1 Cor. 15.56]: and comp. Rom. 7.7, 9, 13, 14.

Reflection on the perfectness of the law only made him more conscious of the carnality of the flesh, which was not of himself, yet which seemed to drag him down. The conflict as represented in the epistle to the Romans ends in a conscious split in his nature: 'I do that I would not' [Rom. 7.16].

At[22] first sight there seems an inconsistency between his frequent denunciation of the law as carnal, and his saying 'the law is spiritual, but I am carnal' (Rom. 7.14).[23] We must however distinguish between the law as it is in itself from what it is to those who 'went about to establish their own righteousness'[24] – a selfish or *carnal* object – by observing it.

Thus the law was the source of death as awakening the consciousness of the carnal separation from God, of moral paralysis – the consciousness of being under a curse or condemnation. 'Who will deliver me from the body of this death?' [Rom. 7.24], i.e. the body to which, as the seat and source of sin, death (or separation from God) attaches.

It is easy to understand how one burdened with this consciousness would at first seek to overcome it by 'more abundant zeal' for the law. Across this zeal came the preaching of Christ by Stephen: the preaching of him as the true Messiah, who had borne the penalty of the law because he had declared that the privileged Jewish worship of God was to give place to a universal and spiritual worship, and whom God had declared to be the true Messiah by raising him from the dead [Acts 6.1–7.60]. It was because Paul saw that the acceptance of such a Messiah involved the falsehood of the Jewish idea of righteousness, as consisting in the special observance of a special law, that it provoked him. But the conception of the Messiah as manifested under conditions of the extremest carnal humiliation, and as bearing the curse[25] of the law, (when his own consciousness of the burden of those conditions, and of being under that curse, came to a head) suddenly took a new character.[26] He found that that conception was just what he wanted.

The subjection of the Son of God to the death in which he found himself was his own deliverance from it, as shewing[27] that God was not the giver of an external law which could not be obeyed, but a God who communicated himself to man under conditions which had seemed to separate from him. Thus the death wrought by the law – wrought by it, though spiritual in itself, owing to the relation in which it stood to our carnal nature – through the *participation of Christ* in it becomes death unto the law; that is, the deliverance of man from the attitude in which he stood to God as servant to taskmaster, and the substitution for this of the consciousness of communion with God. (Gal. 4.4).[28]

This deliverance from the law has two aspects, corresponding to the two aspects of the 'works of the law.' [e.g. Rom. 9.32, Gal. 3.2, 3, 5, 10] It is the extinction of the imaginary legal righteousness of the Jew: it puts an end to 'works' as the Jew understood works. On the other hand it is the condition of the true fulfilment of the law. The substitution of the consciousness of the presence [of] God as 'working in us' [2 Cor. 4.12] enables us to fulfil the law through love, as it could not be fulfilled when regarded as imposed from without.

Being 'under the law' [Heb. 7.11] is with St. Paul equivalent to being 'in the flesh' [e.g. 2 Cor. 10.3]. The carnal man is the selfish man, and the Jew, 'going about to establish his own righteousness' [Rom. 10.3], feeding his pride on the consciousness of his separation from other men, is living 'after the flesh' [Rom. 8.3] almost in the sense of living selfishly. But the man who has passed out of this pride into the state of bitter humiliation described in Rom. 7, is still in bondage to the flesh, because, owing to his sensuous nature, he presents God to himself merely as an external law-giving power. As from the death under the law, so from 'the flesh' (or 'body of this death' [Rom. 7.24]) Christ delivers us by sharing it: sharing, that is not in actual sin,[29] but in the consciousness of alienation from God.

'Sin'[30] arises from the relation of the law to the flesh. Did Christ, according to St. Paul's idea, even as he was born of a woman and born under the law whose penalty he also bore, share our sin? 2 Cor. 5.21. 'he made him sin for us, who knew no sin'. This idea is best expressed by saying that 'sin' = to sin in principle, that is the flesh: or that in taking flesh the Son of God was in that sense made sin: comp. Rom. 8.3.

The spiritual revulsion, the deliverance from the death which he was conscious of carrying about and with him, came to Paul under certain accidents of vision and ecstasy on his journey to Damascus, when he recognized God in the crucified Jesus whose claim to Messiahship had provoked him [Acts 9.21–20].

As the negative side of this revelation was the extinction of legal righteousness, its positive side was the mission to the Gentiles. A controversy may be raised as to the objective reality of the appearance of Christ to Paul. What is objective reality? An actual picture on the retina and agitation in the tympanum of the ear? The only available evidence of this would be that of his companions. If the others had heard and seen what he did, then we should say that it was not merely that his state of mind affected his nervous system, but that there was some physical operation on his sensitive organs. As to such evidence we cannot say much: there is a discrepancy between Acts 9.7 ('hearing a voice') and 22.9 ('they heard not the voice').[31]

The question being thus understood, if there was such a picture, at any rate its only meaning and reality arose from the ideas associated therewith, a state of mind of which we have certain knowledge, whereas there is no corresponding evidence about the objective reality.

Without those associated ideas the sensuous impression was practically nothing. Thus the true objective reality lay in the truth of those ideas to law and grace, which truth was proved by the success of Paul's apostleship to the Gentiles. Thus, though he appeals to the vision of Christ, yet he says the seal of his apostleship is found in the congregation he founded [1 Cor. 9.2].[32]

Was the Galatian congregation (a) composed of Gentiles, or (b) did it contain an admixture of proselytes to Judaism, or even of born Jews?

4.8, 5.2, 6.12 can only be addressed to Gentiles, and are conclusive on one side: on the other hand 3.2 and 13, 4.3 and 21, are appealed to as evidence of a Jewish element. At any rate, it is said, an acquaintance with the Old Testament and the Jewish interpretation of it supposes the presence of proselytes. As external evidence, 1 Peter 1.1 (ἐκλεκτοῖς παρεπιδήμσις διασπορᾶς Πόντου, Ἰαλατίας, Καππαδοκίας, Ἀσίας καὶ Βιθυνίας ['to the strangers scattered throughout Pontus, Galatia, Cappaocia, Asia, and Bithynia.']) is appealed to: comp. the beginning of the Epistle of James ταῖς δώδεκα φυλαῖς ταῖς ἐν τῇ διασπορᾷ ['to the twelve Tribes which are scattered abroad' (Jam. 1.1)]. But who are the παρεπίδημοι διασπορᾶς? That the first Epistle of Peter is addressed to the Gentiles appears from [1 Peter] 1.14 and 18, 2.9 and 10, 3.6, 4.3: the explanation of these words then must be that the author of the Epistle had come to regard the Christians as the true Jews, according to a habit of thought which can be shewn to have existed later. (For an external indication of the existence of a Jewish population in Galatia, see Lightfoot's Essay, especially p.11).[33] 4.21. ('ye who wish to be under the law, do ye not hear[34] the law?' implies no more acquaintance with the Old Testament than would naturally follow from the influence of Judaizing teachers, to say nothing of Paul's own; who, to judge from his constant language about the Gospel as the 'fulfilment of the law,' would expect some study of the Old Testament from his converts: comp. 1 Cor. 15.3 and 4 ('according to the Scriptures').

3.2. (ἐξ ἔργων νόμον τὸ Πνεῦμα ελαβετε ἢ ἐξ ἀκοῆς πίστεως ['received ye the spirit by the works of the law, or by the hearing of faith']) – does not imply that those to whom it is addressed had tried 'salvation by the works of the law' before they had received the Spirit 'from the hearing of faith'.[35] The words of the following verse ('having begun in the Spirit') would rather imply the contrary.

3.13 and 4.3 present more difficulty. (Χριστὸς ημᾶς ἐξαγόρασεν ἐκ τῆς κατάρας τοῦ νόμου: ἡμεῖς ὅτε ἦμεν νήπιοι ['Christ hath redeemed us from the curse of the law' (Gal. 3.13): 'we, when we were children' (Gal. 4.3)].) Must not 'us' refer to Paul's fellow-Jews, and can those be said to be redeemed from the curse of the law who had never been under it? On the other hand, if the Jews as such are referred to in v.13, how are we to explain the transition to the Gentiles in v.14?[36] That no opposition is intended between ἔθνη ['Gentiles'] and ἡμᾶς ['us'] is clear from the return to the first person in λάβωμεν ['we might receive']: and it may be observed that, although the Corinthian Church was clearly regarded by St. Paul as Gentile (1 Cor. 12.2) he uses the expression *all our fathers were under the cloud* (1 Cor. 10.1).

The explanation is to be found in Paul's conception of the Jewish law as representing the régime of the law, as opposed to grace, in general. Comp. 3.22 'the scripture included all under sin'; and Rom. 3.9; 11.32.

The antithesis in his own experience he transferred to the history of the world, as two stages or periods in the order of God's dealing with man. With what truth? St. Paul's experience was no doubt special. Numberless Christians since have felt it to be their own, but because they have been acted upon by the system of thought which Paul originated: to which, at least, he first gave distinct shape. But there is this truth in his view of the divine economy, that a change in the conception of God, a change from the conception of him as an external law-giver to the conception of him as an indwelling spirit, not excluded from us by our human limitations, has been effected by Christianity, that is, by the life and teaching of Jesus, as interpreted by St. Paul and the author of the fourth Gospel. Thus 'we' here and in v.23, etc. does not imply the writer's identification of himself with some of those whom he was addressing, *as fellow Jews*, but the identification of all mankind with himself in his experience of the effects of the law. As the 'law' is the expression for the régime prior to the Gospel under its Jewish aspect, so τὰ στοιχεῖα τοῦ κόσμου ['the Elements of the world' (Gal. 4.3)] is the expression for it under its Gentile aspect: or moral and metaphysical aspects: and as St. Paul treats the Gentile conscience as having been under the law, so he treats the Jewish religiosity as having been in bondage to the elements of the world. 4.3, and 8.10. V.8 [Gal. 4.8] would seem to have only a Gentile application; but v.10 transfers its significance to the Jews. Note that the first person is used in v.3, the second in v.8. The adoption of Judaism is a *return* to a previous state: not because the Galatians had been Jews and proselytes before they received the Gospel, but because the Gentile and Jewish religions were alike as systems of bondage to the 'elements of the world', and thus in adopting Judaism they were resuming their bondage. The common element of the Gentile and Jewish religions, according to St. Paul's view, is the externality or materialism of their presentation of God, in which they are alike opposed to the revelation of God 'in the Spirit'. Hence both alike are exclusive.

Στοιχεῖα τοῦ κόσμου ['the Elements of the world' (Gal. 4.3)], v.v. 3 and 9. Some would take these words as representing a rudimentary stage of education, comparing Hebrews 5.12. But in that passage στοιχεῖα ['Elements'] acquires this meaning from the words joined with it, στοιχεῖα τῆς ἀρχῆς τῶν λόγων τοῦ Θεοῦ ['the first principles of the Oracles of God']. It is doubtful whether it could mean this by itself; certainly it could not when qualified by του κόσμου ['of the world']. And how could *bondage* to such rudiments be spoken of? Is οτοιχεῖα τοῦ κόσμου, then, to be taken (a) as = the earthly, fleshly elements, or (b) more precisely of the powers of nature, the heavenly bodies etc, as identified according to the common notion of that age, with the subordinate, created Gods who mediated between the highest God and matter? In the latter case the point of the passage will lie in the assimilation of the Jewish religion as 'ordained by angels', and by its observance of days and months, etc. allowing the powers of nature to regulate the soul's access to God, to the Gentile worship of 'Gods many and lords many' (1 Cor. 8.5) resident in those powers of nature.

Probably with St. Paul the phrase does not convey so definite a notion. The ideas of στοιχεῖα τοῦ κόσμου as = τὰ σαρκικα ['the flesh'] and as = the divinized powers of nature were not thoroughly distinguished: comp. 1 Cor. 2.6 where πνευματικὴ σοφια ['spiritual wisdom'] is opposed to the wisdom of the rulers of this world, δαίμονες, that is, according to the notion of Plato and the Gnostics.[37] In Col. 3.8, 20 he says that we are freed from the στοιχεῖα τοῦ κόσμου by the death of Christ: because death with Christ means the communication of God to us under the conditions of humanity which seemed to separate us from him, and thus produced a bondage to the στοιχεῖα τοῦ κόσμου – the powers of natural and material rites – as the only medium of approach to him.

They are 'weak and beggarly' [Gal. 4.9] because they only allow a stinted and narrow conveyance of God to the soul: whereas in Christ dwells 'the whole fullness[38] of the Godhead bodily'. (Col. 2.9).

3.1. Does ἐν ὑμῖν σταυρωμένος ['crucified among you'] refer to the 'crucifixion of Christ' as involved in falling from Grace? Lachmann, on the authority of A and B, omits ἐν ὑμῖν ['among you'].[39] If retained, the words are most naturally taken with σταυρωμένος ['crucified']: they can only be taken with προεγράφη ['was set forth'] on the supposition that the writer virtually forgot how he began the clause when he had written προεγράφη ['was set forth']. If taken with εσταυρωμένος, they can scarcely mean anything but the above; but there is no parallel to such a notion except in the Epistle to the Hebrews.[40] Without ἐν ὑμῖν ['among you'] the passage is quite simple: depicted as crucified, and the crucifixion annulling the law. (προεγράφη ['was set forth']: the proposition has no reference to the time when he was among them). 2. ἐξ ακοῆς πιστεως. Ἀκοὴ πίστεως may mean (1) 'hearing which comes of faith'. So Lightfoot, who compares ὑπακοὴ πίστεως ['obedience to the faith'] of Romans 1.5, 16.26.[41] If so, the sense is first the converse of that of Rom. 10.17 'faith comes by hearing'. Without taking ἀκοὴ as = ὑπακοὴ ['obedience'], one may understand it as 'the apprehension which comes of faith'.

(2) The apprehension of, or becoming acquainted with the faith: 'faith' used as = the matter believed: comp. 1.23, and *perhaps* 3.23.

(3) The announcement (or preaching) of faith (as means of justification). For ἀκοὴ = φήυη ['message'] comp. Matth. 4.24 with 9.26: and see other references in the concordance.[42]

Does not πίστεως ['faith'] express the *manner* of hearing – the state of mind of the hearer? 'Hearing (not which comes of faith, but) which faith qualifies'?

'Hearing' and 'preaching' pass into each other in St. Paul's mind as together forming the channel of grace, the receptivity of God, as distinguished from the effort to do something for oneself: comp. 1 Cor. 1.21 (διὰ τῆς μωρίας τοῦ κηρύγματος ['by the foolishness of preaching']). Through such ἀκοὴ πίστεως the believer 'begins in the Spirit': receives the Spirit as αρραβὼν ['a pledge'] or ἀπαρχὴ ['a first act of sacrifice'] : becomes conscious of a principle of spiritual life, which is progressively actualized in the spiritual walk, in the active love through which the δικαίωμα νόμου ['the righteousness of the law' (Rom. 8.4)] is fulfilled (comp. Rom. 8.4, Gal. 5.6, 25). How is it that 'faith' is the beginning of 'life in the Spirit'? The answer is to be found in the beginning of Rom. 8. Christ is the manifested God, the Spirit is the indwelling Christ. The manifestation by God of himself in Christ renders possible his communication of himself as Spirit: made under conditions which seemed to separate man from him, it renders possible the conception of God as operative in the moral life of man, so that henceforth man does not indeed cease to work, but works as of God that worketh. The νοῦς ['mind', 'spirit', 'intellect', or 'reason'], which had before struggled in vain against the flesh, because slavishly and 'in fear', having now become conscious of its union with God, having become (1 Cor. 2.16) the 'mind of Christ', – a union which always *existed* but which is quite different when *recognized*, can prevail where it could not prevail before. It is no longer simply νοῦς, (which is St. Paul's term for reason as merely human, i.e. as not recognizing its union with God) but 'spirit', with which 'the Spirit bears witness that it is born of God'.

Thus the 'hearing of faith', 'beginning in the Spirit', 'delivery from the curse of the law', represent a change of consciousness wrought by the belief that God is manifest in the crucified Christ, which results in an altered mode of moral life called 'spiritual walk' or 'walk κατ᾽ ἀγάπν ['charitably']' (Rom. 14.15).[43] This change is followed also by certain ecstatic effects, to which St. Paul occasionally refers as σημεῖα ['signs'] comp. v.5; and also 2 Cor. 12.12, Rom. 15.18, 1 Cor. 12.28, 31: 14.18, 37: Gal. 6.1 {? 6.17? *H.N.*}

The same distinction is represented in another form as that between the '*imputation* of righteousness' and the *fulfilment* of the δικαίωμα νόμου ['the righteousness of the law'], which is the sequel of such imputation; equivalent now to 'justification' and 'sanctification': but Paul uses them indifferently, sometimes as completed and sometimes as in process (Rom. 5.9, 18; 8.24: 1 Cor. 15.2; Eph. 2.5).

The real distinction is between righteousness in principle, i.e. as imputed, and righteousness as realized: so a distinction is drawn between sanctification as imputed and as realized. [Gal. 3.]v.v. 6, 14 ἐλογίσθη, [=] imputed. The point is that through faith in Christ, i.e. by believing in God as manifested under conditions which seem to separate man from him, man is counted righteous, though he has not yet fulfilled the δικαίωμα νόμον ['the righteousness of the law']: just as Abraham, without doing the works of the law, before there was a law to fulfil, was counted righteous in virtue of his faith [Rom. 4.5], and received a blessing in which 'all nations' were to share, and which they do share in receiving through faith the gift of the Spirit [Gal. 3.8]. The notion conveyed in 'imputation' may be explained if we remember its equivalent expression 'reconciliation': see 2 Cor. 5.19.

From Paul's language on this subject have arisen *three*[44] notions of popular theology (a) that through the work of Christ a change takes place in the mind of God towards man: (b) that in 'counting him righteous' God treats man as being what he is not: (c) that God punishes Christ in a character that does not belong to him (viz: as a sinner) that he may be able, compatibly with his justice, to treat man as what he is not, namely righteous.

These notions have grown out of certain accidents of Paul's language, which again are due to the difficulty of representing a change in man's consciousness, by which his relation towards God is altered, except as implying some change in God's relation towards him.

The conception of this imputation and of faith as the condition of it gets its character from the Judaic consciousness with which Paul contrasts it and which yet conditions it. Suppose a man seeking, glory, honour, and immortality[45] through the works of the law and fearing tribulation and anguish if he fails; he finds that he cannot do them, the notions of sin remain only quickened into clearer consciousness of opposition to the law: God seems to be his enemy and angry, and he has upon him the load of past transgression, the penalty due for which must for ever prevent his starting fair on the new life, because it prevents the good will of God. To him Christ's death appears as the paying of this *penalty*: he has only to abandon his own pretension and accept God's promise by faith, and he is justified, put straight with God, reconciled. Thus righteousness is imputed to him (as opposed to worked out by him) on the negative side as freedom from wrath, on the positive side as the transfer to him of Christ's perfect obedience, a transfer which qualifies him for the good will of God (Rom. 5.18). But this imputation of Christ's δικαίωμα ['righteousness'] with Paul is only preliminary to its realization: the thought of its imputation, that God has worked out for us a perfect righteousness in the flesh, which is already complete, and we have only to appropriate, renders possible a fulfilment of the righteousness of the law in the walk according to the Spirit, which was not possible under the law.

Thus the essential part of this conception of imputation is, (not that God regards him as righteous when he is not, but) a change in man's consciousness towards God, through which for the first time righteousness seems possible for him, and its thus seeming possible is the condition of his becoming in the highest sense morally good. There is no change in God's mind towards man: this is implied in Paul's speaking of the previous history of man as leading up to the manifestation of Christ: the law is given that sin may abound, and so the new life of the Spirit becomes possible.

As to point (c): Gal. 3.13, 2 Cor. 5.21. 'he made him to be sin for us, who knew no sin' (this = the manifestation in the flesh, for that is the source of sin): 'sin for us' means 'sin in principle': 'no sin' means 'no active sin', no consciousness of a broken law. The question arises: did Christ, in his death, really undergo God's wrath as represented by a *quantum* of suffering adequate to what is due for the sins of all men, or did he relieve the smitten conscience from the sense of God's wrath by bringing God near to it in reconciliation even under its sinful conditions? Once get hold of this and see that the 'wrath of God' is a transfer from our consciousness, and no doubt can remain. To Paul the distinction between the two views did not present itself clearly: but the second view represents his spirit, and Paul's whole conception of the scheme of the world implies that 'while we were sinners God loved us', which goes against the first view, and that his wrath against us was only on the part of our conscience 'reconciling us to God', not God to us. He does not say the Son 'meets his Father's wrath', nor does he quantify the suffering due for sin.

But he certainly did regard Christ in his crucifixion as bearing the curse of the law, and so bearing it as that henceforth he should be exempt from it: comp. Rom. 3.25, 26. ὃν προέθετο ὁ Θεὸς ἱλαστήριον...εἰς ἔνδειξιν τῆς δικαιοσύνης αὐτοῦ.[46] He regarded him further as making a payment of the penalty required by the law: *as vindicating[47] God's righteousness against the supposition that he was careless of sin. This passage of the Romans is the only one where this view appears distinctly. The drift of it is: for God to have justified man, i.e. given him such a consciousness of a proper relation to God as can alone set him free to walk after the Spirit, without a previous payment of the penalty due for sins, would have been against his justice. The penalty of sin, however, cannot be separated from sin, and is borne in the consciousness of alienation from God which sin produces: there is no other moral penalty but this, and this is not transferable, and the only deliverance from it lies in the transformation of the consciousness of alienation from God into the consciousness of his love through the abandonment of personal pretension. Such a change Paul himself had experienced, and the condition of the change had been the conception of God as manifested in Christ under the circumstances which had seemed to separate from him. Sometimes Christ's death is spoken of as 'a death by which the penalty of sin was paid': but essentially it is conceived as a death *unto* sin, in which we ideally partake (2 Cor. 5.14 foll.), while at the same time, by the new consciousness of God's mind towards us which it gives, it enables us gradually to actualize this ideal death to sin in a new spiritual walk.

In 3.13; [and] 2 Cor. 5.15, does ὑπὲρ mean *on behalf of*, or *instead of*? No doubt strictly the first. But does not bearing a penalty *on behalf of* another imply bearing it *instead* of him, and did not Paul think of the curse of the law as a *penalty*? a penalty analogous to that inflicted by the civil law, distinct from the sin for which it is inflicted as punishment is from crime? In 2 Cor. l.c. (ὑπὲρ πάντων ['died for them' (2 Cor. 5.15)]) there is no notion of penalty. We being dead unto the law and to the flesh, Christ shares that death, and through his sharing it this universal death under the law and to the flesh became a death to the law and to the flesh, and the beginning of a new life, not unto self, but unto God. But the word 'curse' seems to imply a civil penalty, distinct from the crime for which it is inflicted. Is it not so with death then?

St. Paul could not invent a language. He had to use terms carrying with them a significance derived from their original application, which could not be wholly got rid of in their new application, and which may have reacted somewhat on Paul's thought, as, much more, it did on his readers'. But when he speaks in detail of the 'curse of the law', as in Rom. 7, it is not as a penalty in the ordinary sense, (as distinct from that of which it is the penalty), but as a state of mind, the consciousness of separation from God and spiritual impotence, wrought by the law. ('By the law is the knowledge of sin' [Rom. 3.20]: 'the strength of sin is the law' [1 Cor. 15.56].)

Just so far as 'the curse of the law' is thus thought of, Christ's redemption of us from it by bearing it 'for us', ceases to appear as the paying of a penalty – as so much suffering which we should otherwise have had to endure. His death is not 'substitutory' *in that sense*. It is so only as that submission of himself, the manifested God, to our conditions, by which his life in us, as the indwelling God or Spirit, becomes possible: a life which is the 'substitution' of the new and spiritual for the old and natural man.

But is there not just as great a difficulty about God's submission of himself, or subjection of his Son, to our conditions (a difficulty made none the less by the phrase 'submission of himself in *the person of Christ*') as about his bearing the penalty for sin committed by others? At any rate the former difficulty is only metaphysical, while the latter is moral. The doctrine that Christ bears a penalty for sin of which he is innocent cannot be held without lowering morality. The other is the standing difficulty, how the eternal and perfect God can communicate himself under conditions of time and progressively: and the conception of such communication is further embarrassed by that form which has yet given it practical power over men, as conditioned by, and somehow having taken place in, a past historical event.

Reverting to v.5 ἐπιχορηγῶν...καὶ ἐνεργῶν δυνάμεις ['He therefore that ministereth to you the Spirit, and worketh miracles among you, doeth he it by the works of the law, or by the hearing of faith?' (Gal. 3.5)] must be God. (For δυνάμεις ['powerful deeds'], see p.l l)*[48]

[Gal. 3] V.14–end. V.14. 'The blessing of Abraham' is the gift by which the promise to Abraham is fulfilled: the 'promise of the Spirit' is the promised spirit: comp. Rom. 8.24.

The intermistic function of the law. God's government of the world is one long regime of grace. It appears as such in the promise given to Abraham, and the law is not against the promise, but the condition of its fulfilment. It is so as producing that consciousness of sin which renders us receptive of the Spirit through self-annihilation. The law was added in order to produce transgression (comp. Rom. 5.13, 20.): the law causes the imputation of sin, or actualizes ἁμαρτία ['sin'] (which is there in the flesh) into παράβασις ['transgression'], the condition of a new life.

There are two aspects of the law to St. Paul. It is one thing in itself, and another in relation to our flesh. In itself it is just, good, even spiritual: but in relation to our flesh its office is to give the consciousness of sin, to produce παράβασις ['transgression'] (Gal. 3.19). Both views are blended in v.21. The law is not against the promises of God, because (a) if it could have given life – and it was only our flesh that prevented this – the promised blessing would have been given through it: and (b) because the 'death' which as a matter of fact it produced was the condition of the receptivity of the Spirit.

3.20. 'The mediator is not a mediator of one'. The Law, as is shewn by its requiring a 'mediator', implies a separation between God and man which is not yet overcome. Salvation under the law, if it were possible, would not be 'all of God'. It would be the achievement of man, fulfilling on his part and by his own act (without God working in him) the conditions of a contract made with him by God through a mediator, according to which blessedness is to be attained if the conditions are fulfilled. But this is not possible. The real condition of 'blessedness' or 'life' being attained is the removal of that separation between man and God which the law supposes and continues, so that 'all things may be of God' (2 Cor. 5.18)[49] – the 'one God' who promises the blessing and communicates himself to us in the Spirit, as the sole means of attaining the blessing, which indeed is nothing else than that communication. Hence (v.21) if the law could have given life, it would have been against the promise, for the inheritance cannot at once be of the law and of promise (which is almost equivalent to 'of grace?') But the law (a) cannot fulfil the blessing, convey the 'inheritance', and (b) prepare the way for its fulfilment by the quickening consciousness of sin.

The promise is fulfilled by the act of God in so 'sending forth his Son' under the conditions of flesh and the law, as that our identification with the Son by faith (faith, that is, in Jesus as the manifested God) becomes possible, and we thus in him *become* sons of God, (receive the *adoption*), and, having become sons receive the spirit of the son which cries 'Abba, Father'. [Gal.4.6]

[Gal. 3] V.26. 'Faith' means trust in Jesus as the manifested God, and to Paul, whereas Christ is the Son from eternity, we *become* sons in him. It is thus in the Son of God, as having become the seed of Abraham (Heb. 2.16), and in us as by adoption into his sonship having become the 'seed of Abraham' likewise – the seed κατ᾽ ἐπαγγελίον ['after promise'] and not κατὰ σάρκα ['after flesh'], that the promise to Abraham is fulfilled.

Upon this arise three questions: (a) Were not men already sons of God, before God sent forth his Son? (b) Is not the adoption constituted by our *becoming conscious* of such sonship? (c) If so, if the adoption consists in our receiving the Spirit, namely this new consciousness, how can it be *because we are already sons* that God sends forth the spirit of his Son into our hearts? ([Gal. 14] v.v.4, 6.)

If St. Paul's statement stood thus: 'Because you were already sons, God by manifesting himself in the flesh gave you the *consciousness* of sonship', we shall find no difficulty. But the words ὅτι ἐστε υἱοί ['because ye are sons' (Gal. 4.6)], as following v.5, express that which we *first become* through the 'sending of the Son', etc: and if our becoming sons in this way means merely a change in our consciousness, our receiving the consciousness of sonship, how can the gift of the Spirit 'whereby we cry *Abba Father*', be spoken of as '*a further consequence of our having thus become sons*'? Does not such language (it may be asked) show that it is a mere philosopher's gloss upon St. Paul to make the change, wrought by the incarnation and crucifixion, a mere change in man's consciousness?

No doubt St. Paul did not distinguish the change in the relation between man and God, as it is for God, from such a change as one on the part of consciousness, so sharply as we do. Still it is not Pauline to suppose a 'transaction', apart from and prior to the change in man's consciousness, by which, not having been so before, he becomes the son of God: by which his adoption becomes possible, and which is then followed by the communication of the Spirit.

The only *essential priority* with St. Paul is that of the adoption (and communication of the Spirit involved in it) to the fulfilment of the law by love, which is only possible as its result. We cannot become sons of God by first doing good works. – But (a) because in his own experience (as in that of suddenly 'converted' persons now) the acceptance of Christ by faith appeared rather as a single act, and the *consciousness* of sonship (expressed in the cry 'Abba', and in the fulfilment of the law by love) as continuous: (b) because the ideal is naturally thought of as prior to the actual, and thus the ideal adoption in Christ as prior to the actualization thereof in the new consciousness; and (c) because he regards the condition of the new consciousness as certain historical events; he is apt to speak of the fact of adoption – which so far as it means something else than an eternal relation of man to God, is constituted by a change of consciousness – as if it were an event in time which preceded and caused that change.

Observe that in the Fourth Gospel the relation of sonship to God on man's part appears as antecedent to the manifestation of the Word in flesh, and the condition of the Word, when manifested, being received. (John 1.13, 11.52: *[* is the last reference right? H.N.]*[50] The greater distinctness of this view goes along with the more distinct view of the pre-existence of the Son from eternity, which implies the adoption in him, from all eternity, of all who should be manifested as sons of God in time. Comp. 1 Cor. 15.21, 47. The Pauline notion is not of the Son as becoming man for the first time when born of woman, but as man from eternity: so in Philo.[51]

Comp. Rom. 1.4; 5.14. 1 Cor. 15.47: 10.4: 2 Cor. 8.9: Phil. 2.6. But just as the idea of Christ's eternal existence is not prominent in St. Paul, so our sonship is apt to appear as having come into existence for the first time with the manifestation of Christ.

The distinction between the ideal completeness of our righteousness or new life as it is in Christ, and its gradual actualization in us, appears also in the expressions which represent the Spirit as not fully communicated. The language of the Spirit in us is represented as a 'cry' or a 'groan' (Gal. 4.6; Rom. 8.11, 23, 24: comp. 2 Cor. 5.4. Philipp: 2.11, etc).[52]

The fact that we are still only saved in the way of hope, that we only have the Spirit as an ἀῤῥαβὼν ['pledge'], may explain the fact that the same struggle is in Gal. 5.17, represented as going on in those who have received the Spirit, which in Rom: 7 appears as terminated by the communication of the Spirit.

Νοῦς is the reason not conscious of its relationship to God; πνεῦμα ['Spirit'] [=] reason transformed through this consciousness. But in Gal. 5 one cannot make πνεῦμα = the spirit before the consciousness of sonship, nor is the struggle between two principles in the world: it is *in* the individual between the Spirit of God and the flesh, and the apparent contrast with Rom: 7 must be explained by the adoption being incomplete.

---

[1] Prof. Nettleship makes a cross (*) when there is anything he can not quite make out. [Henry Nettleship was Professor of Latin at Corpus Christi College, Oxford from 1878 until his death in 1893. His brother, Richard Lewis Nettleship (usually credited as editor of Green's *Works*), was never elected professor.]

[2] [Green adopts Lightfoot's divisions and headings, although Lightfoot does not refer to the non-existent Gal. 10 (Joseph Barber Lightfoot, (ed.), *Saint Paul's Epistle to the Galatians* (London and New York: MacMillan, 1890), pp.65–7. First published 1865.]

[3] [MS reads '10' even though Galatians has only six chapters.]

[4] ['Stand fast therefore in the liberty wherewith Christ hath made us free, ...' (Gal. 5.1). 'If we life in the Spirit, let us also walk in the Spirit.' (Gal. 5.25).]

[5] [I.e., Gal. 6.11–18.]

[6] [Lightfoot, *Epistle to the Galatians*, p.80.]

[7] [MS del.: 'Jews'.]

[8] ['And I went up by revelation, and communicated unto them that Gospel which I preach among the Gentiles, but privately to them which were of reputation, lest by any means I should run, or had run, vain.' (Gal. 2.2).]

[9] ['To reveal his son in me, that I might preach him among the heathen, immedi-

ately I conferred not with flesh and blood:/Neither went I up to Jerusalem, to them which were Apostles before me, but I went into Arabia, and returned again unto Damascus.' (Gal. 1.17).]

[10] ['And that because of false brethren unawares brought in, who came in privily to spy out our liberty, which we have in Christ Jesus, that they might bring us into bondage.' (Gal. 2.4).]

[11] ['And when James, Cephas, and John, who seemed to be pillars, perceived the grace that was given unto me, they gave to me and Barnabas the right hands of fellowship; that we should go unto the heathen, and they unto the circumcision.' (Gal. 2.9).]

[12] [Curled brackets are given as square brackets in HN's MS.]

[13] [Possibly a reference to the 'letters' delivered by Judas, Silas, Paul, and Barnabas to the church at Antioch (Acts 15.23). See Acts 16.4.]

[14] [MS alt.: '? rite'.]

[15] ['And the other Jews dissembled likewise with him; insomuch that Barnabas also was carried away with their dissimulation.' (Gal. 2.13)]

[16] [This is the beginning of the extract in Green, *Works* 3, pp.186–9:. RLN 'Gal. ii. 15–21.–'.]

[17] [RLN (p.186) 'believed'.]

[18] [RLN (p.186) 'was'.]

[19] [RLN (p.186) omits this and the two subsequent paragraphs.]

[20] [Probably Gal. 1.11–16.]

[21] [RLN (p.186) 'His belief involved negatively …'.]

[22] [RLN (p.187) omits this paragraph.]

[23] [MS reads: '(Rom. 7.17)'.]

[24] ['For they being ignorant of God's righteousness, and going about to establish their own righteousness, have not submitted themselves unto the righteousness of God.' (Rom. 10.3).]

[25] [MS orig.: 'penalty'.]

[26] [RLN (p.188) '… and as bearing the penalty or curse of the law, suddenly took a new character when his own consciousness of the burden of those conditions, and of being under that curse, came to a head.']

[27] [RLN (p.188) 'showing'.]

[28] [RLN (p.188) substitutes Gal. 4.3–7.]

[29] [RLN (p.189) 'vice'.]

[30] [RLN (p.189) omits this paragraph.]

[31] [RLN (p.189) omits both quotations.]

[32] [End of RLN's extract (p.189).]

[33] [Lightfoot, *Epistle to the Galatians*, p.11.]

[34] [MS orig.: 'bear'.]

[35] ['This only would I learn of you, Received ye the Spirit by the works of the law, or by the hearing of faith?' (Gal. 3.2).]

[36] [These references are to Gal. 3.13–14.]

[37] ['Howbeit we speak wisdom among them that are perfect: yet not the wisdom of the world, nor of the princes of this world, that come to nought.' (1 Cor. 2.6) Plato, *Republic*, 474b–480a. Second century Gnosticism was characterised by the belief that special, divine knowledge ['gnosis'] was revealed to man through secret traditions originating in the Apostles as well as through the insight of the leaders of the various Gnostic sects.]

[38] [MS reads: 'fulness'.]

[39] [Lightfoot omits these words 'in deference to the best authorities' (*Epistle to the Galatians*, p. 134b).]

[40] [Possibly an allusion to Heb. 6.6: 'If they shall fall away, to renew them again unto repentance; seeing they crucify to themselves the Son of God afresh, and put him to an open shame,']

[41] [Lightfoot, *Epistle to the Galatians*, p.135b.]

[42] [This concordance has not been identified.]

[43] ['But if thy brother be grieved with thy meat, now walkest thou not charitably. Destroy not him with thy meat, for whom Christ died.' (Rom. 14.15).]

[44] [MS reads: '*two*'.]

[45] ['To them who by patient continuance in well-doing seek for glory and honour and immortality, eternal life:' (Rom. 2.7).]

[46] ['Whom God hath set forth to be a propitiation, through faith in his blood, to declare his righteousness for the remission of sins that are past, through the forbearance of God./To declare, I say, at this time his righteousness: that he might be just, and the justifier of him which believeth in Jesus.' (Rom. 3.25–26).]

[47] ['Vindicating' is queried in the MS.]

[48] [The missing reference may be to Lightfoot, *Epistle to the Galatians*, p.136.]

[49] ['And all things are of God, who hath reconciled us to himself by Jesus Christ, and hath given to us the ministry of reconciliation.' (2 Cor. 18).]

[50] ['And not for that nation only, but that also he should gather together in one the children of God that were scattered abroad.' (John 11.52).]

[51] [Possibly an allusion to Philo's commentary on Gen. 4.6 in his *Quod Deus Immutabilis Sit* [*On the Unchangeableness of God*], 7–11 (§§33–50).]

[52] ['Is this right' written on the opposite page against the last reference. While 'crying' appears in Gal. 4.6 and 'groan' in 2 Cor. 5.4 and Rom. 8.23, the words are found in neither Rom. 8.11 nor 24, nor Philipp. 2.11.]

Lectures on the Fourth Gospel[1]
[Remaining text.]
[ca.1877]
[Edited by Henry Nettleship and Colin Tyler]

Doctrine of the λὸγος ['Word'] according to Philo   P.1
Theology of the Fourth Gospel (general sketch)   P.2
Commentary on the Prologue vv. 1–11[2]   P.9–18[3]

'The[4] growth of the theological notion of the λὸγος ['Word'] may be seen in the Old Testament, and still more in the Apocrypha. Origen on Genesis I, where the Creation is ascribed to divine utterance, 'let there be light'.[5] This word is Hebraically personified, and so appears in the Psalms, e.g. Ps. 33.6 quoted in Heb. 11 'By the word of the Lord were the Heavens made', etc., and to it are ascribed the moral attributes of the divine nature.[6] In Isaiah 55.11 a personal agency is ascribed to the word (comp. 40.8). Also in the Old Testament the notion appears that God in his own essence is unapproachable, and deals with us through manifestations; sometimes through a mediating angel, e.g. Exod. 33.12 foll. where presence = angel of his presence, as distinguished from the unapproachable essence; comp. Exod. 23.20. In the Targums[7] the word is often presented as this mediating angel between God and man and God and the world. (The Targums represent the old tradition, though composed later than Christianity). In Proverbs and Apocrypha 'Wisdom' takes the place of the Word. Prov. 8 and 9, 8.22–30; Job 28.12 etc. In 'Wisdom' and 'Ecclesiasticus' (?and the beginning of Ecclesiastes??)[8] 'wisdom' and the 'word' are combined ([Exod.] 24.8). In Wisdom 7.22 we have μονογενὴς ['only-begotten'] (the title of Son in the fourth Gospel), and 25, like the beginning of the Hebrews. In the Greek λὸγος the two notions of 'Wisdom' and the 'Word' are combined, and in Philo, the source of the complete doctrine, the points are as follows:–'[9]

Doctrine of the λὸγος [Word][10]
(Philo.)[11]
With Philo the content of God's thought, or the Divine thought as object, is expressed by λὸγος ἐνδιάθετος ['intelligible order']; this

135

again = κόσμος νοητός ['intelligible world'],[12] ἀσώματος ἀόρατος ['incorporeal invisible'],[13] ἰδέα τῶν ἰδεῶν: Philo De Vita Mosis p.672: De Mundi Opif. pp.6, 7.[14] This λόγος ἐνδιάθετος ['intelligible order'] becomes, by the process of γέννεσις [generation], προφορικός, or ὁ λόγος γεγωνός ['the proclaimed Word'] (De Post. Cain. p.245).[15] As such the λόγος is called ὁ δεύτερος Θεός [the second God], or Θεὸς δὲν καταχρήσει, in opposition to ὁ ἀληθεία Θεὸς ['the truthful God']. Other titles are υἱὸς πρεσβύτατος [elder son], εἰκὼν τοῦ Θεοῦ [image of God], or πρωτόγονος τοῦ Θεοῦ ['firstborn of God'] (Comp. Coloss. 1.15 εἰκὼν ['image'], πρωτότοκος ['firstborn']). Μονογενης ['only-begotten'] seems not to be applied to the λόγος ['Word'] in Philo.   As substance to attributes, as thinking and willing self to thoughts, so is God to the Word as His expression in the κόσμος νοητός ['intelligible world'], to the world as a system of ideas.   If one asks, what is any substance, one can only define it but its attributes: ask what is in one's self, you can only define it by thoughts and acts.   So if the question be asked, 'What is God?', the only answer is to be found in His expression in the intelligible world.

The antithesis of sensible and intelligible necessitates the further notion of an *expression of His expression*: of a manifestation of the κόσμος νοητός, (which is itself a manifestation of God as hidden substance) in a κόσμος αἰσθητός.

The 'Word' as προφορικός ['as He emanated from God'] is not (by Philo) identified with the visible world, but is the maker of it, (δὶ οὗ σύμπας ὁ κόσμος ἐδημισύργέπο, or κατεσκευάσθη).[16]

The λόγος προφορικὸς, considered as traces of Divine power and wisdom appearing up and down in the world, is also called σπερματικός ['that which contains the seeds of things'].

Another epithet is τομεὺς ['sharp'] (comp. Hebr. 4.12 τομώτερος ὑπέρ κᾶσαν μάχαιραν ['sharper than any sword']) and δημιουργὸς ['the Maker', sc. of the world (Heb. 11.10)].

The Theology of the Fourth Gospel.

The λόγος of the Fourth Gospel, as identified with the Person of Jesus, is of course infinitely different from the λόγος of Philo.   If again the λόγος of the Fourth Gospel is to be distinguished from that of Philo as apart from and pre-existent to this identification, the difference must lie in this: that the relation between God and the Word, according to Philo, is not so much one of distinct persons in one substance, as that between substance and essence; in other words between unknown substance and cognizable qualities.

(a) *The Idea of God in the Fourth Gospel*, considered apart from his relation through the λόγος to the Church.
1.18 Θεὸν οὐδεὶς ἑώρακεν, etc. ['No man hath seen God at any time: the only begotten Son, which is in the bosom of the Father, he hath declared him.']
4.24 Πνεῦμα ὁ Θεός [etc.]. ['God is a Spirit, and they that worship him must worship him in spirit, and in truth.'] This implies that he is not local or visible:
5.37 οὔτε φνὴν αὐτοῦ πώποτε ἀκηκόατε, etc. ['Ye have neither heard his voice at any time, nor seen his shape.'] Comp, 6.40, 46; 8.26, 28; 1 Epist. 4.12, 20.
(On the corporality of God, see Clementine Homilies 17.7,10,11:[17] Tert. De Carne Christi II, 'omne quod est, corpus est sui generis; nihil est incorporale nisi quod non est ['Everything that exists is body of some kind or another. Nothing is incorporeal except what does not exist.'];[18] comp. adv. Marc. 1.25, 2.27.)[19]
Again. 5.26 ὁ πατὴρ ἔχει ζωὴν ἐν εαυτῷ ['the Father hath life in himself']: 1 Epist. 5.20 καὶ ἐσμεν ἐν τῷ ἀληθινῷ ἐν τῷ υἱῷ αὐτοῦ Ἰησοῦ Χριστῷ, οὗτός ἐστιν ὁ ἀληθινὸς Θεὸς καὶ ζωὴ αἰώνιος. ['and we are in him that is true, *even* in his Son Jesus Christ. This is the true God and eternal life.' (1 John 5.20)]: comp. Evang.17.3 αὕτη δὲ ἐστιν ἡ αἰώνιος ζωή, ἵνα γινώσκωσιν σὲ τὸν μόνον ἀληθινὸν Θεόν, etc. ['And this is life eternal, that they might know thee the only true God, and Jesus Christ whom thou hast sent.']
According to Evang. 1.4 'the life' (as in the λόγος) is 'the light of men'.
According to Epist. 1.5 ὁ Θεὸς φῶς ἐστι ['that God is light' (1 John 1.5)].
Again: Epist 1.4, 8 and 16 ὁ Θεὸς ἀγάπη ['God is love' (1 John 4.8)]. The primary object of His love was (according to Evang.17.24) 'the only-begotten Son': ὅτι ἠγάπησάς με πρὸ καταβολῆς κόσμον. ['for thou lovest me before the foundation of the world.' (John 17.24)]
(b) The relation of the λόγος ['Word'] to the ἀληθινὸς Θεὸς ['God of truth'].
It does not appear that the Evangelist distinguishes between a λόγος as ἐνδιάθετος ['intelligible'] and προφυρικὸς [manifest]; his only distinction is between the λόγος as before and after the incar-

nation (σὰρξ ἐγένετος ['was made flesh' [John 1.14]).²⁰ Passages bearing on the pre-existence of the λόγος. 1.2 ἐν ἀρχῇ πρὸς τὸν Θεὸν ['in the beginning with God']: 1 Epist.1.2 τὴν ζωὴν τὴν αἰώνισν, ἥτις ἦν πρὸς τὸν κατὲρα ['that eternal life, which was with the Father' (1 John 1.2)]: Evang. 1.18 ὁ μονογενὴς υἱὸς ὁ ὢν εἰς τὸν κόλπον τοῦ πατρὸς ['the only begotten Son, which is in the bosom of the Father']: 17.5 παρα σεαυτῷ, τῇ δόξῃ ᾗ εἶχον πρὸ τοῦ τὸν κόσμον εἶναι παρὰ σοί ['with the glory which I had with thee before the world was.'].

For ἐν ἀρχὴ ['in the beginning'] in the sense of πρὸ τοῦ τὸν κόσμον εἶναι comp. Philo De Mundi Opif §7 on the words: 'In the beginning God made the heaven and the earth';²¹ where it is explained that the ἀρχὴ ['beginning'] is not κατὰ χρόνον ['in a chronological sense'], since time is διάστημα τῆς τοῦ οὐρανοῦ κινήσεως ['measured space determined by the world's movement'],²² and therefore πρὸ τοῦ κόσμον ['before there was a world'] there could be no time. One may at first sight compare the words of Irenaeus (Adversus Haereses 1.1.1) about the βὺθος of the Valentinians,²³ ὑπάρχοντα δ᾽ αὐτὸν ἀχώρητον καὶ ἀόρατον, αἴδιόν τε καὶ ἀγέννητον, ἐν ἡσυχίᾳ καὶ ἠρεμίᾳ πολλῇ γεγονέναι ἐν ἀπείροις αἰῶσι Χρόνου. ['Invisible and incomprehensible, eternal and unbegotten, Christ remained throughout innumerable cycles of ages in profound serenity and quiescence.']²⁴ But in the Fourth Gospel such negative designations of the unmanifested God scarcely appear: on the contrary, its view is better expressed by such passages as 5.17 ὁ πατὴρ μου ἕως ἄρτι ἐργάζεται κἀγὼ ἐργάζομαι ['my Father worketh hitherto, and I work'].

Comp. Wisdom 9.4: τῶν θρόναν αὐτοῦ πάρεδρος ['that sitteth by thy Throne'].²⁵

What is the relation expressed by πρὸς τὸν Θεὸν ['with God' (John 1.1)], and by μονογονὴς υἱὸς ['only-begotten son']?

Πρὸς τὸν Θεὸν ['with God']. Πρὸς ['with'] at any rate does not express simple immanence, but some distinctness analogous to that between persons of whom one is the object of communion to the other; who yet may be of 'one mind'.²⁶

The next clause, Θεὸς ἦν ὁ Λόγος ['the Word was God' (John 1.1)], being only connected by καὶ ['and', 'yet'] with the preceding one, cannot be adverse to it, so as to mean, *'though* a distinct person from God (the Father), *yet* the Word was perfect God.' It rather heightens the meaning of the previous words, 'The Word, in this eternal relation to God, was itself God.'

Two questions arise here. Is Θεός ['God'] subject or predicate, and is there any distinction between Θεός ['God'] and ὁ Θεός ['the God']? Θεός without the article can quite well stand as subject. Indeed, from the nature of the case Θεός can scarcely ever occur as predicate; and probably does so occur nowhere in the New Testament except here. As predicate we find ὁ Θεός Evang. 4.24 πνεῦμα ὁ Θεός ['God is a Spirit'], and 1 Epist. 4.8 ὁ Θεός ἀγάπη ἐστιν ['for God is love' (1 John 4.8)]. It would seem also as if a uniformity of subject were intended throughout vv.1 and 2. What would be the meaning of 'God was the Word?' That the word was the essence, the 'exhaustive predicate', of God? Theological interest would be against this interpretation, as it would tend to obliterate the 'distinction of Persons.' But in any case it is probably not the true interpretation. It is more consistent both with the context and with the doctrine of the Λόγος as developed by Philo and the Gnostics to take Θεός as predicate. Does Θεός then mean *a* God? No, yet it is not the same as ὁ Θεός. It expresses the Godhead not as *primary*, but as *partaker* of, tho' *fully* partaken of: the Θεός ἐν καταχρήσει, or δεότερος Θεός, of Philo.

Origen ad.1 (Hom. in Joann. 2 §2 sub fin.) says πᾶν τὸ παρὰ τὸ αὐτόθεος μετοχῇ τῆς ἐκείνου Θεότητος Θεοποιούμενον, οὐχ ὁ Θεός, ἀλλὰ Θεός κυριώτερον ὂν λεγοπο ['Does the same difference which we observe between God with the article and God without it prevail also between the Logos with it and without it?']...Ἀληθινὸς οὖν Θεὸς ὁ Θεός, οἱ δὲ κατ᾽ ἐκεῖ νον μορφῦύμενοι Θεοί, ὡς εἰκόνες πρωτοτυπου ['The true God, then, is "The God," and those who are formed after Him are gods, images, as it were of Him the prototype.'] (in this sense Origen quotes Ps. 50.1 Θεὸς Θεῶν κύριος ἐλάλησε ['The mighty God, *even* the Lord, hath spoken,']), ἀλλὰ πάλιν τῶν πλειόνων εἰκόνων ἡ ἀρχέτοπος εἰκὼν ὁ πρὸς τὸν Θεὸν ἐστιν λόγος ['But the archetypal image, again, of all these images is the Word of God'].[27] Comp. 10.34.

Μονογενὴς υἱὸς ['only-begotten son']. This title belongs to the Word as such, not to Jesus as such; that is, to the Word antecedently to and independent of its manifestation in Jesus Christ. This appears from v.18.

Υἱός ['Son'] and τέκνον ['child'] are indifferently applied to believers elsewhere in the New Testament, but in the fourth Gospel they are called only τέκνα ['children'], To Christ God is ἴδιος πατὴρ [his own father], 5.18. On the *derivative* relation of Christ (i.e. the Word manifested in the flesh) to the Father, see especially 5.43 ἐγὼ ἐλήλυθα ἐν τῷ ὀνόματι τοῦ πατρός μου ['I am come in my Father's name']; 7.28 ἀπ᾿ ἐμαυτοῦ οὐκ ἐλήλυθα, etc. ['I am not come of myself, but he that sent me is true, whom ye know not'] 8.28 ἀπ᾿ ἐμαυτου ποιῶ οὐδὲν ['I do nothing of myself']. So 8.42. The great passage is 14.28 ('My Father is greater than I');[28] but it is difficult to decide there whether the joy of the disciples was to be on their own account (because henceforth they would have direct communication with God through the indwelling Spirit instead of through the veil of Christ's flesh), or on Christ's own account.

μονογενὴς ['only-begotten']—πρωτότοκος ['firstborn']. Coloss. 1.15 ὅς ἐστιν εἰκὼν τοῦ Θεοῦ τοῦ ἀοράτου, πρωτότοκος πάσης κτίσεως ['Who is the image of the invisible God, the firstborn of every creature.']—Μονογενὴς is more than πρωτότοκος.

The negative conception of God, as the unknown or hidden, is really got rid of by ascribing to him the title of 'Father.' It is true that primarily he stands in this relation to the Word, and that his revelation of himself is to the ἴδιος υἱός ['only-begotten son']; but of this revelation the Son (partly through the works done in the lifetime of Jesus Christ, and in a further way through the communicated Spirit,) is the reflex to us.

Hence, though the Evangelist retains the metaphysical doctrine of his time that the αὐτὸ Θεος [being of God] was unknowable, yet by the conception (a) of a perfect reciprocity of knowledge and love between him and the μονογενὴς υἱός ['only-begotten son'], and (b) of a perfect exhibition of the Son's nature and the communication of his life to man, he really vindicates for men an intelligible and personal relation to God. (See especially Evang. 5.17; 20.31; 6.46; 8.38; 9.4; 14.7–9, 12).

The Relation of God to the world antecedently to the Incarnation.
Such a relation is certainly described in vv.3–5 of the Prologue. There may be a doubt whether this is so in the case of vv.10–13; but πάντα ['all things'] of v.3 = κόσμος ['the world'] of v.10: comp. τὰ πάντα ['of all things'] 1 Cor. 8.6; Coloss.1.16. Note that the

word used is ἐγένετο ['became'], not ἐκτίσθη ['were created']²⁹ (as in Coloss. 1.16.) How is this κόσμος [world], as made by the Word, and as an exhibition of him, as that in which he is, related to the world which is spoken of as necessarily evil? The word κόσμος has the following different meanings:

(a) It is used simply of the 'sensible world', neither as necessarily bad, nor as specially the world of *man*: e.g. 11.9 τὸ φῶς τοῦ κόσμον τούτου βλέπει ['because he seeth the light of this world']; 17.5 πρὸ τοῦ τὸν κόσμου εἶναι ['which I had before the world was']; [17.]24 πρὸ καταβολῆς κόσμου ['before the foundation of the world'].

(b) From this we have a transition to the notion of the 'world' as specially that in which man lives, which he knows and cares for, and which is evil: 13.1 ἵνα μεταβῇ ἐκ τοῦ κόσμου τούτου ['he should depart out of this world'].

12.25; 17.11; in 8.23 τὰ κάτω ['the thing below']; in 3.31 ἡ γῆ ['earth'].

(c) A further transition is to the idea of the 'world' as 'human kind' in its evil; as not cognizant of God through the Word. 1.29 αἴρων της ἁμαρτίαν τοῦ κόσμου ['which taketh away the sin of the world']: 4.42 ὁ σωτὴρ τοῦ κόσμου ['the Saviour of the world']: 6.33; 7.7; 16.20; 17.14.

The three meanings are all combined in 1–10. (b) and (c) are constantly combined; e.g. 3.19 τὸ φως ἐλήλυθεν εἰς τὸν κόσμον ['that light is come into the world']; 15.19; 16.33; 18.16; and again where the διάβολος ['devil'] is called ἄρχων τοῦ κόσμου τούτου ['ruler of this world'].³⁰

The real distinction is not between two worlds, but between the world as thoroughly known, and the world known under the first impressions, which are mistaken for truth. Nor again (morally speaking) is the distinction between the world of sense which is evil, and the spiritual world which is good, but between the world as it is to us, and the world as it is in its truth, and *as it becomes to us*; between the world in which we practically suppose the senses to be ends in themselves, and surrender ourselves to their satisfaction, and the world in which the simple senses are but as letters to an intelligible world.³¹

The Prologue.

In the Prologue are concentrated all the leading ideas which are afterwards exhibited in the words and acts of Christ as related by this Evangelist. It states summarily the manifestation of God through the Word (1) as eternal life and light, which is in the world and man, whether recognized by man or no; (2) as specially conveyed to the Jews, though not originally received by them; (3) as completed through the incarnation of the Word; the incarnation through which the word is presented to us as 'grace and truth'. [32]

To these three stages of manifestation correspond severally (1) [John 1.]vv.3–5: (2) vv.11–13; (3) v.14.

In each case the manifestation meets with an antagonistic element: in v.5 σκοτία ['darkness']: in v.11 οἱ ἴδιοι αὐτὸν οὐ παρέλαβον ['his own received him not']. The antagonism to v.14 (ὁ λόγος σάρξ ἐγένετο ['And the Word was made flesh']) is not here mentioned, but all the rest of the Gospel is an account of it.

The above statement is based upon the view that vv.11–13 relate to the special manifestation of the Word to the Jews through the law and the prophets. But it is not certain whether this is the right interpretation. We may question (a) whether τὰ ἴδιοι ['his own' (John 1.11)] means the Jews, or all mankind; in which case vv.11–13 are merely (as vv.9 and 10 undoubtedly are) a more explicit re-statement of vv.4 and 5; (b) whether ἦλθεν ἐς τὰ ἴδιοι ['He came unto his own' (John 1.11)] can refer to anything but the coming of the Word *in the flesh* as Jesus Christ, in which case these vv. will be an anticipation of what is stated more fully in vv.14 and following.

If the latter interpretation is right, though we may still say that three stages of manifestation are indicated by the Prologue, the second will consist simply in the testimony of John; whereas according to the former view this testimony would be regarded as a continuation of the special manifestation to the Jews referred to in v.11.

To return to (1). The manifestation of God through the Word is a communication of life, which to man is light. This life, as in the Word (a Son) though here spoken of as simple and absolute (just as in v.1 'The Word was God') is yet derived, according to 5.26 (οὕτως καὶ ἔδωκε τῷ υἱῷ ζωὴν ἔχειν ἐν ἑαυτῷ ['so hath he given to the Son to have life in himself']). [33]

The 'light' is a further differentiation of the 'life'. It is the 'life' as it becomes in relation to man, as the source of knowledge of

God. This knowledge is afterwards ([John]17.3) spoken of as constituting 'eternal life', and generally in this Gospel, since Divine life, as is natural, is only considered in reference to such a moral and intellectual being as man. The notions of life and light pass into each other (see e.g. 8–12 'the light of life') except so far as 'life' is especially determined by antagonism to the mortality of 'the flesh'.

And even in this regard, since, according to the Evangelist 'life', which delivers us from mortality, consists in that knowledge of God which is conveyed by the 'light' of the Word, the distinction is no sooner made than it disappears.

Here, however, in the Prologue, the Word has in v.3[34] been spoken of as the source of all 'becoming' in the world, not of moral or spiritual activity merely. This general operation in the world is summed up in the words 'in him was life', and then the Evangelist proceeds to a further determination of the same active principle, by stating that it is to man as 'light' – as a moral and intellectual principle.[35,36]

In v.5 the *part* of the light becomes *present* again. Light and darkness appear as eternal principles according to the Alexandrian, and Gnostic notion of an eternal ὕλη ['mass of fuel'] on which God works, but which resists him. There is a return however to the past in οὐ κατέλαβε ['comprehended it not']. 'As a matter of fact, the darkness (of men) was not illuminated by light'; there is no statement of an inherent and eternal impossibility of illumination.

'Darkness did not make it its own'[37] ('so as to be illuminated by it', not 'so as to get the better of it'.)

How is the notion of antagonistic darkness, which light does not penetrate, to be reconciled with the strong assertion of v.3? Is the darkness a thing δι᾽ αὐτοῦ γιγνόμενον ['made by him'], by him in whom is life, which is the light of men? Comp. Isaiah 45.7 'I make light and create darkness'. The same difficulty arises out of v.10, where the paradox is repeated more explicitly, where the world is spoken of as not knowing the Word who yet is in it; the 'world' there answering to 'darkness' here.

One may say that the Evangelist thought of darkness (or, more precisely, a world which cannot know the Word) as that which becomes (? comes into existence, γίγνεται ?) through the Word, in order to the full exhibition of the light; that the existence of a world which knew him not was a[38] condition of true knowledge of him on the part of those who are in the full sense children of

God (v.12). So a modern philosopher might say that a certain antagonism to or abstraction from the 'natural' is a[39] condition of the development of the moral and spiritual; that thus Nature, though not God, and unable to comprehend God, is yet that without which God would not be what he is, and thus is necessary to God: an outcome from him, necessary to his return to himself.

Perhaps this is reading into the Evangelist's words what is not in them – What his interpreter has properly to do is to note (a) the exclusion in v.3 of 'Manichaeism' and 'Dualism': of the notion that there is such a thing as matter not originating in God and antagonistic to him; and (b) the way in which he conceives the alienation of the world from God.

Κόσμος ['world'] has, as we have seen (p.7 foll. above) three senses in this Gospel. In the third sense there mentioned it would be incapable of true knowledge: comp. 17.6–9 οὐ περὶ τοῦ κόσμον ἐρωτῶ ['I pray for them, I pray not for the world' (John 17.9)]: 3.3; 8.23; 14.17. The incapacity arises from being born of the 'flesh', (3.6) of the devil (8.44) who (12.31, 14.30, 16.11) is the 'prince of this world'. It is not the result of the Divine will (3.17 οὐ γὰρ ἀπέστειλεν ὁ Θεὸς τὸν υἱὸν, etc. ['For God sent not his Son into the world to condemn the world: but that the world through him might be saved.']).

Is then the purpose of God baffled? Is it that he sent light into the world for its salvation, but that owing to the nature of the world light meant for salvation serves merely for κρίσις [condemnation']? (3.18, etc.). Perhaps an answer may be found in Epist. 1 2.8 and 17, ἡ σκοτία ['the darkness' (1 John 2.8)], ὁ κόσμος παράγεται ['the world passeth away' (1 John 2.17)]. The 'world', as such, cannot know God, but the 'world' is not final; it ceases to be the world. Not the world, but those 'chosen out of the world', in other words, delivered from the worldly mind; hence we obtain a reconciliation with the statement in Romans 11.32 συνέκλεισεν γὰρ ὁ Θεὸς τοὺς πάντας εἰς ἀπείθειαν, ἵνα τοὺς πάντας ελεήσῃ ['For God hath concluded them all in unbelief, that he might have mercy upon all.'].

The account of the shining of the light and its relation to darkness naturally leads to the introduction of John the Baptist, as the most notable medium through which the light was thrown upon the darkness prior to the incarnation of the Word.

The characteristic ways in which the Evangelist conceived the relation of the light to the darkness that would not appropriate it are represented by (a) μαρτυρία ['testimony'], (b) κρίσις ['judgement']: both being operations of the λόγος ['Word'].

(a) The object of μαρτυρία ['testimony'] is that all should believe, and in believing receive the light into themselves. But to those who, because 'of the world', cannot receive it, it serves merely as κρίσις ['judgement'] (comp. Hebr 4.12) a word which has the double meaning of 'discernment' and 'judgment'. The highest μαρτυρία ['testimony'] is that of the indwelling spirit, and of the works 'greater' than those done by Christ on earth (14.12) which should result from this indwelling (13.[40] 26). The works of Christ[41] done on earth rank below this as a witness; see 14.11. After this comes the witness of John (5.33, etc). Then that of the Scriptures, then that of Moses (5.45).

(b) For κρίσις ['judgement'], as arising out of μαρτυρία ['testimony'] of the Old Testament, see 5.45: as arising out of Christ's words, 12.47, 48: out of his works, 15.24: out of the witness of the spirit, 16.11.

The communication of the Spirit, rendered possible by the glorification of Jesus through his death and resurrection, convinces the world of judgment, ὅτι ὁ ἄρχων τοῦ κόσμου τούτου κέκριται – 'because the Prince of this world is judged' [John 16.11] – words which further explain what it is in which the ἔλεγχος ['test'] consists. The world is compelled to recognize that the power of evil has been exhibited in its proper nature and thus condemned; has been shown not to be the proper law of the world, inasmuch as the self-surrendering principle of love has triumphed through the return of Jesus to the Father. The world, when this conviction is complete, is delivered from evil. But as thus convinced and delivered it ceases to be the world in the sense in which the Evangelist conceives it. This very conviction is a passing away of the world: it amounts to τὸ τὸν κόσμον παράγεσθαι [the passing away of the world].[42]

From the mention of John as a witness to the light about to be more fully manifested through the action of the Word made (in the) flesh the Evangelist, instead of at once proceeding to speak of the incarnation, reverts to a more explicit assertion of the continuous presence of the Light in the world, prior to and independent of the incarnation. This, at least, is the purport of v.9 according to the most likely interpretation of it. 'The true light...was actually and constantly coming into the world', namely, through 'providence', or the divine ordering of the history of man, and through the conscience (Rom. 2.15). And not only was the 'Light' thus constantly coming into the world; he was never not in it. He did not make it like a workman and leave it to 'spin round his finger'. He was in it, and it came to be (ἐγένετο) what it was through his continuous action ('my Father worketh hitherto, and I work'), yet it recognized him not.[43] Nay, when he came to his own people, (his own in virtue of the special revelation) – when he came to them through the law and the prophets, etc., they received him not; they did not take the light into their own souls. Yet among them were a people who were his own in a higher sense, not as 'children of Abraham after the flesh' (8.33, etc., comp. Rom. 9.8, 11.7 etc.) not in virtue of any natural origin, but in virtue of an adoption by the divine will. There he enabled them to recognize their true relation to him, and thus to become children of God in the higher sense of being of one mind with God, of 'knowing what their Lord doeth'; knowledge of God constituting true Sonship (17.6–8) and true love (15.15, 17.25–6).

We now come to consider the interpretation (a) of ἦν τὸ φως τὸ ἀλη θινόν, ὁ φωὶτζει πάντα ἄνθρωον, ἐρχόμενον εἰς τὸν κόσμον, (v.9) ['That was the true light, which lighteth every man that cometh into the world' (John 1.9)]; (b) of τὰ ἴδια ['came unto'] (v.11); (c) of ἐξουσίαν τένκα Θεου γενέσθαι ['to become the Sons of God'] (v.12).

(a) ἦν τὸ φῶς, etc. [John 1.9]. The interpretation given by the old Authorized Version, ('that[44] was the true light *that* lighteth every man that cometh.') is now given up by all, because it is agreed that τὸ φῶς τὸ ἀλη θινὸν ['that was the true light'] must be subject. Ἰωάννης ['John' (John 1.6)] having been the subject of the previous sentence, φῶς ['light'] could not be *understood* as subject in this sentence, unless represented by a pronoun. Meyer, admitting this, still retains the old way of taking ερχόμενον ['that cometh'] with πάντα ἄνθρωπον ['every man']: 'Vorhanden war das Licht, das wahrhaftige', etc. ['*That* was the true Light' (John 1.9)]; quoting for ἦν ['was'] = 'vorhauden war' ['existed']. 7.39 οὖπω γὰρ ἦν τὸ πνεῦμα δεδόμενον ['For the holy Ghost was not yet *given*']. The objection to this is that to qualify ἄνθρωπον ['man'] by ἐρχόμενον εἰς τὸν κόσμον ['that cometh into the world'] is otiose. Meyer rightly holds that from its position stress must be laid upon ἦν ['was']; but this is quite compatible with taking it with ἐρχόμενον ['coming'], if ἦν ἐρχόμενον is construed 'was in truth constantly coming'. Meyer's objections only have any force as against taking ἦν ἐρχόμενον as simply = 'came', or 'was about to come'.[45] It will not do, as he rightly says, to make it an act successive upon John's witness: comp. v.26. But this objection does not apply to taking it as in the foregoing paraphrase (foot of p.14), or even as = 'was *then* (in the act of) coming into the world. If ἦν is taken with ἐρχόμενον, it must mean either (as Ewald and Baur)[46] 'was *constantly coming*', with reference to a state of things prior to the incarnation, or 'was then in process or act of coming', (as Hilgenfeld takes it).[47] The decision between these two renderings depends on whether v.11 is taken of the incarnation, or of comings prior to the incarnation.

(b) First, however, the question about τὰ ἴδια ['his own things'] and ἴδιοι ['own people'] must be settled [John 1.11]. There is not much doubt that the reference is to the Jews, not to the world in general. The only ground for questioning this lies in the way in which the Jews are spoken of *in this Gospel*. Elsewhere plenty of passages can be found when they are treated as in a primary sense the people of God (e.g. Exod. 19.5; Deut. 14.1; Matth. 8.12; 15.26). The Christ of St. John, however, always specially detaches himself from the Jews and their law (7.19, 22; 8.17; 15.25). Again, our Lord's breaches of the law are emphasized; 5.18; 7.22; 9.14. Again, the denial to the Jews of any knowledge of God is put in the most general way; 7.28; 8.19; 54–5; 15.21; 16.3. Again, the Jews are thoroughly identified with the 'world' which knew not God; 15.19, 21: 7.23.[48]

Still it is quite natural that the Evangelist, by way of heightening the shamelessness of their rejecting the Light, should pass into the received way of thinking in regard to the Jews as ὁ λαὸς περιποιήσεως ['the saved people']. Just so according to Paul's view the object of the law is to make 'sin more exceeding simple',[49] so that the special dealing of God with the Jews, in virtue of which they were a 'peculiar people', heightens the tragedy of their ignorance of him.

There is no particular difference between ἴδια ['things'] and ἴδιοι ['people']; the former represents Israel rather as the *im*-personal property of the Word, while the latter represents the nation personally.

ἦλθε ['came']. Can this be taken of anything but the coming in the flesh? Would anything but this have been spoken of in the aorist as if it were a coming once for all? The tense may be explained by supposing that the Evangelist, having expressed the continuity or repeatedness of the coming of the Word into the world by ἦν ἐρχόμενον ['was coming'], used the simple aorist to express the revelation to the Jews as having more by comparison, of the single historical event about it.[50] This helps to remove the objection to taking it of comings prior to the incarnation. The positive reason for so taking it is that otherwise v.14 ὁ λόγος σὰρξ ἐγένετο, etc. ['And the Word was made flesh, and dwelt among us (and we beheld his glory, the glory as of the only begotten of the Father,) full of grace and truth.' (John 1.14)] would be a mere return to what has been said before, whereas if we do so take it, the whole previous passage leads up to v.14.

(c) {12. 'As many as received him', to them he gave 'authority' (ἐξουσίαν) to become sons of God; even to them that believed on his name. In the face of these words can the interpretation above given be maintained?} Can τοῖς πιστεύουσιν εἰς τὸ ὄνομα ['to them that believe on his Name' (John 1.12)] be understood of anything but belief in Jesus as the incarnate Λόγος? and if not, does not this compel us to take ἦλθε ['came'] of coming in the flesh? (? comp. 8.56). For the meaning of ὄνομα ['sign'] comp. 17.6, 26: ἐφανέρωα σοῦ τὸ ὄνομα τοῖς ἀνθρώποις, etc. ['I have manifested thy Name unto the men which thou gavest me out of the world: thine they were; and thou gavest them me; and they have kept thy word.' (John 17.6)] ἐγνώρισα αὐτοῖς τὸ ὄνομα σον καὶ γνωρίσω ['I have declared unto thy Name, and will declare it' (John 17.26)]. To 'believe on the name' of the Lord or of Jesus Christ would originally mean to believe that Jesus was the Messiah, 'the Son of God' in the special sense, not merely as Israel generally, or David and the prophets, were so.[51] In this Gospel, with the idea of Jesus as the incarnate Word, 'belief in his name' comes to have a higher sense. His 'name' is the manifestation of God's 'name', of God's nature and attributes. To believe in his name is thus to accept God's manifestation of himself through him (1 Epist. 5.20 ὁ υἱὸς τοῦ Θεοῦ ἥκει καὶ δέδωκεν ἐμῖν διάνοιαν ἵνα γινώσκωμεν τὸν ἀληθινὸν ['the Son of God is come, and hath given us an understanding that we may know him that is true' (1 John 5.20)]), to know God, and in knowing to become one with him through that communication of the Divine Spirit of which the incarnation and glorification of Christ are the condition. It is thus, in St. Paul's language, to receive 'the spirit of adoption', or the consciousness of oneness with God; as the Evangelist puts it in this place, 'to be authorized or entitled to become his children. Could this be said of anyone under the 'old dispensation'? Probably, according to the view of this Evangelist, it could: comp. 8.56; 12.41 (of Abraham and Isaiah).[52] They 'saw the glory' of the Son – anticipated the complete manifestation of God through his finished work, and in this sense 'believed on his name', just as the disciples did after his return to the Father. It is quite possible, however, that the Evangelist, though thinking primarily in vv.11 and 12 of a 'coming' and 'receiving' prior to the incarnation, should yet pass into the thought of 'the receivers of the Word' as one body, without distinction of the periods before and after the incarnation, and should thus use language which he would more strictly employ only of those who believed after the full manifestation.

v.13 ἐξ αἱμάτων ['of blood' (John 1.13)] conveys the notion of blending of two 'bloods' or 'stocks', according to the idea that 'the blood is the life'. The Evangelist wishes to put the antithesis to the sonship through the Divine will in the fullest way – Such sonship could result neither from the simple operation of the principle of life, nor from animal desire, nor from human volition.[53,54]

(Is it that because ἐκ Θεοῦ ἐγεννήθησαν ['[of] God were born' (John 1.13)] they received the Word, who ἔδωκεν αὐτοῖς ἐξουσίαν τέκνα Θεοῦ γενέσθαι ['to them gave he power to become the sons of God' (John 1.12)], or in Θεοῦ εγεννήθησαν ['[of] God were born'], the explanation of the sense in which they were entitled, etc.?).

v.14 ὁ λόγος σαρξ ἐγένετο ['And the Word was made flesh']
[...]

[On p.207, l.12, after 'gospel', there is the following note:]
In the earlier drafts of these lectures Mr. Green begins as follows:-
'σάρξ ['flesh'] (on the whole) in the New Testament means (a) sense and appetite; (b) the subject of sense and appetite; (c) the object thereof.'

[On p.207, l.29, after 'selfishness', there is the following note:]
Philosophical analysis had not then been carried far enough to
discover that is the divine principle (πνεῦμα) in man in its
elementary form, which renders man capable of delusion and
selfishness.

[On p.210, last line, after 'calamity.' appears:]
(! T.H.G.)

[On p.211, l.20, after 'knowledge', there is the following note:]
{In the first draft of the lectures occurs the following:}
The manifestation, which, as such, is a salvation or redemption,
is of *the person* of the 'only begotten Son' as the 'Word' or
expression of God under the three attributes of 'light', 'life', and
'love'. During the life of Christ in the flesh, it is made (1) through
ἔργα and σημεῖα, which, however, are an essentially inferior form
of manifestation: (2) through words, which however are not understood while Christ is on earth: (3) through his death and resurrection: (4) through the Spirit, which is the sole complete manifestation. The condition (on the side of man) of the manifestation is
faith, which becomes knowledge (7.17; 8.32).

[On the verso of the text printed at pp.211–212, is written the
following text, headed 'From the first draft':]
{Passages illustrating the manifestation of Christ's person.}
   3.15 foll.; 8.32–36; 10.8 foll.; 12.46. (In 13.34 he *teaches* the new
duty of Love, but as a communication of *his own love*, and imitation
of his own act: 13.15; 17.23. The Person however to be believed
in is not his own person as in the flesh, though the flesh is the
means of communication; not his person as Jesus of Nazareth but
the eternal Person, for ever manifest in the world, if we could but
see it, in beholding whom with the spiritual eye we behold the
eternal God (l l.9.). The flesh of the 'historical Jesus', according to
the view of 'St. John', is merely the *means of the manifestation* of
the eternal 'Jesus Christ' (1 Epist. 4.2 παν πνεῦμα ὁ ὁμολογεῖ τὸν
Ἰησοῦν Χριστὸν ἐν *σαρκὶ ἐληλυθότα* ἐκ τοῦ Θεοῦ ἐστὶ ['Hereby
know ye the Spirit of God: every spirit which confesseth that Jesus
Christ is come in the flesh is of God' (1 John 4.2)]): therefore Jesus
Christ is prior to his coming in the flesh .... The withdrawal of the
'Word' from the fleshly tabernacle is the necessary condition of his
communication as the Spirit and Paraclete.[55]

{Passages illustrating the value of σημεῖα *['signs']}:*
4.48; 10.38; 14.11; 20.29.
{Passages illustrating the exhibition of works and utterances of words}:
9.4; 14.10; 5.22–24.
{Passages illustrating the power of 'words'}:
3.34; 6.63, 68; 8.47; 12.47; 15.2.
Light means manifested truth: the truth is God: in 17.3, 6, 17
it is the Son, as the expression of God: 17.18; 14.6, 9.
'Truth' is the eternal in which God lives; only by participation
in this can there be community with him through prayer (4.24).

Popular philosophy confines 'truth' either to a *proposition* as
the correct expression of thought, or to a *conception*, as a
combination of thought, or qualities in thought according to
their combination in 'nature': the agreement of thought with its
object. What can be meant by calling God 'truth'? 'Truth' as
the conception of this or that man, may be described as 'the
agreement of thought with its object', but what is this object?
An *intellectual system* which he appropriates. This system =
objective truth, and this again must be relative to a mind (ἰδέα
ἰδεῶα) which = God as the truth: the unity in which all the
distinctions and oppositions of the manifold are reconciled: the
unity of the *moral*, not merely of the physical life: consequently
a unity, the attainment of which on our part at once presupposes and issues in a moral life.
According to strict Alexandrianism this 'mind' would be the
λόγος, as distinct from the αὐτόθεος.
This Evangelist, though retaining this conception, yet merges
it in the conception of the one *manifested God*.

This 'truth' is derived from the Father by the μονογενής υἱός
['only-begotten son'] by an act described as one of 'seeing and
hearing': 5.20, 30; 6.46; 8.26, 38; 12.50. From the Son to
believers it is derived by a like act, which must be understood in
the latter case in the same sense as in the former: 6.40; 12.45;
14.9; 20.29. Without the sensuous metaphor, the act is described
as one of believing and knowing; 12.44; 14.1; 7.17; 8.32; 1 Epist
5.20.
Is such an 'abstract philosophical' conception of truth viz: a
conception of it as the personal spiritual unity of the moral and

intelligible world, which unity = the manifested God, what the Evangelist means by God as truth in knowledge of whom standeth eternal life, of whom knowledge gives life and freedom? To say that God was 'truth' to one who had the Alexandrian way of thinking, would mean nothing but that God was an *Idea*. The mere, the abstract, etc. are modern prefixes derived from a wholly different way of thinking. The *Idea* in question is conceived as active and *morally* active: as *life* and *love*. Its appropriation by us is the source of life and love and freedom in us. But this appropriation is not *our* act, in the sense of being one for which we may take credit to ourselves. (So far as we are individuals, exclusive of each other, and thus capable of 'taking credit' for anything, we are incapable of such appropriation. 'How can ye believe, who receive honour one of another' [John 5.44].) The appropriation of the Idea by us is the self-realization of the Idea in us. The Son (or manifested Idea) exhibits the truth (*14.21.*) He again gives *liberty*, which comes with the knowledge of the 'Truth' (8.32, 36). He again gives *life* (5.21, 26). The true point of view for understanding the 'Johannine' view of the Word as *life* is given by 17.2. The Word is Life, as manifesting the 'true God' or 'truth' of whom knowledge is life eternal.

{What has made the conception of 'truth', as presented in this Gospel, practically potent, while the philosophical conception of truth has been practically impotent?
(a) The antithesis must not be made too strong. Has Christendom ever practically got hold of the conception of God as 'truth'? Has it not rather explained it away, and put in its place the conception of an arbitrary will, revealing itself in an artificial 'scheme of salvation', through a priesthood, through sensuous signs,[56] through a 'letter which killeth'. [2 Cor. 3:6]}
(b) One reason is that in this Gospel the Spiritual principle in question was identified with that Jesus, who was already believed in as the true Messiah who had been raised from the dead; and was represented as manifesting Himself through the acts of this Jesus. The 'philosophical conception' thus becomes potent with the strength of the developed belief in a crucified and risen Messiah, and with the practical life of the society resting on that belief.

(c) Another reason is that the 'truth' of this Gospel, though intellectually apprehended, is moral; gives life and *loves*: is realized in the *love* of the congregation'. And the condition of its appropriation by us is that doing my commandment which is already incipient love. The antithesis between the speculative and moral which had been the weakness of philosophy is thus overcome. The historical condition of this moralizing of the conception of Divine Truth, however, was the establishment of the belief in Jesus as the risen Messiah (and therefore not merely Jewish), and of the Christian society resting on this belief.

This knowledge (see on p.IV.)[57] according to 14.21 is equivalent to community of love between the believer and God through the Son as the personal means. The condition of this again is 'doing my commandment': comp. 7.17. But no 'commandments' are mentioned in this Gospel, and scarcely any in the other. What can this really mean then, but living the highest life of Christian society?

The 'life' then, which Christ is, and which he communicates, is an 'amor intellectuallis'. At the same time the Evangelist certainly conceived of the restoration of physical life as a σημειαν ['sign'] of this spiritual life, and sometimes the two kinds of life seem blended. Yet in 12.25 they are distinctly opposed. So it is conversely with death.

The words of the communication of this life are ζωοποιεῖν ['quickening'], ἐγείγειν ['awakening'], ἀνιστάναι ['arising']. It is a communication of Christ's person (6.33) through the contemplation of and faith in him (6.40). The act which renders the communication possible is Christ's death (1) as a perfect act of love which draws all men: (2) in the withdrawal of the *sensuous* presence, which is the condition of the coming of the 'Comforter' [John 16.7]. This coming results in that 'dwelling in me and I in you' which is the condition of 'bearing much fruit' (15.5: comp. 4.13 (?)).
{An explanation of 6.51 follows different from that given in the second draft. Mr Green in the first draft too the words 'to partake of the body' to mean 'to be in active and conscious communion with the Christian society; the Church being 'his manifested person or body.'}

[On p.213, l.9, after 'supper.', there is the following note:]
To understand v.53 of a command to receive the communion as
a condition of salvation is intrinsically absurd, and directly
against the tenor both of v.v.47 and 56 (where 'eating' represents
an indwelling state), and of v.63.

[On p.215, end of first paragraph, after 'man.':]
If we ask by what process according to this Gospel [of John],
the incarnation was effected, no direct answer can be given; but
taking it by itself, we should conclude that the 'flesh' of Christ was
born in the ordinary human way,[58] and v.32 of chap.1 rather
points to the notion that the Word was incarnate through a
descent of the Spirit upon this 'flesh'. It is true that 'Word' and
'Spirit' may be distinguishable notions – probably the Evangelist
would hardly have written πνεῦμα σαρξ ἐγένετο [the spirit
awakened the flesh] – but so far as the Word is the divine principle
in Jesus, it is identical with πνεῦμα ['spirit'], which, in the rest of
the gospel, after the prologue, is the regular word for this
principle. Πνεῦμα was the regular term in the Christian society
for the communicated God in Jesus, as in the Church. The
Evangelist having borrowed from the outside the Church
conception of the Word, as incarnate in Jesus, drops it again in
favour of πνεῦμα.

The context of v.32 scarcely allows us to suppose that the
Evangelist regarded the Spirit as communicated to Jesus for the
first time on the occasion of the Baptist's Θεωρία νοητικὴ [intellectual
apprehension]; for unless it was previously communicated, what
meaning is there in 'I knew him not' ([John 1.] v.33)? which must
mean 'I knew him not (prior to this vision) as being what he really
was', namely, either as the Messiah, or as the eternal being who 'was
before me'. What the Baptist saw, the Spirit descending and abiding
upon him, was already a constant fact: compare the last verse '*from
henceforth*[59], ye shall see the heavens opened,' etc.

Here the ascent and descent of angels' represent the constant
intercommunication of the Spirit between the Father and Son: an
intercommunication, however, which did not begin when Nathaniel
first saw it, any more than it did when John first saw it.

Ἐσκήνωσεν ἐν ἡμῖν ['dwelt among us' (John 1.14)]
This further illustrates the mode in which the Evangelist
conceived the incarnation. The 'flesh' is a temporary resting

place of the Word or Spirit, in which he dells *with* us (14.17 παρ᾽ ὑμιν μένει ['he dwelleth with you']):⁶⁰ which the Spirit must occupy, but from which it is equally necessary that he should withdraw, in order to his communication to men. [...]

[On p. 217, l.9, after 'impossible.', appears:]
The beholding of Christ's glory by Isaiah (14.14) can only have been a Θεωρία νοητεκή ['intellectual perception']. [...]

[On p.220, the text continues after the end of extract:]
The mere word ἐθεασάμεθα, then, does not prove that the writer meant to represent himself as one of the original disciples, who 'saw' Jesus of Nazareth. It merely expresses the identification of himself with the believers in whom the contemplation of the 'Word' was continued after its manifestation in the flesh had come to an end; who saw the glory of the Word spiritually, when the world no longer saw Jesus (14.19), and who received of his fulness (πλήρωμα, 1.16). Compare the first verse of St. Luke.

The passages within the Gospel which are thought to imply that the writer was the apostle John are 13.23 ἦν ἀνακείμενος εἷς ἐκ τῶν μαθητῶν αὐτοῦ ἐν τῷ κόλπῳ τοῦ ῾Ιησοῦ, etc. ['Now there was leaning on Jesus' bosom one of his disciples, whom Jesus loved' (John 13.23)]: 18.15 ἄλλος μαθητής ὁ δὲ μαθητής ἐκεῖνος γνωστὸς ἦν τῷ ἀρχιερεῖ ['another disciple: that disciple, which was known unto the high Priest']; 19.26 ῾Ιησοῦς...ἰδὼν...τὸν μαθτὴν παρεστῶτα ὃν ἠγάπα ['Jesus ...saw...the disciple standing by, whom he loved']: 19.25 [sic] καὶ ὁ ἐωραὼς μεμαρτύρηκεν, καὶ ἀληθινὴ αὐτοῦ ἐστιν ἡ μαρτυρία, etc. ['And he that saw it, bare record, and his record is true, and he knoweth that he saith true, and that ye might believe' (John 19.35)]; 21.24 οὗτός ἐστιν ὁ μαθητής ὁ καὶ μαρτυρῶν περὶ τούτων καὶ ὁ γράψας ταυτα, etc. ['This is the disciple which testifieth of these things, and wrote these things, and we know that his testimony is true.']

Throughout these passages, as in 1.35–41, there is a reference to a disciple whose name is uniformly withheld, and who is probably meant to be the apostle John himself, as his [is] the apostolic name most conspicuous by its absence in this Gospel.⁶¹ It is thought then that the apostle John, being himself the writer of the Gospel, suppressed his own name out of modesty. On the other hand it is urged that there would be but little modesty shown by the apostle, if he were himself the writer, in describing himself as specially the object of Jesus' love, especially after our Lord's warning, apparently connected by Church tradition with a certain self-assertion on the part of John (Matth. 20.20 foll.; Luke 9.46–9): that in doing so and at the same time witholding his name, he would have shown a very unlovely self-consciousness. 19.25 and 21.24 both rather seem to convey an appeal indeed to the eye-witness of the beloved disciple, *but* an appeal made to it by one who was not[62] the apostle himself. Those who take the apostle John to have been himself the writer say that ἐκεῖνος is the speaking subject objectified ('das objectivierte redende subject sellst' ['speaking subject objectified']. Meyer), and say that this 'objectification' is of a kind with the writer's uniform suppression of his own personality:[63] with his unwillingness to intrude it upon a theme so exalted. Others (as Ewald) explain it by supposing that the apostle John dictated the Gospel, and that the scribe thus came to put him into the third person. Anyhow, one must admit that the writer, if other than the apostle, meant to convey the notion that he was appealing to the evidence of the apostle, as that of an authority still living and present (οἶδεν, etc. ['he knoweth that he saith true, that ye might believe.'] 19.35).

Those who reject the Johannine authorship of the Gospel hold that it represents a school of disciples of John in Asia Minor, who retained a special reverence for his name, and for the tradition of his distinctive ideas, but had, more or less unconsciously, given quite a new significance to these, and wished to gain currency for their own new spiritual interpretation of the Johannine tradition under the Johannine name. All that is known of the apostle John points in the direction of his having retained strongly Judaic ideas of Christ and the Church; that he was full of the apocalyptic spirit, looking for the return of Christ in glory to restore the kingdom to a purified and enlarged Israel. Apart from dogmatic consideration, the case is much stronger for ascribing the Apocalypse to the Apostle John than for ascribing the Gospel to him. Now in certain dominant phrases the Apocalypse has a likeness to the Gospel. The Apocalypse dwells much on special revelations through 'the spirit': speaks of Christ as 'the Word of God' (19.13): as 'the Lamb that was slain' (cap.5): and looks for a second coming of Christ to 'make all things new'. At first sight such notions seem to reappear in the Gospel, but they reappear wholly altered. The revelation of the Spirit is not a revelation of things to come (except once, 16.13) but a communication of perfect love and knowledge. Christ is the 'Word', but not merely as the utterance of God in the judgment of the world (Rev. 19.13), but in a much more complete and metaphysical sense. He is the 'Lamb slain', but is so in a far more spiritual sense than in the Apocalypse: in a sense of having a perfectly devoted will, which is expressed by 'Laying down his life': he 'comes again' to make all things new, but he does so through that communication of himself as the Spirit,[64] by which the believer is 'born from above'. Does not all this look like the work of one who was putting new wine into the old vessel of traditionary Johannine doctrine; of one who had imbibed Pauline ideas, especially as these are represented by the Epistle to the Ephesians, Philippians, and Hebrews, and who, without being a Gnostic, had shared in the sort of speculation about the relation between God and the World in which Gnosticism originated? It would have been quite according to the spirit of these times for such a one, while availing himself of the words of the master whose disciple he took himself to be, to give them, without knowing it, quite a new significance, and in doing so to identify himself with his master, as the writer of 19.35, if he be not John, indirectly does.

With the question whether 19.35 is really written by the person whose eye-witness it purports to convey, is involved the question of the significance which the writer attached to the efflux of blood and water.

(a) One view is that the efflux was natural; as such it is explained on the supposition (1) that Jesus was not previously dead, but died through the spear piercing the *pericardium*, from which would flow 'lymph', and the chamber of the heart, from which would flow blood: or (2) that he was already dead, and that the blood in the corpse had decomposed itself into 'serum' and 'crassamentum', (clot): the spear on this hypothesis not piercing the heart; or (3) that Jesus had died of a broken heart, and that, the spear having reached the heart, the peculiar efflux is thus to be accounted for.

But whether the efflux was natural or no, it is quite clear that the writer regarded it as having a supernatural significance: ἀληθὴ λέγει ἵνα ὑμεις πιστεύητε ['he saith true, that ye might believe' (John 19.35)]. The mere announcement of the natural efflux could have no relation to belief. The writer evidently regarded it as a σημεῖον ['sign']; a σημεῖον which, as it is his characteristic to consider all manifestations of God to sense – is indeed to produce belief but presupposes belief as the condition of its being read aright. It is a σημεῖον of the shedding abroad of the spirit as the spirit of self-devotion and purity (comp. Hebrews 9.14; 1 Pet. 1.19) which ensues on the glorification of Jesus through death, and his return to the Father (7.39; 12.32: 1 Epist. 5.6). It may be held then either –

(b) That the efflux was itself supernatural (whatever that may mean) as well as rightly interpreted by the on-looking apostle; or

(c) that it was *natural*, but was spiritually interpreted by the apostle himself under the divine inspiration: or

(d) That it really occurred (as a natural event), and was described by the apostle, but received a spiritual interpretation from a writer who was not the apostle; or

(e) That the belief in the event having happened is itself the result of the idea under which the event was interpreted according to (c) and (d).

The importance attached to the spiritual interpretation of the efflux is probably the reason of the iteration in v.36.[65] What is the meaning of ἀληθινή ['true' (John 19.35)]? Does it mean that his testimony accords with the facts of the case? 'I that saw it give evidence of what I saw, namely, that the legs of Jesus were not broken, that the soldier pierced his side, and that there flowed out blood and water'. Would not such reiterated assertion be very unmeaning, and what would it convey that would be of such importance to be believed?

To this it may be answered that what was to produce the belief was the correspondence between what happened in regard to Jesus as testified to by the apostle, and the type and prophecy mentioned in the following verse, ἐγένετο γὰρ, etc. ['For these things were done, that the Scripture should be fulfilled, A bone of him shall not be broken.' (John 19.36)] This is, in a certain sense, true; but the correspondence which the Evangelist had in view was not one of a peculiar event with a prediction, but one of that which the pierced side and efflux of blood and water symbolized, with the type and prophecy of the following verse. And that which was symbolized was (a) the voluntary self-sacrifice of the Messiah, which should draw all to him who spiritually gazed on the pierced side, and spiritually fed on him as the true Paschal Lamb, and (b) the consequent communication of his spirit to them, as a 'river of living water' [John 4.10–11].

Evidently in the mind of the Church from which this Gospel
and the Epistle originated (whether that was the mind of the
Apostle John or a later mind) 'water' and 'blood' had come to be
charged with a spiritual significance, in which their natural
meaning was quite lost. In the case of 'water', this probably arose
out of the use of it in baptism; in the case of 'blood', partly from
that association of the shedding of blood with sacrifice which
(though sacrifice had ceased in Christian congregations) the use
of the Old Testament kept alive, and which made it natural to
speak of Christ's devotion of himself as the shedding of his blood;
partly through the drinking of wine at the memorial supper,
which had come to be considered, as early as St. Paul's time, as
a drinking of Christ's blood, and thus as the representative of
participation in his sacrifice.

As used in the Gospel they seem inextricably blended, jointly
or indifferently representing the operation of the Divine Spirit,
primarily in Christ, and through communication from him in the
believer, as the source of unselfish energy, purity, and love.
'Water' is spoken of in a way which does not correspond to its
symbolical use in baptism, but rather to the use of wine in the
Lord's Supper. So in the conversation with the woman of
Samaria, and in 7.37 etc. Conversely, *blood* is used symbolically
for *purification*, which the water of baptism seems more naturally
to represent (1 Epist. 1.7; comp. Hebr. 9.14) οὗτός ἐστιν ὁ ἐλθὼν
δι᾽ ὕδατος καὶ αἵματος (1 Epist. 5.6 ['This is he that came by
water and blood,' (1 John 5.6)]).

'Water and blood' really represents the mode of operation of
the Spirit, which is Christ, in the Church; therefore the mode in
which Christ comes (Evang. 14.18.) But this present and
continuous coming being thought of as presented and conditioned by the historical coming of Christ in the flesh, it is put as
a past: while immediately afterwards (v.8) they are spoken of as
present influences, (still 'witnessing') which combine in one result
with[66] the Spirit (εἰς τὸ ἓν εἶσον ['these three agree in one' (1 John
5.8)]: comp. τετελειωμένοι εἰς ἓν Evang. 17.23 ['the world may
know that thou hast sent me' (John 17.23)]. The 'water and
blood' through which Christ came are doubtless the water of his
baptism and the blood of his cross, but they are these as
converted in the writer's conception into the spiritual processes
which they represent and which are continually going on in the
Church.

The whole passage shows, perhaps more strikingly than any other, how completely the symbol and the thing symbolized, past and present or eternal, historical and ideal, outward and inward, are merged in the Johannine writings: how all logical lines between them disappear. 'Water and blood' having been first spoken of as the past mode in which 'Jesus Christ came', are immediately co-ordinated (nay, reduced to unity with) the Spirit as present 'witnesses'. 'It is the Spirit that witnesseth', yet the 'water and blood' witness too. The 'witness', which naturally means the testimony of the senses to a fact (and does not here lose this meaning) becomes the witness of the spirit. God *has* given the witness to his Son in order to produce belief, yet the belief itself is the witness, which each may have in himself. The witness again consists in the eternal life which he has in himself, who has the Son in himself. The witness to the Son is the Son himself as indwelling. This may help us to understand the significance which the μαρτυρία ἀληθινή ['true record'] of 19.35 would have to the Evangelist's own mind. Let us consider the usage of ἀληθινός elsewhere: ἀληθινὸν φῶς ['true light'] 1.9: ἀληθινοὶ προσχῦνται ['true worshippers'] 4.23: τὸν ἄρτον τὸν ἀληθινὸν ['true bread from heaven'] 6.32; ἄμπεος ἡ ἀληθινή ['the true vine'] 15.1; μόνον ἀληθινὸν Θεὸν ['the only true God'] 17.3. Primarily of course its meaning is 'genuine' as opposed to 'spurious', and this meaning is not lost in the above passages; but owing to the Evangelist's way of thinking that the spiritual alone is genuine, it comes almost to = *'spiritual'* as opposed to *'carnal'*. 'The true light' is the spiritual light which sensible light signifies, or opposed to that which signifies it. So with the 'bread' and the 'vine'. So here 'his witness is a *genuine* witness', in the sense that it is a witness to events which indeed were sensible, but which were σημεῖα ['signs'] of spiritual matters: these realities being the eternal self-devotion of Christ of which the sacrifice of the Paschal Lamb had been the figure: of which believers partake as Israel ate of the Lamb, and in partaking of it receive the purifying spirit.

The importance which the Evangelist attaches to the 'witness' lies in this spiritual significance of it, which is what constitutes it[s] ἀληθινή ['truth']. He continues ἐγένετο γάρ ['For these things were done,' (John 19.36)]– this higher spiritual belief was what these signs were given to produce, for they were done to show that Jesus was the true Paschal Lamb, and the suffering Messiah, of whom the Scriptures spoke.

To him it is not, at least not merely or chiefly, the ocular evidence of a sensuous witness. It is the witness borne by the Spirit, which is alone the true witness (1 Epist. 5.6) to spiritual realities: to that self-sacrifice of Christ, and the efflux to believers of his self-sacrificing spirit, to which the Spirit can properly witness, because they are really identical with it. The like juxta-position of water and the spirit meets us in 3.5. Nicodemus is probably meant to be regarded as one of those who according to 2.23 had 'believed on the name' of Jesus from 'seeing the signs', etc; whose idea of the Messiah and the 'kingdom of heaven' which he was to establish consisted in the expectation of outward manifestations of power, and who, seeing the σημεῖα ['sign'] wrought by Jesus, 'believe on his name', or believe that he is the Messiah according to *their own idea of the Messiah*. Jesus knows what this belief is worth (2.24). Its value depends on its capacity for passing into the higher belief in his Person, as God manifested not in any outward glory, but in humiliation and death, and coming to his people, not as king or judge, but in the Spirit of love and knowledge. It only does so in those who are 'born from above'. Therefore the works of Christ act as a κρίσις ['condemnation'], 3.19; 5.24. Apparently, however, the effect of 'birth from above' in regard to faith admits of degrees. The true sort of faith in the person of Jesus, as manifested God, in some anticipates the σημεῖα ['sign'], for whom the words, through which his divine nature speaks are sufficient. So (in 4.42) it is with the Samaritans in contrast with the Jews: so with the βασιλικός ['nobleman'] (4.48 etc.) In this latter case Jesus says reproachfully (v.48) 'Except ye see signs and wonders, ye will not believe'. The βασιλικός simply renews the prayer, showing that his faith was independent of the σημεῖον ['sign'], and accepts the simple declaration of Jesus that his son liveth without the σημεῖον ['sign'] (v.50). Then a σημεῖον ['sign'] is granted him, and having believed before, he now believes (presumably) in the sense of higher assurance (v.53).

The 'words' of Jesus, it is to be observed, in this differ from the σημεῖα ['sign'], that having nothing 'carnal' about them,[67] they only appeal to the spiritual nature. So far as they touch the carnal nature at all, it is only to offend it. Thus in 6.66 the lower faith which has been attracted by the σημεῖα ['sign'] is repelled by the 'words' which are 'spirit and life'. Thus, though the 'works' and 'words' of Christ are alike manifestations of his divine nature, the latter one, so to speak, a purer manifestation. The 'works' have two sides. (a) They are examples of divine activity dwelling in him; expressions of the divine will with which his own is identical (4.34; 5.36; 9.3, 4; 14.6). In order to exhibit the power, in virtue of which they are done, as no other than the eternal power of God, and thus antecedent to, and unlimited by, institutions even of divine authority, he heals on the Sabbath (c.5) and vindicates himself by the words 'My Father worketh hitherto and I work'. Works in this sense are inseparable from the person of Christ. But (b) they have a sensible side, as σημεῖα ['sign']; and, as such, manifest the true person of Christ only to those who are born of the Spirit, the πνευματικοί ['he that is spiritual'] of St. Paul (1 Cor. 2.15; 3.1). Hence whereas a belief founded on σημεῖα ['sign'] may turn out only to be another form of unbelief, when tried by ῥήματα ['words'], in which their true import (the true nature of the Persons they exhibit) is explained (as at the end of ch. 6) belief in Christ's words can be no other than true belief in his person (6.63 and 68; 8.47; 12.47, etc.; 15.7).

Jesus, 'knowing what was in man', distinguishes the demand for a σημεῖον ['sign'] which springs from a true though elementary faith (as in the case of Thomas) from that which represents the merely carnal mind. The latter he meets not by granting a sign, but by a 'scandalizing' assertion of the Divine personality. So in 2.19 'The sign of my authority is no mere sign, but that of which all my works are signs, even myself, or the eternal life which is in me, and which, when my carnal body is destroyed, will appear in my spiritual or risen body, which is the Church (1 Cor. 3.16 & 17). Comp. 10.17 & 18 (where ψυχή ['life'] changes its meaning from the carnal life 'laid down' to the 'spiritual life' resumed, or, more properly re-manifested).

It may be asked what justification there is for taking the 'body raised in three days' of the Church? Must it not mean the body which according to this Evangelist was seen on the third day after the crucifixion? The answer to this is that to the Evangelist it no doubt did mean this body, but this body was the σημεῖον ['sign'] of the communication of Christ as the Spirit to, and his presence in, the Church (comp. 20.23). Only by thus regarding the risen body could the Evangelist hold together his account of the appearances in ch. 20 with the announcement of the spiritual coming again 'in a little while' of the discourses in ch. 14–16.

It is sometimes doubted whether the Evangelist understood our Lord's words aright in the interpretation he gives them in 2.21. 'Is it likely', it is asked, 'that our Lord would have used words in a sense in which he could not possibly be understood by his hearers? Was he not really speaking of the substitution, which he would effect, of a spiritual religion for a local Jewish one? But we cannot at once accept the Evangelist's account of the words as authentic, and at the same time reject the interpretation he gives them. The words τρισὶν ἡμέραις ἐγερῶ αὐτὸν ['wilt thou rear it [the Temple] in three days?' (John 2.20)], if actually spoken, could have no reference except to the resurrection. The words quoted against Christ by 'false witnesses' (Matt. 26.61) would naturally be understood simply of the Temple. If they were used by our Lord, the probable reference was to the establishment of a new worship on the ruins of the Temple-worship. In Mark 14.58 the words used are still appropriate to building, but the temple to be built in three days is ἀχειροποίητες ['made without hands'], which naturally represents the new spiritual society, originating indeed in the resurrection, but not identified with the risen body of our Lord. In John 2.19, in the second clause all words appropriate to building have disappeared. The reference can only be not to the establishment of a spiritual worship or church by means of the resurrection, but only to the resurrection itself. As to this Evangelist the resurrection is not merely a means to, but is identified with, the communication of the spirit, to believe, so the new Temple, the Spiritual Church, is identified with the risen body.[68]

In 6.30 the unbelieving demand for a sign is met by Christ's 'scandalizing' assertion of his personality, as the spiritual bread came down from heaven, and who would return thither, as the son of man whose flesh must be eaten and whose blood must be drunk: words expressive of his spiritual personality as communicated to believers, which could only be 'spiritually discerned' (1 Cor. 2.14). In the case of Nicodemus the faith founded on σημεῖα ['signs'] is a *possibility* of higher faith (7.50; 19.39); but, as it is, he is looking for a kingdom of heaven that 'cometh with observation' (Luke 17.20); and this expectation speaks through his works. Hence our Lord's reply, v.3 [John 3.3]. Nicodemus understands γεννήθη ἄνωθεν of a second birth. The true sense is shown by 1 Epist. 5.1, 4 πᾶν τὸ γεγεννημένον ἐκ τοῦ Θεοῦ νικα τὸν κόσμον ['whatsoever is born of God, overcometh the world' (1 John 5.4)], and by Evang. 8.23 and 44.

There are three different ways of thinking in our Lord's discourses which have contributed to form the theological notion of regeneration. The first is represented by Matth. 18.3. 'Except ye be converted and become as little children', etc. The second by Matth. 19.28 'in the regeneration, when the Son of man shall sit upon the throne of his glory'. The third by this passage. It would be with 'regeneration' in the second sense that baptism would be associated in the earliest Christian mind. It was by the initiatory rite into that Christian society which was to attain the final triumph and remodel the world when Christ came again to make all things new (Rev. 21.5). As with St. Paul 'regeneration' takes a new meaning, so does baptism as a symbol of 'regeneration'. With him γέγονε καινὰ ['they have become new'], the renewal is already accomplished, but it is a renewal of the individual soul, consisting in that death in Christ to flesh and the law, which on its other side is the new life (2 Cor. 5.17; Gal. 2.19, etc.). Baptism is associated with this change as the symbol of the 'burial with Christ' (Rom. 6.4). This it may be said, is a return to the first notion of the new birth; and it is in a way; but St. Paul's struggle with flesh and the law has given a peculiar cast in his mind to the thought which with Jesus, as represented by Matth. 18.5, was simply one of trustfulness and self-surrender. In our passage 'born again' has become 'born from above', which is explained to mean 'born of water and the spirit'. 'Water' no doubt refers to the water of baptism, the 'mark of difference' between Christian society and those outside it, which is identified with that which it symbolizes; as instead of 'regeneration', whether in the Judaic sense of the Messianic kingdom or in the Pauline of a breach with the legal life, we have now got the notion of a principle of spiritual life which need imply no change in time at all, so the water of baptism, which is the symbol of regeneration, has come to be thought of as representing this principle of life, as in 4.14; 7.38.

Three questions have suggested themselves: (a) Is it true that the 'birth from above' need 'imply no change in time', need not take place in time, at all, according to the meaning of this passage? Do the words (v.6) τὸ γεγεννημένον ἐκ τῆς σαρκὸς

['That which is born of the flesh' (John 3.6)] and τὸ γεγεννημένον ἐκ τοῦ πνεύματος ['That which is born of the spirit' (John 3.6)] refer to two originally different classes of men, or to two successive epochs of life? Probably, if we looked to this passage simply, apart from other considerations, we should take the former view (comp. 8.47; 12.39). The immediate reference would seem to be two classes of men (St. Paul's πνευματικοὶ ['those of the spirit'] and σαρκικοὶ ['those of the flesh']); whether *originally different*, there is nothing in the passage to determine; and while there is nothing here or elsewhere in St. John amounting to a statement that the 'carnal' can never become 'spiritual', it does seem to be implied that there are 'spiritual' persons who have never been carnal: who, because already 'born of God', hear God's words as uttered by Christ (8.47).

(b) Is it certain that there is any reference to baptism at all in ὑδαπος ['water' (John 3.5)]? The reference cannot be to John's baptism; yet of what other baptism could Nicodemus if the reference was to baptism at all, be expected to understand it? In the Synoptics there is no appearance of either Jesus or his disciples during his lifetime, baptizing all. Nor from this Gospel should we gather that Jesus at the time of this conversation had begun to baptize: see 3.22; 4.2. There is certainly a great difficulty in supposing that Jesus, as a matter of history, thus at the outset of his career, where (even supposing that he had already baptized) baptism had not yet become the distinctive mark of a Christian society, should have thus referred to it. On the other hand, there is equal difficulty in supposing that ὕδατος ['water'] here does not refer to baptism. There is a corresponding difficulty about 6.53, with regard to the Lord's supper.

(c) According to the interpretation given above, 'water' does indeed convey a reference to baptism, but the baptismal water is regarded simply as a symbol which had become perfectly fused in the mind of the writer with the communication of the 'Spirit' symbolized'. What then, it may be asked, is conveyed by ὕδατος καὶ πνεύματος ['*water and* spirit'] which would not have been conveyed by πνεύματος ['spirit'] simply? The answer is that though πνεῦμα ['spirit'] gains no further significance by being associated with πνεῦμα ['spirit'].[69] If Christ used the words, we must suppose that, intending baptism to be the

initiatory rite of Christian society, he means it to be understood
that the reality which this signified was – not a rational or
sectarian difference such as circumcision represented – but
participation in the Spirit, which was the Father's and his.

If
the words are merely put by the Evangelist into the mouth of
our Lord, the explanation of the addition of ὕδατος ['water']
will be that the Evangelist, finding baptism established as the
initiatory rite of Christian society, wished to gain for it a purely
spiritual significance (as in c.6 for the institution of the Lord's
supper). Perhaps it was the insertion of ὕδατος ['water'], with
such reference and motive here, which led him to represent
Jesus as baptizing in v.22; a representation which, with the
Synoptics before him he bethought himself of correcting in
4.2.

3.8 οὕτως ἐστι πᾶς ὁ γεγεννημένος ἐκ τοῦ πνεύματος ['So is
everyone that is born of the Spirit']. A comparison with wind
must be intended: πνεῖ ['blows'] would not be said merely of
the Spirit. In every one born of the Spirit the operation of the
spirit resembles wind, as described above: since (a) it acts upon
whom it will: Rom. 9.16; 1 Cor. 12.11; below 5.21: (b) its
effects are outward and sensible 'those hearest the same
thereof': comp. Rom. 15.19; 2 Cor. 12.12; Gal. 3.5. (c) but not
so its source and ultimate result; 'thou canst not tell whence it
cometh', etc.

3.12 εἰ τὰ ἐπίγεια (what exists or takes place on earth) εἶπον
ὑμῖν ['If I have told you earthly things'] cannot refer specially
to what goes before, but must refer to the previous teaching of
the Jews generally. It is commonly supposed that τὰ ἐπίγεια
['the earthly things'] refers to the new birth of which our Lord
has already spoken, and which may be called 'earthly' in the
sense that its effects are matter of experience in the world;
while τὰ ἐπουράνια ['heavenly things'] refers to the heavenly
mysteries of which he speaks in the following verses.[70] Meyer,
though he admits this, still thinks that what is described in
vv.5–8 would fall under the designation of ἐπίγεια ['earthly'].
But it is very odd that the 'birth from God' should be described
as an earthly in opposition to a heavenly operation. If it is so
in virtue of effects which are matter of experience to those
living on earth, why should not the same be said of what is
described in vv.13 foll.? Probably in the words τὰ ἐπίγεια
εἶπον ['I have told earthly things'] the writer means our Lord

to be referring, not to any teaching of his recorded in this Gospel, but generally to such exoteric teaching of his as is given in the Synoptics, with which is contrasted such assertion of our Lord's 'heavenly existence' or divine personality as is contained in v.13.

'No one hath ascended up to heaven, but he who had no need to ascend' because he was never not there; even the 'Son of Man' who has descended from heaven, indeed, in the sense of 'becoming flesh' or becoming apprehensible to the senses, but who still, even as you see him and hear him, is in heaven'.

v.14. What is the significance of ὑψωθῆναι ['lifted up']? Does it merely arise out of the comparison between the lifting up of Christ on the cross and the holding up of the brazen serpent before the eyes of Israel? Is the crucifixion here merely thought of as the means by which we are to be delivered from[71] sin? comp. 8.28; 12.32 foll.. And does this delivery, as conveyed by the Evangelist, imply a *substitutory* sacrifice on the part of Christ, a bearing of the penalty for the broken law?

The Evangelist avails himself of the ambiguity in ὑψωθῆναι ['lifted up'] to associate the glorification of Christ in death with the elevation on the cross. The death on the cross is the glorification of Christ as constituting his triumph over the flesh: his return through most intense fleshly humiliation to the Father (7.39; 12.16; 13.31; 17.1 and 5). It is at the same time the deliverance or healing of man, because it is the condition of the communication of the Spirit. In this Gospel death = glorification = resurrection = communication of Spirit: which last is itself spoken of as the glorification of Christ. (16.14). The conception of the death of Christ as a *bearing of our sins* in our stead does not appear in this Gospel. In 1.29 αἴρων need only mean 'taking *away*'. The figure of the lamb is probably taken from Isaiah 53 (whether mediately through the Apocalypse or no,) and the sin is 'taken away' through that communication of the Spirit which comes of, or is identical with, the love born of the sight of the Son exalted through death on the cross to unity with the Father (12.24).

The Evangelist wishes to represent the death of Christ as identical with his return to the Father, which was to be coincident with the sending of the Spirit. Hence he makes the final appearance of the risen Lord an appearance of him as *in process of ascending*[72] (20.17), while the next is accompanied by the gift of the Spirit.

Meyer's interpretation of 20.17 ('Touch me not, for I am not yet ascended to my Father') is that Mary, with an instinctive doubt whether it is Jesus in the flesh that she saw, or only a 'vision', is putting out her hands to feel him, as afterwards Thomas, and that Jesus anticipates her by saying 'Touch me not: you have no need to touch me, for I have not ascended, and hence am not a glorified spirit, which has ascended and descended again, but am still tangible.[73]

This would imply that the ascension made the difference to our Lord between being bodily or tangible, and not being so. Is there any reason to suppose that this was (a) either the fact, or (b) the belief of the early disciples, or (c) the belief of the evangelist?

(a) This question cannot be discussed with any result, because it carries us into a region of miracle in which it is impossible to say what might not be. The account of the ascension, however, (Mark 16.19; Luke 24.51; Acts 1.9–11, especially the latter) represent it as a local removal of our Lord's risen body.

(b) As to the belief of early disciples, the account of St. Paul's conversion implies a belief in a continued existence 'in heaven' of the body with which our Lord rose. It is evident from 1 Cor. 15 that St. Paul believed himself to have seen, long after the 'ascension', just the same body which the apostles saw, i.e. according to the Gospel narrative, the risen body as it was before the ascension.

(c) As to the belief of the Evangelist, he gives no account of any ascension as distinct from the 'return to the Father' which was to be accompanied by the gift of the Spirit, and which it is therefore to be presumed that he considered to have already taken place when our Lord breathes on the disciples and says 'receive ye the Holy Ghost' (20.22). There is nothing corresponding to this in the Synoptics. In the Acts, the gift of the Spirit is the sequel (though not immediate) of the return to the Father as accomplished in the ascension, but this return is quite distinct from the death and resurrection.

The following is a possible explanation of the case. The Evangelist's own conception of the person, life, and death of Jesus implied that his elevation to the Father, of which his return in the Spirit to the believers was but the other side, was accomplished in the death on the cross. The work for which the Word was made flesh was finished. Hence the word τετέλεσται ['It is finished' (John 19.30)], peculiar to this

Gospel. According to this conception, our Lord's death was *ipso facto* resurrection and ascension. But the Evangelist had to deal with a tradition which represented our Lord as appearing under fleshly conditions after the resurrection, and returning to the Father only after an interval of time. Accordingly he reads his own conception into the tradition as best he may, giving it such a form as to represent the return to the Father as *in process* immediately after the tomb was found empty, 'Seek not to hold me with a fleshly grasp,[74] for my ascent, my return to the Father, is not yet accomplished, though it is in process, as you are still my disciples'.[75] In 20.22 this announcement, which was to be made to the disciples, is verified by our Lord's coming to them, according to the promise in 14.18: coming to them in a mode which admitted of no more separation (because he would come as that Spirit of truth which should abide with them for ever), and which implied that our Lord's ascent to the Father was accomplished (16.7). Hence he breathed on them and said 'Receive ye the Holy Ghost' [John 20.22].

Thus the Evangelist, by rendering it symbolical, spiritualizes what was carnal in the tradition of our Lord's appearances after death. The fleshly manifestation to Thomas is turned into a rebuke of the carnal mind which requires such signs. Just as the resurrection and ascension of Christ himself are identified, so far as the tradition of the Church would allow, with the communication of the Spirit, so it is with the resurrection and glorification of the believer. The belief of the early church would seem to have been that Christ was to 'come again' at some point of time, either raising from their graves or bringing with him the righteous or believing dead, finally establishing the Messianic kingdom, from which the wicked are excluded either into torture or destruction. (Daniel 12.2–13; 1 Thess. 4.14 foll.; 2 Thess. 1.8 etc.; Rev. 20.4; 5.12).

In the Epistles to the Romans and Corinthians, no mention is made of any resurrection of the wicked (except in 2 Cor. 5.10). The bodily resurrection is there conceived solely as the complement of the Spiritual, already wrought for those in whom in Christ lives and who live in him (1 Cor. 15.22; 52; Rom. 5.5; 8.11).

So in this Gospel the prevailing idea is (3.36; 5.24; 6.54) that the eternal life, conveyed in the communication of Christ's person, as the Spirit, has some 'quickening of the body', so that it shall never die, for its sequel.

The chief passages to be considered are 11.25 foll., and 5.25–29; 11.22: here Martha has some vague expectation, which she scarcely ventures to express, that Jesus can recall Lazarus from the dead. He replies in a manner which is probably meant to have a double meaning, as at once a statement of the general truth that a quickening of the body is a consequence of the faith which conveys eternal life, and an announcement of the raising of Lazarus to be wrought immediately afterwards, as a sign of this truth; but which, as she understands it, baffles her hope. Hence v.24, which is in effect the expression of resignation in the dashing of her hope. A resurrection 'at the last day' was a regular article of her creed, but was little comfort to her. Jesus then meets her despair by telling her of a present resurrection and life, which he himself is, and which is thus conveyed in that communication of his spiritual person of which faith is the medium. In the following words notions of what we should call physical and spiritual life, and likewise physical and spiritual death, pass into each other.[76] Meyer takes these words to mean 'He that believeth in me, though he be already dead in the body, shall yet live uninterruptedly – before the resurrection, in Paradise, after it eternally; and every one who, being still alive in the body, believes on me, shall live eternally'. This interpretation makes eternal life virtually no more than a continuance of fleshly or physical life, which yet is mysteriously independent of physical death. If the life referred to in ζήσεται ['live'] were eternal life, in the highest spiritual sense (that of 17.3 'this is eternal life, that they may know thee', etc.)[77] The *future* tense would be inappropriate. It is better to take it of that revived bodily life, the quickening of the mortal body[78] (Rom. 8.11) which is indeed (according to the conceptions of St. Paul and this Evangelist) an effect of spiritual life, but is future while the latter is present. Conveying in the words ζῶν καὶ πιστεύων ['*life* and faith'] the life thought of is probably the spiritual life which faith conveys. It is the way of this Evangelist to coordinate verbally ideas which are to him correlative or identical; so with 'water and the spirit'. He who has this principle of life, which is nothing else than myself, – the life, as appropriated by Faith, – is proof against death (in both its forms) for ever.'

To *believe on* Christ, observe, according to this Evangelist, is to receive Christ; to have Christ take up his abode in one as the Spirit: which again is to know God, or the truth which is God: which again is to have eternal life and to be *free.* Comp. 1.12; 5.43; 14.23 for 'receiving' Christ, and for the converse attitude of 'coming' to him 6.37; 7.37.

He in whom (as in Christ) God thus dwells by the Spirit does the works of Christ, which are God's (14.10–12): which = keeping his commandments as he kept the Father's (15.10), which again = sharing the love with which he loved the Father (14.15.).

The Spirit is the Spirit of truth, as Christ is the Truth (14.6 and 17). To be of the truth = to be of God (18.37; 1 Epist. 2.21; 13.19). He that 'doeth truth' is of 'the truth', and accordingly comes to Christ as manifested truth (3.21).

To know the truth (8.32) is to know God (17.3) which is eternal life. To worship God in Spirit and in truth (4.23) is to worship him in virtue of his own presence in us: as St. Paul puts it, to 'pray to him with groanings of the Spirit' (Rom. 8.26).

{*The following notes on the* παρουσία [literally, 'coming'], *or second coming of Christ, are added from the first draft.*}

1. What was the belief of the early disciples as to the 'second coming' of Christ?

2. How, in their belief, was this coming connected with a *resurrection*?

3. What was to be the nature of this resurrection: was it to be of the good only, and how, in their belief is it connected with 'judgment'?

4. How far was their belief in these matters the application to Jesus of a Messianic doctrine received among the Jews?

5. In what sense did Jesus Christ announce a *second coming* of himself to judgment and resurrection (a) according to the Synoptics (b) according to St. John?

In answering (5) the question as to the sense in which Jesus took to himself the title 'Son of man' must be previously settled.

(1) The παρουσία ['coming'], in the shape of the descent of the Lord from heaven is sometimes anticipated during the writer's own life-time: e.g. 1 Thessal. 4.15; 1 Cor. 15.51; it is not so, however, in Phil. 1.23 'to depart and be with Christ'. Sometimes language is used which is applicable to the present and the future

blended: e.g. 1 Thessal. 2.19; 3.13; 5.23 (so James 5.7). The believers are spoken of as already risen Eph. 2, 5 and 6; Coloss. 3.1; as yet to rise Rom. 6.5; 8.11, 17; 8.23; Phil. 3.21; 2 Tim. 2.11. The coming of Christ is distinctly spoken of as future 1 Cor. 11.26 ... τὸν θάνατσν τοῦ Κυρίου καταγγέλλετε, ἄρχις οὗ ἔλθῃ ['...ye do shew the Lord's death till he come']: 1. Cor. 1.17 τὴν αποκάλυψθη τοῦ Κυρίον απεκδεχόμεοι:[79] so Col. 3.4 ὅταν ὁ Χριστὸς φανερώθῃ ['When Christ, who is our life, shall appear,']: 2 Cor. 5.2–4.

According to the Pauline view the import of this 'presence' or 'revelation' of Christ as future to the believer in the full realization in him of the 'Resurrection'. To be raised with Christ is the complement of death with Christ. The believer is already *dead with Christ* in the full sense, and 'quickened' also with him in the Spirit: but there yet remains the 'vile body' to be quickened. *This* quickening is the resurrection which accompanies or is the παρουσία ['coming'] of Christ.

According to Josephus (Ant. 18.11.4, Bell Jud. 2.8.14) the doctrine of the Sadducees was that 'souls die with their bodies': that there is no future existence 'in Hades' with rewards and punishments.[80] The Pharisees and Essenes[81] held otherwise, but said nothing about a *resurrection*. The Sadducees 'say that there is no resurrection', neither angel nor spirit: their question, however, to Christ (Luke 20.27 foll.) is about the *resurrection*, and this they put as if it was future, 'Whose wife shall she be?' In Christ's answer, however, there are no futures: οἱ καταξιωθένες τοῦ αἰῶνος εκεινοῦ ... ἐγείρονται.[82] His 'proof' refers to eternal life, not to a bodily resurrection at all. The ἀνάστασις ['resurrection'] spoken of seems to be only that of the 'just'.

In Luke 16.31 (οὐδὲ ἐὰν τις ἐκ νεκρῶν ἀναστῇ, πεισθήσυνται ['neither will they be persuaded, though one rose from the dead']) the notion is that of a reappearance to those living on earth, which must be 'bodily'...[83]

As to 'judgment', the rewards and punishments which the Pharisees expected were, according to Josephus, to be in *Hades*.

It would seem that the notion of the *resurrection*, as distinct from *immortality*, and as followed by judgment, was at least very vague, except so far as determined by the Messianic belief (Daniel 12. 2–13; Matth. 11.5). 'Judgment', appertaining to the Messiah as the true king of the house of David, may, on the strength of the passage from Daniel, have been by some anticipated as involving a judgment of the raised dead. But it is doubtful whether such an anticipation had any power until the Messianic belief had been partly de-temporalized by the death of Jesus. To the disciples he was the true Messiah; yet not glorified, but humbled, on earth. He is glorified in being raised from the dead; yet this glory is only shown to a few (Acts 10.41). It has yet to be exhibited to all men in the rising of all from the dead through the same communicated power which had raised Jesus. Then the rule and *judgment* of Christ will be exhibited as universal over quick and dead. This faith, however, is still so far temporal that this full glorification of Christ was looked for as a 'second coming' at a definite future moment.

The idea of the kingdom of heaven involves that of judgment. But (1) did Christ himself represent this as coming at some definite future moment? (2) as a personal reign of himself as distinguished from the Spiritual reign of God in the heart.

In Matth. 7.22 Christ represents himself as the judge of fitness to enter the 'kingdom of heaven' 'at that day'. On the other hand (20.23) Christ can promise the sons of Zebedee to suffer with him, but not to *reign*. That shall be given to them for whom it is prepared by his Father. Contrast however with this Matth. 19.28; Luk. 22.29. In Matth. 26.29 he points to a future kingdom when he will drink the wine new, but the kingdom is *his Father's* (comp. Luke 22.18).

The most distinct passage as bearing on a future judgment by Christ is Matth. 25.31: So Matth. 26.64: but here it is ἀπ᾿ ἄρτι ['henceforth']. '*Henceforth* begins the true glory of the Son of man', as reigning spiritually over men *because* put to death in the flesh. This will be a glory which in its effects even you must see.

The *coming* of Christ, even where spoken of as future, is never spoken of as a *second* coming. There is only one coming, which is identical with the full manifestation of the kingdom of God. Where this is placed in a definite future, this future is very near (Matth. 10.23; 24.29 and 34).

We should get a different notion of the 'kingdom', the institution of which is the same as the 'coming of the Son of man', from such passages as Matth. 13.31–33; 6.34; 9.38 (??), Mark 4.27; Luke 17.20 foll.[84] and again from Matth. 12.28; 4.17; 5.10; 18.4.[85]

We are justified in taking these passages of the Synoptics in which our Lord speaks of the kingdom of heaven as spiritual and present – as a ruling consciousness of God – as expressing his essential meaning. From what we know of the Apostolic age these passages were least likely to find their way into Christian tradition, unless they were actually spoken by Jesus Christ. Whether these passages in which he takes to himself, as founder of this kingdom, the Messianic glory described by Daniel the glory of a judge to come in the clouds – where they found their way into the tradition as it was pondered over by men who knew him 'after the flesh', and still thought of his 'glory' as temporal though future, we cannot say.[86]

That the passages from Daniel were what determined the conception of the coming in glory is certain.

In all the passages of the Synoptics, the coming to judgment or in glory is that of the Son of Man. How did Christ apply this title to himself? It first occurs Matth. 8.20 ('the Son of man has not where to lay his head'). It is clear from Matth. 16.13 that he did not use it primarily to indicate the Messianic office: (this is expressed by the title 'Son of God' or 'Christ') though he came to declare that he, as *Son of man*, was the true Messiah (Matth. 26.64).[87]

The title (leaving out of consideration the fourth Gospel) under which Christ presents himself as Messiah is 'Son of God'. The title 'Son of man' did not carry with it the idea of his being the Messiah (Matth. 16.13 etc.) The knowledge that the Son of man was the Son of God was specially commended in Peter. That with the Jews it was understood that the Χριστός ['Christ, anointed one'] was Son of God is certain (Matth. 26.63). Some try to make out that this was not so, because they think that 'Son of God' carried with it all the theological associations that it now does. But it is clear that they understood the Messiah as simply equivalent to the 'Son of God'. In the fourth Gospel, from the association of Christ with the title μονογηνὴς υἱός ['only-begotten son'] the words 'Son of God' do carry the ideas of pre-existence and all the ideas associated with the λὸγος ['Word'], but not so to the Jews. In the Old Testament we have Genesis 6.2, 4, where the 'Sons of God' was identical with the children of Seth, or good people. In Job 1.6; 2.1 {the 'sons of God' are the angels.} 'Israel' as one person is spoken of as the son of God (Exod. 4.22, 23; Hosea 11.1). In Psalms 2.7; 45.5, 6[88] the righteous king is spoken of as God, and Jehovah as God of him. In Psalm 81.6 (referred to in John 10.34) it refers to the rulers of Israel. (Comp.

Is[aiah] 9.6). It is clear that the scribes meditating on such passages might naturally think of the Messiah as the Son of God, without attaching our significance to the title, having the idea of the eternal sonship of the λόγος. It was not by them associated with any idea other than that of an earthly and temporal rule.

The characteristic title which Christ takes to himself is 'Son of man'. Using the title of himself, and also coming to assert himself as the Messiah, though not at first, the title 'Son of man' would then recall Daniel 7.13: comp. Rev. 1.13; 14.14. According to the Synoptics he ultimately applied to himself the language of Daniel (Matth. 26.63). Then, after his rejection, crucifixion, and resurrection, the title 'Son of man' would carry the notion of coming again in glory to judgment: but whether he so meant it is another question. He no doubt spoke of himself as introducing a kingdom of heaven, carrying the idea of judgment as to fitness to enter it: but whether he represented it as coming at some definite future time, or as a personal reign of himself as distinct from a spiritual reign in the hearts of men, is doubtful. On the one hand we have Matth. 20.23, on the other 19.28: comp. Rev. 2.26; 3.21. In Matth. 26.29 he points to a future kingdom, but it is his Father's. Here certainly the kingdom, the institution of which he is the coming of the Son of Man, is future; but elsewhere it appears as present (12.28; 5.10; 18.4; Luke 17.30 etc.) The coming of the Son of man, then, in the Synoptics is equivalent to the establishment of the kingdom of heaven; there is no mention of another coming.[89]

The παρουσία ['coming'] of the Fourth Gospel.

The notion of the παρουσία ['coming'] in the Apostolic age, determined partly by the received ideas of the Messianic reign [of Christ] in judgment and transferred to the crucified and risen Jesus, is considerably modified in the transference, partly by our Lord's own language, which is sometimes present, sometimes future. We may suppose that our Lord, growing in wisdom, having first spoken of himself (the true Son of man) as introducing a true kingdom of heaven by his life on earth, afterwards conceived of this kingdom as a reign in the spirits of men which should first begin upon his death, and in this sense applied to himself the words of Daniel. If this was his meaning, it was not apprehended by the original disciples, who expected a half-spiritual, half-sensible return in the clouds of heaven. Then St.

Paul gives a new meaning to the παρουσία ['coming'] by treating it as that full and final manifestation of Christ which is to complete the work of the resurrection by the 'redemption of the body'.

In the fourth Gospel (omitting all mention of 5.28–29) the παρουσία ['coming'] is represented as the present indwelling of the Spirit, the gift of the παράκλητος ['advocate'], which is the return of Christ in glory without the veil of the flesh, present and in the Spirit, not future and outward. And all the notions of the παρουσία ['coming'] in the Apostolic age, judgment, resurrection, the αποκάλυψις ['manifestation'] of divine glory, the φανέρωσις ['evidencing'] of God, are all involved in the gift of the spirit. The true meaning of παράκλητος is advocate, a person who represents another ('We have a παράκλητος with the Father, Jesus Christ the righteous', etc.): thus the Spirit is the παράκλητος as representing at once God to the believer and the believer to God.

In chapter 14.3 the present tense πάλιν ἔρχομαι ['I come again'][90] is represented in vv.16 and 18 as the giving of ἄλλον παρακλητον ['another Comforter' (John 14.16)], the Spirit, which already dwells in the person of the believer, or the coming of both the Father and the Son in the Spirit (v.23, 'we will come' etc). That what is communicated in the mind of Christ (which is the mind of God) is clear from 16.14; and 1 Cor. 2.16; 2 Cor. 3.17 ('we have the mind of the Lord': 'the Lord is the Spirit', etc.).

As Christ, as the Eternal Son, the Word, is the presence of the παράκλητος ['Comforter'], so the παράκλητος is Christ, as in bringing us into relation with God (comp. 1 Epist. 2.1; Rom. 8.26). This coming of Christ in the Spirit takes the place of the manifestation to witness of Acts 10.41, and of the manifestation to all men in the final coming to judgment and resurrection. There is only one 'seeing again', and that is a permanent one, identical with the presence of the Spirit of Truth (16.22 and 23; comp. vv.15 and 16). This manifestation is to be 'at that day'. This is the received word for the time of the 'second coming' (2 Thess. 1.10; 2 Tim. 1.12; Acts 2.20). According to the representation of this Evangelist, however 'that day' is to come immediately on the withdrawal of Christ in death to the Father (16.17; comp. vv. 20, 23).

Here we are met with a difficulty. Whereas in this Gospel Christ, as the Son, has a perfect continuity of consciousness with the Father (14.28; 17.5). If we ask was this a separation to our

Lord's own consciousness (which would seem inconsistent with the full immanence of God), or only to the consciousness of believers, who could not fully see the Father in him, we must answer that the two notions are blended. The glory of Christ is only full as a recognized glory; his presence to the Father and the Father's to him is only complete when it means the presence also of gathered mankind in Christ to the Father, and the Father's to them (14.2, 3; 17.24). This presence is realized through the indwelling of Christ.

The gift of the Spirit comes directly upon Christ's sacrifice, through the communication in the flesh (σὰρξ ἐγένετο) was necessary as the condition of the reception of the true light, yet it is only through the withdrawal from the flesh that this spirit becomes fully communicable. The death of Christ is thus conceived of under two modes: (1) as such a withdrawal from the manifestation in the flesh to the fullness of the divine life, as draws with it into that higher element the belief set upon him while in the flesh, and (2) as a perfect act of love (15.13) which is the condition of the attraction conceived of in the first mode.

On his death follows the communication of the Spirit, symbolized in the *efflux of blood and water*.[91]

Then the coming of the Spirit follows without any distinct separation on the withdrawal from the flesh and takes the place of the carnal παρουσία ['coming']. It is a coming to *judgment* (16.8, 11). The Spirit as the full manifestation of Christ convinces of *sin*, by setting his glory in full contrast to the darkness which prevented its recognition. The world, *as the world*, has to recognize its darkness, but cannot be rid of it.

Of *righteousness*, namely of the perfect righteousness of the Son, vindicated by his withdrawal to the Father away from *fleshly* sight. This righteousness is primarily that of the Son, but *communicated*: not however to the world *as the world*: to it, it remains an external righteousness to be convinced of.

Of *judgment*, because the power of the evil one is broken in that which is the very element or vehicle of his power, namely 'this world', or 'the flesh'. It is broken (1) by the manifestation of the Son in that element; (2) by the demonstration that the Son, though *in it*, is not *holden of it*: but through *death*, through the process in which his dominion of the earth seemed most absolute, passes to the Father. In this passing he carries the believers with him. In one sense they are still in the world, and have tribulation in it: but it is *overcome* even for them. They are for ever passing from it to God, and God to them, in the Spirit.

The piercing of the side is related as explanatory of the fact that the limbs were not broken, as was usual, and thus showing the anti-typal relationship of *Christ and the Paschal Lamb*, of which no bone shall be broken. No doubt this is one great purpose of this Gospel, connected with the controversy at the beginning of the second century as to the continuation of the Passover. Note that whereas in the Synoptical account Christ eats the Passover, is apprehended that evening, and not crucified till the next morning, here there is no mention of the Passover: the supper takes place before the feast, and the crucifixion is regarded as taking place on the day of the Passover (18.28) on the morning of which Christ is taken from Caiaphus to Pilate, but the Paschal supper was not yet eaten.

This fact is made much of in the controversy as to the authorship of the Gospel, because the sect among the Judaic Christians who recognized the obligations of continuing to keep the Paschal supper on the evening of the 14th Nisan pleaded the authority of John, who was said to have kept up the custom which he had observed with Christ. So far as it can be made out that John was the authority for the Quartodecimanus,[92] it follows that he cannot have written this account.

There is a dispute as to the reference in 1.29 of the words 'Lamb of God'. Is the Paschal lamb meant, or is there merely a reference to Isaiah 53.7, where the expression is φέρειν ['to bring'], not αἴρειν ['to take away'], τὰς ἁμαρτίας ['the sins']? Αἴρειν in this Gospel means everywhere 'to take away' 2.16; 10.18; 11.39, 48; 15.2; 16.22; 17.15; 19.15, 38. The comparison of Christ to the Paschal lamb is found again 1 Cor. 5.7; 1 Pet. 1.14.

Thus it might be expected that the Gospel, according to its main idea, would end with c.19 [i.e. John 19]. But the writer had to deal with the received tradition of the appearance of Christ under fleshly conditions after the resurrection.

These are related with three main purposes. (1) To illustrate the spirituality of the risen body. St. Paul conceived of a σῶμα πνευματικὸν [spiritualised body], and so does this writer. (2) To reprove the carnal nature which requires a sensuous testimony as represented by Thomas. (3) To represent the risen Christ as the imparter of the Spirit.

(1) The appearance to Mary Magdalene (20.13 foll.) v.17 ('Touch me not') must be considered with reference to Matthew 28.9 ('they

took hold of his feet and worshipped him'). Probably the writer had this account before him, and wished to give it a different character, to illustrate the spirituality of the risen body, and his own idea that the return to the Father took place all but immediately upon the death of the flesh. So μήμου ἅπτου seems to represent a haste to be away: he will not be holden in a fleshly grasp in the process of passing to the Father which is regarded as now going on. But the disciples are to be told that he is in that process.[93]

Probably the Gospel ended at 20.29, and most characteristically. It is generally admitted that ch. 21 is an addition, not from the hand of the original writer. The writer of ch. 21 evidently (from v.22) expected a 'second coming' in the ordinary sense. That he was not the author of the rest appears (1) from vv.30, 31 of the previous chapter. These must obviously form the original ending. If the continuation had been by the original author, he would, on continuing, have cancelled these verses. (2) In v.24 the writer speaks of 'him who wrote these things' as another person: '*we* (that is some collection of disciples) know that his testimony is true: contrast the words '*he* knoweth', of 19.35, where the author is speaking of himself. (3) In v.20 the designation of 'the disciple whom Jesus loved' as 'he that leaned on his breast' is clearly by a later hand. To the original author such a designation would have been superfluous: comp. 13.25; 18.15; 19.26; 20.3. It appears from Irenaeus Adv. Haer. 3.1 and elsewhere that in Asia Minor ὁ ἐπὶ τὸ στῆθος αὐτοῦ ἀναπεσών ['he who had leaned upon His breast'][94] was a standing appellation for John: taken, probably, from 13.25. If so, it (? implies) a use of this Gospel. (4) The scene of ch.21 is laid in Galilee: and yet no explanation is given of the shifting from Jerusalem. Elsewhere the author of this Gospel is very precise about local transitions (comp. 1.44; 2.12; 4.3 and 43; 6.1; 7.10; 10.40; 11.54).

V.25 is admitted to be apocryphal: yet Origen took it as belonging to the original.[95]

The phraseology of this chapter varies in several particulars from that of the rest of the Gospel.

Most critics are agreed on the spuriousness of ch. 21; but if ch. 21 is an appendix, we may carry the spuriousness back to the 30th and 31st verses of ch. 20, which are feeble, and have the air of being written by an editor wishing to conciliate this Gospel with the Synoptics.

The Gospel however is found in all MSS in the form in which we possess it, with the exception of the beginning of ch. 8.

May not the editors or appended ch. 21, have made other additions such as 5.29?

For, apart from this passage, as (according to this Evangelist) spiritual life carries physical, so it would seem that spiritual death carries physical (see 8.21; 24; 12.25; 15.6; 6.27). What is it that should live in the wicked? That which 'is from above?' But they have it not. 'The earthly' element? But that 'passes away' (παράγεται, 1 Epist. 2.17). It may be said that even wicked men have something in them 'from above'. So far as they have they are not wicked.

In 8.56 ('your father Abraham rejoiced to see my day') there is no mention of a *Hades.*

In 5.20 the 'greater works' which are to incite marvel are the giving of spiritual life, in contrast with the physical σημεῖον ['sign'] of a miracle (as in 14.12). In v.28 the 'marvel' is to be excited by a future resurrection from the tomb, in contrast with the spiritual resurrection.

It is true that in v.25 the physically dead are represented as to live (in the future): but this is a physical revival following on the spiritual one of v.24; and it is a revival *continuous and already in the act of beginning* (ἔρχεται ὥρα και νῦν ἐστι ['The hour is coming, and now is']: comp. 4.23; 14.20. 23 (?). So in 11.25 those already dead (in the body) will live *physically* in virtue of that belief which already is equivalent to eternal life. The raising of Lazarus is an instance of this. According to St. Paul those who were already dead (in the body) would be raised to partake in that glorified bodily life which to those who were 'alive and remained' would mean exemption from physical death. With Paul, however, this is a complement of work already done. So with this Evangelist. But as with him the expectation of a παρουσία ['presence'] at a definite future time is replaced by a belief in a παρουσία already begun in the coming of the Paraclete [John 14.16; 1 John 2.1], so the expectation of 'change in the vile body' [Phil. 3.21] of those physically alive and the revival of the physically dead as *future*, gives way to a belief in a present eternal life, which already in some way involves a *physical* life. The σημεῖον ['sign'] of this is the raising of Lazarus [John 11.1–45].

But in 5.29 the ἀνάστασιν ζωῆς ['resurrection of life'] of believers is only a consequence upon that future physical revival which they are to share with the wicked. This, in contrast with the view uniformly presented elsewhere in this Gospel; is ὕστερον πρότερον.

With the φυνή of 5.29, contrast 10.16 (they (the sheep), have my voice).

Elsewhere in this Gospel 'the last day' (ἐσχάτη ἡμέρα) is already spoken of in connection with the raising of believers, except in 12.48 ('he that rejecteth me, and receiveth not my sayings, hath one that judgeth him: the word that I have spoken, that shall judge him on the last day'). In the passage in ch.6 (vv.40, 44, 45) it does not seem wanted, because eternal life has been spoken of as already given, and may merely mean some final manifestation of this life, according to the Pauline notion.

---

[1] [Headed: 'Copies of Lectures made by C. B. Green & Mr. Ormerod.' Charlotte Byron Green (1842–1929), social activist and reformer, sister of Green's great friend, John Addington Symonds, married Green in 1871. Probably Rev. George Thomas Bailey Ormerod (1846–1916), educated at Harrow, then Balliol 1864–7, barrister, 1870, ordained 1872.]

[2] [The Prologue is identified at the beginning of this piece as John 1:1–11, however in fact Green deals with vv.1–14.]

[3] [These lectures go far beyond these three areas, running to a total of 102 pages in the fair copy from which the present text is taken.]

[4] {*Insert at the beginning (from Mr. Bradley's article.)*} [Presumably the author is Andrew Cecil Bradley. The article has not been identified.]

[5] [Gen. 1.3. Origen, 'In Genesum. Homiliae Prima' ['Commentary on Genesis. First Homily'], in J.P. Migne (ed.), *Patrologiae cursus completes, series graeca: Col. 12 Origenes Opera Omnia, Tomus Secundus* (Paris: Garnier, 1862), pp.146–7. Origen, *Contra Celsum*, trans. H Chadwick (Cambridge University Press, 1965), bk 2, chap. 9, p.73.]

[6] ['Through faith we understand that the worlds were framed by the word of God, so that things which are seen were not made of things which do appear.' (Heb. 11:3).]

[7] [Targum: 'The name, meaning 'translation', given to the Aramaic interpretative translations of the O[ld] T[estament] made when Hebrew has ceased to be the normal medium of speech among the Jews.' EA Livingstone (ed.), *The Oxford Dictionary of the Christian Church*, 3rd ed. (Oxford University Press, 1997), p.1577.]

[8] [Probably a reference to two prologues of the apocryphal book 'Wisdom of Jesus the Son of Sirach, or Ecclesiasticus'.]

[9] [The quotation from Bradley ends at this point.]

[10] *{The words actually written by Mr. Green have been exactly repeated except in a very few cases where a slight alteration appeared necessary.*

The second set of lectures has, where necessary, been supplemented by the first. PP.1–8 are almost entirely from the first set.

The references have been verified, sometimes rearranged, and, in one or two instances, corrected, except in two places where I have as yet been unable to lay my hand on the passages quoted.

Matter obviously parenthetical has generally been put into a note: matter apparently subordinate to or illustrative of the main current of the lectures has been written a little distance off the margin. H.N.}

[The words 'as yet' in the third paragraph of this note imply that HN intends these comments to be used by RLN as editor. Clearly HN envisages doing more work on the notes, and the copyist did not feel the notes were for her, or else she would not have included them in this fair version.]

11   [For Philo of Alexandria (c.20BC–c.40AD), Hellenized Jew. Green's references are to the marginal numbers in Mangey's edition of Philo's writings where Mangey includes them. Otherwise he gives pages references in the relevant volume of Mangey's edition. (*Philonis... Opera Omnia Graece et Latine. Ad editionem Th. Mangey collatis aliquot MSS. edenda curavit AF Pfeifer*, 5 tom. (Argentoati: Erlangae, 1785–92).)]

12   [Philo, *De Opifico Mundi* [On the Creation], in *Philo*, with English trans. by FH Colson and GH Whitaker, 10 vols. (London: William Heinemann, 1929), vol. 1, §35 (pp.26, 27).]

13   [Philo, *De Opifico Mundi,,* §29 (pp.22, 23).]

14   [Philo *De Vita Mosis* [On The Life of Moses], in Mangey, ed., *Philonis*, p.672.]

15   [Philo, *De Posteritate Caini* [On the Posterity and Exile of Cain], in *Philo*, with English trans. by FH Colson and GH Whitaker, 10 vols. (London: William Heinemann, 1929), vol.2.]

16   [This refers to the Stoic distinction between λόγος ἐνδιάθετος (the Word as He was in God) and λόγος προφορικὸς (the Word as He emanated from God).]

17   ['Pseudo-Clementine', 'The Clementine Homilies', in Alexander Roberts and James Donaldson, eds., *Ante-Nicene Christian Library: Translations of the Writings of the Fathers: Volume 8 The Twelve Patriarchs ...,*. (Edinburgh: T & T Clark, 1870), Homily 17 (pp.257–273) has the chapter headings: chap. 7 'Man in the Shape of God' (pp.261–2), chap. 10 'The Nature and Shape of God' (pp.264–5), and chap. 11 'The Fear of God' (pp.265–6).]

18   [Quintus Septimius Florens Tertullianus, *Treatise on the Incarnation*, ed. and trans. Ernest Evans (London: SPCK, 1956), chap. 11, §§20–21, pp.42–43.]

19   [QSF Tertullian, 'The Five Books Against Marcion' [aka *Adversus Marcionem*], in Alexander Roberts and James Donaldson (eds), *Ante-Nicene Christian Library: Translations of the Writings of the Fathers: Volume 3 Latin Christianity. Its Founder, Tertullian. Three Parts: 1. Apologetic; 2. Anti-Marcion; 3. Ethical* (Edinburgh: T & T Clark, 1870), bk 1, chap. 25 'God is Not a Being of Simple Goodness; Other attributes Belong to Him. Marcion Shows Incosistency in the Portraiture of His Simply Good and Emotionless God'; bk 2, chap. 27 'Other Objections Considered. God's Condescension in the Incarnation Nothing Derogatory to the Divine Being in this Economy. The Divine Majesty Worthily Sustained by the Almighty Father, Never Visible to Man. Perverseness of the Marconite Cavils.']

20   ἐξῆλθον παρὰ τοῦ πατρὸς ['I came forth out of the Father'] in 16.28 need not be taken of the process by which the λόγος, from being ἐνδιάθετος ['intelligible'], became προφορικὸς [manifest]; it probably only refers to the other side of the same act as ἐλήλυθα εἰς τὸν κόσμον ['I am come into the world'], namely manifestation in flesh.

21   [Philo, [*De Opifico Mundi*], §2, pp.21–23.]

22 [The Loeb edition (from which this translation is taken) has 'κόσμον' rather than 'οὐρανοῦ' (Philo, *De Opifico Mundi*, §7, pp.20, 21).]

23 [The Valentinians were followers of Valentinus (fl. 120–160AD), whose Gnostic doctrines were condemned by the Church Fathers, including Ireaneus.]

24 [Irenaeus, 'Against Heresies', in Alexander Roberts and WH Rambaut, trans., *The Writings of Irenaeus* (Edinburgh: T & T Clark, 1868), bk 1, chap. 1, pp.4–5. I have slightly adapted the translation, to better reflect Green's text.]

25 ['Give me wisdome that sitteth by thy Throne, and reject me not from among thy children:' (Wisdom 9.4). Luther, among others, attributed the apocryphal Book of the Wisdom of Solomon to Philo. Martin Luther, '[Comment on] Hebrews 11:3', in Jaroslav Pelikan (ed.) *Works of Martin Luther*, 55 vols. (Saint Louis: Concordia Publishing House, 1958–86), vol. 29, p.231.]

26 In many passages of the New Testament πρὸς with accusative seems to be used in the same sense as παρὰ with dative in classical Greek: e.g. Matt. 13.56 (= Mark 6.3): Mark 9.19: 1 Cor. 16.6: Gal. 1.18: 4.18.

27 [Origen, 'Commentary on the Gospel of John' (trans. Allan Menzies), in A. Menzies (ed.), *The Ante-Nicene Fathers, translations of the Fathers down to AD325: Volume 10 The Gospel of Peter...* (Edinburgh: T & T Clark, 1887), Book 2, §2.]

28 ['Ye have heard how I said unto you, I go away, and come again unto you. If ye loved me, ye would rejoice, because I said, I go unto the Father: for my Father is greater than I.' (John, 14.28)]

29 Philo's notion of a primary ὄλη δυμαμένη πάντα γενέσθι, and παθητικὸν: this κινηθὲν καὶ σχηματισθὲν καὶ Ψοχωθὲν ὑπὸ τοῦ νοῦ; μετέβαλεν εἰς τὸ τελειοτάυτον ἔργον, τὸνδε, τὸν κόσμον. This κόσμος ['world'] is opposed to κόσμος νοητὸς ['intelligible world'], which = ὁ κατὰ τὴν γένεσιν κόσμος [since the start of the world]. Philo, however, by no means confines himself to γίγνεσθαι ['come into existence'] to express the origin of the world, but also uses κατεσκευάσθη ['built', or, as here, 'compounded']: De Cherubim §35 εὑρήσεις, αἴστον μὲν του κόσμου τὸν Θεὸν, ὑφ' οὗ γέγονεν ὕλην δὶ τὰ τέσσαρα στοιχεῖα, ἐξ ὡν συνεκράθη' ὄργονον δὲ λόγου Θεοῦ, δὶ οὗ κατεσκευάσθη' τῆς δὲ κατασκευῆς αἰτίαν τὴν ἀγαθότητα τοῦ δημιουργοῦ. ['We shall see that its [the Universe's] cause is God, by whom it has come into being, its material the four elements, from which it was compounded, its instrument the word of God, through which it was framed, and the final cause of the building is the goodness of the architect.' Philo, *De Cherubim* ['On the Cherubim'], in *Philo*, 10 vols., trans. FH Colson and Whitaker (London: William Heinemann, 1929), vol. 2, §35, p.83.]

30 [The phrase occurs at John 16.11, but Green may also have in mind Eph. 6.11–12: 'Put on the whole armour of God, that ye may be able to stand against the wiles of the devil./For we wrestle not against flesh and blood, but against principalities, against powers, against the rulers of darkness of this world, against spiritual wickedness in high *places*.']

31 {See note on p.15. H.N.} [Page 144 here.]

32 This is Ewald's view of the sequence of thought in the Prologue. [Georg Heinrich August Ewald (1803–1875), Professor of oriental languages and exegesis at Göttingen and Tübingen. See his *Geschichte des Ausgange Des Volkes Israel Und Des Nachapostolischen Zeitalters*, 2nd ed., 7 vols. (Göttingen, 1858–9), vols. 5 and 6.]

[33] Comp. Epist. 1 5.20 [1 John 5.20], a passage about which there is an old controversy as to whether οὗτος ['this'] represents the immediately preceding 'Son Jesus Christ', or the Father, 'him that is true', of the previous clause. No doubt the latter is the true interpretation. The notion of the Father as 'the true God', revealed in the Son, governs the whole passage, and οὗτος would be the most naturally referred to it, apart from other considerations. But it is quite against the 'Johannine' way of thinking to speak of the Son directly as ἀληθινὸς Θεὸς ['the true God'], or immediately as eternal life. Eternal life is in him, he manifests it to us, through him we have the 'eternal life', which consists in knowledge of God through Christ (17.3); but nowhere, not even in 1.4, or Epist. 1.2 [1 John 1.2] does he say 'the Word or the Son is eternal life'. The only passage which favours the other view is 11.25 'This – the God in whom we are through being in his Son Jesus Christ, and whom, through the Son we Know, is the true God and eternal life'.

[34] The object of v.3 may be to oppose the Gnostic and Alexandrine notion of a ὕλη ['fuel'] not originating in God, though worked on by him (or rather of the δημιουργὸς ['builder'] under limitation arising from its inherent nature. (See note on p.7.)

[35] In Epist. 1 1.5 we have the expression ὁ Θεὸς φῶς ἐστι ['that God is light' (1 John 1.5)] – But in the Gospel the *light* is always assigned to the Word or Son, naturally, as the manifestation is especially the (this, the?) Word as incarnate.

[36] This is all based on the punctuation followed in the English version, 'in him was life'. There are however two other ways of punctuating the passage (v.3) ['any thing that was made in him was life' (John 1.3–4)] (a) οὐδὲ ἑν΄ γέγονεν ἐν αὐτῷ, ζωὴ ἦν. (b) οὐδὲ ἐν ὃ γέγονεν ἐν αὐτῷ, ζωὴ ην. (a) is the Valentinian way of taking the passage, adopted by Bunsen and Hilgenfeld (Einleitung, note on p.710). According to the Valentinians ζωὴ ['life'] and λόγος ['the Word'] were συζύγες begotten by νοῦς ['spirit'] and ἀλήθεια ['truthfulness'], as these again were by Βύθος ['depth'] and σιγὴ ['silence']. With this reading, life is presented as a γένεσις by or out of the Word; as the summary of the πάντα γιγνόμενα ['all things ... that were made' {John 1.3}] of the previous verse, instead of as (with the reading of the English translation) immanent in the word. Hilgenfeld (I suppose) would consider the object of the passages as of the rest of the Prologue, adopting Valentinian terminology, to concentrate all the Valentinian συζυγίαι [bonds], the whole eternal γένεσις ['birth'] represented by them, in the 'Word'; which again is identified with the person of Jesus, and through this identification becomes a presentation of God under moral and spiritual attributes.

Meyer's objection to this reading chiefly depends on the impropriety of the tense ἦν ['was']; but this is removed by the reading of the [Codex] Sinaiticus, ἐν αὐτῷ ζωὴ ἐστιν ['In him life is' (John 1.4)]. If however ἐστιν ['is'] be adopted for ἦν ['was'], what difference is intended between it and the following ἦν ['was']? Perhaps ἦν ['was'] would indicate the historical manifestation to man – a manifestation which took place in time, whether at the creation of man, or in the 'providences', or in the incarnation of the Word, as opposed to the eternal subsistence of life in the Word. [Christian Carl Josias von Bunsen (1791–1860), German diplomat, prolific amateur theologian, and critic of FC Baur. Adolf Bernhard Christoph Hilgenfeld, *Histor-kriticshe Einleitung in das Neue Testament* (1875). Hilgenfeld (1823–1907) was a moderate member of the Tübingen school so greatly admired by Green. Heinrich August Wilhelm Meyer, *Das Neue Testament Grieschisch nach den besten Hülfsmitteln kritisch revidirt* ..., 2 vols. (Göttingen: Vandenhoeck und Ruprecht, 1829). Meyer (1800–73) also edited *Kritisch-exegetischer Kommentar zum Neuen Testament*, 16 vols. (Göttingen: Vandenhoeck und Ruprecht, 1832–1859; English trans., 20 vols. 1873–95). Green's copy of the German New Testament (*Das Neue Testament…sterotypirt nach der Hallischen Ausgabe* (London: Samuel Bagster, ca.1840?)) survives among his papers at Balliol (see Thomas, *Moral Philosophy of TH Green*, p.386).]

37 Probably not 'understood', although it might be argued from οὐκ ἔγνω ['knew him not' (John 1.10)] of v.10 that this was the meaning. Doubtless, what the two verses are intended to convey is the same, but οὐ κατέλαβ conveys it under a different figure, while οὐ κατέλαβε conveys it directly. There is in v.10 no idea of 'light'. Καταλαμβάνειν means to 'understand' only in the middle in the New Testament (Acts 4.13, 10.34, 25.25, and Eph. 3.13); but in classical and Alexandrine Greek, the active is also so used. In Evang. 12.35 ἵνα μὴ σκοτία ὑμᾶς καταλάβῃ ['knoweth not wither he goeth'], it means 'to get the better of': so Rom. 9.30. In Phil. 3.12 and 13 to 'attain', 'overtake'. Origen (Tom. 2 §22) suggests the idea that καταλάβε here may mean 'did not overtake when pursuing it': or 'did not catch it when lying in wait for it'. [*The Commentary of Origen on S. John's Gospel*, ed. A.E. Brooke, 2 vols. (Cambridge University Press, 1896), vol. 2, Book 2, §27 (22) pp.92–3.]

38 [MS alt.: 'the?'.]

39 [MS alt.: '?the'.]

40 [MS alt.: '?14?.']

41 5.36, 10.25.

42 [Possibly an allusion to 1 John 2.17: 'And the world passeth away, and the lust thereof: but he that doeth the will of God abideth for ever.']

43 This may be taken to explain in what sense, according to this Evangelist, the κόσμον ['world'] is evil. Not 'evil' as it is to God, as that which is what it really is only 'through him', or in relation to him; only evil as it is for the consciousness of man, who does not recognize the God in it, but regards it simply as a means of satisfying his own selfishness. The world then as 'necessarily evil' means really for the Evangelist either the world as misunderstood and misused by man, or man as thus misunderstanding and misusing it.

44 [MS alt.: '?which?'.]

45 In all passages where ἦν is used with the present participle it expresses a continuous act or state. {*The Revised Version translates* 'There was the true light, even the light which lighteth every man coming into the world.' H.N.}

46 [Probably references to Ewald, *Geschichte des Ausgange.*, and FC Baur, *Geschichte der christlichen Kirche*, 5 band (Leipzig: Tubingen, 1863).]

47 [Probably Adolf Hilgenfeld, *Das Evangelium und die Briefe Johannis nach ihrem Lehregriff Dargestellt* (Halle: CEM Pfeffer, 1849).]

48 In 4.22 ἡμεῖς προσκυνοῦμεν, etc. ['Ye worship ye know not what: we know what we worship: for salvation is of the Jews'] is commonly taken, as of the Jews generally (in opposition to the Samaritans) with whom our Lord for the time identified himself. But it is more likely that ἡμεῖς ['ye'] means our Lord and his disciples, who knew the Father through him, in opposition to ὑμεῖς ['ye' plural], which includes both Jews and heathens. 'For salvation is of the Jews' will then mean that salvation has its outward origin with the Jews, since I that speak unto you, who bring the true knowledge of the God whom you (Jews and Samaritans) unknowingly worship, am according to the flesh a Jew (comp. Rom. 1.3). It would be against the tenor of the passage above quoted, and in particular of 8.54–5, to take 'we know' etc as implying a knowledge of God on the part of the Jews as such

in virtue of the Law or Old Covenant. The whole idea of the Gospel is that it was an unknown God who was worshipped till the Son declared, 1.18.

49 ['Simple' is the MS reading, but what is probably intended is '…that sin by the commandment might become exceeding sinful' (Rom. 7:13).]

50 Compare the change of tenses in v.4 according to Tischendorf's reading, ζωὴ ἐστι ['is life'] ζωὴ ἦν ['was life']; and in v.5 φαίνει ['shines'] κατέλαβε ['comprehended']. [Constantinus Tischendorf, *Novum Testmentum Graece* (Lipsiae: Giesecke & Devrient, 1870–1), vol. 1, fasc.1.]

51 The words 'Son of God' were not originally understood to imply any 'equality with God' (comp. 5.19 οὐ δύναται ὁ υἱὸς ποιεῖν ἀφ' ἐαυτοῦ οὐδὲν ['The son can do nothing of himself']), but meant merely the 'Messiah' as the King who should be the son: who should be fully what David had only been partially. Comp. 10.33 *{? As compared with 10.36? H.N.}*

52 That there are fuller and less full degrees or realizations of Sonship appears from 1 Epist. 3.2.

53 *{These words are marked with notes of query by Mr. Green. H.N.}*

54 Meyer says that the plural αἱμάτων ['bloods'] is only used for the singular by the substitution for the material of the elements of which it is composed.

55 ['Paraclete' is a broad transliteration of the Greek word παράκλητον (also 'the Comforter') (John 14.16; 1 John 2.1), and means 'one sent to assist.']

56 [MS orig.: 'sensuous signs'.]

57 [Pages 151–2 from 'This "truth"…'.]

58 See 1.46; 6.42 (the Son of Joseph): 2.12; 7.3 and 5 (his brethren).

59 *{These words, ἀπ' ἄρτι, are not in the best MSS. and are omitted in the revised version. They occur Matth. 26.64: ἀπ' τοῦ νῦν ['hereafter'], Luke 22.69. H.N.}*

60 Here [i.e. John 14.17] πὰρ ὑμῖν ['dwelleth with'] is explained as = ἐν ὑμῖν ['dwelleth among']: on p.24 the two phrases have been contrasted. The force of a preposition is not a fixed quantity, but depends on contrast and connection. Here (1.14) the force of ἐν ['among'] is determined by ἐσκήνωσεν ['dwelt']: in 14.17 it is determined by the contrast with παρά. In 14.17 Ewald would read μενεῖ with [the] Vulg[ate]. There is a doubt about the meaning of ἐντὸς ὑμῶν Luke 17.21.

61 The Church tradition that John was the disciple who lay on Jesus' breast at supper, proves nothing, for it may have been derived from the Gospel.

62 [MS alt.: 'did not mean to pass for'.]

63 [MS reads: 'personally'.]

64 [MS alt.: 'Paraclete'.]

65 [John 19.35] ἵνα πιστεύητε ['that [ye] may believe'] must be taken either directly with λέγει ['he saith'], or καὶ ἀληθινὴ ['and is true'] – λέγει ['he saith'] being taken as a parenthesis, with μεμαρτύρηκε ['bare record'].

66 [MS orig.: 'came to the same thing'.]

67 Justin, Apol. 1.61 ὁ Χριστὸς εἶπεν, ἂν μὴ ἀναγεννηθῆτε, οὐ μὴ εἰσέλθετε εἰς τὴν βασίλειαν τῶν οὐρανῶν. Ὅτι δὲ καὶ ἀδύνατον εἰς τὰς μήτρας τῶν τεκουσῶν τοὺς ἅπαξ γεννωμένους ἐμβῆναι φαμερὸν πᾶσιν ἐστι. ['Christ said, "Except ye be born again, ye shall not enter into the kingdom of heaven." [John 3.3] Now, that it is

impossible for those who have once been born to enter into their mothers' wombs, is manifest to all.' Justin Martyr, 'The Apologies', in Alexander Roberts and James Donaldson (eds), *Ante-Nicene Fathers*. *Volume 2 The Apostolic Fathers with Justin Martyr and Athenagoras*, trans. M Dods, G Reith and BP Pratten (Edinburgh: T & T Clark, 1867), Apology 1, chap. 61 ('Christian Baptism'), p.59]

68 Those who consider this Gospel to be the work of a disciple combining the materials furnished by the Synoptics into a connected whole, so organized as to represent the disciples idea of the person of Christ, find materials for John 2.19 in the passages above quoted, and in Matth. 12.39: with which comp. Luke 11.29.

69 [Green may have intended this sentence to read: 'The answer is though that πνεῦμα gains no further significance by being associated with πνεῦμα.']

70 {It is however difficult to explain the words in this way.}

71 [MS orig.: 'healed of'.]

72 [MS orig.: *'returning'*.]

73 [MS orig.: 'bodily.']

74 Comp. ἐκράτησαν αὐτοῦ τοὺς πόδας ['with fear and great joy'], Matth. 28.9.

75 ['Jesus saith unto her, Touch me not; for I am not yet ascended to my Father: but go to my brethren, and say unto them, I ascend unto my Father, and your Father;' (John 20.17).]

76 {*'I am the resurrection and the life: he that believeth, etc.'* ['Jesus saith unto her, I am the resurrection, and the life; he that believeth in me, though he were dead, yet shall he live:' (John 11.25)]}

77 ['And this is life eternal, that they might know thee the only true God, and Jesus Christ whom thou hast sent.' (John 17.3).]

78 Such quickening belongs to the full φανέρωσις ['manifestation'] of Christ, which is also the φανέρωσις ['manifestation'] of the believers as of him in whom Christ lives Col. 3.4.

79 [These words do not occur in 1 Cor. 1.17. They mean (very roughly indeed) 'expect the revelation of the Lord.']

80 [Ant. 18.11.4: 'The Sadduces hold that the soul perishes along with the body.' Josephus [*Jewish Antiquities*], trans. Louis H. Feldman, 9 vols. (London: William Heinemann, 1965), vol. 9, 16:4, p.13). Bell Jud. 2.8.14: 'As for the persistence of the soul after death, penalties in the underworld, and rewards, they [the Sadducees] will have none of them.' Josephus [*The Jewish War*], trans. H. St. J. Thackeray, 8 vols. (London: William Heinemann, 1927), Vol. 2, 14, p.387.]

81 [MS reads: 'Eseenes'. The Essenes were a highly-organised communistic sect of Jewish ascetics which lived in Judea from approximately the second century BC. Possibly the authors of some of the Dead Sea Scrolls.]

82 ['...The children of this world marry, and are given in marriage:/But they which shall be accounted worthy to obtain that world, and the resurrection from the dead, neither marry, nor are given in marriage./Neither can they die any more; for they are equal unto the Angels, and are the children of God, being the children of the resurrection./Now that the dead are raised, ... (Luke 20.34–37).]

83 [Ellipsis in original.]

84 {*where the coming of the kingdom is spoken of as quiet and gradual*}

85 *{where in one way or another it is spoken of as already present.}*

86 ['I saw in the night visions, and, behold, *one* like the Son of man came with the clouds of heaven, and came to the Ancient of days, and they brought him near before him./And there was given him dominion, and glory, and a kingdom, that all people, nations, and languages, should serve him: his dominion *is* an everlasting dominion, which shall not pass away, and his kingdom *that* which shall not be destroyed.' (Dan. 7.13–14.)]

87 *{From this point I copy mainly from Mr. Bradley's Notes.}* [Presumably AC Bradley's notes, although these have not been located.]

88 ['Wrong' is written in above 45.5, 6.]

89 *{See above p.| |, which contains the substance of Mr. Bradley's note here.}*

90 [This translation is from the Revised version of the New Testament. The King James version reads 'I will come again'.]

91 *{see above second draft, p.| |., for the discussion of this and of the words* ἀληθινὴ μαρτυρία.*}*

92 [Quartodeciman was the early Church's practice of celebrating Easter on the fourteenth day of Nisan, which is the day of the Jewish Passover: Nisan was the seventh month in the Hebrew calendar (now the first).]

93 *{See second draft of the lectures, p.| |.}*

94 [Slightly adapted from Irenaeus, 'Against Heresies', in Alexander Roberts and James Donaldson (eds), *Ante-Nicene Christian Library: Translations of the Fathers Down to AD 325: Volume 5. Irenaeus 1* (Edinburgh: T and T Clark, 1868), Bk 3, chap. 1, p.258.]

95 [Origen, 'Commentary on the Gospel of John', in Menzies (ed.) *Ante–Nicene Fathers: Volume 10*, Bk 1, chap. 11.]

Part 2
Bernard Bosanquet

Undergraduate Essays.

[1.] Asceticism.

From one point of view nothing is more to be lamented than the exaggerations which have distorted so many truths, and deprived them of the value which once was theirs, by bringing them into disrepute. But looked at in another light these same exaggerations which arise sometimes from a true but mistaken zeal, sometimes from mere party spirit, are most precious as preserving from obliteration and oblivion the characteristic features of the truth, which, however imperfectly, they represent.

Our very word heresy means a 'choosing' of a particular truth as doctrine,[1] and is seldom applied to new and original forms of error, but rather to the doctrines of a day gone by, which their advocates, having chosen for themselves, cling to with most obstinate pertinacity. So we may see the usefulness of investigating old forms of error, both of belief and practice, whether they ever reached the stage of heresy or not. It cannot but be useful to drag out the truth which lies buried under its own abuses, and by comparing the results of the enquiry with the present state of things, to test the amount and propriety of the attention paid to that particular truth in our own time.

Now it is evident that the wide range of meanings which the verb ασκεω possesses are not all covered by our word asceticism; the received meaning appears to be that of, training, disciplining, and so finally, mortifying, the body. But this idea is by no means confined to our own religion; we are familiar in one at least of the greatest heathen philosophers, with the notion of the body as a bar or clog, to be separated and removed from the soul as constantly and as widely as possible.[2] We are also accustomed to an apparently identical idea in the works of our greatest apostle,[3] 'keeping under the body and bringing it into subjection' [1 Cor. 9.27] where the language of the original is far stronger than that of our Version. Now the idea of mortifying, of annoying, and of subduing the body has been of such universal existence, that it would be well to examine if there is any fundamental difference

191

between the notions of our own religion and those of heathendom on this subject.

We should notice first the object of the discipline in each case; does Plato propose to purify the body to elevate it, and fit it for immortality? His object is rather to put it out of the way; to let the soul sit so loosely by it as to take no impression from it during life, and leave it without a wrench or struggle at death. But this though analogous to our object, [it] is not the same. We rather propose to educate the body by discipline, than to tame it and break its influence, to raise it to be a fit place for the soul to be in, rather than to make it a place that the soul shall rejoice to escape from. Yet the self-tormenting power of the human mind has carried asceticism to a point utterly inconceivable to a mind like Plato's; the satisfaction of suffering in body in compensation, as believed by some, and held distantly possible by others who dare not confess their belief, for one's own misdeeds, has been more powerful in those regions to which our religion has not yet penetrated, than in our own country.[4] This apparently instinctive feeling of the possibility of propitiating a superior power by suffering is one of the most degraded emotions of our fallen nature, and is rightly put by Mr Browning into the mouth of Caliban on the island, as a part of his philosophy, in the following words, uttered in terror of a sudden storm 'Lo, 'lieth flat, and loveth Setebos, maketh his teeth meet through his upper lip, Will let those quails fly, will not eat this month One little mess of whelks, so he may 'scape.'[5] But besides this degraded asceticism, the worship of the Indian Devotee and of the Eastern Dervish, there is a true asceticism; a disciplining of the body in conformance with the hints of St Paul, which all our great names in saintliness have constantly practised, but not as anything in itself, for here is the point; it must be a matter of expediency or nothing. It must recognise the fullness[6] of our belief in a future state, and not militate against common sense and religion by aimlessly and constantly thwarting and injuring that which we believe will in some form or another, reproduced as a new and higher organisation from the relics of the old as a corn stem from the grain, be our companion through eternity. The truth then of which asceticism is in one case a gross perversion, in the other a tremendous exaggeration is, that our body is by no means in a perfect harmony with our soul; and the more the soul is improved the wider will the discrepancy become, unless checked by a corresponding improvement in the body, and accommodation of it to the soul. But in the heathen mind consciousness of the discord, and ignorance of the body's future developement, produced despair of anything but destroying the body's influence by continual discipline; in the Christian mind the endeavour to prepare the body for its final developement has been too often superseded by a wild endeavour to procure favour by uncalled for not meritorious asceticism, leading to the evils of seclusion, and also to the few advantages of the monasterial system.

[Initialled by tutor: 'RS'][7]

[2.] The Conception of Historical Causes in Thucydides Compared with that in Herodotus.[8]

The difference between the whole style and tone of thought of Herodotus and Thucydides, is far greater than can be accounted for by the short space of time which intervened between the writing of their histories.[9] If we can trace the cause of this different colour of thought, we shall find the results of our investigation very useful in determining the mutual relations of their historical conceptions. It is remarkable that Grecian literature appears to have migrated from Asia Minor westwards. Homer, if there was a single Homer, was probably an Ionian colonist; Hesiod indeed was born in Boeotia, but was of very recent Asiatic extraction; the first famous school of Greek philosophy was that known as the Ionic school, while the last great Greek philosopher, Aristotle was a native of Chalcidice,[10] further removed than any other from Asia both in place and in thought; and nearer than any other to the thought of modern Europe.[11] Herodotus was of Carian origin, Thucydides an Athenian by birth; this ought to furnish the clue to much that is remarkable in their writings.[12] The work of Herodotus is as much like a great epic poem as a history; it is enthusiastic, quaint, poetical, and often untrustworthy; it shews a slightly modified belief in Homer's notion of the Deity; conceding to it unity of action and purpose, and depriving it of the heterogeneous elements of sensuality and human infirmity of all kinds, which accordingly [?] so disfigure Homer's conception of the gods. The parallel between Agamemnon's vision in Il. 2[13] and the account in Herodotus of the manner in [which] Xerxes's wavering resolution to attack Greece is confirmed,[14] is too obvious to be overlooked, and too interesting to be left without some comment.

It is evident that the Διος βουλη ['divine will'] plays as important a part with Herodotus as it did with Homer; And that the same idea that figures so largely in the tragic poets, namely that of an ατη or judicial infatuation pursuing excessive prosperity, is at the root of Herodotus' conception of his subject. The Persian power was too great, was to be humbled; the Greeks were, for no particular merits of their own, but simply on account of the will of heaven, to be the instruments of its downfall; the Persian king is reluctant, is distracted by conflicting advice, but at last he is made to decide in favour of the expedition, and the principal opponent of the scheme is deterred from saying more against it, by a vision.[15] Now to compare this with Thucydides' conception of the causes of the great war the history of which he undertakes to write. We at once pass from a story consisting of legendary fables coloured and woven together by the historian, to a searching and condensed analysis, partaking of the character of our most highly finished modern history, just as the other does [?] of ancient Thucydides will, he tells us,[16] examine the causes and quarrels which led to the war; then he mentions in three lines what he considers to have been the true cause, and in the next chapter proceeds to give at length the alleged causes, connected with the Corcyraean alliance.[17]

But the true cause first mentioned is a not a Διος βουλη or a judicial infatuation; it is a perfectly modern and familiar idea, simply that of international jealousy between Sparta and Athens; and instead of a vision ordering one side or the other to prosecute the war, we have the whole chain unfolded link by link, how Epidemnus began the quarrel, how the corcyraeans were called in one party of Epidemnians and the Corthinians by the other; how when the thing was referred to Athens she sided with the Corcyraeans, thereby driving the Corinthians to seek the aid of their natural allies, the Peloponnesian powers; this is a very different style of history to that of Herodotus. The Persian war was in fact semi-heroic; it was not at that early time a subject for dispassionate history; accordingly, though Herodotus had acquired some power of testing evidence, his work is that more of a chronicler than a historian; Thucydides was as modern as any writer of the present day; perhaps Mr Froude's manner is as fairly to be compared with his as any, whereas Froissart may be compared with Herodotus, though the Greek historian was perhaps considerably his superior in candour and accuracy.[18]

[Initialled by tutor: 'T.H.G.'][19]

[3.] The Social and Economical Evils Produced by the Increase of Population.

There appears to be a radical difference between these two kinds of evil, the social and the economical. The social evils, those that is which apply to the social system which is arbitrary, and different in different places, are for the most part uncertain in extent and in action, and difficult to trace to their proper source. Many of the minor ones are traceable to other causes besides the one now under investigation, and have their roots as well in the original defects of the particular social system to which they belong, as in the additional abuses caused by an application of that system to a greater mass than it was originally intended to suit. But the economical evils, those which relate to the great laws which regulate the position of labour with regard to capital, and of produce both to consumers and to labour, these are universal, easily traced, and everywhere produce results little varied by the idiosyncrasies of the nations and countries where they exist. Of the social evils the one which calls for most notice at the present moment, is the acknowledged inadequacy of our representative system as at present organised to give any fair voice in the government of the country to many who are only deprived of it[20] because the last step, corresponding to the increased numbers of the censuses during the last thirty-four years, has not yet been taken.[21] The parochial system, both as regards pauper relief and spiritual teaching, has in like manners been entirely left behind, and is now struggling helplessly especially in London, against the via inertiae of the constantly increasing masses it has to deal with.[22]

It is obvious that in some cases the social and economical evils are closely allied, as in the case of one which we venture to mention, as, though properly a small matter of detail, it lately assumed alarming proportions. We allude to the practice of child-murder.[23] This is evidently a social evil in one sense, but hand-in-hand with the strictly economical evils of which we shall speak presently, of lowness of wages, high price of necessaries, and so forth. Another small matter in theory, but very serious in fact, is the overcrowding of our great towns, which also has relation to the lowness of wages produced by an oversupply of labour. For, to enter on the second half of our subject, it is evident that the price of labour that is wages, the room for labour, and the power of supporting labour must diminish in the inverse ratio of that in

which the supply of labour increases; supposing, that is, that the capabilities of the country are not improved by the increased amount of labour expended in it. But it of course does happen that by an increase of commerce, of manufactures, and even of agricultural inventions, the self-supporting, that is labour-supporting, power of a country becomes greatly reinforced. This however does not do more than disturb, it can never destroy entirely, the proposition mentioned above; except of course in the case of a young country, whose resources have never been fully developed by a sufficient expenditure of labour. It is therefore noticeable that many of these so-called evils contain a self-righting power; as for instance; a certain increase of population will reduce wages to a certain point; when they are there, the effect must be to check the increase of population; it is in open defiance of this principle of self-adjustment that strikes and Trades Unions exist, and, by artificially keeping up the level of wages, check production, thereby again checking consumption, and thus once more checking the demand for labour which it is their true interest to encourage.
[Initialled by tutor: 'RS']

[4.] The Proper Functions of Universities

We presume that it will not be questioned that the first and special function of a University is to provide for the teaching of its members. Now as it is a debated question how far it is bound to provide for their education as well, if we understand that term in its fullest sense, it will be as well to speak, first, of teaching proper, and secondly education and how far it is the office of a University to supply it.

The question that faces us at the opening of the first part of our subject is the much debated one of classical education; is it to continue to hold the first place? if so, in what form, scholarship or philosophy, or a mixture? if not, how is its place to be supplied? It is unnecessary, when the discussion has been before the world so long, to clear the ground of the old fallacy that classical education is useless because it isn't practical, and does not immediately assist men in what some choose to call the business of life. It has been observed with regard to this point that an illustration much to the purpose may be drawn from natural history; those animals which belong to an inferior organisation are the first to attain their full developement; to branch off from the main highway by which one species above another grows and developes, and to declare by assuming their peculiar characteristics to what special class of organisations they belong; but the higher kinds remain longer undecided; they combine or rather superadd to one another all the characteristics between the acquirement of which the lower orders turned away one by one to their own completed nature; thus the whale is a mammal; but its chief characteristic as such is that it does not generate by incubation; it turns off before the land quadrupeds, which have lungs, and limbs formed instead of rudimentary, [sic] for it is a very low order, nearly a fish. Now this applies very exactly to our point; a low style of education pronounces almost directly for what special pursuit it is going to fit a man; the very polypus [sic] of education is too often the agricultural labourer; he is sent into the fields at thirteen, having learnt to add, to write, arts that may be useful to him; often not to read, though in our more enlightened counties that is usually taken care of now; now compare him with Mr Gladstone; he has just got a backbone and fins; while Mr Gladstone is indeed a man.[24] So really there is no antecedent improbability in the profitableness of a classical education, arising from the fact that it usually turns men out at about twenty-four fitted for no calling in particular; for it is in the nature of things that the highest education in the world should remain undecided in its object for the longest period; and there is no necessity for this reason, though there may possibly be for some others, to admit even Natural Science or Mathematics to a share in University teaching, much less Law and Modern History, which verge suspiciously on the practical. But it would seem that University teaching should be made comprehensive enough to afford benefit to minds, and there are many good ones, which make no response to classical thought. Of course as a matter of convenience, Universities, where there is more or less money and leisure, are the place to keep learning stored up for the benefit of the country, and there can be no conceivable objection to members of the University profiting by the existence of these professors; but how far it is wise or would be safe to relax the rules which requires a preliminary modicum of classics, before allowing a degree to be conferred for other acquirement it is very hard to say. The study of classics has a very exclusive effect upon the University; and it does seem lamentable that a fine intellect should be excluded from a training in Mathematics and Physical Science such as may be obtained at either of our great

Universities from inability to appreciate or understand the niceties and refinements of scholarship, and the incorrect and clumsy system of grammar which is now learnt as a kind of enigma, the solution of which is to be imparted gradually at a later age. The ground on which many objections to classical education put themselves will be quite cut away the moment we get a simple and harmonious grammar of the Indo-Germanic languages, with some theory of philology in which all scholars of authority can be got to agree. It appears as to philosophical reading, that it is the true consummation of a first rate classical training, but ought not to supplant the accurate and laborious scholarship training which it very rightly and logically follows in our University, while in the other the foundation is left unbuilt upon, though it is indeed a very first rate foundation.

Now as to education; the social life of our Universities is constantly said to be an integral and most advantageous part of their training; it is quite a truism among some people that University life fits a man to live in the world, prepares him for the temptations of the world and so on. Now is it indeed the true function of an University to supply this kind of education? It belongs of course to our collegiate system,[25] but if we consider the waste of funds to which this system gives rise, and the attractions offered by the University to young men who have no interest in the proper objects of the place, it does become a question whether we are not contemplating a mighty abuse. Ought there to be a society at a University that makes it worth a man's while to spend three or four years at it with the view of a mere pass at the end?[26] True, the good done to the passmen, many of whom are doubtless our country gentlemen to be, is very great; but the wrong done to our poor but intellectual countrymen is greater. Why have the English so few places in comparison, University London is about the only one, where they can get for next to nothing a positively first rate education; a Scotchman can do it easily.[27] It is ours to see that these men are well-educated; for if a little knowledge is ever dangerous, surely it is when masses of intelligent men are crying for manhood suffrage, merely for want of the training which would make them fit to exercise the suffrage, and eager to withhold it from all whom they would then see to be unfit to possess it. [Initialled by tutor: 'T.H.G.'][28]

[5.] The Conception of Fate in the Ancient Poets and Historians.

It is noticeable that this conception was one which [enjoyed] a much greater place in the Greek mind than in the Roman; the speculative Greek was not satisfied with the machinery of the Pantheon, and so he invented the notion of a supreme power, irresponsible, behind and above all personal Deities. The Roman mind on the contrary busied itself more with the practical ideas of duty, love of one's country, and above all things loyalty to the state, and left things to take their course, not denying, but practically disregarding the influence of a Supreme Power. The notion of Fate is indeed one belonging to an intermediate state of speculation, when the first belief in the omnipotence of certain personified Deities has evaporated, and before taking refuge in atheism the mind turns naturally to the enquiry

'Or is it that some power, too wise, too strong
E'en for yourselves to conquer or beguile
Whirls Earth and Heaven and men and gods along
Like the broad rushing of the insurged Nile?
And the great powers we serve themselves may be
Slaves of a tyrannous Necessity?'[29]

So in Homer we see that the deity is practically supreme; we do indeed catch an occasional glimpse of a Μοιρα ['fate']; the Διος βουλη ['divine will'] even here is not all powerful; it can modify by not annul the decree of fate. Take the instance of Sarpedon; he is to be killed before Troy, this appears to be Μοιρα ['fate']; but Zeus mediates putting off the execution of the decree or even evading it altogether; but is restrained by the complaints of the other gods, who argue that if Zeus could avoid the Μοιρα ['fate'] for his son, they could not for theirs, so it would not be fair upon them to do so.[30] Again, Achilles's Μοιρα ['fate'] is so far unsettled that he has choice of two Κηρες ['Fates'], the idea of whom in Homer apparently is that one is told off to attend every person. This shews us a comparatively undeveloped idea of Μοιρα ['fate']; but now as I cannot examine all poets and historians in this limited space, I will at once turn to Aeschylus, the great expounder and preacher of the doctrine of fate.[31] It is not with him as in Sophocles a mere auxiliary in his development of the plot; it is that for which his plays are formed in a way which is unparalleled[32] by any other author. In fact, if we consider that these plays were the sermons as well as operas of the Athenian people, it will be easily seen how a principle of this kind which was considered by him conducive to the highest morality should be so dwelt upon, by a preacher so to speak of the old school; and again, how Sophocles who belonged to a far more lax generation than Aeschylus should find this tone somewhat overstrained both as regarded his audience and himself; and the same remark applies of course far more strongly to Euripedes.[33] Now the classical place on the doctrine of Fate in Aeschylus is one (PR. V) where the daughters of Oceanus in conversation with the prophetically wise Titan, express a hope that he will be freed soon, and again be a match for Zeus.[34] No replies Prometheus, that is not my Μοιρα ['fate'], I have much to suffer first, for cunning is far weaker that Necessity. 'But who rules Necessity?' 'The three Fates, and the Furies.' Then comes the crucial question; 'Then I suppose Zeus is weaker than them?' Prometheus evades the question, but yet gives a reply very important to our subject 'He can never escape from destiny'. Here we plainly have Zeus inferior, and himself subject to the action of Μοιρα ['fate'].

Now at this point I should notice a curious passage in the Agamemnon. ει δε μη τεταγμενα μοιρα μοιραν εκ θεων ειργε μὴ πλέον φέρειν ['And were it not that one fate ordained of the gods doth restrain another fate from winning the advantage'];[35] which read in conjunction with l[oc.] c[it.] of PR.V would mean 'Unless fore-ordained fate had prevented the gods' decree from bringing aid.'[36] In fact this points to a loose Epic use of μοιρα ['fate'] like Homer's vague one, according to which it might simply mean a Διος βουλη ['divine will']. The Three Fates[37] are entirely a post-Homeric notion, and μοιρα ['fate'] in any pregnant sense is the same. The notion of a god who was personal and material, and yet eternal, omniscient, and omnipotent, was not the notion of Aeschylus, if it was ever that of anyone; therefore Zeus was not a fit head for the universe and a power is invented which is to be a refuge for the human intellect when wearied with contemplating a chaotic infinity of events with no ruling power; Μοιρα shall be accountable for every event, shall rule the universe in cycles marked by the downfall of dynasties of gods, and shall unerringly though tardily punish the wicked and exalt the good, using the machinery of 'An Apollon, a Pan, or perchance a Jove'[38] of the Κηρες ['Fates'] and Έρινύες ['Erinyes' or 'Furies'], some common, some attached to individual men.

[Initialled by tutor: 'T.H.G.']

[6.] Courtesy.

There are some few attributes which appear never to desert man in any country or under any circumstances. Among these may be reckoned the feelings which prompt courtesy. Instead of being, as might have been imagined, non-existent in[39] barbarous nations, courtesy is with them usually exalted into a kind of superstition, and the warmth and energy with which it is shewn are generally-speaking a sign of a low as opposed to a high state of civilization. In the ancient literature we find the most extraordinary reverence for the duties of ordinary courtesy; it may be traced in the scrupulous observance of the relation between host and guest, and in the exaggerated chivalry of Homer's heroes, when they meet in battle and, finding out some connection between their respective ancestors forthwith exchange presents and swear friendship.[40] There is however one instance at least in which this primeval courtesy is shewn in a very beautiful example, and one that proves its utility as well as its beauty. The example in question is the famous visit of Priam to Achilles in the Iliad, where he is received with the most peculiarly graceful sympathy.[41] In modern times courtesy is much less formal as we call it, it is in fact a matter of much less importance than formerly, and is treated as such. The rules of society are less stiff on the one hand, and on the other the moral obligations of hospitality and sympathy have almost disappeared. This all points to the conclusion that external courtesy was a mere fence against outrages to society. In lawless ages therefore, when every man's hand was against every other man, if he had no previous connection of any kind with him, it was natural that people should build up these protections and strengthen them with all the force of superstition in order to defend themselves by a kind of tacit agreement against outrages whether personal or international against which there was no law to protect them. It will be said that if this is a true view, the effect of civilization ought to be to do away with courtesy. It has done away with much of the stiffness of the fence; but there is still remaining a great code of politeness as it is called, which is in the mass of instances courtesy with the feeling lost; and what a still further progress of civilization should effect for us, should be to remove all codes and rules of politeness, and to supplant them by a refinement and security (arising from law) that should render all barriers unnecessary (for they are apt to degenerate into politeness), but leave full play for the moral grace of courtesy, which is a thing we cannot afford to lose the possession and practice of, though all formalities may go as soon as possible. The true spirit of courtesy we may fairly say 'blesseth him that gives' even more than 'him that takes', and is the only thing worth trying for.[42] Those who try to conform to the usages of politeness without having first become imbued with the spirit of courtesy are losing their labour by beginning at the wrong end.

> The churl in spirit however he veil
> This want in forms for fashion's sake
> Will let his coltish nature break
> At seasons through the gilded pale
> For who can always act &c.;[43]

The point to be noticed is that is 'noble manners' should be 'the flower and native growth of noble mind';[44] and if this aspect of courtesy be remembered, it will form a sufficient answer to those who maintain that it is after all a refined selfishness because the world couldn't get on comfortably without it. Of course courtesy is, like honesty, the best policy; but that is no reason that every courteous man should be guilty of selfishness, any more than that every honest man should be so.
[Initialled by tutor: 'RS']

[7.] The Connection of Morality with Art.

It is not by any means an easy question what Art really is. Its distinction from mere empirical taste on the one hand, and from science on the other, cannot be definitely laid down and is hard to discover even approximately enough for purposes of argument. We may say generally perhaps that art consists in a combination of science and something more, call it taste, genius, or what you will, brought into action on something which concerns mankind in a particular way; this way is again hard to define, it is not their intellect or their spiritual faculties; perhaps the word aestheticism comes as near my meaning as any. For though the productions of art, as a picture, or a statue, or a musical composition, may be of such a kind as to appeal either to the intellect or to the moral nature of the spectator or reader, yet they must do so only in a secondary and indirect way, through the medium of this faculty of aestheticism. The above definition has been purposely made wide, so as to admit of poetry being included in the subject, which it appears to have a fair claim to be; though any definition only intended to cover the so-called fine arts would be pretty certain to exclude it from their numbers. An illustration of what is meant by the secondary and indirect character of the appeal made by a work of art, regarded as such, to the intellect and spiritual faculties, is to be found in the common observation made about the prophecies of the Old Testament; namely, that it is quite possible to read them without caring for their prophetic, philosophic or spiritual aspect, and yet to enjoy them greatly as splendid poetry. In such a case, they are regarded purely as works of art; and in this point of view they will be made use of for illustration in the course of the following remarks. Now the subject appears to divide itself as follows. What is the comparative value of the aesthetic effect of a work of art, and of its indirect appeal to the soul and intellect? And, how far is this second function affected by defects or excellencies in the moral nature of the producer of the work of art? Well then, the first question appears to be easily settled; Whatever may have been the case in Grecian times, when art was loved and as it were worshipped for its own sake, in our own days the thought and intention, and even the moral tone of a picture, poem, or musical composition, is with all but the merest art critics, the most important thing. It is not intended to overdraw the distinction here; of course many people would recognise this truth to such an extent that they would judge of the work as a work of art by its intention and meaning; rather than by the more technical merits, e.g., the force, originality, unity or harmony, of its conception and execution. But this is not to judge of it as art, it is to judge of it as art applied to a particular purpose.

Then to come to our second question; it can hardly be doubted, if our first position be admitted, that the goodness or badness of the producer's moral nature has an effect on the value of a work of art. For though it may be possible for a man of bad moral nature to produce a work aesthetically as perfect as that produced by a man of good moral nature, yet it is impossible to believe that its appeal to the moral and spiritual nature of man will be so true or harmonious as that of the man of good moral nature. And for this there seems a definite reason, not because the one is incapable of conceiving characters of as high moral qualities and sentiments of as sublime spiritual import as the other, but because, as his own nature is deficient in these points, he will have so to speak no stimulus urging him to dwell on them in preference to other topics, they will not find a response in his own moral nature, and for that reason, as I believe, he will not understand that they are things which do find a response in the nature of others. It is possible to read the Old Testament prophesies as a work of art; but surely no one, even supposing the poetry to be uninspired, could have written them as a mere work of art, without having some excellence in his own spiritual nature to correspond to their spirituality. A person devoid of such excellence might have been capable of writing them; but would never have known that they would find an echo in the human heart, and would therefore never have written them. I have left to the end one important remark; namely, that people go widely wrong in ascribing 'immorality' as they call it, to men who have produced great works of art, because of certain immoral acts which can be proved against them. For it seems to me that such faults may be accounted for by weakness of will, strength of passions, and so forth, which are merely practical, and may coexist with the most highly developed moral and spiritual feelings.

> Not on the vulgar mass,
> Called work, must sentence pass;
> ...
> But all the world's coarse thumb
> And fingers failed to plumb
> So passed in making up the main account;
> All instincts immature
> All purposes unsure
> That weighed not with his work, yet swelled the man's amount.[45]

These lines of Mr Browning's give one some notion of the impossibility of forming a judgment of the moral nature of a man from his actions; so that to every instance of high moral sentiment quoted against me (if any can be) from Byron for instance, I should say, He did not form that as a pure conception in his mind; but on that point his moral nature was developed, and he had sympathy with the Enthusiasm of Humanity.[46]

[No tutor's initials.]

[8.] What Constitutes Civilization?

When boys pass a certain age, they become men; when nations pass a certain age they become civilized. Some boys are slower to become men than others; some nations are behind others in the race of civilization. Only, the periods which different nations require to become civilized, appear at first sight to be entirely out of proportion to each other; the fact is, that some races live slower than others; and many are only capable of receiving a very partial civilization, so that it is extremely hard to say which are to be taken as examples of perfect civilization.

For instance, it is a common paradox that the great empire of China has stood still for many centuries and has been passed by younger nations, in spite of having had the start by possessing a considerable amount of civilization before they began to be civilized at all. But then if we look into this so-called civilization of theirs, we find it to be mere artificiality, in the means of existence, without the least pretension to a notion of a state or public duty, which are to us among the fundamental conceptions of civilization. Now this will not satisfy any one who examines it candidly; we cannot give it the name of anything but a hideous and painful burlesque of civilization. For the true progress of nations is, we think, towards a more perfect form of the state, which must indeed mould itself according to the idiosyncrasies of particular races; but whatever its final shape is, must have for its chief characteristic the utilization of the masses. By utilization we mean, not providing for their good merely, according to the short-sighted plans of a so-called paternal government; but a system which by imparting responsibility and authority as far as possible to all classes and individuals, puts them in the way of helping themselves, and of being advantageous to others by reason of the life such a process instils, instead of a dead weight upon the nation.

By the side of this action of civilization, and tending towards and harmonising with it, is that which is burlesqued by the state of things in China, which has imitated but half the truth, and that badly. Of course the progress of physical and social science has a tendency to make the individual life more artificial and complex; and this is a result which is not to be deprecated, but met and dealt with by our better lights. For instance; clothes are better than the woad of our ancestors; but clothes represent tailors; tailors apparently just now mean Trades Unions;[47] this is not the place to discuss the merits of these combinations; but their existence and enormous extent form one among the many phenomena to which our artificial individual life has given rise.

It would seem then that the action of civilisation is twofold and complementary; first, its action on the nation and on public relations is to simplify and reduce to nearer conformity with first principles; representation of the people, free trade, finally we hope, the abolition of pauperism and systems of poor relief, are some of its chief results in this field; the second and complimentary action, which works into depending on and being depended on by this, is the more refined artificiality of individual life; for example, improved education, increased comfort, speed in locomotion; to spread these benefits from the few to the many is the highest work of civilisation; and it is obvious that the more every individual partakes of them the fitter he will be for a share in the simplified public government.

As Trades Unions have been mentioned as complications arising chiefly from the artificiality of individual life, and apparently standing in opposition to one feature of simplified public life, namely free trade; it is fair to note that this opposition is only imaginary; every master, though an individual, is in fact a corporation in his own person; so that the only possibility of stopping him, when he begins to tamper with the labour market, is by an actual combination of men, who can only thus become equivalent to him; and these adverse combinations are no doubt not free trade, but they are less opposed to it than one-sided monopolies having it all their own way; and are essentially temporary in their action, for when one side becomes reasonable the occupation of the other will be gone, and we shall have free trade.
[Initialled by tutor: 'T.H.G.']

[9.] The Use of the Expression 'Things, not words,' in the controversy about Education.

Perhaps the oldest antithesis we have is that of 'words and deeds.' Achilles in Homer is to be carefully framed as 'a doer of deeds and a speaker of words'.[48] The great philosophic historian of Greece gives us this antithesis usque ad nauseam in every page; but the meaning of the expression he uses has in its[49] time become more modern and more varied; his antithesis may be either that of 'theory and practice' or of 'report and fact'. One cannot help thinking that many people who use the expression 'Things not words' in the present day, are led away by a deceitful resemblance between the antithesis they use, and the expressions of Thucydides and Homer. Now, as might be expected, Homer's antithesis is the broadest and plainest; and a great part of the usage of Thucydides is nearly as plain. There could be no mistake about the distinction, in early times when diplomacy was a thing unknown, between what a man does and what he says; nor in later times between what you hear and what actually takes place. But when in more complicated thought, men come to substitute 'things' for 'deeds' or 'fact'; and when, as we shall see to be the case, certain writers appear to confuse all that can bear the name of 'theory' with 'words' one may be excused for looking about one with a slight suspicion that the meaning of language has here as in many cases undergone a radical perversion.

It should be admitted however that we fully agree with the great bulk of what is said by the latest writers on Education; and it is only the overstrained use of this antithesis, which appears to us likely to produce great confusion, that we wish to criticise.

No one, we should suppose, will deny that there is a verbal criticism and mere verbal acquaintance with literature, for we cannot call it knowledge, which is worthless when obtained in full perfection, and particularly useless for the purpose of education, 'We require the knowledge of things and not words', says Mr Farrar in his Essay on Latin and Greek.[50] Verse composition, 'of the truths which great men have to tell us, and not of the tricks and individualities of their style' and so on. Now this is very true in itself; but if we look back at Mr Farrar's Essay will shall be startled at finding what he apparently includes under 'words'. 'In the age of Nero,' we are told, 'Grammar and Philology were everything, Philosophy nothing'.[51] This is a very curious statement; if the Philosophy was nothing, one would think the Grammar and Philology were very little; but the fact is, the statement about Philosophy merely fills up the antithesis, when Grammar and Philology have passed to the 'Words' side of the equation, Philosophy may follow as soon as anything can be got to fill the side she would leave empty. Here is a specimen of the contrast that may be drawn in this way. In Germany before the middle of the last century[52] there were existing Classical schools. But they were accused of not supplying 'Useful' knowledge, the knowledge of 'things'; so we have, in opposition to these 'Verbalschulen',

'Reaschulen' founded, for combining the knowledge of 'things' with that of 'words', and a liberal training with the knowledge of 'breeding silkworms' or 'ninety kinds of leather'.[53]

This throws some light on the meaning of the term 'things' in the mouths of these gentlemen; now let us look at another example.

The French system of Bifurcation was introduced about 1854 and lasted ten years.[54] In this, boys were divided into Humanists (word students) and Realists (Things students). The Humanists were excused from 'higher mathematics and higher physics', the Realists 'in part from *philosophy* and Latin, and entirely from Greek'.

When students of *things* are to be released from philosophy to study 'ninety kinds of leather' or even the higher mathematics and physics, which are after all but the sciences of things as they are; and are to do this *because of* and not *in spite of* or in addition to being students of *things* distinctly, one wonders what has become of Plato's notions about the world of things that *are*; not by any means our world, he would say.[55] Are not ideas things? Are not words the embodiment of ideas? We come pretty much to this then, that people are always in danger of forgetting, as Dr. Arnold did, the connection of words and things;[56] and because ideas are inseparable from words, they thereby run a worse risk, that of forgetting that ideas are things; of forgetting truth, and clinging only to fact. Surely when words cease to embody ideas, it is immoral to deal with them; if indeed they ever do cease to embody ideas. The laws of language and the laws of thought; a faith in them is a faith in thought; the object of education in language is twofold; 1.[57] to give power over language as the embodiment of thought, 2. to exercise and strengthen faith in law, whether law of language or law of thought. 'What God has joined let no man put asunder'.[58]

In fact he cannot; but he may persuade mankind that he has and so do them the greatest wrong imaginable, by shaking their faith in human thought. Let us by all means try to have education that teaches things, but instead of 'Things not Words' let our cry be 'Words that are Things'.

[Initialled by tutor: 'T.H.G.']

[10.] The Chief Points of View in which the Relation Between the Church and the State May be Regarded.

The ideal State, it will hardly be denied, represents the people whom it governs. In the greater or less divergence of the real State from this type, appears to lie the secret of the difficulty found about this question of Church and State, and many others. For the individuals who form the ruling body to combine in selecting for establishment and in maintaining at the public expense the Church which appears to them best deserving of such confidence, is, as long as they represent the subject people, a sufficiently safe course. But as practically no existing government does or can feel certain that it fairly or perfectly represents the people it governs, while many must feel certain that they do not, a strange practical difficulty arises in dealing with the question of a National Church.

Before however going into this branch of the subject, it may be as well to mention the reasons for which it seems that this is henceforward to be the predominant form of Church. Doubtless the Catholic Church which professed to be and was for some time, a power coordinate with and independent of, that of the State, was ideally a very perfect conception of a Church system. And it is possible that the Catholic Church might have longer retained its power and purity, had it not been for the fatal infatuation which ever loaded it with the incubus of the temporal power. It was not however, as we at least believe, the church for the ages from the middle age onwards; and the magnificent conception of the coordinate and independent, or rather equally interdependent, Catholic domination of the Emperor and the Pope, one secular, the other spiritual, has gone never to return.[59] For the tendency of modern times is to nationality, both in civil and religious matters, first the Empire broke up; then the Papacy; and though there is something cosmopolitan in the high civilization and perfect intercommunication of modern life, yet the cosmopolitanism is that of toleration, not of absolute agreement, and finally, we hope, of unity, not of uniformity.

From this point of view then, however much we may regret it, it is now fruit*less* to look at the Church question. Our idea of the relation must now vary with the amount of divergence of the government from the true type. Were the government an unanimous government of an unanimous people, whose wishes and opinions it fully represented there would be no difficulty about its establishing a National Church, *as* it would a National and Endowed System of Education, on the plan most approved to its own ideas and consequently to those of the people.[60]

But immediately we depart from this position of affairs we face a difficulty: Is the government to follow its own conscience in this important matter, and provide for the people such a church as it believes to be the best possible; Or is it, considering itself as their servant, and the steward of the money it collects from them, to take as it were their suffrage, and provide each man, or each considerable division of men, with the worship and religious instruction they like best?   Or, for a third course is possible, is it to regard religion, as governments have been too ready to regard Education, as something that might be left to take care of itself? and so grant no endowment to any persuasion whatever.   To the first we may give a decided negative, unless it have one condition attached, viz. that if the State feels bound in conscience to provide what it considers wholesome religious instruction to a part of its subjects who profess another religion it must then put this Church on a strictly missionary footing; That is to say, none of those, for whose unwilling benefit it is intended, must directly or indirectly, be made to contribute to its support.   The third course is that to which matters in Great Britain seem now hastening; but it may be hoped a more fully organised system of State Education may bring with it the conviction that it is easier than is now imagined to make religious instruction of two or three denominations work harmoniously in the same establishment, and that by the insertion of this small end of the wedge (i.e. paying both R. Catholic and Protestant chaplains in State schools) the different persuasions may come to accept endowments, which must be regulated by the number of their members, and will be of incalculable use in England in grappling with our constantly increasing population, and inert mass of pauperism.

[Initialled by tutor: 'RS']

[11.] The Advantages and Disadvantages of Commercial Prosperity.

In dealing with the results of Commercial Prosperity, the usual difficulty of distinguishing between Effect and Cause presents itself with immense force.   For example, are we to say, if the Carthaginians were rich commercial and illiterate, the Athenians rich commercial and literary, the Athenian character refused to be deadened by its forces, and the Carthaginians succeeded in resisting its activity?[61]

We shall look at the earliest and simplest effects of Commercial Prosperity first; hoping that from them we may deduce its relative advantages and disadvantages. Wherever it begins to arise, it soon shews a tendency to dethrone the aristocracy in favour of a plutocracy.[62] It is soon felt that wealth is a power in the State, and that unpleasant mixture of the power of wealth and of birth, which for instance under the later Roman Emperors offended Juvenal,[63] is merely the effect of not recognizing the transition, and of forcing wealth, if it will be recognized as a power, to be so by aping the privileges of birth. Now the aristocratic spirit is not one to be dispensed with by a nation, unless something very good is to be given in its stead; what this good is we must enquire. The Aristocratic spirit is chivalrous, patriotic, impatient. The Commercial is calculating, cosmopolitan, persevering. The first of these tempers is suited to Action, the second to Science. Here we think is the point, if Carthage failed to be more than a very wealthy town; it was because not having, except in one magnificent family,[64] the aristocratic spirit, she must also, possibly from her Semitic origin, have been unscientific; An Aristocracy without action, and a middle class or still more a presiding commercial class as without Science are nothing worth. The people will quickly demand powers and representation in their government, where great commercial prosperity inspires all classes with a desire of bettering their lot; unless the upper classes have liberality enough, to concede these demands when just, and wisdom enough and political science enough to grant them in due manner and proportion, the pressure which should have been onwards will become downwards. We cannot, one would think, attribute the great intellectual life of Athens to her commercial status; but we may say that it was that which saved Athens, in spite of her splendidly adapted position, from becoming merely the market of the world of that time. Of course the accessories of commerce would immensely contribute to this intellectual life; the contact with other nations and attrition of mind against mind which can be traced in the Greek tragedy (Aeschylus particularly is alluded to also Euripides) apparently is to be accounted for by commercial intercourse. Commerce is to civilized times what war is to earlier times; it rubs nation against nation, and is an outlet for energy and restlessness; but it is better than war, the commerce of aristocratic nations, because it does not, or where it is wise it does not, foster the narrow and exclusive patriotism which Dr Arnold considered so great a bane to any country.[65] And this one would think is a slight answer to such complaints as that sufficiently magnificent one of Wordsworth;

> When I have borne in memory what has tamed
> Great nations; how ennobling thoughts depart
> When men change swords for ledgers ...
>   Some fears unnamed
> I had, my country, am I to be blamed?[66]

If the middle class were, as its true commercial interest would teach it to be, in accordance with Mr M. Arnold's view 'the stronghold of science',[67] there would be great cause for confidence that such fallacies as that of Protection for example, which is hardly yet, one would fear, expelled from the middle class mind, must die a speedy death. The cosmopolitan spirit of true commercial enterprise is very useful; as above remarked, it tends to overthrow the narrower patriotism, which is too justly charged against the English. Again, the mere tendency to brand and stamp everything with its money value, which obtains in a commercially prosperous [nation] is useful, as a rough though inadequate means of stigmatizing what is unproductive. Though culture might fall under this censure in an unenlightened community, many more things must do so that are bad; and the mere realization in practice of the old commercial axiom 'Them as orders pays' and especially its converse 'Them as pays, orders' as applied to government is probably the effect of commercial prosperity and its influence on men's minds.
[Initialled by tutor: 'T.H.G.']

[12.] The Contrast Between Ancient and Modern Tragedies.

It would hardly be too much to say that the conception of a drama or tragedy in our sense of the words is essentially modern and entirely distinct from the conception which we must look to find realized in ancient tragedies. The pure objectivity which we consider so great a beauty in Shakespeare of whom it is truly said that his own ideas (of religion for instance) are not to be gathered from his plays, is not a characteristic of the ancient drama. The last thing that Aeschylus wished to do was to be entirely absorbed in his characters, and to have his individuality merged in theirs; Sophocles probably wished it very little, Euripides a good deal. Any life or motion, vigour or appearance of reality that the characters have, is the result of an artistic necessity not of a many-sided sympathy with the complex forms of life. (This statement again must be modified with regard to Euripides.) A practical test is readily formed. The chief beauty of ancient Tragedy lies either as in Aeschylus, in the sublimity of the lyrical passages, and some of the dialogue and semi-epic narrative, or in the artistic arrangement of a complex plot, with a correct catastrophe or succession of catastrophes, as in the Oedipus Rex, which is in some way the masterpiece of Sophocles.[68] Now all this artistic progress on the one hand, and the genuine earnestness of a writer like Aeschylus on the other, no doubt demand as much consistency and completeness in the characters as suffices to a certain extent to excite the interest of an audience. Still they are examples of character more than human beings, Oedipus is not a man we know by that name, he is the proud but rash and morally unstable tyrant, who will, Sophocles seems to be teaching the Athenians, under such and such circumstances act in such and such a way. The reasons for this are of course numerous, and beyond our subject; is there not however something in the mere isolation of the Greek mind, its proud eminence, as it thought, among a sea of barbarians, which is sufficient to explain this or a greater deficiency? One must know more of the existence of mankind, and their relations to ourselves and to each other, before one can be filled with the Enthusiasm of Humanity, which if not the root, is at least a necessary condition, of absolutely first rate dramatic power. A self complacent patriotism even if carried to a sublime or romantic pitch, like that of Aeschylus or Demosthenes, is but a poor substitute for such an Enthusiasm.[69]

But to turn to modern tragedies, one feels there (in the plays of Shakespeare I mean) in the middle of a multiform world. In spite of the first rate artistic force and finish which authorities tell us are displayed in Shakespeare's plays we do not all attribute their influence over us to any purely artistic qualities. Indeed technically speaking, fault has been found with the catastrophe of one (I believe more than one) of the leading plays, a statement which could not be made about Sophocles. Besides, few people appreciate the finish of art, though no educated man almost fails to enjoy

a scene of Hamlet. The characters seem instilled[70] with life; in fact all this has almost become cant, it is now so commonly insisted upon. As a real test and illustration one might offer the following. Let a man equally familiar with both languages read Shakespeare and Sophocles by way of comparison, let him be so far educated as to look for more than the glitter of commonplaces but not trained by a specialized education to overadmiration for faultless though frigid art, and he is certain to take immensely more pleasure in Shakespeare than in Sophocles. We have sermons and political treatises and philosophical works, and we don't want them put into our dramatic literature forms; the Athenians were not so provided, and consequently did. The contrast is perfect if we merely look at the fresco representations we have of the performance of an ancient tragedy, with the actors looking very monotonous in their gorgeous sacred robes, arranged in a kind of tableau vivant on the narrow stage, giving the effect it has been said, more of a group of statuary than of a set of actors. Then if one could imagine them intoning their solemn iambics in the great theatre that held thirty-thousand people, where no modulation of voice or expression of face (generally prevented by a huge mask) could have any effect, one would gain a conception of the religious grandeur of the whole ceremony, and the suitableness to it of such eulogia as the οὐ γὰφ δοκεῖν ἀριστος [literally, 'the thing that does not seem best'] – to us rather commonplace – and such sentiment as that in Antigone's speech,[71] in which there is a distant echo of the assertion made centuries after 'We ought to obey God rather than men.' [Acts 5.29] This gives a clue to the extraordinarily angry reception with which the great critic Aristophanes hailed the true dramatic power and liberality of Euripides; it was to a Greek as if one had expected a sermon and received a chapter of Mr Dickens or a poem of Tom Hood.[72]
[Initialled by tutor: 'T.H.G.']

[13.] The Influence of Endowments on Education.

The first effect of endowments on Education is to render it independent, or nearly so, of the amount and nature of the demand for it. Education is thus taken out of the class of commodities, which, if their production is to be lucrative or even self-supporting must be produced in quantity and quality to suit the appetite of the consumer. This characteristic influence of endowments may be regarded from two points of view, which represent the two opposite poles of opinion on the subject of education at the present day. The first is the theoretical or scientific, the second the Practical or Utilitarian. The first is on the side of knowledge for the sake of knowing, the second on that of knowledge for the sake of its usefulness. With regard to the first of these points of view; it will hardly be denied that classical education in its more refined forms, as well as philosophy, and pure science, would be at an immense disadvantage wherever and whenever the demand for education was regulated solely by the real or fancied needs of the class to be educated. We probably owe the preservation of a philosophic spirit in this age of applied science and utilitarianism in a great degree to our university endowments. And from the nature of education it seems desirable that the educating power should not be entirely dependent for subsistence on the popularity of its method, as it is from the nature of the case a better judge of what is required than its customers. Connected with this part of the subject is the liber- alizing effect of an educational system calculated not with a view to immediate preparation for success in life, but rather with the purpose of letting us behind the scenes, to have a notion of the true objects of success, and of any truths that may pervade all the phenomena of life in which are soon to take an active part, thereby necessarily sacrificing our extent of view. The very conception of an educational endowment is that of providing for the teaching and learning of something, which is implied by the means resorted to, to be unlikely to find general attention and support without artificial help.

With regard to the second point, that of Utilitarianism; it is no doubt a great detriment to endowments that they do often, from the indolence or degeneration of the educating power and the absence of competition, fail to secure their object. They often do not provide for anything but what is really antiquated and worthless; or rather, what is antiquated and worthless is often mixed up in their arrangements with what is merely high and noble. This vice, acting with the increasing practicality of the age, a practicality and impatience of speculation which we are told is extending itself even to philosophy, has produced a strong feeling that education should be practical, should be in fact what people can feel they get their money's worth out of. For the reason here hinted at, this kind of education can get on well enough without endowments, though the theoretical part even of physical science is likely to suffer from such short-sighted practicality. But no doubt the independence of endowed institutions may be carried too far, and they may become witnesses to what is high and true or mere ruins of what once was great, according to the wisdom of their directors. Instances of the effect of endowments may be seen where it is still doubtful which party has most truth on its side; Eton, the most largely endowed of our public schools except perhaps Charterhouse, has not yet admitted, or has only just admitted, the principle of education by physical science; Harrow has done so for a longer period; and Rugby for longer still.[73] Endowments may of course by utilized to give education to those who cannot afford it otherwise, and this is a very worthy aim; indeed it may almost be classed with that spoken of above; for in both cases the education is more or less provided independently of the person's own exertions; and in both cases, had he been obliged to choose an education without any preference arising from endowments, he would have chosen the cheapest and that the profit of which could be most immediately realised. Lastly, it is a great characteristic of endowments in England at least, that they have been answerable for putting education to a great extent in the care of the clergy. As many thanksgivings for founders remind us 'godliness' and 'good learning' used at one time to be thought of in conjunction; and probably people did not very accurately distinguish whether they left money to a church or a college.[74] This has doubtless, from the conservative nature of church institutions, added to the tendency of endowed education to withstand progress good as well as bad, and finally has exposed those who would make the Universities undenominational to the charge of secularizing church property.

[Initialled by tutor: 'T.H.G.']

[14.] The Greek Idea of Citizenship.

This, it must be remembered, only deal with free and equal members of a community. The extensive employment of slaves in ancient Greece both set free the members of every state from much of that drudgery which is the sole occupation of a large portion of a modern commonwealth, and also caused this drudgery to be despised. From this along with other causes, it followed that the true field for the energies of every citizen worthy of the name was placed in the affairs of the state. Taking into consideration, besides this, the smallness of the scale of all the Greek cities, each of which formed a state, we shall see a further reason for this tendency to exalt the common welfare and the art of the statesman above private life. For, every citizen could in a Greek city take a fair share in the public business, without even the intervention of a representative; so that he might be sure in theory of exercising influence proportioned to his abilities. The state being therefore as fully as possible identified with the whole body of its members partaking of all their sympathies, and representing every individual perfectly, had a right to consider itself as qualified and bound to provide for the highest wants as well as the merest conventional necessities of the people. It was not as in a modern community where the government is to a greater or less extent dissociated from the members of the state, and a most mutilated and imperfect representative of them. For in this case the maximum that can safely or hopefully be attempted by a government is that modicum of protection and advice which one man can afford to another without danger of going wrong, when he has no means of communication with him whom he protects. But in the ancient commonwealth, though Plato's theory and Pericles' practical statement[75] may differ as to the means, both the philosopher and the true statesman venture to put before themselves as an object the highest good of the ruled. The subordinate condition of the inferior classes in the Republic is not really an exception to this rule, it is only a mechanical way of effecting that predominance or reason in the government which Pericles proposes to attain by perfect freedom of discussion and legislation, so that all intellects may find their level. Plato proposes in addition that they shall be forcibly retained there for fear of obstructing the others.[76] The government was according to this idea the expression of the higher mind of the community, not as some now would have it, of its lower necessities. Now rejecting the hypothesis of Plato, that the individual is the unit of which the state is to be constructed, and accepting as this unit, the family; we shall have a safeguard against the utter destruction of individual life effected by the constitution of his ideal 'Republic.' For while the family remains untouched, the head of it is naturally supreme; and the state will not interfere with his control in that sphere. So each citizen will have vital interests and responsibilities of two kinds; for his family to the State; and for the State to his family. Having in his charge a portion of the rising generation, whose culture is above all things important to the State, he will feel it his first duty and anxiety to provide for their mental and moral perfection in every way in his power. And for their moral perfection at least the domestic atmosphere gives a better chance than that of public education. Again, the head of the family as a full citizen will have an appreciable influence in the conduct of the State, and as Pericles says it is then profitable to the state that he should have a family, for he will be doubly anxious to give no unwise counsel, to sanction no immoral measures. This idea coincides well with the action of the highest specimens of the Greek citizen that are recorded, Socrates for instance and Demosthenes; the untiring patriotism, jealousy of the honour of the state, and noble self-sacrifice, which are displayed in the lives of these two great men, are worthy fulfilment of so grand a conception of citizenship.[77]

[Initialled by tutor: 'RS']

[15.] The Constitution of Sparta Compared with the Ideals of Plato and Aristotle.

The Spartan constitution is mentioned and criticised both by Plato and Aristotle, more severely by the latter.[78] In certain points however it approaches more nearly to the ideal states of these two philosophers, than any other among the cities of Greece.

To begin with those points in which it resembles the ideal of both of these philosophers. It is an attempt at government by persons who have received an education in harmony with the chief aim of the state. That this aim is a bad one is nothing to the point here. It is a constitution which satisfies the different elements of which it is compounded. Here again, though it satisfies them by unworthy means, yet it is a point gained that they should be satisfied. It realises one great postulate of both Plato and Aristotle, indeed of every Greek, that the citizens are to be exempt from the labour of agriculture, of mechanical arts, and of trade. Its institution of the syssitia[79] is one which for different objects and under different regulations would be adopted by both Plato and Aristotle. Next, to compare it with the ideal republic of Plato, which we have complete. They agree in the very great extent to which the system of public education and discipline is carried; but the Spartan is not so thorough going; for while it makes the concession to the natural feeling which Aristotle appears to require, by omitting to break up entirely the family life; yet as Aristotle points out, by this omission it contravenes the spirit and intention of its own system, and so implants the germ of disorder and destruction.[80] However revolting the Platonic ideal may appear to us, it, at all events, is open to no such censure. The community of women and children in which Aristotle finds so many insuperable difficulties, at all events leaves no disturbing element in light [?] of domestic establishment. They agree also in the importance attributed to music and gymnastic as a means of education, and to the development by this means of a high spirited and soldierlike temperament. Another point of resemblance is the trust reposed in the ruling power, as shown by the absence of written law, for which is substituted the perfect system of education. The great point of different us that of the community of property. There is not sufficient evidence to prove that so much as the equalization of property was ever a feature in the Spartan system; while at a later time the disparity of wealth was certainly very great. Another point of difference was the object of the state. This separates the Spartan system from the ideals of both Plato and of Aristotle. Its end was war; a kind of πλεονεξια ['greed']. This bad aim had a powerful influence on the disposition of the citizens, and had no doubt a share in the formation of that character for φιλοχρηματια ['covetousness'] which belonged to the Spartans of a late period.

Thirdly, the comparison between Sparta and the ideal state of Aristotle cannot be made quite so definitely. It must be gathered to some extent from his criticism of Sparta herself. His own ideal state was an aristocracy in the Platonic sense. Sparta was a closed[81] oligarchy. There was therefore some resemblance between their methods, but the aim was different. The predominant importance given to the question of education, the syssitia, the contentment of all the elements which made up the state, are in his eyes good points. But he would have the syssitia supported from public property; and regards it as a dangerous vice that, as the test of citizenship is the subscription to the syssitia, increasing wealth among the few tends to lessen the numbers of citizens. In fact at the time of Leuctra there were less than a thousand Spartan citizens.[82] The kings had indeed in early times a power of deciding the destination of Levilsies, [?] but there is no proof that they used it to keep down the monopolies of land. Also the influence of the women, proceeding from the fundamental omission to legislate for the household was a great fault in Aristotle's opinion, and tended to produce φιλοχρηματια ['covetousness']. The position of the Helots he also considers a dangerous mistake.[83]

It is apparently a question to what form of ideal state Aristotle does incline; but assuming, as above stated, that it is to the theoretical aristocracy, he yet considers that practically a μιγτη [?] πολιτεια ['mixed constitution'] is as useful as any likely to be found, and it is with this, his second or third best state, that we should really compare the Spartan constitution.[84] He would have such a state composed in such a way as to satisfy its three elements, αρετη ['virtue'], πλουτος ['wealth'] and the people; At Sparta the βασιλευς ['king'] and Gerontes would represent the αρετη ['virtue'], and the ephors the people; the plutocratic element was not legitimately recognised; as it forced its way in to the subversion of the morality of the state. It represented itself in the kings, corrupting ephors, who were often poor men and so venal, just as at Carthage we are told, the people having no true share in the government were kept quiet by the action of wealth upon them.

The chief resemblances of Sparta to the philosophic type then were,

[1.] The pursuit of a single aim by a system of education and social organization.

[2.] The power being in the hands of those who were in theory qualified by education to act without direction of law.

[3.] The obedience to this power, obtained by satisfying all the elements in the state.

And the great defects were. [1.] The half measures by which the social organization left the household untouched.

[2.] The lowness of the aim set before the state, which reacted on its members.

[3.] The unwise political narrowness which excluded citizens for poverty, and refused to admit new ones.

[Initialled by tutor: 'RS']

[16.] Legislation and Morality.

Does the question of the proper sphere of legislation practically depend on the aim theoretically assigned to the state? For this aim has been differently defined in ancient and modern times according to theories of politics varying with the notions of philosophers. Is the End of the state that the individual should live well, as Aristotle says, or should be protected from aggression as Mr Herbert Spencer and Mr Mill would have it; and does this problem make any difference in the theory of legislation?[85] Perhaps this is in some ways analogous to the question whether it makes any difference to practical morality which of the two great theories of its origin is accepted? Both seem to demand a negative answer. The Utilitarian (if we accept for the moment his basis of morality as sound) extracts from the gratification of our sentiment of sympathy all those higher manifestations of self-denial for which his theory at first seems inadequate to account. And thus if a sufficiently large interpretation be given to the duty of securing freedom of individual action, the state in the view of the Utilitarian shares all those responsibilities which a higher ideal only might seem justified in casting upon it. For if no virtue can be purely self-regarding, but all must be capable of analysis into conduct in social relations; and if all social relations as potentially containing elements of coercion, come under the cogniscince [sic] of the state, then on this view no other limitations to legislation can be recognized than those practical ones to which, on any theory, law making must be subjected. Thus for instance there would be no theoretical diffi-culty about legislating against field sports, as being simply a fraud-ulent expenditure of entrusted revenue, and as tending to mar the good effects of education on the lower classes. The only objection in fact is one which applies equally on either view of the case, that in the present state of public opinion no such measure could pass. Again on Mr Spencer's own shewing the State is responsible for the protection of class against class, as for instance from those manifes-tations of Trades Unionism which he holds to be the result of bad Political Economy; if so, the surest and only sound remedy is, as he says, that of Education.[86] But if the state once takes charge of the education of the mass of the people, it becomes responsible for the nature of that education, and consequently to a very great extent for the popular morality of the kingdom. Thus the principle of protection from aggression, or the mere administration of justice may be carried out to any possible extent; and the advance of popular morality may render it possible to legislate on this system against any violations of duty that could possibly be attached by any other.

There is indeed one direction in which a difference may be made. It has been acknowledged by many as an unquestionable benefit that the State and the Church should where possible be closely allied. If the course of time should lead to destruction of the formulae on which Churches now exist, it may be worth consid-ering whether functions analogous to those of Churches may not come to be lodged in the State. That every member of a community should, by his connection with the state, ipso facto be understood to belong to an organization embodying as far as practicable the highest known morality, so far from being a violation of personal liberty, might without paradox be held almost necessary to it. Only the State would do what no Church ever could; for it would not merely, perhaps not at all, express the need of external and united worship; but it would provide a discipline for its citizens in accordance with the best ideal of life, and in its principles of action and legislation it would only differ by the least practicable amount from the best known morality. It would seem that functions like these could never in truth be exercised by a State nominally directed on the principle of mere protection, however great the similarity between special enactments might be between communities with these different aims.

The practical limitation to legislation in a such a community is the impossibility of producing moral action by political or social machinery. That is to say, all that legislation can do in this respect, is to remove all material obstacles and false ideals, and to provide good education. It may include in this education such materials of an artistic training, as may be be [sic] developed into something analogous to religious worship by any who have the power and feel the necessity. The ordinary rules applicable in all governments to legislation with a view to moral and social well-being, are that it must be such as can be enforced without producing greater evils that those it would cure; it must be impartial not running the risk of forbidding in the lower classes what is freely allowed to the upper; this applies strictly if what is said be true, the enactments about betting houses, which extend apparently to every house where men meet for betting, except Tattersall's;[87] (no doubt this must be from some oversight in framing the clauses); and it must always be borne in mind that all extraordinary public expenditure is quite so much added to taxes, which even in Education itself is a serious difficulty.
[No tutor's initials.]

[17.] A Sense of Beauty as an Element in Morals.

If what is meant by Morals be the effort to bring life under the dominion of Reason, or in other words, to express or manifest Reason in the actions of practical life, it is impossible but that whatever is commonly known as an elevating influence in life should be in some way connected with this Reason and its expression, Beauty may be considered as the expression of Reason, Law, Unity or whatever we like to call it, in the Universe, and the Sense of Beauty therefore as the recognition of this Reason or Law by the similar principle in the individual; to which the artist adds a peculiar power of eternalising[88] and universalising the recognitions or impressions of Beauty that fall to his lot as an individual. Brilliant but untrustworthy attempts have been made to show in details how those undefined impressions which to most people constitute a sense of beauty, may be analysed into perceptions of the manifestations of a principle of reason; there are however one or two considerations which tend to show that the view stated above is a just one. The beauty which most easily and obviously excites in the mind a sense of unity, is that of the human form. Now this is the earliest type of beauty recognised by Art; while the development of that wider sense of Law which can recognise the unity of a landscape, has required an immense increase of knowledge, and a greater complexity and variety of life. And no doubt for the average of civilized men, it would still be impossible to feel more than a vague impression of delight on looking at a sunset or a storm; though when translated from an artist the highest beauty of such scenes is now not above the appreciation of the average mind. And in all art it would seem that the line of progress is towards the recognition of unity in greater complexity; though the art of painting is more or less behindhand [sic] in doing for human life what Turner has done for landscape, or again what Shakespeare has done in a different art; and probably the art of music might be adduced to complete the parallel.[89]

The great difference between the Sense of Beauty and the Moral life, is one from which it follows that the former is a necessary complement of the latter. Our reason, in the endeavour to express itself in practical morality is curbed and thwarted on every side by the condition of human life; and the very cause of our striving after an ideal at all, is also perhaps the cause why our ideal is never attained to the full. But with beauty this is not so. Whether to an infinite Reason the universe as at present existing were an adequate expression of beauty is a question that must be let alone, or perhaps answered in the negative; but the beauty that we may recognise in the universe is limited for us only by our powers of recognition. In the actual representation of beauty by the artist there is indeed a perpetual imperfection; but this again depends on the condition of all human work, which is that of failing to satisfy an insatiable self. Though imperfect to him, to others the artist's work may be perfect enough. But to have at command as it were an inexhaustible series of visions of perfection, cannot fail to be an important adjunct to a life the characteristic of which is perpetual failure. Perhaps there is no greater assistance and stimulus to the work of organising our life in accordance with reason, than the perpetual recognition of the highest result of organised life in external nature, or in man.

The impression of beauty in the mind of an artist is probably not different in character from that in the mind of individuals; but owing to his wider and deeper life, and a power of expression which is perhaps only an accident of it, his recognitions are so to speak available for others, while those of ordinary men are always unexpressed, and often transient. And although the nature of these revelations renders it impossible for them ever to be translated from the artist's work into words, for they are not discovered by reasoning though dependent on reason, yet their influence is distinctly perceptible in practical action. The spirit of harmony love is strengthened by direct contact with their laborious and more perfect manifestations. And the religious spirit which [...?] to pause for the refreshment of devotion during the labour of life finds no safer outlet than the worship of perfect beauty, whose freedom is one with Law.

[Initialled by tutor: 'RS']

[18.] Plato's Conception of Justice in the Individual and State

Our own notion of Justice fluctuates between the corrective and the distributive Justice of Aristotle. The first is our theoretical notion of Criminal Justice, the rectification that is of conscious wrong done by man to man; The second approaches more nearly to our notion of Justice as a moral principle which consists in rendering to all their dues; including the rectification of wrong done, not consciously, but from a mistaken notion of what is due to self or to another. It is only with the latter Justice that Plato has to do. Equally by the ideal nature of his state, by his axiom that no man knowingly does wrong, he was forbidden from introducing Corrective or Criminal Justice the true basis of which is the repression of conscious and premeditated injury. His justice in the individual is merely the perfect state of moral freedom, without which indeed justice in the highest sense is impossible, but which aims at being an unmanifested, that is as good as a nonexistent, virtue. And even in the action of the State the only manifestation of Justice would be in rectifying mistaken assumptions of functions and their instruments or rewards; for, excepting in such a display, his justice would merely be the harmonious performance of duties, the perfect organization of all the relations of society; with regard to which we should say either that in a condition so perfect there would be perfect justice, or there would be no justice at all. It is the old question of the existence of virtue in a state of perfection. Plato however is describing not heaven, but only a heaven on earth; and therefore there is this distinct function, of what we should all agree to call justice, left to his governing class; that they should regulate the positions and functions of individuals according to their deserts; and though he does not suppose men to transgress the limits of their class, or aspire to the honours of another, without the belief that it is their right to do so, yet it is just such conflicting claims to what both parties believe to be a right, that form the subject matter of civil law.

It is to be observed however that in one point Plato's justice differs materially from our civil law, and approaches more to the criminal. He does not give us to understand that in cases of conflicting right, or rather conflicting duty, the state is merely to act as mediator between the two parties. It is distinctly regarded as the office and responsibility of the state to see that the functions are properly allotted and the material necessaries for their performance suitably assigned. In fact, if we call this distributive justice, it is necessary to explain that Plato does not contemplate, any more than we could possibly contemplate, the adequate apportionment of reward to the fulfilment of duty; it is merely the allotment to each kind of duty of the things necessary for its performance, and of each kind of duty to those competent for its performance, of which he speaks.

[No tutor's initial.]

[19.] The Notion of Evil Among the Ancients.

It is a common saying that the Hellenic notions of good and evil were in the main artistic; and, no doubt, the endeavour after symmetry of external form was one method by which the love of proportion manifested and intensified itself. In fact however, Hellenic art was but one side of Hellenic life. Probably the political conditions of Hellas had as much to do with the conceptions of good and evil which prevailed there, as the artistic aspiration of her inhabitants; or still more accurately it might be maintained that both are traceable to the primary conditions of Hellenic life and society, in their constant action and reaction on the Hellenic mind. It is unnecessary to enlarge on the artistic conditions surrounding men

> Whose lot fell in a land where life was great
> And sense went free, and beauty lay profuse;[90]

for this has now become a commonplace.

Perhaps it may be worth while to notice influences of an analogous nature in Hellenic society. The smallness of the states of Greece, due perhaps mainly to the geographical conditions of the country, rendered disorganization at once possible and alarming. To this fear of disorganization anything like presumption on the part of one of the citizen body added a sudden stimulus, far different from anything that could be experienced in the cumbrous fabric of a modern community. Thus the root of all evil to a Greek in politics and society as in art was the transgression by any member of the limits assigned by its proportionate relation to the whole. To violate any of the primitive relations on which society depended, the ties of family, or the rights of a guest or a king, was the most terrible crime known to the earliest Greek poetry. Of an analogous nature was the horrors of 'Insolence, the child of impiety'[91] to which the two earlier tragedians gave expression; and with which they, as well as the former of the two great historians, associated the peculiar curse of heaven. In its more practical form of πλεονεξία or Selfishness this tendency to self-aggrandisement is stigmatised by Thucydides as the cause and aggravation of the horrors of the Peloponnesian war.

It was from a language penetrated with thoughts like this that Plato took the phraseology which embodied his idea of Justice, the foundation of all virtue in the state and in the individual; and it was on the one hand as an offence against social and civic ties, and on the other as a derogation from the dignity of the perfect man, that all evil was regarded by him and by Aristotle. It is hard to say how far in the time of the latter the word καλὸν which is generally regarded as the meeting point of Greek art and morality, may have lost its artistic meaning, and become a general term to express the end of action. However, it seems fair to conclude both from the stress laid on the doctrine of μονὶτγτες, [?] together with the description of the μεγάδοξος, [?] ['glorious'?] that artistic conceptions were not entirely absent from the mind of Aristotle; and it is doubtful whether καλὸν would be so fairly rendered by 'duty', as by 'nobleness' or some such equivalent.

It is thus difficult to extract from the strange formulae of Plato an idea of evil at all commensurate with our own. The conscious violation of the law of reason had for him no existence. The reason might well[92] be overcome by the lower parts of man's nature, but then apparently the man became a brute, and as such incapable of what we mean by wrongdoing. With Aristotle and Euripides this was not so. Aristotle holds that for particular actions done from the influence of evil habits, men could not be held responsible, were it not that for the formation of their habits they are fully accountable.

But the vindication of the Law of reason is by far most complete in Euripides. His two greatest heroes die for an idea which they maintain with all the powers of heaven and earth against them, excepting, in the case of Hippolytus, his patron goddess.[93] She is in fact a personification of Chastity; and her hero's intercourse with her is one of the most exalted notions of religion in all Greek literature. 'He is beside her, hears and answers her, listening to her voice, but not beholding her face.'[94] For such a hero, any wavering in his allegiance would have been little short of sin, and his death in the cause of his goddess is not far removed from martyrdom. [Initialled by tutor: 'RS']

Thecet: 176 & 7.[95]
Timaeus, 29.a.
—— 86.a.[96]
Rep: 380 etc.
    617.[97]

1   [The roots of the word 'heresy' are found in the Greek word 'hairiome' or 'choose'.]

2   [Plato, *Phaedo* 82d–84b.]

3   [Of course, Saul of Tarsus (d. ca.65AD), who became known as Paul following his conversion to Christianity on the road to Damacus (Acts 9.1–19, 22.5–16, 26.12–18). The author of many books of the New Testament, he was sainted as 'the Apostle to the Gentiles'.]

4   [The 'Indian Devotees' and 'Eastern Dervishs' referred to a little later in this essay. By 'Indian Devotee', Bosanquet is probably referring to Hindu ascetics, the most extreme of which gave up all earthly comforts so as to live a quasi-monastic life in caves and forests. A dervish (or 'Darwīsh') was a member of a Sūfī tariqua, an Arabic Muslim mystic brotherhood community, the first of which grew up in the twelfth century. Dervishs sought to induce a spiritual trance through vigorous physical exercise, especially whirling dances.]

5   [Robert Browning, 'Dramatis Personae: Caliban upon Setebos; Or, Natural Theology in the Island', in John C Berkey, Allan C Dooley and Susan E Dooley (eds.), *Complete Works of Robert Browning*, 16 vols. to date (Athens: Ohio University Press, 1969–), vol. 6, p.270, l.292–5. Poem first published 1864. Caliban, a savage, is Prospero's slave in Shakespeare's play *The Tempest*.]

6   [MS reads: 'fulness'.]

7   [Robert Scott (1811–87), divine, graduated First in Classics from Christ's Church, Oxford in 1833, Master of Balliol 1854–70, Dean Ireland's professor of exegesis 1861–70. Later, dean of Rochester 1870–87.]

8   [Cf. TH Green, 'The Nature of Historical Narrative in Thucydides and Herodotus' earlier in this volume.]

9   [Herodotus is believed to have written his *Histories* between 445 and 426BC. Thucydides (c.460–c.400BC) wrote his history of the Peloponnesian War between c.431 and 400BC.]

10 [MS del.: 'Macedonia'.]

11 [Homer is thought to have been born in the eastern part of the Aegean Sea, possibly at Chios or Smyrna. Hesiod (fl. c.700BC) grew up in Ascra, Boeotia. Aristotle (384–322BC) was born at Stagira in Chalcidice. His father was court physician to Amyntas II of Macedon.]

12 [Herodotus came from Halicarnassus (now Bodrum on the Aegean coast of Turkey). Thucydides was an Athenian.]

13 [Homer, *The Iliad*, Book 2, l.1–38.]

14 [Herodotus, *Histories*, Book 7, §§12–8.]

15 [Herodotus, *Histories*, Book 7, §§ 12–8.]

16 [Thucydides *History of the Peloponnesian War*, Book 1, ch. 21–2.]

17 [Thucydides *History of the Peloponnesian War*, Book 1, ch. 23:6: 'The truest explanation [for the origin of the Peloponnesian War] although it has been the least often advanced, I believe to have been the growth of the Athenians to greatness, which brought fear to the Lacedaemonians and forced them to war.' Thucydides *History of the Peloponnesian War*, trans. C. Foster Smith,

4 vols. (London: William Heinemann, 1919), vol.1, p.43. For the lengthy explanation, see *ibid.*, Book 1, ch.24–87.]

18 [James Anthony Froude (1818–1894), English historian. Jean Froissart (c.1335–c.1405), French chronicler of Europe during the Hundred Years War.]

19 [Of course, Thomas Hill Green (1836–82), Fellow of Balliol College 1866–78. Later, Whyte's Professor of Moral Philosophy, 1878–82.]

20 [The Second Reform Act had been passed in 1867, expanding the electorate to 2.4 million by 1869, an increase of a little of a million on the 1866 figure. The 1867 Act retained a £10 lodger-qualification as well as residence requirements and other subsidiary conditions.]

21 [Censuses of the English, Scottish and Welsh populations began in 1801, and were held every ten years thereafter (as they continue to be).]

22 [The 1834 Poor Law (Amendment) Act had been modified in 1865 by the more centralised and in many ways harsher Union Chargeability Act, although pressure for reform of the inconsistent and increasingly costly system continued throughout the rest of the century.]

23 [A number of child murders had come to light over the previous few years, with *The Times* reporting either the arrest, trial or execution of James Longhurst (17 April 1867), Jane Jarron (10 October and 9 December 1867), Margaret Ward (16 March 1868), Isabella Davidson (25 May and 1 June 1868), Lucy Buxton (27 July 1868), and Jane Cox (8 February 1869).]

24 [William Ewart Gladstone (1809–1898), statesman and man of letters, Prime Minister at the time of this essay (1868–74), and was again in 1880–5, 1885–6, and 1892–3).]

25 [The University of Oxford had twenty colleges in 1868, operating as 'independent corporate bodies' to which most but not all students belonged. Each (with certain caveats for All Souls, Christ Church, and Keble) had 'a Head, Fellows and Scholars in various numbers' (*Oxford Ten-Year Book A register of University honours and distinctions completed to the end of the year 1870* (Oxford: James Parker, 1872), pp.50–1).]

26 [The majority of Oxbridge undergraduates did not read for Honours degrees at this time, but for a 'Pass' or 'Poll' degree. For example, when Bosanquet gained his First in *literae humaniores* in the Michelmas term of 1870, out of two hundred and thirty, one hundred and seventy students (74%) were awarded only pass degrees. (The examiners were Mark Pattison, George William Kitchin, Thomas Hill Green, and John Richard Magrath (*The Oxford Ten-Year Book*, pp.397–8).]

27 [Only four English universities existed in 1869: Oxford, Cambridge, London, and Durham. Scotland had the same number catering for a much smaller population: Glasgow, Edinburgh, St. Andrew's, and Aberdeen.]

28 [The tutorial discussion of this essay may have been the occasion later recalled by Bosanquet: 'in speaking of man's function, his 'work,' his *raison d'être* and hope or right of continuance, the student is apt to fix his eye on the leaders of mankind in great vocations, and on their nearest followers. Though well aware that their work is *for* mankind he finds a difficulty in exhibiting the value or values that come by and through mankind. Perhaps the present writer may tell a story against himself which illustrates this

weakness of the scholar. In a youthful college essay on some such topic as the extension of the franchise he had given vent to extreme hopes and theories respecting general education and the 'ladder from the elementary school to the university.' But from his college tutor, the sturdy democrat, T.H. Green, his speculations only elicited the remark: 'If you imply that no one is fit to have a vote who has not had a university education I don't agree with you." (Bernard Bosanquet, 'Unvisited Tombs', in his *Some Suggestions in Ethics* (London: MacMillan, 1918), pp.69–70). See Colin Tyler, 'TH Green, Advanced Liberalism and the Reform Question, 1865–76', *History of European Ideas*, vol. 29, no. 4 (December 2003), pp.437–58.]

²⁹ ['Or is it that some Force, too wise, too strong,
Even for yourselves to conquer or beguile,
Sweeps earth, and heaven, and men, and gods along,
Like the broad volume of the insurgent Nile?
And the great powers we serve, themselves may be
Slaves of a tyrannous necessity?'

Matthew Arnold, *Mycerinus*, in Kenneth and Miriam Allot (eds.) *The Poems of Matthew Arnold*, 2nd ed. (London: Longman, 1979), p.28, l.37–42 [first published 1849.]]

³⁰ [Sarpedon, son of Zeus and Laodamia, commanded the Lycian contingent in the Trojan War. Homer, *The Iliad*, Book 16, l.430–461.]

³¹ [Sophocles (c.496–406BC), Aeschylus (c.525–c.456BC), Athenian playwrights.]

³² [MS reads: 'unparallelled'.]

³³ [Euripedes (d. c.407BC), Athenian playwright.]

³⁴ [Aeschylus, *Prometheus Bound*, l.286–525.]

³⁵ [Aeschylus, *Agamemnon*, in *Aeschylus*, 2 vols., trans. HW Smith (London: William Heinemann, 1926), vol. 2, l.1025–7).]

³⁶ [The intended passage from Aeschylus' *Prometheus Bound* is probably: 'Not thus, nor yet, is fulfilling Fate destined to bring this end to pass.' (*Aeschylus*, trans. Herbert Weir Smyth, 2 vols. (London: William Heinemann, 1922–26), vol. 1, p.261, l.511–2.]

³⁷ [By the eight century BC, the three Fates were named Κλωθώ, Λάχεσις, and Ἄτροκος, having reference severally to the thread of life, to allotment, and to inevitability.' (St George Stock, 'Fate (Greek and Roman)', in James Hastings (ed.) *Encyclopaedia of Religion and Ethics*, 12 vols. (Edinburgh: T & T Clark, 1908–26), vol. 5, p.787).]

³⁸ ['some one of the powers supreme – Apollo perchance, or Pan, or Zeus' (Aeschylus, *Agamemnon*, pp.10, 11, l.56).]

³⁹ [MS reads: 'any'.]

⁴⁰ [The heroes are Glaucus and Diomedes (Homer, *The Iliad*, Book 6, l.120–236).]

⁴¹ [Priam king of Troy comes to Achilles' tent to ransom the body of Hector (Homer, *The Iliad*, Book 24, l.468–691).]

⁴² [Portia addresses the court of Venice in answer to Shylock: 'The quality of mercy is not strained,/It droppeth as the gentle rain from heaven/Upon the place beneath. It is twice blest:/It blesseth him that gives, and him that takes'

(William Shakespeare, *The Merchant of Venice*, Act 4, Scene 1, l.180–5).]

43 ['The churl in spirit, howe'r he veil
His want in forms for fashion's sake,
Will let his coltish nature break
At seasons through the gilded pale:

'For who can always act? but he,
To whom a thousand memories call,
Not being less but more of all
The gentleness he seem'd to be'

Alfred, Lord Tennyson, *In Memoriam AHH*, in Christopher Ricks (ed.) *The Poems of Tennyson* (London: Longmans, 1987), vol. 2, p.432, stanza 111, ll.5–12 [first published 1850]. Bosanquet quotes ll.5–9.]

44 ['To noble manners, as the flower
And native growth of noble mind;' (*Ibid.*, p.432, ll.15–6).]

45 [Robert Browning 'Dramatis Personae: Rabbi Ben Ezra', in Berkey et al (eds.), *Complete Works of Robert Browning: Volume 6*, pp.231–2, ll.133–4, 139–44, from stanzas 23 and 24 [poem first published 1864].]

46 [George Gordon, Lord Byron (1788–1824), English poet and libertine.]

47 [Since 1866, a number of strikes by tailors' unions had taken place in many cities, including Edinburgh, Cork, Limerick, Paris, New York and particularly London.]

48 ['For this cause sent he [Peleus] me [Phoenix] to instruct thee [Achilles] in all these things, to be both a speaker of words and a doer of deeds.' Homer, *Iliad*, Book 9, l.442–443 (Vol. I p.415).]

49 [MS reads: 'his'.]

50 [FW Farrar, 'On Greek and Latin Verse-Composition as a General Branch of Education', in FW Farrar (ed.) *Essays on a Liberal Education*, 2nd ed. (London: MacMillan, 1868), p.239. First published 1867.]

51 [*Ibid.*, p.234.]

52 This information all comes out of Mr [Charles Stuart] Parker's Essay 'On the History of Classical Education' [*ibid.*, pp.1–80.]

53 ['The cry of 'Things, not words,' gathered strength, and useful was opposed to liberal education. It was thought that boys intended for trade were out of place in the classical schools (Verbalschulen). The first Realschule was opened by Semler, at Halle, in 1739. At Berlin (1747) a Realschule, with a classical department, was founded, in which a liberal education might be combined with the study of any special subject, such as 'breeding silkworms,' or 'ninety kinds of leather." *Ibid.*, p.60]

54 [For 'Bifurcation', *ibid.* pp.70–1.]

55 [Famously Plato held that the physical world was unreal, being merely an imitation of the eternal, real world of the Forms (*Republic*, 478e–480a, 523a–525b, 596a–597e).]

56 [Possibly a reference to Thomas Arnold, *Introductory Lectures on Modern History*, 4th ed. (London: B Fellowes, 1849), pp.13–4.]

57 [MS reads: '1ˢᵗ'.]

232 Unpublished Manuscripts in British Idealism

58 [Matt. 19.6; also used in 'The Form of the Solemnization of Matrimony', *Book of Common Prayer (1662)*.]

59 [The position of Holy Roman Emperor evolved from Pope Leo III's installation of Charlemagne as Emperor of Rome in 800. The papacy and imperial office clashed frequently over the following centuries over the boundary between temporal matters (the proper concern of the Emperor) and spiritual one (the proper concern of the Pope). The positions of both the pope and the emperor were weakened by the Treaty of Westphalia of 1648, which shifted power and authority to states and away from both the Roman Catholic church and Holy Roman Empire. In 1806, Napoleon Bonaparte formally abolished the Holy Roman Empire as well as the office of 'Holy Roman Emperor'. The position of the pope was more secure. Bosanquet's essay was written a little over a year prior to Italy's annexation of Rome (and hence the Vatican) in 1870.]

60 [Following the Schools Inquiry Commission (1864–8) (for which Green served as a Commissioner), the Endowed Schools Act was passed in 1869. The Act led to the creation of the Endowed Schools Commission which was tasked designing a national schools system based on the endowed schools that were then in existence. In January 1870, Green spoke in support of the National Education League, which was lobbying for 'free, compulsory, secular elementary education, run by boards of rate-payers.' (Peter Nicholson, in Green, *Works*, vol. 5, p.236n13; see also Green's speech, *ibid.*, pp.236–8).]

61 [Carthage, a Phoenician colony on north African coast, was destroyed by the Romans in 146BC.]

62 [MS reads: 'ploutocracy'.]

63 [Juvenal, 'Satire Five' and Satire Eight', in Juvenal and Persius, *Satire*, trans. G.G. Ramsay (London: William Heinemann, 1950), pp.69–83, 159–181, respectively.]

64 [Probably a reference to the family of Hannibal (247–183/2BC), particularly his father Hamilcar (d.229BC) and Hamilcar's brother-in-law Hasdrubal (d.203BC).]

65 [Possibly a reference to Thomas Arnold, *Christian Life: Its Course, its hindrances, and its helps* (London: B. Fellowes, 1859), Lecture 16. First edition published 1841. Bosanquet may also have in mind JM Wilson's 'On Teaching Natural Science in Schools', in Farrar, *Essays on a Liberal Education*, essay 6. Wilson was a teacher at Rugby School in 1868, although his essay is obliquely critical of certain aspects of the Arnoldian curriculum.]

66 ['When I have borne in memory what has tamed
Great Nations, how ennobling thoughts depart
When men change swords for ledgers, and desert
The student's bower for gold, some fears unnamed
I had, my Country! – am I to be blamed?'

William Wordsworth, 'When I have borne in memory what has tamed', in Paul D Sheats (ed.) *Poetical Works of Wordsworth. Cambridge Edition* (Boston: Houghton Mifflin, 1982), p.288, ll.1–5 [first published 1807].]

67 [Possibly an allusion to Matthew Arnold, *Culture and Anarchy. An essay in political and social criticism* (London: Smith Elder, 1869), chapter 3 *passim*.]

68 [Catastrophe: *OED* [primary definition] 'The change or revolution which

produces the conclusion or final event of a dramatic piece'. Sophocles [*Oedipus Rex*] trans. F. Storr, 2 vols. (London: William Heinemann, 1912), Vol. 1, pp.1–140.]

69 [Demosthenes (384–322BC), Athenian orator.]

70 [MS very unclear.]

71 [Probably Antigone is arguing with Creon:

'Yea, for these laws were not ordained of Zeus,
And she who sits enthroned with gods below,
Justice, enacted not these human laws.
Nor did I deem that thou, a mortal man,
Couldn't by a breath annul and override
The immediate unwritten laws of Heaven.
They were not born to-day nor yesterday;
They die not; and none knoweth whence they sprang'.

Sophocles [*Antigone*] trans. F. Storr (London: William Heinemann, 1912), 451–459 (p.349) (Cf. Caird's citations of this passage in *Social Ethics*, vol. 2 of this set.)]

72 [Probably a reference to Aristophanes, [*Thesmophoriazusae*], trans. Benjamin Bickley Rogers, 3 vols. (London: William Heinemann, 1927), vol.3 pp.130–241. Charles John Huffam Dickens (1812–1870), alcoholic British journalist and novelist; Thomas Hood (1799–1845), comic poet.]

73 [Eton College (founded 1440), Charterhouse School (founded 1611), Harrow School (founded 1571), Rugby School (founded 1567), English public schools.]

74 ['Godliness and good learning' were the guiding principles of Thomas Arnold's headship at Rugby School (1828–42). 'Outward order, regularity, nay, even advancement in learning, may be, up to a certain point, enforced; but no man can force another to be good, or hinder him from being evil. It must be your own choice and act, whether indeed, you wish this place to be "unavoidably a seat or nursery of vice" or whether you wish to verify the words of our daily thanksgiving, that, by the benefit of our founders, "you are here brought up to godliness and good learning".' Thomas Arnold, *Sermons*, 6 vols. (London: Longmans Green, 1878), vol. 2, p.122, quoted in David Newsome, *Godliness and Good Learning. Four Studies on a Victorian Ideal* (London: John Murray, 1961) p.32. See also *ibid.*, vol. 5, pp.65–7.]

75 [Pericles (c.495–429BC), Athenian statesman. Probably referring to the 'Funeral Speech' reported in Thucydides, *History of the Peloponnesian War*, Book 2, ch.35–46, vol.1 pp.319–41.]

76 [Plato, *Republic* 414b–415d.]

77 [Socrates (469–399BC), Athenian philosopher who unsuccessfully defended himself from charges of impiety, arguing that he should be honoured for trying to bring Athenians to a reasoned allegiance to their polis. Demosthenes (384–322BC), Athenian patriot, pupil of Plato, orator, statesman and military commander.]

78 [Plato, *Republic*, 544c, 547–548. Aristotle, *Politics*, 1265b8–1266a2, 1269a29–1271b19.]

79 [The various syssitia or 'mess groups' formed the bedrock of Spartan society.

Every male Spartans lived within such a group between the ages of 20 and 30.]

[80] [Possibly an allusion to Aristotle, *Politics*, 1269a12–1270a10.]

[81] [MS reads: 'close'.]

[82] [The Battle of Leuctra (371BC) at which the Thebesians broke the military power of Sparta.]

[83] [Aristotle, *Politics*, 1269a37–9.]

[84] [Aristotle advocated a constitution with a mix of oligarchic and democratic elements in *Politics* (1293a35–1297a13). The Gerontes or *gerousia* was the Spartan council of elders.]

[85] [The idea that the primary duty of the State is to protect the individual from aggression (whether from his own countrymen or foreign states) frequently occurs in Spencer's writing, e.g. *Social Statics* (1851 edition) in Herbert Spencer, *Collected Writings*, 12 vols. (London: Routledge/Thoemmes, 1996), vol. 3, p.269. See also 'Over-Legislation' (reprinted from *Westminster Review*, July 1853) in *ibid.*, vol. 11, p.236.]

[86] [Probably 'Parliamentary Reform: the Dangers and Safeguards', *Westminster Review* April 1860, reprinted in Spencer, *Collected Writings*, vol. 11 pp.358–386. In this essay Spencer discusses the misdeeds of the trades unions on pp.362–5 and offers education as the necessary concomitant of parliamentary reform on pp.375–9]

[87] [Tattersall's was the world's first bloodstock auction house. It was founded in London sometime between 1765 and 1773. (It moved to Newmarket in 1939.)]

[88] [MS reads: 'eternising'.]

[89] [Joseph Mallord Turner (1775–1851), British landscape painter. William Shakespeare (1564–1616), British poet and playwright]

[90] [Robert Browning, 'The Ring and the Book', in Roma A King jnr. and Susan Crowl (eds.), *Complete Works of Robert Browning. Volume 9* (Ohio University Press, 1989), bk 10, l.1702–3, p.131, l.142 [poem first published in 1868–9].]

[91] ['I give utterance to a timely truth: arrogance/Is in very sooth the child of impiety.' Aeschylus [*Eumenides*] trans. Herbert Weir Smyth, 2 vols, (London: William Heinemann, 1957), vol.2, p. 321, l.529–531.]

[92] [MS reads: 'willed'.]

[93] [Euripedes, *Hippolytus* (first produced 428BC). A play of great power and, in its closing scenes, pathos and beauty, which especially attractive to those Victorian who, like Bosanquet, saw Hippolytus as a martyr to the cause of chastity.]

[94] ['That I may be with thee, and converse with thee,/Hearing thy voice, yet seeing not thy face.' Euripedes, *Hippolytus*, trans. AS Way, 4 vols. (London: William Heinemann, 1912–16), vol. 4, pp.167–9, l.85–6.]

[95] [Plato, *Theaetetus*, 176–7 examines the intrinsic and divine worth of the good life.]

[96] [Plato, *Timaeus*, 29a examines the construction of the cosmos; 86a the causes

of diseases lies in an imbalance of the vital elements.]

97 [Plato, *Republic*: 380 only those poetry which convey God's goodness should be allowed in the city; 617 the 'vision' of heaven.]

Report on a Dissertation entitled 'The Metaphysical Basis of Ethics' by Mr. G.E. Moore.[1]

[19 September 1898]

The Dissertation which has been submitted to me presents, in my opinion, an exceedingly difficult problem. I will state in general terms the question on which, if I am right, the electors must make up their minds, and will then give some reasons for my opinion, in order to expose it to criticism.

In considering the claim of undergraduate candidates for a scholarship or for a place in the class list, it is enough I suppose to be satisfied of the ability and knowledge displayed in their work. It is not expected that they shall make a serious contribution to the science with which they are dealing. If they shew what is called 'promise' in a marked degree, their claim is taken to be made out. But I presume that a Dissertation offered to the electors for a Fellowship is judged by a somewhat higher standard. The electors, I imagine, would desire to be satisfied that the candidate has begun to turn his promise into performance, and has not merely shown even a brilliant capacity for a certain kind of study, but has taken up a line of work which has begun to be fruitful in his hands. Of course it must be borne in mind that in philosophy a critical or sceptical attitude is no bar to the achievement of highly valuable results.

In the present case, to the best of my judgement, the above distinction applies in its fullest force. It would hardly be possible, within the limits of the subject chosen, to display more knowledge, ingenuity, and power of continuous persistence in a line of argument, than the writer of this dissertation has displayed. As a piece of controversial pleading his work would do credit to any living author. And I do not mean to imply that he is deficient in strictly philosophical acumen. On particular points, especially in the discovery of difficulties and discrepancies, his insight is remarkably keen. And his conception – to make one observation in detail – of the duties of a historian of philosophy seem[s] to me to be thorough and just. I was therefore all the more disappointed when I found myself almost wholly unable to appreciate the theoretical point of view which the author has adopted. It appears

236

to me to lie beyond the limit of paradox which is permissible in philosophy. It may be suggested that a disagreement with his positive views should be no bar to an independent judgment of the criticism of Kant, of which, as explained and supported by the author, the Dissertation consists. But here, as I am glad to point out, it is by his own merit that he suffers. His just conception of the duty of the historian of philosophy[2] has the effect of marrying his positive views so closely to his critical standpoint, that it is wholly impossible to estimate them separately. His view of what Kant can have meant is controlled by his view of what there was for Kant to mean, and he analyses what he takes to be Kant's errors and misapprehensions into what he takes to be the truths at which Kant was aiming. Thus the whole weight of the work rests upon the author's theoretical position; and if this position seems altogether inadequate, the value of the exposition of Kant, which depends upon it, is destroyed. This observation only applies to matters of principle in philosophy, and not to what may be called the philological aspect of the author's criticism. I believe that so far as regards the citation and immediate interpretation of passages from Kant his comprehensiveness and candour are unimpeachable.

This then is the general statement of the problem which in my view lies before the electors. If they are of opinion that ability and intellectual distinction, with great knowledge, and, I may add, with great earnestness in the pursuit of truth, are sufficient qualifications, then I think they will be absolutely safe in electing the author of the dissertation; and it is quite possible that they may secure in him a considerable philosopher. But it is my duty to point out that I have never met with a stronger case of the paradox that a man may be exceedingly able and devoted, and yet, for some inexplicable reason, may fail to take up a sound position in his science. As to what future development may bring with it I can see no sure ground for predicting. Only it occurs to me that constant work under high pressure at a limited subject may have had to do with the one-sidedness which I complain of. If this is so, the author of the dissertation might be able in the future to justify himself in a way which does not now appear.

It is obvious that my conclusion is based on a difference of philosophical opinion between the author and myself. When we get beyond the mere estimate of ability and promise, and begin to consider the value of contributions to philosophy, I do not know how this is to be avoided. All I can do is to indicate some specific points to which my opinion refers, so that the electors may know how to discount my judgment. Of course I am only referring to points in the Dissertation, and am not giving an account of them which would be complete if taken by itself. In sum, the intellectual motive of the Dissertation, as I read it, is to dissociate truth from the nature of Knowledge, and Good from the nature of the Will, so as to free Metaphysic from all risk of confusion with Psychology. The theory of the proposition and the concept which harmonises with the dissociation of Truth from the nature of Knowledge is set out in ch.2.[3] I confess that I feel a difficulty in regarding it as serious. It is necessary no doubt to distinguish, in the processes and products of cognition, between their nature as knowledge and their psychological genesis. But the theory here propounded seems to reduce the world of truth to an immutable framework of hypostasised 'propositions' or 'concepts' in relations, which are indeed possible objects of thought, but are entities not dependent upon thought, nor partaking of any character which distinctively belongs to thought. Truth and falsehood depend on the nature of the relation between the 'concepts' which constitute a 'proposition' (neither of these entities necessarily implying mental formulation); and their nature, (that of truth and falsehood), cannot be further defined, but must be immediately recognised.

Here it seems to me clear that 'the child has been thrown away in emptying the bath'. To get rid of mere psychology, the essential idea of consciousness and cognition as an endeavour towards unity has been abandoned, and relational truth has been hypostatised as a self-subsistent form of Reality. The hostile criticism upon Kant's Copernican attitude,[4] and the inability to find an interpretation for his 'personification' of Reason as 'a creature with claims',[5] or to treat the rationality of ethical action in any adequate way, are the natural consequences of this abandonment.

The divorce between the 'good' and the nature of the will, as also between Reason with its law and this same nature, seems to me to indicate an equally hopeless surrender of the most important connections. It seems a verbal question whether the idea which acts as cause in volition is to be counted as a natural cause, and whether Reason can be Practical; but it would appear that to disconnect the nature of actual will from that of its object and its law must make any account of the ethical self or of ethical freedom impossible. The impossibility of finding a meaning for Kant's Autonomy,[6] except in a sense in which it applies to all natural objects, results from this disconnection, which, as I understand it, is a mere case of the author's general separation between the nature of consciousness on the one hand, and Truth and Goodness, as simple or unanalysable concepts, on the other.

To make my meaning clear, I ought to add that I do not complain of the rejection of the Free Will of Indifference, either in itself, or as ascribed to Kant, and the writer's defence against objections based on moral responsibility seems to me successful. But I do think it a serious matter that views should be adopted by an interpreter of Kant which wholly preclude him from giving a positive significance to the idea of Freedom which underlies Kant's whole philosophy. I put my complaint in this form, because I agree with the writer that his views leave him no alternative so far as his representation of Kant is concerned. In making Kant consistent, I suppose, some of his statements must in any cause be rejected or explained away, and the interpreter's views of what it was possible for him to mean decide which are to be so treated.

I ought in fairness to call attention to a reservation under which the author seems to propound his views throughout. He is speaking as 'from the common point of view, which takes the world of experience as ultimately real'. And he maintains this ground, I gather, as an argument *ad homines*: as he rightly considers it to be the ground taken by both Determinists and Indeterminists, in their controversy.[7] It may be that his views would be better able to justify themselves if they were liberated from this assumption, than they appear to be while it is accepted.

I have not allowed this Report to expand into a complete philosophical discussion of the Dissertation, because such a discussion would involve requiring the electors to act as judges in a philosophical controversy. I have stated the opinion which with great reluctance I have been obliged to form, and the question, which, if I am right, is presented to the electors for decision. I have also, I think, given sufficient indications of the grounds for my opinion to enable the electors to allow for any bias which may have affected it. The above are my principal objections. If I have exaggerated their importance, my estimate of the dissertation is not trustworthy.

It may illustrate the situation if I state what my treatment of the work would have been, if it has been sent me for review by 'Mind',[8] I should have treated it respectfully as a brilliant essay by a very able writer, but should have endeavoured to point out that its positive stand-point and consequently its treatment of the subject were hopelessly inadequate, that is to say, that the writer was not successful, to any appreciable extent, in[9] representing the real nature and interconnection of the factors involved in the problem with which he was concerned.

I do not think that I can make my judgment clearer by any further observations.

Bernard Bosanquet,
Sept. 19 1898.

---

[1] [Bosanquet's title. George Edward Moore, 'The Metaphysical Basis of Reality', dissertation for 1898 Trinity Fellowship competition. See further the introduction to this volume (pp. xxiii–xxv). George Edward Moore (1873–1958), English philosopher, gained Firsts in both the classical and the moral sciences tripos from Trinity College, Cambridge (1894 and 1896, respectively), appointed Fellow of Trinity in 1898, later university lecturer (1911–25) and then professor of philosophy (1925–39) at Cambridge before moving to the United States. His few writings, together with those of Bertrand Russell and Ludwig Wittgenstein, caused a sea-change in Anglo-American philosophical fashion in the early decades of the twentieth century.]

[2] [Moore's method of intellectual history appeared to have consisted in attempting to discern the elements of the 'correct' solution to a philosophical problem in the author he was studying, and explaining, in light of this 'correct' answer, what the author really meant to assert.]

[3] [The draft of the 1898 dissertation which survives in the Wren Library is highly fragmentary and lacks the chapter to which Bosanquet refers. That chapter appears to have been published as 'The Nature of Judgment', *Mind* (April 1899), 8:30 ns, pp.176–93, although possibly in a revised form.]

[4] [Immanuel Kant, *Critique of Pure Reason*, trans. and ed. by P Guyer and AW Wood (Cambridge University Press, 1998), pp. 110 (B xvi–xvii), 113 (B xxii).]

[5] [Kant, for example, 'Critique of Practical Reason', in I Kant, *Practical Philosophy*, trans. and ed. M Gregor (Cambridge University Press, 1996), pp.153–8 (Prussian 5:19–21).]

[6] [Immanuel Kant, 'Groundwork of the Metaphysic of Morals', in his *Practical Philosophy*, pp.81–6 (Prussian 4:430–7), 88–9 (Prussian 4:439–40), 94–108 (Prussian 4:446–63).]

[7] [See GE Moore, 'Freedom', *Mind*, 7:26 ns (April 1898), pp.179–204.]

[8] [The first issue of *Mind. A Quarterly Review of Psychology and Philosophy* was published in January 1876 under the editorship of George Croom Robertson. It remains one of the world's leading philosophical journals.]

[9] [MS del.: 'did not make a serious attempt to'.]

Part 3
David George Ritchie

My dear Sir,

I hope you will excuse my writing to you about the interesting review of my last book[2] which you publish in *Mind* for this month.[3] Unlike most reviews it gives real criticisms and has supplied me with materials for reflection. When I expressed a hope in the *Preface* that the book might be of use to 'the special student of ethics and politics',[4] I was not thinking primarily of persons reading for examinations, but of persons like myself who are trying to find out what is true and to whom a short statement of problems (theoretical and practical) is sometimes more helpful than an elaborate dogmatic system. I should not indeed hesitate to recommend the book – such as it is – to candidates reading for the two examinations I have most acquaintance with, viz., *Lit. Hum.* and Mod. Hist. at Oxford.[5] Knowing the kind of teaching they get and need, I don't think the book would do them any harm. In Scotland as yet, unfortunately, no such subject as Political Science is recognised. Elsewhere I should be cautious in recommending the book!

The book, I may explain, grew out of a popular lecture;[6] but behind that lay a good many years' study of the American and French Declarations of Rights.[7] I was tired of the vague criticisms generally given. And as you see these Declarations are responsible for the order and grouping of subjects. In treating the idea of 'natural rights' as 'an element of current thought',[8] I have thought it quite as important to deal with popular writers (e.g. Henry George)[9] as with an expositor of the *Lex Naturalis* like Father Rickaby[10] or of the doctrine of *Naturrecht* like Prof Lorimer[11] or of his own special views like Mr. Spencer.[12] As to the last of these I thought the criticism of his fundamental formula of Justice in pp.141–147 dispensed me from minuter treatment of the edifice erected on what seems to me so rotten a foundation.[13] Besides I have written a good deal about Mr. Spencer in a little book called *Principles of State-Interference* (where I also attempted to grapple with the terms 'social organism', etc.)[14] and so I made the mistake

243

of not repeating what I had said elsewhere. I may be quite wrong in my opinion of Mr. Spencer, but it is my honest opinion, and I believe (rightly or wrongly) it will ultimately prevail.

However, to come to the two matters – which are really my excuse for troubling you with this letter – the historical statements. I am indeed very fully 'conscious of the limitations of my knowledge',[15] especially in regard to mediaeval history. I can only say that I used the most scrupulous care to verify my statements as to matters of fact and my references to the opinions of writers, and I submitted many points to judgments of those more specially qualified than myself. As to the two examples of my inaccuracy which you give, I have gone over the passages again and I am afraid I do not acknowledge error, although my statements might certainly be improved and made fuller and less ambiguous. The passage from Filmer is very familiar to me: it used to be a stock-quotation in my lectures at Oxford.[16] In tracing the theory of natural rights to the Protestant revolt against authority, I do not say that the theory cannot be traced farther back also. I do trace it farther back e.g. on p. 7, and in chap. ii. Mediaeval writers on the ecclesiastical side did assert the sovereignty of the people and the right of resistance to tyrants – *when the Church (or the Pope) declared them such.* What Protestantism does is to leave the people (and that ultimately comes to mean individuals) to decide: that seems to me to make an immense difference and it is that which makes Protestantism the logical parent of the French Revolution. I do not assert this because Hegel said so. That Hegel (practically) said so proves, in my judgment, his historical insight.[17] On p. 240 fl. I have referred to the difference introduced by Protestantism into the 'right of resistance'[18] – one particular illustration of what I say in general terms on p.13.[19]

As to Locke and Rousseau – Locke leaves 'the people' to judge *when* the established government is faithful to the trust reposed [in] it and *when not*, so that I think I am right in regarding Rousseau's theory *on this particular point* as simply Locke's theory expressed by a more lucid writer.[20] I do not ignore differences between Locke and Rousseau. I have referred to the matter more fully in *Darwin and Hegel &c* (Essays on 'Social Contract' and 'Sovereignty') p. 254, p. 220 &c; *Principles of State-Interference* p.164;[21] and in the translation of Bluntschli's *Theory of the State* 2nd edit. p. 294 *footnote*.[22] (My note in 1st Edit. was not quite accurate.)[23]   Probably I ought to have qualified my emphatic contradiction of the usual contrast between Locke and Rousseau more carefully.[24] By 'identical' I only mean 'identical' as one may say Kant's form of the Social Contract theory was identical with Rousseau's.[25] One only asserts identity on a basis of difference; but perhaps you will disallow that ordinary practical procedure as 'suspect' of Hegelian logic!

Of course I do not ask you to reply to my Apologia; but if you or any of your pupils or friends – who may have looked into my book – should send me any jottings of passages (even if only the part of the page were indicated) when *statements as to matters of facts or interpretations of authors* seem inaccurate or in need of revision, I should be very grateful. My present work here may keep me from a long time from taking up the study of political theories again; but I hope I may sometime be able to resume it. And these details as to matters of fact seem to me as important as are his 'specimens' to the biologist or geologist.

Again asking you to excuse this letter and its length and thanking you for the trouble you have taken with my book

    I am

            Yours faithfully
            David G. Ritchie

To Prof. H. Sidgwick.

---

[1] ['University/St. Andrews, N.B.' is printed on both sheets of headed notepaper. 'N.B.' denotes 'North Britain', a.k.a. Scotland.]

[2] [David George Ritchie, *Natural Rights: A criticism of some political and ethical conceptions* (London: George Allen and Unwin, 1894) (hereafter *NR*).]

[3] [Henry Sidgwick, Critical Notice of D.G. Ritchie, *Natural Rights*, *Mind*, vol. 4, no.15 ns (July 1895), pp.384–8.]

[4] [*NR*, p.x.]

[5] [Ritchie taught students taking *literae humantiores* (i.e., classics and philosophy) and Modern History during his early career at Oxford. He was Fellow of Jesus College (1878) and a tutor at Balliol (1882–86).]

[6] [Ritchie gave this lecture to the Fabian Society in London, on 20 November 1891. The *Fabian News*, vol. 1 (1891/2), p.38) carried a brief summary of it. See Peter Nicholson's introduction to Ritchie's *Collected Works*, ed. P. P. Nicholson (Bristol: Thoemmes, 1998), vol. 1, p.x, n.10. See *NR* p.x.]

[7] [*NR* (pp.287–300) reproduces the Virginian Declaration of Rights (12 June 1776), an extract from the 'Declaration of Independence of the United States of America' (4 July 1776), the French 'Declaration des Droits de L'Homme et du Citoyen' (1789), the 'Declaration Prefixed to Constitution of June 24, 1793', and 'Declaration

Prefixed to the French Constitution of ... Aug. 322, 1795', and the preamble to the 'Constitution de la République Française' (4 November 1848).]

8   [Sidgwick uses the phrase 'an element of present thought' ('Critical Notice', p.385).]

9   [*NR*, pp.270–1.]

10 [Father Joseph Rickaby, *Moral Philosophy, or Ethics and Natural Law*, 2nd ed. (London: Longmans Green, 1889). Discussed *NR*, pp.40, 88, 89, 90, 126, 162n, 163–66.]

11 [James Lorimer, *The Institutes of the Law of Nations. A treatise of the jural relations of separate political communities* (Edinburgh: William Blackwood, 1872; 2nd, enlarged edition 1880; 3rd ed. in 2 vols. 1883–4). Discussed *NR*, pp.61n, 92, 94, 128n, 233. Ritchie appears to be using the 2nd edition.]

12 [Herbert Spencer, particularly *Principles of Ethics*, 2 vols. (London: Williams and Norgate, 1879–93), and *The Man* versus *the State* (London: Williams and Norgate, 1884). Discussed *NR*, pp.14–15, 24, 45–46, 113, 139, 141–142, 187, 234n, 235n, 249.]

13 [*Justice* was the name of Part 4 of Spencer's *Principles of Ethics*, and was first published in 1891.]

14 [David George Ritchie, *The Principles of State Interference: Four Essays on the Political Philosophy of Mr. Herbert Spencer, J.S. Mill, and T.H. Green* (London: Swan Sonnenschein, 1891), chaps. 1 and 2 ('Mr. Herbert Spencer's Individualism and his Conception of Society', and 'The State *versus* Mr. Herbert Spencer', respectively). The discussion of Spencer accounts for a little under half the book.]

15 [Sidgwick claims that Ritchie is not conscious enough of the limitations of his (Ritchie's) historical knowledge in certain areas ('Critical Notice', p.386).]

16 [' "Since the time," says Sir Robert, "that school divinity began to flourish there has been a common opinion maintained, as well by divines as by divers other learned men, which affirms–

'Mankind is naturally endowed and born with freedom from all subjection, and at liberty to choose what form of government it please, and that the power which any one man hath over others was at first bestowed according to the discretion of the multitude.'

This tenet was first hatched in the schools, and hath been fostered by all succeeding Papists for good divinity. The divines, also, of the Reformed Churches have entertained it.' (Robert Filmer, *Patriarcha*, chap. 1, §1, quoted in Sidgwick, 'Critical Notice', p.387). See Robert Filmer, *Patriarcha and other writings*, ed. JP Sommerville (Cambridge University Press, 1991), p.2.]

17 [Sidgwick implies that Ritchie is simply parroting Hegel, when he writes 'this is a dangerous mode of applying the principle of the 'Rationality of History' ('Critical Notice', p.387). Hegel links the rise of the Protestant spirit with the French Revolution in his *Philosophy of History*, trans. by J Sibree (London: Dover, 1956), pp.442–9. First English edition published in December 1857.]

18 [*NR*, pp.240–1. Chapter 9 (pp.238–43) is entitled 'Resistance to Oppression.').]

19 [*NR*, pp.13–4.]

20 [John Locke, *Two Treatises on Government*, ed. P Laslett 2nd ed. (Cambridge University Press, 1967), pp.424–46 (i.e., *Second Treatise*, chap. 19). Jean–Jacques

Rousseau, *Social Contract*, trans. M Cranston (Harmondsworth: Penguin, 1968), for example, bk 3, chaps. 13–15.]

21 [David George Ritchie, *Darwin and Hegel with other philosophical studies* (London: Swan Sonnenschein, 1893), pp.254, 220 ('Contributions to the History of the Social Contract Theory' (pp.196–226), and 'On the Conception of Sovereignty' (pp.227–264)); *State Interference*, p.164.]

22 ['It should be noted that the Theory of Contract is applied in different ways by Hobbes, Locke, and Rousseau. According to Hobbes (*Leviathan*, ch. 17) men only pass from the "state of nature" to the social state by surrendering their rights to a sovereign (one, few, or many). Locke (*Treatises on Government*, Book ii. ch.ii. §6) supposes rights, e.g. of liberty and property, to exist in the state of nature: by the "original compact" (Locke uses the term "compact," not "contract") a form of government is instituted to secure these rights (c. viii). According to Rousseau men pass from the state of nature to the social state by the social contract (as on Hobbes's theory), but the sovereign to whom each surrenders his rights is "the people," so that each is sovereign as well as subject (*Contr. Soc.* i. c. 6). This sovereignty is inalienable (ii. c. 1): a government is not instituted by a contract (iii. c.16); the government is only the minister of the General Will. Thus, according to Hobbes, a revolution against the *de facto* government, which he identifies with the sovereign, implies a return to the state of nature, anarchy, and is quite unjustifiable. According to Locke, a revolution might be justifiable, where the government had ceased to fulfil the trust reposed in it, i.e. to protect personal rights. According to Rousseau, a revolution would be a change of ministry. Contrary to what is very commonly supposed, Locke does not speak of any contract between government and people. His theory is almost identical with that of Rousseau. Cp. T.H. Green, *Works*, ii. pp.366–396.' Johann Caspar Bluntschli, *The Theory of the State. Authorised English translation from the sixth German edition*, trans. DG Ritchie, PE Matheson, and R Lodge, 2nd ed. (Oxford: Clarendon, 1890), pp.294–5, note a.]

23 [The note in the first edition reads 'quite different' in its opening sentence; does not include the comment '(Locke uses the term "compact," not "contract")'; includes ', as on Locke's theory' after '(iii. C.16)'; reads 'a revolution may be justifiable' instead of 'a revolution might be justifiable'; reads 'where the government has ceased to fulfil its part of the contract,' rather than 'where the government had ceased to fulfil the trust reposed in it,'; and reads 'Such seems a fair interpretation of the views of these three writers; but the language, especially of Locke, is not always consistent.' Instead of the final three sentences of the second edition (i.e. 'Contrary to what … 396.'). JC Bluntschli, *The Theory of the State. Authorised English translation from the sixth German edition*, trans. DG Ritchie, PE Matheson, and R Lodge (Oxford: Clarendon, 1885), pp.276–7 note a.]

24 ['[Rousseau's] views about the sovereignty of the people and about the justification of revolution are identical with those of Locke, expressed indeed in more telling language, and addressed to an audience that was suffering graver and older evils than those which had induced the English Whigs of 1688 to change the government of their country.' (*NR*, pp.50–51). Sidgwick, 'Critical Notice', pp.387–8.]

25 [Immanuel Kant, 'Metaphysics of Morals', in his *Practical Philosophy*, trans. and ed. M Gregor (Cambridge University Press, 1996), pp.456–8 (Prussian Academy Edition 6:313–315). Rousseau, *Social Contract*, bk 1, chap. 6.]

Appendix
The Contents of Bosanquet's Undergraduate Notebooks.

This appendix supplements the discussion of Bosanquet's undergraduate notebooks that is given in the introduction to this volume (see pp. xxii–xxiii above).

Notebook A

This notebook includes twenty-four essays written in English and fourteen Latin exercises, as well as two sets of Logic exercises. The latter begin from the back of the notebook and are written upside-down. Tutor's initials are given at the end of the English essays (Robert Scott accounts for eleven and TH Green accounts for eight, with five essays not initialled). Of the Latin exercises, eight are initialled by Scott and five by Green, with one essay not initialled. No tutor is identified for the Logic exercises. Each of the sixteen essays from this notebook that are included in this volume is marked on the following list with an asterisk. Presumably, the English and Latin essays run in chronological order, although the relative date of the Logic exercises is unclear. The English essays appear in the following order.

1. Asceticism.* [RS]
2. The Conception of Historical Causes in Thucydides Compared with that in Herodotus.* [THG]
3. The Social and Economical Evils Produced by the Increase of Population.* [RS]
4. The Proper Functions of Universities.* [THG]
5. The Origin of Mythology. [RS]
6. The Conception of Fate in the Ancient Poets and Historians.* [THG]
7. Courtesy.* [RS]
8. The Connection of Morality with Art.* [No initials.]
9. The Genius and Character of Sir Walter Scott. [RS]
10. What Constitutes Civilization?* [THG]
11. The Use of the Expression "Things, Not Words," in the Controversy About Education.* [THG]

12. The Advantages and Disadvantages of Anonymous Writing. [RS]
13. The Connection Between Novel Writing and Poetry. [No initials.]
14. The Chief Points of View in which the Relation Between the Church and the State May be Regarded.* [RS]
15. The Advantages and Disadvantages of Commercial Prosperity.* [THG]
16. The Influence of Rhyme upon Poetry. [RS]
17. The Contrast between Ancient and Modern Tragedies.* [THG]
18. The Influence on Endowments on Education.* [THG]
19. The Greek Idea of Citizenship.* [RS]
20. The Contrast Between Homeric and Historical Greece. [No initials.]
21. The Place of the Early Tyrannies in the Constitutional History of Greece. [No initials.]
22. The Comparative Permanence of the Gentile Tie at Rome and in Greece. [RS]
23. The Constitution of Sparta Compared with the Ideals of Plato and Aristotle.* [RS]
24. Legislation and Morality.* [No initials.]

Upside down from back of this notebook:
25. Logic Questions [1] (6pp.)
26. Logic Questions [2] (9pp.)

Notebook B
This notebook contains thirteen essays, all written predominantly in English. Presumably they are in chronological order. Scott has initialled seven of these, with six not being initialled at all. Each of the three essays from this notebook that are included in this volume is marked on the following list with an asterisk. The contents of this notebook is as follows.

1. A paraphrase of the process by which Aristotle arrives at the[1] conception of ἀνδρώπινον ἀγαδόν. [No initials.]
2. The method of the practical science in Aristotle. [RS]
3. Office of ἐθιδμος in Moral Education acc. to Aristotle. Difference between his view and Plato's. [No initials.]

4. The conceptions of faculty, function, & final cause, as determining Aristotle's moral theory. [No initials.]
5. Epicureanism in Aristotle. [RS]
6. The relation of πράζὶς and δεωρία in Plato & Aristotle. [RS]
7. Contrast of φνσικα and σίχα in Aristotle. [No initials.]
8. A Sense of Beauty as an Element in Morals.* [RS]
9. The Sophists in Their Relation to Popular Morality. [RS]
10. Plato's Conception of Justice in the Individual and the State.* [No initials.]
11. The Notion of Evil Among the Ancients.* [RS]
12. The Difficulties Presented to Ancient Philosophy by the Phenomenon of ἀκρασία ["incontinence (to use a literal though inaccurate translation of the Aristotelian word ἀκρασία)" from Bosanquet's essay]. [No initials.]
13. The Relation of Plato to the Eristics. [RS]

---

1 ['his' substituted, in the unknown tutor's (?) hand.]

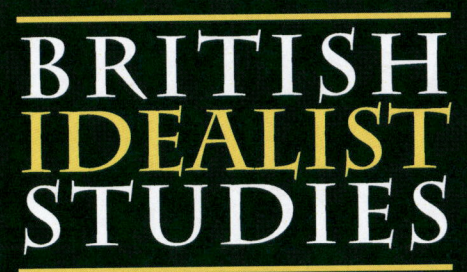

A monograph series reflecting the renewed interest in the British idealists.

All titles are priced at £30/$49.90 and cloth-bound. Please check website for full details, sample chapters and updates:

imprint-academic.com/idealists

'An excellent series', *TLS*

Series 1: Michael Oakeshott

Luke O'Sullivan: Oakeshott on History

- 'A very helpful and welcome volume.' Michael Bentley, *English Historical Review*
308 pages £30/$49.90 978-0907845294

Roy Tseng: The Sceptical Idealist

- 'Meticulously reconstructs Oakeshott's views.' Graeme Garrard, *Political Studies Review*
320 pages £30/$49.90 978-0907845225

Ian Tregenza: Michael Oakeshott on Hobbes

- 'A skillfully posed and smartly analysed work.' Steven Gerencser, *Hist. Political Thought*
250 pages £30/$49.90 978-0907845591

Efraim Podoksik: In Defence of Modernity

- 'This is an excellent and illuminating book.' John Charvet, *History of Political Thought*
260 pages £30/$49.90 978-0907845669

Kenneth B. McIntyre: The Limits of Political Theory

- 'Ably written and cogently argued.' **James Mellon**, *Political Studies Review*
210 pages £30/$49.90 978-1845400101

Suvi Soininen: From a 'Necessary Evil' to an Art of Contingency: Michael Oakeshott's Conception of Political Activity

- 'Well researched and intellectually engaging.' **David Boucher**, *Political Studies Review*
300 pages £30/$49.90 978-1845400064

Glenn Worthington: Religious and Poetic Experience in Oakeshott

- 'Well-ordered and systematic.' **Bob Cheekes**, *Intellectual Conservative*
180 pages £30/$49.90 978-0907845621

Andrew Sullivan: Intimations Pursued: The Voice of Practice in the Conversation of Michael Oakeshott

250 pages 978-0907845287 September 2007

Kevin Williams: Education and the Voice of Michael Oakeshott

250 pages 978-1845400552 September 2007

Erik Kos: Michael Oakeshott, the Ancient Greeks and the Philosophical Study of Politics

250 pages 978-1845400750 December 2007 *[continued overleaf]*

Series 2: R.G. Collingwood

Editor: David Boucher (Cardiff). **Board**: W.H. Dray (Ottowa), Gary Browning (Oxford Brookes), Bruce Haddock (Cardiff), Rex Martin (Kansas), Guido Vanheeswijck (Antwerp), Jan van der Dussen (OU, Netherlands)

James Connelly: Metaphysics, Method and Politics: The Political Philosophy of R.G. Collingwood

- 'Exegesis of the highest quality.' Andrew Lockyer, *History of Political Thought*
346 pages £30/$49.90 978-0907845317

Stein Helgeby: Action as History: The Historical Thought of R.G. Collingwood

- 'An impressive piece of writing.' Peter Johnson, *History of Political Thought*
250 pages £30/$49.90 978-0907845577

Marnie Hughes-Warrington: 'How Good an Historian Shall I Be?' R.G. Collingwood, the Historical Imagination and Education

- 'In short, to this reviewer's mind, Hughes-Warrington has written an exemplary book'
Peter Johnson, *History of Political Thought*
260 pages £30/$49.90 978-0907845614

Richard Murphy: Art, Metaphysics and Dialectic: R.G. Collingwood and the Crisis of Western Civilisation

260 pages £30/$49.90 978-1845401061 December 2007

Florin Lobont: Religious Experience and its Modes in Collingwood

260 pages £30/$49.90 978-1845400088 [postponed to 2008]

Series 3: T.H. Green

Editor: Peter Nicholson, University of York (retd.). **Board:** G.F. Gaus (Tulane), John Morrow (Auckland), Lord Plant (King's College, London), Avital Simhony (Arizona State), Geoffrey Thomas (Birkbeck), Andrew Vincent (Sheffield)

Matt Carter: T.H. Green and the Development of Ethical Socialism

- 'This book is a great service to the Labour movement.' Roy Hattersley, *New Statesman*
230 pages £30/$49.90 978-0907845324

Denys Leighton: The Greenian Moment: T.H. Green, Religion and Political Argument in Victorian Britain

- 'Impressive and scholarly.'**Colin Tyler**, *European Journal of Political Theory*
380 pages £30/$49.90 978-0907845546

Ben Wempe: T.H. Green's Theory of Positive Freedom

- 'Essential reading.' **Roy Hattersley**, *The Guardian*
250 pages £30/$49.90 978-0907845584

Alberto De Sanctis: The 'Puritan' Democracy of Thomas Hill Green

- 'An excellent discussion.' **Thom Brooks**, *Times Higher Educational Supplement*
240 pages £30/$49.90 978-1845400385

Imprint Academic, PO Box 200, Exeter EX5 5YX, UK
Tel: +44 (0)1392 851550   Fax: 851178   sandra@imprint.co.uk
imprint-academic.com/idealists
Imprint Academic, Philosophy Documentation Center
PO Box 7147, Charlottesville, VA 22906-7147, USA
Tel: 800-444-2419   Fax: 434-220-3301   order@pdcnet.org

UNPUBLISHED MANUSCRIPTS
IN BRITISH IDEALISM

Volume 2

UNPUBLISHED MANUSCRIPTS IN BRITISH IDEALISM

Political Philosophy, Theology and Social Thought

Edited and Introduced by

Colin Tyler

Volume 2

ia

imprint-academic.com

First published by Thoemmes Continuum 2005

This edition published in the UK by
Imprint Academic, PO Box 200, Exeter EX5 5YX, UK

and in the USA by
Imprint Academic, Philosophy Documentation Center
PO Box 7147, Charlottesville, VA 22906-7147, USA

ISBN 9781845401252

A CIP catalogue record for this book is available from the
British Library and US Library of Congress

Contents

Introduction

Excuse this scrawl. When I try to think as I write, I get too careless. I hope that you will be able to make me out.[1]

The idea of publishing more idealist texts occurred to me in 1998 while I was preparing *The Collected Works of Edward Caird*.[2] I was struck by the fact that while Caird himself published very little regarding his own positive theory of ethical and political philosophy, many manuscripts on these subjects were preserved in his archives at the University of Glasgow. Most notable in this regard were a series of professorial lectures on social ethics that Caird appeared to have given as part of his moral philosophy course, and a lecture on political economy. The archive also contained a number of unpublished but well-developed pieces on religion, metaphysics, and psychology. Two of the religious manuscripts are included here. Further research yielded two referee's reports at Trinity College Cambridge, one regarding GE Moore and the other JME McTaggart. Both are historically significant and philosophically developed, and so are included here as well.

Finding the texts was one thing, but turning them into a critical edition was another. Sir Henry Jones once described Caird's written comments on the essays of his undergraduates as 'for most part either illegible to the student or decipherable only by exhausting all the probabilities.'[3] Unfortunately, most of Caird's manuscripts are in a similar condition. Nevertheless, one does get used to his hand, and I believe that a laborious process of checking and re-checking numerous times has produced texts for this volume that are at least as accurate as those found in the preceding one. I hope that you find them as interesting and revealing. The remainder of this introduction addresses the specific issues of the individual manuscripts.

1. Reform and Reformation.' [ca. 1866]
[Title and location of manuscript: 'Reform and Reformation.' MS
Gen. 1294, Special Collections Library, University of Glasgow.]
   This long essay survives in fair copy in Caird's papers. The
manuscript appears to be complete, and may have been submitted
by Caird early in 1866 as part of his application for the Chair in
Moral Philosophy at the University of Glasgow.[4] Caird was
successful against a large and strong field of candidates.[5]

2. Lectures on Moral Philosophy: Social Ethics. [1877–93?]
[Title and location of manuscripts: 'Social Ethics.' MS Gen. 1294,
Special Collections Library, University of Glasgow.]
   This piece consists of eight lectures from what appear to be the
course on moral philosophy that Caird gave each year at Glasgow.[6]
Lectures one and four, and all of lecture two except for four folios,
are written on numbered pages ripped from notebooks, while the
remainder are written on numbered pages taken from quarto
volumes of a type commonly used by Caird.[7] No trace has been
found of the missing text (lecture three, the bulk of the first two
pages of lecture five, all of lecture seven, and the concluding pages
of lecture six).
   One might wonder whether Caird would have approved of the
publication of these lectures. After all this was the man who sued
a former student, WS Sime, for publishing notes made from his
(Caird's) course, partly on the grounds that one's thought
developed so quickly that any unauthorised set of notes was almost
bound to misrepresent the lecturer's current position. Indeed,
even his own lecture notes functioned more as a guide than a
statement of principle. Jones described Caird's practice in the
following terms.

> He was in the habit of constantly recasting his lectures - even
> when the course as a whole followed the same main lines. And,
> further,…he by no means confined himself to his MS. when he
> was lecturing. He omitted and he amplified, interpreting at the
> moment as a great teacher must the degree in which his students
> were following his thoughts, and catching inspiration in their
> companionship. Of all Professors he was one of the least likely
> to find himself anticipated in his class by students possessing
> ancient manuscripts of his lectures.[8]

Jones' characterisation is supported at least in certain respects by the surviving sets of student notes, which show that the curriculum of Caird's moral philosophy lectures changed little throughout the 1870s and 1880s (see the appendices to volume for an indicative curriculum from the 1876-77 session).[9]

Yet, there is a significant justification for publishing Caird's own lecture notes on social ethics. Muirhead identified the key point, mentioned above, when he observed that, 'It may seem surprising that though engaged during a long life in teaching Moral Philosophy Caird left no systematic work upon Ethics.' He expanded on this point in the following terms,

> Even his public class teaching in Glasgow was mainly historical, and consisted rather in a review of older theories than in an independent development of one of his own. This omission indeed towards the end of his life he intended to supply, but it is doubtful whether he would have added anything material to what may be read by the attentive student between his criticism of others. He believed in Jowett's dictum that 'moral philosophy should be largely historical,' and seemed always to find himself more at home in bringing out the essential truth that underlies the great classical writers than in developing his own ideas in detail.[10]

To some extent, a preference for the historical approach is evident in the lectures on moral philosophy that survive in his papers, both in his own manuscripts,[11] and in the surviving lecture notes of his Glasgow students.[12] Nevertheless, Caird explicitly rejects the historical method in his 'Social Ethics', and it is indeed very easy indeed to draw out Caird's own positive position from these lectures. For example, in the discussion of marriage and the family, Caird traces a clear and independent path between the thought of Hegel and Comte (lecture two). Similarly he spends a long time on Montesquieu and JS Mill's writings on the constitution, but only as a means for developing his own theory (lectures nine and ten). There are some surprises in the positions Caird adopts. For example, while he emphases gender equality to a far greater degree than Hegel and even Comte, he retains a belief in the natural spiritual differences of the sexes of a type that one may not expect from someone who worked so hard during his life for the opening up of university education and degrees to women, as well as for the strengthening of female employment rights.[13]

Nevertheless, these lectures on social ethics would need to be worked on before they would be in publishable form for a living author. Caird did plan to write a book on *The Theory of Ethics* for the third series of Muirhead's 'Library of Philosophy' (to be published by Swan Sonnenschein, and MacMillan). We know this because the book was advertised as being in preparation in the front matter of various books published between at least 1893 and 1906.[14] We know also that Caird agreed to write this book while Professor of Moral Philosophy at Glasgow, because the advertisement refers to him in that capacity rather than as Master of Balliol (which he became in November 1893). We know that the book was to be a statement of Caird's own position because the third series in Muirhead's 'Library' contained 'original contributions to philosophy'.[15] Nevertheless, what appears here are clearly identified as lecture notes rather than book chapters (p. 98). It may be that Caird shelved the book project when he was appointed as Master of Balliol in 1893 in spite of the fact that the work was still advertised as in preparation even after that date.[16]

3. Lecture on Political Economy [ca. 1887-8?]
[Title and Location of Manuscript: Untitled. MS Gen. 1294, Special Collections, Glasgow University Library.]
   Caird was Professor of Moral Philosophy at the University of Glasgow from spring 1866 until winter 1893, and we know that for 'a considerable part of this time', 'he taught Political Economy as well as Moral Philosophy.'[17] This manuscript is the text of the final lecture of the first series of lectures that he gave on political economy (see p. 162 below). I date its delivery tentatively to 1887 or 1888, primarily on the grounds that Caird refers to an address that he is hoping to write within the next year on questions arising out of the course (see p. 160 below). Assuming that Caird actually did go on to write the promise address, then the most likely candidate is *The Moral Aspects of the Economical Problem* which was delivered and published in 1888.[18] Caird's final lecture on political economy is useful in that, while it offers few substantive reflections on political economics, it does summarise the preceding course in some detail. It shows that Caird was developing some of the themes that he had introduced in his lectures on social ethics (see lecture four in particular).

4. Essay on Mysticism.' [1890s]
[Title and location of manuscript: 'Essay on Mysticism.' MS Gen. 1294, Special Collections, Glasgow University Library.]
Caird's untidy handwriting and frequent deletions in this manuscript imply that he was thinking with his pen in his hand. Nevertheless, it is a wide-ranging and very detailed piece of historical scholarship, indicating that it comes from late in Caird's life.

5. Report on Mr Moore's Essay.' [Late 1897]
[Title and location of manuscript: 'Report on Mr Moore's Essay': Add. Ms.a.247/2(1)-(13), Wren Library, Trinity College, Cambridge.]
Two versions survive of Caird's report on GE Moore's dissertation for the 1897 competition for a Fellowship at Trinity College Cambridge. The draft is preserved amongst Caird's papers at Glasgow. The version that is published here is the final, fair copy held at the Wren Library, Trinity College, Cambridge. Moore was unsuccessful this time, but was appointed in 1898. Bernard Bosanquet was one of his examiners on this second occasion, and Bosanquet's (highly critical) report is reproduced in the first volume of his edition (pp. 236–40).

6. Reference for JME McTaggart's D.Litt [1902]
[Title and location of manuscript: Untitled. MS Gen. 1294, Special Collections, Glasgow University Library.]

This text appears to be the 'unprinted manuscript' mentioned by Muirhead in the biography of Caird.[19] It is almost certainly a draft, with terrible handwriting and many deletions. The fair copy has not been found.
Caird and John McTaggart Ellis McTaggart were on very friendly terms for many years. Mc Taggart lauded Caird's writings, and Caird commented on McTaggart's work and encouraged him to develop his thought further.[20] Despite certain philosophical reservations, Caird was certain of McTaggart's brilliance, and wrote to his friend Mary Sarah Talbot on 31 March 1902 in the following terms.

I have been looking over McTaggart's works, on the 'Dialectic' and 'Cosmology.' He has applied for Cambridge D.Litt. and I was asked to report on him. It was a good deal a matter of form,

I suppose, with a man of his standing, but I had some difficulty in doing justice to him, and yet pointing out his perversions of Hegel. He has very curiously turned Hegel upside down, and proved to his own satisfaction that Hegelian dialectic leads to a system of mysticism - in some points not unlike that of Plotinus. Of course, *that* also was in Hegel as an element, but McTaggart has curiously selected it out again.[21]

Caird was correct to see McTaggart's application as a mere formality.

Conclusion
The works published in this edition cover a wide range of issues, and offer numerous insights into previously obscure areas of British idealist thought. Hopefully, scholars will find them of use.

Colin Tyler
University of Hull, 2005

[1] Letter to Mary Sarah Talbot, 3 June 1891, in Sir Henry Jones and John Henry Muirhead, *The Life and Philosophy of Edward Caird* (Glasgow: Maclehose, Jackson, 1921), p.170.

[2] Edward Caird, *Collected Works*, 12 vols., ed. C Tyler (Bristol: Thoemmes, 1999). There is a small amount of material at Balliol College, Oxford, mostly on administrative matters related to Caird's tenure as Master (1893-1907) and some correspondence of largely biographical interest.

[3] Jones et al, *The Life and Philosophy of Edward Caird*, pp.84-5.

[4] For the background to this application and Caird's tenure, see Jones et al, *Life and Philosophy of Edward Caird*, chap. 3. Cf. Amelia Hutchison Stirling, *James Hutchison Stirling. His life and work* (London: T Fischer, 1912), pp.177-9, and Green, *Works*, vol. 5, pp.454-5.

[5] Jones et al, *Life and Philosophy of Edward Caird*, p.47.

[6] William Martin's list of Caird's lectures is reproduced below as Appendix A (pp. 209–13).

[7] Similar quarto volumes survive as MS Gen. 1544 to 1554.

[8] Jones et al, *Life and Philosophy of Edward Caird*, pp.109-10.

[9] A different set of student notes do survive from the 1893-94 with a markedly different curriculum ['Lectures on Moral Philosophy' [1893-94], notes taken by James Dick (MS Gen. 827)]. While these are still historical in a sense, nevertheless unlike the earlier 'thinker-based' approach, this later set of lectures are concerned far more with tracing the general sweep of History in a Hegelian sense. Extracts

from these lectures appear in Caird, *Collected Works*, vol. 1, pp.ix-xi, and vol. 11, pp.xi-xii, xii-xv.

[10] Jones et al, *Life and Philosophy of Edward Caird*, p.304.

[11] Roughly two thousand pages of Caird's own notes for the historical portions of the lectures on moral philosophy survive in a series of hardbound notebooks (MS Gen. 1544, 1546-8, 1550-3). They cover various sessions during his tenure at Glasgow, including 1883-4, 1886-7, and 1887-8. Other lectures survive on psychology (MS Gen. 1549 (front) and 1554) and logic (MS Gen. 1545 and 1549 (back)). All appear to be superseded by the notes published in this volume.

[12] The following student notes of the either part or all of the course on moral philosophy survive in the Caird Papers: 1870-71 session, 3 vols., taken by James Bonar (MS Gen. 104); 1874-75, J.B. Douglas, 3 vols. (MS Gen. 478-9); 1876-77, 3 vols., William Martin (MS Gen. 278-80); 1879, John Lennox, (MS Gen. 498); 1881-82, 3 vols., Robert A. Moody (MS Gen. 105); 1881-82, Edward Henry Steel, with abstracts (MS Gen. 740-1).

[13] See lecture two below; and Jones et al, *Life and Philosophy of Edward Caird*, pp.96-101, 118-25, 150-2.

[14] Otto Pfleiderer, *Development of Theology in Germany since Kant, and its Progress in Great Britain since 1825*, 2nd ed. (London: Swan Sonnenschein: 1893; New York: MacMillan, 1893), p.iii, where the front papers carried an advertisement of a 'work in preparation': '*The Theory of Ethics*. By Edward Caird, LL.D., Professor of Moral Philosophy in the University of Glasgow.', as part of the Third Series of 'The Library of Philosophy' (General Editor, J.H. Muirhead). The same details were repeated in the front matter of FH Bradley, *Appearance and Reality*, second edition [fourth? impression] (London: Swan Sonnenschein: 1906; New York: MacMillan, 1906). The first volume in this series was Erdmann's *History of Philosophy* (1890).

[15] Pfleiderer, *Development of Theology in Germany*, p.ii. The first, second and fourth series dealt with 'the development of particular schools of Philosophy', 'the history of theory in particular departments', and 'translations of valuable foreign works', respectively.

[16] Aside from the collection of occasional lay sermons and addresses that was published shortly before his death, the only book that Caird wrote as Master was *The Evolution of Theology in the Greek Philosophers* (Glasgow: James MacLehose, 1904), which were the Gifford lectures for the 1900-1 and 1901-2 sessions..

[17] JS MacKenzie, 'Edward Caird as a Philosophical Teacher', *Mind*, vol. 18, no. 72 ns (October 1909), p.511n.

[18] Edward Caird, *The Moral Aspects of the Economical Problem. Presidential Address to the Ethical Society* (London: Swan Sonnenschein, Lowrey, 1888), reprinted in Caird, *Collected Works*, vol. 11. See p. 163 for a further discussion of an alternative date.

[19] Jones et al, *Life and Philosophy of Edward Caird*, p.298n.

[20] JME McTaggart, Review of *The Evolution of Religion*, *Mind*, vol. 2, no. 7 ns (July 1893), pp.376-83, G Lowes Dickinson, *J. McT. E. McTaggart* (Cambridge University Press, 1931), p.36-7.

[21] Jones et al, *Life and Philosophy of Edward Caird*, pp.237-8; also *ibid.*, pp.196-7, 297-8, 353.

UNPUBLISHED MANUSCRIPTS
IN BRITISH IDEALISM

Volume 2

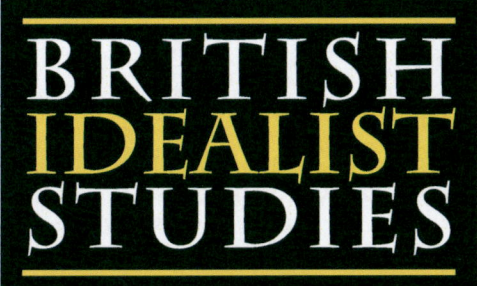

A monograph series reflecting the renewed interest in the British idealists.

All titles are priced at £30/$49.90 and cloth-bound. Please check website for full details, sample chapters and updates:

imprint-academic.com/idealists

'An excellent series', *TLS*

Series 1: Michael Oakeshott

Editor: Noël O'Sullivan (Hull). **Board:** Wendell John Coats Jr. (Connecticut), Richard Flathman (Johns Hopkins), Paul Franco (Bowdoin), Robert Grant (Glasgow), John Gray (LSE), John Kekes (SUNY, Albany), Kenneth Minogue (LSE), Terry Nardin (Wisconsin), Lord Parekh (Hull), Patrick Riley (Harvard)

Luke O'Sullivan: Oakeshott on History
- 'A very helpful and welcome volume.' Michael Bentley, *English Historical Review*
  308 pages £30/$49.90 978-0907845294

Roy Tseng: The Sceptical Idealist
- 'Meticulously reconstructs Oakeshott's views.' Graeme Garrard, *Political Studies Review*
  320 pages £30/$49.90 978-0907845225

Ian Tregenza: Michael Oakeshott on Hobbes
- 'A skillfully posed and smartly analysed work.' Steven Gerencser, *Hist. Political Thought*
  250 pages £30/$49.90 978-0907845591

Efraim Podoksik: In Defence of Modernity
- 'This is an excellent and illuminating book.' John Charvet, *History of Political Thought*
  260 pages £30/$49.90 978-0907845669

Kenneth B. McIntyre: The Limits of Political Theory
- 'Ably written and cogently argued.' **James Mellon**, *Political Studies Review*
  210 pages £30/$49.90 978-1845400101

Suvi Soininen: From a 'Necessary Evil' to an Art of Contingency: Michael Oakeshott's Conception of Political Activity
- 'Well researched and intellectually engaging.' **David Boucher**, *Political Studies Review*
  300 pages £30/$49.90 978-1845400064

Glenn Worthington: Religious and Poetic Experience in Oakeshott
- 'Well-ordered and systematic.' **Bob Cheekes**, *Intellectual Conservative*
  180 pages £30/$49.90 978-0907845621

Andrew Sullivan: Intimations Pursued: The Voice of Practice in the Conversation of Michael Oakeshott
250 pages 978-0907845287 September 2007

Kevin Williams: Education and the Voice of Michael Oakeshott
250 pages 978-1845400552 September 2007

Erik Kos: Michael Oakeshott, the Ancient Greeks and the Philosophical Study of Politics
250 pages 978-1845400750 December 2007 *[continued overleaf]*

Part 4
Edward Caird

Reform and the Reformation
[ca. 1866]

Contents

1. The nature of reform as carried out by *man* depends upon a progress carried out by God.
2. Is there such a progress? How did the fall affect it? How does it go on in spite of the fall. Two-fold aspect of history in consequence.
3. In what field is this progress? Not in the individuals but in humanity. A progress of the *race*.
4. How is it right that the individual should be sacrificed to the progress of the race?
5. How does his sacrifice help the race?–the *law of human progress*–action and reaction of the individual and the universal.
6. The function of men of action–and of men of thought in progress. The intuitional class in which the universal and the particular find their synthesis.
7. The Conservative and the Reformer–the rational basis of their respective creeds–their union and the origin of their separation. Progress only safe which it holds by the past.
8. Spiral course of human development.
9. Is there a moral progress of humanity? Buckle's false philosophy.
10. Religion the source and law of human development. Yet Religion must not interfere directly with politics. Church and State.
11. The hopes of Progress.

I shall divide this essay into two parts–considering in the first of these, the general principles of human progress, and reform: and in the second–some of the illustrations, which these principles receive from the History of the German Reformation.[1]

[§1 The nature of reform as carried out by *man* depends upon a progress carried out by God.][2]
If we consider reform as comprehending all those agencies which man can use to improve the condition, or aid the advance of his race, our view of it will necessarily be dependent upon a deeper question. Man cannot create; all his success is dependent upon his striking in with mighty agencies already at work. His highest effort is to place himself directly in the path of some irresistible law, and then let himself be borne forward by it to the certain execution of his purpose. So here. Reform, the work of man, is dependent upon progress the work of God, and according to the view which we take of the design which He has been, and is accomplishing in the course of history, must necessarily be the nature of the efforts which *we* can make to further that design. Is there, then, a progression toward some higher state discernible in human history, or is it all the record of an ever-repeated struggle between the same forms of good and evil, with none but accidental variation. If we suppose any period in the past–be it the first Christian century, be it the Paradisal state,[3] which can be taken as the high water mark of the human soul–the standard by which all other periods can be judged–and conformity to which is in all points, the test of rightness and wrongness–then all that the most sanguine can hope for is simply *re*formation of the old in the strictest sense of the word:–all that the most zealous reformer could legitimately aim at, would be in some degree to correct the innovations of time, to force back the current of life, and bank it anew, so far as may be, into the channel from which it has diverged, and from which it is ever tending to diverge. Then be all history, except the record of that happy bygone time,[4] is deprived of its main interest, exhibiting but a series of repetitions of the same fact:–a weary succession of struggles of humanity to regain its lost level, with varied success at different times, but ever more or less foiled by the same corruptive tendencies. And for the future all that would be left for us, would be to repeat the same efforts, which our fathers had made, and which our descendants must make again in their turn–if indeed, we had still heart for the unending struggle, after the infinite hope, which is our spur and incitement, was taken away.

If on the other hand the past be the record of a never ceasing advance;–if the tread of an ever-growing purpose is heard through all the ages; if men's gradual loosening from the old forms of his life be not corruption, but the influence of a heavenly voice which is ever calling him forward, and making him feel that all he has done is but the promise of what he yet will do–then there is for man a higher task than to 'remodel moods' that have spent their force: or to look back and long for the former days that were better than these. History, indeed, we will read with new eyes, because every page of it contains some new lineament of the purpose of God in man, which is yet proceeding towards its accomplishment. But we will not consider the best era it records as diviner than today: seeing that all that is good on the past is immortal, and still lives with and in us. Above all, we can then look round hopefully, and watch for the signs of the times that we may find the new element, which is seeking entrance into man's life now–'the spirit of the years to come striving to mix itself with life'.[5] and true reform will consist in uniting and submitting ourselves, as willing servants to a Higher Power, whose glorious purposes for humanity, it is the blessedness of man to further by his obedience, the curse of man to further by his rebellion and self-seeking.

[§2 Is there such a progress? How did the fall affect it? How does it go on in spite of the fall. Two-fold aspect of history in consequence.]

It is evident, then, that all special investigations into the nature of reform must be postponed till this deeper question has been answered. The former answer has often been given: and still oftener it has lain unconsciously at the root of many of those schemes of reaction, which have emerged from time to time both in politics and in religion. According to this view the unfallen state of man is the highest he has hitherto attained, and all history is little more than a struggle to regain the point then abandoned. The paradisal state–the world's baptismal purity–stands ever highest[6] above is, and our best virtue or holiness is some feeble analagon of it.

Now both from reason, and from the records which remain to us, it is evident that the primeval state of man can, at best, have been nothing higher than the negative purity of innocence that has never known temptation. And, putting as high a price, as is possible, upon such a state, we must still rate higher any goodness, however imperfect, that has borne the proof, and confirmed itself against every false allurement. The almost instinctive shrinking before evil, which characterizes the child, may be a tender and beautiful thing, but who would compare it, for worth or elevation, to the tried manly resolve that can look evil in the face, yet hate it with a perfect hatred–that has sought and found the right through the stern paths of duty and self-sacrifice. And so, it would be absurd to think the state of God's church now, when it has passed through all the influences for good and evil that have come to these latter times–when it has been receiving into itself all the mighty inspirations of culture and religion for so many ages, and still brought them to bear in some measure upon all the widened problems of life–it would be absurd to think that such a disciplined goodness–even though it be stained with the long conflict–were inferior to, or even on a level with the childlike stainlessness of Eden.[7]

It is true, indeed, that the fall brought tremendous evil consequences upon man. Had man not fallen, his development might have proceeded peacefully according to its idea without the hard struggles and forcible breaks of continuity which it actually presents. Like a plant that advances silently according to the germinal idea of its nature–to unfold the lower form of seed–into the higher form of leaf and so on to the highest forms of flower and fruit so the development of humanity might have gone on in unbroken unity to the full cultivation of its powers. This possibility of undisturbed normal development was lost. And by this loss, labor [sic] and struggle and pain became the condition of man's advance. But though disturbed and retarded this advance was not stopt. The fall has not changed God's design for humanity. Man has only made the execution of that design hard and painful to himself. He has brought on himself many a scar and stain from which he would have been free, if innocence had passed with holiness, without succumbing to sin. Still amid all confusions and darkness, amid storm and struggle,[8] he is led onwards by the hand of God through the same path of development–to unfold the same capacities and enter into the same spiritual consciousness, which once might have been his by the calm and natural process of growing life. The way has become rough and stony: but the goal is that same everlasting blessedness in God which would have been the lot of man, had he never fallen.

The circumstances of the fall itself when we look closer afford a marked illustration of this principle. It was necessary that the consciousness of good and evil should be developed in man, if he were ever to rise to the dignity of his nature–and to this end it was necessary that temptation should be presented–that the possibility of a course in opposition to the Divine command should be suggested to him. But it was not necessary that he should fall. If he had resisted, he would have received into himself the distinction which was to be taught him. The consciousness, which is at the foundations of man's moral nature might thus have been evolved, without the antithesis of good and evil being received into his character. And thus a commencement of an undisturbed normal development had been made.

On the other hand his fall did not altogether defeat the purpose of God in so tempting him. Man gained, after all, the first step in the development of his nature: and became conscious of moral distinctions. And though he suffered the fearful consequences which follow from disunion with his creator: though he ceased to be fellow worker with God for his own good: yet, in the plan of God, his rebellion was made to serve the same purpose which obedience might have done–and the advance of universal history was commenced.

In this first transaction therefore we perceive the twofold aspect which man's development every where presents: and at the same time we see how far the progress of humanity is dependent upon such reforms as man can work. God's design for man must be accomplished, and it will be accomplished whether by his resistance or by his obedience. But it lies in man's hand, whether that design shall be accomplished by his weal or his woe–by the quiet process of growth, or by division and strife and battle. History gives us examples of both. When men have discerned the signs of the times, and harkened to the still small voice[9] that is ever guiding them onward. When with silent constant energy they have modified and adapted the forms of their government, and worship, and dogma to the growing demands of the spirit within them, then the old passes into the new without convulsion or break of continuity. The principle of the future spreads gradually through the old frame of things, and lo! Ere we were aware, a new world hath formed itself around us. When on the other hand men do not obey the voice of the Divine Spirit, but linger clinging to the dead forms of custom, or rush along wildly in self-chosen paths, yet not the less must their acts contribute to the advance of the world's history. Even their fiercest opposition develops in them the consciousness of the principle they oppose. It arouses their own deepest nature against them, and will not let it rest in anything but itself. Surely and firmly it strengthens its hold upon mankind, sinking [?] deeper the longer it is resisted, and at last its compressed strength will burst forth as a destroying force, and will write its name for ever on the page of history, if in no other way it may–by the black characters of ruin, and devastation and war.-

Sad it is that progress is so seldom effected by the former, so often by the latter path: so often by God's educing good out of evil, so seldom by the quiet development of good. Between man's intent for himself–and God's intent for man, there has generally been a wide and almost irreconcilable[10] division. History is the record of a progress of humanity, of which the men who carried it out often knew nothing. They went their own ways, sought their own selfish ends–and out of their falsity, out of their selfishness, beat out of their one-sided and partial endeavours, God made his mighty purpose to unfold itself. It is not thus in what the individual aims and does, so often as in the *result*, that God brings out of the isolated and partial aims and doings of all men, that we recognise an advance to a new stage of development. And though all true reform, all steady and uninterrupted development–must arise out of man's will uniting itself with the plan of God, yet too often that plan has been accomplished by God's making the wrath of man to praise him. And hence the strange twofold aspect of history. If we look at the expressed desires of men–for which they have striven, at the hopes which have led them even to their greatest works, and we can see little worthy of reverence: but contemplate the ultimate results of their acts, and they would seem to be guided by a superhuman sagacity. As in a grand chorus there may not be one voice which, if you heard it distinct and alone, you would pronounce perfect or well cultured. And yet when the tide of song bursts from the multitude, all these feeble individualities are lost, every discord is taken up [in] the harmony of the whole–and we feel as if one great singer were making them all his instruments. So it is with human history.–Go near enough to hear the separate human voices, and there will seem often to be nothing, but strife and confusion and discord–but go further off, and when the distance has lost all the discordant human voices in one, we hear only the full toned utterance of one divine speaker in it all.

[§3 In what field is this progress? Not in the individuals but in humanity. A progress of the *race*.]
But these views already suggest the inquiry what is the nature of this progress–and in what sphere of man's life are we to look for its traces?

Not it is obvious in those interests which specially concern the individual. An eye that looks upon life from the point of view which personal feeling takes, (as in novels usually)–interesting itself in the objects which individuals propose to themselves and reckoning the value of life by the measure in which it tends to secure these objects–such an eye must always find the world a profoundly sad spectacle. So seen all human story [sic] is one record of fruitless effort, or disappointment, of delusion. The brightest lot is crossed with some dark shadows, and if it were not, yet the final doom of every thing earthly were enough to sadden it. And accordingly we find the mournful refrain of Ecclesiastes, the vanitas vanitatum, running through every page of human experience.[11] The fugitiveness of all earthly beauty and strength, the weariness of all earthly delight and the sadness of decay have been sung by poets, and preached by moralists in all ages, so that the theme would long have been threadbare, if it did not receive ever new illustration from fact.

But even in relation to higher than these outward interests, the same tale has to be told, the capacity for all human joy and sorrow, the infinite spiritual want is in each human heart. No thought can move man, but my nature seems to have a right to it. No Power which has been exhibited on the stage of the world, but might in some measure be evolved in me. And when with this thought in our mind we look round and see the stunted development of most men–the feeble degree in which they are conscious of their own deepest nature: when we note the stern limits of space and time that are laid upon the culture of even the most favourably situated: the extent to which all are forced to sacrifice it to mere earthly needs–and to make themselves instruments toward ends in which they cannot partake–we seem at first to be looking on an even sadder spectacle than the former–inasmuch as a higher treasure is cast away or left unimproved.

But though men fail and vanish, *man* does not: though the individual is limited and sacrificed, it is to a spiritual consciousness of the race which is ever advancing. There is a common life of humanity to which all the lives of its members are but means and contributions and which grows on amid their decay. It is the strange problem of providence to which indeed almost all other speculative difficulties are reducible, that the Race of Man is treated as *the Personality*. And indeed, it would sometimes seem as the only Proper Person. The sins, the merits, the deeds and the sufferings of men pass into a common stock, for which (it would seem) not the special doer, but the whole of which he is a part, is held responsible–and receives, as the case may be, the reward or the penalty. And all history would seem to teach that if this great consciousness of Humanity be preserved, and growing to maturity, it matters little what becomes of the tribes or nations of men, in whom for the time it resides. This must develop to ever higher and higher things whatever becomes of them. The individuals may be limited and sacrificed but by means of all their partial developments and perversions, a higher result is matured. A nation may waste itself on some low stage of development and pass away, but what matter, if by this spending of force, another step can be gained for the world's life.

> Augescunt aliae gentes, aliae minuuntur,
> Inque brevi spatio mutantur saecla animantum
> Et quasi cursores vitai lampada tradunt[12]

The torch bearers weary and sink down one after another–but the torch of life is still held up and borne onward by other hands ever nearer and nearer to the goal. The generations like waves, roll upward, one after another, only to subside again spent and broken: yet still the advancing swells over the receding wave; and the tide of life has been heaved one step higher on the eternal shore!

[§4 How is it right that the individual should be sacrificed to the progress of the race?]
That this sacrifice of all particular existence to the universal–is the law of Providence is abundantly clear. Man's acceptation or rejection of it cannot alter the case. Willingly or unwillingly he is made the instrument of an end out of himself. No one can with impunity take himself as the centre, to which all things are to contribute–whether it be to his advantage to his enjoyment, or, in the highest and most dangerous form of this sin, to his culture. He will not even attain best in this manner the narrow aim, which he proposes to himself. The course of things rolls onward, subordinating and when they come in its way, sacrificing all particular interests. For a self-centred man is out of harmony with his own deepest nature as well as with the eternal laws of the universe. Man derives all his force from coincidence with higher universal agencies. He can do nothing alone. The conditions of his success must be furnished in similar lines of tendency coming from all quarters to

meet and help out his act. 'An individual avails not,' says Goethe, 'but only he who combines with many at the proper hours.'[13] The special interest of any one can therefore only prosper, so far as they fall in with the aims of that spirit which bears up the course of history, and which concentrates all the strivings of men to one goal. No doubt a measure of success has often been attained by selfish men. And it might be thought a conclusive answer to such reasonings as the above, to point to great conquerors and kings, such as Alexander, Caesar, or Napoleon, who were undoubtedly men, that prized their personal ambitions above every other interest however sacred.[14] But the exceptions are only apparent. The effect which such men produced is not to be attributed to their talents, nor to their steady pursuit of their objects–though these were instrumental, and enabled them better than others to use the favourable circumstances. But the reason why any [?] talents could be successful in attaining so prominent and powerful a position lay in the fact that the special desires and aims of the man prompted him to deeds that gave expression to some want of his time. And the proof of this lies in the fate of such characters when they are no longer necessary to the world. A time comes to them, as to all selfish men, when the ends of their ambition begin to diverge from the course demanded by the spirit of the time,–with which all along they have been only in *outward* harmony. And then they can no longer maintain themselves. The invisible force which bore them in irresistibly has deserted them, they have lost the charm-word with which they called forth the spiritual powers of the universe to do battle for them. They may try the old means, but somehow the old effect does not follow. Humanity has other work, which needs other agents, and they are cast aside like broken tools, no longer to be wielded by the Master's hand.

But if this be all true, it might be said, does it not need some explanation that man's individual nature should be sacrificed to any end lying out of itself? Do we not feel as if the life of human soul were something too precious to be used merely as a means? And do we not reduce man to a level inconsistent with his moral and spiritual elevation by demanding such a sacrifice?

Now I might answer this difficulty by saying that man best cultivates even his special talents, the gifts which distinguish him individually from other men, not when he makes it his aim to develop them, but when he strenuously uses them for the good of the whole. If a man's eye is fixed on himself–if his efforts are directed immediately to the education and improvement of his own nature, he may certainly make some progress–and attain a certain useful command over all his faculties and attainments. But he will not thus draw out the deepest voices of his being, nor reveal to himself or others the full scope of his capacity. But if he lose thought of himself–devote himself to some higher object with all his heart and soul so that his own individuality shall seem a paltry thing compared with *that*–suddenly the fountains of his life are unlocked–and the dilettante[15] becomes a deep thinker or manful doer. To make one's special gifts an end in themselves is, therefore, to limit and dwarf them:–to spend them for general objects on the other hand is the best way to evolve, and elevate them to the highest pitch of perfection. Even in this lower sense it is true that he that loveth his life shall lose it, that he only that hateth his life shall in the end preserve it.[16]

But this argument is only partially satisfactory. To recommend self-sacrifice, because it is the dictate of enlighten[ed] self-interest is a suicidal proceeding. The motive destroys the virtue it was intended to prompt. If we had no better ground on which to call man to self-sacrifice than, that thus he will best consult the welfare of his own personal being: the self-reference would render true self-sacrifice impossible. A vicious moral circle would be generated as when some rationalist theologians have recommended prayers on the ground merely of its subjective influence.[17]

The deepest justification of the sacrifice demanded is to be found in the fact that it is not a foreign nature to which man is thus subordinating himself. He is only making his individuality an instrument to the higher universal nature [of] which he partakes with all men. He is sacrificing Himself to the purely Human: to the development of the image of God in man–the most precious element in all and in each. Man ever feels in noble moments that he has a deeper stake in the universal good–the prevalence of Human Love and Human Truth, than he has even in his own personality. This is his dearer Life of life, which gives him whatever value he has in his own eyes: and he is willing to live and die for its success: to be its organ while he may, to be swept away when his work is done. Can we not feel with John the Baptist, when he said, not with envy but with joy, 'He must increase, I must decrease' [John 3.30]? He had done his life-work manfully and truly. He had exercised a powerful influence on the Jewish nation, by the simplicity and grandeur of his character–and now his popularity gone, his voice quelled in prison, and the doom of the tyrant visibly drawing near, he hears of the great new Teacher, who has taken up his work.[18] He feels that he is no longer needed; but must give place to a higher. 'Well then', he seems to say, 'my feeble individuality with its weak strivings–its darkness–its insufficiency is passing away. But what matters! The truth, which it represented, and in which lay its only value, has not gone with it. It has prepared the way for the world's Life that will not pass away. What though I depart, if he remain.–All that I struggled and hoped for is safe for ever for, though I must decrease, *He* must increase.' [John 3.30]

Thus limitation and sacrifice of the individual finds justification in the fact that by this he will best subserve the interests of universal humanity–the common self of all men, if we may so call it. Still there is a further truth. Sacrifice cannot be the last thing under God's government. 'He that hateth his life in this world, shall save it unto life eternal.' [John 12.25] Those universal realities, to which we are called to make ourselves subservient here, we shall enjoy in full measure hereafter. The limitations to which our culture, our knowledge, the development of our being, are subjected, must ultimately be done away with. If this were not so, the ends of life might as well have been fulfilled by beings who could not partake in them. Every capacity must find its due food: all the treasure of humanity must be opened to us. We must be no more narrow fractions of men, hedged in by the bounds of one nationality, one frame of life, one round of thought, but the full stature of man such as it is seen not in any one human figure, must be attained by each of us. Here we sacrifice our individuality to the whole: but there we must receive back the whole into our Individuality.

[§5 How does his sacrifice help the race?–the *law of human progress*–action and reaction of the individual and the universal.] But such reflexions would take us too far from our special subject–and I cannot dwell upon them further. The essential fact is that humanity progresses by the sacrifice of individuals. But, granted that this law is just and right, as I have attempted to show, how does it operate? How does individual life subserve the universal, or, in other words, how does man progress as a whole, by means of the stern limits set round the development of the separate parts of his race? How is it that the course of life has not to begin over again with every new generation, but can take its departure from the acquisitions of the past? This question brings us to the kernel of the subject: and on the manner of its resolution will depend all our conclusions with regard to the nature of reform. Now I find a solution of the problem in a fact of human experience—viz. that truth must be *particularized* in order afterwards to be *generalized*. This point will demand a little explication.

Truth must approach the human mind in the *first* instance, not in general but in particular form—not abstractly in a proposition, but concretely in a phenomenon. In other words the symbol must precede the thought, and evolve it. Abstractions mean literally nothing to a man, who has not some experience of his own or others, by which to interpret them. We have not the faculty, which Swift gives his Laputan projectors of building downwards from the air.[19] There must be a solid basis of fact for all our structures. Not that I mean by this, that spiritual truth is a mere induction from experience. Far otherwise. Experience, facts, only furnish the occasion for our spiritual intuitions. I only assert that the occasion is necessary: or in other words, an outward symbol, a body, is necessary for every human thought, and till the thought is, in some measure, embodied outwardly, it cannot be realized inwardly. But this point I have fully discussed in another Essay.[20]

Applying this to the subject, it is evident that the truth of humanity—the fullness of its power and meaning can only be evoked in all men, so far as it has been realized in history, so far, that is as each of its capacities of thought or feeling has found a particular *form* in which to clothe itself. A truth, therefore, never comes to humanity except as the kernel, the precious ideal contents of some individuality—whether the individuality of a person or of a race: incarnated in some series of facts, and by them manifested to the world.

On the other hand, the body, though necessary is never adequate to the spirit. It 'half reveals and half conceals it'.[21] Sensible form, however perfect it be, can never more than suggest the life beneath, which is struggling to speak through it. Turn it as you will, matter, which is under the law of space and time, will never be fully sufficient to manifest and express that which is above these limits. Hence, though the symbol is necessary to evolve, and suggest the truth, it is a hindrance to its *full* apprehension. The fact must come before the thought but if we rest in the fact, or if we set the fact as a limit to the thought, all progress is stopt. The fact must be removed, its accidents must be dropped, and the principle it contains must be liberated and generalized, that it may produce its true effect. And if the spiritual essence be not thus freed, by the abstracting powers of the mind, from the fleshy[22] and corruptible garment which it wore, the mortal part would drag down the immortal and become its grave.

From this principle it follows that a symbolic fact, after it has served its purpose in evoking some thought or experience in humanity, is best withdrawn to allow such thought to develop its general meaning. Hence death is the great generalizer for by it the fact is removed to a sufficient distance to allow us to transmute it into thought. Ordinarily, e.g., we do not consciously recognise the value[23] we do not recognise the symbolic value of the human beings around us: their presence is too over powering. The fact is too dominant for us to see the spiritual meaning which it contains in its true independence. Death cuts the tie and leaves us the spiritual presence alone. And then only do we come to feel that the human being we lookt [sic] on only represented something which exists also in us. Even Christ has declared, that his outward sensible presence if it had continued on earth, would not have been an open way to the Father but an obstruction. 'It is expedient for you, that I go away: for if I go not away, the Comforter will not come to you, but if I go, I will send Him to you.' [John 16.7] And if this be true of Christ, how much more those earthly individualities which far less perfectly manifested in their outward life the ideal principle with which they were charged. How certain is it, that the many obscurations and perversions, which they mingle with their idea would altogether, or almost altogether, shut us from the knowledge of it–if they were not removed by their passing away from the living scene, to a distance where only the ideal features are clearly visible, while the disproportions of their actual life have been thrown into the shade?

A spiritual principle first enters into Humanity embodied in an individuality–in a single person or more generally in a race or nation: but when it has reached maturity–it is let loose, by the passing away of its earthly embodiment, from the confinement that was necessary to its early growth, that in free universality it may enter into combination with other elements of spirit, and germinate the nobler future. 'Except a corn of wheat fall into the ground, and die, it abideth alone: but, if it die, it bringeth forth much fruit.' [John 12.24] Thus if we contrast the three most prominent nations from whom we have received our religious, and intellectual culture, and examine how they have produced such marked effects on mankind, we trace this principle very clearly.

Note how the Jews were separated from all other influences however good in themselves, in order that there might grow up in them that deep sense of moral distinction and of their religious root which is the characteristic feature embodied in their literature and history. While the empire of aspiration, of beauty, of the ideal, is just as decidedly and exclusively given to the Greek, and the empire of law, of government, of political rights to the Roman. Each was limited as it were to a part of our common nature that he might develop it better: that he might perfectly evolve it and bring it into consciousness–and might chronicle it in symbolic acts for all the world.[24] It would be difficult, or rather impossible to explain these things, if we looked at man as an isolated self-centred being, but, from the point of view of universal History, these limitations justify themselves as the means by which the good of the whole will ultimately be best answered. These consciousnesses of sin and holiness, of ideal beauty, of political right, would never have been so fully developed in Humanity–would never have been felt in their full import as universal elements of man's being, had they not first formed the distinctive aim of a particular nation. The national individual, if we may so express it, is elected for a special work; it is confined to him, and he is confined to it in the first instance, only with a view to the ultimate participation of all: only with a view to the better diffusion of that consciousness which he has acquired through the length and breadth of the race.

But in order to this spiritual influence, the nations themselves had to pass away, and affect man no longer in mere outward relations, but spiritualized and generalized through their literature and history. These nations themselves could never have combined to form a higher whole: where they *were* brought in contact, they exhibited themselves *only* as mutually destructive. But,[25] when the specialities, which in actual life mingled with, and obscured the idea that underlay them; when the earthen vessels which contained the heavenly nectar, were removed, then the universal principles which they represented, combined with perfect freedom, and from their union was generated the richer life of modern Europe, which comprehends all these separate principles acting in living union, and is thus a fuller representation of the idea of humanity than ever existed before.

Perhaps a still grander illustration of the principle is furnished by what Bunsen and others have seen remarked with regard to the relation of the Semitic and Japhetic mind.[26] All the great religions have arisen in the East, and have travelled westward.[27] The great lever in the world's progress has been the mental toil necessary to assimilate the records of Semitic national religion–and national life amid the far different inward and outward conditions of the tribes of Japhet. Now religion in the east was *particular*: that is, man was there conscious of his relations to God, not as universal truth, but (for the most part) only in relation to himself, his caste, or his nation. Hence he never clearly separated between what was required in general, and what was required of *him*. And in his literature, and history, we find national peculiarity and universal humanity–truths of reason and ordinances, which could only have a temporal significance, entwined together as they are in actual life, and scarcely the first lines of separation drawn between them. Only in the words of our Saviour, who was 'neither Jew nor Greek',[28] but in whom all the developments of humanity flowed together, does the universal truth rise clear of the particular. Now when the Semitic race had passed away from its prominent place, and when the standard of human progress, fallen from its failing grasp had been taken up by the tribes of Japhet, the records of the past of the east, its literature, and especially the Bible, in which all its highest worth is represented, became the foundation on which the West had to build. But the transference of ideas could not be effected directly. We can only attain a common ground of sympathy with the records of eastern religion, by letting drop and eliminating the national and special elements they contain, and fixing upon and evolving the universal element, the Purely Human and Divine in them. And accordingly it has been the task of western philosophy in all ages, to elevate to general abstract from the ideas which are concretely presented in Eastern life. *There* truth first combined itself with fact, and clothed itself in symbol: but it has been the task reserved for us to release it from symbolic form, and exhibit its higher Universality.

We have seen that symbol is necessary to evoke the spiritual life of man–and that it is only as spiritual principles are realised outwardly that they can be brought into consciousness inwardly. We have seen, likewise that men are apt to rest in the outward realization, and let the symbol conceal that which it is meant to reveal, if it were not for the abstracting power of thought, which is ever engaged in disentangling the idea from the accidents of its temporal embodiment, and asserting its independence of it. We have now to note that as fact needs thought for its complement, so thought needs fact. Thought itself can never fully attain the spiritual reality which it seeks, can never comprehend it.[29] In Platonic language, the idea that lies behind a thing can never be completely embraced in any one logical concept of it. Only by a thousand efforts of conception do we approximate ever nearer and nearer to the centre of truth, which we can never perfectly attain. If then, instead of looking again and again at the fact, and so finding a basis for ever more perfect generalizations, and correcting the falsity that attaches to our best concept by applying it to reality–if, instead of this, we take any such partial concept, and reason it out to all consequences, as if it were the *only* principle involved. Then we will necessarily reduce life and truth to a simplicity which they have not. And we will end by confining ourselves in a prison of abstractions, which leaves truth almost on the outside.

Hence it follows that not only are symbolic facts necessary to awake in us the corresponding spiritual consciousness, but further, the only way to evolve such consciousness is again and again to return to the facts, and investigate their deeper significance. Until a higher realization of spirit or of any spiritual principle has come, our minds must rest in and start from the lower. We must hold by the symbols of the past, even while we separate ourselves from them and advance beyond them, if we would not lose the benefit of our place in the development of the race. Symbol and idea[30] are united, like soul and body which we can distinguish, but not divide. We can only cut the tie which binds the soul to any particular body, so far as we provide for it a new one. And so we can only separate the idea from any particular symbol, in so far as we give it higher embodiment. Mere thought therefore cannot eliminate this symbolic element. It can only prepare the way for a higher embodiment of truth by loosening the connection which binds it to the lower form. We can only elevate ourselves from dependence on the symbols of the past in so far as our own actions and the institutions which we establish represent and symbolize spiritual reality more perfectly.

Thus effect becomes cause, and cause becomes effect in its turn. I said before, that truth must be *particularized* in the first instance in order afterwards to be *generalized*;[31] I now add that truth is *generalized* in order to be again particularized. Action dissolves itself into thought, that thought may again concentrate into higher action. And humanity advances, not straight forward, but pulsing from side to side, (like a steam engine), its negative force of thought, alternating with its positive force of action:–placing a limit, and then removing it, when it no longer affords room for the advancing spirit: at one time devoting all its energy to incarnate a truth in outward symbolic acts and institutions, and again with equal energy sapping and destroying them. So by ever grander achievements and ever grander sacrifices, man sounds on his wondrous way to God,–not like a plant, which, once born into life, pursues an even course of development to its highest point, and then falls to rise no more–but by a continual death-birth, where the spirit remains permanent, and the dissolution of one earthly tenement only leaves it free to weave for itself a higher resurrection body.

[§6 The function of men of action–and of men of thought in progress. The intuitional class in which the universal and the particular find their synthesis.]
These remarks lead me to notice a contest that is ever going on between two classes of men–the men of action[32] and the men of theory. The man of theory, looking at experience from a distance, by means of his abstracting power separates the symbol from the thing signified by it, the letter from the spirit, and is thus led to declare that the latter is the only thing valuable, and that, if it be preserved, all matters of form are non-essential and indifferent. The man of action, on the other hand, regarding his experience without the medium of reflective thought, or even distrusting it as hostile to feeling, knows that the symbols are the channels of all his spiritual feeling, and thinks that, if they are lost, all is lost: the symbol is to him identical with the truth, and he considers anyone who touches the former as much the enemy of religion, as if he attacked or denied the latter. One of these tendencies predominates in every man, and this forms perhaps one of the most marked lines of distinction in human character. But they also lie deeper than the peculiarity of individuals; they form two poles of character in universal Humanity, of which all partake. Every theorist is at times a man of facts, every practical man at times a theorist. In calm periods, when the depths of man's spirit are untroubled, we have an almost overpowering tendency to the concrete–to rest in facts: we then see truth, if at all, only when it presents itself in some strong outward form. And if this tendency were to go on unchecked, the end could only be, that either, the symbol would be elevated to the place of the spiritual reality, for which it ought to witness, which is superstition: or faith would be utterly lost in any realities except those of sense, which is materialism. On the other hand, in times of agitation and change, when man's inmost nature is strongly moved, and feels its superi-

ority to all the outward things by which it is awakened and revealed: then the most abstract principles come into prominence, and are on the lips of all. The spirit feels independent of all its usual supports and can scarce be prevented from casting them all aside. And we shall see from the history of the Reformation that it is as difficult *then* to preserve the necessary forms of religious and social life, as at other times it is to prevent them from becoming all in all. And this tendency is as fatal as that, if it were allowed to reach its climax. The abstract possibilities of spirit are set in opposition to all institutions, and forms of thought by in which they are realized. And the result necessarily is, in speculation, an abstract idealism, in which all reality is lost in the forms of the mind, and in practice an absolute anarchy of the senses.[33] These extremes can never be quite reached, but there is ever in society a tendency to one of them, which again calls forth a reactive tendency toward the other. So long however as they qualify each other, and combine to produce one result, the danger is not great. The danger lies in their separating one from another, and acting as antagonists–and we may see in the French Revolution a clear exhibition of the length to which both may go, when they are thus opposed. For there was seen, on the one side, the actual institutions of the past, but corrupted and no longer acknowledging any spiritual basis–and on the other abstract theories of the rights of man, but altogether denying any external or concrete Revelation of these. And the awful consequence of this separation and opposition of theory and fact, was that both shewed their worst results; and tyranny, superstition and materialism only gave way, when they were swept aside, to the more desolating agencies of rebellion, anarchy and infidelity.

But the very destructive nature of these agencies when opposed, shows that they were meant to work in union; as the centripetal and centrifugal forces combine to keep the stars in their courses. The action and reaction of fact and thought[34] are, as we have seen, very necessary means for the development of spirit. Each is imperfect in itself and finds its complement in the other. They are not really contradictories, mutually destructive, though they may be made to appear so by the selfishness of man: they are rather opposites, like the negative and positive electricity of the magnet, opposites necessary to each other, and separable only in idea.[35] They cannot exist independently–though they may be differently proportioned in different times and persons. The generalizing tendency is like the wind that causes the kite to soar; the realizing tendency–the tendency which makes man cling to facts and symbols–is like the string that steadies it by holding it to the ground. If either were removed, the necessary balance of things would be destroyed, and progress or permanence would be impossible. And therefore, even it were impossible that both should act harmoniously, though these difficulties should never be quite removed, we still owe a deep debt of gratitude both to the men who assert that spiritual reality is not contained in, or limited by, its symbols: and to the men who assert that it is only attainable to man through symbol, since by their constant struggle and alternate victory man is ever advancing to a fuller and fuller comprehension of its divine idea.

But there are men in whom this division is almost removed. The higher we go, indeed, in these two classes of mind, the more nearly we find them approach to each other: and when we reach the highest minds of either class, Luther or St. Augustine, St. John or St. Paul,[36] we find the distinction almost vanishing, at least in result. Or rather, perhaps, we should include such in a class by themselves: the class of intuitive, emotive, imaginative, minds who see ideas and facts not in their separation but in their unity:–who are in contact with the spiritual reality, which both fact and thought represent–the idea in Platonic sense,[37] which is the union of real and ideal, of soul and body, fact and thought:–and who, therefore, will not and cannot be chained to the triumphal car of a theory–or let the aspirations of their soul be crushed by an institution. When such an one stands still, it is not because the fact is there, but because it is still still [sic] sufficient for the spiritual needs. When he progresses, it is not because logical results force him to do it, but because the voice of God in his soul says 'Forward'. He can neglect consistency of an outward kind, that idol of shallow minds. His course will not be like the iron road[38] made by man, which goes on unswerving through what ever lies before it:–breaking over the ancient landmark, and tearing its way through the sacred recesses of the hills: but it will be like the fluctuations of a mighty river, which, while it rolls on its ever-growing waters steadily to the ocean, bends to every sinuosity of the shore, and, remaining the same, yet adapts its form, its shape, its color [sic] to the soils over which it passes, and the banks between which it moves. While men of facts are obstructive, and men of theory are revolutionary, such an one forms in himself a living connection of the past and the future. By an intuitive glance, which combines the results of the widest theory with the appreciation of the simplest facts, he sees what has reality and worth in it, what can be done and what not, and he will not readily sacrifice a precious germ of truth to preserve a time-hallowed institution, or lose any of the sacred treasures of the past to carry out the symmetry of a Proposition.

[§7 The Conservative and the Reformer–the rational basis of their respective creeds–their union and the origin of their separation. Progress only safe which it holds by the past.]

By these general principles is determined the relation which the past bears to the generation that now occupies the field of the world; And more especially the attitude which we, as reformers should take to the institutions, which the past has left us and which we seek to improve.   These principles are, it is evident, equally hostile to a blind reverence, and to a blind hostility: they strike at once at the slavish adhesion, that dare not alter a time-hallowed form, and the revolutionary fury that would break away from the natural course of development, and begin the world anew.   And what remains to be said under this head will be little more than extension and application of what has already been laid down more generally.

The subject will best develop itself, if we look separately at the positions of the conservative and the reformer and consider the good and evil which they involve, and the rational basis on which they rest.

And first as to the conservative.   The great argument or principle on which conservatism rests is that the present forms of life: the institutions which the past has left us as its ultimate result–that these institutions and forms, (only clear them of the obscurations and corruptions, which the selfishness of man and the friction of time have introduced) are the *highest realized phase of spirit.*   Your reforming institutions are problems; though defended by ever so sufficient a logic, they have not proved a relation to the spirit of the time.   The life of man has not dwelt in them, and it is only an assertion that it can dwell there.   Here is a sufficient dwelling for the soul of man amid the untried dangerous waste.   I will join with you, if you ask me to prop up a mouldering tower: to restore a failing bulwark.   I will even build up a new erection where the old masonry has given way.   But leave my secure home where I have dwelt so long fenced from the wrath of the elements–this one safe spot, amid a world of difficulty won and kept with such toil and struggle by my fathers–leave this spirit-home because of a few unfitnesses, and wants, and venture forth amid the trembling morasses of life, unprotected and unsheltered–merely for the chance of something better–it were child's folly to do that. 'Here is my rest, here will I stay for I do like it well.'[39] The truth that is in this view is obvious and will afterward be more fully developed. The answer to it, if viewed as the whole truth, is that God's law is progress, and man must conform to it. The spirit departs from institutions after a time whether we will or no. The appearance of corruptions in the forms of life is often no sign of man's unfaithfulness, though it may indicate that too: it is rather the indication that the life has passed beyond them, and when this is the case, no patching and mending will restore them.[40] We are seeking to restore bloom to the flowers of last spring, when all nature is arraying herself in a fresh unstained robe of joy:–

The old order changeth, yielding place to new,
And God fulfils Himself in many ways,
Lest one good custom should corrupt the world.[41]

On the other hand the Reformer bases himself on the fact that no realization of truth that has been attained is ultimate. The institutions which express, and satisfy man's deepest[42] wants have no sooner been formed, than he must proceed to *trans*form them into higher and better shapes. While a stage in the progressive realization of spirit remains yet unattained, it may be regarded by those who are striving for it as a lost object and aim: but it is no sooner attained than the spirit of man sinks back into itself, and becomes conscious of its superiority, its infinity:–conscious, at least, of a want beyond which is still unsatisfied. The ideal again separates itself from the real, and the effort of man is again enlisted to fill up the interval between the two. The past can only be the vantage-ground, whence we look forward to a better hope. The culmination of a form of thought and life is only the point whence we descry a still higher eminence to which we must climb. And in all this there is much truth. The spirit has implicit depths[43] in it, which no form of life is sufficient to satisfy or reveal. And if this dissatisfaction urge men to look for and lay hold of the next germ of good–the next element of spirit,–which time brings to them, and to introduce[44] that so far as they are able into the world, uniting it to the agencies already at work there–then it is only exercising its due influence.

But if it lead men to reject all such tentative efforts, if instead of recognising the old as the basis on which it has to build, it claims to reconstruct all things on the ruins of the past–or if–as the ultimate form of this tendency–it reject the influence of all outward institutions as something alien to the perfection of spirit–we must then revive the opposite truth that spirit only possesses it own contents so far as it incarnates them in form–and that therefore it can only progress, not by leaving the field of reality as if it were something inferior, but by striving progressively to introduce some smallest additional element of spirit into it.

I must here notice a misapprehension which has been already indicated, but must once more be pointed out, as it is of vital importance to the subject. A one-sided logic has ever tended to confound *spirit in itself* with *spirit in its idea*. Now spirit in its idea is realized spirit–spirit with all its capacities drawn out and developed. It is strictly speaking not spirit in itself, no more than it is matter in itself, but spirit developed by, and expressed in, matter. But spirit in itself is spirit as it came into the world, unconscious, undeveloped, bearing only the seeds and possibilities of what it afterward becomes. And the doctrine I have all along been declaring is that spirit only passes from its abstract to its concrete state–that is, only attains the knowledge and therefore the enjoyment of its contents, so far as it externalises them–or in other words, makes itself its own object in some institution or form of social union. It is therefore in one sense independent of such forms; in another dependent on them. On the one hand it feels superior to any such form, because its *capacity* is not limited to it–because it feels that such form does not exhaust its possibilities. And hence the conclusion lies open to those who chose to look at this side of the truth only that the form is an obstruction and that spirit is best without forms. Or more generally the logic is not carried so far, but stops short with asserting that spirit has no adequate form in the *past*, but that once the obstructive institutions of the past were taken away, it would produce adequate forms of government, of religion and in all spheres of life. And the practical conclusion is that no terms are to be kept with the actual institutions that prevent this blessed consummation. The first step towards realizing the spirit's aims must be to get rid of these, and then a glorious future will dawn upon man.

But here it is forgotten that spirit feels itself superior to any form or institution, only on the ground of its infinite capacity for growth which is not there satisfied, and not on the ground of something superior which it has realized within itself. When we ask what is to be put in place of the extruded past, we have nothing but certain abstract conceptions, with regards to the rights of man; which could never form the basis of a new constitution of things. And hence comes that terrible contradiction (already noticed), which was seen in the French Revolution in its extremest form.[45] When the absolute infinite capacity of spirit was recognised, yet all hitherto realized contents of spirit were rejected. It was that vacant state of the soul, conscious of its infinite want, yet unsubmissive to the only conditions by which it may attain satisfaction–that vacant state, which the seven devils of passion and greed[46] are only too ready to fill up.

How plausible it looks to say 'Let us tear down the old fabric where falsehood and wrong have dwelt, and get rid of its weakness, its jealousies and strifes for ever. Let us live anew by the light of heaven, uninterrupted by these earth-born clouds. Let the past be behind us a black region of weariness and despair–abolished now for evermore.' The infinite hunger of man's heart awakes and looks eagerly for the new dawn. But not yet–not yet! Narrow conditions hem us in on every side. Our nature has yet much to learn before it is possible for it to be absolutely free. Slavery within is the source of the wrong that is in all of the institutions that [are] without us. ''Tis the blot upon the mind that must show itself without.'[47] And a new constitution, except it were the expression of a new acquisition of internal freedom, could help us little. It is with spiritual enemies, and not with outward wrongs, that humanity has mainly to fight, and the victory in that contest can only be won by continued patient and self-sacrificing effort. *If* that victory be won, outward grievances must fall away, like dust from a living leaf, the vital force rejecting that which has no affinity with itself. But till this be so, we shall merely risk all by snatching too soon at the final prize. We can only help the general progress by accepting the conditions of our place in the world's development,[48] and striving for our part to harmonize them to the needs of the spirit. And therefore, if we are wise, we will not waste our strength in vain longings, or vain struggles with the limits imposed upon us: but with silent fortitude and self-restrained energy, we will concentrate ourselves to our God-appointed work, narrow as it may seem, and keep the infinite hope strong and undying–but shut up within–for a time.

We cannot therefore, throw off the yoke of past ages–or build up from the foundation the structure of social and political life 'as if nothing had been built before'. It is impossible, if it were desirable, to act as if the past were not. If we approach it with a cut-and-dry constitution formed out of our imaginings, we will be certain to destroy the forms that were there before, but we have no security that we will be able to substitute that which we think better. Rather we have the certainty that we will *not* be able. For the plan of the universe never shapes itself by the thought of an individual, but the individual must endeavor [sic] to shape his thought by it. But if we unite ourselves and our working to agencies already working:–if we do not oppose our good to the evil that is in existing institutions, as is so often the injudicious course of reformers, but rather seek points of contact in the old for the new principle which we wish to introduce,–wasting as little strength as possible on conflict; then every step we make will be sure gain. The new will grow up, shaded from the too hastily ripening sun, by the husk of the old–and only when the former has grown to maturity, and found a sufficient covering for itself, will the latter drop away, and allow the full formed kernel to show itself to the light. The best progress in other words, is when the old passes into the new, without break of continuity and by such imperceptible stages that we cannot say where the one begins and the other ends, any more than we can tell where youth ends and manhood begins.

If ever there was a time, when the new light and the old appeared to be in antagonism, it was when Jesus and His Apostles stood face to face with the Pharisees and the Sadducees [Acts 4]. And yet Jesus and His Apostles would not depart from, or oppose Judaism, until they were driven out. They knew that the new truth they witnessed for, was kindred to all the true elements in the old. They claimed to be the truest representatives of the past as well as of the future. And the result was a testimony to their wisdom for they were thus furnished with a basis for their progressive efforts, which nothing else could have supplied, and the Jewish synagogue became the cradle of the Christian Church. 'I come not to destroy the law and the prophets, but to fulfil.'[49]

[§8 Spiral course of human development.]
It is a curious fact that reformers, even while they attack the immediate past as altogether bad; generally appeal to the more distant past against it, and suppose themselves to be vindicating old

institutions from the corruptions that have come over them by time: when in reality they are advocating right and proper innovations. We may partly ascribe this to that confusion of the past with the *ideal*–which ideal is indeed, the basis of human society, but never perfectly realized in it, or rather will be realized only as the ultimate Result of History. This confusion is the same which prompted the dream of a golden age deteriorating through a silver, a brazen,[50] an iron age to the present low state. Man seeks refuge from a present inadequate to the soul's desires by painting in brighter hues, and shaping to his wishes the indistinct memories of the Past. But there is also a deeper basis for this fact. We are ever in our advance taking up again elements which were let drop at an earlier stage of civilization–coming over the traces of lost civilizations, and rediscovering as it were, their discoveries. The curious law observed in family portraits, that features return after the interval of a generation in which they seemed to be altogether lost: so that the son oftener repeats the likeness of his grandfather, than of his father: this law finds its analogy in the history of the race where we see constantly the rise of tendencies, which have no apparent connection with their immediate antecedents: but point back to a period more remote. Thus we seem ever to be leaving the Immediate Past and approximating to the more distant Past. And indication of this we find in the fate of great authors. Thus Shakespeare was understood and appreciated in his own day: but immediately after the world rolled away from him, as it does from the sun, and he was not for long felt in his true greatness, till an age again came, of kindred spirit, when once more he rose to his meridian place.[51]

From this law, which I cannot now stay to illustrate fully, some despairing theorists have been led to adopt the view that history moves in cycles, like nature; in constant change, yet ever repeating the same course with only accidental modifications.[52] 'The thing that hath been, it is that which shall be: and that which hath been done is that which shall be done: and there is no new thing under the sun.' [Eccles. 1.9] Is there anything whereof it may be said: 'Behold this is new: it hath been already of old time which was before us'?[53]

But if we examine more closely we find that though man passes again and again over the same ground, it is every time at a higher level than before. There are no mere repetitions of the past, nor can there be. Thus the Reformers might think, some of them, that their highest aim was to produce a simple copy of the church of the first ages, but they could not annihilate the course of the world's history from that time onwards. Even supposing they had been able, by their deep comprehension of the spirit of the Gospel, and their wide knowledge of the forms in which it was cast by the circumstances of the time when it appeared, to revive a perfect picture of the Apostolic age, and enter into completest sympathy with it: Even though they thus received into their minds the exact spiritual forces which acted on the early Church, and became in all respects, servants of the same principle, yet they had to answer different questions, they had other difficulties which their principle must solve for them. They had received a wider and deeper philosophic culture, and the problem of the world, though still substantially the same, was presented to them in a more advanced and difficult form. In short however faithful they were to the original record of Scripture, their position necessitated and enabled them to develop meanings out of them, which were not present either to the writers, or those whom they specially addressed. Their return to the ancient belief was, therefore not simple return, but involved an altogether new, and unexampled element in the spiritual development of man. And so it is always. There is no advance, which does not imply a deeper comprehension of the past–which does not bring us into relation with thoughts and deeds of the most remote History, and so tighten the cords that bind the race together: but on the other hand, there is no *re*formation, no restoration of the old forms of life, or modes of thought, which does not develop new forces and results–or, what is the same thing, lead to a fuller exhibition of what is included in principles already in operation. Man neither rolls in ever-returning cycles, as some despairing conservatists imagine; nor moves forward in a straight line, as too eager reformers would have it. He moves, it has been well said, in a spiral, which is a composition of these two motions, ever again and again passing through the same round of experience and tendency–yet ever rising to a higher level–ever nearer to the goal.[54] And thus the good that lay in any byegone [sic] form of life, is never altogether lost, even to prepare the way for a higher excellence, but the last result of human development will take up with it, and elevate to a higher pitch every minor beauty or worth that has been exhibited in its course.[55] And, after the long course of ages has rolled, the New Jerusalem will include and more perfectly embody the blind innocence and peace *of the idea of Eden.*

[§9 Is there a moral progress of humanity? Buckle's false philosophy.]

A question has been raised, which I might leave to be answered, in general, by the foregoing investigations, if it did not acquire additional interest from a book which has been lately published—the question viz. whether there is a *moral* progress of humanity. Buckle, a man, I daresay, of wide reading, but of small philosophy, states it as follows. Morality, he declares, must have had extremely small influence on the progress of civilization 'For, there is unquestionably nothing to be found in the world, which has undergone so little change, as the great dogmas of which our moral systems are composed. To do good to your neighbors, [sic] to sacrifice for their benefit your own wishes—to love you neighbor as yourself, to forgive your enemies, to restrain your passions:—these and a few others are the sole essentials of morals: but they have been known for thousands of years, and not one jot or tittle has been added to them by all the sermons, homilies and text-books, which moralists and theologians have been able to produce.'[56] Whence it follows that morality is a constant quantity in human affairs and that all progress must be accounted for by scientific discovery.

Now, allowing for a moment that it is a true representation that morality was as well known from the earliest times, as it is now, this will not bear the inference which is drawn from it (and drawn from, I may remark, by as pure an a priori process as was ever used by the metaphysicians, whom this man of facts so much condemns). But allowing that morality as a knowledge is constant, might there not arise strong personal influences which should raise it from an indisputable proposition to an earnest belief? The soul of man does not move by abstract logical demonstration, but by strong deep currents of feeling: and it is matter of the most ordinary experience, that where all the proof in the world will not move, the influence of a brother-man may. Is it not within the range of possibility that such an influence might be exerted on the whole race, and that the whole current of things should be changed by the permanent admiration and love, which humanity entertains for her good and her great?

But the best answer lies deeper. It is *not true* that morality is stationary as a knowledge: and we may see this if we only make[57] a new application of the principles which have been already developed about the relation of the concrete to the abstract.[58] It is true, indeed, that such moral generalities as have been above exemplified are found in writings of all nations and times, and may be said to be known to all men, however they may interpret them in detail. And it is quite true that, in one sense, these generalities include all that can be known about morals. But then morality is not exhausted by such vague abstractions: but consists rather in the manner in which these are united with life. In the abstract, we may say that we know all things when we know the idea of *being*–for that idea includes all things:–but yet it is only in proportion as the idea is rendered more concrete–i.e. as the space between the vacant abstraction, and the unintelligent fact is filled up–it is only in this proportion that we can be said, in the proper sense, to know anything. So here. Men knew these moral abstractions from the earliest times:–*that* is implied in the fact that morality is implicit in humanity–given in man's very nature. But it was only as morality realized itself outwardly that it could be rendered conscious inwardly. And, if we look to the facts of the case we shall find[59] that moral ideas; the contents of his own moral nature, have been growing in definitiveness: ever becoming more fully developed and determined to the mind of man.

To take but one great example of this. Every one knows the difference which exists between recognising an internal, and an external law: between conforming to moral duty as an outward prescription, and choosing it as the dictate of our own inmost nature. Now, if there is one fact established in History, it is that morality, so far as it was acknowledged at all, was to the early nations of the world a prescribed round of particular acts and duties–which the individual could not question or alter. And here lay the possibility of a perversion which actually in many cases resulted–the possibility of mixing many arbitrary and extraneous prescriptions and customs with the genuine dictates of the moral principle, so that, at last, the sanctions of morality might be given to that which is absurd and unreasonable; or even to that which is utterly wrong and inhuman. And even supposing this was not the case, supposing the law was right and good, it yet came to man altogether as an external bondage–a condition, against which the nature of man always did, and always will revolt. But when morality incarnated itself more and more fully in human Form, till the Highest; the perfect union of God and man, came at last to show the identity of right and humanity. When morality was recognised, not as an external law, but as the substance of man's own nature:–a step, the greatest possible, was attained in human progress. The idea of Conscience, an altogether modern idea, came to supplement the idea of an abstract right. Man, recognised as having a standard of right within him, could no longer have monstrosities permanently imposed on him, *as right*, without protest: and all merely national or temporary elements became more and more purged away from the truth. And highest of all, man recognising the law as his own deepest being and Life, felt that in obeying it, and not in rebelling against it, lay his truest Freedom.

It would be absurd to say that morality was the same thing at the end, or at any advanced point in the course of this process, with what it was at the beginning, but, if so, what becomes of the assertion that morality is a constant quantity in human nature?

[§10 Religion the source and law of human development. Yet Religion must not interfere directly with politics. Church and State.]

Religion is the deepest principle of man's being, the source from which all his other activities receive their direction, and their law. These deepest silences of a man's soul, where he is in contact with the unseen: and which are altogether withdrawn from the stir and bustle of life ultimately give the rule to all the noisy–and apparently important concerns amid which he moves in his outward life. The rushing tide of passion, the brawl of outward interests occupy the foreground of history, and sometimes seem to be the only living agencies in it: but he that looks deeper becomes aware of a quiet constant force which these fitful and violent agencies are utterly unable in the long run, to cope with. Thus when we look closely at the history of Reformation, the wide-embracing negotiations, and contests of Charles and Francis, and the Pope which first attract the eye are really in result of little vital moment to the progress of man.[60] They are little more than a vast system of violent forces, directed in opposite ways, but in the end compensating each other, and furnishing with great noise a result of zero. They merely draw off the attention of the world, and allow the real history of the time to ripen in that quietness which is necessary to the beginning of great events.

And so always. The quiet thought and aspiration and prayer of the religious man–the man who is possessed by a spiritual principle seem to be as it were, nothing in contrast with the storm of war, or the struggles of party. But wait a generation–a century and look again. The storm has raved itself to rest, and its most distant echoes have died away. The parties that divided the world have made an everlasting 'truce of God',[61] and that for which they strove is gone for ever like the shadows on the hills. But the quiet solitary spirit's works and thought is not gone. Quietly it has gathered to itself the agencies of civilization: armed itself with all outward means, and permeated all life with its leaven. It builds constitutions, forms the centre of new political unities, creates a new social world: so that the men who would have been the first to despise it[62] in its simplicity as a faith, are forced to regard it as a fact with respect even excessive:–or even to become its servants.

Perhaps of all the events which teach this lesson, the most impressive is the call of Abraham [Gen. 12–25]. The high line of the faithful, of those who through faith and patience inherit the promises, begins with the early traveller, who, in obedience to the divine command, separated himself from the settled life of his country, and went forth to be a stranger, and a sojourner upon earth in grand loneliness and separation from all national ties. Look for a moment at the contrast between him, and that great empire he came into contact with, as it appeared then, and as it appears now. On the one side was Egypt in the glory of a premature but glorious civilization armed with the widest appliances of art and luxury. On the other a few tents, protected by shepherds and unwarlike men; That was the picture as it appeared then: but how does it look now? The glory of the Pharaohs is silent and gone, and known only by the magnificence of its tombs. But Abraham: his name is in our mouths a household word. His experiences are the lessons of all nations: he is the first great landmark in the world's spiritual history: the father of the faithful in every age and clime. When we turn to this life we see the first gleam of God's revelation breaking in upon the night of a fallen world. The sun is now high in the heavens, and will rise till every dark corner of the earth be flooded by his beams–but till the end of time we must remember and be thankful to the watcher who hailed the first streaks of morning on the everlasting hills. Faith and sight have changed sides, and the ultimate lesson of history is summed up in the familiar text: 'The world passeth away and the lust of it, but he that doeth the will of God abideth for ever.' [1 John 2.17]

If we look at the history of ancient nations we shall find that all the elements which they realized in the course of their existence are already implicitly given in their religions–and that their failure and decay came only when they had reached the point beyond which the limited moral and spiritual principle of their religion could not carry them. And it might in like manner be easily proved that all the systems of polity–all the institutions and forms of social life that have been established,–all the rights of person and property that[63] have been vindicated since the entrance of Christianity have been little more than [several words lost at the bottom of this folio] this right. But the proof of this would require too wide an enquiry to be here developed.

Religion, I have said, contains the rule of all the other activities of man. But it is necessary to guard against an apparent consequence of this, viz. that religion should directly interfere with political rights. On the contrary, there is nothing so dangerous as to combine religious and political reform. For not only will the mixed and impure motives that belong to the sphere of the latter, intrude themselves into the former: but there is a deeper reason. Politics and religion belong to different strata of man's being, if we may use the expression. Politics belong[s] to the comparatively outward interests of man's life. Religion is the deepest principle of his soul. And any attempt to precipitate the gradual process by which a principle beginning innermost life,[64] permeates through all its outward interests and activities, can only end in fastening some external form upon the life which has no vital connection with it. And such an excrescence will be an obstruction rather than a help to the principle which it seeks to communicate. Principles begin to work in the religious sphere, consolidate themselves there, and take possession of the whole mental being before they work outward, and begin to remodel in any extensive degree the forms of government and social life. Thus, as has been said, the whole advances that have yet been made in politics may be said to have comprehended in, or flow, as legitimate consequences from what the Apostles taught as to man and his destiny. But the Apostles did not waste their force on these extraneous matters. Their whole energy was devoted to plant in man's inmost soul the divine principle with which they were intrusted, [sic] and when that was done: they could leave it to time and its own vital force to subdue all the other provinces of his life to itself. Man does not advance all at once but principles begin their work in the deeper silences of his being, and perhaps centuries may come and go, ere it has become clear what consequences they contain, and will produce upon all his life-circle.

Hence it is a very fruitful source of error when men seek to introduce principles, and their utmost logical consequences in all spheres of man's life at once. Even if reformers always[65] apprehended quite rightly the principles they sought to introduce,[66] the course of logical deduction would be too quick for the necessities of human growth. But this is impossible: for principles apprehended merely by the intellect are sure to be misapprehended in some respect, and their results still more. If the early church in their first rough glimpse of Christian principles had carried them out to what they thought their political results, we may be sure that these would not have been the results which we now see to flow from them. The results of a spiritual principle are not to be drawn by logic but by life: they must sink into human hearts, permeate the nature behind the will–and–then only will it become evident in what forms of social life this new spiritual consciousness finds its expression and its support.

He, therefore, who wishes to reform the inmost thoughts of men, must give up all regard to the reform of their outward political relations.[67] And accordingly, we find the Gospel teachers everywhere inculcating obedience and submission to all outward ordinances that did not directly contradict the individual conscience.[68] Slavery and all other institutions they left untouched, if man could enjoy Christian liberty–liberty of soul–beneath them, and only when these institutions intruded into this inner sphere did they authorize resistance. Luther, therefore, was quite right in the principles of submission to the civil power, which he taught–quite right in appealing to the example of the Apostles.[69] Not indeed as though a time would not come, when all the people being permeated by the new principle, they would have a right to conform the government to their inward needs–but simply this–that no forcible means should be used to hasten that time: that it should come as the ultimate result, not of the triumph of one party over another, but of the penetration of society by the new principle. However true the religion was, it had no claim over society, but in virtue of its moral power. So long as society resisted the inward principle, it had a right as the highest authority to resist the outward change, and to impose conformity in political matters[70] upon any minority.

And here lies the decision of the oft-vexed question of Church and State. In the wider and truer sense of the words the church and state can never be separated. Each is made up of the whole body of the nation, only viewed in the one case in relation to its earthly interests and in the other, in relation to the religious principle which is the centre of its unity. In this sense the state is always rightly subordinate to the church, or in other words, man's earthly life is subordinate to his spiritual[71] culture. But these names have been used in a narrower sense to designate the functionaries to whom the offices of government are intrusted–and those to whom the religious culture of the nation is intrusted respectively. And we must carefully distinguish these senses. We cannot too much guard against subordinating the state to the clergy, and that perhaps as much for the sake of the latter as of the former. For if the clergy have domination over the laity, they will no longer maintain their character as clergy. Their pure teaching of principles will be distorted by immediate reference to practical results, and expediency will intrude into their zeal for truth. They will be tempted to neglect their peculiar functions for the lower but more immediate influence of government. They will perhaps relax their efforts in imprinting their principles upon the deepest nature of humanity, being busied mainly in forcing its outward results upon the conduct. They will thus avoid the judgment of God, and the human heart upon what is good and what not in the things they teach, and force raw unmodified abstractions upon the growing life of the world.

Thus after the clergy have defended themselves from intrusion, and have secured liberty of speech and of teaching, they must not attempt to interfere directly or as clergy with the government of the state. It is the business of the government to conform outward institutions to the inward principle of life, when that has penetrated society: and as citizen[s] the clergy may take part in these things. But they can put forth no claim as church to govern, for in this sense the church includes all laity as well as clergy–and it is the spirit in humanity, and not in any class which is the judge of truth, though one class may especially have the function of seeking and of teaching it. Indirectly their influence will be great, though not so much in attaining special results, as in regulating the kind of result sought for: by planting principles that shall ultimately work out their own issues in ways uncalculated.

[§11 The hopes of Progress.]
I had intended to take up several other points and especially I had made preparations for illustrating the principles already determined by a view of the general lines of tendency exhibited in the reformation: and in particular to trace the growing of the principle that lay at the root of the reformation–till it finally embodied itself in the

person of Luther: to show how he guarded it from the obstructive politicians of Rome, by whom he was finally cast off at the diet of Worms–and by the bull which preceded it.[72] And on the other hand from the destructive theorists, in whom the principle had overbalanced itself. I intended to have examined the details of the controversy between Luther and Zwingli, in whom first were showed in any fullness, two tendencies that have since divided Protestantism.[73]

But as I have occupied all the time which I have: and as the essay has extended to almost disproportionate length already, I must leave it at this point.

On the whole the study of history is full of encouragement to faith and active energy, and is the best reconciliation of the two.[74] For on the one hand [we?] see that man's active effort for good is [...?] lost, while man's faithlessness and selfishness may bring almost in [....?] sorrow and evil upon his nation and his [race?]. We see on the other hand, that there [is?] an interest which no man's [failure?] can ultimately imperil–a progress [which?] must go on whether in the hearts [of its?] friends, [or?] over the heads of its enemies. No individual weakness or crime can stop the ultimate triumph of principles in humanity: while each individual may do much to further their quiet and unbroken development.

> Well roars the storm to him who hears
> A deeper voice *across* the storm[75]

With the storm of party debate in our ears and the reins apparently in the hands of unprincipled men, it is well to fortify our faith in the triumph of good, by looking how even these may have been made to subserve the growth of a result, which they hated, or cared not for. And though the discouraging sense of failure may seem to rest on man's best efforts, it is well to remember that [?] the issue is on [the] other [hand,]

> [...] Though we fail indeed
> I–you–a score of such weak workers [–He]
> Fails never.[76]

The hope of progress is for [even?] us whose eyes are too dim for *sight*–not understanding [?] all our [...?]–in the words [of Him who?] said 'Lo, I am with you always, *even* unto the end of the world. Amen.'[77]

1   [The German Reformation ran roughly from the fourteenth to the seventeenth centuries. Caird focuses on two key figures in this reaction against papal authority and the corruption of the Church: namely, Martin Luther (1483–1546), German theologian, and Ulrich Zwingli (1484–1531), Swiss divine, who fostered a more radical form of Protestantism than that advocated by Luther (see pp. 33–4, 39).]

2   [Caird leaves spaces for the sub-headings to sections 1, 3, and 7 to 11 inclusive. I have inserted the remainder according to sense.]

3   [Adam and Eve's life before the Fall is recounted in Gen. 1.27 to 3.5.]

4   [That is, 'the Paradisical state'.]

5   ['The Spirit of the years to come
Yearning to mix himself with Life.'

    Alfred, Lord Tennyson, 'Love thou thy land, with love far-brought', in Christopher Ricks (ed.) *The Poems of Tennyson*, 3 vols., 2nd ed. (London: Longman, 1987), vol. 2, p.38, ll.55–6. Poem published 1842.]

6   [MS may read 'high'.]

7   [Possibly an allusion to: 'That vertue therefore which is a youngling in the contemplation of evill, and knows not the utmost that vice promises to her followers, and rejects it, is but a blank vertue, not a pure; her whiteness is but an excrementall whiteness;' John Milton, 'Areopagitica', in his *Complete Prose Works*. gen. ed. D. M. Wolfe, 8 vols. (London: Oxford University Press, 1953–82), vol.2, pp.515–6.]

8   [An allusion to the *Sturm und Drang* [Storm and Stress] literary movement which flourished in Germany on the 1770s. It was closely associated with Johann Wolfgang von Goethe (1749–1832), man of letters, and emphasised individual feeling and creativity on one hand, and social justice and liberty on the other. Goethe had a very great influence on Caird. Cf. Edward Caird, 'Goethe and Philosophy', in his *Essays on Literature and Philosophy*, 2 vols. (Glasgow: James Maclehose, 1892), vol. 1, pp.54–104.]

9   ['And after the earthquake a fire; but the Lord was not in the fire: and after the fire a still, small voice.' (1 Kings 19.12) The 'still, small voice' is traditionally taken to be conscience.]

10 [MS reads: 'irreconcileable'.]

11 ['Vanity of vanities, saith the Preacher, vanity of vanities; all is vanity.' (Ecclesiastes 1.2)]

12 ['Some species increase, others diminish, and in a short space the generations of living creatures are changed and, like runners, pass on the torch of life.' Lucretius, *De Rerum Natura* [*On the Nature of the Universe*], trans. WHD Rouse (London: William Heinemann, 1975), bk 2, ll.77–9, pp.100–1.]

13 ['Sei ruhig, schönstes Mädchen! ob ich helfen kann weiß ich nicht, ein Einzelner hilft nicht, sondern wer sich mit vielen zur rechten Stunde vereinigt. Aufschieben wollen wir und hoffen.' JW von Goethe, 'Unterhaltungen deutscher Ausgewanderten' ['Conversations of German Immigrants'], in his *Weimarer Ausgabe vom Goethes Werken*, 143 Banden, (München: Artemis, 1987), Abteilung I, Band 18, Seite 257. This quotation recurs in Caird's last book (Edward Caird, *Lay Sermons and Addresses* (Glasgow: James Maclehose, 1907), p.12), as well as his biography (Henry Jones and JH

Muirhead, *The Life and Philosophy of Edward Caird, LL.D, DCL, FBA* (Glasgow: Maclehose, Jackson, 1921), p.254).]

[14] ['For that Spirit which had taken this fresh step in history is the inmost soul of all individuals; but in a state of unconsciousness which the great men in question aroused....World-Historical persons...attained no calm enjoyment; their whole life was labor and trouble; their whole nature was nought else but their master-passion. When their object is attained they fall off like empty hulls from the kernel. They die early, like Alexander; they are murdered, like Caesar; transported to St. Helena, like Napoleon.' GWF Hegel, *Philosophy of History*, trans. J Sibree (New York: Dover, 1956), pp.30–1. First German edition published in 1832. Sibree edition first published in December 1857.]

[15] [MS del. immediately after 'dilettante': 'philosopher'.]

[16] ['He that loveth his life shall lose it; and he that hateth his life in this world shall keep it unto life eternal.' (John 12.25).]

[17] [Possibly a reference to Bausen who is mentioned again on pp.14 above. Rowland Williams, 'Bunsen's Biblical Researches', in F Temple et al, *Essays and Reviews* (Oxford: JH and Jas. Parker, 1860), esp. pp.86–7. Cf. 'Why may not justification by faith have meant the peace of mind, or sense of Divine approval, which comes of trust in a righteous God, rather than a fiction of merit by transfer?' *ibid.*, p.80. If Caird has Bausen and Williams in mind, this sentence might be a covert attack on Benjamin Jowett as well.]

[18] [The remainder of this paragraph is an interpretation of John 3.22–36.]

[19] [Swift's 'most ingenious Architect' in the Academy of Lagado 'contrived a new Method for building Houses, by beginning at the Roof and working downwards to the Foundation' Jonathan Swift, *Gulliver's Travels* ed. Robert A Greenberg, revised critical edition (New York: WW Norton, 1961), pt 3, chap. 5 p.153.]

[20] [Probably a reference to Edward Caird, 'The Roman Element in Civilisation', *North British Review*, vol. 44, no. 88 (June 1866), pp.249–71, esp. pp.263, 271. Alternatively, Caird may be alluding to his 'Plato and the Other Companions of Socrates', *North British Review*, vol. 43, no. 86 (December 1865), pp.351–84, esp. pp.351–2, 358, 362–7 *passim*, 377–80.]

[21] ['For words, like Nature, half reveal
And half conceal the Soul within.'

Alfred, Lord Tennyson, 'In Memoriam AHH', in Ricks (ed.) *Poems of Tennyson*, vol. 2, p. 322 (Prologue, v.5, ll.3–4). Poem first published in 1850.]

[22] [MS reads: 'fleshly'.]

[23] [This word is deleted in the manuscript.]

[24] [Cf. Hegel, *Philosophy of History*, pp.278–9.]

[25] [MS del.: 'But the divine principle.']

[26] [Christian Carl Josias Bunsen, *Egypt's Place in Universal History*, 4 vols., trans. Charles H Cottrell (London: Longman, Brown, Green and Longmans, 1848–1860), vols. 1 and 2. Cited in Williams, 'Bunsen's Biblical Researches', p.53n1. On this basis, the 'others' to which Caird refers include Rowland Williams (see his 'Bunsen's Biblical Researches', pp.53–60). Racial folklore, drawing on Gen. 9.18–11.32, held that the races of men were sprung from the sons of Noah: Shem (the 'Semitic' races), Ham (the 'Negroid' races), and

Japheth (the 'Aryan' races).]

27 [Cf. 'The History of the World travels from East to West, for Europe is absolutely the end of History, Asia the beginning.' Hegel, *Philosophy of History*, p.103; *ibid.*, pp.103–4.]

28 ['There is neither Jew nor Greek, there is neither bond nor free, there is neither male nor female: for ye are all one in Christ Jesus.' (Gal. 3.28)]

29 [Cf. GWF Hegel, *The Logic of Hegel. Translated from the Encyclopaedia of the Philosophical Sciences*, trans. W Wallace, 2nd ed. (Oxford: Clarendon, 1892), §80.]

30 [MS del.: 'fact'.]

31 [See page 12 above.]

32 [MS del.: 'facts'.]

33 [Caird is drawing very heavily on Hegel's analysis of the Terror in the *Phenomenology* (GWF Hegel, *Phenomenology of Spirit*, trans. AV Miller (Oxford University Press, 1977), §§578–95. First German edition published in 1807.]

34 [MS del.: 'life and thought'.]

35 [Cf. Hegel, *Phenomenology of Spirit*, §152.]

36 [Martin Luther (1483–1546), founder of the German Reformation. St. Augustine of Hippo (354–430), Bishop of Hippo and Christian theologian. Of course, St. John and St Paul (d. ca. 65AD), aka Saul of Tarsus, were Apostles, authors of several books of the New Testament.]

37 [Plato, *Republic*, for example, 478e–480a.]

38 [That is of course, a railway track.]

39 ['This *is* my rest for ever: here will I dwell; for I have desired it.' (Ps. 132.14)]

40 [MS del.: 'If we cling blindly to the form of the past refusing to see what what [sic] is accidental and what is essential, the spirit of the past every day is departing further from us'.]

41 [Alfred, Lord Tennyson, 'Morte D'Arthur', in Ricks (ed.) *Poems of Tennyson*, vol. 2, p.17, ll.240–2.]

42 [MS del.: 'spiritual'.]

43 [MS has 'depths implicit', but with the numbers 2 and 1 respectively, written over the words.]

44 [MS del.: 'develop and unite'.]

45 [See page 18 above.]

46 [Cf. Matt.12.45; Luke 11.26.]

47 ['Tis the blot upon the brain
That *will* show itself without.'

Alfred, Lord Tennyson, 'Maud. A monodrama', in Ricks (ed.) *Poems of Tennyson*, vol. 2, p.574 (pt 2, §8, ll.200–1). Poem first published in 1855.]

48 [MS del.: 'history'.]

49 ['Think not that I am come to destroy the law, or the prophets: I am not come

to destroy, but to fulfil.' (Matt. 5.17).]

[50] [The manuscript has 'a brazen, a silver;' with 2 and 1 written above 'brazen' and 'silver', respectively.]

[51] [Caird returned to this broad theme in a lecture that he gave to the Ruskin Society of Glasgow, the text of which was published as 'Some Characteristics of Shakespeare', *Contemporary Review*, vol. 70 (1896), pp.818–34; reprinted in Tyler (ed.) *Collected Works of Edward Caird*, vol. 12.]

[52] [The eternal return is a key notion in Stoic thought, and is founded upon their belief that, for all of the suffering it contains, the world is a providentially-designed ideal. Edward Caird, *Evolution of Theology in the Greek Philosophers. The Gifford Lecture delivered in the University o Glasgow in Sessions 1990–21 and 1901–2,*2 vols. (Glasgow: James Maclehose, 1904), vol. 2, chaps. 17–8; cf. *ibid.*, vol. 2, pp.33–4. (Nietzsche's reintroduction of the idea of the 'eternal return' appears to be ruled out by its late date.)]

[53] [Possibly a reworking of Isaiah 65.17: 'For, behold, I create new heavens and a new earth: and the former shall not be remembered, nor come into mind.']

[54] [Cf. Hegel, *Philosophy of History*, pp.70–3.]

[55] [Cf. TH Green, 'Fragment on Immortality', in his *Works*, vol. 3, pp.159–60.]

[56] [Henry Thomas Buckle, *History of Civilization in England*, 3 vols. (London: Longmans, Green, 1902), vol. 1, p.180. First edition published in two volumes in 1857 and in 1861. Buckle had died on 29 May 1862.]

[57] [MS orig.: 'may'.]

[58] [See page 18 above.]

[59] [This word is deleted in the manuscript.]

[60] [Charles V (1500–58), Holy Roman Emperor 1519–58, King of Spain 1516–56, forced François 1 of France (1494–1547) to sign the Treaty of Madrid in 1526 thereby temporarily ending France's claims to northern Italy. He was confirmed as the Holy Roman Emperor in 1529 having signed the Treaty of Cambrai with France and the Peace of Barcelona with Pope Clement VII (1478–1534), pope from 1523. Charles called Luther to the Diet of Worms in 1521 (see pp. 33–4 below).]

[61] [The 'truce of God' (or *pax, treuga Dei*) was a medieval concept which called for the temporary suspension of all earthly hostilities, especially during the Sabbath, Advent and Lent.]

[62] [This word is deleted in the manuscript.]

[63] [MS reads: 'than'.]

[64] [Illegible interpolation.]

[65] [MS del.: 'men'.]

[66] [MS del.: 'teach'.]

[67] [MS del.: 'circumstances'.]

[68] [Most famously, '...Render therefore unto Caesar the things which are Caesar's; and unto God the things that are God's.' (Matt. 22.21). The sentiment is repeated in Mark 12.17 and Luke 20.25. Cf. Matt. 5.39, 17.27.]

[69] [Martin Luther, 'Temporal Authority: To what extent it should be obeyed',

trans. JJ Schindel and WI Brandt, in Martin Luther, *Works*, gen. ed. J Peliken and HT Lehmann, 55 vols. (Philadelphia: Muhlenberg Press, 1958–86), vol. 45, for example, pp.94–5, 110–1. First published in 1523.]

70 [MS del.: 'outward respects'.]

71 [MS del.: 'higher'.]

72 [The Holy Roman Emperor, Charles V, called Martin Luther to the Diet (governmental or religious session) that took place in the German town of Worms between 28 January and 25 May 1521. Luther defended himself against the Papal Bull *Exsurge Domine* issued by Pope Leo X (1475–1521) on 15 June 1520, which had required Luther to retract forty-one of his *Ninety-Five Theses* (issued in October 1517). Like the original act of issuing them, Luther's defence of the *Theses* at the Diet of Worms became a pivotal moment in the early history of the Reformation.]

73 [Luther denounced Zwingli's denial of the literal presence of Christ's corporeal body at the Eucharist. The pair convened the Colloquy of Marburg in September and October 1529 to seek a resolution, but the issue continued to divide Protestantism for many years afterwards.]

74 [The bottom left-hand side of this folio, with associated text, is missing, hence the state of the remainder of this text.]

75 ['And all is well, though faith and form
Be sundered in the night of fear;
Well roars the storm to those that hear
A deeper voice across the storm'

Alfred, Lord Tennyson, 'In Memoriam AHH', in Ricks (ed.), *Poems of Tennyson*, vol. 2, p.446 (stanza 127, ll.1–4). The poem continues immediately:

'Proclaiming social truth shall spread,
And justice, even though thrice again
The red fool-fury of the Seine
Should pile her barricades with dead.' (*ibid.*, p.447 (ll.5–8)]

76 [Elizabeth Barrett Browning, *Aurora Leigh*, ed. Margaret Reynolds (Athens: Ohio University Press, 1992), pp.528–9 (bk 8, ll.572–4). Poem first published in 1856.]

77 [Matthew 28.20. Jesus says these, the final words of the Gospel of St. Matthew. Only part of this quotation survives in the manuscript as some of the folio has been torn away.]

[Lectures on Moral Philosophy:
Social Ethics.]
[1877-93?]

Social Ethics No. 1
[Abstract Right and Subjective Morality Transcended by Social
Ethics.][1]
The transition from Abstract Right and Jurisprudence to
Morality in the narrower sense gives us no doubt an alteration of
an external into an internal law–but it leaves still an insoluble difficulty in the reconciliation of the universal and particular side of
man's nature.[2] In jurisprudence as we saw the individual has in
virtue of his abstract personality certain claims which he *may* urge
subject only to the respect he owes to the similar claims of other
personal beings.[3] His individuality is thus conceived as
universal–and therefore sacred in its expressions whatever they
may be, while it is an accident of his peculiar desires (which in
themselves have no sacredness) what particular expressions these
shall be. Thus here the particular is absolutely separated from the
universal, though it receives a kind of sacredness from accidental
association with the individual which is itself essential[ly]
universal. But even the unity of the individual and the universal
is imperfect, for the universal nature gives sanctity to the claims
of all other individual and self-conscious beings as well as to me.
And while on the one hand it appears as the ground of absolute
claims, of rights in me, on the other hand it appears as the limit
of these claims. The *limit* is *external* and *negative*. In morality
the limit on the contrary becomes *internal* and *positive*: i.e. the
Universal which limits the ego is identical with it–is its essence as
well as its law. But the contradiction above mentioned
reappeared. The individual as particular as having special
passions is at once identical with and absolutely divided from the
individual as universal. Out of this arises those contradictions
which are expressed in the moral antinomies (as we may call
them) of Kant,–in which the necessary unity of *passion* and *law*
and yet their absolutely equally necessary distinction leads to the
hypothesis of an infinite series of approximations–one endless

40

struggle to attain that which at the same time is postulated as man's essential being.[4] And the same difficulty only reappears in a new form in the infinite series of approximations by examination of which we are to find the absolute and necessary unity of Happiness and Goodness. Morality being thus resolved into a hopeless struggle to find contents for an abstract universal which is reached by abstraction from all content and whose very definition is to have no content, a hopelessness arises of the moral life brooding on itself and finding in itself only emptiness from which some minds are prompted to escape by falling back on authority, on a mere belief in an external code of duties which gives some objective rest to the mind, just as scepticism[5] of private judgement has been followed by slavery to an infallible church.[6] Both reasons have often mingled in the frequent perversions[7] to the Romish Church by which as a kind of back current all the advances of thought for some centuries have been attended.[8] To escape the negative which would [have] hardened itself in mere opposition, and out of which it seems hopeless that any positive should spring–any positive law or doctrine seems welcome. But the only true escape is in that development of thought in which the positive is seen to re-emerge out of the negative in which it was absorbed and lost–in which the particular which is denied in the abstraction whereby we rise to the universal shall be again reproduced by a new negation of the abstract universal.

Now we have therefore to repeat, 1) that the universal–man's consciousness of his nature as universal–was attained by negation of passion. [In so doing, it] implies this which it denies and therefore is bound, or has an affirmative relation to passion, and that 2) the passion which is negated by the consciousness of a man's universal being is itself a form of that universal being–or lies implicitly in it–man's conscious life–which by abstraction is separated from it. And therefore that 3) to live in accordance with that conscious being is not to live in the negation of passion as which it first appears–but to live in the consciousness of that spiritual life which is implicit in the life of passion though manifested by it in a fragmentary and unspiritual way. In this way we arrive at the reconciliation of the individual as particular with the universal, or in other words we make it possible that the higher moral life of man should be realized–nay we make it necessary that it should be realized in and through the gratification of natural desires. The idea of freedom is to be realized *in the world*–and is in fact to *become* an outward world–without losing its purity.

We see then how it may be possible to find a law, which shall be internal without being empty or arbitrary, and at the same time external without being a mere negative limit imposed from without and altogether separate from the tendencies it limits–a law which shall be positive and identical with the tendencies it limits; or in other words shall merely express the inner meaning–the spiritual essence–of these tendencies and shall in fact be related to them simply as the world of laws unfolded by science is to the world of ordinary consciousness–being the same only traced back to its ultimate truth. Let us develop each of these elements a little further.

In the first place in social ethics–in the relations of the family and the state–we find an objectively determined law. The state and the family are each an organization–i.e. a self-maintaining, self-developing unity–in which in the movement of life a multiplicity of parts are continually subordinated to the whole. There is in both a diversity flowing out from and returning to a unity–just as in a living body the change and intercourse of parts–their action and reaction–are subordinated to the common life. Life differentiates itself into members each having a separate function and these separate functions are necessary to each other, and so return again into unity–so that the greater the differentiation, the more complete the concentration and individuality. Now we shall see that in like manner the family and the state are, when we examine them closely, not mere accidental aggregations of atoms determined by individual and accidental passions and desires, but they show in their diversity and unity the manifestation of that unity of Ideal differences–given in the notion of Spirit. Thus we may contemplate the family and the state as higher necessities in relation to which the individuals are to be regarded as accidental, and should so regard themselves. So Antigone speaks of the duty she owes to her brother as laid on her by the essential nature of things–as a part of those divine laws–which are not of today, not yesterday–but eternal–and declares that before them every arbitrary will or command should be silent.[9] 'There is no more necessary'–but in this[10] sense the family and the state are necessary–as the manifestations of spirit, in its essential nature. They are substantial relations in which the life of man as spiritual exists, and apart from which therefore, still more as opposed to which, he has no spiritual value or dignity. Here then we find a positive and objective law–which is independent of and above the individual as such–a law which is not a mere 'ought to be' but which 'is': 'is' in a higher sense than any existence of mere natural things–as here the spirit which is the ultimate truth of nature finds a manifestation not fragmentary and isolated–not above all external, but which[11] while it exhibits even to the outward eye an essential unity of relations, has the consciousness of the individual himself involved in these relations. And this is the second point, that while an external law to the individual, they are also internal. The witness of the spirit to them is given in so far [as] in these relations the individual has the feeling of himself. He lives in them not as relations determined by his caprice–but as determining it. It is in them that he finds himself, the sphere of his activity, its object and its law. They are the presuppositions even of his self-seeking–as they are the law and the end to which self could be sacrificed. For it is out of the unity of the family and the state that he grows to the sense of independence–of self with separate purposes, desires, capacities and will. And again it is [in] losing himself in these that he finds their development and satisfaction.

We may represent, if we please, the determinations of the individual nature and will which flow from the notions of the family and the state–which are involved in his relation to them as a set or system of *duties*–i.e. we may do so if we regard the individual as existing quite independent of these relations–and then as brought under their law. But this way of representing it, we should observe, is based on an abstraction–in so far as the individual out of the family and the state does not show his true spiritual nature, and therefore to regard these as externally binding and limiting authorities of the opposition of ought to be and is, is to fall back on the point of view of abstract morality,[12]–or even on that point of view in which man is regarded merely as a being with various desires and tendencies. Of course if we regard the individual merely as having certain natural appetites, we may regard the law of the family or the state as limiting those appetites–for in the law of the family the appetites are reclaimed from indiscriminate gratification as by the law of the state the rights of others are made strong against individual caprice. Man as the mere abstraction of self-will–or as the complex of natural passions, is restrained. But then this is an imperfect view of man's relation to the family and the state. We should consider on the other hand that in the state and the family the man is truly not bound but freed–the field is given for the development and exercise of his spiritual being. The tendencies of man, it should be observed, find their true gratification and exhibit their essential nature only when their inward rationality is manifested–and the moral will only realizes its freedom when it finds a law in itself and an end. Therefore in both these respects man may be regarded not as limited by the state or the family but as delivered from bondage. For he is a slave when moved merely by natural impulse as such–and the mere negative opposition of law in general to this impulse cannot do more than give him sense of his slavery–since it merely sets the general spiritual nature in opposition to all particular determinations–while again it is only in so far as the general develops again into the particular that the mere externality of the limiting law is removed. Hence therefore, although we may talk of the duties of family and state, we really have transcended the idea of duty–which implies a constraining law over arbitrary caprice with which the individual is identified. The development of the relations of life as they are determined by the notions of the family and the state, and by the idea of freedom manifested therein, gives an *immanent* system of duties, which is shown to be consequent and necessary–and altogether another thing from the vague and fragmentary talk about special duties of humility, truth, etc., which has no necessary limits or order.

There are two other names which are employed to express the general quality of moral excellence in the various relations, and of these it may be well to say a few words to indicate their relation to the conceptions just explained. These are Virtue–and Righteousness or Justice in its wider moral meaning. Virtue is a word applied to moral excellence in so far as it is developed in the individual, on the basis of a certain natural character–is a moral work of art developed out of given materials. If the result of this development be simply that the individual is able to act in accordance with the demands of the circumstances wherein he is placed, we call his virtue specially *righteousness*. But in both these names there is a[n] implicit suggestion that the excellence is not simply man's adequacy to himself–but an artificial and an individual achievement. Hence we use the word virtue more of isolated heroic characters such[13] as Alexander[14]–or the founders of states–in regard to whom the sense of individual achievement–for which the circumstances afforded not favorable materials in present times–rather than of the life of an individual in a settled and ordered society–in which the place gives the materials and the opportunity for the qualities required to be exercised. It is for similar reasons as we have seen[15] that in ancient times *virtue* was the word more frequently used, since by the ancient moral excellence was regarded as the result of the moral genius of individuals, of their particular nature, [rather] than as the adequacy of the particular to the Universal nature of man. For similar reasons again the French are the nation who speak most of *virtue*–because they look on the individual, more to the peculiar temper and natural modes of action than to general life of which[16] he is an organ. We have before seen[17] how this abstract way of looking at the general as external limit and law to the particular–rather than as its informing principle–leads Aristotle to regard virtue as a mean between too great and too little indulgence of a passion,–where however *the* mean is a question of subjective determination.[18]

Here however we have reached that true unity or rather identity of the particular and universal, which is the great characteristic of *spiritual life*. The passions have ceased to be external to the Reason. Habit establishes in man a second nature which is above the immediate life of impulse,–in which the natural life of passion is broken and subordinated to the life of the spirit. In the organic Unity of the family and the civic life the particularity of passion and tendency is at once satisfied and subordinated to the manifestation of a general life–so that here we have the spheres of abstract jurisprudence and subjective morality at once completed and transcended. In abstract right, the particular is given by natural will–in subjective morality there is a demand on the part of the law–a categorical imperative–but the individual will is viewed as independent of this law–as having this law outside it–and therefore as merely capricious. Here the individual determined by his capacities and tendencies to certain employments finds himself in unity with the Universal which differentiated itself to special functions–or we have a complete moral syllogism in which the individual through his particular nature is brought into unity with the universal of the family or state.

Here more-over, in transcending the separate spheres of right and duty, we find their identity. In abstract right I have a right and another consequently a duty–to respect that right. In subjective morality, there is a demand for a unity of right and duty–it is required that I in willing my particular interest shall will the universal law–or in other words that my will and the law on the one side, and the realization of my particular interest and the law shall be one. But here alone is this requirement realized when the universal mediates and is mediated by the realization of the particular.

Freedom demands this *identity*–for while right without duty is the subordination of man's universal nature to man's particular desires–on the other hand duty without right is slavery–or it is a merely negative morality which is opposed to any realization. The attempt more especially to treat either family or state as purely legal or as purely moral contains in it certain immoral results which I have already mentioned. In the first case the relations are lowered to the level of the relations of private right–and the rights over persons by each other which they imply are treated on the analogy of rights over things. It would lead in practice to a neglect of moral duties which [arise] from the set of these relations–as when Cicero would divorce his wife to get a rich portion with a new one.[19]   On the other hand the merely moral treatment of these relations–and the denial of all their outward forms and sanctions–is based on an ignorance of the real importance of the outward manifestation–on a false spirituality that knows not that the spirit is self-expressive that it may know itself–and would lead[20] in practice to [a] life of anarchy and immorality.

One last remark may be made in regard to the social morality of ancient and modern times. The social morality of ancient times was in a sense unconscious. The individual lived in the family, the tribe, or the state as his moral substance–not because he recognized it philosophically as such but because he had grown up with the belief, because he knew no other. On the other hand the modern social ethics cannot have this simple form. The legal stage in which man is isolated as [an] abstract person, the subject of rights and duties–the moral stage in which he views himself as [a] law to himself, have been passed through. The modern sense of individuality has gained so great [a] power that the simple absorption of the Individual in the general life which characterized ancient life is no longer possible–while universal ties have been formed that make it impossible for the good man to be quite lost in the good citizen. We see therefore that the allegiance of the individual to the family–or at least to the state–i.e. the *piety* of the individual in the old sense[21]–must more often in modern times rest on a transcendence of the moral and legal isolation than on the simple absence of both. The individual must transcend the thought of his own isolated *substantiality* that he may regard himself not indeed as [an] accident of the state but as finding in it still his own substance.[22]

Let us now proceed with the development of the social relations in which the idea of freedom realizes itself. And first we regard the *immediate–a natural* organic unity in which man finds himself–the family. Next we consider how, the unity of family being broken up, he appears as [an] independent individual in civic society with others–apprehending himself as [an] independent individual with special wants which unite him to others and so imply a legal order which externally presides over the struggle of opposing interests and brings them back into harmony. Lastly how out of this individualistic community in which individuals are held together by the bonds of interest there grows the higher unity of the state to which the individuals devote themselves–as the highest moral organ of their outward life–as the security at once of their material wants and their higher education.[23]

Social Ethics No. 2

[Marriage and the Family. The Different Natures of the Sexes and their Proper Roles in Society.][24]

In [the] history of consciousness and self-consciousness we saw how the isolation of the individual self-dissipates itself by self-knowledge.[25] How, seeking himself an individual man finds himself universal–necessarily related to other self-conscious beings from whom he distinguishes himself. In the development of the moral consciousness of man, we saw how the knowledge of this spiritual nature as opposed to special passions and desires is at the same [time] the first realization of this nature: but in so far as these passions to which the higher nature of self-consciousness is thus opposed contain in them implicitly the same union of the universal and individual–in as much as, for example, even the appetites have a universal end (which in them as appetites is hidden)–and in so far as this is still more evident in relation to the higher principles of desires selfish and social–in so far there is a possibility of a reconciliation between the *higher* nature and that appetitive life which is opposed to it–there is a possibility of an elevation of desire and even appetite to the point at which the universal is willed in and along with the particular and the particular in and along with the universal. This coincidence of selfish and social tendency, this realization in the form of passion of that self-conscious nature of man which can only know self through the knowledge of others, and seek self in the seeking of others–or in one world can only find life in losing it in the service of a more general unity–finds its first *natural realization* in the ties of the family–the cradle of man's moral life–the first civilizing influence, and in which, the moral and spiritual introduces itself as if by stealth under a natural form, and which indeed forms the type and symbol of all higher moral unities. The problem of all moral life in fact may be described as this:–to extend the affective ties of the family to the nation and the world while preserving sacred the higher moral independence which the individual gains as he emancipates himself from the law of the family–or rather of the first family–that in which he is reared. Comte here speaks almost in the language of Hegel when he says that 'the moral efficacy of domestic life consists in this, that it forms the only natural transaction which can habitually disengage us from pure *personality* in order to elevate us gradually to true sociability.'[26]

The main points then in regard to the family unity are: 1. that in the family the independence of the separate individual is dissolved, so that each member finds himself in the others. 2. That this unity however is one of feeling–a natural unity in the first instance–it is therefore contingent in two ways–[1.] in so far as it is contingent on the natural existence of particular individuals (while the state is elevated above this–and is an independent rational unity which may exist in the complete change of the individuals constituting it):–and 2. as it is contingent on the inward feelings of these individuals and is destroyed by the absence or change of the appropriate feelings.[27]

Let us look at each of these characteristics for a moment. 1. In the Love of the family, the atomic personality of each member of it is denied as Comte says. The husband and wife, the father and son feel themselves each imperfect in himself and find the necessary compliment in the others. Each therefore ceases to claim or has not yet begun to claim to be healed as a person. The family rather as a whole is one moral Personality. Nor is this accomplished in the way of the absolute sacrifice of the different members to the head. It was one of the profoundly immoral conceptions of Roman law, that the family (the wife and children) was made slave of the paterfamilias.[28] It is not that the independence of the individuals is crushed. It is that it is transcended, in so far as each finds in the other the filling up of his own deficiency, first[ly] natural and secondly spiritual. The individual saves his life and freedom by losing it–for the other ceases to be regarded as another, and in the common life each finds the development of his individual capacities and tendencies. It is therefore only in the dissolution of the family–either its natural dissolution by the death of the heads of it–or its moral dissolution by the destruction of the tie of natural affection–that the individual Personality of the members of it appears or reappears. Legal relations, and individual rights as against each other to a share of the common property appear only when love ceases to be the fulfilling of the law toward each other. And this indeed is part of the imperfection of the moral unity of the family–that the individual right and personality is only held in abeyance by a subjective bond–and therefore may easily reappear to dissolve it, by a bond in which the moral element is somewhat more fully developed than the legal.[29]

2. And this takes us to the second point: the contingency of the family unity as a *merely internal unity*–a unity of feeling which is not[30] mediated by knowledge. Personal or selfish feeling is silently dissolved in unselfish sympathy–but there is no constitution, no rational order or law present to the minds of the members, and [by] expressing the nature of their necessarily arbitrary caprice [it] therefore may mingle with, and corrupt without let, an order which to many has yet taken no relevant form. On the side of the children indeed the atomic self-dependence is not really transcended because it has not yet been brought into consciousness. The realization therefore of unity out of difference is not in the family, owing to its mere natural and particular character, complete. The moral element of duty in the form of feeling is more prominent, whereas the legal element of right is as yet in the background: and therefore it is evident that there therefore must be, as already Aristotle notes, a higher differentiation of parts or individuals, etc., [?] [before] the highest moral organization of man can be attained.[31]

Meantime let us consider the family in its origin, in its existence, and in its dissolution–its beginning in marriage–its outward existence in the property of the family, and the care for it–and the education of the children to independent persons into whom it is dissolved.

Marriage contains the two elements or sides outward and inward. On the one side we have the existence of the sexes in their union of whom in man as in all the animal kingdom the natural life of the race is maintained and preserved. This is the first natural negation of the independence of individuals. In the second place and springing out of this we have the spiritual union of the two sexes complementing each other, not only naturally but morally and so forming the means of each others' highest calling.

Here as well as elsewhere that which is Μγενέσει [?] is ιτρώτσυ φὸσδὶ. The obedience to natural desire, leads, because such desires have in them an implicit rationality, to higher satisfactions and higher wants, and in the reaction of these upon the natural union is raised into a form of moral association. (The last becomes first and the first last,[32] and that which was sought πρὸς τὸ ζην subsists πρὸς τὸ [...?] ζηω.) It is by such *reaction of moral results upon natural desires that marriage gained that regular form and order*–which it now has among the civilized nations of Europe–while in savage tribes we have polygamy, polyandry or even worse. There are several views of marriage which have at different times been held, each of which is defective in some one or more of the elements that belong to it as an orderly and moral institution. Lowest comes that which regards it mere[ly] as 1) a *natural relation* of sex and ending in the continuance of the species. But scarcely less degrading is that which regards it as 2) a *purely legal* or juristic relation of contract–which has been almost coarsely expressed by Kant.[33] If we consider the marriage as a mere transaction between absolutely independent persons, we reduce each person into a mere instrument to the other's purposes–for law properly speaking only admits the categories of persons and things (under which last such service of persons to each other as may be classed as things may fall).[34] But to treat in this way the relations of husband and wife–i.e. as a legal relation of contract between independent persons with respect to different services, is profoundly to decimate[35] the relation between them. What the husband and wife give to each other is not definite services but their whole life and being. And this in the view of mere private right, in which the notion of independent Personality is prized, would be nothing less than slavery. But to transcend this notion of mutually repellent Personality without falling into mere slavery of one Person to another–is just the meaning and highest function of the union of the family–or indeed of all social unions in their measure. Marriage begins in a contract springing out of personal inclination, (or it may be out of the arranging of families in an earlier state of society in which the individual will is last [sic] respected–though in this last case at least the individuals interested must finally ratify the agreement by their promise). It begins in a contract, but this contract is no merely legal one in regard to different things or services–such as private right treats of:–it is a contract of two independent Persons–whereby[36] they cease to be independent Persons and become *one Person*.

And yet it is not slavery, for it is not a surrender of the Personality of the one to that of the other–but, it is a surrender of the Personality of both in relation to each other to the higher moral unity of the family which is thus founded. The family is the person and the members are the *accidents* of it–and each finds himself–his substance and moral value–in his position as member of the family. His sacrifice of self-will to the family is therefore only a sacrifice of his baser to his nobler self. In form or limitation it is really a deliverance of his spiritual being from the thraldom of accidental passion–and not a mere negative deliverance by curbing the passion but one in which the accidental passion is made moral, regulated and directed so as to sub-serve the higher ends of life.[37] The marriage contract so-called which relates to the disposal of the property of the two parties is a different thing to which we have afterward to return. Marriage itself in its idea is a contract that terminates all contracts (realizing Hobbes' account of the origin of the state)[38]–in so far as it transcend the independent Personality of individuals; in which their possibility of making contracts is based.[39] It is therefore also *in its idea* an indissoluble contract: but only in *idea*, for there is involved in this special relation an accidental element of a moral kind–of affection which may pass away. The apparently unconditional surrender of self is conditioned by time which may bring about the most violent alteration of feeling–even to the extent that each is ready for the greatest outrages on the other. Hence for 'the hardness of our hearts'[40] divorce is a possibility which must be contemplated–though the law is so far right in holding as firmly to the idea of marriage as circumstances and its own powerlessness in dealing with feeling will permit.

3) Purely moral. Equally degrading in the long run is another view of the institution which comes forward with special claims of purity and spirituality–a view which sees in the outward pledge and promise–the definite and public contract–something that stains the purity of the feeling that leads to the union. This view really tends in its results to concentrate all the importance of the union on the sensual element of it, while it casts that solemn assent of two souls to mutual self-surrender into the background. But as it was a great step gained even in formal right–[in] which the formal sign–the spoken word–were viewed as the real transfer–and not the actual sense of it[41] by the hands. Still more here where the sensible side is secondary and accidental to the higher moral union–should the ceremony in which this union is constituted be viewed as the

essential element that lifts the union above the accidental element of passion into the organ of man's highest moral culture.   This false spirituality finds still another form in the attempt to separate the element of feeling in Platonic love from the sensible altogether–a monkish view which as I have often remarked,[42] beginning with treating the sensible as of no account really raises it into far greater importance as the unconquerable negative of all morality.

The two sexes are complimentary as already said not only as in the animal, but in a higher rational sense–in the sense that their moral and intellectual qualities fit[43] them for being the highest means of moral education to each other, and it is this that makes marriage a truly spiritual union.   At the same time it is not easy to express exactly wherein this complimentary character lies, however much it has been discussed.   The difference has been illustrated in different ways though rather vaguely by the difference of animals and plants[44]–or what is the same thing by the difference of the organic and the animal system in man–in so far as the former exists in self-involved unity, peaceful self-development and absorption, while the latter is the region of antagonism with the outward, of struggle and effort to accommodate self to things and things to self.[45]   The man has generally speaking the clearer sense of individuality and independence–of opposition to other things and persons–hence he feels a call to thought and action, to solve this contrast and division.   His peace is to be obtained by struggle with a discord–by clear conscious plan.   On the other hand this sense of definite opposition is wanting in the woman. She is more [in] unity with circumstances, has that sense of the whole and her place in it which without definite thought generally enables her to act right by feeling. She has tact to anticipate reason–and hence she does not need to generalize so much.   She clings to the individual and particular and is conformed to her surroundings.   And it is this on the whole that seems to prevent her from the highest achievements in philosophy or science.   She has attained very high excellence indeed in art with its unconscious or implicit Universal, but even then not the highest.   And it is probable that her genius is necessarily appreciative rather than productive, even allowing for the great imperfection of her education hitherto.[46]

Now it is easy to see even from this short account that such qualities are complementary.   That unity of feeling in which the woman lives is a sort of prophecy of the unity of Reason–after which the man–who lives in the contrast, is striving; it is therefore adapted to strengthen the faith in that unity and purify the feelings from the selfish element. On the other hand the individualizing tendency of feeling which is so often unjust beyond its own narrow circle is widened and enlarged by contact with the generalizing activity of man. The interest in things and ideas which is most characteristic of man breaks through the narrow concentration in persons which is apt to sink into gossip and family selfishness, while its hardness and ruthlessness of abstract will that pursues its individual purposes–even when they happen to be unselfish–with a carelessness of consequences whose effect is selfish–is drawn out of itself and supplanted[47] into sympathy with individual tendency and motive which ought to be an absolute limit of all personal ambition, and even to modify and restrain the too eager prosecution of the most unselfish designs.

The man has therefore his real substantial life in the state, in reason and the like, or in combat with the outward world and himself–so that out of division he has to win for himself independence, unity and harmony–the principal intuition and the [...?...?] morality of which lies in the family, in which the wife has her substantial Destiny.

Relation to state and family as in Antigone.[48]

What is [indicated?] in this relation is that justice be done both to the absolute limit of nature as spiritual beings–as in the kingdom of heaven there is neither marrying nor giving in marriage[49]–i.e. *in the Spirit* there are no sexes, and on the *other* hand in so far as the Spirit is one which manifests itself and so divides its manifestations between different individuals, in the spirit there are sexes or the distinction can be raised to a spiritual meaning in so far as it is based on different elements in man's life.

In the general we may say that woman's life is less sensible of Contrast, it is more complete in itself. A woman's virtue therefore partakes of the nature of innocence, her intellectual side is apt to confine itself to the expression of feeling.[50] She has a greater grasp of the situation, has tact–where man has to make general rules and to act by them.[51]

On the other hand man does not rest in nature, or find nature guides him, he is at first at war with himself and his world. He does not find the immediate intuitive sense guides him and has to live by general rules, and again his virtue does not consist in maintaining the moral temperature in which he has been born, [so much] as in overcoming the jarring tendencies within him in *self-conquest*.[52]

Hence he rises more into more abstract interests, of the state, and of science–while the woman remains in the region of the family or advances generally not beyond the region of art, at the utmost.

Two remarks have to be made on this.

1. That these contrasts are not absolute–else the common spiritual unity would be denied. For the unity of the sexes consists not in this merely that there are certain general characteristics common to both, but in *this* that the whole nature of man is in each. The woman has implicit in her nature what is explicit in the man, the man implicit in him what is explicit in the woman. Therefore each member is in itself the whole, or we can only say that every man has the womanly nature in him and every woman the manly. And hence it is that the two sexes exercise an influence on each other–because in fact they have one nature, though in each the characteristics of the other sex are latent. And hence we find it often noted that when they are absolutely separated from each other, they develope often each others characteristic–e.g. The feminine surveillances [?] of certain of the old Monks is noted by Froude–*Quote passage.*[53] It has sometimes [been] said that men of genius seem to be of both sexes in their spiritual characteristics–their union of intense receptivity with creative Power.

2. The true solution is however reached by the power in developing each other.[54] In this sense we cannot say that there is any absolute superiority in one sex over another. Fanciful analogies have sometimes been drawn and it has been said that the man stands to the woman, as the animal to the vegetable[55]–but these analogies explain nothing. To say one is superior to another is to neglect those differences which make each stronger on its own ground.

In one way we may say woman is inferior to man–because she is less capable of generalizing, rising to general interests–is more limited by her personal interests. On the other hand in another point of view she is superior in so far as she is more at unity with herself–has more intuitive perception of the immediate relations and requires less the guidance of abstract rules to limit her. She is more at home in her circumstances than man, who is often at war with them. In this way she lives more in the present while man lives in the future. And hence one may say that the perfection of humanity would be that the woman should have her feelings as much as possible widened to those universal[56] interests that engage the man and that the man should be able to attain that unity with himself in these wider interests which is characteristic of the woman. If it is said sometimes that women are more of children than men, it must be remembered that to attain the perfection of manhood is to become again a child and that we must enter the kingdom of heaven *sub persona infantis* ['like little children'].[57] Woman is a prophecy of a *unity* to which man attains by self-conquest, as man is a prophecy of an expansion to which woman attains by *self-development*. And hence it is that their intercourse can be at all conducive to the development of either, which would not be if either were inferior to the other *absolutely*.

The question of the emancipation of woman therefore has a great importance–and is not to be decided *offhand*.[58] Woman cannot be treated as man–her difference must be respected–yet it must be remembered that as the complete man is one who unites womanly gentleness with his struggle, so the complete woman is one who has man's strength *under* her gentleness. And that therefore education *must* to a certain extent aim at making the contrast less marked, less immediate than it is in the natural state.[59]

Marriage to be a truly moral institution–and to make the family such–must be *monogamy* [sic]–and this for many reasons.

Firstly, because it is a union of individuals as individuals; as exclusive persons, whose union must therefore be exclusive. In other words in marriage as the *first* transcendence of mere isolated personality, while there is an absolute surrender of Personality on one side, there must be the same on the other else it is slavery. Polygamy is and involves the slavery of women. The rights of Persons would be violated by a surrender which was not met by an equal surrender on the other side.

Second[ly] this may be expressed in another way by saying that in marriage, as it springs from a purely individual affection on each side, so it[60] tends to an exclusive and individual union. It takes up the selfish passions at their lowest point and gives them a social turn–fuses a social element with them. But this social element is very much destroyed so long as one sex is viewed merely as an instrument to the satisfaction of the desires of the other. The social element comes in only when there is equal sacrifice and equal gain of self–so that the mere personal will of both is transcended in the new unity that is formed–and this leads me to remark lastly,

3. that it is impossible the moral element should subordinate the merely physical–except when the latter is limited so that [it] shall only be the result and the instrument of the former and this only is

the case in monogamy. Hence, there is truth in the legend that connects the institution of marriage in this sense with the institution of property as the work of the founders of social order among the Aryan races.[61] For so long as monogamy is not established, so long the moral equality of women is not recognized, and [so] long her existence is degraded into a mere[62] object of sense—or at best an instrument of rather than a partner in the higher life of her husband. And so long as this is the case, so long the family cannot be a truly moral institution—above man's self-will and demanding the surrender of passion, of self-will—of individual desire—nay, even of [the] life of the individual, to its ends.

We see then that whether we regard the family as the first mode in which the isolation of abstract personality is transcended, and man without ceasing to be free, but rather as the realization of his freedom, loses himself in a higher unity—whether we regard it as the mode in which mere passion is turned into duty—tamed, regulated and made an instrument of the higher life instead of its enemy—whether we regard it as the form in which the woman is elevated from an object of sensual desire or a slave, into a partaker of the higher life of man—or lastly whether we regard it as the means by which the social nature of man first informs and transforms his selfish appetites and desires and so manifests the natural and universal element that is implicitly contained in these desires—in all these points of view marriage is essentially monogamy. The equal union of the two individuals of different sexes self-reverencing each and reverencing each [other] is thus the moral as it is the natural basis of society—and the type of all further moral association, all social morality.

A certain moral feeling has always—always at least among the civilized races[63]—made men shrink from the marriage of members of the same family to each other. It would be attributing too much to outward foresight and to[o] little to other elements of man's nature, if we traced this scruple to an experience of unhealthy results of such unions, their sterility and the like. Rather this outward result only comes in confirmation of a feeling which is grounded in the moral unity of the family itself. The family already is an organism in unity with itself—its members already have certain definite feelings and relations which have grown with their growth and strengthened with their strength: and which would be disturbed and rendered inferior by the intermixture of another train of feelings—their union is complete in its kind through their relation to common parents and through the common atmosphere of life they have breathed. They do not stand therefore in that relation of independence toward each other in the giving up of which a high moral unity is attained. What is to be united must first be separate and the gain of self-surrender to another is feeble, if each did not come to the union with feelings, habits and thoughts which have yet to seek the harmonizing rather than have it already by nature and custom.

Tennyson in the [poem] *In Memoriam* develops a similar thought in speaking of his friendship with the object of the Poem.[64] He had said, 'More than my brothers are to me.'[65] And in a second poem he supposes his brother to remonstrate on this.[66] And he answers that he knows his brother's worth,

But thou and I are one in kind
  As moulded like in nature's mint;
  And hill and wood and field did print
The same sweet forms in either mind.

  ...

At one dear knee we proferr'd vows
  One lesson from one book we learn'd
  Ere childhood's flaxen ringlet turn'd
To black and brown on kindred brows

And so my wealth resembles thine
  But he was rich where I was poor,
  And he supplied my want the more
As his unlikeness fitted mine.[67]

Even the deepest friendship is thus generally won out of difference overcome, and is still more in the case of the highest surrender of personality, which embraces all man's life, it is a true moral feeling that would hinder union between those who are already by nature and custom united—and would demand absolute independence as that out of which absolute mutual dependence is to spring.

The family as a universal and permanent personality needs a permanent and secure means of support—as on the other hand it supplies in itself the first natural division of labour for dealing with each means. Property on the other hand becomes a moral institution when the care for a common want and interest becomes the motive of acquiring it and not mere individual desire or caprice.

Hence we do not wonder that the introduction of private property is usually put along with marriage as an institution of the first founders of states–of ordered social life. The first notions of property we find are of family, and not individual, property vested indeed in the head of the house–who is in early Roman law the proprietor of the family–but in him as the representative of the family rather than as an individual.[68] He is its administrator in the interest of the whole–though of course in the early despotic constitution of the family this easily turns into an administration of the whole for his own benefit. Domestic affection must however always preserve the family from absolute slavery, and in early times the custom[69] of his race has also a binding force to counteract arbitrary will. This dubiety or something like it must of course rest in the family as such in all times, in so far as its morality is not objective–has not taken the form of laws and therefore there are no distinct rights in the members as against each other. The laws exist in the form not of limitations on will–but as embodied in the will of the head and externally enforced on all the other members. Hence the head of the family may act capriciously so as to sacrifice the interest of the whole and yet there are no distinct rights to be alleged against him. This in more developed constitutions is guarded against in various ways: 1. in so far as the state makes certain demands on the head of the house to maintain and educate the children. Here their future destination as independent citizens makes the state their protector against family law. Again the stipulations of marriage contracts in regard to property prime[70] certain rights in anticipation of the possible dissolution of the family, of the destruction of the moral bond that holds it together, or the law does the same by general enactments. In these cases [the] contingency of dissolution which lies in the moral nature of the essential bond of family union is preserve[d] and provided for. It is not a law therefore giving rights to the members of the family as against each other in the family–but it is a reservation against the natural or moral dissolution of it. For in the family and during the subsistence of its absolute unity rights as such are in abeyance: and law is as yet identical with the will of the head. The relapse out of the unity of the family in the independence of juristic persons is shown by the very fact that rights of property come to be spoken of–i.e. the relation of the individuals to things instead of to each other comes into prominence. When that is the case, that unity of affection, that moral [community][71] which constitutes the family life in each–is gone.

The family as a moral unity consists of parents and children. As it is of the essence of marriage that in it two independent Persons find a higher freedom in sacrificing their independence–so it is involved that they are emancipated from the natural union in which they have grown up: so on the other hand the children are only members of the family so long as they have not developed into independent personality. Hence the family principle is really overturned–its real meaning is lost–when the natural bond of race is made to prevail over more generations than one. Then the natural must necessarily more and more take the place of the spiritual bond. The family overthrows itself by its own extension. Hence so-called patriarchal constitutions as they stretch the family beyond its true province end in formalizing it and taking from it its true meaning.[72] This we find for instance in China–where the result of such a gigantic family constitution has been a complete externalizing of morality–in which all depends on the virtue and energy of the emperor, and the individual citizen has no sense of dignity or moral worth in himself. For in widening the family loses its intimate moral tie of individual affection, and custom may, as in China, be expressed as a body of laws, but this law depends entirely for its enforcement on the despotic will of the head. A similar sacrifice of the family to the race is more or less seen in the feudal constitution and the earlier Roman law. This sacrifice of the one family to the other, or the family to the family name is almost necessary whenever the independence of the individual, his personal rights, are not recognized–for it is essential that the man at least should be viewed as independent before he can be the founder of a new family, though the woman may pass from one family to another without such intermediary independence. Whenever however this is wanting the true moral universality of the family is sacrificed to other considerations, for the primacy and the independence of the family life is necessary to its developing its moral office.[73] But this will be clearer if we shew how the family tends by its natural dissolution in the education of the children to maturity and independence.

In the children the unity of the parents which before exists as feeling, is objective–and objective not merely in an outward thing as in the case of formal contracts but in spiritual being whom the parents love, and in whom they love each other. Goethe speaks of all religion as summed up in three reverences, reverence for that which is above us, that which is besides us for our equals, and reverence [for] that which is beneath us.[74] Now all these reverences find their culture in the family. Now we may see that the first reverence grows up in the child's relation to the father: the second finds its beginning in the paternal relation–and being developed in the relations of civic equality finds its culmination in the union of the two sexes, while the third reverence grows out of the relation of parents to the child–in whom they find at once the completion of their own united life and a spiritual being who is to be reverenced for what he can be, rather than for what he is. It is not strictly reverence for what is beneath us, but for what while actually beneath us contains in itself a possibility of equality or of superiority. And it is in this sense that 'maxima debetur puero reverentia' ['you owe the greatest reverence to the young'][75]–for in this reverence humanity itself is reverenced–not as it is as an object of right, but in its possibility as an object of faith. We see then that in various ways in the relations of the family, the first germs of every higher moral element of life are developed and manifested–and under the most individual, the most selfish passions and desires and appetites, under those manifestations of nature which appear most distinctly to belong to the animal nature, the rationality and universality of spiritual life is developed. Hence by the filial affections[76] we are educated to the respect and obedience for the will that is developed into law, and are taught to surrender self-will–and conform our-self to social life subjecting the barbarism of passion,–in that fear of the lord which is the beginning of wisdom.[77] In the paternal[78] affection the one-sided dependence of the child on the parent passes into mutual helpfulness and respect.[79] And the law which was identified with another's will now seems something superior to all individual wills–and mediating their harmony. Finally in the child to whom the parent is embodied law, the parent learns to respect that possibility which is open to all men–and which is higher than any definite manifestation–to respect in fact humanity–and so himself as well as others as the organs and manifestations of it. For as Goethe says, Self-respect is the concentration of the three reverences, and is only possible in the full sense of the term to him in whom they are all developed.[80]

If we look now a little more closely at the relation of parent and child: we may ask what are their natural rights and duties–though the former is only in an imperfect sense present as the family in the true Platonic republic, a socialistic system in which rights are swallowed up in duties.[81] It is the right of the children to be supported and educated by their parents as on the other [hand] it is the absolute right of the parent to be obeyed and served by the child–and to reverence or furnish with absolute sovereignty. But these rights are improper rights–they are only expressions of the fact that it, the family life, has for its end the education of the children to moral freedom and therefore whatever is necessary to that end is to be granted on both sides. The father has [a] right to absolute service and obedience because without this the family can not be *maintained* and *educated.* If the service that the child renders to the father goes beyond this, beyond the point where it is a means to the child's own protection and education, we have then the slavish relation of the family to its head which is the dark side of the Roman constitution of the family.[82] The child is not treated as an end in himself–or as a member of the family–but as an instrument of its head. And the right to unquestioning obedience grounds itself on the necessity of subordinating the natural will of the child–and so awaking in him that sense of defect and longing to advance to maturity which is needful for his education. Always to give reasons to the child is to flatter the natural self-will, it is to treat him as having already attained [maturity] and therefore to awake a premature self-confidence and impatience which prevents all learning. To feel his defeat and be cast on faith and obedience is necessary if the child is to grow to freedom and reason. In the same way the punishments inflicted in childhood are not retributive–they are not therefore disgraceful or slavish as they would be to the grown man. They are directed against the animal self-will–from which the child has to be freed. They are not therefore a dishonour to that humanity which as yet is but a possibility in him. The office of the family toward the children is in fact two-fold–*negative* and *positive*, to break or dethrone the natural will–and to give by custom a moral stamp to the feelings and passions–to teach morality in the form of feeling–identifying it with the subjectivity of the individual and so to ripen the character to that independence of a being who is a law to himself–so that when he emerges from the natural unity of the family he may not be a slave to himself.[83]

The dissolution of the family comes naturally by the death of the parents, morally by the growth of the children to majority in which they attain free Personality–standing in the eye of the law–and become capable of holding property for themselves and of being the heads of new families. Much might be said under the former head about the right of inheritance of the family in the property left by the head which now comes to be divided or on the right of the head to will that property to whom he pleases. The volumes are found in the Code Napoleon which follow[84] out the principle of the family-right to the utmost[85]–and the later Roman law, which is imitated by ours, which looks of course at the individual head as absolute master over his property.[86] The Code Napoleon simply considers the father as an equal possessor of the family wealth with his children, when the family is dissolved. Hence if he has one child, he can dispose of half his property–if two of a third, if three of a fourth, and so on.[87] On the other hand the later Roman law and the German and English only make certain stipulations to secure [sic] that beggars shall not be left on the community.[88] In Rome there was the querela Falcidia?[89] in our law?

There is much to be said on both sides so far as external consequences go. The caprice of testaments–'do I endow a college or a cat', has been carried far enough in this country–and still more immoral consequences appeared as we learn from Juvenal and the corruptive testament-hunting under the Roman empire.[90] And it may be urged that the caprice of individuals has no right to be respected against the superior right of the family. And this at least must be acknowledged in so far as it ought to be secured by the law that no one shall leave his family on the public–or neglect by dispositions for the time after his death, rights which he could not have been allowed to neglect while living. On the other hand the dispositions of French law involves a more real blow to the discipline of the family in so much as it emancipates children from the control of their parents–so far as that depends on their dependent position. This has been often noted by observers in France as discouraging the industrial efforts of the country. The parent has little power to reward obedience or to enforce his will in cases of entail whether this be in favor of one or of all children. And it probably would be the truer policy to take it as the principle of all laws that the parent is bound to provide for the child in such a way as to enable him to make an independent start in life–and that when [this] is done the remainder is a matter of grace.

A deeper question raised by Mill as to the restraint of inheritance beyond a certain size is probably impractible [sic] consistently with the weal of society–as being at least a great business until [?] individual heads have so great a part to discharge in the economic organization of society.[91] But of this and the socialistic idea of the abolition of wills and confiscation of property at death by the state–we cannot further treat here.

Of the moral dissolution of the family a few more words may be said. Majority brings with it a natural emancipation–for the child who has grown to moral equality with his parents can no longer merge his personality in theirs. In this respect there is indeed some little difference between men and women. For women, as their life is more definitely one of feeling and dependence, live often in the unity of one family till they pass from it into another, while the man soon seeks to establish his moral independence by acquiring an independent property and so ceasing to work for the family. Hence the woman is as such the representative of the morality of the family as distinct from the morality of the state. And we find Antigone upholding this sacred law of family duty–as prior to all prescriptions of the state: the implicit law of feeling which has been enacted by no lawgiver to the written and outward law of the state. 'I did not think that your edicts were of such weight as to overthrow the eternal and unwritten laws of the gods, which are not of today or yesterday–but live for ever and no one knows when they first appeared.'[92] 'No one knows' for these are not the dictates of a lone conscious will but of that feeling which is prior to self-consciousness and out of which it in time develops–though to those who discern truly the last is first and the first last.

The Roman prolongater of the patria potestas ['power of the father'] is in itself essentially non-moral.[93] It stretches the principle of the family beyond its true limit–and so stands in the way of that emancipation *for* which the family has to prepare and which at least in the case of man is the true preparation for the foundation of a new family: and still more necessarily to the higher sense of citizenship and of the higher union of state life.

In the first instance however this dissolution of the family gives us the individual educated to the sense of his independence and striving to find his own interest and weal in a society of similarly independent persons.

[Social Ethics No. 3]
[Political and social. Individual Right and Society. Division of Labour.][94]
[No manuscripts found.]

Social Ethics No. 4
[The Divisions of Labour in the Economic and Social Spheres.][95]
We have then to note first what is the natural organization of
society on the basis of the entire independence of the individual
members of it who each seeks the satisfaction of his wants, but at
the same time finds that in doing so he must depend on the others
with whom therefore his relations are those of free contract.

In early times as we have often seen the individual is lost in the
family–and the relation[96] of the members of the family to each other
is the only moral relation–beyond it we find either war or if families
are brought together it is by an external force. The establishment
of wider relations between men is coincident with their emancipation from the family. Hence in the earliest times we have a very
simple economical organization in which in the most favourable
circumstances, [with] men like the Cyclops

[...] θεμιστεύει δὲ εκαστος
παὶδων ἠδ᾽ ἀλόχων, οὐδ᾽ ἀλλήλων ἀλέγουσι᾽
['...each one is lawgiver to his children and his wives, and they
reck nothing one of another.']][97]

and each family must therefore supply all the wants of man for
itself. A limited agricultural civilization is the utmost we can
expect: for of course no proficiency in the finer arts of life can be
expected when each family is struggling for the necessaries for
itself. The primal wants of man may be satisfied in a rough and
ready way–but beyond that little or nothing can be attained. Even
the desire for higher satisfactions will be wanting in a state where
if it were present it could have no prospect of satisfaction. The
division of labour to suit the different capacities, as well as the
production and the distribution of commodities to suit the different
wants of man, must be confined within the narrowest limits.

The independence therefore and supposed virtuous simplicity of
the family life–which by theorists especially of the last century was
set in opposition to the [....?] luxury of society[98]–proves itself,
when we look at it closely, to be a real slavery–a slavery to
nature–and to the mere appetites–since all men's energy and every
man's energy is another stage of society dedicated to the supply of
these desires to the exclusion of every higher satisfaction–and in this
one employment no room is given to the diversity of talents in the
exercise of which each man's individuality finds its freedom and its

cultivation. The Cynic independence which pushed this false idea one step further [....?] man's life even nearer to the beasts [....?].[99] Even the family has a natural division of labour which removes a man one step further from the selfish individual struggle for physical life. But even the family principle must be transcended if we are to find any but the most elementary development of that sociality in which alone lies the possibility of human civilization–of that mutual dependence which is necessary to human freedom.

We are then contemplating that action and reaction of supply and demand out of which the industrial organization of society grows, i.e. we are contemplating how the wants of mankind are more perfectly supplied by a more perfect division of labour according to capacity and how again this division of labour according to capacities as it becomes more perfect furnishes new products or improvements of old products that still further develope and refine the desires of man. Let us look at this progress of the desires on the one hand and of the efficiency and distribution of labour whereby they are supplied on the other–and let us consider the increasing refinement of enjoyment on the one hand–and the continually increasing appliance[100] of Capacity on the other–and the widening association and improved organization of society thence resulting.

First as to the desires and their satisfaction. We have already noted that the animal as such has a very limited range of means for satisfying their desires. Man on the other hand transcends the first animal impulses of his being, as on the other hand he transcends the first means of satisfying these impulses. His spiritual nature–even on this its animal side–even in his dependence on nature–is shown on the one side by a multiplication of his wants–and by multiplication of means to satisfy them. It shows itself further in this that whereas the animal seeks for objects which will immediately and as they are satisfy it, the man considers whether he may not make something to satisfy himself. He therefore as it were analyses his want into parts each of which may be satisfied by some particular natural object and hence these particular elements of the satisfaction of his inward wants become the object of new and more abstract wants. The animal thus has to accommodate itself to its circumstances or find more propitious ones or die. And so we find the animal tribes attracted to single climates, to single kinds of food–we find animals that live in one plant. Man's natural wants are more general, and while he finds nowhere what exactly suits him, while he has to change the form of almost everything except perhaps the water he drinks ere he can find his satisfaction in it, on the other hand he can make circumstances everywhere assume that form. In our former consideration of the desires we saw how the [a]esthetic element introduces variety into the desires and their satisfaction–how the uses and the tastes of men seek ever more perfect satisfaction–how finally the higher tendencies of man mingle with his impulses and give them a wider range and a greater intensity which of course leads to a still greater necessity for new ingenuity–new application of talent in satisfying them.[101] Hegel remarks that even in the very multiplication of want there is implied a certain resolution–a check upon mere animal impulse and appetite–for when men need many things, the pressure towards that which they need at any one time is not so strong and it is in fact a sign that mere necessity is not so powerful over them. Refinement and moderation naturally go together.[102]

The progress of this refinement–even in the direction of mere external convenience–of comfort–is of course an infinite one. For every convenience (says Hegel) has an inconvenience about it which again another convenience has to remove.[103] The resistance of matter is never completely overcome–and the exceptional luxury becomes itself a necessary [sic] from which progress must be made. Another fact which has been noted by Kircher[104] limits in the same direction, viz. that while in the earliest times the efforts of man are dictated and driven by their desires, in the latter times it is rather the new invention of better means of satisfaction that develops his desire. The ingenuity of the producer is constantly on the [hunt?] to invent new objects which shall awaken new tastes and desires in their customers. Thus the activity awakened by human need continually reacts on the desire from which it springs.

One very important point in regard to this refinement is the generality, the social character which is thereby given to the desires. This refinement is attained by constant cooperation of society–by action and reaction of the producer and consumer. Moreover the producer can only produce a special refinement for many purchasers–therefore the desires acquire a social character. Instead of the savage state in which each one though limited to few satisfactions is cast in his own whim to the special form there taken, the desires are now the regulated expression[105] of general species. Hence they take the character of modes or fashions. And thus a harnessing of desire [is] established and in ordinary and indifferent matters every one conforms to the custom of clothing and hooving himself, which have become general in his rank. Fashion is not indeed rational but it is more rational than whim–as the law of honor is not morality in the highest sense–but still is far above caprice. Both substitute the general or the common for the universal–the class or national feeling for Reason–but they are infinitely above that which is lawless. And to protest against either–simply as fashion, or as honor–is of little advantage unless the protest be made in the name of some deeper carnal interest.

Fashion imposes equality–yet is constantly changing–either for change['s] sake among things indifferent–or more rationally because as said above new improvements are made in the means of satisfying wants already existing–or by new discoveries new wants are created. And those which in the first instance form the luxuries of the few rapidly become the desires and necessary requirement or demand of the many–so that the inequality is redressed as soon almost as it is felt.

In all this there is as has been said a liberation from the natural necessity of desire. Man substitutes at least a self-made necessity of life for that which is natural–one grounded in desire and confirmed by habit for the mere natural and instinctive element. For 'To live conformally to nature' in this sense is not a desirable thing.[106] Since it is this 'second nature' which man makes for himself in his habits which only can be the true manifestation and embodiment of his spirit. And as has been often said after Aristotle, philosophy and all the higher employments of life are so far forth luxuries.[107] Still we find a moral difficulty arising here which in so far forth may justify the Cynic protest. The 'second nature' of habit may be as great a slavery as the first–and the freedom which is gained from nature by the mere refinement of the desires and of the means of their satisfaction is yet a[n] imperfect and formal deliverance–which may merely end in great subjection. The *vice of luxury* can exist, though it is not to be corrected by returning to animal simplicity which has no luxuries simply because it never emerges from the circle of the absolute wants and appetites. But the mere multiplication and specification of the wants–the mere indeterminate search for novelty and subtlety to vary and transcend the appetites, when it is not directed by higher ends, may end in the new and worse dependence of the voluptuary–to whom the doubled [....?....?] is pain–and who is as much bound to some narrow region of special excitement, to Pain or boredom–where his own over-stimulated sensibility can be partially satisfied as the insect to its leaf.   A general spread of luxury in this sense–accompanied as it is generally by the loosening of the moral bonds of society and the development of selfishness and avarice in the upper classes–generally has for counterparts the misery and degradation of the lower classes society.   It is this we find especially in times when we have a[108] wealthy class cut off from political life as in later Greece and Rome–and so having no work in which their sense of obligation to the whole might find exercise.[109]   In these cases however the corruption was still further increased by the existence of slavery which rendered the labouring class the absolute instruments of the selfish greed of their[110] masters.[111]   But the bursting[112] of the last and of the beginning of this century in France and even in this country where it was neutralized by a more active political life–with the deficiency, misery and the increase of pauperism which marked the close of the period, and still to some extent subsists, shows that the mere desire of wealth and luxury is not that perfectly self-regulating power, which some Economists have allowed themselves to talk of it as being.[113]   And the Socialistic theories that have arisen–whatever their defects otherwise–are a necessary protest against such a principle.[114]

The other side to this specification of objects of enjoyment is of course the specification of labour.   I have already remarked that nature gives man little or nothing in the form in which he can use it–and he can use the natural object for his wants only so far as he understands it.   To attain therefore greater power over nature–and to separate and combine her materials into a new form suitable to his wants demands labour both theoretic and practical–which must be economized and distributed.   Out of these arises the theoretic and the practical culture of man–his theoretic culture in so far as he must first obey nature ere he can conquer it[115]–and in order to do so he must forget himself and subjective fancies and bend his mind to [an] understanding of things in themselves and in all their manifold relations and connexions.   And his practical culture in so far as he must for the highest efficiency limit his exertions to one field of operations, must engraft on natural talent the specialized habits that are necessary to master special objects and subject them to special wants and desires of man.   It is in this way he becomes master not only of natural objects but of his own power–while at the same time he gains a certain sense of dignity as having a work which he specially can do and which others acknowledge as his work.   He claims the services of all in satisfaction of his wants in virtue of the fact that all claim his service in satisfaction of one special want. Thus we have an organization and division of labour according to capacity and to a certain extent a distribution of the fruits of the labour of all according to wants. We have in fact a reciprocal dependence of men on each other so that each is necessary to the other–none can satisfy himself with the sole fruit of his own labour–and this necessity at a certain point of the division of labour becomes absolute. It may also be noticed that there is a continual[116] tendency in this way to greater simplification of the task of the individual–so that it might seem that there was here as in the case of luxury, a doubt attached to the advantages of division of labour in so far as it finally tended so to divide labour that the workman must lose the view of the whole in the exact discharge of an office relating to a part. And we have writers who lament that increased production should be attained by sacrificing human beings to the work of making[117] the tenth part of a pin,–or of turning a screw–and who look back with regret to the times when each man did everything for himself and so had all his faculties cultivated.[118] But to know something of everything is not such true culture as to know one thing well, and on the other hand it is to be remembered that when the division of labour has reached the point where a work is divided into a number of simple elements and mechanical acts, it is soon transferred to machines while the higher task of intelligent superintendence is reserved for the human workman. Furthermore we are to note the higher moral advantage of a division of labour in developing the social centres of men–in so far as by it the effort of the individual gain, after the securing of individual interests, transforms itself into an effort which contributes to satisfy the wants and interests of all. In this light all resources of society–both the powers of the individuals, and the possessions and objects of their labour–come to be regarded as forming one whole–to which all contribute according to their power–and in which alone each sees the means of his separate well-being in the general Capital [as] we may call it, by and of which alone each can make his special means fruitful to supply his wants. To this point therefore all are equal and have a common interest in increasing the common wealth in which all partake.

It[119] is true indeed that this community is only partial for as each has his claims on the general store regulated by his contribution thereto and this again depends on his own individual resources and his skill (which last depends partly on his resources and on accidental circumstances that favor bodily or mental development, and as these circumstances give rise to a thousand variations both in the quality and the quantity of his contributions to the general wealth, it is obvious that the general fact of equality is not inconsistent with the evident extremes of riches and poverty, or even absolute want. Thus fortune and nature seem to interfere with and cross in many ways the tendency to a perfect organization for the best applications of all human abilities and best satisfaction of all human wants–and to hinder that perfect sense of the solidarity of interests which would arise therefrom. Still the general tendency of this distribution of labour and of the objects of labour is to raise a sense that the occupations of each have a general as well as an individual interest and thus a man's trade gains universal meaning and dignity in his eyes and he takes pride in it for itself and not merely as contributing to his necessities.

We see this sense of dignity and of universal meaning manifested in the organization of professions and trades–which, though never perhaps entirely wanting after society [h]as attained a certain stage of civilization, is more or less definite according to the state of society, and the ideas that pervade it. Every where in fact we see within the greater organizations of the community a tendency to the formation of smaller organizations corresponding to the main divisions of human activity the cooperation of which is necessary to the satisfaction of man's wants. That is, we find the professions and the trades appearing as more or less definitely organized masses–with independent interests and claims which the[y] attempt to make valid as against the other classes and to urge upon the central government. And it is the great danger in fact of civilised society that none of these organized great class interests should overpower and use for its purposes the state whose business it should be to hold the balance by which each and all in the long run will most profit.

Let us therefore first consider what is the ideal division of the various occupations–and secondly let us consider how this division is to be or has been maintained.

We have three great divisions of human occupations marked out by history [which] also are the natural divisions that flow from consideration of objects and interests of men as members of civil society. The contrast of agricultural occupations in which the products of nature are raised to the highest degree of perfection [on the one hand]–and those occupations of trade, commerce, manufacture which may be generally distinguished as occupations of the town as opposed to the country life–since it is with towns that distinct trades arise [on the other]. The object of these occupations is generally to *re*form the products of nature, to adapt them more definitely by division and recombination to human wants and to distribute them to the places where they are wanted. Lastly, we have above the other two the general occupations which are opposed to the others under the name of professions–that is, occupations which have the general interests of the society rather than its specific wants for their objects as the artists, the trades, etc. These have now to be more particularly examined.

First we have the class which Hegel calls the *substantial*–the class that has its property–the object of its efforts in the nature– in [the] product of a given territory–the class best represented by its most numerous and powerful constituent, the agriculturalists.[120] Adam Smith says that nature does more in agriculture than in manufacture (and even explains rent on this ground).[121] But as Mill remarks the part that nature does in every department is not measurable–is infinite–seeing that man can only put things together and separate them[122] and 'caetera natura intus transigit' ['otherwise Nature performs within'].[123] All the process of manufacture as of agriculture simply uses forces and materials given by nature. This is true, still there are several important respects in which we may say that the agriculturalist is more dependent on nature's bounty than on his own exertions and owes his success or failure more to her than the Manufactures. In the first place his labours are determined by the changes of the year. The period of his different exertions and the whole cycle of them is fixed for him therefore by a law external to him. In the next place his success or failure depends on his finding the appropriate weather and other favourable circumstances at each effort. Lastly the product he aims at producing is an organized natural unity–it is in fact a product of nature left to himself–not an artificial unity delivered by human device and art–but for which he tries to create circumstances exceptionally favourable in nature. Thus then both his end and his means are regulated by a power independent of him–and his success more visibly depends on his foreseeing and accommodating himself to a law given independently of his will. Human caprice seems to be more entirely banished from his life and if the need he receives from nature be not greater–it is at least more obvious and more constantly felt. The stability, order and prudence, combined with local attachment and devoted to fixed country which have ever shown themselves as the characteristics of agricultural populations are the natural results of their situations. And hence it was in this life that the first lessons of order were learnt and the first genus of civilization appeared among mankind. In the wandering life of nomadic or hunting tribes[124] as that [...?...?...?...?] there is generally as little definiteness in their ideas on social arrangement as in the place of their abode. And hence such tribes–where they conquer another nation (as in the case of the barbarian invasions of the Roman empire) generally assimilated the religious and social ideas of the conquered.[125] On the other hand agriculture fixed both the abodes and the institutions of men and in early tradition we find even the order of families grows up with it. Marriage and agriculture–volumes also of fixed rights of private property[126]–we find referred to [in] the earliest traditions[127] of the Greek and other nations.[128] But on the other hand as the agricultural settlement of man is favourable to the development of domestic order and morality, so on the other hand it has something of a tendency to limit men's ideas to the range of the family. An agricultural family supplying all its own elementary needs does not need as it cannot well receive much [?] advantage from the labour of other such families, and hence such a population is like to have a strong sense of independence combined with the constant tenacity of its own customs and traditions.[129] It is impervious to foreign ideas–indifferent to association with other men–and often despises the luxuries both higher and lower, luxuries which it might gain by association with them. And oftentimes both in ancient and modern history it has shown a strong inclination to resist any wider political or social idea than that of the family or of the church [or] the tribe. Switzerland in modern times[130] as also the ancient Rome showed always a token of their origin from this state of society–and in their earlier career at least we see many indications that whatever was not of the sword in their manners was of the plough. The Cincinnatus type of patriotism was the first and the basis of all others.[131]

I have spoken of agriculture above,[132] though I might mention a set of occupations that go with agriculture in this [...?] and are only gradually separated therefrom. For hunters, miners, shepherds and the like are also occupied with the immediate products of nature and live more or less under the same conditions–[...?] as these occupations are not till an advanced process disjoined from agriculture. And as even then most of them are of little comparative importance in the general organization of society, it is not necessary to go into details about them.

The description I have given holds in its full sense and strictness only of agriculture in its simpler forms as it exists at first in most European countries, and still maintains itself in many–of domestic agriculture where the land is divided among many small proprietors–and of course does not hold in the full sense of what may be called the modern commercial agriculture–when large farms are united by a great capitalist armed with all the appliances of modern civilization, and employing hosts of men.[133] In such a state of things of course agriculture rather takes the character of manufacture on a large scale and loses something of that simplicity and nearness to nature which it had in earlier times.

All merely natural influences, we may note, become weakened with the course of time. Still the maintenance of the peasant proprietor system[134] in many countries or even its return and the controversy between its advantage and that of the grande culture shows that even now the country life is tenacious of its earlier domestic character–and where this is lost many facts might be mentioned in the history, for example, of landed aristocracies as in this country, which show that the tenacity of custom, the independence, the opposition to wider ideas, which are the characteristics of an independent yeomanry do not necessarily vanish even when the connexions with the land become less immediate–and the husbandry takes more of manufacturing or commercial character.[135]

The proper manufacturing and trading class are however exposed to somewhat different influences. Their business (taking the most prominent and characteristic occupations) which give tone to the others is [to] form the nature product in such as way as to fit it for human needs. Whereas the husbandman respects the synthetic power of nature, and makes his work subservient thereto, the trader or artisan breaks it up into its constituent [parts] and reforms it on a plan of his own to give it adaptation to human wants. Hence that feeling of dependence which is so natural to the husbandman is absent here. The artisan is cast on himself–with sense therefore of personal right–of freedom and order,–order not dictated by the family–but by law–since the free citizen with the sense of his individuality[136] cannot recognize a personal superior without feeling himself a slave. Towns are trades come together–and it is in the towns that the first ideas of liberty and law arise. There are however important differences within this class. In the first place there is to be noticed this, that whereas in earlier times the trades were carried on mainly on a small scale–and according to the orders of customers–now gradually in all departments great manufacturing establishments strive to anticipate the wants of customers, and secure certainty of employment by supplying far greater numbers. This of course has not taken place in all departments–and in some the nature of the case seems more or less to prevent it. But no one can doubt that the great manufacturing Capitalist is driving out [the] small Capitalist[137] who is his own labourer more and more as time goes on. Now with this change there arises the great modern division of labour or artisan and Capitalist classes, which [it] is the great problem of modern society to reconcile in their opposing and yet mutually dependent interests. And with the growth of this great manufacturing system, involving as it does that each manufacturer shall supply a wider extent of [the] country, we see a third class springing into existence the class of traders or commercial distributors who in all their divisions shall mediate in the transference of things from the place where they are produced to the place where they are used–from the farmer to the manufacturer, from one to another and from both to the consumer.

Lastly, there are those who, whether as statesmen, as soldiers and lawyers, as teachers or as scientific and literary men sub-serve the general or common interest of the social state–and some of whom at least must be directly paid by the state as their own occupation is the ground of no special provision–unless indeed as in some ancient and modern states they be by their private wealth lifted above such necessity.[138] These are the professions in the narrower sense–which have for their objects general interests directly as such–and which therefore were conceived to be the only worthy occupations for freemen till the rise of industrial interests and the sense of the *general* value of and dignity of them obliterated the distinction. Christianity on the one hand teaching the worth of the individual as such–and the unity of the human and the divine, and the advance of economical civilization and its theory political Economy on the other proving that every particular interest is also universal–as every universal contains a particular side–gradually forced the professions to moderate their excessive claims while it gave the trader a sense of their importance.

It was for Political Economy to show how the different trades and particularly how the two first great divisions of occupations are related under a free system of exchange. What has to be noticed here is that these separate interests do [tend] continually to organize themselves more or less strictly as imperia in imperio ['empires within an empire']. And that there is in the state as in the body an organization of separate organs. It is slavery and social death where such organization is wanting as when in the later empire of Rome all distinctions were lost in the dead level of slavery.[139] As on the other hand it is equally slavery where as in ancient states either of the great classes makes its interests dominant over that of the others. The professional, the agricultural and the commercial interests must maintain themselves in independence yet in living union or the social body will not be complete and vigorous.

If we look to history for a moment we see however a constant struggle of classes to master the state, and on the other hand a constant struggle of depressed classes to secure their independence. In the towns of Greece we first see the broad division of professions and trades while as yet all other subdivisions were lost. Above stood the military who were also the political class. Below were the industrial class who were slaves or aliens. It was only in the dreams of the philosophers that the universal class was divided into its two great departments of the political or philosophic and the military class and the latter subordinated to the former. And to this end the industrial class were confined in the common dead level of slavery. In Rome we find two great professions of law and war dividing the energies of the citizens while the political career was open to the rivalry of both. And hence when the empire arose the emperor was no mere Eastern despot seeing that he had ready to his hand two great systems of social and military order–and classes of men trained to be the instruments and embodiments of each. And therefore although everything in one sense depended on the virtue and ability of the emperor in whom all power was concentrated–yet that virtue and ability was not confined to mere acts of arbitrary goods but had a great system ready prepared through which it could work for the general good.

In the middle ages the legal order disappears in the chaos of barbarism which feudalism merely systematizes–but a new order appears based on the spiritual interests of man–and therefore independent of birth and station.[140] This order claims to be *the* universal and divine order as opposed to the temporal and particular interests represented by the middle class: and therefore stands out in some sense as the representative of all of the general masses against the worldly powers which had absorbed everything. But it is only in the later period–with the rise of the towns–that the industrial orders appear for themselves as the third estate of the realm gradually through long and painful centuries[141] rising in their claims till Abbé Sieyès published before the French Revolution his celebrated pamphlet Que [sic] est ce que la [sic] tiers état?[142] It is he says answering his own question everything. It ought to be everything, it is nothing.

The organization of the two great industrial and commercial classes has been late in making its appearance. It was only the towns that emancipated themselves from the feudal nobles at first. The country remained subject to them. Nay the towns themselves did not much seek to free the country as they often had serfs of their own, who were not less hardly treated than the feudal retainers of the nobles.

And it was only at the French Revolution that the peasants of France appeared as a distinct class on the scene. In this country[143] things took a somewhat different turn. The nobles were early forced to league themselves with the people against the crown, and never became a mere court as in France but continued to discharge the duties of country magistrates and to cultivate influence in the county. On the other hand the dying out of the yeomanry or small proprietors left the estates entirely in their hands. And hence the nobles subsided into the professional representatives of agricultural interests while on the other hand the weight of the land supported the power of the aristocracy. On the continent the Country proprietors remained in semi-vassalage–while those who were their lords ceased to be their leaders–and hence the peasant proprietor every where arose in place of the emancipated serf–and the country people became either moderate democrats or supporters of the King as against the nobles.

On the other hand the other great class–which in the later middle age formed one united body–has since the Thermidor[144] of last Century whence the mastership of Capital[145] began to take the place of the mastership of talent, split up into the two great divisions of the continiae [?] and the marks capitalists, which do now appear almost as organized hosts in a war under the form of law. The most important classes in the middle ages–the military, and the clerical and the legal have lost their pre-eminent or exclusive position even when taken with the scientific and teaching [?] who are partly their modern representatives. And their weight [is] not so much on their own substantive power as on the influence on the other classes which their knowledge, or character enable them to exercise. And this is their true position for the universal should not be attained by the dwarfing of the individual interests of mankind–but should rather be mediators between them.

The great and important division of the higher class into speculative and practical–represented on the one hand by philosophers and scientific men and on the other by statesmen–with the intermediate classes of teachers and medical men and the like will be better treated when we come to consider the relation of church and state.[146]

How does this division of labour and the consequent organization arise? In ancient times it was more or less a natural organization. In the east we have the system of caste fixing special occupations in special families. In Greece the higher classes–were above and the lower classes were below any distinct subdivision–while their separation from each other was fixed by nature. And even Plato who looked beyond birth to Capacity as the regulator of occupation would have this regulation accomplished by the hand of a paternal government.[147] Under the feudal system the master was no less really bound to the soil than the vassal though in a different way–both having however the escape of the church opened up to them. The growing [workforce?] of the towns organized itself in guilds which at first springing from natural division of labour tended to become fixed and fossilized as time went on, and to interfere with the natural *change* of organization. It is only in quite modern time[s] that the principle of individual choice has been recognized as sufficient in itself to produce the necessary organization of society. Modern Political Economy has made it a commonplace to note how the organized supply of our wants flows from the free choice of individuals seeking each the occupation which capacity and opportunity open up to him. And this as we have often seen has been confirmed and prepared for by the sense of individual right and duty which is the characteristic of modern nations, as on the other hand it is this characteristic that has made the freedom possible without the destruction that followed in ancient states whenever the strict unity of the state was dissolved. The individual cast loose from the state in ancient times was cast loose from social morality and corruption and decay of the whole social organism set in. But in modern times the individual as we have said in his trade and his profession finds a universal meaning. It is not slavish self-seeking–but theirs is a just pride in discharging a useful office for the community. Theirs is a class or trade honor–to a certain extent–in discharging it faithfully–and so far as this is developed, so far the individualness of modern times is not anarchy. The individual emancipated from the family chooses his work and his place in the society and recognizes the laws and obligations incumbent on him therein–so that in seeking the particular he finds the universal in it–finds, that is, a law and not mere capricious individual desire. And in seeking himself he finds others and is formed of them. He finds honor and recognition at their hands as the discharging an office for the community and as submitting himself to the laws and order of that occupation.

On the other hand as this identity of individual right and weal with [the] right and weal of all is partly dependent on subjective caprice–as in the individual this moral recognition of law may be wanting and thus he may attempt to gain advantage over others by breaches of their right, there is necessary at least a public organization of justice. But such limits of individual right may be mentioned later.[148]

Social Ethics 5
[The Administration of Justice.][149]

[...] these laws be made known to those who are subject to them and third that there be organized institutions for appl[150] [...] [...] which have thus to be publicly asserted and maintained. Out of the disturbance of disease the consummation of health and its laws is the result. Out of the troubled simplicity of tradition when particular interest has broken up the formative unity of the state springs the objective universality of law. The systems of law indeed that thus come into existence are but rude collections without unity of principle or at least with no conscious unity of principle–though it is impossible that even the very attempt to write down the customs should not rub off some of the accidental particular and therefore unjust elements that attach to the customs as such. But even such fragmentary, obscure, and formless collections as the twelve tables are a great gain to civilization, and form the first step towards the realization of a state in the proper sense of the term in which the citizens have ceased to be mere individuals or members of families and have, at least in the one point of recognition before the law, found a point of identity and equality.[151] Livy speaks of the legislation of the decemvir as having[152] *equalled* the laws (equates legibus) for though there remained many distinctions of privilege of order, the mere existence of the law in objective form involves in itself one essential element of equality.[153] Law and privilege are ideas which war against each other and the establishment of the one on a firm basis must necessarily ultimately lead to suppression of the other.

2. [...?] But such collections ultimately become insufficient for the growing legal consciousness of a nation–and then a desire springs up to codify the laws–that is to give them[154] a higher generality and order in which it shall be seen to be as far as possible the working out of one principle in application to all the details of life. This demand generally arises when by the progress of time the original law based on isolated custom has by successive enactments swelled to unwieldy bulk and has in these successive additions lost every trace of unity whether in principle, in language, or in structure. English law especially by its curious modes of development had grown in the last generation into a chaos which no mind even of the most experienced lawyer could master and notwithstanding great simplifications which Bentham [was] thus being instrumental in effecting.[155] This result was as I have said occasioned [by] the peculiar circumstances of [the time] and development–for in the first place the moral ideas of men and the customs and constitutions of society have been constantly changing, and these changes were only met by special enactments which reflected their own time, and thus the whole is a conflicting mass of particulars so that, for example, one part of the law reflects feudal, another Roman–a third modern economical ideas.[156] On the other hand as the law has been partly built up by the decisions of judges who while they pretended to interpret really were adding to the law. And as lastly the systems of equity introduced exceptions to the common law which were really contradictory. It follows then that we can only know the law of any point by weighing the bearing of many conflicting enactment[s] and modifying these by consideration of the decisions of a thousand judges–whose validity it may still be open in many cases to the next judge to question.

Now there has been a historical school of lawyers who have ever resisted the attempt to codify the law–to introduce into it order and unity of language and so far as possible principle, and, dwelling on the way in which the uncodified law reflects the development and history of the nation, have spoken of any such attempt as the work [?] of [....?] who do not know that the constitution grows and is not made.[157] And the same school have often denied the existence of any superior principle to custom to which positive law should be conformed. But it is an anomalous state of things–a state of things that must lead to a thousand instances of practical injustice and may give a powerful weapon into the hands of fraud whence no-one not even the most practised lawyer can *know* the law. And it does not matter much whether this ignorance may proceed from its being the secret of a special class–or whether though published its technical and voluminous character makes it impossible for any but adepts, and for even them only imperfectly, to know. The laws are nominally published but really concealed just as when Dionysius the tyrant hung up the laws so high that no one could read them.[158] It is the demand of reason and of justice that the laws should be really generalized expressions of what is binding for [it] is this generality that gives them fixity and lifts them above opinions guided by custom. And this cannot be attained after a certain period without a deeper search for principle–for definiteness of language–for order and system that is found in the mere collections of customs which form the first codes. Hence it is at this point that the effort of the lawyer who seeks to give order, and definiteness and system and comprehensibility to the detailed universality of the laws is met by the effort of the philosopher who examines what are the principles of right, and what is their application. The higher generality of the Roman codes was won from the Stoic philosophy, as in modern times the ideas of individual right that were the springs of the French Revolution expressed themselves in the Code Napoleon.[159] And what approaches to order in the English law have been made partly to Roman law are mainly due to the efforts of Bentham.[160] It is thus that without an unhistoric process of new beginning the principles of right are used to give order to the historical collections of right,–and this cannot happen without the anomalous rights which cannot be reconciled with the principle being weakened, and shown to be anomalous and finally removed. Thus the codification of law involves necessarily its criticism and its improvement.

The same step which is necessary for the perfection of the law is necessary also as already said in order that it may be published.

Blackstone says that it is presumed by the law that every Englishman knows the laws of England[161]–a presupposition which it is absolutely necessary for the law to make–but which cannot be true so long as the law consists as a mass of intricate detail in which no generalization is possible–for what cannot be generalized cannot be communicated, especially to the public who have no time to learn an incoherent collection of isolated facts. The undoubted right to know the laws–which have their value as universally known and acknowledged, and which indeed can only have validity as the expressions of general principles recognised by the conscience of the nation–points therefore to their codification–as the only way in which they can gain that intelligible character necessary to their highest usefulness.

There is of course a sense in which, as it is impossible ever to complete the law, it is impossible ever for it to be generally known. It is impossible to define the individual–and cases must continually arise in which the general rule of the law must be further specified before it can be applied. The nature of the finite matters to which law is applied thus seems to involve the lawyer in an infinite series of specifications and qualifications–and the perfection of a code that shall embrace every case is as far off at the end as at the beginning. The world would not contain the books that must be written ere the casuistry of law could be exhausted. And the [....?] that shall trace out the exact category which every act shall receive seems to be a thing which only the learning of years can give. But this process ad infinitum does not make it necessary that the general principles of law and their main applications should be unknown or unknowable, any more than the impossibility of infinitely dividing a space makes it useless to measure it. Le plus grand science du bien est le mieux ['The greatest science of the good and the best'][162] and thus perfection is impossible from the nature of the case. The real unintelligibility of law–at least the kind of [un]intelligibility that hinders that kind of comprehension of it which is necessary for the general uses of the citizen–is that which arises from the conflict of different and inconsistent principles in the same system or the absence of all expressed principle whatever in a chaos of detail–and generally these two causes are combined. Now it is this kind of imperfection which the[163] codification of the law tends to remove or to limit within clear and understood limits.

The matter of law is given first by the manifold relations and connexions of individuals as independent proprietors in the civil society, and hence the principles of private[164] right already developed should be applied so far as the historical conditions will permit. So far as other elements enter in we have an imperfect system. Next we have those relations which are based[165] on love, faith, mutuality, confidence or natural relationship. But there is only one side of the family and the state on which it is a merely legal relation–and with the other the moral side which is[166] intimately connected with the individuality of the special subject, law may not interfere.[167] Where the Chinese law ordains that a man is to be bastinadoed if he does not love his first wife best, we see one manifestation of the fact that China is an overgrown and fossilized family–in which the distinction of the carnal and the legal is not yet manifested. And it is something very similar to this when Charlemagne and his successors in their Capitularies[168] lecture their people on the evils of avarice and theft or failure[169] in the exercise of hospitality. 'It is necessary', says one Capitulary, 'that every man should seek to the best of his strength and ability to serve God and walk in the way of his precepts; for the lord emperor cannot watch over each person individually, with the necessary care, to keep each man in the proper discipline.'[170] Such exhortations would now be felt to be out of place in laws–and of course the relations of state or family so far as they are moral must be regarded as beyond the sphere of positive law. Lastly the matter of law is supplied by law itself in so far as special rights of action, of suffrage and the like, are given by the organization of justice, or by the constitution of the country.

With regard to the penalty of wrongdoing or of crime–of the violation of rights sanctioned by the law of the community–one may observe that in one sense the crime becomes greater because committed in a civil and organized society–since it is no longer merely an injury of the individual–but of the community. And hence the penalty might be expected to be greater. And this indeed is found to be the case in the early establishment of civil government. The Draconian severity of early municipal law forms a marked contrast to the pecuniary compensations of barbarians for the negation of the right of revenge. In the foundation of society it has often been necessary that the rights of the community should be vindicated against individual violence by the most fearful measures of repression. The punishment must be an example and precedent set against the bad precedent of the crime and, Hegel says, must be more striking in the eyes of the untrained and undisciplined to have its effect.[171] This severity however becomes unnecessary as the law sinks into and becomes fortified in the minds of the citizens–for then the crime is no longer a danger to society itself, to the order of the state. It becomes something merely subjective and accidental–something isolated and without support, for there is no general spirit of violence which it represents or confirms. It has less the aspect of treason to the community, and answers more the aspect of a mere waywardness of particular desire which requires correction. And hence a moderation of punishment, at least to something like equality with the offence, and perhaps in some cases beneath it–so far as that can be allowed without wrong to the moral necessity of the criminal and others–becomes possible. Justice must be ruthless as long as it has to contend with general ruthlessness–to the froward [sic] she must show herself froward [sic]–but she becomes civilized when her dictates reside no longer merely in the bosom of the king and judge–but of the whole people.

Justice we have seen must be expressed *in the laws* in its generality as well as in its speciality. It requires a special organization or court in which it may be applied to the individual case: for only so can it gain independence of the passions of individuals–and be lifted above the perennial contradiction of revenge which commits one crime in compensating for another. It must be the universal and not the particular that avenges–as the Bible says, 'Vengeance is mine.'[172] The judge, as Aristotle says, is as such the ἐμψυχος νόμος ['animated law']–the general law individualized or personified in one who is independent of the particular interests with which the wronged individual is involved. It is only in this mode that the wrongdoer can be made to feel that his punishment is [an] echo or necessary recoil of his crime on himself. By living in a civil society the individual accepts its conditions–and indeed in so far as the law is the expression of reason, his humanity itself accepts it. But at least in a civil society, in a commune, he has a known law before him under which by active and implicit contract he stands–and these being the conditions of his life the punishment is felt as part of his own act, if the court of justice is the mere impartial administration of the law.

In civilized society–in a commune–every one must have the right of calling in the judgement of the court as on the other hand every one must have the duty of appearing before it and submitting to its judgement. The long struggle for the jurisdiction of the courts against the prerogatives of feudalism has gradually established this principle in modern Europe–so that even the most despotic sovereigns make a show of submitting their causes to the ordinary jurisdiction. The freedom of justice is in fact the one criterion, that separates a communal or civil state of society from a semi-barbaric stage, in which the law is not yet separated from the individuals who administer it or to whom it is administered: There are two places where men must be equal in every free state, the court and the church, and if they are equal there, any other inequality still leaves them freemen. For these saved, the individual feels a sense of his own dignity as man, in that the highest is open to him in his inner life–and on the other hand in his outer life he is a sacred personality whom no one–even the highest–can violate with impunity.

In order to secure this liberty it is necessary also that not only the laws should be published, but the execution of them should be public. A hidden court is necessarily a court in which private and particular interests have sway. And the securities of justice cannot be perfect unless that moral sense of the community which is expressed in the laws should also watch over their execution. In this publicity of justice is the security of the individual against personal accusations or political influences unfavourable to his rights, as on the other it is the execution of the laws–their working in practice, that is their test in the eyes of the community. By this experience the popular will receives that education which results in and supports the improvement of the law–for it is essential that the popular conscience and the law should advance pari passu–or else in a free country the law cannot be executed.

In the actual administration of justice as the application of the law to the particular case, two things are necessary: on the one hand there is the determination of fact–on the other the subsumption of it under the law–which includes in criminal cases the determination of the punishment: and these two elements have generally been separated in actual administration of justice wherever that has attained a certain degree of progress.[173] Thus in Rome the praetor was the judge of law–and gave a certain decision in case a certain act was done, or a certain state of matters were present, remitting to a special judge the question of fact. In our country the functions are distributed between the judge and jury,–on the ground that the special determinations of the law can only be known by the adept–but in the general evidence of fact you had best appeal to the common sense of men, and that here your security is best attained by having a number sufficient to protect against individual caprice. Of course this supposes that a certain degree of intelligence and education is diffused among the people from whom the jury is taken, else this confidence must be baseless: for the jury have at least to be able to understand clearly the general nature of the crime–and the conditions of evidence in order that this act of subsumption may be properly confided to them. The judge indeed is intrusted [sic] according to our law with such a power of guiding them by his practised reason in these matters that *their* use is often reduced simply to that of taking the final decision out of his hands–and so guarding against that self-will and partiality or corruption which the continued possession of such a power would probably lead. For after the accuser has made his charge and brought forward his evidence–and the defendant in like manner–the judge then criticizes the evidence as given by both and shows its relation to the law–and [in] general sends the case to the jury with the instruction–that if they believe certain things to be proved, if they trust certain witnesses, then they should find so-and-so, leaving to them therefore the decision as to the credibility of certain evidence and its bearing–though of course it is to be observed that in all this he is instructing them–giving them the data for decision rather than deciding himself–(though of course in particular cases a new trial may be called for on the ground of the jury not attending to this instruction)–finally when the jury have given their decision, it falls to the judge to say what under the law this decision involves–what punishment, damages or the like.

The advantage or disadvantage of jury trial has been much argued about–and there is no doubt that especially in civil cases it often involves substantial injustice–which an impartial judge might avoid, though whether the impartiality of a whole class of judges could in the course of long years have been secured without it may be a question–and it scarcely is a question that jury trial has in political struggles often been the one thing that prevented justice being made the engine of party. But it has to be remembered that jury trial of some kind or other is involved in freedom–and a nation that has justice administered to it is under tutelage. The claim to be judged by one's *peers* or equals is [an] essential right of a free citizen–for only so can he feel that it is his *own justice* that is condemning him or acquitting him. 'It remains for him an external fate.'[174] The same grounds that would justify our expelling the jury from the ultimate decision in administration of justice and giving it over to a special class of learned adepts–would justify the giving over of the government and the making of laws to a bureaucracy whose knowledge must inevitably be greater than the people they govern. But whence thus the people are divorced from interest in the proceedings of the government–particular class interests soon take possession of it–and truth and justice, whenever they become the property of particular individuals, cease to be truth and justice. The knowledge of a class that keeps the keys of knowledge soon becomes [the] mere tradition of the elders–and that knowledge of the rights of all which was the ground of the claim of superiority becomes a reason for refusing any right to other than themselves. Thus it was with the Catholic Church in the middle age and thus it generally has been with all bureaucratic governments. Furthermore as the laws must spring out of the popular morality–must grow with it–it is impossible that any general advance should be made except through that political education of the people which is given by their taking part in the making of laws, and in the administering of them which continually brings the special knowledge of adepts into contact with the conscience of the people, and so spreads the knowledge of legal rights and duties. It is not of course the single acts that the individual takes part in, but the general interests which these acts give to him and to his class–the knowledge that he or his peers are assenting and consenting to what is done–that awakens that patriotism and community of feeling which is the ultimate basis of the state-unity. Thus to defend jury trial we must look further than the mere isolated decision to the whole bearing of the institution on the course and result of freedom–as in fact the necessary expression of that equality before the law without which a civil society–a true commune–is impossible.

We have then as the elements of a[175] civil society a number of independent individuals each seeking his own individual interest but in that seeking necessarily sub-serving the interest of others–so that the general interest only is attained by a *necessity* external to the individual. But then this return of individual into universal interest was only possible in so far the negative limit of abstract justice was observed, in so far as rights of person and property were sacred in each; and as this is here contingent, so it is necessary that the general interest of justice should express itself in an organization of justice by which these rights are protected. Here therefore in the organs of justice there is a unity of the universal and particular will not as an external necessity but as a consciously called Result–or the administrators of justice have for the end of their acts justice as such, in the interest of the whole community–though this interest is not yet viewed as a whole–but only on its abstract side, that of the protection of the negative limits of each in relation to the others. For Persons free properly are secured each in the interest of the whole–but this is only the negative side or condition of the interest of the whole being attained. The positive side arises from the fact that there is an ultimate identity[176] of particular and universal interest–but there is here a certain contingency in so far as the individual only accidentally and externally coincides with the general interest–so that on the one hand as, for example, in [the] case of a competition of two manufacturers to supply particular goods, I may be ruined to the general advantage by another's superiority–and yet again I cannot be ruined without evils from my poverty being brought on the community. Hence a civil society has to advance a step and in some measure [to] give the central power not only the negative universal of justice to maintain but also positively to watch over the individuals, and protect them from harm lest that harm should convert itself into the general loss and injury. And this is the ground of the positive *Polity* of the cooperative.

Social Ethics No. 6
[The Positive Role of the State, and the Social Problem.][177]

In considering the administration of justice we have seen the mere negative conditions of a civil society–for no civil society can exist at all unless there are arrangements by which the authority of the whole shall vindicate the independence and private rights of persons, and shall punish their violators, and enforce so far as possible compensation to the sufferers. But beyond this merely negative action we enter on a very different region of enquiry, viz. how far the central power should be used positively to secure the safety and secure the special well-being of each individual. All civilized societies[178] do so to some extent, though there is the evident difference between the close superintendence of the life and manners of individuals like some continental countries practice and that personal right of caprice as we may call it and intolerance of interference which is shown by the ordinary Briton. This tendency however for each individual to intrench [sic] himself in his rights–or even in his privileges if rights fail him–has been fortified by a misunderstanding of that identity of general and individual interest which political Economy teaches–as if from the principles of political Economy it necessarily followed that if you leave every one to be guided by his interest, the best result must follow and your laws and institutions that interfere with the individual were however well-constructed [?] necessarily productive of more evil than good. No one ever carried out this principle to the extent of wishing to dismiss the police–though Herbert Spencer would invest individuals with the right of declining their services: and of late still further concessions have been made by the upholders of the economical theory of individualism.[179]

The truth is that where we say that the search for individual interest leads to the best results and that interference only hinders these results being attained, we require to add several important qualifications.

In the first place the liberty of individuals to seek their own interest must be proportioned in some degree to their morality or intelligence. Until the elements of social order are impressed on the minds and habits of the citizens, government must be despotic in order to subdue anarchy. And the self-seeking of individuals can only be trusted to produce any good result when it has been made moral by the growth of a sense of individual right and duty. It is the fact that [as] consciously or unconsciously from his own training and the habits of thought of those around him the individual has learned to respect not only the legal claims but in some degree the moral claims that underlie these on the part of others, that makes it possible that self-seeking should ever produce any good result. And we can easily conceive a state of social morality in which the self-seeking of individuals being unlimited by any thing *except* legal penalties would lead to such misery that the only resource against it would a despotism. When on the part of political, [?] etc., [?] attacks are made on such institutions as the guilds of the middles ages–which are indeed alien to our notions of [the] individual right of each citizen to dispose of his labour as he pleases–we must remember that the strict organizations of labour at such a time when the sense of individual right and of the dignity of the individual as a citizen was wanting was the only method of making the labourer respect himself or be respected by others,–i.e. the only method by which he and they could learn his duties and his rights–and therefore perhaps the only way in which his self-seeking could be made moral and so identical with the common good. Now applying this to our present time we must maintain that the extent to which the self-seeking of individuals can be trusted to work out the public good is limited by the social necessity of individuals and classes. And that the only reason whereby it may be maintained that absolute freedom is in this light the best system is that any interferences are likely to be the source of more abuses than they remedy, that to give power to the government or to officials is in itself a dangerous thing because they will be sure to use it for personal or class purposes, and thereby give to certain interests an undue weight, instead of restraining special interests by regard to the interest of the whole, and that finally such interferences even when they were embraced by selfishness have been most often guided by erroneous theories of the public interest and have done more harm than good. Mill expresses it well when he says[180] that 'laisser faire' does many things indifferently–some things well–but nothing with absolute success, but it may be contended that a government will be certain to do most things far worse since 1) it cannot secure in most cases that energetic and enterprizing labour which is the secret of success, and its interference by hampering and restricting the paths of individual energy is apt to quell the life which it would regulate. And 2) because itself is apt to have an interest in its own power in which the public good is lost or absorbed. And 3) because its erroneous theories are apt to be persisted in when failure would have taught prudence to private individuals.

To these considerations it is to be answered however that a free government in which there is a living and continual reaction of the whole body of the people in the central power ceases to have a governing class whose special interests as such are dangerous in any important degree to the interest of the whole: as it ceases to have a class who are specially dedicated to the business of government. And that the danger of such a nation rather is that its government may be invested with too little and too lamentable [?] power to raise them into a position of sufficient independence.[181] And that while individual interest is to be limited to care for itself, what is every body's is nobody's business, and there are certain general functions of society which are apt to be neglected or done in an insecure and unsatisfactory way–or which being in their nature monopolies, are apt to be used as such for private interest when they fall into private hands. That finally in the competition of individual interests, the weak are continually driven to the wall–pauperism, ignorance, and the like all grow up and increase in consequence–and the state will necessarily become loaded with the burden of the faults and the misfortunes of individuals, if it be not ready to step in with measures to prevent it, or to constrain individuals to take such measures for themselves. It would appear therefore that while it must be the effort of the state to withhold its hand as far as possible from interferences that would limit and cramp the energy which can only be secure when individual choice and pleasure is left free–it must yet, 1) take into its hand certain interests of man, 2) must place certain limits on caprice, and 3) must make certain demands or claims on the individual–which he must satisfy whether he will or no.

In the first place under this head comes that detailed administration for the public good which falls mainly under the jurisdiction of the police and the municipal magistracy. In this country the extent of municipal self-government is very great and we take away the appearance of tyranny which a minute police superintendence renders necessary by having the government as it were at our own door and under the influence of our own immediate opinion. In France there is a certain appearance of tyranny superadded to the reality of the wide jurisdiction of police by their connexion with the central government: and it is characteristic that we find the 'administrative law' as it is called occupying such a prominent place in their institutions while it is hidden in ours under the form of 'private bills' or the like.[182] Of course I cannot enter into the details of all this superintendence of the outward life, the trade, the health and the life of the community–merely noticing the important place which it holds in every state. But I would say this, that while the French scheme of centralization has its evils in suppressing the independence of the parts of the country, and arming the government with a power that may as we see be used for very evil purposes–the English too too [sic] often leads to a chaotic and expensive style of government in which we have neither the energy of private interest nor the intelligence and system which *may* be secured by the state. The backwardness in many essential respects of this country in the organization for the spiritual and even for the material interest of the community may be in some degree traced to the obstinate spirit of *particularity* with which every town and sect, and division of local political or religious character maintains its vested right to act according to its own narrow view of its interests, and will concede nothing to the general will of the statesman–so that for liberties we can get no liberty. The general will is thus regarded with suspicion and every particular claim [turns] itself into a right. The very circumstance which has been in some degree the cause of our maintaining our freedom in early times when the government was at war with the people[183] has in later times therefore been somewhat a hindrance to our progress–for we have a still remaining jealousy of any interference from above even with the most narrow and material arrangements–seeing that every such arrangement soon takes the form of a vested interest of some individual or set of individuals and each vested interest claims to be an absolute right. The self-government of this country[184] also has confirmed it as a habit in the central authority in general to wait for local impulse and thus we almost never find a government or a great statesman taking the initiative in a great measure of Reform such as in Prussia is associated with the names of Stein or Hardenberg,[185] who, though supported in the event by the feeling of their nation, had not their course dictated to them beforehand in the way in which a prime minister here waits to be dictated to. There is a consequence of this which is a cause of danger to our institutions at the same time that it is a ground of life–i.e. that our whole system depends for its vitality on the political life of individuals–as the initiative is from them and that consequently we can only expect general to rise above local interests in the mind of the government when they have already done so in the mind of the people. This transcendence of national over local and class feeling–this degradation of the notion of particular interest and right prove[s] the excessive place it has held in our minds, and its subordination to a general will–which at the same time submits to be guided by reason and science–or takes this counsel as the element of patriotism which has been wanting in this country, and by reason of which want we have been of late outstripped in many things by natives to whom we before gave the example of freedom.[186] But as such a[n] absolute dependence of the government on[187] the nation for the collective may delay us for a time so we may hope it will have counterbalancing advantages when the national feeling is awake in a great interest or great concerns among all the simplest citizens which they will not have so long as they wait for the action of trusted ministers from above. For though there is an easier action of science upon a government than upon the people immediately–yet if the people can be got to listen to reason the result has more vitality.

And this leads me to remark that there is an element in modern life which is of increasing weight and which in important ways leads to a harmony between the government and the people, which has not hitherto been realized and that is science. There are departments of the administration that tend more and more to dissociate themselves from the struggle of party: and these are departments concerned with health, with trade and the like.[188] Again political economy though still in the region of controversy because of the complication of its problems with social and ethical difficulties has ascertained for us certain definite principles on which every administration must act. Now so far as an administration is an instrument for applying such principles in the widest and most effective way, no one should be jealous of its influence or power. It may extend its activity without exciting suspicion, if there be a conviction that its activity is guided by science–for private judgment and individual opinion have no claims as against science–and no one should feel it to be tyranny to submit to truth. It was necessary to be jealous of government and to limit it strictly so long as to admit its action was to limit individuals–men with independent[189] power to rule according to their judgement. But as no one [....?] hesitates to submit his body absolutely to the doctor–for he does not submit to him but to the science he is supposed to have learnt–so no one in the long run will be jealous of a wide activity of administration which is based on the application of advancing science.[190] What physics and chemistry recommend, no one can count tyranny who has learnt anything. And though the social problems are of more difficult solution, and from their nature likely always to be complicated by passion, great advances may be expected towards harmony as their nature becomes more clearly understood. And when what opposes the application of a principle is simply individual interest and passion–and does not even pretend to any higher name, men are quite willing as we see in the instance of compulsory vaccination–(and so it is on the continent with the more important case of compulsory education)[191] that individual [interest?] should be forced by the power of the government to submit to that which is imperatively demanded by the general good.[192]

Let us clearly apprehend what is before us in the present constitution of society, and we will best do so by remembering its history. In the later middle age we find a system in which at once the individual and the universal seems lost in the particular.[193] All the organs of social and political life are there–we have the military and the industrial and the spiritual orders–but what is peculiar is that each of the orders stands in an independent position towards the others–is complete in itself and recognises no universal in which its independence is taken up and lost. For even the king, if there be a king, has only the rights fixed by the primitive contract–and this contract he makes only with the general representative of the class–not with the class as a whole. And so it is within the orders themselves. The lord has authority over his vassal but may not interfere with his vassal's vassal. The city government ever deals with the trades–corporations–but not with the citizens as such which have [an] independent Right of self-government.[194] The bonds of society are therefore not organic and vital but dependent on special arbitrary agreement. There was strictly speak[ing] superiority but no sovereignty.

On the other hand the individual had only a right in this system as it was covenanted to him as a member of a guild–as holding a place in the hierarchy of feudalism–or of the church. Out of these orders he is [an] outlaw. Thus the rights with which he is armed become his limit and rule–and he can attain no place or consideration except as the partisan of his order. On the one hand though his order and his occupation become the highest universal he knows–and he does not value it as an organic part of the state–and on the other his individual life as such has no dignity or right or value [?] connected with it.

This constitution of society was destroyed in two different ways in different European countries whose civilizations therefore took a peculiar colour. In France the central government made itself the organ by which the individuals were emancipated from the orders. They curbed the nobility and ultimately even the communes by making themselves the representatives of general interests.[195] It is true that they ultimately used this power for ends in which the people had no share, and became a selfish despotism, seeking glory and luxury at the expense of the public weal, and thereby brought on themselves a frightful retribution.[196] Still they impressed generally on the country that tendency to centralized organization, that wish for comprehensive and enlightened measures for the general good which distinguishes even despotism in France. At the same time it is true they repressed the desire for[197] individual action and taught the people too much to wait for the government: and made them submit to an interference which is apt to be used for tyrannous purposes. On the other hand in England the crown in attempting to extend its particular *rights* to a universal authority forced the orders to unite with the people–but they could only secure that alliance by granting the privileges to the people which they demanded of the sovereign.[198] Thus the individual right of the citizen did not grow out of equality in the eye of the law–or equality as subjects–but by the extension to all of particular privileges wherein they were secured against the interference of government. Thus the rights of Englishmen never became alleged[199] as rights of men. The individual absorbed the particular, but did not identify itself with the universal–and hence it followed that with a constant jealousy of the crown the English liberty was apt to degenerate into caprice and self-will–which finally shows itself in a hatred of order even when the order is dictated by reason.[200] The English are[201] therefore more secure against tyranny than against anarchy–anarchy of particular wills even under the forms of order and law–while the French are in danger of sacrificing individual freedom itself in the desire to absorb the particular in the universal. It is obvious that each has its advantages and defects and that the highest form of polity will not be one in which either the abstraction of individual right is opposed to [the] best interests of the state and made a defence for particular unreason–nor the individual is hindered by excessive jealousy of differences of rank or rights from exercising that freedom of self-organizing and self-governing in which particular capacity and [...?] finds its proper field: and without which indeed the universality of the government is likely soon to lose its true balance and corrective and become an instrument of personal ambition.

What is to be desired then is a free play of that associative tendency which Tacitus noticed as the second great characteristic of the Germans,[202] and as connected with the first great characteristic of freedom–that associative tendency which shows itself so strongly in the creation of all kinds of societies, clubs and unions for literary, communal [or] scientific purposes–and which gives its appropriate organization to every interest and tendency that springs continually out of the free action and reaction of individuals–and thus by their independence secures the national life from being forced from above into a procrustean bed of theory, by an arbitrary despotism and represents and inforces [sic] the claims of each particular interest, while on the other hand the organization of the government which from above descends to meet this spontaneous self-organizing life has for its peculiar function to watch over every weak interest and [guide?] every strong one to that place where it can be most efficient for the good of the whole.

The particular interests in which the action of individuals and the action of the universal authority of the state meet may be divided into these: 1. those relating to the bodily and mental developement of the individuals who are or are to be citizens, 2. those relating to the economy of society, the interest of trade and commerce, etc. 3. The special social interests and difficulties which arise from the misfortunes or faults of individuals. All these are dealt with more or less by the state and more or less also by voluntary organizations of the citizens–and the question of the limit of each is a difficult one.

In the first of these we have to consider the limits of individual liberty and domestic authority which become necessary in a civil society. The family as such claims authority over its members–on the other hand in civil society the family in regard to the training of its members must be regarded as the delegate of the state–since it trains them for a social life–and the state must be regarded as having a right to make such demands on the parents as are necessary for the bodily and the mental development of those who are to have this destination.[203] On the other hand the caprice of adult individuals in a civil society must be limited with reference to the moral as well as the bodily safety of society–though in the former case the limits are of course difficult to draw–and may not be quite the same at different times. And government at once oversteps its function when it forgets that it expresses and does not create or ordain the national life and that it must never constrain in individual cases where the liberty of one would [not] be [a] violation of the personality of another.

Again trade and commerce and agriculture each give rise to many interests–and to voluntary associations to promote those interests: and here again the government is forced to *interfere* with personal liberty–in so far as it would endanger the general interest. And here again individual right to be respected either in its actual or potential state is the concern which leads, for example, to the prohibitions of labor of certain kinds of women or children or to the conditions attached thereto and again to the laws which limit or emancipate the action of unions of masters or men.

Lastly comes the difficulty of society–the poor. Pauperism is the great disease that hangs about our modern societies. As the ranks become more closely ranged–as the division and organization of labour becomes more perfect–the danger of accident or fault losing a man his place in the great organism becomes greater and when he loses it he is apt to lose the power of regaining it. Especially the great and yet uncertain organization of modern trade with its uncertain rises and falls–with its continual and unequal advance–with its commercial crises–is liable to reduce hosts of men suddenly to beggary and to keep them there till they have lost that personal sense of dignity that makes men refuse to be beggars. In a simple state of society every one was sufficient in himself as every one or every family in a rude way provided for itself the commons of life. And if he failed, he could blame no one but himself. But the complicated organization of civil society, while it lifts us above the fierce struggle of individuals, must, at the same time make men dependent on circumstances over which they have no control. And an action that brings victors to society may be fatal to a special trade. Hence as well as from the vice and indolence of individuals, pauperism is ever receiving recruits who become the sewage of the society which rejects them, anticipating its ruin, if the crowd of stragglers is permitted to accumulate around the effective force. For such a pauper population must be essentially lawless and rebellious against a society which offers them no place. Having no feeling of honor or law in themselves, they must be the enemies of all law without. And the lazzaroni of Naples, the old population of imperial Rome, show what is the servile and lawless temper to be expected from such a rabble.[204]

Hence no civil society can continue to exist without some kind of poor law–without in fact taking charge of those who have fallen behind the march of civilized life. It must do so in self-protection, if for no other reason, for it is here that that combination and organization of interests which is the secret of the strength of social and civilized life shows its dark side–and may easily turn to its ruin if the extreme[s] of poverty and riches are allowed to grow continually wider apart, till the end is a war of classes.

Civil society is forced by the mere necessity of its existence to deal in some way with all these subjects or to carry the burdens of each other, and they are forced in one way on the consideration of government and state for common action. It is true that by the free associative efforts of individuals the several difficulties[205] may [....?....?] be met. Thus societies exist for charitable educational purposes–to promote the different interests of social classes–to watch over the health or morals of the community, and in this country there is a certain unwillingness to admit that such societies are inadequate to [do] all that requires to be done. Yet the universal society must at least interfere so far as to moderate between these societies and their fitful and irregular action, guided by tastes and prejudices and interests of individuals and classes, [which] makes it always necessary for the state in some way to extend its superintendence over all these interests–[it] should act[206] at least to secure [sic] that they be everywhere attended to in such measure as is necessary to secure to each citizen what is absolutely necessary for his retaining or recovering the position of a citizen, and to protect against dangers that might be fatal to the common weal. It is not easy to draw an absolute line between those things which a developed community should absolutely take into its own hand and those which it should leave to the work of private individuals and societies, merely controlling and regulating their operations so that they may not transgress on common or individual interests–but experience seems to prove that while special interests–the interests of classes–can take good care of themselves–that the great general interests of the community–health, education, and pauper relief–must inevitably suffer in the long run if left without the active assistance and direction as well as the control of government. The more general an interest is–the more necessary it is for the good of all, while not distinctly appealing to any one or any class in particular–the more it demands the special protection of the government. And it is to be noticed that while the strong organization of particular interests has been everywhere giving way, and thus liberating the individual from feudal or corporate ties, the range of state action has really been increasing in all civilized states rather than diminishing even in our own–where as I have before said the individual has gained most and the state least.

In the corporations men gained a sense of the dignity of their particular occupations, and when the corporations were dissolved this did not take away that sense of dignity–but merely showed that the particular only has dignity as it is absorbed and elevated into the universal–or that the dignity of the class is its function as an organ of the whole. The corporations cease to have independence–have rights as against the state, the sovereign society–but still the free power of forming associations in which their special interests, tastes or the like are represented must be maintained. For it is generally through these associations, be they of lawyers, of doctors, of capitalists or of labourers that the dignity,[207] and so indirectly the class honor is maintained, as well as the professional or trade interest advanced. To take away rights of association for any such object is to prevent the growth of that feeling of importance and relation to the community which elevates a man to look on their occupations not merely as means to gratify their isolated desires. The discussion of *general* interests, even of a particular class, the sense [of] brotherhood with the members of it, is the great means whereby individual self-love is lifted into patriotism, whereby the individual is made to feel himself independent in his dependence; and in his self-seeking an essential involvement of the public good. Without the possession of such a right and the exercise of it, a nation is apt to be a[n] inorganic horde of individuals. And when that is the case, even an advanced civilization will scarcely be a sufficient security for their liberty. Despotism Roman or French has therefore ever been jealous with good reason of the right of association for it [is] the natural discipline of freedom without which it is all but helpless, or destructive. The chaotic character of French revolutions and their relapse into despotism has generally arisen from the repression of this power, and we cannot but therefore regard with hope the tendency shown in France to all kinds of cooperative labour.[208] Socialism and Communism are[209] but the extreme expressions of a longing for organic union in a nation which has in a manner been reduced to atoms: and it shows its weakness in the fact that even in the remedy it proposes, it preserves still the same fatal plan of organizing men entirely from above.

We see in the above sketch how the state in the higher sense rises by a kind of necessity out of the civil society of individuals. If we suppose these individuals each to seek themselves, their highest outward advantage and spiritual culture–we find that in seeking that[210]

[Social Ethics No. 7]
[What is a nation? Montesquieu and Rousseau. Natural and artificial theorists.][211]
[No manuscripts found.]

Social Ethics No. 8
[The Church and the State.][212]

In the last lecture we have seen what is the nature of patriotism–how it is a love of country of which I am inhabitant, of a society of which I am a member, of institutions under which I live–a love that recognises in these the natural and moral basis as on the other side it is the end of my existence and that which lifts it above its transitory insignificance and connects it with the past and the future. We see this latter element in its greatest strength among ancient nations who were also of more homogeneous race[s] than [are] modern [nations]. In nomadic tribes race is the one thing that is paramount–and in the case of the Jews especially we see how this transcendent regard for race, elevated indeed by religious hopes, gives an intensity to national patriotism far surpassing all personal hopes. In modern times the less homogeneous character of nations, and the greater development of the sense of the individual right and interest on the one side and of universal sympathies on the other prevent this exclusive dominion of national feeling. National feeling must arise out of the transcendence, not out of the suppression of difference, and hence it is attained in [a] less direct way and therefore on the whole less perfectly–since many always fall short of any idea higher than personal [sic] right and negative duty–while on the other hand even when attained it cannot occupy that exclusive place which it once occupied. Still this return of family affection in a wider and more comprehensive form and without the suppression of individual independence is one of the highest agents of moral order–and when as in Europe in the thirty years war in Germany the national feeling has been altogether subordinated to other considerations, the result has been a social chaos, the soldier who is not fighting for country soon becomes a barbarian: for a mere abstract tie is soon forgotten–or has substituted for it a mere personal faith in the general which makes him its[213] ruthless instrument.[214] Thus in modern as in ancient times (see Thucydides) the fight of principles has ever been the most immoral of all contentions and the one which most of all dissolved the bonds of social obligation.[215] Where you pass to the higher by mere suppression of lower obligations–you make a few saints and a world of outlaws. The national tie must be like that of the family preserved while it be transcended if the higher ties are to be mere forces of revolution destroying the lower ties and substituting nothing in their place.

Connected with this is the question of the relation of Church and State whose separate jurisdiction[s] was so important a point in medieval history.

The separation or unity and the relations of church and state have formed a great motive; we may say the great motive of civil dissension ever since the Christian church began to acquire power as imperium in imperio ['an empire within an empire'] within the Roman empire.[216] In ancient society the distinction had not yet made its appearance. Either as in the theocracies of the East, the church had absorbed the state, or as in the governments of Greece and Rome, the state had absorbed the church–in one way or other the special organization of each was not allowed to acquire any real independence. But in Paul's charge to the Corinthians not to take one another before the heathen courts, we have the first point of an independent social power–which as the extent of the church increased secured its unity and efficiency by a hierarchical subordination of itself, [of] orders of archbishops, bishops and priests–by definite laws and with regular officers to put them in force.[217] Thus commencing in a number of scattered missionaries[218] who appealed to their individual consciences–and inflicted no rewards or punishments except those which the individual conscience enforces on itself, the church became an organization with great and intimate control of the lives of its members though still so far moral in its operation that the ultimate penalty was not death but merely expulsion. But excommunication took less the character of moral and more that of a civil penalty, the greater were the numbers that were included in the Christian church. Nay, its civil efficiency was often greater than any merely civil penalty since it was inflicted by no definite magistrate but by all the society whose enjoyment constituted the pleasure of life to the criminal–and was not confined to any definite pain or privation–but was an outlawry from all the structures as well as from all the material benefits of existence. When the church by the conversion of Constantine became supported by the power of the state, the civil and ecclesiastical penalty became still more closely confused together; and while the penalties of crime were added to excommunication against the enemies of the church, on the other hand the power of spiritual sanction was often invoked against the enemies of the state.[219] Yet the idea of a separate jurisdiction remained: the church courts and councils assumed a right to pronounce the sentence over spiritual as the civil court [did] over civil crimes, though it was ever more difficult to tell to which category any given case belonged. And according to the feelings of the individual, heresy might be regarded as treason–since the subject who would not respect the religion of the Emperor, would [not] be faithful–must be an actual or possible rebel. While on the other hand, the criminal who rebelled against an orthodox sovereign was assailing the Lord's anointed. Thus there were two supreme societies one of which claimed the jurisdiction of all man's life on its spiritual, the other on its material side. And as there is no act which might not fall under the dominion of the spiritual power because every act is the manifestation of some inward principle or feeling–so again there is no inward principle or opinion or creed which might not be drawn under the surveillance or coercion of the temporal power since every sincere faith will manifest its reality by outward acts, and it seemed wiser to prevent the cause than to deal with mere effects and symptoms. It was impossible that in the course of time as the church and state took more definite form that this great antagonism should not become conscious–and that out of it should not arise an internecine struggle between two powers each of which was animated by the universalism of Rome–and each of which based its claim on a principle whose validity could not be denied. From the time of Charlemagne to the time of the Reformation we see the necessary result of the continually renewed attempt to solve this insoluble difficulty–insoluble because the temporary victory of the one principle necessarily led to the resurrection of its opponent in a new form.[220] The developement of the distinction however involved two consequences, 1. that the church as it defined itself and the spiritual to be that which is *opposed* to the temporal–nay, elevated this opposition into a principle–and warred against social ethics in all its forms. It opposed to the substantial unity of natural affections to the family in which man's appetites are elevated and consecrated by social union and subordination, the duty[221] of renunciation of marriage and established chastity as the first of saintly graces.[222] In opposition to the righteousness, the law-limited energy and independence, and self-respect which belong to the member of the civil society, as one who seeks and receives his subsistence by his own labours, by his services to the others–who by his own exertions earns for himself a possession in which he sees his own will realized, his honor and independent place in society secured, the church in like manner declared this activity to be in itself unholy–declared holiness to be not in laboring for one's subsistence and increasing one's property–but in giving up one's subsistence to the poor, to them who do not labor, and in ceasing from individual property. In like medium, in place of the freedom which belongs to the individual as a citizen finding in a state his own rational will realized in and through the rational will of all the others, they placed the absolute unintelligent obedience to superiors–and the absolute faith in the master of the church. Thus holiness became the abstract opposite of right and morality. And the outward life of man, in all its organized forms, seemed merely the expression of irrational passions. The outward or temporal power was conceived as having none but an accidental existence. And as accidental it ought absolutely to subject itself to the spiritual authority of the church which could loosen the bonds of family and state at pleasure as on the other hand it was its ordinances that gave them all their sanctity. But the inevitable dialectic of this negative movement soon showed itself–the church as thus opposed to the world–as the mere negative of the world–was devoid of positive contents and end except to subdue the world. In emptying itself of all the relative duties of life, it left caprice and the passions to fill the void, and itself became that absolute rule of ambition and passion to which it had degraded its [...?]. Out of the meeting of extremes, the true means of social morality began to arise–or it came to be seen that that negative of universal relations of social life is only the necessary preliminary of a higher positive movement in which they are re-established. And the reformation gave new interpretation to the 'Render unto Caesar, etc.'[223]–by showing that the powers that be in the domestic and civil and political life are ordained of God.[224] In connexion with this it was only natural that the Reformation should re-establish the Civil as superior to the Ecclesiastic power, should maintain that in the government as such, as the manifestation of absolute right, is invested the supreme authority over all the citizens whether laity or clergy–and should deny the absolute validity of the distinction between laity and clergy itself except as a matter of outward arrangement and discipline. Yet in this denial of the claims of the church as a supreme society there lay still a certain ambiguity. It might seem that according to the doctrine afterwards formalized in the theory of the divine right of kings, the actual temporal sovereign had merely stepped into the place of the dethroned spiritual despotism–and Henry the Eighth and the German Elector,–or even the Reformers themselves were pari passu fully comprehending that the principle of spiritual despotism was itself dethroned.[225] The English Puritan revolt however set the individual against the state conscience–and a[226] great leader like the great founder of the Dutch Republic showed a decided tendency, so far as this time should allow, to an absolute toleration by which the religious convictions of the citizens were withdrawn from the cogniscities or at least from the interference of the state, and though a state church has been generally maintained in Protestant countries yet it has less and less been invested with any powers different from those of the dissenting organizations–still less with any absolute rights independent of the state: either over its own members or over the people in general.[227] A church has in fact been for the most part reduced in the eye of the law to a corporation formed by voluntary organization–though in some cases deriving a certain portion of its revenues from the state on condition of adherence to its own laws as well as to the law of the state. And even the right of the state to give such support has been questioned.

Without however entering into these troubled waters, let us look a little at the general principles that lie beneath some common opinions on the subject. In the first place it is maintained that the state has nothing to do with religion: that it has to concern itself with the temporal affairs of man and leave each man to seek his own salvation as his Conscience teaches him–this principle being only modified by the responsibility of the heads of the family for those under their educational tutelage. And this *seems* to follow in its full extent from the principle of protestantism which does not allow two external supreme powers–one to rule over the spiritual, the other over the temporal life of man–but only *one* supreme power external and only ruling over the external life of man, while the other the spiritual life of man can be ruled over by no external power, but only by the power of reason which is in every man equally–though not in every man equally developed. On the other hand there are [so] many difficulties when we take up the view of the state that seems to follow from these principles that in practice we may fall into the same great difficulty of the antagonism of spiritual and temporal which the middle ages had to contend with; for if we fix the notion of the State as merely external, it would seem that the organization which represents the internal ought to dominate over it: if the state as such is not cognisant of the highest end of man, then its dominance must be the rule of the lower nature over the higher. Furthermore as we saw that in pursuance of its outward ends the civil society is gradually forced to interfere with the family and the individual and to enforce upon them whatever may be necessary to secure the existence of the individual as an independent citizen, it is absurd to say that it is not to interfere with the higher life of man seeing that higher and lower are not in this way separable. The existence of an individual as a person so far civilized as to be capable negatively of living in civil society, and positively of discharging some function therein is an end in which spiritual and natural are so intertwined that the power that takes cognisance of the one must regard the other. Even in limiting itself to certain interests, the state must take cognisance of those beyond the limit, for it is the supreme society and this limitation of its own action implies a view as to the nature of the interests so left independent. It has no limit from another society, therefore it must have its limit in its own nature.

If the view we have taken be correct, the state as a moral organism must be considered not merely an external institution for protection of persons and property devised by arbitrary combination–but as arising out of man's spiritual nature–as mediating that natural reformation of man's life as a member of a race by which a nation in the higher sense of the world comes into being. And in this sense it is impossible–whatever be the self-limitation of the direct action of the state–that this should be without regard to these higher ends of the state. If the great educational power of national life is mediated by the state and is the end which the state ever more or less consciously sets before it–which it ought ever to set before it–then its holding of its hand from *direct* action in regard to the religious or the scientific life of man can not be the effect of indifference but [due] to a clear recognition that direct action is hurtful, while on the other hand it cannot treat the temporal interests well except in so far as it recognises that these are also spiritual, and that through them the higher education of the nation is being effected.

Religion in one sense belongs to the inmost sphere of man's being and therefore it is removed from all outward cognisance or government. That another–an external–law should directly interfere with this sanctuary causes desecration and the worst slavery. If property and liberty are sacred interests as the outward expressions of a spiritual and self-conscious nature, it is the utmost of all injuries to invade or attempt to invade the sanctuary of conscience itself. And the state that violates this is committing suicide as assailing the very source of all moral order and life. On the other hand, as I have shown before, this inward life has outward expression–it is developed into forms of art–state customs and institutions, and the state itself is only the highest expression necessary to its self-recognition. In this way it would seem that the religion is of the very essence of the state and that its highest task must be to preserve the religious life of which it is the very embodiment. Hence in ancient states of Greece and early Rome we see the legislator defending the religion as a part of the nationality of the country–and this even after the belief in it had past away. The persecution of Socrates and Anaxagoras and the expulsion of Bacchanals at Rome are different steps in this defence of the νομιμὰ ['orthodoxy']–and though in later Rome the special Roman[228] religion was lost–and, like the special Roman nationality, was submerged in the chaos of foreign rites–yet even then there was one sacred bond in the worship of the abstraction of the imperial power.[229] Christianity was persecuted because it did not make its claim as a national religion among others–and so came into collision with the remaining bonds of superstition in every country–but also and perhaps still more because it refused to worship this gigantic abstraction which had its embodiment in [...?] power–but perhaps [?] most appropriately in the Eagles of the legions–and hence we see that it is the best emperors–those most solicitous for the preservation of the unity of Rome–that persecute it.[230] It was Christianity itself that by its principles vindicated the independence of the main religious life of the outward power and at first in the coarse and external form of the independence of the spiritual power–but then again in the revelation of–nay, nature of–religious life at the reformation (as a self-appropriated life) declared that the meaning of the division [was] already marked in the words 'Render unto Caesar what is Caesars and to God what is God's.' The Christian religion first revealed–at the Reformation–that element in the idea of religion which makes it a contradiction for it to use the state power directly to protect itself or suppress dissidents. Thus a Protestant state cannot persecute without contradiction with that idea of Religion on which it is based: it is by its essential notion precluded from protecting itself in this way, for though sentiments may get to prevail among the people which are adverse to the state and so ultimately its unity might be destroyed, yet for the state so to protect itself would only be to destroy itself with its own hands: to deny that is that principle of individual liberty which is what Aristotle[231] would call its *hypothesis*.

At the same time in the principle of progress in regarding the state as outwardly manifesting a series of connected and progressive phenomena springing from one principle, we find a means of bringing back to law the differences which arise in the freedom of religious opinion. The ancient state founded on a limited and unalterable principle–and being regarded rather as the maker of the morals of the citizens than as continually reproduced thereby–was a moral work of art made once for all and admitting an essential divergence without ruin. The Christian church–with the idea of man's infinite nature, brought in the idea of progress, inasmuch as the deepening penetration of human life with Christian principle involves a continually increasing and perfecting manifestation of it in the organism of social life. The individual conscience is in this sense greater than any outward organism of the state in as much as in the destruction of such [an] organism the moral life returns upon its source in the individual conscience from which it anew issues to rebuild the outward institutions in higher form. This last sanctuary of conscience therefore claims an inviolable respect from the state–which [?] is reaching beyond its proper province when it would interfere therewith.

On the other hand we must be on our guard against transferring this respect to the church as an outward institution–or even of telling the individual conscience whether it put forth its claims on the ground of religious feeling or, as in the right of private judgement, against all the outward organizations of a state as in itself worldly. For as to the former the outward organization of the church, being an organization for a definite end of conforming religious sentiment, is subject to the supreme society that regulates and moderates between all these separate agencies, and keeps each end in its proper place in relation to the general well-being of man. That *Religion* is greater than the state does not necessarily imply that the church is–as an outward organization it comes into conflict with other interests–the clergy are a class among other classes–and they in fact can only preserve their true allegiance to the universal end they seek if they are not permitted to apply in direct command the principles they teach.[232] The very fact that they are addressing themselves to that Consciousness which is above the definite institutions of one state which looks to the past and the future–precludes them from immediate dominion over the present. Thus they have to do with a universal truth which always *is being*, never *is*, realized–and in teaching this, they are cultivating the spiritual life out of which all progressive organizations of the state must flow. But their organization[233] is that of a mere class which must be subordinated to the more perfect organization of the state in which is the highest actual manifestation of eternal principles.

And this leads us to notice the second of the false oppositions above noticed. Those who do not regard the church organization or the clergy as of an authority above all others have yet been often inclined to a false opposition of the religious to the political or social life–in which is involved the same unchristian and irrational opposition of church and world, secular and profane, that was the insoluble difficulty of the middle ages. Religion like science has to do with the eternal–and can *in a sense* look down on the state and its ends as of time–and in this way we often find [the] religious man thinking of the tumults and intrigues, the fierce struggles and party victories which form the *outside* of political life as profane and worldly. They would withdraw from that into the pure sanctuary of the soul and regard religious life as a higher and separated region in which the wicked cease from troubling and the weary are at rest. Yet the purity [of] such a spirit is often all delusive–or it is a purity purchased at the cost of spiritual effeminacy. 'Tis by comparison an[234] easy task earth to despise, but to aspire to heaven that is not easy.'[235] And the spirit that thus withdraws upon itself and thus emptied itself of all content of the actual world finds in this inner saintliness after all no recompense for those active interests which it renounces. The via negativa of spiritual perfection though it produces pure and higher and tender characters in its beginning is yet often–for want of substantial ends of a social or political character–in its end given over to subjective dreams and irrational superstition and the fullness of a soul eternally occupied with the care of its own salvation.[236] And however it [is] a fine spiritualizing and secondary *element* in characters like Dante or Pascal that are otherwise *filled* with material interests–yet as an end in itself it is feeble and imperfect.[237] It has been noticed that even very high monkish Characters, such as St. Bernard or some even of the better Popes, have not really been nobles or statesmen but rather less noble than those who had not passed through the discipline of the will.[238] The very fact that they put such a broad chasm between secular and sacred rendered it impossible for them to see the sacredness of what was secular. And when they were forced to deal with the latter, they could not conceive of pure ways of dealing with the essentially impure. Now the religious man who stands back from the world and looks on the political contest as not concerning *him*, who thinks of the world *but as* the world may, sometimes be really inferior in [regard] of real elevation of spirit to the active political partisan who has at least the welfare of his party blended in some degree with general aims.

The great error of such a view is that it puts a possibility against every actuality–puts the *general* greatness of man's spiritual nature against every organization in which that nature is revealed. It is well that man should be aware of this possibility–and the Christian religion that teaches the essential unity of divine and human in giving man the consciousness[239] of this has given the great essential of freedom and progress–but if this religious consciousness of man's nature as man–that is, of his possibilities which are the possibility of morality and social life–be set against or in hostile antagonism to all actual realization, we have an inactive resignation put in place of the energy of Christian virtue, a solitary self-brooding spirit in place of occupation with social ends–and if, from this negative universality with its being in man's capacities and contempt of his attainment, any activity goes forth–it will be the activity of destruction and revolution. The fanaticism of revolution has always been the counterpart of quietism in all its forms.

Looking then at the general result of these enquiries, we see that religious feeling is the basis and the fundamental bond of the state unity–and that therefore in one sense it might seem the office of the state as such to protect the religion which expresses and secures its patriotic sentiment. But that, however, the idea of Christianity as expressed in the reformation simply involves the freedom of the individual soul–involves the absence of all forcible measures in the propagation of it–involves therefore that the state shall leave the conditions of teaching or of expressing religious truth free–and that whatever end direction it give, it shall give consistently herewith. For I do not see any real objection to the state supporting any kind of moral as of other instruction–provided in the circumstances of the country this can be done consistently with a constant refusal to prescribe to the teacher what is moral or natural or religious truth. Of course it is a practical question of politics in every case whether the state can support such instruction without prescribing what is truth, which essentially belongs to the individual conscience[240] or to Science–or whether the deeper interests of liberty preclude any such support–or finally whether as some say such instruction is sufficiently secured by the great efforts which religion prompts in its votaries.[241] This I say as a question of practical politics depends on the actual state and character of the nation and therefore I do not seek to interfere with them.

Social Ethics No. 9
[Montesquieu, Mixed Constitutions
and the Balance of Powers.][242]

In *patriotism* we have the subjective element of national life, whose[243] object expresses its unity in a *Constitution*. A constitution is that supreme law which determines or declares the organs through which in each case the state or nation shall act–I say 'determines or declares'–for in one sense you may say that the constitution only declares the existence of an order which has already come to exist in the natural operation of the different forces of society. It tells us that a nation, an amorphous mass of people–of the same tribe or of different tribes–has by the agency of force or consent been elevated into an organic unity–in which it faces the *other* nations of the globe as one personality–*collective yet one*. In another sense we may find authority for the word 'determines' in the fact that we have no true state–no *state* in the full and proper sense of the term–till the irregular and inconstant massing of mankind in tribes and armies has ceased to appear as the mere action of individual caprice and has taken definite and objective form in a written law. So long as custom is the only source of order it is vague, arbitrary and uncertain–the general is lost in and easily changes with the particular–but in a written law it is made clear to the consciousness of action and lifted above caprice and accident. The Constitution-making is the decisive chrystallization [sic] of the confused compound, the final expression of what was till then the latent working of unknown affinities. We see then how it is possible to make little or to make much of the written law according to the point of view from which you regard it as *reaching* [?] or as *constituting* the state, for while the law as many experiences of revolution has shown, for example, the French Revolution and still more the excellent constitution given by Napoleon to Spain[244]–is little or nothing in itself–and soon falls away from a national life which is not in harmony with it. On the other hand a nation is still immature if it has not reached that point where it acquires the clear consciousness of its objective unity. The word is nothing in itself but everything as the expression of reason come to the consciousness of itself.

As consciousness generally comes with pain, so a constitution generally arises out of a discord. A discord which is met by the declaration of principles. But if the constitution is to be a permanent[245] one, these principles are mainly drawn from an order which has already shown itself as custom. Thus though Magna Charta, the Bill of Rights, *declares* what are–what have been the rights of Englishmen–[it] does not determine what they shall be.[246] At the same time in this reference to the past there is something delusive in so far as the existence of custom[247] is shifting and exposed to a continual invasion from caprice–and rights supported only by custom are not in the full sense rights. On the other hand a constitution necessarily by its generality somewhat purifies the rude order of habitual morality, and we have many examples in which a very hard discipline has been necessary after the making of the constitution–ere a nation could become thoroughly identified with it. Nations thus had to be as the Greeks in their youth. The Solonian legislation was pressed home even by the tyranny of Psistratus[248] and the despotism of Napoleon gave time for France to confirm itself in those principles of equal right which the revolution brought in, but which the counter-revolution might else have destroyed ere the new interests grew able to protect themselves. Thus it is that law substitutes itself for force and again requires force to makes it valid.

Another point I have to notice is that[249] the Constitution, etc., grows up in parts, as our own constitution is of many fragments–according as in the long struggle of crown and people different rights were questioned, asserted, and determined by a law or treaty. Or there may be as in modern times a universal remodelling of the Constitution in some decisive moments in which Revolution has cast a doubt on every right. And out of this springs a new and complete Constitution in one document. This has only occurred in quite modern times for universal revolutions we do not find before the great French outburst. The Constitutions thus arising might be the most logical and complete in one sense–but these are less likely to be secure–for in such moments constitution-building, being left in the individual workman's hands–and done without much guidance from anything fixed or certain–is apt to produce structures which have no basis but individual opinion and which therefore another individual opinion may easily overthrow. How many constitutions have France–and some other European states, seen born and buried within the last fifty years?[250]

Conceive however a people knit together in that organic unity we call a state by the inner bond of patriotism–by which each citizen identifies himself with the whole–so that before the world, before other states, they constitute one personality. We ask how is the unity of will and acts thus arrived at to be maintained and realized. How is this multiple organism to act as one? It is obvious that this can only be secured in this as in the bodily organism by some distribution of the functions to different organs. The state cannot do everything with each member of it. The offices must be distributed to the different members–according to their capacity–and thus the unity of the life must show itself in manifold ways. And *yet again* all these manifold works of the different members must conspire to one result–else the life will be destroyed by the diversity it uses to realize itself. Now the constitution is that which determines who in each case speaks and acts in the name of the whole. It is in other words the distributor[251] of the state power.

Two things have to be considered:[252] 1. the *necessity* of division of power[253] that the true nature of the state may be realized. 2. the necessity of the subordination of the different organs to one life and Montesquieu's error on this subject.

To Montesquieu, according to his celebrated theory, the great security for liberty is in the division of the different powers which check and limit each other–and above all in this that the executive, the judicial and the legislative powers should be kept distinct–and he attributes the liberty of England to the accuracy with which this balance is adjusted. Here are his words: 'There is no liberty where the legislative power is in the hands that administer the law–for one may find that the monarch or senate may make tyrannical laws in order to execute them tyrannically. There is no liberty if the power of judging is not separated from the executive as well as the legislative power. If it be joined to the legislative, then the power which disposes of the lives and liberty of the citizens will be arbitrary: for the judge will be legislator. If it be joined to the executive then the judge may have the force of an oppressor. All will be lost if the same man, the same body of princes, or nobles or people exercise the three powers of making the laws, executing the public resolutions, and judging the crimes or the civil suits of individuals.'[254] Then going on to the review of actual states he says: 'In the greater number of the kingdoms of Europe, the government is moderated because the prince who has the first two powers, leaves to the people the exercise of the third. With the Turks[255]–where all these three powers are united in the hand of the sultan, there reigns a fearful despotism. In the Republics of Italy[256] liberty is found less than in our monarchies for the three powers are united. The government needs as violent means to maintain itself as that of the Turks–witness the state-inquisitors at Venice and the box in which every informer might deposit his charges against anyone.['] The multitude of magistrates, and tribunals put limits on each other in these republics.[257] Then he goes on to point out the advantages of the English constitution. To avoid the evil of ancient democracies that the people took active and immediate resolve and at the same time to secure the general interests–the people ought only to choose representatives and even these representatives should lay down[258] laws. To secure that the common liberty be not slavery to those distinguished by wealth and honor, the popular assembly in [its] legislative function must have beside it a hereditary house of nobles. And finally as the legislative might destroy the sovereign power the sovereign must have the right of veto. While on the other hand he must have no independent power of legislating else the executive will absorb the judicial. The legislative must however have the power to judge how their laws are executed by the executive, though the person of the sovereign must himself be saved. [?] He is, assisted therefore only by[259] his ministers. The lower house must accuse before the upper. On the other hand the legislature should have no direct power over the executive in its use of the powers committed to it though it keep in its own hand the supplies–in order that the executive may not overthrow it. For similar reasons Montesquieu approves of jury trial as the proper mode of distributing the judicial power.[260]

In all this there is much truth. Montesquieu was the first writer who taught this country to understand itself–who generalizes the principles that underlay its institutions–he is the author of the theory of constitutional government and for a long time his notions about the three powers and their reciprocal limitations ruled over all political speculation, which even to this day owes a great deal to his impulse. At the same time there are important qualifications to be taken along with his doctrine.

1. It is already observable in what has been said that there is no absolute division of organs. For in England the parliament which is the special organ of legislation is also judicial, and executive in so far as it must have the power to carry into effect its judgments. The sovereign who is the executive is also a part of the legislative–and his prerogative of mercy implies a judicial function. While the judicial power again in applying is partly making the law–and is also executive in so far as it bears the direct capacity of using force to carry out its decisions. Through

which there is a division of functions–and each function has its special and appropriate minister or ministers. Yet each organ is a living image of the whole and has all the functions of the whole organism, though its prevailing character may be given by one function. And this obviously is necessary in the nature of the case–for a legislative which was merely legislative would be a powerless name, and an executive which had no legislative function would be itself soon abolished by law. Montesquieu himself notes this while he tells us that under the early monarchy of Greece the kingdoms had both too much power and too little–for the executive or military power was combined with the judicial, so that the law became the instrument of tyranny, while on the other hand as the king had no legislative power he could not defend himself against the legislature.[261] Thus it is clear that the distinction of organs does not involve an absolute independence or distinction of functions–or that each organ should go its own way and discharge its own office. For that is rather the mark of disease and dissolution. In the living body all the organs act in harmony so that their separate actions support each the other. And so it must be in the living state. Each organ of the state must be penetrated by and partake of the character of the other organs so that[262] the functions may go on in harmony with each other.

2. And this leads me to say that Montesquieu's theory looks rather to the outward mechanical construction of the state, than to its organic unity. He regards it under the analogy of [a] carefully constructed machine in which the action of one force is applied to counteract another–[rather] than of a living being in which the whole is in every part. Hence he looks on its unity as springing from the check and counter-check of opposing and balanced powers that are merely outwardly related to each other. But a state which was held together only by such a nice balance of forces would soon lose its unstable equilibrium and incline to one side–and when it did so would have no self-rectifying power to restore it. Montesquieu anatomized the state from without–but he did not enter into its inward formative principles and the spiritual bond of their *defecta membra* ['scattered fragments'] is wanting. It is true that life displays itself [...?] it from the embryo to the adult–from the lowest animal to man–from the simplest aggregate of savage life to the complexity of a constitutional state, by continual differentiation of organism to correspond[ing] different functions–but to

understand this process we trace how unity of life shows itself necessarily in a diversity of function and how this diversity of function is the ground of a diversity of organisms. Whereas Montesquieu only looked to the different organs and tried to construct the state by mechanically putting them together.

3. A constitutional state is presented by Montesquieu as a unity of aristocracy, monarchy and democracy, which respectively have for their characteristics the predominance, of the executive, of the administrative and of the legislative. Montesquieu notes that the principle of democracy is virtue, of aristocracy moderation and of monarchy honor, but we find some difficulty in seeing how these three are to be compounded into one.[263] Let us however before going on look a little more nearly at the meaning of these assertions and the various characters of ancient and modern states manifested thereby. It is true that the ancient states did not develop that complexity of organism which we see in modern states. And though Aristotle already speaks of the danger of excess in the carrying out of the principle of each state, and approves of mixed governments of the least aristocratic aristocracies and of the least democratic democracies and considers it a condition of order that while certain necessary powers (κρίσις και ἀρχαιρεσία ['right of judgement and the election of magistrates']) should be given to the people, there should yet be a career of ambition open to those who by superior[ity] in wealth or ability are naturally led to desire it.[264] Yet he confines such concessions within very narrow limits and demands that above all things the state should be harmonious with its own ὑσὸ θεσις, or fundamental notion.[265] As a matter of fact the principles of aristocracy and democracy in ancient Greece showed themselves as absolutely contradictory and irreconcilable–and their war–the Peloponnesian–was the dissolution of the social order of Greece, while monarchy could after the heroic age appear only as tyranny. In Rome also we find the three principles appearing successively and as mutually exclusive. The early kingdom with the development of civil as opposed to military order passes into an aristocracy at first close[d] and then open–an administrative aristocracy maintained by the national feeling rather than legal privilege and which therefore dissolved when the Roman nationality perished by its own extent–into an anarchic democracy whose hand was only in force of the armies and which therefore soon placed the supreme power again in an imperial executive.[266] Now in this greater simplicity of the arrange-

ments of ancient Constitutions we may see the truth of Montesquieu's derivation. [?] Whereas in Athens the legislative assembly was also the judge over the lives and property of the citizens–and at the same time took into its own hand the direct control over the instant resolves of the executive in the conduct of wars or foreign politics, the machine of government could only work safely so long as a principle of virtue as Montesquieu calls it lay in the minds of all the citizens–for that control of general principle over particular resolves of law, over [...?]–which alone could give continuity and order to the government must be provided by a political identification of the citizen with his state–in which the sense of private interest was lost or absorbed.[267] And this was as Montesquieu remarks only possible in a very small state where each citizen was continually feeling the influence of the whole and reacting on it.[268] Montesquieu well shows how in such a state as at Athens the wealthy must find enjoyment of themselves in being the entertainers of the state, in public festivals and exhibitions–and must submit to what would otherwise be intolerable burdens of taxation–while every citizen being called to spend and be spent in her wars and business can find little scope for particular interests or ambitions. In it he must feel himself rich, while with [sic] it he must become poor. The separation of particular interests–the desire to make the state an instrument to self–must be fatal to such a substantial morality–as we see indeed in Greece it was fatal–for with that the general is no longer present in the particular resolve and the state unity is broken up.

In an aristocracy there are rulers and ruled–there is a separation of general and particular interest–for the general government has become itself a particular interest opposed to the others. Here then we find a continual danger that the government forgetting all general interests should become a selfish oligarchy who administer for their own good–and hence such a government easily passes over into tyranny. This it can only avoid so long as it puts a check on itself–on the individual passions of the members of the aristocracy–and in expending the resources of the state for the chosen end, be it conquest as with the Romans or commercial aggrandisement as with the Venetians.[269] Aristocracies have therefore often exercised a strong and sometimes[270] even a tyrannical and bloody discipline over their members, as in the case of the state-inquisitors of Venice or the censors of Rome. They must force their members into political activity and watch jealously over the use they make of their powers as magistrates. It was the greatness of the provincial commands which took the Roman nobles beyond the reach of the senate that dissolved the bonds of the Roman aristocracy–and made imperialism inevitable.

Montesquieu says that the principle of monarchy is honor as distinguished from despotism in which the principle is fear.[271] Under the name of monarchy he thinks therefore of a[272] hierarchy of nobles with a supreme noble at the head such as we see at the end of the feudal period. This feudal monarchy is of course equally distinguished from the patriarchal and antique monarchy of the Greeks and Romans–or on the other hand from the constitutional monarchy of modern times. The king in the feudal monarchy is the head of a privileged class–whose privileges are proportioned to their nearness to himself. The bond of such a state can of course only be that each one considers his duty as also his right and his honor–as the manifestation of his privileged personality. The sense of importance which the noble has gives him a personal dignity which limits the caprice of the king–who is after all but the first of the gentlemen of his realm. While on the other hand it makes him the natural defender of the throne as the source of his honour.[273] There is therefore here an advance on the simple military and clan leader–who in an early state of society is necessarily, by the necessity of a warlike state of society, exalted into king. We have here not that simple monarchy that takes its place besides the aristocracy and democracy[274] with which Montesquieu deals–but a monarchy that combines [?] again [?] the complexity of modern constitutional government.

We may see however by looking at these three kinds of government that they are not merely qualitatively distinguished by the government of *one, of few* or *of many*–but that they have essential d[ifferences] beneath this.[275] The king represents the unity of the nation–both its national unity as a race and its unity of will. Hence in cases where this sense of unity is strong–especially therefore in warlike stages of society–both because *then* we feel most our unity with our selves and our opposition to others, and because then the unity of executive will is most required, royal government is most common. Again where a continuous *policy* is to be carried out as by the Roman or Venetian, an aristocracy naturally appears–since with them tradition is strongest and individual changes of character that remould a monarchy with each reign are not felt. Here the general purpose of government is regarded as settled–and what is wanted is fit instruments for it. And this is likely to be secured in [the] endless succession required only by a persistent dedication and education of certain families to the task. The administrative in such a case naturally absorbs both legislative and executive powers. Lastly where the nation becomes [an] end to itself–where the enjoyment of liberty of the general resources by each citizen, and not the attainment of an outward end, becomes the object of state life–there a self-legislating democracy naturally arises in which each citizen shares in forming and continually anew forming the state whose development is simply the development of all the citizens.

Now if we speak of a constitutional state as in modern times seeking by a balance of executive administrative and legislative powers to meet [?] all these principles of democracy, aristocracy and monarchy,[276]–we do not mean–as Montesquieu might seem to mean–that we have here a number of independent powers–counterpoising each other as of three states put together–which would be anarchy–but that elements or functions that are implied in every state receive separate development and organization–whereas in ancient states the due development of either executive or administrative or legislative powers tended absolutely to absorb the other two. And so injustice was always done to some necessary element of political life.

You will notice however that I have not adopted Montesquieu's three powers exactly.[277] His three are the legislative, the executive power in things relating to the law of nations, and the executive power in things relating to civil law–but while the legislative is the general *element* in the state–the particular is represented not only by the judicial–but by all that falls under the name of administrative power, i.e. the subsumption of particular under the universal. And the individual, or executive power which finds its representative in the sovereign not only represents the unity of the state as opposed to other states–but the unity of the state as opposed to the individual citizens. The final subjective power of decision which is [the] beginning and end of the whole. We may therefore distinguish the legislative, administrative and the executive or sovereign power. In every state these three elements are represented in some way or other, by permanent or changeable officers [sic] as the case may be–but the development and perfection of the organism and of its several parts as well as their relations depends necessarily on the state of civilization of the nation in question and the character of its union. A *general* theory of the state can only express the character of the three powers in the abstract. Although as it is the highest state which best corresponds to the idea of a state, it may in this way point to an ideal, which can only be approached in so far as the whole social movement supports it.[278]

We have then to consider on the one side the formation of the *permanent* or *universal* will that corresponds to the character of the individual in opposition to his resolves or acts–we have then to consider the judicial and administrative machinery by which this general will is particularized. This in the main corresponds to the habitual actions of the individual in which he simply acts out the principles which have already taken hold on him. And finally we have to consider that immediate decisive power by which the state transcends the imperfect generality of the laws or meets new emergencies by instant act–which corresponds to action of the individual in so far as it transcends the habitual action or action on distinct principles–the element which Socrates referred to the δαιμόνιον τι ['the divine power'] and his countrymen to the creator,[279] but which the modern throws upon the Conscience and will of the individual subject–and which in fact implies a reference to a higher principle that is expressed in law–and its application to a more definite order than can be[280] realized by its mere application.

Social Ethics No. 10
[The Structure of the Legislature.][281]

We must consider then that every state by its very nature as the organized expression of national life involves here three moments or powers–the legislative which is concerned with the formation of definite and conscious principles of action and with the *refor*-mation of these according to the increasing civilization of the nation; the administrative which applies these principles to the concrete case; and last the sovereign power–which has in its hands the instant decision of the national will in cases unforeseen by the law–and has therefore within certain limits the right of suspending or confirming their execution in particular cases. All these three elements are implied in a perfect organic expression of the national will. And every constitution is an attempt more or less perfect to provide such organs of expression. In developing the nature of each of these organs, let us try to keep as far as possible from definite criticisms of actual politics and simply ask what are the ideal requirements to be satisfied–the principles to be fulfilled in each of these and the means necessary to fulfil them–the one never however to forget [is] that there is one national will which is seeking expression in all these and that the organism is subordinate to the functions and continually modified by them.

The legislative will of the nation requires expression–how shall it best be expressed–by what organs, is the question before us. Let us first consider what that legislative will includes. It must include specially two elements: the making of the laws by which the duties of the government are determined towards the citizens, and those by which the duties of the citizens are determined to the government. In the former of these is included not only the specification of the constitution or the application of the general principles of justice which are[282] necessary to reduce vague generalities into rules capable of application by the administrative [organ]–but also that progressive modification which in the end will result in a new constitution. For if the legislative organ of society is at all perfect in its working, there need to be no sudden break or transition in the development of a new constitution. The legislature will itself then reflect and express the changes of the society and will modify itself and all the other powers of the government gradually and certainly in conformity with them. Thus Hegel notes that the 'means of the princes and their families were at first private property but were gradually altered into regal domains–i.e. the public property attached to the *office* of king–because the kings felt the needfulness of stopping the continual division of estates that ruined their families, and sought the guarantee of this indivisibility for the estates of the realm–thereby giving up their own right to dispose of them at their pleasure. In like matter the emperor was formerly a judge and went round the empire judging right, till gradually by the advance of civilization, he was obliged to transfer this office to many substitutes and so the judicial power fell into the hands of citizens.'[283] In England the increase of the power of the lower house has had some great and violent transitions as at the two revolutions[284]–but generally its development has been peaceful–and the greatest change whereby the government of a ministry responsible to parliament was made the rule[285] of the constitution has come in almost imperceptibly and without even being fixed by any definite law, though implied in many.

With regard to the other department–the laws that regulate the judicial and administrative powers–we may have something more to say when we treat of these powers–but in the mean time I would notice that the line between law and administration is not an absolute one. Of course it would not be enough for a lawgiver to lay down the ten commandments[286] as his law–yet the progressive specifications of crime and injury can never be complete, and while the judge is nominally applying a rule, he must really be givin[g] it greater definition and so enacting a new rule. The confusion of the two reaches its highest point when we come to what are called private bills, which seem really administrative decisions of particular cases, and take in this country the place of the actions of administrative officials in France and Germany–but of this again [later].[287] The point where administration begins and legislation ends is therefore a shifting one which must be determined by the circumstances, needs and habits of each country.

Passing to the second great department of legislative power–the determination of the duties of subjects to the state. The most important point to note is the great difference in the way in which provision is made for the requirements of the state in ancient and modern times. In ancient times the state addressed a direct command to the subject, fitted by his character, ability or wealth for it, to do a particular service. The picture of the Platonic republic in which the guardians select special individuals according to their talents and distribute them to particular offices and ranks was simply an ideal exaggeration of the direct claims the state made on the citizen–to fight, to judge, to furnish ships or even one's slave to the state.[288] This ancient ideal is still preserved in the main in feudalism where vassals held their estates in virtue of particular offices and services–and where taxes were generally levied in kind. But modern governments do not in the main ask anything but money of their citizens. The only exception is among continental nations the military service–and with us the service of juries. And often where the former is enforced, it is allowed to be commutable for money. This is the legitimate result of the principle of the modern world in which the choice of his occupation and profession is left to the individual will. We reserve the right of the state in the absolute necessity of war to make itself independent of the accidents of particular choice–but we consider it as the most valuable organization which[289] arises out of freedom–and we would if possible try to make the discharge of state duties consistent with this mediation. To this end we must allow the individual to free himself of his obligation by money–as the general representative of value[290]–trusting that therewith again the state can attract and purchase the service it requires. It is a secondary advantage of this method that it can be more easily just, since the claims of the state are referred to a general standard and are not dependent on the accidental estimate of individuals. But the great point is that the subjective freedom of the individual is respected: the state is satisfied with the general discharge of obligations and only takes special services from the individual when he offers himself to perform them. Any further claims which the state makes require special [justification] ([....?]–right to refuse current taxes) as they involve a sort of tutelage of the state over its subjects; and no tutor ought to exist except of a minor. Toward criminals, paupers and the like the state justifiably stands still in somewhat of its ancient attitude and may lay special commands and duties on them just as the parent may on the child who is only a potential and not an actual person.

The duties then of the legislative power as such are then [sic] to fix and alter the laws and the taxes–what is or should be its constitution. This cannot again be definitely arrived at in any country without regard to its circumstances and traditions. Whether there should be one or two chambers–and in what relation the sovereign power, the king or president, should stand to them, it is impossible to say in the abstract–but we may perhaps arrive at some general views in relation thereto by considering how best the permanent national will can find expression.

The first point to notice is that there are especially two things to be considered in the determination of the laws–one is their scientific perfection as expressions of the principles desired to be expressed [and] the purposes desired to be served–and with this we may combine as also a matter of science in some sense their approximation to some ideal standard in those purposes and principles. Another is their adaptation to the wants, the wishes, and the state of civilization in the nation to which they are applied. In other words their absolute and their relative value.[291] Now while the former may seem to be best secured by the action of men of special administrative training–whose minds by education and occupation have been continually directed to the principles and application of law, the latter can only be secured by the free action upon legislation of all the different interests of the country. In lawgiving, in other words the special administrative ability from above, with its universality must meet with, and give unity and system to, the claims of all particular interests from beneath in order to produce a law which is at once universal and particular, at once guided by correct principles and relative to the existing state of society. Now it is the defect of all despotic or aristocratic systems that, 1) only the first of these requirements can be satisfied, and 2) for that reason not even it is satisfied well–for the universal separated from the particular becomes itself particular. Let us look at each of these points in succession.

In the first place a good despot–or an aristocracy animated by good ends, cannot however it strive really adapt its institutions to the life of the people as a whole with that precision which is necessary if the people are to feel themselves identified with the law and the constitution. In the movement of society new interests are continually arising–new combinations and separations of interest and, with these, new problems which even the utmost experience and thought cannot anticipate. These problems and difficulties therefore will never be expressed in their fullness unless we give a voice to such interests and let it speak for itself–and when they are not expressed, they can never be solved. Nay, when there is no natural political outlet–no call for expression–tendencies and feelings at utter variance with constituted authority may long work in the minds of classes or even of whole populations without clear consciousness on their own part. And thus revolution[292] may grow to ripeness without the consciousness of the most intelligent observers, of those who have most to fear from it–or even of the future revolutionists themselves. What they had been obscurely driving at was first revealed to the French Constituent [Assembly] only at the very moment when they were doing it.[293] Thus even with no evil intentions on the part of the rulers, the gulf between the feelings of the people and their institutions may grow continually wider, and no one may be fully aware of it till the moment when the evil is too far gone to cure by any means but violence. The same danger lies in every case–whether of a whole nation or of a class in it which is unrepresented and where the laws are made for it–but not in any way by it. Give a class or a nation an organization first that it may become conscious of what it wants, second that it may express and promote it–and its working[s] become orderly and regular. Leave it inorganic, and it is for long inactive and dumb till like a volcanic force it gathers itself for a destructive outburst.

2. But in the second place, as I noticed, the universal separated from the particular becomes itself particular. Just as the church when absolutely opposed to the world became finally itself a mere hopelessly corrupt world[294]–so we find that when a particular class by reason of their training or otherwise become the special depositaries of the science of law and administration–they soon come to regard this universal science as the special property of[295] their class and the sanction for any claims it may choose to make. They become a bureaucracy who use their science as a means of extending their power, till that science utterly loses all universal meaning and aim. Their possession of the keys of knowledge become[s] the means of shutting out every one else and finally themselves from its possession. Or if it be a despot who as in Rome gains his author[ity] as the executor and minister of a universal system of jurisprudence–the minister of law is soon lifted above all law and makes and remakes it at his will. The security therefore for the influence of practical knowledge of the science of legislation, administration, and government–is that the class that devotes themselves thereto should not themselves be the irresponsible despositaries but should have a voice rather in limiting the exclusive and contradictory claims of different[296] interests and bringing them back into systematic unity.

Now it would appear that what we substantially want in a legislative power is that knowledge and representation of particular interests and classes combined with and modified and corrected by the experience and skill of those who have had special training in the science of government, or special practice in administration. The former however supposes a discipline of peace and order, a capacity for general interests and discussion, an ease of communication and mutual intercourse that has only of late become realized in countries of any size. Hence in all earlier states, in so far as they extend beyond [the] form of the commune or municipality, this element–the representation of particular interests–has been wanting, and the business of government has been thrown generally on a monarch assisted by a more or less qualified aristocracy[297] trained in the theory and practice of government. The Roman emperors were thus but the head or centre of two great professions of law and arms–who were the instruments of the government of the Roman world. In later times the church took to a great extent the place of the profession of law as the representatives of the science of government, until with the revival of learning and the reformation, the lawyers again reclaimed their place on the one side, and the landed aristocracy ceased to confine their energies to war, and acquired sufficient culture to become instruments of peaceful administration.[298] In all these cases the legislature was in the hands of a class–who by having or having added to birth were in theory at least the representatives not of any particular interest but of the general good–who had their authority not as interested individuals–but as alone possessing the qualifications of experience and position necessary for law-giving. And who often (and especially we may notice in the bureaucracy of Prussia)[299] did really and with no little effect represent the public interest; while they often in the excellence of their administration contrasted favourably with the awkward action of freer institutions and might cast a doubt upon the latter if we did not remember that no machinery can in the long run replace or compete with the power of life. Still in all cases as already said, the legislature suffered and must suffer from the want of that clear comprehension of the subjects' interest which can only be secured by their effective representation–and in all cases the temptation to put the interests and power of the lawgiving class in place of the perfection of the law produced many evil results: and the progress of[300] justice in law and administration is coincident with, if it may not entirely be measured by, the advancing power of the representation of particular interests in opposition to the predominance of an aristocracy of skilled administrators or those whose claim is that they are such. There have[301] indeed been two concurrent lines of change by which on the one hand the representation of particular interests has continually been more perfect–and on the other hand by which the general influence of knowledge and experience has been more and more purified from all class interests. In the former line of progress, England with its traditions of freedom and self-government has most distinguished itself while in the other, in the training of what we may call an official or administrative aristocracy enlightened by all scientific aids–no country perhaps has been so forward as Prussia. The *ideal* of a legislative body would involve the full development of each with the harmonious unity–would demand the widest extension of representative institutions combined with the highest scientific and practical culture of a special class of legislators–and their united action in such a way that the national will uttering itself in the somewhat discordant voice of particular interest through the representative body should be moderated, enlightened and checked till it assume a harmonious and well-considered form by the operation of those tried [organs of] service and knowledge the nation has learned to respect, as on the other hand the too abstract and wide plans of those who look to the nation only as a whole will be moderated and conformed to the needs of society by the power of particular interests.

In connection with this arises the question of *one* or *two* chambers in the legislative assembly which has been greatly agitated especially by continental theorists.[302] There are two points of view from which their necessity has been urged, with a view to a proper balance of interests–and with a view to counter-posing a more thorough and careful deliberation, or rather a deliberation from a new point of view, between the proposal and the final result. On the former argument, Mill has some good remarks–that if one house be intended as a check on the other–'its efficacy in this respect wholly depends on the social support it can find[303] outside the House. An assembly which does not rest on the basis of some great power in the country is ineffectual against one which does. An aristocratic House is only powerful in an aristocratic state of society. The House of Lords was once the strongest power in our Constitution and the Commons only a checking body: but this was when the Barons were almost the only power out of doors. I cannot believe that in a really democratic state of society, the House of Lords would be of any practical value as a moderator of democracy. When the force on one side is feeble in comparison with that on the other, the way to give it effect is not to draw out both in line and muster their strength[304] over-against one another. Such tactics would ensure the utter defeat of the less powerful. It can only act with advantage, by not holding itself apart, and compelling every one to declare himself either with or against it, but taking a position among rather than in opposition to the crowd,[305] and drawing to itself the elements most capable of allying themselves with it on any given point; not appearing at all as an antagonistic[306] body, to provoke a general rally against it, but working as one of the elements in a mixed mass, infusing its leaven, and often making what would be the weaker part the stronger by the addition of its influence. The really moderating power in a democratic constitution must act[307] through the democratic House'. p.241.[308]

The idea of an external checking influence in favour of one special interest or the other predominant interests of the country belongs to that false view of the constitution as merely a system of balancing forces which Montesquieu gave rise to.[309] And as a proper representative body must contain representatives of all the special interests of the country in proportion to their strength, such additional representation of one interest would involve a practical unfairness, which might easily lead even to a reactionary unfairness on the other side from the jealousy excited by the interest then artificially supported. When the stronger party has resolved on a course which it has judged favourable to its interests–it is not likely that it will listen with respect to a new opposition from the interests it has already set aside. There is only one voice that can be opposed to it with effect and that is the voice of reason that looks beyond particular interest to the general good on which *they* are all dependent. Such a voice, if its utterance can be secured, will have weight not only with[310] the representatives of special classes and interests, but what is still more important with those citizen[s] whom they represent. While every suspicion that the voice *is* the voice [of a] particular and not of general interest–every suspicion in fact that the second Chamber speaks for a class and not for the whole–will necessarily weaken its natural influence. Now if in any way a second chamber be secured whose voice *is*, and will be received by the country *for*, the utterance of experience and science–we may expect that such a chamber–just in proportion to the extent of its real independence of interests–will be able not indeed to thwart the confirmed will of the country, but to give pause to the short-sighted impulses of strong classes, and on the other hand to originate measures of a more universal aim. In the ultimate resort the victory is to the strong–and an absolute checking power on a representative body can only be allowed permanently to exist on condition that it is not *used* as absolute. But on the other hand [that] no nation is fit for representative institutions that is not willing to take means that the voice of universal Reason may come on the one hand between the impulse of particular interests and this enactment of law–and on the other may initiate movements for which particular interests are not urgent; [?] and there seems no better way in which such a voice may gain the weight and authority of organization–and the definite opportunity of making itself felt–than by gathering into a separate chamber those whose character, circumstances and training raise them above special interests–and direct their minds to the considerations of the national life as a whole.

'The consideration which tells most', (says Mr. Mill p.239) 'in my judgment in favor of two Chambers (and this I do regard as of some moment) is the evil effect produced upon the mind of any holder of power, whether an individual or an assembly, by the consciousness of having only themselves to consult. It is important that no set of persons should[311] be able, even temporarily, to make their *sic volo* prevail, without asking anyone else for his consent. A majority in a single assembly–when it has assumed a permanent character–when composed of the same persons habitually acting together, and always assured of victory in their own House–easily becomes despotic and overweening, if released from the necessity of considering whether its acts will be concurred in by another constituted authority. The same reason which induced the Romans to have two consuls, makes it desirable there should be two chambers: that neither of them may be exposed to the corrupting influence of undivided power, even for the space of a single year. One of the most indispensable requisites in the practical conduct of politics, especially in the management of free institutions–is conciliation; a readiness to compromise; a willingness to concede something to opponents, and to shape good measures so as to be as little offensive as possible to persons of opposite views; and of this salutary habit, the mutual give and take (as it has been called) between two Houses is a perpetual school (useful even as such[312] now and its utility would probably be more felt, in a more democratic constitution of the legislature.)'[313]

I think this reasoning is true–that there is the necessity of an opposition for freedom–that above all in the business of lawgiving–which has in it essentially the two sides of the universal and particular, the[314] application to particular in the spirit of with a view to the general–that it is well that these two sides should receive separate organization so that they may both be duly attended to. This is a case in which the division of labour is a great gain. Of course if you grant a legal equality to two bodies, you make *possible* a collision and a permanent state of war between them. But this bare possibility may be met by some legal arrangements for the ultimate overpowering of the non-representative body such as are found in the reserved powers of the sovereign in England. Generally however you may rely on such a *permanent* state of war being avoided by a properly constituted second chamber–for those who look to the general interest must desire in the Duke of Wellington's phrase that her majesty's government may be carried on[315]–and must see that no resolution however partial can be so destructive to the common weal as the continued warfare of the different organs of the commonwealth. If reason be ever so much against the course taken by the assembly that represents the interests of the country, yet ultimately reason lies in [a] correcting and not a commanding voice–and the fact that after a full utterance of reason and a recommitment of the question for deliberation–the representatives and the country refuse to listen, seems to show that the country is not yet ripe for the course it recommended. The universal in fact must give way for the time to the sum of the particulars through whom alone it can be realized, for only so can it hope for ultimate triumph. The same reasons that prove therefore that the church must be subordinate to the state, prove also that the second chamber, though it be in one sense the representative of a higher interest or even because it is such, must give way to the first. Its power is given it that it may make reason fully heard, but it is not yet time for reason to prevail if it prevail not by being heard alone. (This subject has to be further explained when we come to consider the sovereign power.)[316]

At the same time, this superiority of the lower or representative chamber is dependent on two conditions.[317] These are, 1) that society has[318] reached the point at which particular interests acknowledge the limit of their claims. In the later feudal constitution the various estates of the realm were organized in themselves in some degree. The defect was that they imperfectly recognised their subordinate character. The state did not include and absorb them all and annihilate the possibility of war between them. It was simply a loose general bond under which they still preserved their independence–or armed neutrality. And as every step in progress is generally the extreme opposite of the previous one–so the decay of these particular powers gave place to the crushing of all particular powers by the universalism of monarchy, under which the rule so far as it was not capricious was not checked in its caprice by the representatives of the people but guided by the wisdom of statesmen. In such a state of things and before the particular interests and classes, giving up their claim to absolute independence, were organized as effective powers in the state, as members of its unity–the powers of legislation must be in the hand[s] of statesmen whether collected into an upper chamber or no. For the pressing need was to make the universalism of the state triumphant, and as the representatives could not yet recognise this as a law or limit of their action–it had to be imposed on them from without. (As Plato[319] says that the highest good for a man is to have justice enforced on him, for without it he has not it within.)[320] It is therefore not an unlimited opposition or contradiction that we suppose to subsist between our ideal upper and lower chamber[s] of statesmen and of representatives–for until each has acquired something of the nature of the other, no harmonious action is possible. Until the representatives have learned to acknowledge that the state is above all particular interests, there can be no real efficiency of the state bond consistent with their free action or at least their predominance; and then in order to escape anarchy, we have to run the danger that great statesmen, by their arbitrary method of carrying through abstract plans of improvement without regard to the particular wants of the community as sometimes happened with Richelieu and Colbert in France[321] [will ensure] that[322] the universal interest shall be often made subordinate to the interest of the ruling aristocracy who properly should be the organ of abstract statesmanship. In order to dispense with that overriding power of an aristocracy of statesmen which either is used in defence and furtherance of class interest–or at best in too great reliance on abstract theory as opposed to facts–we require a really organized and civilized body of constituents, who recognise in some degree at least the general weal of the state as supreme and elect the representatives of special interests–with the recognition of this, that their interests must support their claims on general grounds.

2. The predominance of the lower chamber is not [an] absolute and universal thing. Coming from the people immediately, their spirit is likely to be more immediately the expression of the actual tendencies of the people at the worst in their broad general outline. But this by no means excludes the fact that in the progress of the debate even on these questions, the maturer

statesmanship of the other house (such an ideal house as we are describing) would gain the greater support of public opinion–and it is even possible that in certain questions, especially such as have not become prominent in the elections, the statesman who looks more to the whole may, for the first [?] [time] be more truly in harmony with the national will than the accidental majority gained by the combination of particular interests in the lower house. There will therefore always be a certain dubiety in the case of two such chambers–where there is really an upper house of statesmen that gets the credit of being such [as] we have described–as to *where* the national will is in each particular case–notwithstanding the representative character of the lower house, and that [will be the case] even in the most democratic constitutions. And therefore there will be less fear of reducing such a chamber into shadow. Nay, one can conceive times, when the universal is more present to the minds of all than [the] particular–times of war or other incidents that makes the unity of the state rather than its manifoldness the predominant motive–when greater power would almost necessarily be thrust on the upper chamber.

In criticising actual governments and the degree in which they have realized their ideal, I must here be silent. We find actual two chamber governments here, in the U.S.–and during the existence of constitutional government in France, in Prussia and some other states.[323] Here the house of Lords did in some degree correspond to the ideal in so far as its members had very often a great administrative career, and as the representatives of Church and Law and by their enoble[ment], the aristocracy of the sword have had place in it. The facts of the times of its feudal origin however, necessarily led to the house being in the main composed either of peers by inheritance or of royal nominees; and while the latter were often chosen for other reasons than merit, the former whose independent position in some degree gave them the necessary prestige–and enabled them when really able and patriotic, to be true organs of the universalism of statesmanship, yet had the disadvantage of being dependent on the accidents of birth–and in later times when the growth of commerce reduced agriculture from the main interest of the country to only *one* of its main interests, their connection with the land made them appear to be the organ of a class rather than of a whole.

In France the aristocracy before the Revolution had sunk into a mere set of comitiers divorced from all the interests of the comites on the one hand and equally divorced from the business of statesmanship in which they had been supplanted by administrative officers of humble birth (so de Tocqueville).[324] And when at the Restoration and under Louis-Phillipe it was attempted to make an upper house of them, such a house appeared merely as an instrument of the crown and could therefore gain no weight whatever in the country.[325]

In America a happy device has been suggested by the federal constitution of the Republic as a union of many states. For while the members of the house of representatives are chosen by people directly in proportion to numbers, the members of the senate are chosen by the governing bodies of the several states and in equal number for each state of the union without regard to its numbers.[326] And as these small governing bodies naturally and for their own interest are led to send those members who have proved already their talents in separate state government for a considerable time, the senate contains much statesmanship and experience. And in fact has as great weight in the eye of the people as the representative body chosen by themselves; and in fact often resists its will as is well-known from recent events.[327] This device of union is one which is only possible to a federal state though excellently elected therefore.

Of course in approximating to any ideal such as we have laid down, it is necessary to build on the foundations already laid in each country, and to have constant reference to the social conditions thereof. And it is always better as it is easier gradually to remould an old institution in a new sense than to create one afresh. A dissolution of an upper chamber actually existing would be apt to deprive a country of the two chamber system altogether, whereas it might be easy to suggest changes by which the old might transform itself into the new–and inherit its past prestige without hindering its future usefulness.

Lecture One: Abstract Right and Subjective Morality Transcended by Social Ethics

[1]   [Martin's title (p. 213 below): '[Lecture] 92. Ancient and modern morality. Family. Marriage.']

[2]   [Caird's lecture course follows Hegel's *Philosophy of Right* at this and many other points, see *ibid.*, §141 et sub. English translations of this work are from GWF

Hegel, *Philosophy of Right*, trans. TM Knox (Oxford University Press, 1967; first edition 1952), unless otherwise stated. First German edition published in 1821.]

3   [Possibly a reference to what Martin (p. 213 below) calls '[Lecture] 88. Alienation of Property, Civil injury. Fraud. Crime.']

4   [Immanuel Kant, 'Critique of Practical Reason', in his *Practical Philosophy*, trans. and ed. M Gregor (Cambridge University Press, 1996), pp.231-6 (Prussian Academy edition 5:113-9).]

5   [MS. reads: 'just as out of scepticism'.]

6   [The Roman Catholic doctrine of implicit faith holds that believers can attain salvation by honouring church dogma and decisions, even where the justification for that dogma or those decisions is not understood by the believer him or herself.]

7   [The term 'perversions' was sometimes used in the stricter forms of Protestantism as a synonym for 'conversion'.]

8   [Caird may well have in mind Newman, Manning and Manley Hopkins, among others. John Henry Newman (1801-90) was a leading Tractarian before converting to Roman Catholicism in 1845. He was ordained a Catholic priest in 1846, and was created Cardinal of St. George in Velabro in 1879. Henry Edward Manning (1808-92), another leading Tractarian, converted to Roman Catholicism in 1851. He was appointed Roman Catholic Archbishop of Westminster in 1865 and Cardinal in 1875. Gerard Manley Hopkins (1844-89), the poet, was known personally by TH Green, Lewis Nettleship and Henry Scott Holland. He converted to Catholicism in 1866 and became a Jesuit in 1868. On Manning and Newman, see Caird's letter to Mary Sarah Talbot, 15 April 1896, in Henry Jones and John Henry Muirhead, *Life and Philosophy of Edward Caird* (Glasgow: Maclehose, Jackson, 1921), pp.213-4. On Manley Hopkins, see Green's letters to Scott Holland, 29 December 1868 and 9 January 1869, printed in Green, *Works*, vol. 5, pp.424-5, 425-8, respectively. Jowett reflected on 'Newmanism' in 1894 (Evelyn Abbott and Lewis Campbell, *Life and Letters of Benjamin Jowett, MA*, 2 vols. (London: John Murray, 1897), vol. 1, pp.176-7).]

9   ['Yea, for these laws were not ordained of Zeus,
And she who sits enthroned with gods below,
Justice, enacted not these human laws.
Nor did I deem that thou, a mortal man,
Coulds't by a breath annul and override
The immediate unwritten laws of Heaven.
They were not born to-day nor yesterday;
They die not; and none knoweth whence they sprang.'

Sophocles, *Antigone* trans. F Storr (London and New York: William Heinemann, 1912), p.349, ll.451-9. Caird also quotes this passage on p. 63 below.]

10   [MS reads: 'these'.]

11   [MS reads: 'which is while'.]

12   [MS del.: 'Jurisprudence'.]

13   [MS reads: 'just'.]

14   [Alexander of Macedon ('the Great') (356-323BC), pupil of Aristotle, king of Macedon 336-23BC, who conquered most of the known world during his short life.]

[15] [Lecture 16 ('Socrates and the Sophists - Virtue - Socrates and Anaxagoras - Plato and Aristotle'), and lectures 32-6, on Aristotle.]

[16] [MS reads: 'which which'.]

[17] [Apparently, a reference to an earlier, lost lecture in the series.]

[18] [Aristotle, *Nicomachean Ethics*, 1095a7-29.]

[19] [In 47-6BC Cicero divorced Terentia, his wife of thirty years, and soon afterwards married a younger woman. The allegation that he did so for the sake of another marriage settlement ('portion') is one of several motivations put forward by his biographers. Plutarch, 'Cicero', in his *Lives*, trans. B Perrin, 11 vols. (London: William Heinemann, 1949), vol. 7, p.187 (§41).]

[20] [MS reads: 'leads'.]

[21] ['Piety' [Lat. *pietas*] originally denoted dutiful conduct towards one's family, country or benefactors.]

[22] Erdmann puts it thus–Vorlesungen über den Staat, p.26-7

'The state is that manifestation of objective [MS orig.: 'social'] ethics (Sittlichkeit) in which morality and legality are one. This unity may bear more the character of commanding, so that the moral and legal are not yet separated–and there it assumes a naïve and childlike aspect. Thus it is in antiquity when as yet there was no talk of universal rights of man, nor of a Conscience with dictates at variance with the laws of fatherland and when personal honour and political fame were synonymous; and when it was thought natural that the Furies should leave Orestes when the Areopagus had acquitted him [Aeschylus, *Eumenides*, ll.754-77] just as a child obtains peace of Conscience when the mother forgives it. It is otherwise with modern (objective) morality. It has the character of something *re*gained and produced by reflexion–it is related to the simple ethics of Antiquity as the born again to the new born, as sanctity to innocence. And if in this it has lost the attractive character of naïvety–it need not therefore be *intensively* weaker. But just because in Antiquity the objective morality was the primitive state out of which afterward Right and subjective morality proceeded–while in modern times the opposite is the case–for that very reason the generality of men *then* showed more objective morality in the form e.g. of Patriotism, and only the most distinguished individuals upheld the claims of subjective morality while in modern times those who are backward in moral education fall short mainly in objective morality though from the point of view of subjective morality and of abstract jurisprudence they may be good men.' [Johann Eduard Erdmann, *Philosophische Vorlesungen über den Staat* (Halle: HW Schmidt, 1851), pp.26-7.]

[Caird adds in pencil:] Hence to Plato it is Oath [...?] that the state has first appeared.

[23] Moral element more developed in family
Legal element [more developed] in state
Unity in State.   [Caird's pencil addition.]

Lecture Two: Marriage and Family. The Different Natures of the Sexes and their Proper Roles in Society.

[24] [Martin's title (p. 213 below): '93. Social Ethics continued.   Marriage. Characteristics of the Sexes.']

25   [Lectures 60 to 67 (pp. 211–2 below).]

26   ['The moral value of the Domestic life consists in its being the only natural medium, through which mere Personal life is gradually enlarged into a truly Social life.' Auguste Comte, 'Social Statics, or the Abstract Theory of Human Order', in his *System of Positive Polity*, trans. F Harrison, 4 vols. (London: Longmans, Green, 1875), vol. 2, chap. 3, p.155. Following Caird's translation of this passage in his *Social Philosophy and Religion of Comte* (Glasgow: James Maclehose, 1885), p.45, the word 'mediation' has been adopted here also. The manuscript appears to use a different word (possibly 'transaction'), but Caird's letters are very poorly formed. Cf. Auguste Comte, *General View of Positivism*, trans. JH Bridges (London: Trubner, 1865), pp.100-3. First French edition published in 1848. Later addition between paragraphs at this point: 'As the self grows it is [...?]'.]

27   A unity in which the moral is in the form of the *natural*. [Placing uncertain.]

28   No duties, rights or virtues. [Placing uncertain.]   [*Four Commentaries of Gaius on the Institutes of the Civil Law*, 7:109-120, in SP Scott (ed.) *The Civil Law*, 17 vols. (New York: AMS, 1973), vol. 1, pp.97-9.]

29   A unity in which the moral is in the form of the *natural*. [Placing uncertain.]

30   [Illegible interpolation.]

31   [Aristotle, *Politics*, 1261a10-1261b15, 1328a21-1329a39.]

32   ['But many that are first shall be last; and the last first.' (Mark 10.31)]

33   ['For the natural use that one sex makes of the other's sexual organs is *enjoyment*, for which one gives itself up to the other. In this act a human being makes himself into a thing, which conflicts with the right of humanity in his own person. ... [I]t is not only admissible for the sexes to surrender to and accept each other for enjoyment under the condition of marriage, but it possible for them to do so *only* under this condition.' Immanuel Kant, 'Metaphysics of Morals', in his *Practical Philosophy*, trans. and ed. M Gregor (Cambridge University Press, 1996), p.427 [Prussian Academy edition 6:278].]

34   Hegel shows the impossibility of bringing family union under those categories which are the categories of Roman law by calling the [...?] of marriage persons over each other. Deylich personaliat Recht founded on contract. [Placing uncertain. Hegel, *Philosophy of Right*, §180. Caird himself fails to close this parenthesis in the manuscript.]

35   [MS. reads: 'desomate'.]

36   [MS del. interpolation: 'realizing Hobbes' idea of a contract that ends all contracts'; see p. 51 below.]

37   'Die Ehe ist dabei in sich so zu bestimmen, dass sie die rechtlich sittliche Liebe ist, wodurch das Vergängliche, Launenhafte und bloß Subjektive aus derselben verschwindet.' [This is a slight misquotation of Hegel, *Philosophy of Right*, §161A, which Knox translates as: 'Marriage, therefore, is to be more precisely characterized as ethico-legal (*rechtlich sittliche*) love, and this eliminates from marriage the transient, fickle, and purely subjective aspects of love.' Hegel, *Philosophy of Right*, §161A (p.262).]

38   [Thomas Hobbes, *Leviathan*, chaps. 17 and 18. First edition published in 1651.]

39   To many [MS del.: 'marriage'] is just this: to start from the standpoint of contract, of two person in independence first [?] in order to establish that standpoint.

[Placing uncertain.]

40 ['And when he had looked round about on them in anger, being grieved for the hardness of their hearts, he saith unto the man 'Stretch forth thine hand.' And he stretched it out: and his hand was restored whole as the other.' (Mark 3.5)]

41 [MS orig.: 'apprehension'.]

42 [Presumably in the preceding lectures.]

43 [MS reads: 'fitt'.]

44 [Cf. Hegel, *Philosophy of Right*, §166&A. See p. 54 below.]

45 Marriage [MS del.: 'Family'] not merely embrace [?] it, nor […?] it nor moral. Not all 3 in one.

Ancient conception of women as undeveloped men–Plato vindicator of piece [?] at expense of the difference of nature. [Placing uncertain. Aristotle believed that the naturally free man possess an active 'deliberative faculty', the latter 'is present but ineffective' in women (*Politics*, 1260a12-4). Caird may have in mind Plato's claim that certain women could properly develop the same skills as male guardians (*Republic* 453e-455a).]

46 [Together with his brother Principal John Caird and others, Edward worked hard and successfully to secure access to higher education women at Glasgow and Balliol. See Jones et al, *Life and Philosophy of Edward Caird*, pp.96-101, 150-2.]

47 ['Transformed' or 'transcended' would seem more appropriate.]

48 [For Antigone, see p. 63 below. This note and the preceding paragraph appear on the reverse of the folio. Immediately above both, Caird has written in pencil, 'See book for fuller development of this.' Four larger sheets, from Caird's notebooks, immediately follow these folios (see editorial introduction, p. vi above). These larger sheets are reproduced here as the next eight paragraphs (i.e. up to 'in the natural state.']

49 ['For in the resurrection they neither marry, nor are given in marriage, but are as the Angels of God in heaven.' (Matthew 22.30)   See also Mark 12:25, Luke 20:35.]

50 Unity with nature *in munia affecta* ['possessed of duties'] [Marginal note.]

51 He easily accepts the situation and conforms to it. [Marginal note.]

52 [Illegible marginal note.]

53 [The allusion is unclear. Probably to James Anthony Froude (1818-94), English historian and author of the twelve-volume *History of England from the Fall of Wolsey to the Defeat of the Spanish Armada* (1856-70), but possibly to his elder brother Richard Hurrell Froude (1803-36), Tractarian divine.]

54 The family is an organic unity in which the equality of the members […?] not [?] […?…?…?]. [Marginal note.]

55 ['The difference between men and women is like that between animals and plants. Men correspond to animals, while women correspond to plants because their development is more placid and the principle that underlies it is the rather vague unity of feeling. … Women are educated–who knows how?–as it were by breathing in ideas, by living rather than by acquiring knowledge. The status of manhood, on the other hand, is attained only by the stress of thought and much technical exertion.' (Hegel, *Philosophy of Right*, §166A).]

[56] [MS del.: 'widened'.]

[57] ['[Jesus] said, Verily I say unto you, Except ye be converted, and become as little children, ye shall not enter into the kingdom of heaven.' (Matt. 18.3)]

[58] In the relation of man and woman we leave Mr Taine['s] contrast of individual and U[niversal] [?] which we find in eye [?] [Marginal note. Caird may have in mind Hippolyte Taine's analysis of 'The Jacobin Programme', as set out in the latter's *The French Revolution*, trans. J Durand 3 vols. (Indianapolis: Liberty Fund, 2002), vol. 3, bk 6. The first French edition was published in 1878.]

[59] [This folio ends: 'We are obliged to anticipate much that should properly come in the further'.]

[60] [MS reads: 'its'.]

[61] [Possibly an allusion to the opening pages of the second part of Rousseau's *Un Discours sur l'Origine de l'Inégalité* (Jean-Jacques Rousseau, *A Discourse on Inequality*, trans. M Cranston (Harmondsworth: Penguin, 1984), pp.109-14 First French edition published in 1755). Another possibility is William Edward Hearn, *The Aryan Household: Its structure and its development: An introduction to comparative jurisprudence* (London: Longmans, Green, 1879). For Caird's ultimately rather damning assessment of Rousseau and his thought, see his 'Rousseau', in Edward Caird, *Essays on Literature and Philosophy*, 2 vols. (Glasgow: James Maclehose, 1892), vol. 1, pp.105-46.]

[62] [MS. reads: 'merely'.]

[63] [MS del.: 'of Europe'.]

[64] [Alfred, Lord Tennyson, 'In Memoriam AHH', in Christopher Ricks (ed.), *The Poems of Tennyson*, second edition, 3 vols. (London: Longman, 1987), vol. 2, p.392 (stanza 79, l.1.). The poem was first published in 1850. The poem is about Arthur Henry Hallam (1811-33), Tennyson's close friend from his undergraduate days at Trinity College Cambridge (see *ibid.*, pp.304-15).]

[65] [Tennyson, 'In Memoriam AHH', in Ricks (ed.), *Poems of Tennyson*, vol. 2, p.392, stanza 79, l.1.]

[66] [Tennyson quotes this line at the beginning of stanza 79 of 'In Memoriam AHH', it having first appeared in stanza 9:

'My Arthur, whom I shall not see
Till all my widowed race be run;
Dear as the mother to the son,
More than my brothers are to me.' (stanza 9, ll.17-20)

Tennyson described stanza 79 as being 'Addressed to my brother Charles (Tennyson Turner)' (*ibid.*, vol. 2, p.392n). Alfred was the fourth of seven sons of George Tennyson, rector of Somersby.]

[67] [Tennyson, 'In Memoriam AHH', p.392, stanza 79, ll.5-8, 13-20.]

[68] [Cf. Sir Henry Sumner Maine, *Ancient Law. Its connection with the early history of society and its relation to modern ideas*, introduction and notes by F Pollock (London: John Murray, 1906), pp.170, see also *ibid.*, pp.143-52. First edition was published in 1861, tenth edition 1884.]

[69] [Conjectural. MS may read: 'cartem'.]

[70] [MS reads: 'primes'.]

71 [MS illegible.]

72 [Maine, *Ancient Law*, pp.131-3.]

73 Cf. what Comte says about the analogy between spiritual power in state and wife in family–moderating the individual's self-assertative [sic] and possibly selfish tendency, by the affections and their *implicit* generality) the spiritual by its *explicit* generality regulates the temporal power–in whose hands as with the man the ultimate practical decision must rest.

These interest not absolute.

For every man has implicit in him, etc., and apart [...?] stands to develop each others characteristic. [Placing uncertain. See p. 48 above. Cf. Comte, *A General View of Positivism*, pp.249-52, 257-60, and Caird, *Social Philosophy and Religion of Comte*, pp.44-5.]

74 [Johann Wolfagang von Goethe, *Wilhelm Meisters Wanderjahre*, in his *Werke*, vol. 10 (Stuttgart: Cattaschan Buchhandlung, 1882), bk 2, chap. 1, pp.150-5. See further Edward Caird, 'Goethe and Philosophy', in his *Essays on Literature and Philosophy*, 2 vols. (Glasgow: Maclehose, 1892), vol.1, pp.98-9. Goethe refers to three types of reverence, the first and third of which Bell translates as 'ethnical' (= 'above us'), and 'Christian' (= 'below us'). Bell translates the second as 'Philosophic' reverence, however this is not love between equals as such, as it refers to the philosopher's need to draw down all that is above him and raise all that is beneath in order to understand the true significance of the whole. See Goethe, *Wilhelm Meister's Travels*, second edition, trans. and ed. E Bell (London: George Bell, 1885), pp.155-6. Cf. Caird, *Social Philosophy and Religion of Comte*, pp.26-7.]

75 [Juvenal, *Satires*, in *Juvenal and Persius*, trans. GG Ramsay (London: William Heinemann, 1950), 'Satire 14', pp. 268, 269, l.47.]

76 [MS reads: 'filial the affections'.]

77 [Prov. 9.10.]

78 [MS. del.: 'and conjugal'.]

79 For the moral element in the family, the mutual love–is love for actual present individuals, not for an abstraction–and in feudalism we see therefore *the family as rule* accepted that *this* family may be maintained. [Placing uncertain.]

80 [Goethe, *Wilhelm Meisters Wanderjahre*, bk 2, chap. 1, pp.154-5.]

81 [Plato, *Republic*, 460b-6d. See Caird's lectures earlier in this course (p. 52 below).]

82 [*Laws of the Twelve Tables*, Table 4 *passim* and Table 6, Law 5, in S.P. Scott, ed., *The Civil Law*, 17 vols. (New York: AMS, 1973), vol. 1, pp.64-65 and 68, respectively. See also pp. 78–9 above.]

83 Each bears *testament* whereas [?] only as idea of individual right extended. [Placing uncertain.]

84 [MS reads: 'follows'.]

85 [The first three books of the *Code Civil* (aka *Code Napoléon*) concern the rights and obligations of persons, while the remaining two concern property. The Code was first issued under the Consulate between 1799 and 1804.]

86 [A reference to the principle of *patria potestas* ['the power of the father'] in the Roman law, which granted the eldest father of a family rights over his children and other male descendants (by blood or adoption) of that family. See Maine,

Ancient Law, chap. 5. The first edition was published in 1861. See p. 63 below.]

[87] [*Code Napoleon; or, The French Civil Code. Literally Translated from the Original and Official Edition, Published at Paris, in 1804. By a Barrister of the Inner Temple*, trans. George Spence (London: William Benning, Law, 1827), bk 3, title 1, chap. 3, §1 (arts. 731-8) and §3 (art. 745). The first version of this section of the Civil Code was decreed on 19 April 1803.]

[88] [Welfare support in Germany was minimal at this time, with a combination of very low levels of state poor relief and the patchy coverage usually associated with charitable provision. In 1883 Bismark the Chancellor of the newly-united Germany introduced the first scheme for national health insurance. In Britain, what became known as the New Poor Law operated from 1865, following the passing of the Union Chargeability Act. It sought to overcome problems of perceived needless claims, expense and pauper migration by restructuring the institutions of poor relief and imposing somewhat harsher conditions on claimants.]

[89] [The *querala inofficiosi testamenti*, or plaint of the unduteous will, was an action that could be brought in Roman law against an instituted heir. In the late second century, Gaius sketched the change of the principles of this action through the Law of the Twelve Tables, the *Lex Furia* and *Lex Voconia*, to the *Lex Falcidia* and *Lex Fufia Caninia*. In the course of his brief history, Gaius observes: 'Then the *Lex Falcidia* was enacted, by which it was provided that no more than three-fourths of an estate could be bequeathed; and therefore it was necessary for the heir to have a fourth part of the same, and this is the law at the present time.' Gaius, 'The Four Commentaries of Gaius on the Institutes of the Civil Law', in SP Scott, (ed.), *The Civil Law*, vol. 1, 'Third Commentary', §227 (p.143); see *ibid.*, §§224-8 (pp.142-3).]

[90] ['And so the Provinces supply our kitchens; from the Provinces come the fish for the legacy-hunter Laenas to buy, and for Aurelia to send to market.' Juvenal, 'Satire 5', ll.96-7 (p.76).]

[91] ['The parent owes to society to endeavour to make the child a good and valuable member of it, and owes to the children to provide, so far as depends on him, education, and such appliances and means, as will enable them to start with a fair chance of achieving by their own exertions a successful life. To this every child has a claim; and I cannot admit, that as a child he has a claim to more...[Usually, a child has no legitimate grounds for complaint] if the remainder of the parent's fortune is devoted to public uses, or to the benefit of individuals on whom in the parent's opinion it is better bestowed.' John Stuart Mill, *Principles of Political Economy*, in his *Collected Works*, 33 vols., gen. eds. FE Priestly and JM Robson (University of Toronto Press, 1963-91), vol. 2, bk 2, chap. 2, §3 pp.221-2. First edition published in 1848, eighth edition published in 1909.]

[92] [Sophocles, *Antigone*, ll.451-9. Caird alluded to this passage in the first lecture (p. 42 above).]

[93] [See note 86 above.]

Lecture Three: Political and Social. Individual Right and Society. Division of Labour.

[94] [Title from Martin's lecture 94 (p. 213 below).]

Lecture Four: The Divisions of Labour in the Economic and Social Spheres.

95 [Martin's title (p. 213 below): '95. Division of Labour contd. Ancient classes. The agricultural state. Trades.']

96 [MS reads: 'relations'.]

97 [Homer, *The Odyssey*, trans. by AT Murray (London: William Heinemann, 1919), bk 9, ll.114-5, p. 310. Caird appears to be drawing on Maine here, with the latter quoting a slightly longer Greek passage from the *Odyssey* in his *Ancient Law*, and translating it as follows: 'They have neither assemblies for consultation nor *themistes*, but every one exercises jurisdiction over his wives and his children, and they pay no regard to one another.' Homer, quoted in Maine, *Ancient Law*, p.133.]

98 [For example, Jean-Jacques Rousseau, 'Discours sur les Sciences et les Arts' ['Discourse on the Sciences and the Arts'] (1750). David Hume, 'Of Commerce' and 'Of Refinement in the Arts', in his *Essays Moral, Political and Literary*, eds. TH Green and TH Grose, 2 vols. new edition (London: Longmans, Green, 1882), vol. 1, pp.287-99, 299-309, respectively. First published in 1752. Adam Smith, *An Inquiry into the Nature and Causes of the Wealth of Nations*, 2 vols., gen. eds. RH Campbell and AS Skinner, textual ed. WB Todd (Oxford University Press, 1976), vol. 2, pp.869-78, 886-7, 895-6. First edition published in 1776.]

99 [Cf. Edward Caird, *The Evolution of Theology in the Greek Philosophers*, 2 vols. (Glasgow: James MacLehose, 1904), lecture sixteen.]

100 [MS reads: 'apliance'.]

101 [Possibly a reference to lecture 64 and lectures 81-3 (see pp. 212–3 below).]

102 [Hegel, *Philosophy of Right*, §§5-26, especially §§17-20.]

103 [Possibly a reference to Hegel, *Philosophy of Right*, §195.]

104 ['Kircher' is a conjectural reading. May be a reference to Athanasius Kircher (1602-80), German Jesuit polymath.]

105 [The word 'expression' is deleted in the manuscript.]

106 ['To live in accordance with nature' was the basic principle which Stoicism took from Cynicism. Caird later credited its first expression to Cleanthes (331-232BC). Edward Caird, *Evolution of Theology in the Greek Philosophers*, 2 vols. (Glasgow: James Maclehose, 1904), vol. 2, pp.121-9.]

107 [Aristotle, *Politics*, 1334a11-b29, 1337b33-1338a12.]

108 [MS. reads: 'an'.]

109 [Cf. Edward Caird, 'The Roman Element in Civilisation', *North British Review*, vol. 44, no. 88 (June 1866), pp.261-9, reprinted in his *Collected Works*, 12 vols., ed. C Tyler (Bristol: Thoemmes, 1999), vol. 12.]

110 [MS reads: 'of the their'.]

111 Effect of luxury in the east still more destructive–from the *substantial* character of their ethics?–from want of element of mediation. 'Es ist den Asiaten nicht gegeben, Selbständigkeit, Freiheit, gediegene Kraft des Geistes mit Bildung, dem Interesse für mannigfaltige Beschäftigung und der Bekanntschaft mit den Bequemlichkeiten zu vereinigen; kriegerischer Mut besteht nur in Wildheit der Sitten, er ist nicht der ruhige Mut der Ordnung, und wenn der Geist sich mannigfaltigen Interessen eröffnet, so geht er sogleich zur Verweichlichung über, läßt sich sinken und macht

die Menschen zu Knechten einer schwachen Sinnlichkeit.' [G.W.F.] Hegel[, *Vorlesungen über die Philosophie der Geschichte*, ed. E Gans (Berlin: Duder und Humblot, 1840) [Hegel, *Werke*, Neunter Band], pp.230; cf. denunciation of the prophets. [Placing uncertain. Caird highlights this passage in his copy (now held in the Glasgow University Special Collection) and underlines the words, 'kriegerischer Mut besteht nur in Wildheit der Sitten, er ist nicht der ruhige Mut der Ordnung'. The complete passage translates as, 'It was not given to the Asiatics to unite self-dependence, freedom and substantial vigor of mind, with culture, *i.e.* an interest for diverse pursuits and an acquaintance with the conveniences of life. Military valor among them is consistent only with barbarity of manners. It is not the calm courage of order; and when their mind opens to a sympathy with various interests, it immediately passes into effeminacy; allows its energies to sink, and makes men the slaves of an enervated sensuality.' G.W.F. Hegel, *The Philosophy of History*, trans. by J. Sibree (New York: Dover, 1956), p.188.]

112   [Conjectural reading. Caird have in mind the French revolution of 1789 and the resultant civil unrest in Europe, including Britain.]

113   [The assumption that perfectly free markets produce an equitable distribution is an axiom of classical economics, finding its most famous expression in the writings of Adam Smith (see, for example, his *Wealth of Nations*, p.116.]

114   [Cf. Edward Caird, *The Present State of the Controversy between Individualism and Socialism. Being the inaugural address to the Civic Society of Glasgow* (Glasgow: James Maclehose, 1897); reprinted in Caird, *Collected Works*, vol. 11.]

115   ['*Natura enim non imperator, nisi parendo.*' Francis Bacon, 'Novum Organon', in his *Works*, 14 vols, eds. J Spedding, RL Ellis and DD Heath (London: Longman, 1857-74), vol. 1, bk 1, aphorism 129, p.222. In English: 'For Nature is only governed by obedience.' Francis Bacon, *Novum Organon; or A true guide to the interpretation of nature*, trans. GW Kitchin (Oxford University Press, 1855), p110. The first Latin edition was published in 1620.]

116   [MS reads: 'continually'.]

117   [MS. reads: 'make'.]

118   [John Stuart Mill, *Principles of Political Economy*, vol. 2, pp.122, 127, quoting Smith's famous pin-making example (Adam Smith, *Wealth of Nations*, pp.14-5)]

119   [Caird marked this paragraph for possible deletion.]

120   [Hegel, *Philosophy of Right*, §203.]

121   [Smith, *Wealth of Nations*, pp.363-4.]

122   [Mill, *Principles of Political Economy*, bk 1, chap. 1, §3; cf. *ibid.*, bk 1, chap. 7, §1.]

123   [An adaptation of 'Ad opera nil aliud potest homo, quam ut corpora naturalia admoveat et amoveat; reliqua Natura intus transigit.' Bacon, 'Novum Organon', in his *Works*, vol. 1, pt. 1, p.157, aphorism 4. In English: 'With a view to results man can do nothing but apply and remove natural bodies; everything else Nature performs within.' Bacon, *Novum Organon*, p.12.]

124   [MS del.: 'a fixed constitution can scarcely appear'.]

125   [Caird, 'Roman Element in Civilisation', pp.252-5.]

126   [Caird adds this subclause by caret.]

127   [MS. orig.: 'lawgivers'.]

[128] [Maine, *Ancient Law*, pp.14-6. Maine refers to the Hindu 'Laws of Manu', in addition to 'the Attic Code of Solon'.]

[129] [MS del.: 'its conservative instincts'.]

[130] [A reference to Switzerland's system of government through self-determining canons.]

[131] [According to a story told by Livy, in 458BC, at a time of military crisis, Cincinnatus was called from his farm and appointed dictator. He raised an army, defeated the enemy, celebrated his triumph, resigned his office, and returned to his farm. All this happened within fifteen days. See Livy Bk. 3, xxvi, 6–xxiv, 7, pp.89-99.]

[132] [Caird marked this paragraph for possible deletion.]

[133] [Cf. Mill, *Principles of Political Economy*, bk 1, chap. 9, §4 (pp.142-52).]

[134] [MS del.: 'petite culture.']

[135] [Cf. Mill, *Principles of Political Economy*, bk 1, chap. 9, §4 (pp.142-52); bk 2, chap. 6, §7 (pp.275-7); bk 2, chaps. 6 and 7 *passim*.]

[136] [MS reads: 'indiv'.]

[137] [MS reads: 'Capitalists'.]

[138] Comte distinguished earlier to later as warlike and traditional. [Placing uncertain. Cf. Edward Caird, *Social Philosophy and Religion of Comte*, pp.39-41.]

[139] ['Rome crushed and levelled all. The only powers left standing in the world were the majesty of the emperor and the imperial government, on the one hand, and on the other, the individuals of the subject population. The free life of the city, which had absorbed the energies of an earlier time, was gone. Men were, as we may say, isolated and *individualized*.' Caird, 'Roman Element in Civilisation', p.267.]

[140] At first this organization [...?] innovation.
1. Caste–Brahman, Kshatriyas, Venas or Viasyas ([...?] and [...?]), Sudras
2. Ranks in ancient and feudal [ages]
3. Classes–
[...?] of Individual liberty on one side and elite as other.
Individual liberty elite retained by custom -

[Placing uncertain.]

[141] [MS orig.: 'struggle'.]

[142] [Emmanuel Joseph, abbé Sieyès (1748-1836) became famous his pamphlet of January 1789 *Qu'est-ce que le Tiers état?* [*What is the Third Estate?*], in which he called for the abolition of all special privileges and the creation of a popularly-elected national assembly to govern France.]

[143] [MS orig.: 'England'.]

[144] [This word is very poorly formed. Caird may intend the word 'Thermidor'. The Thermidoreans dominated the French National Convention from 9 Thermidor 1794, when they issued their formal accusation against Robespierre's faction. They favoured the middle classes while retaining an intense dislike for the established church and the former nobility.]

[145] [MS reads: 'C.'.]

[146] [See pp. 98–108 below.]

[147] [Plato, *Republic*, 412a-415d.]

[148] 1. Social organization is in modern times separated from political i.e. the developed relation of class to each other for their relation to the whole.
2. It is an organism of organisms in three classes.
3. Principle [sic] freedoms as opposed to individual party and [....?] caste.
4. As freedom comes in more necessity of [....?] idea of state.

[Placing uncertain.]

Lecture Five: The Administration of Justice.

[149] [Martin's title: 'The development of civil law.   State interference.' (see p. 213 below)]

[150] [MS del.: 'conveying'. The first folio of this lecture is lost completely, and only this fragment from the top of the second folio survives.]

[151] [The 'Twelve Tables' were the result of an attempt to codify Roman law, and are usually dated to ca.450BC. The fragments that survive are chaotic. See p. 61 above.]

[152] [MS reads: 'have'.]

[153] [Livy, bk 3, §§32-4 recounts the collation of the Twelve Tables by the ten magistrates of Roman, who were otherwise known as 'the decimvir'.]

[154] [MS reads: 'it'.]

[155] [Jeremy Bentham (1748-1832), legal reformer and polymath. The need to replace common law with a codified system of simplified laws was a constant theme of his writings on the law. See Jeremy Bentham, *'Legislator of the world': Writings on codification, law and education*, eds. P Schofield and J Harris (Oxford: Clarendon, 1998). Maine, *Ancient Law*, pp.84-5.]

[156] [Final clause added by caret.]

[157] [The leading exponents of the historical school were Sir Henry James Sumner Maine (1822-88), William Edward Hearn (1826-88) and Henry Thomas Buckle (1821-62), each of whom Caird mentions in these lectures.]

[158] ['To hang the laws so high that no citizen could read them (as Dionysius the Tyrant did) is injustice of one and the same kind as to bury them in row upon row of learned tomes, collections of dissenting judgements and opinions, records of customs, &c., and in a dead language too, so that knowledge of the law of the land is accessible only to those who have made it their professional study.' Hegel, *Philosophy of Right*, §215R. Dionysius II (ca.395-43), tyrant of Syracuse 367-57 and 353-44.]

[159] [See p. 138 above. Caird, 'Roman Element in Civilisation', pp.269-71.]

[160] [Cf. Maine, *Ancient Law*, pp.83-5.]

[161] [Sir William Blackstone, *Commentaries on the Laws of England*, 4 vols. (Oxford: Clarendon, 1765), vol. 1, Introduction, §1, especially, pp.34-7. First edition published from 1765 to 1759. Blackstone (1723-80), legal writer, Vinerian Professor of English Law (1758-66) and Justice of Common Pleas. He was a particular target for the young Bentham (see his *Comments on the 'Commentaries'; and, A Fragment on Government*, eds. JH Burns and HLA Hart (London: Athlone, 1977).]

[162] [Possibly a quotation from Auguste Comte.]

[163] [MS reads: 'which by the'.]

[164] [MS orig.: 'individual'.]

[165] [MS reads: 'bases'.]

[166] [MS reads: 'are'.]

[167] Moral and Legal side becomes determined into civilization [...?] first. [Placing uncertain.]

[168] [The capitualaries are most associated with decrees issued by Charlemagne to his magnates, although as Guizot, Caird's source, notes, 'The *capitula*, "little chapters," equally applies to all the laws of the Frank kings.' François Pierre Guillaume Guizot, *History of Civilization from the Fall of the Roman Empire to the French Revolution*, trans. W Hazlitt, 3 vols. (London: Bogue, 1846), vol.2, p.212.]

[169] [MS reads: 'faiure'.]

[170] See Guizot, *Hist. Civ.* 2. 222. [Guizot, *History of Civilisation*, vol. 2, p.222, from which Caird quotes Hazlitt's translation of Cap. a. 802 §3.]

[171] [Cf. Hegel, *Philosophy of Right*, §96R.]

[172] ['Dearly beloved, avenge not yourselves, but rather give unto wrath: for it is written, Vengeance is mine; I will repay, said the Lord.' (Romans 12:19; see Deut. 32:35; Psal. 94:1; Heb. 10:30).]

[173] [Caird is following Hegel very closely here. (Cf. Hegel, *Philosophy of Right*, §§225-8.)]

[174] ['...the justice they receive remains in their eyes a doom pronounced *ab extra*.' Hegel, *Philosophy of Right*, §228R.]

[175] [MS reads: 'an'.]

[176] [MS del.: 'positive tendency'.]

Lecture Six: The Positive Role of the State, and the Social Problem.

[177] [Martin does not have a discrete heading for this lecture. It seems to fall under the 'State interference' aspect of his name for the previous lecture ('The development of civil law. State interference.').]

[178] [MS reads: 'society is'.]

[179] [Herbert Spencer (1820-1903), philosopher and social theorist, who sought to derive social and political prescriptions from Lamarkist evolutionary thought. His mix of a crude form of materialist psychology and the justification of minimal state action was one of the most influential targets for British Idealist social criticism. Caird attacks Spencerian and other forms of individualism in various of his published lectures. For example, see his *Ethical Philosophy. An introductory lecture* (Glasgow: James Maclehose, 1866); *The Moral Aspect of the Economical Problem. Presidential address to the Ethical Society* (London: Swan Sonnenschein, Lowrey, 1888); *The Present State of the Controversy between Individualism and Socialism* (Glasgow: James Maclehose, 1897); and several of his *Lay Sermons and Addresses. Delivered in the Hall of Balliol College, Oxford* (Glasgow: James Maclehose, 1907), for example, 'The Nation as an Ethical Ideal', pp.97-122.]

[180] [Mill, *Principles of Political Economy*, bk 5, chap. 11.]

[181] [Caird marks the paragraph up to this point for possible deletion.]

[182] [France experienced a period of significant centralisation and authoritarian rule following the election of Napoleon III (1808-70) in December 1848, and particularly after the coup that he staged in 1851 to seize total control of the state. The situation was easing somewhat as Caird wrote, following Napoleon's death in 1870 and the establishment of the Third Republic shortly thereafter. In Britain, private bills (as opposed to private members' bills) are introduced to Parliament by a local authority or public corporation that wishes to be granted a special power in the form of a by-law.]

[183] [Possibly a reference to the Magna Carta, the pledge which King John signed at Runnymede on 15 June 1215, in which the King formally acknowledged the authority of the feudal laws, thereby abrogating certain of his rights in favour of the barons and other feudal orders.]

[184] [MS. orig.: 'England'.]

[185] [Heinrich Karl vom Stein (1757-1831) and Karl August von Hardenberg (1750-1822), Prussian statesmen, consecutively responsible for wide-ranging reforms of the Prussian state between 1807 and 1822. Ultimately, they 'achieved the abolition of serfdom, administrative reorganization of the government and the army, and the partial emancipation of a capitalist economy from feudal and guild encumbrances.' (GWF Hegel, *Elements of the Philosophy of Right*, ed. AW Wood (Cambridge University Press, 1991), p.388n18. Cf. Edward Caird, *Hegel* (Edinburgh and London: William Blackwood, 1883), p.67.]

[186] [Caird seems to have the reforms of Stein and Hardenberg in mind.]

[187] [MS del.: 'people may delay hinder our'.]

[188] [At this point, trade fell under the remit of the Board of Trade. The Poor Law Board handled health matters until 1871 when it became the Local Government Board.]

[189] [MS reads: 'indep'.]

[190] [MS interpolation: 'At the same time there is for [?] as yet for [...?] such respect for knowledge in mind of public–for [....?...?] a [....?....?] things that are [...?].']

[191] [Compulsory state education at the primary level was introduced Saxony in 1769, Austria in 1794, in Prussia in 1798, in France in 1795, in Prussia from 1806, and Belgium in the 1840s. The principle held sway throughout most of the continent by the 1870s, and was usually provided without charge.]

[192] [In reality, there was considerable opposition to compulsory vaccination based on fears about contaminated vaccine and the poor practice of the (usually unqualified) men who carried out the process, particularly among the poor. See Francis Barrymore Smith, *The People's Health 1830-1910* (London: Weidenfeld and Nicolson, 1990), pp.162-70.]

[193] [Cf. Hegel's discussion of this aspect of feudalism (*Philosophy of History*, pp.369-71).]

[194] [MS del.: 'It is true that each corporation has its place and receives its jurisdiction over itself in virtue of a special office which it discharges to the community–but while the right of the class as such is maintained not only as against other classes but as against even the sovereign power–so long there can be no duty coextensive

with the right. Or the class stands in a special relation in subordination but as to the rest of its being and after discharge of this obligation is free.']

195 [Cf. Hegel's analysis of the Terror which followed the French Revolution (Hegel, *Phenomenology of Spirit*, trans. AV Miller (Oxford University Press, 1977), §§578-95.]

196 [Caird may have in mind Hegel's thoughts about 'World-Historical Individuals' (Hegel, *Philosophy of History*, pp.29-34).]

197 [MS reads: 'of'.]

198 [Caird may have in the signing of the Magna Carta in 1512, the first English Civil War of the early 1640s, the Glorious Revolution of 1688, or a number of other occasions.]

199 [MS. reads 'alledged'.]

200 Nor is there any supreme judge to determine when the orders have trespassed [?] on each others functions–or to determine the higher and lower when dispute arises as to the rightful [...?] of their material obligation. So that there is ever a recourse [?] to fear [?] in place of law. [Placing uncertain.]

201 [MS reads: 'is'.]

202 [Tacitus, *Germania*, §§21-22.]

203 The state recognises the family in its sphere–and as I said that the family only in its breaking up becomes legal–so the state watches or we may say [...?] the family to turn its moral into legal, if the moral unity of the family–the love that is the fulfilling of the law. Here its [...?] is of course the regard to the individual rights as such of the persons or particular persons included in the family.

In Athens, the individual had to give account of how he lived–so Bavaria–law of marriage especially. This we think concerns no one. But while the personal will should be respected yet the state that would require to maintain the pauper and would suffer for his vices has a right to protect itself against ire of the proletariat. If the state undertakes a responsibility toward individuals in general also a right [...?...?]. [Placing uncertain.]

204 [The lazzaroni were the idle poor of Naples, named after the Hospital of St Lazarus where they were based. The meaning was extended to include the poor of other European cities, including Paris. *The Times* carried a report from its Naples correspondent regarding the lazzaroni on 2 November 1876 (p.12a), which read in part: 'Their trades are equivocal, and, when without work, in desperation they pick a pocket, or snatch a gold chain (we have heard several cases lately of wrenching earrings out of the ears of women), steal fruit from an ambulatory ass, ... Throughout and without an elementary idea of honesty, when they find work, however, they work well and are ill-paid. With difficulty you will find a lazzaroni who can read or write, and very strange are his notions of morality.... [I]t is no exaggeration to say that in the '*bassi quartieri*,' the distinction between good and evil is unknown. Jealous in love, the lazzaroni slashes the face, not only of the woman who is unfaithful to her promise, with razor, but of her whose parents prohibit marriage;...But the most terrible feature in the lives of the lazzaroni is prostitution, which does not bear the same ill repute among this class that it does in other parts of the world....[I]t has been ascertained that among girls from 12 years of age and upwards, not one was a virgin...']

205 ['Difficulties' is deleted in the manuscripts, but replaced with an illegible alternative.]

[206] [MS reads: 'ac'.]

[207] [MS reads: 'dignity or class honor and'.]

[208] [Presumably, a reference to the French revolutions of 1789 and 1848 as well as the coup of 1851 which led to authoritarian rule of Napoleon III (see p. 144 above). By 'cooperative labour' Caird may well have in mind Comtean Positivism, Fourerism and the socialism of Saint-Simon.]

[209] [MS. reads: 'is'.]

[210] [Subsequent sheet(s) lost.]

Lecture Seven: What is a nation? Montesquieu and Rousseau. Natural and artificial theorists.

[211] [Martin's title (see p. 213 below). On this subject, see Caird, 'The Nation as an Ethical Ideal', in his *Lay Sermons and Addresses*, pp.97-122.]

Lecture Eight: The Church and the State.

[212] [Martin's list does not contain a corresponding title (pp. 213 below).]

[213] [MS reads: 'his'.]

[214] [Germany descended into civil war during the Thirty Years War (1618-48) with principalities fighting either for or against the Holy Roman Emperors, Ferdinand II and then Ferdinand III, both of whom came from the Habsburg dynasty.]

[215] [Thucydides, *History of the Peloponnesian War*. Cf. Green, 'The Nature of Historical Narrative in Thucydides and Herodotus', vol. 1 of this edition, pp. 78–81 above; and Bosanquet, 'Undergraduate Essays: 2. The Conception of Historical Causes in Thucydides Compared with that in Herodotus', vol. 1, pp. 193–4 above.]

[216] [Caird, 'The Roman Element in Civilisation', pp.270-1, where he cites James Bryce, *The Holy Roman Empire* (Oxford: Shrimpton, 1864).]

[217] [1 Cor. 6.1-7.]

[218] [By the 'scattered missionaries', no doubt Caird means primarily the Apostles and St. Paul.]

[219] [Constantine the Great (d.337), Emperor of Rome (306-37), converted to Christianity in 312. He took an active interest in church matters, for example giving judgements in the controversy of the Donatist schematics in 313, the Arian dispute of 325, and the banishment of St. Athanasius in 336. He christianised Roman law and indeed the empire, whose capital he moved in 324 to Byzantium, which he renamed Constantinople in 330.]

[220] [Charlemagne (ca.742-814), from 800 first Holy Roman Emperor, who centralised and rationalised the administrative structures of his expanding territory. The beginning of the Protestant Reformation is usually put at some time between the fourteenth and sixteenth centuries. See Caird's 'Reform and Reformation', pp. 1–39 above.]

[221] [MS reads: 'virtue'.]

[222] [The celibacy of the clergy has been a (controversial) principle in certain sections

of the church since the Council of Elvira in 306. The four cardinal virtues (or graces) are temperance (or chastity), prudence, fortitude and justice. They entered Christian thought from Plato and Aristotle. (The four theological virtues (or graces) are faith, hope and charity (or love).)]

223 ['... Render therefore unto Caesar the things which are Caesar's; and unto God the things that are God's.' (Matt. 22.21). Also, Luke 20.25.]

224 [See p. 32 above.]

225 [The 'divine right of kings' held that the authority of the sovereign derived from his (alleged) descent from the line of rulers instituted by God. The principle was articulated in *The Homily against Wilful Rebellion* (1569), although it can be found in earlier defences of royal authority. Henry VIII (1491-1547), King of England from 1509, parted with the Church of Rome in 1533, after which time he attacked its position in England, not least through the Dissolution of the Monasteries in 1536 and 1539. Frederick William ('the Great Elector') (1620-88), a staunch Calvinist, elector of Brandenburg-Prussia from 1640 to 1688. During that time, he transformed the Hohenzollern dominions from a weak province of the Holy Roman Empire into a centralized Protestant bulwark against the papacy.]

226 [MS reads: 'at'.]

227 [The Puritan Revolt refers to the period of English history from 1640 to 1660, a period characterised initially at least by an almost complete freedom of the press. Prince William I of Orange ('the Silent') (1553-84), who laid the ground for the Dutch republic (1588-1795) though died before it became a reality. He worked tirelessly to establish a principle of toleration of Catholicism in the Protestant territory although the dream finally eluded him in the summer of 1579. See Jonathan Israel, *The Dutch Republic. Its rise, greatness and fall* (Oxford: Clarendon, 1995), pp. 202-3.]

228 [MS reads: 'Rome'.]

229 [Socrates (c.470-399 BC), Greek philosopher, was executed in 399 BC for impiety and corrupting the youth of Athens. Anaxagoras (c.500-428 BC), Greek philosopher, was prosecuted for impiety probably in 437-6, after which he settled in Lampsacus. The Bacchanals (an adjunct of the worship of Dionysius) were suppressed in Rome in 186 BC.]

230 [The eagle was a symbol of Rome, and increasingly, Roman power, and appeared on the standards of the legions of the Roman army. Regarding the 'best emperors', in all likelihood Caird has in mind Marcus Aurelius (121-80), Stoic philosopher and Roman Emperor, who although renowned for his civilisation, learning and humanity in other regards, brutally suppressed Christianity in the Empire during his rule.]

231 [MS reads: 'A'.]

232 The Christian church is an organization to teach spiritual truth. The state is the organization in which it embodied so as far as it has been discovered and brought home to consciousness of nation. [Placing uncertain.]

233 [MS del.: 'as an organization they are themselves a mere...'.]

234 [MS reads: 'and'.]

235 [William Wordsworth, 'The Excursion', in his *Poetical Works: Cambridge edition*, revised by PD Sheats (Boston: Houghton Mifflin, 1982), p.449 (bk 4, ll.130-2).]

236 [Cf. Caird, 'Essay on Mysticism', especially pp. 167–8 below.]

237 [Dante Alighieri (1265-1321), Italian poet and philosopher, most famous for the epic *Divina Commedia.* Cf. Edward Caird, 'Dante in his Relation to the Theology and Ethics of the Middle Ages', in his *Essays on Literature and Philosophy,* 2 vols. (Glasgow: James Maclehose, 1892), vol. 1, pp.1-53. Blaise Pascal (1623-62), French mathematician and theologian. Cf. Edward Caird, *The Evolution of Religion,* 2 vols. (Glasgow: James Maclehose, 1893), vol. 1, pp.333-4, vol. 2, pp.32-4, 286, 292, 306.]

238 [St. Bernard (1090-1153), Abbot of Clairvaux, rejected the comfortable life of the noble French family into which he was born, and become a Cistercian monk of a particularly acetic cast. See Caird, 'Essay on Mysticism', pp. 167–9 below.]

239 [MS reads: 'C.'. MS del.: 'sense'.]

240 [MS reads: 'C.'.]

241 [One such person was John Stuart Mill in his 'Inaugural Address Delivered to the University of St. Andrews', in his *Collected Works,* 33 vols., (eds.) JM Robson et al (University of Toronto Press, 1981-91), vol. 21, pp.247-51. This address was given on 1 February 1867. Caird could have been present as he was then Professor of Moral Philosophy at the relatively-nearby University of Glasgow, although this is speculation.]

Lecture Nine: Montesquieu, Mixed Constitutions and the Balance of Powers.

242 [Martin's title: '98. Montesquieu contd. Moral bonds of Aristocracy. Monarchy. Despotism. Mixed governments. United States. Value of Montesquieu's book.' (see p. 213 below).]

243 [MS reads: 'which'.]

244 ['The state in its constitution must permeate all relationships within the state. Napoleon, for instance, wished to give the Spaniards a constitution *a priori,* but the project turned out badly enough. A constitution is not just something manufactured; it is the work of centuries, it is the Idea, the consciousness of rationality so far as that consciousness is developed in a particular nation. No constitution, therefore, is just the creation of its subjects. What Napoleon gave to the Spaniards was more rational than what they had before, and yet they recoiled from it as from something alien, because they were not yet educated up to its level.' Hegel, *Philosophy of Right,* §274A. Knox adds, 'When he expelled the Bourbons from Spain and put Joseph Bonaparte on the throne under the Constitution of Bayonne in 1808. With the breakdown of the Napoleonic régime in 1812-13, the Bourbons were restored together with the constitution. A liberal document, the Constitution of Cadiz, was drawn up in 1812, but it remained a dead letter.' (*Ibid.,* p.286n).]

245 [MS orig.: 'vital'.]

246 [Under the terms of the Magna Charta (1215), King John acknowledged the authority of the customary rights of Englishmen, and especially of the baronial families.]

247 [MS orig.: 'as an existence'.]

248 [Solon (fl. ca.600-560BC), poet and archon at Athens, replaced the law-code of Draco with a new constitution for Athens in 594. Pisistratus (or Psistratus) (d. ca.528BC) retained Solon's reforms when tyrant of Athens in 560-556 and 546-528.]

[249] [MS reads: 'notice that is that'.]

[250] [The Second French Republic saw new constitutions following the revolution of 1848, the coup of 1851. The Third Republic was established following the overthrow of Napoleon III in September 1870. This unstable regime lacked a formal constitution, although it was underlain by certain enabling laws that were passed in 1875. Spain, Germany, Portugal and many other European countries also changed their constitutions quite significantly throughout this period.]

[251] [MS reads: 'distributive'.]

[252] [MS del.: '1. Montesquieu's idea of the distribution of power - the *balance of powers* in the state, 2.'.]

[253] [MS del.: 'in the organs of power.']

[254] [Caird's own translation, of Charles-Louis de Secondat, Baron de Montesquieu, *De l'esprit des lois*, livre 11, chaptre 6 ('De la Constitution D'Angleterre'), in Montesquieu, *Oeuvres Complètes*, 7 tomes, ed. Édouard Laboulaye, (Paris: Garnier Frères, 1875-1877), tome 4 [1877], pp.7-23. Montesquieu, *The Spirit of the Laws*, eds. Anne Cohler, Basia Miller and Harold Stone (Cambridge University Press, 1989), pt. 2, bk 11, chap. 6, p.157.]

[255] [MS. alt. 'In the East'.]

[256] [MS insert: 'Venice'.]

[257] [Montesquieu, *Spirit of the Laws*, pt 2, bk 11, chap. 6, p.157.]

[258] [MS orig.: 'only prescribe'.]

[259] [MS reads: 'in'.]

[260] [Montesquieu, *Spirit of the Laws*, pt. 2, bk 11, chap. 6, pp.158-9.]

[261] [Montesquieu, *Spirit of the Laws*, pt. 2, bk 11, chap. 11, pp.169-70.]

[262] [MS. reads 'that so'.]

[263] [Montesquieu, *Spirit of the Laws*, pt 1, bk 3.]

[264] [Aristotle, *Politics*, 1281a39-1283a22.]

[265] [Aristotle, *Politics*, 1283a23-1284b34.

[266] [Caird, 'The Roman Element in Civilisation', *passim*.]

[267] [Montesquieu, *Spirit of the Laws*, pt 1, bk 3, chap. 3.]

[268] [Montesquieu, *Spirit of the Laws*, pt 1, bk 8, chap. 16, p.124.]

[269] [Montesquieu, *Spirit of the Laws*, pt 1, bk 5, chap. 8, p.52.]

[270] [Conjectural, MS reads: 'sts'.]

[271] [What follows is a selective précis of Montesquieu, *Spirit of the Laws*, pt 1, bk 3, chaps. 5-7; *ibid.*, pt 2, bk 11, chaps. 7 and 8.]

[272] [MS reads: 'an'.]

[273] [The spelling is 'honour' not 'honor', for once.]

[274] [MS reads: 'Ay & Dy'.]

[275] 'If the d[ifference]s have abstract and independent existence, it is obvious that two independences cannot constitute a Unity–but must produce combat whereby either the whole is broken up, or the unity is restored by force. So in the French

Revolution the legislative at one time swallowed up the called Executive–at another the Executive swallowed up the legislative.' Hegel p.347 [Caird's translation from Hegel, *Philosophy of Right*, §274A, in GWF Hegel, *Werke*, 19 vols., 3 Aufl. (Berlin: Duncker und Humblot, 1854), vol. 8, p.347. Placing of note uncertain.]

276 [MS reads: 'Ay & My'.]

277 [Montesquieu, *Spirit of the Laws*, pt 2, bk 11, chap. 6.]

278 1. Necessity of patriotism expressing itself in constitution
2. Constitution–result of a struggle after [?] understood in [?] another's [?] country
3. *Montesquieu's analysis*
    Three powers
Objections
4. [...?] each by itself, and then [...?] and [?] [...?] out highest
5. Real fact is that 1. all features [?] of life not [?] be developed–2 get [...?] to common whole. [Placing uncertain.]

279 [Plato, *Crito*, 50a-54e.]

280 [MS reads: 'by'.]

Lecture Ten: The Structure of the Legislature.

281 [This lecture corresponds with the final parts of Martin's title for lecture 98: 'Montesquieu. Moral bonds of Aristocracy. Monarchy. Despotism. Mixed governments. United States. Value of Montesquieu's book.' (p. 213 below.) See the previous lecture for the first parts of Martin's title. If Martin's list applies, the lecture course moved on to consider the philosophy of religion.]

282 [MS reads: 'is'.]

283 [Hegel, *Philosophy of Right*, §298A. Hegel is discussing Germany in particular. Caird omits silently some clauses from Hegel's original text.]

284 [A reference to the English Civil Wars that erupted sporadically between 1642 and 1660, and the Glorious Revolution of 1688.]

285 [MS del.: 'and law'.]

286 [Exod. 20.]

287 [For 'private bills', see p. 144 above.]

288 [Plato, *Republic*, 374a-376c.]

289 [MS reads: 'whi'.]

290 [MS reads: 'V.'.]

291 [MS reads: 'V.'.]

292 [MS del.: 'as the French Revolution'.]

293 [Louis XVI (1754-93), king of France from 1774, signed the Tennis Court Oath on 20 June 1789, thereby transforming the Estates General into the National Constituent Assembly. The latter's primary task was to draw up and implement a new constitution for France, which it did by 1 October 1791. Many of its reforms arose as pragmatic responses to unpredicted events and problems, and there implications far outstripped the goals originally envisaged.]

294 [See Caird, 'Reform and Reformation', pp. 1–39 *passim* above.]

295 [MS del.: 'existing for the support of'.]

296 [MS del.: 'private'.]

297 [MS reads: 'aristocracies'.]

298 [Cf. Edward Caird, 'Reform and Reformation', pp. 29–33 above.]

299 [See pp. 91, 144 above for discussions of the Prussian reforms instigated by Stein and Hardenberg.]

300 [MS del.: 'civilisation justice laws'.]

301 [MS reads: 'has'.]

302 ['Of all topics relating to the theory of representative government, none have been the subject of more discussion, especially on the Continent, than what is known as the question of the Two Chambers.' Mill, 'Considerations on Representative Government', in his *Collected Works of John Stuart Mill*, 33 vols., gen. eds. FE Priestly and JM Robson (University of Toronto Press, 1963-91), vol. 19, p.511.]

303 [Mill has 'command', not 'find'.]

304 [Mill includes 'in open field' here.]

305 [Mill replaced 'the crowd rather than opposed to it' with this sub-clause from the second edition of *Considerations* onwards (both the first and second editions were published in 1861), so Caird cannot be using the first edition.]

306 [Mill has 'antagonist', not 'antagonistic'.]

307 [Mill includes 'in and'.]

308 [John Stuart Mill, *Considerations on Representative Government*, second edition (London: Parker, 1861), pp.240-1; reprinted in his *Collected Works*, vol. 19, pp.514-5. Caird's punctuation has been retained.]

309 [Cf. the preceding lecture in this series.]

310 [MS reads: 'only in with'.]

311 [Mill added ', in any great affairs' to the third edition (1865). When combined with note 305 above, this implies that Caird was using the second edition.]

312 [Mill has 'as such even'.]

313 [Mill, *Considerations on Representative Government*, pp.239-40; reprinted in his *Collected Works*, vol. 19, p.514. Caird's punctuation has been retained.]

314 [MS reads: 'then'.]

315 [Wellington, Arthur Wellesley, duke of (1769-1852), soldier, conservative statesman and prime minister.]

316 [MS del.: 'Let us look for a moment at the different constitutions of some of the foremost civilized lands in the light of what has been said.']

317 [MS del.: 'and even where these conditions are present it is subject to important limitations'.]

318 [MS reads: 'have'.]

319 [MS reads: 'P.'.]

320 [Plato, *Republic*, 518b-521b.]

321 [Armand Jean du Plessis, Cardinal and Duc de Richlieu (1582-1642), French

statesman, Minister of State (1624) and Louis XIV's Chief Minister (1624-42) although he wielded real independent power through the Bourbon state, renowned for his intrigues and brutal suppression of the Huguenots, among others. Jean-Baptiste Colbert (1619-83) was Louis XIV's *contrôleur général* (finance minister), who as a merchantilist emphasised international trade while effectively neglecting domestic growth.]

322 [MS read: 'France or that'.]

323 [For the fortunes of the various constitutional settlements of France in the nineteenth century, see p. 149 above. Frederick-William IV, king of Prussia (1840-61), introduced a new limited, constitution in November 1848 which created a bicameral diet modelled on the British House of Lords. This constitution lasted until 1918.]

324 [Alexis Charles Henri Clérel de Tocqueville (1805-59), French historian, political sociologist and politician. Born into the petit noblesse, de Tocqueville made his name from his monumental *Democracy in America* (1835).]

325 [Louis-Phillipe (1773-1850), King of France (1830-48).]

326 [This arrangement continued until 1913, when direct elections for the Senate were introduced.]

327 [Unfortunately, this reference to the people supporting the indirectly-elected Senate over the directly-elected House of Representatives is rather too vague to tie down.]

[Lecture on Political Economy.]
[ca.1887–8]

Let us in this concluding lecture take a glance over the field we have traversed and the results we have arrived at.

We started with the idea of man as a being with many needs and desires for the satisfaction of all which he is dependent on nature. On the other hand nature does not spontaneously offer to man this satisfaction. In rare cases she may supply the barest necessities of life–but all beyond these must be won from her by labour. Men have indeed at all times dreamed of a Solomonian age[1] in which nature offered no resistance to man's wishes, in which without labour men lived on her spontaneous bounty and we might readily imagine that if such a state were possible to all men, the result would be a higher civilization. We might imagine that in such a[2] state, men relieved from the hard struggle for existence to which so many even at this advanced age of the world are sacrificed, would have more time and opportunity for those higher enjoyments and pursuits in which the worth of human life consists. But the few instances in which we have a partial realization of this paradisical state should undeceive us. The savage of the south sea islands into whose mouth the Banana[-tree] almost drops its breadfruit is a slave and a cannibal–while those European nations to whom nature has been most grudging and sparing in her gifts are the leaders of the civilization of the world. It is in the struggle for the first necessaries of life that men and nations acquire that momentum, that energy of movement, that carries them forward to higher wants and satis-factions. Struggling with the elements for daily bread, man awakes to a hunger that bread alone cannot satisfy,–and this new hunger again stirs him to new efforts to subdue the earth to its satisfaction. And thus the very difficulty of the first struggle with nature brings into play energies that more completely subject it to man's ever extending desires.

As therefore the earth is not in its first state suited to the satis-faction of man's desires, a process is necessary whereby it may be so subjected and it is with this process that Political Economy has to do. And as these desires grow–as man progresses and new

153

wishes and processes are developed in him, there is an economy corresponding to every stage of human progress. In a moral and intellectual as well as in a merely physical point of view man's elevation is dependent on or is connected with the way in which he husbands his powers and expands them in subjecting nature to his will. His power over nature is the measure as it is at once cause and effect, of his power over himself. It is scarcely possible therefore to consider the economy of man's life without reference [to] the moral and intellectual characteristics of the particular stage of civilization which his ever changing spirit has attained–as on the other hand it is scarcely possible rightly to estimate the civilization of a nation, the social and political relations of its members to each other and to other nations–the degree of its intellectual culture–or its prevailing standard of morals, without reference to the character of the economical organization which is the necessary concomitant of all this. For it is knowledge of nature that gives power over her, and on the other hand it is by the successful struggle with nature that the desire of knowledge is awakened and the means of gratifying it are obtained. Again political economists have generally presupposed the freedom of the individual and the acknowledgement of absolute rights of persons and property as residing [?] in him. And they have considered it often solely their business to reason out and the organization of society on the presupposition of such rights. But here again we must acknowledge that such freedom and such rights are not acknowledged prior to the economical development of society–but are partly its consequence. The growth of freedom and of the sense of freedom and right in man goes parallel with the increase of his power over nature. The ancient civilizations were built upon a basis of slavery because a high culture was then only possible to the few and at the expense of the many, for in the absence of machinery–of knowledge of natural process, of extended intercourse of nations, it was only at this sacrifice that the necessary leisure of a culture could be obtained even for the few. The medieval civilizations again rested on a basis of serfdom–though already in the organization of the church the higher principle of freedom was partially recognized–since in the church peasant and noble were equal–and the aristocratic order so far as it prevailed was independent of birth. And it was a consequence or a concomitant of this [....?] that the church led the way in all the higher as well as in all the lower elements of civilization–in tilling the earth as well as in [...?] the natives. Civilization economical as well as intellectual radiated from and concentrated itself in the monasteries.[3] With the renaissance and the reformation new paths were opened at once to thought and to industry.[4] The labourers at least in towns and then in the country gained a more independent position. The commercial enterprize of England and of the Netherlands at once expressed and confirmed the principles of freedom of which the Reformation had made them the representatives.[5] That overthrow of feudalism again which culminated in the assertion of the rights of man in the French revolution[6] was the counterpart and concomitant of the great development of modern industry and commerce which bound the nation together by new ties, opened the possibility of wealth or at least of comfort to the many as well as to the few and rendered that close warlike organization of society necessary in the middle ages for safety an encumbrance. It was by no mere chance that Rousseau and Adam Smith came together, for that same strong sense of individual right [which] led the former to explain the state as a social contract, was only possible at a time when free contract was the principle of the economical organization of society–as on the other hand it is presupposed in that organization.[7] Political Economy in fact arose as a science out of the attempt to analyze the commercial relations of modern times into their simplest elements. And this should ever be remember[ed] else we shall be in danger of laying down as universal principles what really has only been true even partially within the last century. Political Economy has been too much divorced from history and to forget history in dealing with the life of a progressive and changing being like man almost necessarily leads us to suppose the universality of maxims and principles which have only value for the present time, and to introduce an artificial [...?] of theory at the sacrifice of truth. It leads us besides to forget the essential relation between the material and the spiritual wellbeing of man and therefore ultimately to produce an insufficient theory [of] both. For though it is convenient in study to place barriers between the sciences, yet it is not good to respect such barriers too much. And this is specially true in the present case–for the complete theory of the economical relations of men could only be attained together with the complete theory of their social and moral relations. The two are separable only by an ideal boundary–but there is no real division between them–subjugation of nature and himself would only be completed by man at one and the same moment.

These considerations may enable us to determine the place of political Economy relatively to the other sciences. It stands on the same ground with moral or political philosophy, it deals with the same subject: man. It presupposes the natural sciences which deal with the objects in which man finds the satisfaction of his desires and even with the physical nature of man himself. It presupposes also psychology, or that science which deals with the nature of man in itself. It contemplates like Ethics the relations into which man's desires, tendencies and powers bring him toward the outward world and toward other men. But while moral and political philosophy regard these relations from within, political economy looks at them from without. While moral and political philosophy consider the outward relations as relative to the nature of man which they manifest, in relation to the higher ends of moral and spiritual life–of the highest education of the human race–attained by them, Political Economy regards them from the external or material side as one might call it. It asks not what are the highest ends of human life or forms of human society–but simply taking these ends as given, by what material means may they be best attained. Given nature–the outward world and what it contains–and given the desires and wishes of man–how may man best husband and direct his efforts so as best and most easily to utilize the former with a view to gratify the latter? That is the problem of political Economy: Seeing the conquest of nature is necessary for the gratification of man's desires–what is the shortest way to the conquest of nature?–or, in other words, how with the least possible labour to obtain the greatest result in commodities and in consum[p]tion by the least possible expense of such commodities or goods to secure the greatest furtherance to human ends.

The term *political* Economy already points to the first necessity towards such husbandry, viz. union: and hence in Adam Smith's great work as in almost all scientific treatises on Economy the principle of division and combination of labour takes the first place.[8] It is by the combination of men and nations with each other, each supplying for the general weal the resources in themselves or in natural objects which circumstances have placed in their command, that the greatest enjoyment is secured with the least trouble–the greatest victory over nature with the easiest struggle–'The Camuoli [?] economy of 10 millions of men working for each other produces 10,000 times as many goods as if there were ten million separate economies side-by-side acting independently'[9]–without combination these were scarcely anything that could be called an Economy at all. And the development of the Economy of the world is more than any other circumstance conditioned by the closeness of the cooperation of all men and nations together. From division of labour by which peasant labour is made to cooperate together, we past [sic] next [?] to the subject of capital or the cooperation of past labour with present. And we considered how the circulating capital which constantly perishes in one application and is reproduced, is related to the fixed capital which it maintains as a possibility of many acts of production. Lastly under this head we considered what are the limits to human production–and we found them to consist on the one hand in the relative limitations of the field of employment–which in advanced nations tends, unless neutralized by other influences–to make capital and labour continually unproductive and on the other hand in the state of practical science at any given time–in so far as by this is determined the limit to which profitable applications of capital and labour on a given field can be extended. The continual increase of man's wealth is only possible therefore on the one hand as he occupies a wider and wider field till the whole earth is so appropriated–and as he continually advances in that knowledge of the powers of nature and the modes of turning them to account.

After thus discussing production so far as is possible apart from distribution: that is considering only the best modes in which human force may be disposed so as to overcome the resistance of nature–we go on to ask in what way this disposition or organization of human effort is to be secured. Is it by leaving each individual to seek himself and his own interests in the confidence that these jarring interests will neutralize each other so far as they are antagonistic–that 'out of the eater will come forth meat'[10]–and that the universal well-being will be the result of the selfish struggle–or are we to seek refuge from individual selfishness in a strong central authority which acts in the interests of all?

There is as we saw sometimes a tendency in Political Economy to separate too absolutely between the self-seeking of individual interest which actuates the trader and that devotion to the general good which should actuate the head of a family in relation to its members, the statesman in regard to the nation he serves, or the philanthropist in regard to man in general. But in the first place the notion of self-interest is a general name under which many motives

are included, reaching from the mere struggle for the means of gratifying appetites up almost to the patriotism of the hero whose self
is identified with his country. And in the next place while political
economy demonstrates that the ultimate good of the individual,
even taking it in the sense of mere material wealth, can only be
secured by means which also tend to the general good, the freedom
of the individual to seek himself cannot produce good results except
in so far as he recognizes this identity of general and particular
interests. And as this identity only holds in regard to ultimate and
not to individual interests, as it often is far from holding good in
regard to the individual,–as the individual on the contrary must
often find opportunities for a success which is gained at the expense
of others–so we find that the principles of sound economy are
constantly endangered by selfishness and will not be observed
probably to their full extent by any one who is not actuated by
higher than economic motives. What sound economy teaches–that
no one can benefit himself who does not benefit others–is the
converse of a proposition that holds good of all efforts for the
general good that no one can benefit others without benefiting
himself. The casual charity that brings back no blessing to the giver
brings no blessing to the receiver just as an unscrupulous desire of
wealth that never recognizes any limit in the interest of others ends
by cheating itself. If therefore we recognize a distinction between
the action that is prompted by self-love and that which is prompted
by regard to the general good–we must at the same time remember
that in the long run they are identical and that Political Economy
proves that the self-love that leads to the highest economic result
is one that recognizes the identity of self-interest and general interest
just as the highest Ethics is a proof that in order to save our lives
we must lose them.[11]

The question for political economy then is not as some have
represented it simply this–given the selfish instinct, what results
would it lead to?–but simply this –whether the highest result in
production is to be obtained by leaving men in absolute freedom
and independence of each other, allowing each of them absolute
rights of property in his own labour and its results, and allowing
them freely to exchange the products of that labour,–or whether
such result will be best obtained by their submitting their individual
wills to some strong compulsive organization of the state or some
other authority which shall direct their energies to the appropriate
objects.

Now this is a question which is susceptible of being answered from two different points of view: historical and scientific. On the one hand we may regard the past history of mankind–and we may consider how the realization of the conceptions of individual right and liberty has been rendered possible by the progress of civilization. The first necessity of men in their struggle with nature is unity, and while social morality is yet undeveloped, unity can only [be] attained[12] by the sacrifice of liberty. The circumstances of a warlike time in which a stranger is an enemy, or even of a time in which as yet–as in ancient nations–no higher principle of unity than the municipal state [exists], exclude the free relations of contract on which a developed industrial economy depends because they exclude that sense of mutual obligation which is necessary to confidence that free trade–or the free action of competition may produce good results: it is necessary that social morality and the civilization of nations have attained at least a certain degree of advance–else it will lead only to war of all against all only less deadly than that of savage life, and an oppression of the weak by the strong under the form of law.[13] No one who has any historical sense now refuses to admit that feudal rights and the strict organization of the guilds may for their day have been as necessary and useful as free trade is for ours, and that the attempt to introduce free trade at that time might have had fatal consequences where society was not yet ripe for it. In the growth of nations as of individuals, the process of emancipation must keep pace with the progress of intelligence and morality, if freedom is not to mean anarchy.

In this point of view then free trade and individual competition has been constantly gaining a larger field for itself as society has advanced–and has invaded one after another [of the] many spheres of human existence which had before been reserved to the state, to the family or the corporations. Now there are as we have seen at least, no important spheres of existence in which the restrictions on individual competition remain except to some small extent the land.[14] In this point of view the principle of freedom seems to have its victory confirmed by the whole tendency of history during the last two centuries. We may however look at the question also from a scientific point of view and ask whether there are not certain departments of the economy of nations which not merely temporarily but permanently and by their nature are withdrawn from the salutary influences of competition–where in fact the great problem of economy–how with the least expense to produce most–and how to use the given production most effectively and economically for the satisfaction of human purposes–cannot be so well solved by the individual: and where therefore[15] sound economy dictates that the state or some other power representative of general and not of special interest should come in. This is perhaps one of the greatest problems of political Economy and one that is as yet far from being satisfactorily solved. There are allowed by all to be certain functions–the protection of person and property at the least–which must be abandoned to the state. There are others which are of the nature of monopolies from the immense scale on which they must be done and because for this or [any] other reason it is impossible that competition should produce its full result, and in regard to these again it is generally allowed that the state should either take them into its own hands or at least closely watch and regulate the proceedings of those who do. But how far the state should go in its interference in regard to such enterprizes as railways–or in regard to the maintenance of the poor or in regard to education–how far it should act and how far it should merely regulate the actions of others–and how far again such regulation should go–are questions which can only be settled by slow experiment. Political Economy has to consider such questions only from one point of view–and to use only one test in deciding them, viz. Can the greatest result be obtained by least expense in the way of competition or of state action?–And of course there are other tests and considerations that have to be taken into account–though it is probable that we should find that the limits of state action as determined by economical and by moral considerations are ultimately the same.

In the lectures just ended I have confined myself entirely to those enterprizes in which the principle of free competition has the first place. The consideration of the economical objects and limits of state action I must for the present omit. I hope to write something about it before another year.[16] And if so I will make it the subject of the concluding lectures of another course at which I will be glad to see any of this class. In the foregoing lectures however we considered first those individual rights of property and person presupposed in free competition and exchange–then we went on to consider the nature of Exchange Value and its relation to what is called Value in use. We examined the laws that determine Exchange Value of commodities [in the] market and use [?] permanently. We considered how the value as determined by free exchange is distributed between all the various persons who contribute to production, the proprietor of natural objects, the Capitalists and the Labourer–and in connexion with the last two of these we considered some of the difficulties that arise from the present modes of association between capital and labour and the practical attempts to solve these difficulties. Lastly we consider[ed] in some detail the nature of the measure of value and medium of exchange–money. The various ways in which its use is economized by our present organization of credit–by the banking system–and weighed the validity of the arguments by which the present restrictions on notes have been maintained.

A French writer said that Political Economy was a science 'guided by[17] facts' and Senior in opposition to him maintained that it merely involved the correct and accurate reasoning out of a few abstract principles.[18] But if the view above given be correct, and if economical science be not limited to the mere deductions from a selfish instinct, but the laws of the process by which nature is subjected to human purposes, then the French view is true. Economical science is of equal extent with moral science–it is in fact its complement and can only partially be separated from it. And as man is a progressive being–so all the sciences that analyze his life must be progressive–must be constantly accumulating new facts and evolving new principles. If this be kept [in] view, Political Economy will be delivered from one of its greatest dangers, a danger which popular Political Economy has seldom escaped–the mistaking of tendencies for facts. How often have we heard deductions drawn from, e.g., the law of supply and demand which are as rational as it would be to argue from the law of gravitation that every stone must fall to the ground, forgetting that it may be stopped on its way thither. Abstract laws express tendencies and therefore we must ever remember that as we can apply them to the concrete, we need to be sure that we have considered all the laws that have a bearing on the case–and this can only be done by the most careful analysis of all the facts of the case. Political Economy is it seems to me even yet in its infancy. It, like the social life it attempts to analyze, is developing so rapidly, discovering so many new problems every day, and as yet so many of these problems want an exact solution, that it will probably require the efforts of many minds or generations of minds ere it finds its completed form. The accurate and far reaching collections of statistics however of all kinds that are accumulating on all branches of human industry are materials which yet wait for another Adam Smith or even a greater mind to arrange them.[19]

I have finally to thank you for the attention with which you have listened to these lectures which I am conscious have all the imperfections of a first attempt to lecture on this difficult subject. Examinations on Tuesday and Thursday next week–after which farewell.

---

1   [MS del.: 'paradisical state'. King Solomon ruled over a vast territory, stretching from the Euphrates to the Nile. His age was one of universal peace and immense affluence (1 Kings 1.10–11.43, 2 Chron. 1–9).]

2   [MS del.: 'paradisical'.]

3   [Christian monasticism spread from Egypt to the West in the fourth century. Its guiding principles were poverty, chastity and obedience, and monasteries soon became centres for the preservation and exploration of knowledge. The Benedictine form held sway from the eighth to the twelfth centuries, although the types of monasticism proliferated from the twelfth to the sixteenth centuries. Monasticism declined as the Reformation grew in power.]

4   [The Renaissance was the period of revival of classical forms of art and literature in fourteenth to sixteenth century Europe. The Reformation began in the sixteenth centuries under the influence of Martin Luther. It was a reaction against the corruption of the mediaeval church and had as its most significant result the rise of Protestantism in Europe. Cf. Edward Caird, 'Reform and Reformation', pp. 1–39 above.]

5   [Protestantism's emphasis on the individual's personal relationship with God through conscience and reflection on Scripture was seen by many as linked to the rise of capitalism, especially among the northern Germanic peoples.]

6   [The French Constituent Assembly passed the 'Le Déclaration des Droits de L'Homme et du Citoyen' ('The Declaration of the Rights of Man and the Citizen') on 26 August 1789. It also formed the preamble to the 1791 French constitution.]

7   [Jean-Jacques Rousseau (1712–1778), Genevan political philosopher, author of *Du Contrat Social* (first published in 1762). Adam Smith (1723–1790), Scottish political economist and philosopher, author of *An Inquiry into the Nature and Causes of the Wealth of Nations*, eds. R.H. Campbell, A.S. Skinner and W.B. Todd, 2 vols. (Oxford: Clarendon, 1979) (hereafter, WN) (first published in 1776).]

8   [The first three chapters of WN, on the division and combination of labour, heavily inform the remainder of that work.]

9   [This passage does not appear in Smith's *Wealth of Nations*.]

10 ['And he [Samson] said unto them, Out of the eater came forth meat, and out of the strong came forth sweetness. And they could not in three days expound the riddle.' (Judges 14:14).]

11 [The imperative to 'die' as a selfish being in order 'to live' on earth as spiritual one is a recurring theme in EC's writings: see, for example, 'Salvation Here and Hereafter' in his *Lay Sermons and Addresses* (Glasgow: James Maclehose, 1907), pp.45–72.]

[12] [MS del.: 'at the expense of slavery or'.]

[13] [A revealing revision of Hobbes' famous characterisation of life *without* effectively enforced law. Thomas Hobbes, *Leviathan*, chap. 13.]

[14] [For a broadly contemporaneous liberal examination of 'the Land Question', see Herbert Samuel, *Liberalism. An attempt to state the principles and proposals of contemporary Liberalism in England*. (London: Grant Richard, 1902), chap. 5. Cf. Green, LLFC.]

[15] [MS del.: 'the principles of supply and demand can not produce the highest result'.]

[16] [Probably Edward Caird, *The Moral Aspect of the Economical Problem. Presidential address to the Ethical Society* (London: Swan Sonnenschein, 1888). He revisited this theme in his *The Present State of the Controversy Between Individualism and Socialism. Being an inaugural address to the Civic Society of Glasgow* (Glasgow: Maclehose, 1897). Both pamphlets are reprinted in Colin Tyler (ed.) *Collected Works of Edward Caird*, 12 vols. (Bristol: Thoemmes, 1999), vol. 11.]

[17] [MS reads: 'of'.]

[18] [The 'French writer' may well be Jean-Baptiste Say (1767–1832), French economist. See, for example, the 'Discours Préliminaire' to his *Traité D'Économie Politique: ou, simple exposition de la manière dont se forment, se distribuent, et se consomment les richesses*, 2 tom., 3rd edition (Paris: Deterville, 1817), tom. 1, pp.vii–lxxix. First edition published in 1803 Nassau William Senior (1790–1864), English economist and essayist, defended something like the position Caird attributes to him throughout his career. He claims that 'the general facts on which the Science of Political Economy rests, are comprised in a few general Propositions,' although contra Caird he continues, that these are 'the result of observation *or* consciousness.' (emphasis added) These four 'elementary propositions' are: 'the general desire for wealth'; that population 'is limited only by moral or physical evil' and fear of a lack of one's particular customary 'articles of wealth'; the indefinite possibility of the increase of labour productivity through technological innovation; and the law of diminishing returns in agriculture (Nassau W Senior, *Outline of the Science of Political Economy* (London: George Allen and Unwin, 1938), p.26, see *ibid.*, pp.26–56). First edition published in 1836.]

[19] [Cf. Caird, *The Present State of the Controversy between Individualism and Socialism*, p.30.]

Essay on Mysticism
[ca. 1890s?]

'Care is taken', says a wise German proverb, 'that the trees do not grow into the sky.'[1] Neither in nature, nor in history is any one tendency allowed to carry all before it: each existence calls for the forces that limit and complete it. The highest example of this law may be found in the way, in which, again and again in the course of History, the spirit of man breaks the fetters of custom and convention which itself has forged, and irresistibly asserts its freedom. Custom is ever unspiritualizing the outward and logic the inward life of man; but the straitest framework of dogma is burst asunder, the firmest structure of law and convention is undermined by this irrepressible activity. In the middle ages, if ever, it might have seemed that the prison house was closing upon the human soul. Vast systems of formal thought which claimed to explain everything, and really explained nothing tended [?] to chain down the intellectual energies of man, just as the untamed activity of barbaric life was subdued under the yoke of the church.[2] On every side some dead barrier shut man in from the freedom and greatness, the complexity and infinity of nature. Yet just *then* do we meet with the most forcible, and almost revolutionary proclamation of the independence of man's spirit,–an independence that rises above the need [of?] any outward institution, or rite, or dogma. Retiring into himself from the confusions and restrictions of life, into the inner life of feeling, where he is alone with God, the devotee finds that all the outward forms of ritual, all the logical limits of dogma have at once ceased for him to exist. All this apparatus of doctrine and worship seems but a half-expression of the infinite fullness, which he finds in this dim region of pious feeling,–but broken gleams of that light, which[3] shines within him. How can such merely outward things limit him? At once his chains drop off: and at a step he passes from the language of the narrowest slavery to the letter of church authority to language which casts contempt on all letter or form whatsoever, and scarcely shrinks, in its proclamation of the infinite nature[4] of man, from identifying him with God. In other words a hard scholastic theology gives rise[5] to, and finds

164

its natural complement in, a vague and daring mysticism. The spirit of man compensates for its bondage by an unfettered liberty, and the whole by weight of dogma and formality that had fixed and petrified around it, is loosened and dissipated in the penetrating solvent of feelings, to which all limits are lost, and all distinctions confused.

Mysticism first took firm root in the Western Church in twelfth century. In one sense it presented itself as the natural enemy of the scholastic divinity, then coming into existence: in another sense both may be said to have their origin in the same causes, and to be different expressions of the same spirit. The vita contemplativa ['contemplative life'] did for devout minds the same service which the modified Realist[6] tendencies of Abelard did for those of a more intellectual and less spiritual order.[7] It opened up to them a way of escape from the prison of petrified dogma, and formal worship. Abelard had raised almost without [...?] it the standard of revolt against church authority, and subjected the church doctrines, hitherto received with implicit faith, to a minute dissecting and analyzing logic, which respected nothing. This was the secret of the enthusiasm with which he was followed and listened to by crowds of eager pupils, as he unfolded his paradoxes of unreal dialectic. He seemed to the rising intellect of the time, just awakened to a sense of its power and its rights like a new Moses leading them out of Egypt into the promised land.[8] He seemed to translate unintelligible formulae, which had hitherto been accepted with vacant awe and wonder, into an order and system, which had a meaning for man's mind and a relation to its wants. The endless subtlety of his dialectic, its hairsplitting distinctions, its argument within argument, and reason for reason, did not repel them. Rather all this delighted them with a strange new sense of power, of which they had never before been conscious. All these wonderful freaks were but the exulting play of the intellect in the first joy of its deliverance from the house of bondage.[9] It is this youthful and sanguine spirit that still casts some faint ray of interest over the barren waste of logical puzzles.[10] 'How could men have studied and listened to all this', we are inclined to say, 'without an unutterable feeling of weariness? How could they have rejoiced[11] in weaving and unravelling these endless puzzles, in tracing out these blind ways that led to nothing?' The answer is not far to seek. Here we have the intellect of man, *not* employed on the earnest tasks of manhood, *not* really bracing itself to investigate the problems of the world, but rejoicing in its youth and new-felt strength. What wonder if that strength is mainly shown, like a child's, in tearing every-thing to pieces. It is not to gratify an appetite for destruction, but to feel and test its own powers that it seeks. Nor need we think it strange if there be a want of reverence in its mode of dealing with that which is sacred,[12] if nothing seems too holy or too sacred for its curious probings, if the intellect awaking from its long sleep, recognizes at first no law in its wanderings, and the spiritual faculties that should limit it, are for the moment silent and leave it the whole field to itself.–*Still* the character of this result[13] was such that it naturally set the devout minds of the time against it. Its irreverence, its unspirituality, its disregard of authority made the saints its natural enemies. Nor is it wonderful that, seeing in the whole movement so much to disgust them, they overlooked its rightful expression of the claims of the intellect. Reason must show a purer and steadier light than the brilliant fireworks of Abelard ere its claims can be recognized by Faith. St. Bernard, who in his life and character most purely represents the religion of the time, at once declared against it.[14] And he was supported by the strongest sympathy of all religious men in putting down the new theology and its doctor.

Yet, unable as the more spiritually-minded were to recognize or sympathize with Abelard's emancipation of the intellect from the dogma of the church, they too felt the need of something freer and more inspiring, they too sought an escape from the externality and formality of a dogmatic church. They could not any more, like their barbaric ancestors, repeat with unenquiring assent the words which mother church puts into their lips.– They wished not to rebel: they could not but long to be free. And what they wanted, they seemed to find in mysticism. This afforded them the means of reconciling an outward obedience with an inward liberty,–of accepting all the limits laid down by the church, and yet not being really cramped or confined by them. Dogma might be fixed and unchangeable: church order might be narrow and inflexible: but by mysticism they were enabled to rise [above?] both into an atmosphere of pure feeling, which like the air was too impalpable to be limited or fixed, which overpassed and penetrated all barriers as if they were not. No form of words, no rule of life, draw it carefully as you will, can hinder the extravagances of the mystic. He is too far from the earth to be affected by those fences of mere material wood and stone wherewith we mark off and separate one field from another. He may sign all the creeds and confessions, but what they affirm and what they deny is equally left behind him when he retires into his own soul.

The Latin church carried among its own traditions the means whereby mystic thoughts could take form in the West.[15] Among the other legacies, which it had received from the Eastern church before its separation, was that curious half-Christian, half-Neoplatonist forgery of the fifth century, which bore the name of Dionysius the Areopagite.[16] France had identified its author with her apostle St. Denys;[17] and Scotus Erigena had translated it into Latin.[18] Much of its contents might well have shocked and alarmed the more practical and dogmatic spirit of the Western Church, if it had not been partially protected from censure by the title of saint and father. As it was, its strange thoughts and forms came in, as it were under licence, and were eagerly received into the religion of the cloisters. It became a sort of text-book of the religious life, and was commented on almost as much as the Sentences.[19] It brought the awe and passion of Asia, the Neoplatonist's longing for the infinite, into the worship of the West. Living amid the endless Greek dialectic of the Trinitarian controversy,[20] its author had seen how little real knowledge of God can be got from definitions and therefore his words bore weight with those, who were shrinking before the shadow of Scholasticism.[21] They think to know by their understanding he says, Him who hath made darkness His hiding place. 'Of Him', to use the similar language of Hooker, 'our fittest eloquence is our silence when we confess without confession that his glory is inexpressible and beyond our reach.'[22] We must leave behind all the truth of the understanding, and even separate ourselves from ourselves, and be merged in the darkness of ignorance, in order to approach the sacred inviolable silence of God. The world is not His revelation, but a veil between us and Him. He is above truth and error, above Being and Not-being, above every contradiction. We can not call Him Perfect, but Over-Perfect: not God, but Overgod. Neither by His outward service and worship, nor by ordinary duty, nor by the teaching of Scripture can we approach Him, but only by the path of mystic Initiation. What then, is this Initiation? There are, says Dionysius, two ways to the knowledge of God, the via affirmativa and the via negativa, by affirming predicates or by denying of them of Him.[23] The former breaks up the unity of God into variety, and loses his simple essence among the multiplicity of his creatures, so that we can attain to no real knowledge. The latter leads us back from the variety of the changeable world to a mystic ενωσις ['union'] or union with God, in which we come under the rays of His light which is unsearchable. In this union a divine and exstatic [sic] love fills the soul of the worshipper οὐ μόνον μαδὼυ ἀλλὰ υἱι παδὰν τὰ θεια·–and in this love is lost all distinction between the lover and the beloved.

A curious inconsistency of the mystic spirit reconciles this theory of union with the church system. The unapproachable unnameable God is bound to His meanest creatures by a successive series of emanations. God lives in love, and therefore must create. The overflowing beams of his light stream out to animate rational spirits of the highest angels, and these again pour out the powers which they receive from Him into other souls in the second stage of emanation, and these again communicate of their fullness to others.

'And so the whole round world is everywhere,
Bound with gold chains about the feet of God.'[24]

A sacred hierarchy arises in heaven and on earth with three orders of angels in the one corresponding to the three orders of clergy in the other: and through this long descending chain the life and light of God flows forth to the lowest of his Offspring.[25] Each creature can only receive this influx by remaining in his place and order: if he leave it, he is nought, for he thus separates himself from the life of God and from union with Him.

The very logical inconsequence of this scheme fitted it for its work. Its Neoplatonic insertion of a series of emanations and mediators between God and man might seem the very antithesis of the Christian doctrine of the Incarnation, but this very defect enabled it to be received without suspicion into a church now become hierarchical. Its exultation of the clerical office only secured, against the suspicion of heresy, its doctrine of mystic union, and the via negativa, whose ultimate tendencies were fatal to the claims of the church.

Such was the mysticism which St. Bernard called in for his ally, when in his contest with Abelard, he was pleading the claims of faith against reason. He argued that logic was unable to weigh the deep things of God, and that it only misled its students when it attempted to [several words lost] 'How can we believe', says Abelard, 'what we do not understand? Must not our professions of faith be mere words without intelligent assent?' We cannot understand, answers Bernard, except we first believe.[26] All intellect can do is to unroll and examine the treasure of truth which it has received from the church as it were wrapped up in a bundle (involatum). Yet even St. Bernard was forced by the spirit of the time to demand a higher kind of spiritual satisfaction than was involved in implicit faith. The negative expression, the via negativa of mysticism seemed to him consistent with the doctrine of the transcendent incomprehensibility of God to the ordinary reason of man, which he was maintaining. Its theory of ecstatic union through love seemed to promise a kind of knowledge of which faith could not be jealous. Accordingly we find him maintaining that there are three stages of perfection in the religious life.[27] Lowest comes that of the ordinary Christian who lives by faith a practically pious life, making a moderate use of the things of sense. Higher than this is the stage of fides quaerens intellectum ['faith seeking understanding'][28] in which a faith which he calls 'propalatio graedam necdum propalatae veritatis' is developed into an intelligent assent to known truth. It corresponds to that philosophic attitude of mind which passes from the variety of phenomena to contemplate things in the unity of their causes, and detects the essence beneath the qualities. Highest of all stands the mystic, who, withdrawn from outward things, stripping off the images of the senses, and divesting himself of all that[29] is [less than?] human, dwells solely in the beatific vision [words lost] he dies not to life, but to all the fetters of life that bind 'our aspirant souls',[30] and enjoys a pure exstasy [sic] of love. But St. Bernard scarcely allows the possibility of anything but a faint and far off foretaste of such a state in this life,–a caution in which the later mystics did not imitate him. We may also find in him some germ of the religious sweetnesses, as we may call them, which the school of St. Theresa carry so far.[31] For it is a curious feature of mysticism, that while it seems to stretch the language of the intellect, and allows only negatives to be spoken of its God,–on the other hand it indulges at times in the very extreme of sensuous metaphor. Its favourite book is the Song of Solomon,[32] and it uses the language of earthly passion almost to audacity. But we never in these earlier writers meet with that spiritual sensuality, as it sometimes deserves to be called, which is exemplified by St. John of the Cross and later Roman Catholic mystics.[33]

All these tendencies of Bernard are developed in [the] mystics of St. Victor.[34] Hugo[35] and Richard[36] of St. Victor give an elaborate analysis of the steps whereby the soul, at first lost in things outward and sensible, learns to return upon itself, and lose its hold of the world that it may find all in itself. So far they allow philosophy may guide men. But there is a higher stage to which neither Plato nor Aristotle attained. The pure intuitive gaze of the mystic seizes at once and in its fullness all that the slow and laborious powers of thought can only reach in faint and imperfect measure. 'Sensus nortii corporis vertentus in rationem, ratio [...?] intellectum, intellectus transibit in deum.' The end is always the [....?], an exstasy in which thought and feeling, love and intelligence [are?] one, and in which all distinction ceases [?] between the soul and God.[37] The Victorines describe the psychology of the religious life and its development, with a subtlety that is analogous to the logic of the schools.[38] The spirit of the schools influences them even while they deny and protest against it. But they do protest and with ever increasing vehemence, as time opens the breach wider between the mystic and scholastic tendencies. On the one hand the great doctors Aquinas[39] and Scotus[40] uniting the logic of Abelard with the orthodoxy of Bernard went on developing these immense systems of logic, which as it were covered all life with a web of subtle distinction spun out of the dogma of the church. On the other hand the voice of the mystic was ever becoming more threatening and revolutionary. Already Hugo denounces the labor [sic] of the schools as at once dangerous and ineffectual for the investigation of sacred truth, and denies that either by direct or by analogical reasoning we can pass from the human to the divine.[41] We cannot speak of the soul from the analogy of the body, and God is higher above the likeness of man's spirit, than the spirit is above the flesh. Richard declares that the highest kind of truth is not only above reason but against it, and, the highest state of the soul one of passive absorption in God, where thought is not.[42] The culmination of this tendency we find in Gerson whose nominalism seems to free him from all fetters [word lost] the comprehensibility of God.[43] He lived at a time when [?] the scholastic systems had almost exhausted all the possibilities of refined distinction, and he felt therefore the more strongly the unsatisfying nature of the results thus to be attained. 'It is granted,' he says, 'that the nature of God is one and simple: to what end then these distinctions which men make in His essence except for a vain play of imagination. The schoolmen are like men, who have cultivated the senses of sight and hearing, and allowed the other spiritual senses to get dull. But what avails this culture, when it is just by these other senses that divine things are apprehended.'[44] Gerson finds even the precept 'Believe that ye may understand' too liberal to the understanding. We cannot understand God. We know Him only by experience, by enjoying Him: and to ask for reasons for this experience is vain curiosity. Reason can give no addition to the bliss of love, whose darkness is perfect light.

The name of Gerson reminds of the level[l]ing tendencies of mysticism: yet the French mystics were generally the obedient servants of the church. Mysticism could not but withdraw men's minds from the outward service and ritual: it always warred against the logical development of dogma: but within the church[45] it was generally kept within some limits by the discipline of the monastic orders, among whom it flourished. It was long partly the instinct, partly the policy of the Church of Rome to adopt, modify and regulate principles, which were at bottom its deadliest enemies, so that they became allies and servants. The poor preaching friars were a living protest against the magnificent hierarchy, of which they were the chief support. They were forces of revolution tamed and harnessed to the car of despotism. Scholasticism[46] was the fruit of the resurrection of intellect against the authority of the church. But Aquinas seemed to divert the attack by employing its utmost subtlety in the development of dogma. And so too, that intensity of the religious life, which finds expression in mysticism, and which was the natural enemy of a religion that set the church between God and man, seemed to find vent merely in increasing the subtle refinement and intensity of its devotions. Yet there are not wanting signs in all these cases that the truce which bound such opposite principles together was but hollow and temporary. The intellect that developed and subtelized [sic] the doctrine of the Latin church soon began to undermine it. The more fervent of the Franciscans, the new democracy of Rome, early showed symptoms of insubordination to the hierarchy.[47] And mystic piety could not live and grow without casting contempt on an outward and ceremonial worship. Even Hugo of St. Victor speaks of these outward means of approaching God as a humiliation imposed on man, because he had degraded the spiritual beneath the sensual. Gerson dares to cast doubt on the superior sanctity of the so-called religious life. It is however, as has been already indicated, a characteristic of French mysticism, that they preserve a sort of balance and harmony between the inward and outward life, and rarely allow the revolutionary tendencies of their principles to appear. Their works are distinguished by an exquisite sweetness, but at the same time a certain want of vitality and energy, as of men who found in their own souls a refuge from a world they did not seek to reform. In Germany on the other hand Mysticism breaks through in the direction of higher speculation.[48] The more independent spirit of German piety had never to the same extent been subdued under the yoke of Latin Christianity and it was the first to attempt to emancipate itself. Even the friar's vow was no security against this spirit of revolt, and beyond the circle of the monastic orders there early arose in western Germany certain lay or partially lay societies, called variously Lollards, Beghards, Friends of God, Brethren of the common lot, etc.–which were far less obedient to the hierarchy, and guided far more by the spirit that was within them.[49] Many of them were heretics or in suspicious connexion with heretics. Amid such influences it was that the Dominican preacher Eckhart, and his scholars Tauler, Suso, and Ruysbrock developed their mystic teachings.[50] Among them we hear again the full and more than the full tones of the Eastern Dionysius[51] again renewed. The works of Eckhart were condemned by the pope after his death, and some of his more extreme disciples were burnt. At this we do not wonder: but what we do wonder at is that he and they should have been allowed for a moment, much more for a long series of years, to preach as they did. No German Pantheist or Hegelian of the present day has ever used more emphatic and bold language than Eckhart in describing the mystic union of man with God. God, he says, is that Eternal Rest from which all things come, and to which they long to return.[52] Spiritual life consists in this that God pour Himself without reserve into[53] man, and that man change into God.[54] In order to this he must rise above self. 'Many men desire to love and see God', he says, 'as they love a cow for the milk it gives them.'[55] But not only must we renounce selfishness, we must even divorce ourselves from our own identity, that emptied of self, we may be filled with God. For who is the God that is sought by this self-renunciation? He is a God without self. He is *no thing*, not this, nor that; he is above all being and naming, a substance without substance. We approach Him not by affirmation, but by negation: he is above all distinction, one in all things, in grass and stones, and men: Creature and Creator are lost in one: for all things are eternal in Him. 'Ere the creatures came into being', he says, 'God was not God, therefore I pray God to make me rid of God. In the beginning I existed, and willed to produce the man I am. That which I was in eternity, I am and will remain for ever, while that which I am in time will pass away with time itself. If I were not, God would not be'.[56] The Trinity is, as it were, repeated in the life of every individual soul, who goes forth from God into the flesh, and returns to Him in the spirit. The soul, the Reason is God's son, and in thinking, we become one with God, from whom we become separated so far as we identify ourselves with our corporeal nature. 'It is', he repeats, in language whose vagueness well suits the meaning, 'it is out of the desert of a vague infinitude that the son of God must rise.' The later German mystics altered and softened these words into a more practical shape: they infused into them more direct moral purpose for popular exhortation: they raised cautions against their dangerous ambiguity: but they were in substance true to their teacher. Ruysbrock, one of the most cautious yet ventures to say, 'There is a highest state of knowledge to be attained, the state of ignorance, where there is neither God nor Creature as respects distinction of persons, but where we in God and God in us form one blessedness, provided only we have altogether lost ourselves, and been diffused through or even dissolved in the unknown Obscurity.'[57]

Their historical notices will better explain for us the nature of mysticism than any direct definition could do. Mysticism is a word which has sometimes been applied to every fullness of feeling which passes the limits of exact thought. But such transcendence of feeling must pass into the 'via negativa' ere we can properly call it by this name. A negative tendency is what unites the mystics of all ages and places, Indian and European; Buddhist and Christian. It is interesting to ask what is the source of this common characteristic.

Its source[58] seems at the first aspect of it to be a disgust [?] with the immediate forms in which man's spiritual life is expressed together with a[n] inability to get beyond that merely negative [...?] to a new positive. Negatives take the place of affirmatives because we are unable to affirm enough. The path of thought is as it were, reversed to attain its goal the sooner. In the region of religious experience, where men have most often to grapple with 'thoughts beyond the reaches of their souls',[59] where shadows of truth not yet ripe for the wisest often enter minds of little or no culture, little or no means of mastering them, we naturally find mysticism most frequent. The expression, the symbol, the word for the half-revealed thought is not yet present, and men 'search what or what manner of time the spirit that is in them doth signify'.[60]

The soul outruns history with its forecastings, and learns to despise the insufficient present. It would, if it could, rise above time and space, which seem unable to contain an adequate symbol of its infinity. It turns to asceticism in practice, to abstraction and negation in thought. It rejects all the slow-earned gains of the past, whether they take the form of outward institutions, or of systems of ideas. It thinks that it possesses an inner light, which these, limited and formal as they necessarily are, can only darken and confuse. And so it learns to cast contempt on human knowledge, and to elevate instinct and feeling above thought. All rules are useless, all forms superfluous, all doctrines but the vain babbling of those who have never seen the central light of truth. The soul withdraws into itself into a divine darkness which is excess of light, and stripping itself of all the gathered wealth of tradition, for the first time feels truly rich.

It is not without significance that these men have been called reformers before the reformation. As surely as the French Revolution was contained in germ in the abstract theories of Rousseau and Voltaire, so surely did this withdrawal of the spirit of man from the outward institutions into itself forbade that their fall was near.[61] These gentle peitists,[62] as they generally were, may seem to have little in common with the stormy forerunners of Revolution, but yet both equally were uttering the spells that can wake the slumbering[63] forces of man's nature to insurrection against all that is fixed and established. Narrow is the line that separates the saint who retires from the world into his own heart as into a cloister from the enthusiast who revolutionizes it, and often in history has that line been crossed. Flanders, the chosen home of mysticism, was also the birthplace of democracy, and from the workshops of its weavers came that subversive anabaptism,[64] that followed the reformation every where like a dark shadow. The mystic like the revolutionary set man's Consciousness of the infinite possibilities of his nature against the actual framework of life: and the temper of mind that treated the church with all its gigantic apparatus of ritual and dogma as mere nonessential externalities easily passed into the temper of those who swept it away.

And here we come upon the weak side of mysticism. It is *only* negative, only destructive. It sets, as has been said, the possibilities of the soul against all that is actual, all that is already attained;–and these possibilities, though infinite, are still no more than possibilities. It sets a formless hope against a formed reality. It seeks to rise above a limited present to that which is eternal and unlimited. Yet it is not able to emancipate itself from its place in history, and seeking to escape from all form, it sinks to the barrenest of all forms, *negation*. And, just as the worth of asceticism depends on what we renounce, so the worth of mysticism depends on what we deny. It is inextricably bound up with that which it despises; and by the height of the object contemned is to be measured the elevation gained by contemning it. What makes all the vast difference between the void tautology, with which the Buddhist expresses his immersion in the Infinite Nothing,[65] which is all things, and the riches and variety of the Christian mystic of the middle ages? It lies simply in this, that it is a richer and more concrete form of life from which he turns away. His language and his thought is enriched to spiritual fullness by the dogma, the ceremonies, and the life of that world and that church, which he abandons and condemns.

There is besides an awful danger which lies very near to mysticism, in that its language may mean either the very highest or the very lowest that is possible to man. It talks of negation, or a divine ignorance which is above knowledge, of a divine emptiness which is true fullness, of a darkness which is excess of light, of a death and apathy which alone is true life. These words may be understood of a sacrifice of self to God,[66] of the old man to the new. They may bring before us that death of nature which is the birth of spirit. But they may also be understood of an ignorance, which is ignorance indeed, of a death which is death indeed. If the language of faith easily passes into the language of antinomianism,[67] still more easily does the language of the mystic pass into that of the Anabaptist. The mystics are ever guarding their doctrines against this abuse, yet their negative form ever leads them again close to it.[68] Tauler, Suso and Ruysbrock, and the author of the Theologia Germanica[69] are ever protesting against the false lights of men who deified every impulse, who proposed to have transcended all moral obligation and authority, and who resigned themselves to a stupid apathy which they called poverty of spirit. Luther had to lift up his lion voice in constant protest against a set of prophets who talked [word lost] the language of a spiritual experience while they had [never?] passed through its pains and self-sacrifices.[70] 'Do you wish', he says, 'to know the times, and the manner in which God holds converse with men? Hear then,–' "as a lion, so hath He crushed my bones" '.[71] And again, 'I am cast out from before thy face', and again 'my soul is filled with plagues, and my life draweth nigh into the gates of hell'. If [words lost] to you of a spirit emptied of self, ask them whether [?] they have felt these spiritual agonies, these divine pangs of birth, these deaths and hells. If you hear only of calm and joy and exstasy, and exaltations to the third heaven, believe them not. Tenta ergo, et ne Ihesum quidem audias gloriosum, nisi prius videris crucifixum.'

If we had only the mystic to oppose to the dogmatist, the world might swing for ever between anarchy and stagnation. The mystic awakes the world from its sleep of death, but he can give little or no direction and guidance to its reviving energy. He overturns, but he cannot reconstruct. The real Reformers of the world, the men who have guided it from the Old to the New, have been made of a different stuff. Whether they have been called poets like Dante,[72] or philosophers like Plato, or preachers like Luther, they have ever been men, whose main tendency was affirmative, not negative, toward form and not away from it. Hence it has oftener been their error to cling too closely to the past, than to let it go too easily. But while preserving the forms of the past, they have poured such a tide of new life into them, that these were forced to develop[73] to something greater and better. Thus in Plato's Republic, we have a dream of the future under the form of the past. The ideas of an aristocracy in which birth shall have no weight, of a spiritual nature in man that is deeper than the distinction of sex, of a communion between man and man which transcends all the[74] natural ties, and in which each and all feel themselves but organs of the whole, are combined with the unnatural restrictions and bonds of the Greek state, with its oligarchic contempt for labor, [sic] and its immolation of the lower classes.[75] All this shows us, how a man may be beyond his own time, while he is yet of it. It exhibits the higher and better way in which we can prepare for the future, though it be but pouring new wine into old bottles [Matt. 9.17]. The bottles may burst, at last must burst, (as the old Greek life did burst asunder with the force of the new spirit), but only to pour it out upon the world. For, if we do not pour it into old bottles, we have none to pour it into. 'The soul is form and doth the body make.'[76] The formless life must speak through inadequate forms, till its new garment of mortality be woven. Elseways it must be left unattired, or in other words, uttered only in negations. The mystic devotee may be satisfied with this, but not the true artist or reformer. It is the[77] constant and barren accusation of bigots against such men, that they are using words in new meanings, that they are perverting the natural sense of terms, that they are appropriating the phrases and forms of the past to meanings that the past never knew, that, in short, they are pouring new wine into old bottles. Those whose chief care is for the bottles have indeed good reason to be alarmed. But so long as the world has any hopes that go beyond a repetition of the present, so long as it is not content to express these hopes in a creed of mere negations, so long is this so-called sophistry the greatest service that men of genius can render to their fellowmen.

The two extreme poles of the spiritual life of man may be called *mysticism* and *art*. But in this use of the word art, we express something wider than that term generally implies. We mean all that constructive power, whereby man models and remodels his outer life and its circumstances after the image and according to the mode of his inner life; by which he tries to give local habitation and name to that which eye hath not seen nor ear heard. The ages of faith are the periods, in which this constructive power is active, in which the eager mind of man, rejoicing in the fresh impulses that flow into it from without in a constant tide of revelation, and freely reacting upon these influences, builds for itself a spiritual temple wherein to it may dwell. A new light has come from heaven, and makes all things new. St. Paul breaking from the power of Judaism,[78] and laboring [sic] to build up the edifice of the Christian Church, wherein all nations should sit down together;[79] Luther, armed with the principle of the modern world, the principle of individual faith, changing in a few years the religious associations of centuries, show the mighty stimulus to construction, which works on the human mind in such an age. They show to what intense activity the spirit is urged under the pressure of a new principle.[80]

---

[1] [Caird may have in mind the German proverb: 'Auch Bäume wachsen nicht in den Himmel' ('Trees do not grow into the sky either.') Champion records two further possibilities: 'God cuts down all trees before they reach the sky' (p.165, no.480) and 'God prevents trees from growing into heaven' (p.183, no. 1355) (Selwyn Gurney Champion, *Racial Proverbs*, second edition (London: Routledge and Kegan Paul, 1950).) All three are aimed at any person who has arrogant aspirations (i.e. whose ideas 'grow into the sky') and so deserves to be brought back to earth.]

[2] [Scholasticism, the dominant school of medieval Christian thought, was renowned for its complexity and aspiration to produce a systematic expression of divine truth. It declined as the Reformation gained in strength, although it still

informs much Roman Catholic theology. The Inquisition into those believed to have heterodox beliefs took on increasingly tyrannical character in 1232, when Frederick II (1194–1250) formally ordered the hunting down of heretics throughout the Holy Roman Empire. Its last vestiges were destroyed only with the suppression of the Spanish Inquisition by French forces in 1820.]

3 [MS del.: 'in its fullness wholeness'.]

4 [MS del.: 'freedom'.]

5 [MS. reads: 'riser'.]

6 [MS del.: 'partially nominalist'. MS reads: 'Realism'.]

7 [Pierre Abelard (a.k.a. Abailard) (1079–1142), French theologian and philosopher, whose *Sic et Non* (*For and Against*) collected contradictory statements by Scripture and the Church Fathers, as a challenge to believers to unpack the respective paradoxes within orthodox doctrine.]

8 [Exod. 12:31 et sub.]

9 [MS insert: 'The […?] was really inadequate to the Caste [?] […?] it.' Caird marks from here to '…dealing with that which is', for possible deletion. See note 12 below.]

10 [MS del.: ', which we find in Abelard's 'Sic et hon', in which every imaginable reason seems to be collected for and against every possible opinion.']

11 [MS reads: 'rejoicing'.]

12 [Illegible interpolations at top of this folio, possibly replacing the passage marked for possible deletion. See note 9 above.]

13 [MS del.: 'movement'.]

14 [St. Bernard, (1090–1153), Abbot of Clairvaux, theologian and monastic reformer, long-time opponent of Abelard's perceived attacks on orthodoxy which he condemned at the Council of Sens in 1140. Bernard was renowned for his extreme piety.]

15 [The 'Great Schism' between Greek church of the East and the Latin church of the West is usually dated to 1054.]

16 [In 533, the Monophysites attributed to the mystical theologian, Dionysius of Athens (whose conversion is recorded in Acts 17:34) a body of written work including *The Celestial Hierarchy*, *The Ecclesiastical Hierarchy*, *The Divine Names*, and *The Mystical Theology*. This inaccuracy of the attribution was quickly recognised when the texts were shown to date from approximately the year 500. The texts are now attributed simply to Dionysius the Pseudo-Areopagite. Neoplatonism was the dominant philosophical school between the third and thirteenth centuries. It sought to supplement Christian theology with Platonism, although it tended to favour ritual magic over intellectual insight. Its major statements were in the works of Plotinus (ca. 205–70) and then Iamblichus (ca. 250–ca.325).]

17 [St. Denys, (a.k.a St. Dionysius of Paris) (ca.250), patron saint of France, who is sometimes claimed to be Dionysius the Pseudo-Areopagite.]

18 [John Scotus Erigena (c.810–c.877) Irish philosopher and translator of the Pseudo-Areopagite texts.]

19 [Peter Lombard, *Sententiarum libri quaruor* (written ca. 1155–8), which became

the standard textbook of medieval Christian theology.]

20 [The Trinitarian controversy concerned the correct understanding of the Trinity, and raged from the second century AD through the Council of Nicaea in 325 and afterwards.]

21 [Characteristically, Scholasticism employed reason, analogy, and definition to understand and systematise, with increasing complexity, the revealed truths of Scripture.]

22 ['our safest eloquence concerning him is our silence, when we confess without confession that this glory is inexplicable, his greatness above our capacity and reach'. Richard Hooker, *Of the Laws of Ecclesiastical Polity, in The Works of Mr. Richard Hooker*, arr. John Keble, 3rd ed., 3 vols, (Oxford University Press, 1845), vol. 1, bk 1, chap. 2, §3, p.201. First edition published in 1593.]

23 ['D[ionysius] is here contrasting the Affirmative Path of Knowing with the Negative Path of Unknowing. The former has a value as leading up to the latter; but it is only safe so far as we keep within the bounds of Scripture. Unscriptural conceptions of God are false: Scriptural conceptions of God are true so far as they go; but their literal meaning must be transcended.' *Dionysius the Areopagite on the Divine Names and the Mystical Theology*, trans. CE Rolt (London, 1940), p.51 n.7. First edition published in 1920.]

24 ['For so the whole round earth is every way
Bound by gold chains about the feet of God.'

Alfred, Lord Tennyson, 'Morte D'Arthur', in Ricks (ed.), *Poems of Tennyson*, vol. 2, pp.17–8 (ll.254–5).]

25 [The 'number and order [of angels] were only fixed by Dionysius in his 'Celestial Hierarchies', where they are arranged in three hierarchies containing three choirs each, in the order of Seraphim, Cherubim and Thrones; Dominations, Virtues and Powers; Principalities, Archangels and Angels.' FL Cross and EA Livingston (eds.) *Oxford Dictionary of the Christian Church*, 2nd edition (London: Oxford University Press, 1974), p.53. At this time, the three orders of the church were the priesthood, the deaconate and the sub-deaconate.]

26 [Caird appears to be reconstructing the essentials of, for example, a letter sent by St. Bernard to Haimeric in 1140. St. Bernard, *Life and Works of Saint Bernard, abbot of Clairvaux*, eds. J. Mabillan and S.J. Eales, 2 vols., second edition (London: Burns and Oates, 1800), vol. 2, pp.871–3, esp. p.872.]

27 [St. Bernard distinguishes three devotional attitudes, 'the three-fold kiss': 'the kiss on the feet' (penitence), 'the kiss on the hands' (the promise to continue seeking to grow in devotion to God), and 'the kiss on the mouth' (the ecstasy of grace), in his *Commentary on the Song of Songs*, sermons 2 to 4.]

28 [The concept originated with St Anselm (1033–1109), Scholastic theologian, born in Aosta, Archbishop of Canterbury from 1093.]

29 [MS reads: 'than'.]

30 ['To muse upon eternity's constraint
Round our aspirant souls'

Elizabeth Barrett Browning, 'Cheerfulness taught by Reason', in *The Poetical Works of Elizabeth Barrett Browning* (London, 1914), p.188. First published in 1844.]

31 [St. Teresa of Àvila (1515–82), aka St. Teresa of Jesus, Spanish Carmelite nun.

Founded the convent of St. Joseph at Àvila in 1562. Her combination of ascetic mysticism and practical work still exerts a profound influence over certain sections of the Carmelite Order.]

[32] [The twenty-second book of the Old Testament, renowned for its sensuous imagery. Commentaries on it were written by Origen, St Dionysius the Pseudo-Areopagite, St. Theresa of Avila, St John of the Cross and most famously St Bernard.]

[33] [St. John of the Cross (1542–91), mystic and in 1579–80 co-founder of the Discalced Carmelites, who traced the methods and stages of spiritual purification in three main works: *Spiritual Canticle* (written 1578), *Ascent of Mount Carmel* (c.1579), and *Living Flame of Love* (c.1583–4).]

[34] [The Victorines were the canons regular of the Abbey of St. Victor founded c.1115 under the influence of the thought of St. Bernard, by William of Champeaux. They included Adam of St. Victor (d. between 1177 and 1192) and Walter of St. Victor (d. after 1180), as well as Hugh and Richard (see below).]

[35] [Hugo (or Hugh) of St. Victor (d.1142), French theologian, who entered the Abbey of St.Victor in Paris in 1115, and particularly well-known for his book *De sacramentis Christianianae fidei.*]

[36] [Richard of St. Victor (d.1173), Scottish theologian and mystic, who entered the Abbey of St. Victor in 1159, and whose major work was the six volume *De Trinitate.*]

[37] [The gaps and query in the original Latin and the English translation are the result of damage to the manuscript.]

[38] [The Schools is of course a common name for the Scholastics.]

[39] [St. Thomas Aquinas (c.1225–74), Dominican theologian and philosopher, who massive *Summa Theologiae* did more than any other text to combine Aristotelianism with Christianity.]

[40] [John Duns Scotus (c.1265–1308), Scottish Franciscan, Scholastic theologian and philosopher.]

[41] [Hugo of St. Victor defends this position in many of his works, including *De arca Noe*, *De vanitate mundi*, *De sacramentis* and *De laude caritatis.* The Christian should progress from study to meditative devotion and eventually a state of contemplation.]

[42] [Richard of St. Victor set out six stages of mystical devotion in his works *Benjamin Minor* and *Benjamin Major.* The soul moves from worship inspired by things which are visible, to the rapture of the soul that has been carried beyond itself and into the 'Divine Presence'.]

[43] [Jean Le Charlier de Gerson (1363–1429), French theologian, mystic and cleric, who rejected what he saw as the excessive intellectualism of Scholastic theology, a trend which he traced back to Duns Scotus, and which he saw as undermining true faith.]

[44] [Cf. 'God is simple and one, and one ought to seek Him in simplicity and unity of heart', Jean Gerson, 'La Montaigne de contemplation', in Jean Gerson, *Ouevres complètes*, ed. P Glorieux, 10 vols. (Paris: Desclée and Cie, 1960–73), vol. 7, p.38, as quoted in D Catherine Brown, *Pastor and Laity in the Theology of Jean Gerson* (Cambridge University Press, 1987), p.287n75. Belief in the

unity and simplicity of God was common among nominalist theologians such as Gerson.]

[45] [MS. del.: 'in France'.]

[46] [MS. reads: 'Scolasticism'.]

[47] [St Francis of Assisi (ca.1181–1226) founded the Franciscan order, or 'Order of the Friars Minor', in 1259. Their founding principle was one of individual and institutional poverty. Over time, splits developed between those 'Spirituals' who upheld a literal interpretation of this ideal, and the bulk of the Order who reinterpreted the principle more pragmatically. The latter were accepted by the papacy eventually. Yet from the fourteenth century, the dominant strand of the Order came under sustained attack for their alleged corruption.]

[48] [MS orig.: 'It is to Germany we must look for the full development of these negative tendencies.']

[49] [From the fourteenth to the seventeenth centuries, 'The Lollards' was the name for followers of John Wycliffe (c.1330–84) English philosopher, theologian and reformer, who rejected papal authority in favour of personal devotion and the authority of Scripture. The Beghards spread from the Netherlands across northern Europe from the twelfth century, surviving until the French Revolution. They were men, who lived in communities without a common rule or private property. (The female equivalent were 'Benguines'.) Their lives were dedicated to philanthropic work and mystic devotion. The 'Friends of God' (or 'Gottesfreunde') were fourteenth century mystics predominantly from Austria and Switzerland who stressed the need for a more perfect union of the individual soul with God. They were inspired by Eckhart, Tauler and Suso. The 'Brethren of the common lot' probably refers to the Brethren of the Common Life (*Fratres Communis Vitae*), a spiritual movement founded in the fourteenth century by Geert de Groote (1340–84) in the Netherlands, although their influence spread to Germany prior to their final decline in the seventeenth century. They stressed the importance of education and the life of unforced, yet deep, piety.]

[50] [Eckhart (or 'Meister Eckhart') (c.1260–1327), German mystic Dominican, many of whose beliefs were declared heretical by Pope John XII in 1329. Sometimes controversially seen as a forerunner of Kantianism and Hegelianism. Johann Tauler (c.1300–61), German mystic Dominican and student of Eckhart and Suso at Strassburg. Henry Suso (c.1295–1366), German Dominican mystic, disciple of Eckhart, whose greatest work was *Das Büchlein der ewigen Weisheit* (*The Little Book of Eternal Wisdom*) (c.1328). Jan van Ruysbroeck (1293–1381), Flemish mystic, who was heavily influenced by Eckhart. Caird consistently spells his surname as Ruysbrock.]

[51] [Dionysius of Alexander (d. ca. 264), follower of Origen.]

[52] [A recurring theme in Eckhart's writings (e.g. 'Peace' from *Sermons and Collations*, in Pfeiffer (ed.) *Meister Eckhart*, pp.102–4. The phrase 'Eternal Rest' is much less common though than 'the Eternal Birth' and 'the Eternal Word' (e.g., *ibid.*, pp.20–5, 38–39).]

[53] [MS reads: 'into to'.]

[54] [Cf. Eckhart, 'This is Another Sermon', from *Sermons and Collations*, in Pfeiffer (ed.) *Meister Eckhart*, pp.10–11.]

[55] ['Some people think to see God with their eyes as they would see a cow, and they expect to love him as they would a cow. This thou lovest for its milk and for its

cheese: for its profit to thyself.' Meister Eckhart, 'Sermon 14, in Franz Pfieffer (ed.) *Meister Eckhart*, trans. C de B Evans (London: John M Watkins, 1924), p.52.]

[56] [Cf. Meister Eckhart, 'Tractate 19 The Beatific Vision', in Pfeiffer (ed.), *Meister Eckhart*, p.410.]

[57] [Cf. Jan van Ruysbroeck, *The Book of the Twelve Beguines*, trans. J Francis (London: John M Watkins, 1913), chap. 12.]

[58] [MS del.: ', if we would say all in a word, is defect of expressive power, and that mental capacity of realizing one's thought, which is the complement of expression,–of the inward and the outward λὸγος ['Word'].']

[59] [William Shakespeare, *Hamlet, Prince of Denmark*, Act 1, scene 4, ll.54–6.]

[60] ['Searching what, or what manner of time the Spirit of Christ which was in them did signify, when it testified beforehand the sufferings of Christ, and the glory that should follow.' (1 Pet. 1:11).]

[61] [Jean-Jacques Rousseau (1712–1778), French romantic philosopher. François Marie Arouet de Voltaire (1694–1778), French Enlightenment polymath. The thought of both exerted decisive influences on the French Revolution of 1789. For Caird's attitude to Rousseau, see 'Rousseau', in his *Essays on Literature and Philosophy* (Glasgow: Maclehose, 1892), vol. 1, pp.105–46. Cf. 'Wordsworth', in *ibid.*, pp.147–89. It is unclear why this 'forbade' the fall of these institutions rather than, say, 'foretold' what would happen.]

[62] [A devotional movement which grew out of seventeenth century Germany. Its founder, Phillip Jakob Spener (1635–1705), sought to reinvigorate Lutherianism by focusing worship around devotional meetings and stressing the equality of all believers before God.]

[63] [MS del.: 'revolutionary'.]

[64] [The 'Anabaptists' was members of a loose collection of religious groups which flourished in sixteenth century Europe. They recognised the baptism of adults only.]

[65] [Cf. Caird's comparison of Buddhism and Stoicism, in his *The Evolution of Religion. The Gifford Lectures Delivered Before the University of St Andrews n Sessions 1890–91 and 1891–92*, 2 vols. (Glasgow: James Maclehose, 1893), vol. 1, chap.13.]

[66] [MS del.: 'nature to spirit'.]

[67] [Antinomianists hold that believers are not bound by moral laws as believers are saved through grace. This view was associated with Anabaptists, among others.]

[68] [MS del.: 'when they seem to have escaped it.']

[69] [An anonymous fourteenth century German mystic treatise thought to have been written by a member of the Teutonic Order.]

[70] [Martin Luther (1483–1546), German theologian, whose 1517 Ninety-Five Theses against the Indulgences of Pope Leo X, inspired the German Reformation.]

[71] [The quotations in this paragraph are Caird's own translations of parts of a letter which Luther wrote to Philip Melanchton on 13 January 1522 (Martin Luther, *Werke. Kritische Gesamtausgabe. Brieswechsel 2. Band*, Weimar: Hermann Böhlaus Nachsolger, 1931), p.425). Caird rearranges the parts silently. The

sequence given in the standard English translation of Luther's works is as follows: 'In order to explore their individual spirit, too, you should inquire whether they have experienced spiritual distress and the divine birth, death, and hell. If you should hear that all [their experiences] are pleasant, quiet, devout (as they say), and spiritual, then don't approve of them, even if they should say that they were caught up to the third heaven. ... Do you want to know the place, time, and manner of [true] conversations with God? Listen: "Like a lion has he broken all my bones" [Isa. 38:13 Vulgate]; "I am cast out from before your eyes" [Ps. 31:22 Vulgate, but RSV numbering]; 'My soul is filled with grief, and my life has approached hell." [Ps. 88:3 Vulgate, but RSV numbering] ... Therefore examine [them] and do not even listen if they speak of the glorified Jesus, unless you have first heard of the crucified Jesus.' Martin Luther, *Works, vol. 48 Letters I*, ed. and trans. by G.G. Krodel (Philasdelphia: Fortress, 1963), pp.366–7 (words inserted by Krodel; Biblical references inserted by the current editor from Krodel's notes). In a note, Krodel gives the literal translation of the final sentence (the one which Caird fails to translate from the original Latin) as 'Therefore examine [them] and do not even listen to the glorified Christ, unless you have first seen the Crucified [in them].' (*ibid.*, p.367n28).]

72 [Dante Alighieri (1265–1321), Florentine poet. Caird explores the background to this claim in his 'Dante in his Relation to the Theology and Ethics of the Middle Ages', in his *Essays on Literature and Philosophy* (Glasgow: Maclehose, 1892), vol. 1, pp.1–53.]

73 [MS. reads: 'developed'.]

74 [MS del.: 'bonds and limits of nature'.]

75 [These are recurring themes in Plato's *Republic*, but key statements include: meritocracy 415b–c, 423c–d; gender-neutrality 454d–456b; communion in an organic community 414b–415b; labour 415b–c.]

76 [Cf. Plato, *Phaedo*, for example, 79–80.]

77 [A single vertical line appears at this point, although its meaning is obscure.]

78 [Acts 9:1–16]

79 [Possibly an allusion to Psalms 86:9: 'All nations whom thou hast made shall come and worship before thee, O Lord; and shall glorify thy name.' Cf. Psalms 22:27; Jer. 10:7; Rev. 15:4.]

80 [MS del.: 'Every year at [words lost].' Any subsequent sheets have also been lost.]

Report on Mr. Moore's Essay.
[Late 1897]

I have carefully gone over Mr. Moore's Essay and his article in Mind,[1] and intend to criticise it so far as it is possible to do so without going into too great detail; but I should first wish to express my appreciation of his philosophical ability. This is the more necessary, as it is difficult to criticise without unduly emphasizing what one thinks to be defects.

I wish therefore to say that I think very highly of Mr. Moore's philosophical powers, especially of his power of following out his ideas to their ultimate results. What one has most to fear in philosophy is that this should not be done, and therefore the weakness and strength of ideas should never be distinctly seen, but hidden under some plausible compromise. It is therefore very high praise to say that a writer on philosophy can, and does realise fully the consequences of his principles. By such thinking he may make a great contribution to philosophy, even if the result is that the principles break down; for they cannot do so without throwing light upon the relations of the element of truth which they exaggerate to the other elements of it.

Partly in consequence of this, but partly I think, because Mr. Moore has not sufficiently studied how to be clear to those who are not looking at things at his precise angle; he is extremely difficult to understand. It has cost me much trouble to do so, and I do not think the fault is entirely mine. This fault, however very natural in a young philosopher, who has not had much experience of teaching, and should not be counted as taking much from the merit of the essay.

The difficulty however, I should add, partly arising from the from the fact, that Kant is read so much through the eyes of Bradley and Lotze,[2] which leads I think, to an imperfect realisation of the best points in Kant's work, and an exaggeration of his inconsistencies. Sometimes it is not quite easy to see whether Mr. Moore is interpreting Kant, or expressing his own views.

At the same time, I think that, in spite of these defects, Mr. Moore shows himself to be a thinker of no ordinary power, and that he has established his claim to any reward that is given for such work.[3]

Of the *Introduction*, I need not say much. Mr. Moore rightly contends I think, that such predicates as 'true', 'real', 'good', cannot be explained without metaphysical enquiry, and he objects to the division of 'Philosophy' or 'Reason' as theoretical and practical. Kant's full phrase is '*criticism* of Pure and Practical Reason'.[4] That is, he aims in his Transcendental Regress, at the *Theory* of Knowledge and the *Theory* of Morality or Practice, these being the two great facts of human life. Mr. Moore, for reasons afterwards given, holds that the reason that knows cannot be *practical*, i.e. cannot create motives for itself. But this is no legitimate criticism upon Kant's division from Kant's point of view.

Perhaps however, I may take occasion from what he says p.XII ('He himself says that freedom of the will rests upon transcendental freedom, which latter is a speculative notion.') to correct an error as to Kant's meaning, which frequently appears in the Essay (see p.64 seq.)[5] Kant defines practical freedom as the power of acting upon motives not derived from desire, and says that we have empirical evidence of it in our consciousness of the moral law as a motive.[6] This however, might be explained away, if we were able to conceive the ego as a mere phenomenon, as merely one object among the other objects of experience, or if its consciousness were limited to its own status as such an object. But both of these assertions, Kant attempts by his transcendental regress to shew to be untrue.[7] The attempt therefore to prove that Kant is inconsistent *from his own point of view,* rests upon a misunderstanding. Kant's point is just that this is an experience which cannot be explained on the principles on which we usually explain objects of experience, i.e. without taking account of their relation to the subject. There is no doubt, a difficulty in speaking of the moral consciousness as experience at all, considering Kant's narrow definition of experience: and Kant shews that he is quite aware of this, when he speaks of the moral law as only a *quasi factum*. (See e.g. K.P.R. p.50.)[8] But the point is that we have here also an immediate unreflected consciousness, of which we have transcendentally to explain the possibility. (I may refer to my Kant, vol. II, p.123.)[9] There is a sense in which it is true that no object of experience can be explained without taking into account its relation to the subject;

and Mr. Moore, (p.50 seq.) maintains that this is true of all objects equally; but this is not Kant's view. This point we shall have to discuss hereafter.

The first chapter of the Essay begins with a comparison of Kant's statement of the question of Freedom with that of Mr. Sidgwick,[10] which is at least misleading. Kant holds that there is a necessity according to the law of Nature, but that that necessity pre-supposes a principle, which at once explains and limits it, and which also we must take into account in order to explain the moral consciousness. So far as I see, the words quoted from Mr. Sidgwick,[11] do not bring in this distinction at all, and to make Kant answer the question in a form in which he has not asked it, cannot tend to clearness. Again, to call Kant a *'determinist'*, because he says that moral actions cannot be understood by taking them as merely a succession of states in an object,[12] is surely misleading. The contrast that what must be possible because it ought to be done, need not be capable of appearing and indeed cannot appear, is necessary to Kant; but the action viewed objectively as an event, and viewed in reference to the subject as its action, is not strictly the same thing. The contrast holds in much the same way as if I should say that a line without breadth is possible in Mathematics, but not in physical reality. If one has to take an abstract view of things, and then a point of view that does away with the abstraction, it is impossible to put the abstract on a level with the concrete view. The only defect in this analogy is that Kant, for reasons to be mentioned hereafter, does not think that we can ever understand *how* the real includes the appearance.

There is nothing that directly contradicts the above in Mr. Moore's statement, but I think that the way he puts the distinction, is somewhat misleading.

The section that follows, p.5 seq. is perhaps the most important in the Essay, as it shows how Mr. Moore understands Kant's view of reality and freedom, and what view he opposes to it.[13] There are two particular mistakes, which I may first get rid of.

1. (p.8). What Kant says of the third Antimony is that *both*, not merely *one*, of the alternative may be true: one horn of the dilemma referring to the world of appearance, the other to the world of reality.[14] This is not much more than a verbal mistake, due to Mr. Moore's not noticing the way in which Kant puts the Antimony.

2) Mr. Moore states (p.26 seq.) that Kant only applies the idea of freedom or of an unconditioned cause to *some* things or beings

within the system of appearance (i.e. to men), and *not* to the system as a *whole*.[15] This is incorrect; for in stating the antimony, Kant deals in the first instance with the necessity of a free cause for the *whole* system; although he goes on to speak more fully of free causes which are partial existences *within* the system, because of the special interest of this question in relation to morality. (See K.R.V p.320 'Nun haben wir diese Notwendigkeit', etc. and following sentences.)[16]

Passing now to Mr. Moore's general argument, let us first see what is his view of Kant. Kant, according to Mr. Moore, confuses the *epistemological* view of things, after which he is striving, with a *psychological* view of them as determined by their relation to man's peculiar kind of subjectivity. He therefore (p.16) is unable to answer the question: 'How do we know that these conditions imposed by our knowing faculty are universal?' All we know is, that our peculiar subjectivity imposes these conditions on any reality that is presented to us; for it is only as the given matter is brought under them, that it becomes an object for us. Kant, indeed, assumes a *Ding an sich* ['thing-in-itself'] as a cause for the affections of our subjectivity which constitute this matter. But therein he makes an illegitimate use of the category of cause; for, in this application, the category of cause must lose its schema, and be reduced to the merely analytic relation of reason and consequence (p.10).[17] Now, as Kant holds, (quite correctly, according to Mr. Moore) that all the *a priori* forms that we apply to the given, are merely relational, and as he has surrendered, or never adopted, the notion[18] that in the given we are in contact with reality, he is reduced to a merely subjective view of experience. His only escape from this is through the ideas of reason; ideas which represent, on the one hand, the mind's dissatisfaction with a merely relational experience (such as alone we can have through the categories as applied to a matter under the conditions of space and time); and on the other hand, its demand for a *res completae*, in which the universality of thought should be really united with the particularity of sense, and not externally applied to it as is the case in our experience.[19] And this, for Kant, remains, at least so far at least as theoretical reason is concerned, a mere demand, a problematical conception. For the idea of totality thus introduced, cannot be legitimately combined with the idea of the *Ding an sich* ['thing-in-itself'], whose existence was originally assumed, or was justified only by the illegitimate application of the category of causality. We are, therefore, left with, on the one hand, a *demand* for totality which cannot be satisfied, because of the essential universality and relational character of thought; and with, on the other hand, an experience which as it is constructed according to such relational forms out of the matter of sense, is purely subjective. Now Mr. Moore holds that this view, (which he attributes to Kant) is quite accurate, in so far as it asserts the abstractly universal and relational character of our thought; and therefore of the experience or knowledge which we construct by means of it. But he maintains that it is quite untrue as regards the matter to which our thought is applied. He holds, p.23, that reality directly *appears* in intuition, though it does not appear *as it is*; for the moment we go beyond the fact *that* it appears, we connect it as in space and time with other things according to the relational forms of our thought, and construct an appearance which is necessarily subjective, as is shown by the Antinomies to which it leads.[20] The *thing* that appears, on the other hand, must be taken as an individual and unconditional totality, a self-determined whole, and in that sense as free. Thus for Mr. Moore, its negative unconditionedness as a mere *'that'*, converts itself at a stroke into complete self-determination. This seems like saying that 'O = the absolute', but Mr. Moore, I think, would answer, that in the intuition, the something perceived is given not as a mere *'that'*, but as qualitative–holding, as he does, that qualities can be sharply distinguished from relations (cf. p.24).[21]

This view seems to me untenable, and the criticism of Kant by which it is introduced, unfair, or at least reached by unduly emphasizing Kant's weaknesses. His *main* weakness is, I agree, the introduction of the *psychological* point of view into *epistemology*, or rather as I should prefer to put it, his stopping at *epistemology*, and not going on to *metaphysics*: for it seems to me that epistemology is essentially a mere compromise between psychology and metaphysics. Kant tells us that his criticism has not to do with the 'the origin of experience', but aims at discovering 'what lies *in* experience' (Proleg. p.52).[22] But as Mr. Moore sees, in working this out, Kant often falls back–and still oftener I think appears to fall back–on the process of constructing experience out of elements previously conceived in separation, as *our* understanding and *our* sensations. Mr. Moore, as I understand him, accepts this view, only putting intuition for sensation, but maintaining the essential disparateness, and therefore coming to the same conclusion that what we know is merely appearances; though, as it is in *intuition* and not in *sensation* that the object appears, what appears is objective reality, the *thing* in its unconditioned individuality.

Now this seems to me to be *exactly* Kant's point of view in the *Aesthetic*, where he goes on the supposition that individual things are given in perception, though the forms through which we apprehend them are subjective, and therefore we do not know them as they are.[23] (Cf. the *Dissertation* in which the ideas of the *Aesthetic* were first expressed.)[24] In the *Analytic*, however, Kant brings in the further criticism that the forms also through which we determine them *as objects* are *a priori*, and further that this determination is not possible unless there is also a synthesis of imagination, (in conformity with the pure synthesis of understanding,) whereby the manifold–which is now all that is attributed to sense–is brought together in an image, to which the conception can be attached as a predicate (K.R.V. p.99).[25] The result towards which Kant is now working, therefore, is that the image is nothing without the conception, and the conception nothing without the image. We are thus brought to the conclusion that perception involves a judgment in which the subject and the predicate are necessarily distinguished, but at the same time necessarily related; a judgment which *therefore* is objective (a fact which Kant considers to be expressed by the use of the verb of existence as the copula) (K.R.V. p.121).[26]

Kant thus rejects as inadequate the view which Mr. Moore finally adopts, and in the *Analytic* he is developing[27] a quite different view, especially in the chapters on the *Transcendental Deduction*, and the *Schematism*, though with some imperfection, owing to his never completely giving up the point of view of the *Aesthetic*.[28] I have tried in my treatise on Kant (see especially I. p.594 seq.)[29] to show how he fails to bring the two sides together. So far, however, as this new view is worked out by Kant, he is not constructing experience out of pre-existing factors, but simply taking our perception of things as in time and space, and showing that such perception could not exist for us without conceptions, which determine the images of perception as objective, and connect the objects so determined in one experience. In other words, we cannot even imagine the world in space and time, except by the use of the categories of quantity and quality, and we cannot determine it as an objective world, unless all its elements are necessarily combined into one experience by the principles of substance, causality, and reciprocity.

But again, Kant cannot stop here; for, in speaking of the synthesis by means of the categories, he has brought to light another element of experience; viz. the unity implied in this connecting process, a unity of which we become conscious when we become conscious of the self. Hence Kant says that all our experience is subject to the condition that we must be able to combine it with the '*Ich denke*' ['I think'].[30] It must, in other words, be capable of being combined with self-consciousness, else its elements could not be combined with each other in one experience. Instead, however, of taking in this new element, and asking how it modifies the results so far gained,–which he must have done if he had been faithful to his programme of simply enquiring what is in experience,–Kant treats consciousness which the Ego has of itself, as utterly disparate from that which it has of objects, and that, in spite of his confession that the consciousness of self is mediated by the consciousness of objects. The judgment of self-consciousness is, he holds, analytic, though it presupposes a synthesis (a view which is equivalent to saying that it is, and is not, a synthesis). Hence it follows that the ideal demand of a self-conscious being, for an object corresponding to itself, as it is a demand which springs out of the bare analytic unity of self-consciousness, can never be satisfied in experience, which has only a synthetic unity. In other words, it is impossible to bring together abstract unity with abstract difference. Hence the demand [of] reason takes the paradoxical form on which Mr. Moore has insisted in p.14. The error, however, lies not in the demand of reason for an intelligible world, but in its being put in such a way which would make its satisfaction an absurdity. It is not merely that we do not see how it is possible, but that we see that it is impossible. Now it seems to me that whole subsequent difficulty of Kant's philosophy, and especially of his view of freedom and morality, just arises from the fact that he is obliged to treat the ideal of reason and the moral law (which is the form the ideal takes in Ethics) as at once synthetic and not synthetic, as a fruitful idea and yet a mere tautology, as a new principle for the explanation and, experience, especially moral experience, and yet as a mere 'A is A', a formal principle, which would not authorise us to draw from premises any conclusion which was not explicitly contained in them. Mr. Moore, however, accepts this deadlock as the truth about human reason, whenever it attempts to go beyond our immediate contact with reality in intuition. Hence he is obliged, so to speak, to read Kant backwards, and to empty Kant's use of the ideas of reason, in relation to knowledge and practice, of all its meaning. But it seems to me that the only legitimate way of correcting the deficiency in Kant's procedure, is to reconsider his analytic view of reason, a correction which Kant himself suggests when he speaks of the analytic unity as implying a synthesis.[31] What however I am more concerned to point out in this place is that, if the problem how we were to reach knowledge of reality, meant that the abstract particular had to be identified with the abstract universal, without either of them ceasing to be what they are, it would not only be insoluble in the sense that we cannot see how it is to be done, but in the sense that we see clearly that it cannot be done. On the other hand, I think Mr. Moore is right in holding that the very beginning of knowledge implies the highest ideal of it, though he gives no reason for this supposition, such as is given by Kant when he points out that all experience implies, and must be interpreted in relation to, the unity of self-consciousness.[32]

Mr. Moore goes on in p.28 to the discussion of the application of the idea of freedom to the will of man in the two forms 1) of *liberty of indifference,* as maintained on the ground of the immediate affirmation of consciousness; and 2) of *self-determination* as maintained by Kant.[33] Of the former, Mr. Moore tries to show,–and I think, shows–that when we endeavour to state the nature of the freedom to which consciousness testifies, we can get no distinct deliverance in favour of a *motiveless decision between motives.* And he points out the ambiguity of the question when we merely ask whether man can act rationally, and not whether he can act either rationally or irrationally, since the former necessarily brings in the other view of freedom as *self-determination.*[34] I have not Mr. Sidgwick's book[35] with me, and am not able to say whether Mr. Moore's criticism upon his statements on this point, are valid. But I should like in passing, to advert to Mr. Moore's statement[36] that the consciousness of an end may change the character of that end, and that in a *processus ad infinitum*; and that therefore, 'the results of human volition alone among causes, must remain incapable of prediction', though they are really determined like other effects. If consciousness thus changes our motives, it must be because it brings with it some new idea which continually reconstitutes them; and if this be admitted it will be difficult to maintain that the conscious self is not free, so far as it thus determines its own motives. Such a process would be impossible, if we merely looked at ourselves and what was happening in ourselves, as, to use Kant's simile, a conscious *Bratenwender* ['roasting-fork'] might look at its own movements.

Mr. Moore then goes on to deal with the Kantian notion of self-determination. He thinks that Kant's great error was that he did not see that every thing is unconditioned or free from our point of view, and determined by its relations from another; but that he conceived some things or beings in the phenomenal world as organic wholes, and so free, and others as not free (p.50). Freedom and necessity indeed are combined in the phenomenal world; for we can not only say that the existence of one thing is necessarily connected with the existence of another, but also that the quality belonging to the one is necessarily connected with the quality of the other, although as a quality it cannot be explained by this relation, and is therefore, free. Hence Kant was right in maintaining that the phenomena in their particularity must be such that the principles of the understanding can be applied to them.[37] It is quite different, however, with the ideas of reason, which have no such necessity of application; and Kant confused the two points when he said that the world of experience as a whole must be taken (even regulatively) to be such that we can realise the idea of totality-in-unity or organic unity in it.[38] *A fortoiri* he was wrong when he supposed that that idea could be used even as a regulative conception to determine any *particular* existence within the world. The only point according to Mr. Moore at which thought and reality meet, is the immediate intuition in which reality is given to us, yet not as it is, but as it appears. Whenever we go beyond the something intuited, the idea of the unconditioned can only be applied to the whole, and, as so applied, it remains a mere idea; for it is impossible to make an experience conditioned in time and space, into a whole. If we take anything less than the whole, e.g. an animal, or a man, it is impossible to treat it as a whole at all: for the line of division between it and other things is quite 'arbitrary' (p.54). And this applies to a mind quite as much as to an animal organism, for 'there is no special form to fix the limits of a unity anywhere between the smallest distinct element and the whole mental world' (p.55). And thus though it is true that 'consciousness is itself an element in mental processes, so that here the form which determines the change knows itself'.[39] What we have in consciousness is merely a series of presentations, and this is equally true of the willing consciousness; for will merely means that the presentation of an idea is the cause of the presentation of that of which it is the idea.

Even if we can act, as Kant asserts, in view of a law which prescribes what ought to be done, this merely means that the presentation of the law is causally related to the presentation of the action as done. And Kant was confusing the *content* of the former presentation which is universal, with the *form* of its individual presentation as an event in the psychical series, when he spoke of moral action, as action determined by a 'mere conception'. A conception, as universal, may be the ground of another conception *analytically*, but it cannot *synthetically* be the ground or cause of an existence either in inner or outer sense. And Mr. Moore attempts to show that Kant confused these two things by reference to the way in which he speaks of the relation of practical to transcendental freedom.

Now I have already spoken of what I take to be Mr. Moore's misunderstanding of Kant's assertion that practical freedom is *experienced*, but that the *explanation* of its possibility must be *transcendental*. We are conscious of being able to act not only in view of the objects of our particular desires or the pleasures they bring us, but in view of the idea of law or of a possible kingdom of ends.[40] But how can we justify this consciousness, or prove that this is not an illusion, involving as it does practical freedom, i.e., the power of acting irrespective of the limitations of our individual being, as parts of a world in space and time essentially related to the other parts? How can we vindicate an experience which seems, if we take it as it presents itself to carry us beyond what can be experienced? Kant's answer is, that the self or ego is not an object like other objects, but the principle of unity in knowledge, a principle implied in the synthetic functions (by which objects of experience are determined for us as such objects), and which also, as we become conscious of its pure unity, gives rise to the ideas of reason in contrast with which experience is found wanting.[41] So far, however, it might be said, as Kant says, that the self is merely the subject of knowledge which we cannot determine as an object; and, on the other hand, that the idea of an object to which it gives rise, is merely the abstract counterpart of its own formal unity. This might fairly be said, if the idea of a whole, or totality-in-unity, which thus arises, did not become a motive or principle of action. We might then possibly contemplate the play of our passions, as we contemplate the succession of events without us (like the conscious '*Bratenwender*' ['roasting-fork']); and then we should not be conscious of freedom, for we should not attribute the acts to ourself at all. For in the theoretical consciousness, the consciousness of self is essentially the consciousness of the unity to which experience is referred, and which also is the source of the ideas that make us dissatisfied with experience. In our practical consciousness, however, this ideal does not merely come last to make us strive after an impossible completion of experience; it comes *first* as a consciousness of totality, which is bound up with the consciousness of the acting self. And although in one sense this is a 'mere conception'; which we cannot objectify without typifying it as a law of nature, yet this does not prevent it from being a motive.

I should, however, at once state that there is a defect in Kant which partly justifies Mr. Moore's representation of him, a defect which I have already pointed out. This is that the consciousness of the self, as the unity underlying experience, is taken as *purely analytical*. But Kant himself, as we have seen, shows us the way out of this difficulty, when he says that it *involves* a synthesis, which really means that it *is* a synthesis. For, if the unity on which we return from the synthesis of experience, becomes by that very return conscious of itself *as a self*, this surely is a synthetic process. The correction to be made in Kant is, therefore, to acknowledge this, and to consider how the acknowledgement of it will transform experience, i.e. how far the fact that experience exists only for a self, gives a new point of view for the interpretation of experience. It is because Kant views the unity of self-consciousness as analytical, that he considers it only capable of suggesting a *regulative* idea, and not an idea that *reconstitutes* experience for us. And it is for the same reason that he conceives the moral idea as a conception, which may be typified, but cannot be known as realised. Another defect which is the counterpart of this, lies in his imperfect doctrine of inner sense, with which Mr. Moore deals [on] pp.66–7. This doctrine is greatly modified in Kant's second edition, but he is unable quite to transform it without altering his view as to the unanalytic character of self-consciousness. (I may refer to my discussion of this in my Kant I p.605 seq.)[42]

In pp.74–5 we see how Mr. Moore presents the opposition of analysis and synthesis. Either, he thinks, we have a synthetic relation of causality between presentations or an analytic development of conceptions and there is no third possibility. This is a dilemma for Kant, just so far as he conceives the judgment of self-consciousness with the ideas of reason and the moral law, as all expressing an analytic unity. But just so far as he points to a better idea, and suggests that view of experience which we get by looking only to the connections of objects with each other, is essentially abstract, and that we have to correct this view by the idea that the object is essentially an *existence-for-a-self*, we can reject both horns of the dilemma. And yet we are not reduced to a mere impossible 'combination of the notion of causal dependence into that of logical dependence' p.75. In other words, the truth is not to be reached *either* by treating time-conditioned experience as absolutely real, *or* by taking refuge in the mere timelessness of abstract laws, but only when on the one hand we correct the abstractness of ordinary experience and of science by the consideration of its relativity to a unity not in that series; and on the other hand, correct the abstractness of that unity by viewing it as essentially related to, and manifesting itself in, an experience of which time is one of the elements.

And this seems to me the main point of importance in relation to the discussion in 'Mind'.[43] We cannot say simply that reality *is*, or that it *is not*, in time. It is not in time in the sense that we cannot rest upon our first [?] conception of reality as a time-series, without considering that time, like objectivity generally, is *for a self*. On the other hand, we cannot take the unity of the ego as simply timeless; that is, its unity with itself in knowledge and action cannot simply be opposed to, or severed from, the time process of the objective world which exists for it; for self-consciousness is only possible through the consciousness of an objective world. To say simply that it is in time, would be to confuse it with one of its own objects; to say simply that it is not in time, might be taken to mean that it does not relate itself to, or realise itself in, an objective world. In particular, such a view would make it impossible to conceive how a self, which as such, is as Aristotle said a universal δύναμις ['capacity' or 'potential'] should be also a particular part of the world he knows.[44] From this point of view then, the question whether reality is, or is not in time, cannot be answered by a simple 'yes' or 'no'.[45] I do not deny that there are great difficulties in working out this view, but it seems to me the only view that offers any kind of solution of the problem.

Though I have been too lengthy already, I must notice another difficulty of which Mr. Moore frequently speaks; a difficulty which presses heavily upon Kant, but on which I think some light is thrown by this view. Are we to say that will, if free, is essentially rational, or that if free, it may be *either* rational *or* irrational? I do not think the question can be answered when simply so stated. To Kant, it is a great difficulty that the rational being should have any other motive than reason, and he tries to get over it by speaking of him as 'taking up' into his will, the motives of particular desire.[46] But ultimately he is forced to think of these motives,–or something that makes us capable of being affected by them,–as taken up into the Will, prior to experience, (i.e. as a sort of original sin). According to the view I have suggested above, there would be no purely objective or sensuous motives at all. I never seek to gratify my desires, but always to gratify myself. I always act *sub ratione boni*, and therefore in all I do, I am in some way determined by the idea of the whole,[47] which is the counterpart of the self. I am free however, in the highest sense, only so far as I have organised my conflicting desires by this idea which is always involved in them; just as I know in the highest sense, only when I have recognised the unity that underlies all my experience, and have re-organised my knowledge in view of it. Mr. Moore, (p.82) quite rightly argues that no such transformation, or reconstitution, of our motives could come out of the abstract idea of self-consistency, which seems to be all that is expressed in Kant's first formula for the Moral Law.[48] But Kant reinterprets this formula as equivalent to consistency with the ideas of the self, and of a kingdom of ends; and this shows that he is trying to express the idea of the whole, as involved in the consciousness of self, though continually checked by his view of self-consciousness as analytic.[49] Agreement of Will with its own nature as rational is, if it be taken in this sense, not an empty idea, but one which is capable of being used as a principle to reorganise our desires; and which in fact, always does in a rational being enter into the constitution of them. The worst and the best will so far agree, as there is no Will of a rational or self-conscious being which is not for the good. This may be a sufficient reply to what Mr. Moore says, p.83. We cannot have absolute badness any more than absolute error. The 'ought' arises out of the contrast of the particular end sought with the idea of the good or end involved in self-consciousness; and the consciousness of this contrast may often precede, and always in the long run, follows, the attainment of ends which are unworthy. It is upon the growing sense of this discord, that moral improvement mainly depends.

In the last ten pages of this chapter of the Essay, Mr. Moore seems to be trying to get back some of the ideas which he has rejected. Thus his general theory would lead us to say that, if good can be taken as a predicate of reality at all, it can be so taken only in a sense that excludes all evil; What is real is, as such, good. If, on the other hand, we apply the idea of goodness to the phenomenal, we can only say that all phenomena are good or evil according to the point of view we take up; good, as the *real* appears in them, and evil as it only *appears* (p.90). But in this way there is no room for a better or a worse: and Mr. Moore, as we have seen, has excluded the idea of any relative whole either in man or animals, as 'arbitrary' (p.54). But in p.91 he brings back just this arbitrary conception, and bids us regard a good will as the best of things, and a bad will as the worst, assuming that a systematic unity is realised or realisable in the will, as an end in itself. For 'more of the subordinate objective ends contribute in the good will as means to a result, which is also an end in itself, and in the bad will are emptied of the goodness which they possess in their own right, by being united into a whole, which is the most complete negation of an end in itself'. The idea of the self as an end in itself, is thus supposed to be an organising principle, which brings the natural goods of life–i.e. all particular ends of desire–into a systematic or organic whole. This, indeed, seems to be explained as merely 'formal completeness', or 'inclusiveness'; but obviously it cannot be meant merely that there is a larger aggregate of particular ends brought together in the good than in the bad will. If further we reject the idea that natural goods are determined as such by the relation to pleasure and pain, as Mr. Moore rejects it (p.92) there seems to be nothing left except that each of them is good as real, and all are equally good. Now a 'sum of pleasures' may be a doubtful conception, in itself and in so far as it characterises the whole by reference to one element, but a 'sum of reals', into which every element entered on equal terms with the others, would be meaningless. And how could the abstract idea of reality or goodness supply an organising principle for such a sum?

Mr. Moore thinks we may treat freedom and goodness as conceptions, each of which implies the other (p.92), so that in the case of things determined as natural goods, we can argue to their free causation from their goodness, while, in regard to moral goods, we can argue to their goodness from the conception of their cause as free. But as to natural goods, we can only say on Mr Moore's principles, that as *appearances* they are bad, and as appearances of the *real* they are good; while as to moral goods, we can only say that they imply freedom if we can take the subject for which they exist, as a self, which as self-conscious has an idea of the whole, and can use that idea as an organising principle, for the particular ends of desire.

Mr. Moore tries to explain this reciprocal implication of the good and the free, by reference to the Hegelian categories[50] which, (p.93) he supposes all to imply each other, and all to embrace the whole extension of appearances, though they nevertheless express different degrees of reality in appearance. I think Mr. Moore has not quite seen the bearing of Hegel's view. In a sense it is true that all the categories which we can apply to any thing, we can apply to everything; just as we cannot understand fully the 'flower in the crannied wall', without knowing 'what God and man is'; according to Tennyson's epigram.[51] But taking a flower or a stone by itself, apart from its relations to higher forms of reality–which is the quite legitimate abstraction of science,–we can explain them satisfactorily without the use of the higher categories. And the categories sufficient for Mathematics are not sufficient for Physics, and those sufficient for Physics are not enough for Biology; and so on through all the scales of existence. We can of course apply the category of quantity to a man's body or to his mind: or, if you like, to the absolute; but it becomes increasingly inadequate, and its application (without reference to the higher categories) takes the meaning out of the object in question. Hegel conceives the categories and the existences to which they are applied as graduated, so that we cannot fully explain the lower except through the higher; but the lower does not imply the higher *as* the higher implies the lower. And in the ascent, extension and intension grow together; for the higher category, like the higher object that calls for its application, at once includes and transcends the lower. At the same time, Mr. Moore's assertion has an element of truth in it as applied to such categories as 'free' and 'good'; for the highest categories–what Hegel calls the categories of the *Begriff* ['concept'][52]–involve organic relations between different elements, so that each reciprocally implies the other.

In chapter II, Mr. Moore criticises the basis of Prof Sidgwick's Hedonism.[53] He attacks 1) the doctrine that we cannot attribute the character of goodness to anything out of relation to some consciousness; and 2) the doctrine that in relation to consciousness there is ultimately no reason to prefer one thing to another, except as it produces a greater pleasure or a less pain.

In regard to the former point, Mr. Moore asserts that, so far as we can abstract from the relation of consciousness at all, we can prefer, or count it good, that e.g. things should be beautiful, though no one has consciousness of them. He has 'not given any strict argument on these points, as Prof. Sidgwick gives none'. (p.100) He puts it simply as an appeal to 'intuitive judgment'. It seems to me that, if we take the idea of good, as simply expressing the completeness of an organic system, we can judge that an object has good uses more or less without reference to any consciousness; i.e. we can abstract from the relation to consciousness, and still so judge. On the other hand, in so far as neither the world nor any part of it can ultimately be taken as a complete whole without reference to consciousness, and when we speak of good in morals–good that is willed–we are necessarily regarding the whole in that relation. I think that Mr. Sidgwick's view is, for Ethics, the true one.

As to the second point, it seems to me that Mr. Moore is right in saying that, if good be taken in this latter sense,–i.e. if we think of the good as Aristotle does in the Ethics, as something perfect and self-sufficient, and to which nothing can be added from without,–we cannot take it as pleasure, or as any other particular element of life, though we *can* say that neither it nor any other element can be left out. The organising principle, however, cannot be found in the mere abstract idea of the sum of all things, each of which, as real, is an element in the good; it must, as Aristotle urged,[54] be found in some positive conception of the whole, derived from the nature of the self who is to realise it–some conception that puts pleasure and everything else in its place as a means to, and at the same time element in, the whole. I rather think that Aristotle would justly have directed against Mr. Moore's view, one of the criticisms which (whether justly or not) he directs against Plato's idea of the Good: viz. that an abstract idea of the good,–the idea of that which is common to all things, to which the predicate good is applied,–cannot supply a principle of unity in the moral life.[55] At least I do not see how Mr. Moore would answer such a criticism.

Edward Caird

1   [George Edward Moore, 'The Metaphysical Basis of Ethics', Dissertation for a Fellowship at Trinity College Cambridge, 1897. George Edward Moore, 'Freedom', *Mind*, vol. 7, no. 26 ns (April 1898), pp.179–204. No fair copy of this dissertation has been found. The final draft (with directions to the copyist) is archived at the Wren Library, Trinity College (Add. Ms.a.247). The draft has very different pagination from that given in Caird's report. Caird's references to the fair copy occur in the text. Where 'Freedom' echoes without repeating the draft dissertation, the reference is given in the editorial notes in the form "Cf. Moore, 'Freedom'," followed by the number of the relevant folio of the draft. The notes supplement Caird's references to Kant (again, marked 'Cf.'). No attempt has been made to produce a systematic collation of the draft and 'Freedom'.]

2   [Francis Herbert Bradley (1846–1924), English idealist philosopher. Caird probably has in mind the position Bradley sets out in his *Appearance and Reality* (1893). Rudolf Hermann Lotze (1817–81), German post-Hegelian metaphysician. Cf. Moore, 'Freedom', p.202.]

3   [Moore failed to get the Trinity Fellowship with this application. See vol. 1, pp. xxiii–v, and vol. 2, p. ix.]

4   [Immanuel Kant, *Critique of Pure Reason*, trans. P Guyer and AW Wood (Cambridge University Press, 1998) (first edition published in 1781; second edition 1787). Immanuel Kant, 'Critique of Practical Reason', in his *Practical Philosophy*, trans. M Gregor (Cambridge University Press, 1996). First German edition published in 1788.]

5   [Moore, 'Draft 1897 Dissertation', p.7 ('Introduction'); *ibid.*, p.35 (chap. 1, §2). Moore, 'Freedom', pp.194–204.]

6   [Kant, *Critique of Pure Reason*, pp.533–4 (A533/B561–A534/B562).]

7   [Kant, *Critique of Pure Reason*, pp.411–25, 445–58 (A341–67; B397–432).]

8   [Caird uses the following abbreviations: KPR = *Kritik der praktischen Vernunft* [*Critique of Practical Reason*]; KRV = *Kritik der reinen Vernunft* [*Critique of Pure Reason*]. In line with Moore's dissertation, Caird's references in this report seem to be to the Hartenstein edition of Kant's *Werke*. Cf. Kant, 'Critique of Practical Reason', pp.164–5 (Prussian 5:31).]

9   [Edward Caird, *The Critical Philosophy of Immanuel Kant*, 2 vols. (Glasgow: Maclehose, 1889), vol. 2, p.123.]

10 [Moore, 'Draft 1897 Dissertation', pp.1–2 (chap. 1) is repeated verbatim in Moore, 'Freedom', p.180.]

11 ['Is the self,' he says, 'to which I refer my deliberate volitions a self of strictly determinate moral qualities, a definite character partly inherited, partly formed by my past actions and feelings, and by any physical influences that it may have unconsciously received; so that my voluntary action, for good or for evil, is at any moment completely caused by the determinate qualities of this character, together with my circumstances, or the external influences acting on me at the moment – including under this latter term my present bodily conditions? or is there always a possibility of my choosing to act in the manner that I now judge to be reasonable and right, whatever my previous actions and experiences may have been?' Henry Sidgwick, *Methods of Ethics*, 5th ed. (London: MacMillan, 1893), p.61, as quoted on Moore, 'Freedom', p.180.]

12 [Cf. Moore, 'Draft 1897 Dissertation', chap. 1, pp.2–3. Cf. Moore, 'Freedom',

pp.179–85.]

¹³ [Cf. Moore, 'Freedom', pp.182–4.]

¹⁴ [Thesis: 'Causality in accordance with laws of nature is not the only one from which all the appearances of the world can be derived. It is also necessary to assume another causality through freedom in order to explain them.' Antithesis: 'There is of freedom, but everything in the world happens solely in accordance with the laws of nature.' (Kant, *Critique of Pure Reason*, pp. 484 (A446/B474), 485 (A447/B475), respectively.]

¹⁵ [Cf. Moore, 'Freedom', pp.185–94.]

¹⁶ ['We have really established this necessity of a first beginning of a series of appearances from freedom only to the extent that this is required to make comprehensible an origin of the world, since one can take all subsequent states to be a result of merely natural laws. But because the faculty of beginning a series in time entirely on its own is thereby proved (though no insight into it is achieved), now we are permitted also to allow that in the course of the world different series may begin on their own as far as their causality is concerned, and to ascribe to the substances in those series the faculty of acting from freedom. One should not, however, be stopped here by a misunderstanding, namely, that since a successive series in the world can have only a comparatively first beginning, because a state of the world must always precede it, perhaps no absolutely first beginning of the series is possible during the course of the world. For here we are talking of an absolute beginning not, as far as time is concerned, but as far as causality is concerned....' Kant, *Critique of Pure Reason*, pp.486, 488 (A449/B477–A450/B478).]

¹⁷ [Cf. Moore, 'Freedom', p.183–5.]

¹⁸ [Reading uncertain: 'm' has been written in above the first 'n'.]

¹⁹ [Kant, *Critique of Pure Reason*, for example, pp.264–5 (B165–8).]

²⁰ [Cf. Moore, 'Freedom', p.191. Kant, *Critique of Pure Reason*, pp.459–550 (A405/B432–A567/B595).]

²¹ [Cf. Moore, 'Freedom', pp.191–2.]

²² [Immanuel Kant, 'Prolegomena to any future metaphysics that will be able to come forward as science', in his *Theoretical Philosophy after 1781*, ed. H Allison and P Heath (Cambridge University Press, 2002), p.79 (Prussian 4:283). First German edition published in 1783.]

²³ [Kant, *Critique of Pure Reason*, pp.153–92 (A19–49/B33–73).]

²⁴ [Immanuel Kant, 'On the form and principles of the sensible and intelligible world (Inaugural Dissertation)', in his *Theoretical Philosophy, 1755–1770*, ed. David Walford (Cambridge University Press, 2003). First German edition published in 1770. See Caird's *Critical Philosophy of Immanuel Kant* (vol. 1, chap.5) for his full discussion of the relation of Kant's *Critique of Pure Reason* to what Caird calls the '*Dissertation of 1770 on the Form and Principles of the Sensible and Intelligible World.*' (*ibid.*, vol. 1, p.160).]

²⁵ [Kant, *Critique of Pure Reason*, pp.224–6 (A92/B124–A94/B129).]

²⁶ [Kant, *Critique of Pure Reason*, pp.251–2 (B140–2).]

²⁷ [MS del.: 'striving after'.]

²⁸ [Kant, *Critique of Pure Reason*, pp.219–66 (A84–A130 and B117–69); and

ibid., pp.271–7 (A137/B176–A147/B187).]

29 [Caird, *Critical Philosophy of Immanuel Kant*, vol. 1, p.594–9. Caird traces this consequences of resolving this contradiction in the remainder of the first volume of his work (*ibid.*, pp.600–54).]

30 [Kant, *Critique of Pure Reason*, pp.411–22, 445–58 (A341/B399–A361/B432).]

31 [Kant, *Critique of Pure Reason*, p.248 (B135).]

32 [Kant, *Critique of Pure Reason*, pp.248–50 (B136–40).]

33 [Moore, 'Draft 1897 Dissertation', p.4 (chap. 1, §2).]

34 See, however, on this point what I say on p.20 of his paper. [Moore, 'Draft 1897 Dissertation', p.20 has Caird's marginal note: 'Is the Ding an Sich an object of intuition?']

35 [The fifth edition of Sidgwick's *Methods of Ethics* (see p. 200 above).]

36 [MS del.: (p.30–31)'.]

37 [Kant, *Critique of Pure Reason*, pp.271–337 (A137/B176–A235/294).]

38 [Kant, *Critique of Pure Reason*, pp.520–550 (A508/B536–A567/B595).]

39 [Caird's punctuation has been retained here, although the next sentence should run on from this one.]

40 [Kant, 'Groundwork of the Metaphysics of Morals', in his *Practical Philosophy*, ed. MJ Gregor (Cambridge University Press, 1996), pp.83–9 (Prussian 4:433–40).]

41 [Kant, *Critique of Pure Reason*, pp.234–44 (A110–30), and pp.245–66 (B129–69).]

42 [Caird, *Critical Philosophy of Immanuel Kant*, vol. 1, pp.605–6.]

43 [That is, Moore, 'Freedom'.]

44 [Possibly a reference to Aristotle, *De Anima*, 412a–13a.]

45 We might say 'the whole is not in time, but time is in it': but this without further explanation, would not help us much.

46 [Kant, 'Groundwork of the Metaphysics of Morals', pp.100–1 (Prussian 4:453–5).]

47 [MS del.: 'or the good'.]

48 ['...*act only in accordance with that maxim through which you can at the same time will that it become a universal law.*' Kant, 'Groundwork of the Metaphysics of Morals', p.73 (Prussian 4:421).]

49 ['For, all rational beings stand under the *law* that each of them is to treat himself and all others *never merely as means* but always *at the same time as ends in themselves.* But from this there arises a systematic union of rational beings through common objective laws, that is, a kingdom, which can be called a kingdom of ends (admittedly only an ideal) because what these laws have as their purpose is just the relation of these beings to one another as ends and means.' Kant 'Groundwork of the Metaphysics of Morals', p.83 (Prussian 4:433).]

50 [GWF Hegel, *The Logic of Hegel. Translated from the Encyclopaedia of the*

Philosophical Sciences, 2nd edition (Oxford: Clarendon, 1892), for example, §§24–25, 79–83.]

51 ['Flower in the crannied wall
I pluck you out of the crannies; –
Hold you here, root and all, in my hand
Little flower – but if I could understand
What you are, root and all, and all in all
I should know what God and man is.'

Alfred, Lord Tennyson (1809–1892), 'Flower in the Crannied Wall', in his *The Holy Grail and other poems* (London: Strahan, 1870), p.204. This volume actually appeared in December 1869. It is also an epigram, being inscribed on the statue of Tennyson which still stands in the grounds at the back of Lincoln cathedral. Caird quotes the poem in full in his *Hegel* (Edinburgh and London: William Blackwood, 1883), p.180.]

52 [Hegel, *Logic*, §§160–244.]

53 [Once again, Moore's target is the fifth edition of Sidgwick's *Methods of Ethics* (see pp. 186, 200 above).]

54 [Aristotle, *Politics*, 1252a1–1253a39.]

55 [Aristotle, *Politics*, 1261a10–1262a24.]

[Reference relating to JME McTaggart's Application for a D.Litt. at the University of Cambridge.]
[March 1902]

The work which Mr McTaggart[1] has submitted may be classified under two heads. The Studies in Hegelian Dialectic and the articles in 'Mind' are mainly expository of Hegel's system.[2] The Studies in Hegelian Cosmology, on the other hand, though connecting themselves closely with Hegel are on the whole more free in their treatment of the subjects and might be regarded rather as an exposition of the author's own views.[3] This difference, however, is not so marked as it at first seems, for in his Studies of Hegelian Dialectic, Mr McTaggart introduces – as legitimate criticisms or developments of Hegel's thought – very great alterations of Hegel's actual view, and it is these mainly that lead to what is most original in the 'Cosmology'.

There are, therefore, two questions which one would wish to keep separate – and I find it somewhat difficult to point out what I think the defects of Mr McTaggart's work as an exposition of Hegel without seeming to deny the value of it as a criticism and as an independent discussion of important philosophical questions. In order to do justice to him, therefore, I shall first mention, as shortly as I can, the main points in which I disagree with his interpretation of Mr Hegel and then very positively what I think he has succeeded in doing.

In the first place I think that the separation that he makes between what is given in experience and which is done by thought, between the immediate and the mediate is not Hegelian. Hegel, I venture to say, never thinks of a minimum of empirical postulate with which he may start his logic ('something is'). He has two introductions to the Logic, one in the Encyclopaedia, where he renders the point of view of the Logic, through the immediately previous development of philosophy,[4] and another in the Phenomenology where he attempts to shew that every form of thought which is dualistic or fixes any difference or distinctions as absolute must be abandoned and that the point of view of philosophy from the[5] start must be that in which such distinctions are abolished – i.e. the prime self-reference of being – in which so to speak the copula has swallowed up both subject and predicate.[6] Cf. what he says of the Spinozaistic point of view as his extential other.[7] Mr McTaggart thinks that it was by an oversight that Hegel did not begin with something like the transcendental argument of Kant[8] or the ontological argument of Des Cartes.[9] If he had done so, he would have committed the very error which he objects to in the [...?][10] arguments for the Being of God – the substitution of a process which is purely positive for one that is mediated by negation. For Hegel to say that anything was purely mediate or purely immediate would have been to commit two errors: 1) to make up a difference which cannot be transcended, 2) to deny the relation of [im]mediacy [?] and mediation which he is continually asserting. (Mr McTaggart quotes several passages where he holds [?] that[11] a *positive postulate* of the Logic is clearly excluded, but he seems to explain them away pp.37, 45 etc.).[12] This again leads him to think that at the end of the Logic the idea of experience is simply reinstated by an external addition to the Absolute Love.[13] But for Hegel the reinstatement really takes the form that Nature in its [....?] is uncovered as the meaning[14] of that Idea in its pure unity into itself.[15]

In the second place, while Mr McTaggart exaggerates the positive aspect of the relation of thought to experience, he commits the opposite error of exaggerating the negative aspect of the relation between the categories and the different stages of being – or 'degrees of reality' as Mr Bradley calls them.[16] All these he regards as 'absorbed' and negatived [sic] in the Absolute which alone is real. He turns Hegel's 'circle'[17] into a straight line, and makes the Absolute not the self-maintaining God of Christianity, which reveals itself in the finite, but a transcendental timeless Absolute in which the finite is lost. This view Mr McTaggart attempts in the fourth and fifth chapters to draw from Hegel but it is really the reverse of his [Hegel's] view.[18] The result is seen in the end of the Cosmology wherein we have an Absolute in which (as with Mr Bradley)[19] all the differences of reality are 'aufgehoben' ['transcended'] in some unity which is not rational but like the One of Melissus[20] is above reason. Mr McTaggart only stops short of this as he uncovers the absolute as a community of absolute selves[21] with whom intellect and will are lost in love. – He holds indeed that they are incarnate selves, because will and reason are taken up into love in some way we cannot understand.[22]

This[23] way of looking at things may be true – I do not discuss this – but it is the reverse of Hegel and I do not think it can be connected legitimately with Hegel. The error I think lies in not seeing that for Hegel, the lower 'degree of Reality' is at once negated as independent and reinstated as the necessary condition of the higher. Thus when Hegel says that Philosophy goes beyond religion what he means is merely that a religion which is conscious of its principles is higher than one which is not so conscious.[24] To suppose that religion dies out in philosophy or a purely intellectual state or process is from the point of view of Hegel a mistake.

There are other points as to the nature of the dialectical movement etc. which I do not agree with, but these are sufficient to show my point of view in regard to the expository part of Mr McTaggart's work.

On the other hand I think in spite of what I have said Mr McTaggart's work has great value 1) as a criticism and 2) as an independent philosophical theory.

As a criticism I consider that the misunderstandings I have mentioned do not take away from its value. Mr McTaggart is the first writer in English at least who has gone over all the main ideas of the system and has endeavoured to weigh correctly the objections, that can be taken to turn on the points in which theory requires explanation and development. He has given us a very full collection of Hegelian ἀπορίαι ['difficulties'] which must be solved, if his philosophy has to be maintained. He has also done much to bring the ideas of Hegel into relation with more recent speculations which must test and be tested by them. I have often found his criticisms very suggestive even when I did not agree with it.

On the other hand Mr McTaggart has given us a philosophical theory of his own which though worked out in connection with Hegel, is not it seems to me so closely bound up with that system. It is a theory which is more akin to the mysticism of Plotinus[25] than to any other philosophy I know – though of course it differs from that philosophy in many very important points, and I do not think that McTaggart has been directly influenced by Plotinus. Or perhaps I should say that that his elective affinities for one side of Hegel have led him to work it out apart from and in opposition to other elements of the Hegelian philosophy.

I consider Mr McTaggart's books as an important contribution to philosophical enquiry and as in every respect worthy of the Degree.

In any case the effort to work out a system of mysticism from a modern point of view is interesting and instructive.

[1] [John McTaggart Ellis McTaggart (1866–1925), idealist philosopher, College Lecturer (1897–1925) and Fellow (1902–25) of Trinity College, Cambridge. The University awarded McTaggart his D.Litt in 1902. Henry Jones and JH Muirhead, *Life and Philosophy of Edward Caird, LL.D., D.C.L.* (Glasgow: Maclehose, Jackson, 1921), pp.188, 196–7, 237–8, 297–8, 332, 353. G Lowes Dickinson, *J.McT.E. McTaggart* (Cambridge University Press, 1931), pp.49–50.]

[2] [JE McTaggart, *Studies in Hegelian Dialectic* (Cambridge University Press, 1896). It is unclear which *Mind* articles McTaggart submitted in support of his application. His four most recent had been: 'Hegel's Treatment of the Categories of the Subjective Notion [Parts I & II]', 6 ns (April & July, 1897), 164–81, 342–58; 'Hegel's Treatment of the Categories of the Objective Notion', 8 ns (January 1899), 35–62; 'Hegel's Treatment of the Categories of the Idea', 9 ns (April 1900), 145–83; 'Hegel's Treatment of the Categories of Quality', 11ns (October 1902), 503–26.]

[3] [JE McTaggart, *Studies in Hegelian Cosmology*, 2nd edition (Cambridge University Press, 1918). First edition published in 1901.]

[4] [GWF Hegel, *The Logic of Hegel. Translated from The Encyclopaedia of the Philosophical Sciences*, trans. by W Wallace, 2nd edition (Oxford: Clarendon, 1892), §§7, 13–5. First German edition published in 1817.]

[5] ['from the' is deleted in the manuscript.]

[6] [GWF Hegel, *Phenomenology of Spirit*, trans. AV Miller (Oxford University Press, 1975), §§48–72. First German edition published in 1807.]

[7] Gesth. der. Phil III [MS del.: 337]. [Caird adds this note at top of the folio. It appears to refer to the following: '[For Spinoza] The negative is conceived altogether as a vanishing moment – not in itself, but only as individual self-consciousness;...Self-consciousness is born from this ocean, dripping with the water thereof, *i.e.* never coming to absolute self-hood; the heart, the independence is transfixed – the vital fire is wanting. This lack has to be supplied, the moment of self-consciousness has to be added. It has the following two special aspects, which we now perceive emerging and gaining acceptance; in the first place the objective aspect, that absolute essence obtains in self-consciousness the mode of an object of consciousness for which the "other" exists, or the existent as such, and that what Spinoza understood by the "modes" is elevated to objective reality as an absolute moment of the absolute; in the second place we have the aspect of self-consciousness, individuality, independence.' GWF Hegel, *Lectures on the History of Philosophy*, ed. and trans. ES Haldane and FH Simson, 3 vols. (London: Routledge, Kegan and Paul, 1896), vol.3 , p.289. First German edition published 1831.]

[8] [Immanuel Kant, *Critique of Pure Reason*, trans. P Guyer and AW Wood (Cambridge University Press, 1998), pp.219–66 (B116–B169). First German edition published in 1781, second in 1787.]

[9] [René Descartes, *Meditations on First Philosophy with selections from the Objection and Replies*, trans. J Cottingham (Cambridge University Press, 1986), pp.45–8 (Fifth Meditation), 95–102 ('Objections and Replies'). First Latin edi-

208   *Unpublished Manuscripts in British Idealism*

tion published in 1641. Cf. Edward Caird, 'Anselm's Argument for the Being of God', *Journal of Theological Studies*, vol. 1 (1899), pp.23–39; reprinted in Colin Tyler (ed.) *Collected Works of Edward Caird*, 12 vols. (Bristol: Thoemmes, 1999), vol. 12.]

10 [MS del.: 'Ontological'.]

11 [MS reads: 'of' or 'by'.]

12 [McTaggart, *Studies in Hegelian Dialectic*, pp.37, 44.]

13 [Mc Taggart, *Studies in Hegelian Cosmology*, chap. 9.]

14 [MS orig.: 'correlate'.]

15 [Hegel, *Logic*, §244. Cf. Caird, *Hegel* (Edinburgh and London: William Blackwood, 1883), pp.182–3.]

16 [Francis Herbert Bradley, *Appearance and Reality: A metaphysical essay* (Oxford: Clarendon, 1893; 2nd ed. 1897), chap. 24 ('Degrees of Truth and Reality').]

17 [Hegel, *Logic*, §17.]

18 [McTaggart, *Studies in Hegelian Dialectic*, chaps. 4 and 5.]

19 [Bradley, *Appearance and Reality*, e.g., chap. 26.]

20 [The name 'Melissus' is conjectural as the text is particularly indistinct at this point. Melissus of Samos (fl. mid-fifth century BC), Greek Eleatic philosopher, who argued that all reality, which he calls the 'One', is homogenous, eternal, unchanging and present everywhere without exception.]

21 [MS del.: 'eternal self'.]

22 [McTaggart, *Studies in Hegelian Cosmology*, pp.209–230.]

23 [This word runs on from the preceding sentence in the manuscript, although Caird precedes it with 'NP' which appears to denote 'new paragraph'.]

24 ['Philosophy has been reproached with setting itself above religion; this, however, is false as an actual matter of fact, for it possess this particular content only and no other, though it presents it in the form of thought; it sets itself merely above the form of faith, the content is the same in both cases.' GWF Hegel, *Lectures on the Philosophy of Religion, together with a work on the proofs of the existence of God*, trans. EB Speirs and J Burdon Sanderson, 3 vols. (London: Kegan Paul, Trench, Trubner, 1895), vol. 3, p.148. First German edition published in 1832. Hegel, *Logic*, §§1–2, 28–31, 36, 68.]

25 [Plotinus (c.205–70 AD), Egyptian neoplatonist philosopher, whose works were edited by his disciples as the *Enneads*. See Caird's letter to Mary Sarah Talbot, 31 March 1902, in Jones et al, *Life and Philosophy of Edward Caird*, pp.237–8; cf. letter to same, 26 September 1893, *ibid.*, pp.196–7. Caird examined the thought of Plotinus at great length in *The Evolution of Theology in the Greek Philosophers. The Gifford Lectures 1900–1 and 1901–2*, 2 vols. (Glasgow: Maclehose, 1904), lectures 22 to 26 inc. Caird was rewriting these lectures at the time he wrote this reference for McTaggart.]

[Appendix A]
[Edward Caird's Lectures on Moral Philosophy. The University of Glasgow, 1876–77]

[The following is a verbatim transcription of the tables of contents of William Martin's three volumes of notes on Caird's moral philosophy lectures.[1] Martin's Roman numerals for the lectures have been converted into Arabic.]

Moral Philosophy
Profr. Caird's Lectures
1876–77
Volume 1
Bench XVII–I
William Martin
Glasgow[2]

1. Philosophy. The general department to which it belongs.
2. The use and abuse of metaphor in Philosophy.
3. The unity after which Philosophy seeks – its concrete nature.
4. The progressiveness and developement of philosophy. The true meaning of developement.
5. The nature of developement in animals, man and the state.
6. Reflection and Action.
7. The nature of the Law of development in Philosophy. Ancient and moral Philosophy – contrast.
8. Philosophy and History. The likeness between the history of events [?] and the history of Philosophy. The one-sided nature of the unifying and separating minds.
9. The search after unity. Anaxagoras. Progress to and in Philosophy.
10. The Philosophy of Greece compared with that of Egypt, Persia and India. Pantheism. The Greek's freedom.
11. Greek religion contrasted with Asiatic and other forms.
12. The origin of the State in Greece.
13. The Greek state – Athens – population and conditions.
14. [The Greek] Measure. The Sophists.

15. Casuistry. The Relation of Socrates to the Sophists.
16. Socrates and the Sophists – Virtue – Socrates and Anaxagoras – Plato and Aristotle.
17. Socrates.
18. The Megarics, Cynics and Cyrenaics.
19. Plato.
20. Plato. Idealism. What Plato meant by ideas. Abstraction. Common element species.
21. Plato. The ideal theory – his mysticism – his morals – the 'Republic.'
22. The Platonic Republic. Social theories of Hobbes, Locke, Rousseau and Spinoza. Plato and Rousseau.
23. Social theories contd. Division of Labour. Greek idea of justice.
24. Socialism and Individualism.
25. Socialism contd., Plato's system of moral and intellectual education.
26. Platonic education contd.. The Mythological element. The idea of good.
27. Plato. Socialism. Defects. Immortality.
28. Aristotle and Plato. Aristotle's view of sense. Two kinds of progress in knowledge.
29. Aristotle and Plato. Aristotelian and Christian conception of God.
30. Aristotle. Two kinds of progress in Knowledge. Form and matter. Psychology. A priori and a posteriori Knowledge.
31. Aristotle's psychology and ethics. Happiness.
32. Aristotle's idea of virtue. Its relation to that of the Stoic and Solon.
33. Aristotle's Virtue. The mean. Habit. Reason and the passions. The extent of habit. The form the idea of habit takes in modern times. The opposition between habit and self-developement.
34. Aristotle. Virtue. Habit. Its good and bad side.
35. Aristotle's list of virtues. Its exposition and nature.
36. Aristotle. The idea of an end. Delicate tact in contingencies. Mill. Self-consciousness. The narrowness of Aristotle's definition. Two modern definitions of it.
37. Aristotle. Freedom. Will, Reason and Passion. Contingent and eternal truth. Eudamonia. [sic] The relation of please to happiness. Justice. General and particular Justice. Ethics and jurisprudence. Distributive and corrective justice. The highest state. Friendship - three kinds.

38. The Sophists, Plato and Aristotle, in relation to individualism. The criterion. The Stoics, Epicureans and Sceptics.

Moral Philosophy
Profr. Caird's Lectures
1876–77
Volume II
William Martin
Glasgow[3]

39. The Stoics, Epicureans and Sceptics.
40. [The Stoics.] Speculative and ethical philosophy.
41. [The Stoics.] The onesidedness of Stoic philosophy. Comparative [?] uses and relation to Roman law.
42. [The Stoics] and the Epicureans. Atomic theory, Ethics.
43. Stoicism and Epicureanism. Scepticism its inconsistency.
44. The Sceptics. Tropes. The doctrine of the relativity of Knowledge.
45. Scepticism. Its relation to Christianity.
46. Christianity. The combination of the monotheistic and pantheistic conceptions of God. The notion of Mediation.
47. Christianity. Scholasticism.
48. Ancient and modern civilisation. Scholasticism, its nature and method.
49. Scholasticism. Its method and results. The revolt against it. The church and the world. The Revival of latter. The Lawgiver.
50. The Reformation. The 'right' of private judgment.
51. The 'right' of private judgment. Its relation to morality and religion. Luther and Erasmus. Modern philosophy.
52. Luther and Comte. Hume, Kant and Berkeley.
53. Philosophy and Science. Bacon, Locke and Berkeley. Kant, ordinary consciousness. Huxley.
54. Science and Philosophy. Hume. Spencer.
55. [Science and Philosophy.] Indestructibility of Matter. Force and Correction of Force. Laplace. Cause.
56. Science and Philosophy. Hume's notion of causality. Animal life. Spencer.
57. Science and Philosophy. Evolution.
58. Soul and body. Theory of occasional causes.
59. Soul and body. Aristotle's classification.
60. Soul and body. Consciousness. What is involved in

Consciousness? Theories of Sir Wm. Hamilton and Prof. Ferrier.
61. Nature of Consciousness.
62. Sensuous Consciousness. Observation and reflection or understanding.
63. The three stages contd. The infinite.
64. Self-consciousness. The life of desire. Savage life and morality. Slavery.
65. Master and Slave. Universal Self-consciousness. Expressions of higher Self-consciousness.
66. Consciousness contd. Descartes and Spinoza. 3 periods in modern philosophy.
67. Consciousness contd. Descartes, Locke, Leibnitz, Berkeley and Hume – Kant; moral results of his philosophy. 3 main theories of morality in modern [...?]
68. 3 periods of modern philosophy. 3 theories of morals. Utilitarianism. Paley.
69. Utilitarian theory of pleasure.
70. The other [?] side of the hedonist theory. The pleasure of the [...?]
71. Hedonism and Bentham.
72. Utilitarianism contd.
73. Benthamism.
74. Mill and Bentham.
75. The theory of the moral sense. Hobbes, Shaftesbury and Maurice.
76. Sentimental School contd. Shaftesbury, Mandeville, Hutcheson and Butler.

Moral Philosophy
Prof. Caird's Lectures
Volume III
William Martin
Glasgow[4]

77. Sentimental theory contd. Butler, Hutcheson, Hume.
78. Hume contd. Theories of Freedom.
79. The idea of Freedom contd. Kant.
80. Kant's idea of Freedom. Jacobi.
81. Kant. Appetite in man.
82. The desires contd.

[Appendix B]

[This appendix is a verbatim transcript (with contractions silently expanded) of two folios in the hand of either of Caird's biographers, Henry Jones or JH Muirhead.][5]

List of Caird's [Oxford] Lectures [1894–1906]

(Most of his lectures were specially marked 'for fourth-year students.' He gave few elementary courses. The general scheme seems to have been to lecture on 'Logic' in the first term; then on ethics, either speculatively or historically, for the next two terms.)

Michaelmass 1894	Logic (especially Aristotle's Logic).
Hilary 1895	Principles in Ethics.
Easter and Trinity 1895	Philosophy of Plato.

Michaelmas 1895	Logic.
Hilary 1896	History of Greek Ethics.
Easter and Trinity 1896	History of Modern Ethics.

Michaelmas 1896	Logic.
Hilary 1897	Principles of Ethics.
Easter and Trinity 1897	Philosophy of Plato.

Michaelmas 1897	Logic (with special reference to the development of the Forms of Thought)
Hilary 1898	Moral Philosophy of Aristotle.
East and Trinity 1898	Post-Aristotelian Philosophy (Stoics, Epicureans, etc.).

Michaelmas 1898	Logic (with special [reference to the development of the] forms of Thought).
Hilary 1899	Principles of Ethics.
Easter and Trinity 1899	Philosophy of Plato.

Michaelmas 1899.	Logic (with special [reference to the development of the] Forms of Thought).
Hilary 1900	History of Modern Ethics (Hobbes to Kant).
Easter and Trinity 1900.	Philosophy of Plato.

Michaelmas 1900	Logic (with special reference etc.)
Hilary 1901	Moral Philosophy of Aristotle.
Easter and Trinity 1901	Post-Aristotelian Philosophy.

Michaelmas 1901	Logic (etc.)
Hilary 1902	British Moralists (Hobbes to Hume)
Easter and Trinity 1902	Philosophy of Plato.

Michaelmas 1902	Logic (etc.)
Hilary 1903	Moral Philosophy of Aristotle, and its relation to his Metaphysics.
Easter and Trinity 1903	Philosophy of Plato.

Michaelmas 1903	Logic (etc.)
Hilary 1904	History of Ethics – Hobbes to Kant.
Easter and Trinity 1904	The Principles of Ethics.

Michaelmas 1904	Logic
Hilary 1905	The Philosophy of Kant.

Easter and Trinity 1906	Moral Philosophy of Aristotle.

[1] [William Martin (1856–1924), knighted in 1919, leading Glasgow Liberal. 'Hon. Representative of the Royal Humane Society,...President of Toynbee Hall, Glasgow; Hon. Vice-President, National Citizens Council', *Who was Who,...1916–1928* (London: A & C Black, 1929), p.708.]

[2] [MS Gen. 278. This text is from the title page of Martin's first notebook.]

[3] [MS Gen. 279. This text is from the title page of Martin's second notebook.]

[4] [MS Gen. 280. This text is from the title page of Martin's third notebook. Above it is written: '2nd examn./5 classes/2nd class/____/3rd exam/5 classes/2nd class.']

[5] [MS Gen. 1475/29. Sir Henry Jones and JH Muirhead, *The Life and Philosophy of Edward Caird, LL.D., D.C.L.* (Glasgow: Maclehose, Jackson, 1921).]

Bibliography

Abbott, Evelyn and Lewis Campbell, *Life and Letters of Benjamin Jowett, MA*, 2 vols. (London: John Murray, 1897).

Aeschylus, *Aeschylus*, 2 vols., trans. H.W. Smith (London: William Heinemann, 1926).

Aristophanes, *Aristophanes*, trans. B.B. Rogers, 3 vols. (London: William Heinemann, 1927).

Aristotle, *Nicomachean Ethics*, trans. H. Rackham (London: William Heinemann, 1926).

———, *Poetics*, trans. W.H. Fyfe and W.R. Roberts (London: William Heinemann, 1927).

———, *On the Soul [De Anima]*, trans. W.H. Hett (London: William Heinemann, 1935).

———, *Politics*, trans. H Rackham (London: William Heinemann, 1950).

Arnold, Matthew, *The Poems*, 2nd ed., eds. K. and M. Allot (London: Longman, 1979).

———, *Culture and Anarchy. An essay in political and social criticism* (London: Smith Elder, 1869).

Arnold, Thomas, *Introductory Lectures on Modern History*, 4th ed. (London: B. Fellowes, 1849).

———, *Christian Life: Its Course, its hindrances, and its helps* (London: B. Fellowes, 1859).

———, *Sermons*, 6 vols. (London: Longmans Green, 1878).

Augustine of Hippo, *The City of God Against the Pagans*, trans. W.M. Green, 7 vols. (London: William Heinemann, 1957-1968).

Bacon, Francis, *Novum Organon; or A true guide to the interpretation of nature*, trans. G.W. Kitchin (Oxford University Press, 1855).

———, *Works*, 7 vols, eds. J. Spedding, R.L. Ellis and D.D.

Heath (London: Longman, 1879-87).

Baur, Ferdinand C., *Geschichte der christlichen Kirche*, 5 band (Leipzig: Tubingen, 1863).

Bentham, Jeremy, *Comments on the 'Commentaries'; and, A Fragment on Government*, eds. J.H. Burns and H.L.A. Hart (London: Athlone, 1977).

————, *'Legislator of the world': Writings on codification, law and education*, eds. P. Schofield and J. Harris (Oxford: Clarendon, 1998).

Bernard of Clairvaux, Saint, *Life and Works of Saint Bernard, abbot of Clairvaux*, 2 vols., eds. J. Mabillan and S.J. Eales, 2nd ed. (London: Burns and Oates, 1800).

Blackstone, Sir William, *Commentaries on the Laws of England*, 4 vols. (Oxford: Clarendon, 1765)

Bluntschli, Johann Caspar, *The Theory of the State. Authorised English translation from the sixth German edition*, trans. D.G. Ritchie, P.E. Matheson and R. Lodge (Oxford: Clarendon, 1885; 2nd ed. Oxford: Clarendon, 1890).

Bosanquet, Bernard, *Some Suggestions in Ethics* (London: MacMillan, 1918).

Bosanquet, Helen, *Bernard Bosanquet: A short account of his life* (London: Macmillan, 1924).

Boswell, James, *Life of Samuel Johnson*, new edition, ed. J.W. Croker, 5 vols. (London: John Murray, 1831).

Bradley, Francis H., *Appearance and Reality: A metaphysical essay* (Oxford: Clarendon, 1893; 2nd ed. 1897).

Brown, D. Catherine, *Pastor and Laity in the Theology of Jean Gerson* (Cambridge University Press, 1987).

Browning, Elizabeth B., *The Poetical Works* (London: John Murray, 1914).

————, *Aurora Leigh*, ed. M. Reynolds (Athens: Ohio University Press, 1992).

Browning Robert, *Complete Works*, eds. J.C. Berkey, A.C. Dooley and S.E. Dooley, 16 vols. to date (Athens: Ohio University Press, 1969-).

Bryce, James, *The Holy Roman Empire* (Oxford: Shrimpton, 1864).

Buckle, Henry T., *History of Civilization in England*, 3 vols. (London: Longmans, Green, 1902).

Bunsen, Christian C.J., *Egypt's Place in Universal History*, 4 vols., trans. C.H. Cottrell (London: Longman, Brown, Green and Longmans, 1848-1860).

Butler, Joseph, *Analogy of Religion to the Constitution and Course of Nature: Also, Fifteen Sermons* (London: Religious Tracts Society, n.d.).

Caird, Edward, 'Plato and the Other Companions of Socrates', *North British Review*, vol. 43, no. 86 (December 1865), pp.351-84.

————, 'The Roman Element in Civilisation', *North British Review*, vol. 44, no. 88 (June 1866), pp.249-71.

————, *Ethical Philosophy. An introductory lecture delivered in the Common Hall of Glasgow College on November 6, 1866* (Glasgow: James MacLehose, 1866)

————, *Hegel* (Edinburgh and London: William Blackwood, 1883).

————, *Social Philosophy and Religion of Comte* (Glasgow: James MacLehose, 1885).

————, *The Moral Aspect of the Economical Problem. Presidential address to the Ethical Society* (London: Swan Sonnenschein, Lowrey, 1888).

————, *The Critical Philosophy of Immanuel Kant*, 2 vols. (Glasgow: James MacLehose, 1889).

————, *Essays on Literature and Philosophy*, 2 vols. (Glasgow: James MacLehose, 1892).

————, *The Evolution of Religion. The Gifford Lectures Delivered Before the University of St Andrews in Sessions 1890-91 and 1891-92*, 2 vols. (Glasgow: James MacLehose, 1893).

————, 'Some Characteristics of Shakespeare', *Contemporary Review*, vol. 70 (1896), pp.818-34.

————, *The Present State of the Controversy Between Individualism and Socialism. Being an inaugural address to the Civic Society of Glasgow* (Glasgow: James MacLehose, 1897).

———, 'Anselm's Argument for the Being of God', *Journal of Theological Studies*, vol. 1 (1899), pp.23-39.

———, *The Evolution of Theology in the Greek Philosophers. The Gifford Lectures Delivered in the University of Glasgow in Sessions 1900-1 and 1901-2*, 2 vols. (Glasgow: James MacLehose, 1904).

———, *Lay Sermons and Addresses. Delivered in the Hall of Balliol College, Oxford* (Glasgow: James MacLehose, 1907).

———, *Collected Works*, 12 vols., ed. C. Tyler (Bristol: Thoemmes, 1999).

Champion, Selwyn Gurney, *Racial Proverbs*, 2nd ed. (London: Routledge and Kegan Paul, 1950).

Code Napoleon; or, The French Civil Code. Literally Translated from the Original and Official Edition, Published at Paris, in 1804. By a Barrister of the Inner Temple, trans. George Spence (London: William Benning, Law, 1827).

Comte, Auguste, *General View of Positivism*, trans. J.H. Bridges (London: Trubner, 1865).

———, *System of Positive Polity*, trans. F. Harrison, 4 vols. (London: Longmans, Green, 1875).

Cross F.L. and E.A. Livingston (eds.), *Oxford Dictionary of the Christian Church*, 2nd edition (London: Oxford University Press, 1974).

Descartes, René, *Meditations on First Philosophy with selections from the Objection and Replies*, trans. J. Cottingham (Cambridge University Press, 1986).

Dionysius the Areopagite, *On the Divine Names and the Mystical Theology*, trans. C.E. Rolt (London: SPCK, 1940).

Erdmann, Johann E., *Philosophische Vorlesungen über den Staat* (Halle: HW Schmidt, 1851).

Euclid, *Elements*, ed. R. Simson, 5th ed. (Edinburgh: Nourse, 1775).

Euripedes, *Hippolytus*, trans. A.S. Way, 4 vols. (London: William Heinemann, 1912-16).

Ewald, Georg H.A., *Geschichte des Ausgange Des Volkes Israel*

Und Des Nachapostolischen Zeitalters, 2nd ed., 7 vols. (Göttingen, 1858-9).

Farrar, F.W., 'On Greek and Latin Verse-Composition as a General Branch of Education', in F.W. Farrar (ed.) *Essays on a Liberal Education*, 2nd ed. (London: MacMillan, 1868), pp.205-39

Feuerbach, Ludwig A., *Das Wesen des Cristenthums* (Leipzig: Wigand, 1841).

———, *The Essence of Christianity*, trans. by G. Eliot (London: John Chapman, 1854).

Filmer, Robert, *Patriarcha and other writings*, ed. J.P. Sommerville (Cambridge University Press, 1991).

Froude, James A., *History of England from the Fall of Wolsey to the Defeat of the Spanish Armada*, 12 vols. (London: Longmans, Green, 1856-70).

Gaius, 'The Four Commentaries of Gaius on the Institutes of the Civil Law', in ed. S.P. Scott, *The Civil Law*, 17 vols. (New York: AMS, 1973), vol. 1, pp.79-219.

Gellius, Autus, *Attic Nights*, trans. J.C. Rolfe, 3 vols. (London: William Heinemann, 1947).

Gerson, Jean *Ouevres complètes*, ed. P. Glorieux, 10 vols. (Paris: Desclée and Cie, 1960-73).

Goethe, Johann Wolfgang von, *Werke*, ed. K. Goedeke, 36 vols. (Stuttgart: Cattaschan Buchhandlung, 1867-82), vol. 10.

———, *Weimarer Ausgabe vom Goethes Werken*, 143 Banden, (München: Artemis, 1987).

Green, Thomas H., 'The Philosophy of Aristotle', *The North British Review*, vol. 45, no. 89 (September 1866), pp.105-44.

———, 'Popular Philosophy in its Relation to Life', *North British Review*, vol. 48 (March 1868), pp.133-63.

———, 'General Introduction', in T.H. Green and T.H. Grose (eds.) *A Treatise of Human Nature...and Dialogues Concerning Natural Religion by David Hume*, 4 vols. (London: Longmans, Green, 1874), vol.1, pp.1-299.

———, 'Introduction to the Moral Part of the Treatise', in T.H. Green and T.H. Grose (eds.) *A Treatise of Human*

Nature…and Dialogues Concerning Natural Religion by David Hume, 4 vols. (London: Longmans, Green, 1874), vol. 2, pp.1-71

——, *Lectures on the Principles of Political Obligation and other writings*, eds. P. Harris and J. Morrow (Cambridge University Press, 1986).

——, *Works*, eds. R.L. Nettleship and P.P. Nicholson, 5 vols. (Bristol: Thoemmes, 1997).

Griffin, Nicholas (ed.) *Selected Letters of Bertrand Russell. The Private Years 1884-1914* (London: Routledge, 1992).

Guizot, François P.G., *History of Civilization from the Fall of the Roman Empire to the French Revolution*, trans. W. Hazlitt, 3 vols. (London: Bogue, 1846).

Hearn, William E., *The Aryan Household: Its structure and its development: An introduction to comparative jurisprudence* (London: Longmans, Green, 1879).

Hegel, Georg W.F., *Werke*, 19 vols. ed. E. Gans (Berlin: Duncker and Humblot, 1834-1887).

——, *Lectures on the Philosophy of Religion, together with a work on the proofs of the existence of God*, trans. E.B. Speirs and J. Burdon Sanderson, 3 vols. (London: Kegan Paul, Trench, Trubner, 1895).

——, *The Logic of Hegel. Translated from the Encyclopaedia of the Philosophical Sciences*, trans. W Wallace, 2nd ed. (Oxford: Clarendon, 1892).

——, *Lectures on the History of Philosophy*, ed. and trans. E.S. Haldane and F.H. Simson, 3 vols. (London: Routledge, Kegan and Paul, 1896).

——, *Philosophy of History*, trans. J. Sibree (New York: Dover, 1956).

——, *Philosophy of Right*, trans. by T.M. Knox (Oxford: Clarendon, 1967)

——, *Philosophy of Mind*, trans. W. Wallace and A.V. Miller (Oxford: Clarendon, 1971).

——, *Phenomenology of Spirit*, trans. A.V. Miller (Oxford University Press, 1977).

——, *Elements of the Philosophy of Right*, ed. A.W. Wood

(Cambridge University Press, 1991).

Herodotus, [*Histories*] trans. A.D. Godley, 4 vols. (London: William Heinemann, 1920-24).

Hilgenfeld, Adolf B.C., *Das Evangelium und die Briefe Johannis nach ihrem Lehregriff Dargestellt* (Halle: CEM Pfeffer, 1849).

————, *Historisch-kriticshe Einleitung in das Neue Testament* (Leipzig: Fues, 1875).

Hobbes, Thomas, 'Tripos; in Three Discourses. I. Human Nature: Or the fundamental elements of policy', in T. Hobbes, *English Works*, ed. W. Molesworth, 11 vols. (London: John Bohn, 1839-45), vol. 4, pp.1-76.

————, 'Tripos; in Three Discourses. II. De Corpore Politico: Or the elements of law, moral and politic, ...', in T. Hobbes, *English Works*, ed. W. Molesworth, 11 vols. (London: John Bohn, 1839-45), vol. 4, pp.77-228.

————, *Leviathan*, in T. Hobbes, *English Works*, ed. W. Molesworth, 11 vols. (London: John Bohn, 1839-45), vol. 3.

Homer, *The Odyssey*, trans. by A.T. Murray (London: William Heinemann, 1919).

————, *The Iliad*, trans. A.T. Murray, 2 vols. (London: William Heinemann, 1924).

Hooker, Richard, *The Works of Mr. Richard Hooker*, arr. J. Keble, 3rd ed., 3 vols. (Oxford University Press, 1845).

Hume, David, *Philosophical Works*, 2nd ed., 4 vols. (Edinburgh: Adam Black, William Tait and Charles Tait, 1826).

————, *Essays Moral, Political and Literary*, eds. T.H. Green and T.H. Grose, 2 vols., new ed. (London: Longmans, Green, 1882)

Hutcheson, Francis, *An Essay on the Nature and Conduct of the Passions and Affections with illustrations on the Moral Sense* (London: J. Darby and T. Brown, 1728).

Irenaeus, 'Against Heresies', in Alexander Roberts and James Donaldson (eds.), *Ante-Nicene Christian Library: Translations of the Fathers Down to AD 325: Volume 5. Irenaeus 1* (Edinburgh: T. and T. Clark, 1868).

Israel, Jonathan, *The Dutch Republic. Its rise, greatness and fall* (Oxford: Clarendon, 1995).

Jones, Sir Henry and John H Muirhead, *The Life and Philosophy of Edward Caird, LL.D, DCL, FBA* (Glasgow: MacLehose, Jackson, 1921).

Josephus, [*The Jewish War*], trans. H. St. J. Thackeray, 8 vols. (London: William Heinemann, 1927).

——, [*Jewish Antiquities*], trans. Louis H. Feldman, 9 vols. (London: William Heinemann, 1965).

Justin Martyr, 'The First and Second Apologies', in Alexander Roberts and James Donaldson (eds.), *Ante-Nicene Christian Library: Translations from the Writings of the Fathers down to A.D. 325. Volume 2. Justin Martyr and Athenagoras*, trans. M. Dods, G. Reith and B.P. Pratten (Edinburgh: T. and T. Clark, 1867), pp.1-84.

Juvenal, *Satires*, in *Juvenal and Persius*, trans. G.G. Ramsay (London: William Heinemann, 1950).

Kant, Immanuel, 'Grundlegung zur Metaphysik Der Sitten', in Karl Rosenkranz and Friedrich Wilhelm Schubert (eds.), *Immanuel Kant's Sämmtiliche Werke*, 12 vols. (Leipzig: Voss, 1838-42), vol. 8.

——, *Kritik der Praktischen Vernunft*, ed. K. Vorländer (Leipzig: Verlag von Felix Meiner, 1922).

——, *Practical Philosophy*, ed. and trans. M. Gregor (Cambridge University Press, 1996).

——, *Critique of Pure Reason*, trans. P. Guyer and A.W. Wood (Cambridge University Press, 1998).

——, *Theoretical Philosophy after 1781*, ed. H. Allison and P. Heath (Cambridge University Press, 2002).

——, *Theoretical Philosophy, 1755-1770*, ed. D. Walford (Cambridge University Press, 2003).

Keene, Carol A.. and William J. Mander (eds.), *The Collected Works of F.H. Bradley*, 12 vols. (Bristol: Thoemmes, 1999), vols. 1-5.

Laws of the Twelve Tables, in S.P. Scott, ed., *The Civil Law*, 17 vols. (New York: AMS, 1973), vol. 1, pp.57-77.

Lightfoot, Joseph B., (ed.), *Saint Paul's Epistle to the Galatians*

(London and New York: MacMillan, 1890).

Livingstone, E.A. (ed.), *The Oxford Dictionary of the Christian Church*, 3rd ed. (Oxford University Press, 1997).

Locke, John, *Two Treatises on Government*, ed. P. Laslett, 2nd ed. (Cambridge University Press, 1967).

——, *An Essay Concerning Human Understanding*, ed. P.H. Nidditch (Oxford: Oxford University Press, 1975).

Lorimer, James, *The Institutes of the Law of Nations. A treatise of the jural relations of separate political communities* (Edinburgh: William Blackwood, 1872; 2nd, enlarged edition 1880; 3rd ed. in 2 vols. 1883-4).

Lowes Dickinson, G *J.McT.E. McTaggart* (Cambridge University Press, 1931)

Lucretius, *De Rerum Natura* [*On the Nature of the Universe*], trans. W.H.D. Rouse (London: William Heinemann, 1975).

Luther, Martin, *Werke. Kritische Gesamtausgabe. Brieswechsel 2. Band* (Weimar: Hermann Böhlaus Nachsolger, 1931).

——, *Works*, gen. ed. J. Peliken and H.T. Lehmann, 55 vols. (Philadelphia: Muhlenberg Press, 1958-86).

MacKenzie, J.S., 'Edward Caird as a Philosophical Teacher', *Mind*, vol. 18, no. 72 ns (October 1909), pp.509-37.

McTaggart, John M.E., *Studies in Hegelian Dialectic* (Cambridge University Press, 1896).

——, 'Hegel's Treatment of the Categories of the Subjective Notion [Parts I & II]', 6 ns (April and July, 1897), pp.164-81, 342-58.

——, 'Hegel's Treatment of the Categories of the Objective Notion', 8 ns (January 1899), pp.35-62.

——, 'Hegel's Treatment of the Categories of the Idea', 9 ns (April 1900), pp.145-83.

——, 'Hegel's Treatment of the Categories of Quality', 11 ns (October 1902), pp.503-26.

——, *Studies in Hegelian Cosmology*, 2nd edition (Cambridge University Press, 1918).

Maine, Sir Henry Sumner, *Ancient Law. Its connection with the early history of society and its relation to modern ideas,* introd. F. Pollock (London: John Murray, 1906).

Mant, Rev. D.D. (ed.) *Book of Common Prayer, and Administration of the Sacraments, and Other Rites and Ceremonies of the Church, and According to the Use of the United Church of England and Ireland...*, (Oxford: J Parker; London: F.C. and J. Rivington, 1820).

Meyer, Heinrich A.W., *Das Neue Testament Grieschisch nach den besten Hülfsmitteln kritisch revidirt ...*, 2 vols. (Göttingen: Vandenhoeck und Ruprecht, 1829).

Meyer, Heinrich A.W. (ed.), *Kritisch-exegetischer Kommentar zum Neuen Testament*, 16 vols. (Göttingen: Vandenhoeck und Ruprecht, 1832-1859).

Mill, John S., *Considerations on Representative Government*, 2nd ed. (London: Parker, 1861).

——, *Collected Works*, gen. eds. F.E. Priestly and J.M. Robson, 33 vols. (University of Toronto Press, 1963-91).

Milton, John, *Complete Prose Works*, gen. ed. D.M.Wolfe, 8 vols. (London: Oxford University Press, 1953-82).

Monk, Ray, *Bertrand Russell, 1872-1921: The Spirit of Solitude* (London: Jonathan Cape, 1996).

Montesquieu, Charles-Louis de Secondat, *Oeuvres Complètes*, 7 tomes, ed. É. Laboulaye, (Paris: Garnier Frères, 1875-7).

——, *The Spirit of the Laws*, eds. A. Cohler, B. Miller and H. Stone (Cambridge University Press, 1989).

Moore, George E., 'The Metaphysical Basis of Ethics' [Dissertation for a Fellowship at Trinity College Cambridge, 1897].

——, 'Freedom', *Mind*, vol. 7, no. 26 ns (April 1898), pp.179-204.

——, 'The Nature of Judgment', *Mind*, vol. 8, no. 30 ns (April 1899), pp.176-93.

Nettleship, Richard L. 'Preface of the Editor', in T.H. Green, *Works*, eds. R.L. Nettleship and P.P. Nicholson, 5 vols. (Bristol: Thoemmes, 1997), vol. 3, pp.v-vii.

——, 'Memoir', in T.H. Green, *Works*, eds. R.L. Nettleship and P.P. Nicholson, 5 vols. (Bristol: Thoemmes, 1997), vol. 3, pp.xi-clxi.

Neue Testament...stereotypirt nach der Hallischen Ausgabe (London: Samuel Bagster, n.d.).

Newsome, David, *Godliness and Good Learning. Four Studies on a Victorian Ideal* (London: John Murray, 1961).

Nicholson, Peter P., *The Political Philosophy of the British Idealists: Selected studies* (Cambridge University Press, 1990).

———, 'Introduction', in D.G. Ritchie, *Collected Works*, ed. P.P. Nicholson, 6 vols. (Bristol: Thoemmes, 1998), vol. 1.

Novum Testamentum, ed. C. Lloyd? (Oxford, 1847).

Origen, 'In Genesum. Homiliae Prima' ['Commentary on Genesis. First Homily'], in J.P. Migne (ed.), *Patrologiae cursus completes, series graeca: Col. 12 Origenes Opera Omnia, Tomus Secundus* (Paris: Garnier, 1862).

———, 'Commentary on the Gospel of John' (trans. Allan Menzies), in A. Menzies (ed.), *The Ante-Nicene Fathers, translations of the Fathers down to AD325: Volume 10 The Gospel of Peter...* (Edinburgh: T & T Clark, 1887).

———, *The Commentary of Origen on S. John's Gospel* ed. A.E. Brooke, 2 vols. (Cambridge: Cambridge University Press, 1896).

———, *Contra Celsum*, trans. H. Chadwick (Cambridge University Press, 1965).

Oxford Ten-Year Book A register of University honours and distinctions completed to the end of the year 1870 (Oxford: James Parker, 1872).

Parker, Charles S., 'On the History of Classical Education', FW Farrar (ed.) *Essays on a Liberal Education*, 2nd ed. (London: MacMillan, 1868), pp.1-80.

Pfieffer, Franz (ed.), *Meister Eckhart*, trans. C. de B. Evans (London: John M. Watkins, 1924).

Pfleiderer, Otto, *Development of Theology in Germany since Kant, and its Progress in Great Britain since 1825*, 2nd ed. (London: Swan Sonnenschein: 1893; New York: MacMillan, 1893).

Philo, *Philonis... Opera Omnia Graece et Latine. Ad editionem Th. Mangey collatis aliquot MSS. edenda curavit AF Pfeifer*, 5 tom. (Argentoati: Erlangae, 1785-92).

————, *Philo*, trans. F.H. Colson and G.H. Whitaker, 10 vols. (London: William Heinemann, 1929).

Plato, *Euthyphro, Apology, Crito, Phaedo, Phaedrus*, trans. H.N. Fowler (London: William Heinemann, 1926).

————, *Theaetetus, Sophist*, trans. H.N. Fowler (London: William Heinemann, 1921).

————, *Timaeus, Critias, Cleitophon, Menexenus, Epistles*, trans. R.G. Bury (London: William Heinemann, 1929).

————, *Republic*, 2 vols., trans. Paul Shorey (London and New York: William Heinemann, 1946).

Plutarch, *Lives*, trans. B. Perrin, 11 vols. (London: William Heinemann, 1949).

Prawer, S.S., *Heine The Tragic Satirist: A study of the later poetry 1827-1856* (Cambridge University Press, 1961).

'Pseudo-Clementine', 'The Clementine Homilies', in Alexander Roberts and James Donaldson (eds.), *Ante-Nicene Christian Library: Translations of the Writings of the Fathers: Volume 8 The Twelve Patriarchs ...,*. (Edinburgh: T. and T. Clark, 1870).

Rickaby, Father Joseph, *Moral Philosophy, or Ethics and Natural Law*, 2nd ed. (London: Longmans Green, 1889).

Ritchie, David G., *The Principles of State Interference: Four Essays on the Political Philosophy of Mr. Herbert Spencer, J.S. Mill, and T.H. Green* (London: Swan Sonnenschein, 1891).

————, *Darwin and Hegel with other philosophical studies* (London: Swan Sonnenschein, 1893).

————, *Natural Rights. A criticism of some political and ethical conceptions* (London: George Allen and Unwin, 1894).

Rousseau, Jean-Jacques, *A Discourse on Inequality*, trans. M. Cranston (Harmondsworth: Penguin, 1984).

Ruysbroeck, Jan van, *The Book of the Twelve Beguines*, trans. J. Francis (London: John M Watkins, 1913).

Samuel, Herbert, *Liberalism. An attempt to state the principles and proposals of contemporary Liberalism in England* (London: Grant Richard, 1902).

Sanctis, Alberto de, *La democrazia 'puritana' di Thomas Hill*

Green: Con alcuni scritti inedite (Florence, 2002)

Sandars, T.C., 'Hegel's Philosophy of Right', in *Oxford Essays. Contributed by Members of the University* (London: John W. Parker, 1855), pp.213-50.

Say, Jean-Baptiste, *Traité D'Économie Politique: ou, simple exposition de la manière dont se forment, se distribuent, et se consomment les richesses*, 2 tom., 3rd ed. (Paris: Deterville, 1817).

Senior, Nassau W., *Outline of the Science of Political Economy* (London: George Allen and Unwin, 1938).

Shaftesbury, Lord Anthony A.C., *Characteristicks of Men, Manners, Opinions, Times*, ed. P. Ayres, 2 vols. (Oxford: Clarendon, 1999).

Sidgwick, Henry, *Methods of Ethics*, 5th ed. (London: MacMillan, 1893).

———, Critical Notice of D.G. Ritchie, *Natural Rights*, *Mind*, vol. 4, no.15 ns (July 1895), 384-8.

Smith, Adam, *The Theory of Moral Sentiments*, ed. D.D. Raphael and A.J. Macfie (Oxford: Clarendon, 1976).

———, *An Inquiry into the Nature and Causes of the Wealth of Nations*, eds. R.H. Campbell, A.S. Skinner and W.B. Todd, 2 vols. (Oxford: Clarendon, 1979).

Smith, Craig A., 'TH Green's Philosophical Manuscripts: An annotated catalogue', *Idealistic Studies*, vol. 9 (1978), pp.178-84.

Smith, Francis B., *The People's Health 1830-1910* (London: Weidenfeld and Nicolson, 1990).

Sophocles, *Sophocles*, trans. F. Storr, 2 vols. (London: William Heinemann, 1912).

Spencer, Herbert, *Principles of Ethics*, 2 vols. (London: Williams and Norgate, 1879-93).

———, *The Man* versus *the State* (London: Williams and Norgate, 1884).

———, *Collected Writings*, 12 vols. (London:Routledge/ Thoemmes, 1996).

Stirling, Amelia H., *James Hutchison Stirling. His life and work* (London: T. Fischer, 1912).

Stock, St. George, 'Fate (Greek and Roman)', in James Hastings (ed.) *Encyclopaedia of Religion and Ethics*, 12 vols. (Edinburgh: T. and T. Clark, 1908-26), vol. 5, p.786-90.

Suetonius [*The Twelve Caesars*] trans. J.C. Rolfe, 2 vols. (London: William Heinemann, 1924).

Swift, Jonathan, *Gulliver's Travels* ed. R.A. Greenberg, revised critical edition (New York: WW Norton, 1961).

Tacitus, *Agricola, Germania, Dialogus*, trans. M. Hutton and W. Peterson (London: William Heinemann, 1970)

Taine, Hippolyte, *The French Revolution*, trans. J. Durand 3 vols. (Indianapolis: Liberty Fund, 2002).

Tennyson, Alfred, Lord, *The Holy Grail and other poems* (London: Strahan, 1870).

———, *The Poems*, 3 vols., ed. Christopher Ricks, 2nd ed. (London: Longman, 1987).

Tertullianus, Quintus S.F., *Treatise on the Incarnation*, ed. and trans. E. Evans (London: SPCK, 1956).

———, 'The Five Books Against Marcion' [aka *Adversus Marcionem*], in Alexander Roberts and James Donaldson, (eds.), *Ante-Nicene Christian Library: Translations of the Writings of the Fathers: Volume 3 Latin Christianity. Its Founder, Tertullian. Three Parts: 1. Apologetic; 2. Anti-Marcion; 3. Ethical* (Edinburgh: T. and T. Clark, 1870), pp.318-83.

Thomas, Geoffrey, *Moral Philosophy of TH Green* (Oxford: Clarendon, 1987).

Thucydides, [*History of the Peloponnesian War,*] 4 vols., trans. C Forster Smith, (London and New York, William Heinemann, 1919-23).

Tischendorf, Constantinus (ed.), *Novum Testmentum Graece*, 2 vols. (Lipsiae: Giesecke & Devrient, 1870-1).

Tyler, Colin, 'TH Green, Advanced Liberalism and the Reform Question, 1865-76', *History of European Ideas*, vol. 29, no. 4 (December 2003), pp.437-58.

Wempe, Ben, *TH Green's Theory of Positive Freedom: From metaphysics to political theory* (Exeter: Imprint Academic, 2004).

Who was Who, a companion to 'Who's Who', containing the biographies of those who died during the period 1916-1928 (London: A & C Black, 1929).

Williams, Rowland, 'Bunsen's Biblical Researches', in Frederick Temple et al, *Essays and Reviews* (Oxford: J.H. and Jas. Parker, 1860), pp.50-93.

Wilson, J.M., 'On Teaching Natural Science in Schools', in F.W. Farrar (ed.) *Essays on a Liberal Education*, 2nd ed. (London: MacMillan, 1868), pp.241-91.

Wordsworth, William, *Poetical Works: Cambridge edition*, revised by P.D. Sheats (Boston: Houghton Mifflin, 1982).

Index

Groups of Arabic numerals refer to pages in the first volume when following 'I' and the second volume when following 'II'.

142, 146, 147, 211-2 (see 'Code Napoleon')
Lazarus, I 170, 180
lazzaroni, II 96, 145-6
legislature and legislation, I 21, 217, 219, 220-2: II 79, 104, 110, 111-5, 117, 118-31, 142, 149-50
Lennox, John, II xi
Leo X (pope), II 39, 182
Leuctra, I 219, 234
Lightfoot, Joseph B, I 121, 124, 132, 133, 134
Livy, II 79, 141, 142
Local Government Board, II 144
Locke, John, I 35, 41-3, 45-7, 49, 67, 82, 86, 87, 244-7 *passim*: II 210, 211, 212
logic, I xxiii, 1, 3, 4, 11, 55, 57, 58, 160, 198, 244, 245, 248, 249: II xi, 16, 19, 20, 22, 27, 32, 110, 164, 165, 168, 170-1, 195, 204, 205, 214-5 *passim*
Lollards, II 172, 181
Lombard, Peter, II 178-9
Lorimer, James, I 243, 246
Lotze, Rudolf H, II 184, 200
Louis XIV (France), II 152
Louis XVI (France), II 150
Louis-Phillipe (France), II 6, 152
Lucretius, II 35
Luther, Martin, I 10, 183: II 19, 32-9 *passim*, 162, 175-7 *passim*, 182-3, 211

Macan, Reginald W, I xxii, 107
Maine, Sir Henry Sumner, I 76: II 136-42 *passim*
MacKenzie, JS, II xi
Magdelene, Mary, I 178
Magna Carta, II 110, 144, 145, 148
Mander, William J, I xxv
Mandeville, Bernard de, I 47, 68: II 212
manichaeism, I 144
Manning, Henry E, II 132
Martha, I 170
Martin, William, II x, xi, 131, 132, 134, 139, 142, 143, 146, 148, 150, 209-13, 215
Maurice, FD, II 212
McTaggart, John ME, II v, ix-x, xi, 204-8